Adam Goodheart

1·8·6·1

Adam Goodheart is a historian, essayist, and journalist. His articles have appeared in *National Geographic,
Outside, Smithsonian, The American Scholar, The Atlantic,* and *The New York Times Magazine,* among others,
and he is a regular columnist for *The New York Times*'s
acclaimed online Civil War series, *Disunion.* He lives
in Washington, D.C., and on the Eastern Shore of
Maryland, where he is the Hodson Trust–Griswold
Director of Washington College's C. V. Starr Center
for the Study of the American Experience.

www.adamgoodheart.com

Union rally, San Francisco, 1861

"Goodheart's history is filled with many scenes and tiny details that transport readers through time . . . told with passion and remarkable scholarship that puts flesh on the dry bones of familiar historical fact. It's a compelling, captivating read."　　　　—*The Philadelphia Inquirer*

"[Goodheart] offers a lyrical work of literary nonfiction. . . . With [the] opening sentence of *1861*, we are placed in the hands of a storyteller."　　　　—*Reviews in American History*

"You can practically hear the drums rolling as you turn the pages of *1861*. . . . [Goodheart] brilliantly evokes the dread and anticipation that warred in the hearts of the American public."

—*Washingtonian*

"Goodheart's book stands out . . . for the author's deft narrative style and vivid description. . . . [He] conjures a remarkable cast of individual Americans—from slaves and foot soldiers to the occupant of the Oval Office—using their stories to evoke a national watershed."

—*The Times-Picayune* (New Orleans)

"Engrossing. . . . Tension is palpable on every page. . . . Goodheart's book is an impressive accomplishment, a delightful read, and a valuable contribution that will entertain and challenge popular and professional audiences alike."　　　　—*Harvard Magazine*

"With boundless verve, Adam Goodheart has sketched an uncommonly rich tableau of America on the cusp of the Civil War. The research is impeccable, the cast of little-known characters we are introduced to is thoroughly fascinating, the book is utterly thought-provoking, and the story is luminescent. What a triumph."

—Jay Winik, author of *April 1865* and *The Great Upheaval*

I·8·6·I

The Civil War Awakening

Adam Goodheart

VINTAGE BOOKS
A Division of Random House, Inc.
New York

FIRST VINTAGE BOOKS EDITION, FEBRUARY 2012

The Library of Congress has cataloged the Knopf edition as follows:
Goodheart, Adam.
1861 : the Civil War awakening / Adam Goodheart.—1st ed.
p.   cm.
Includes index.
1. United States—History—Civil War, 1861–1865—Causes.   2. United States—
Politics and government—1861–1865.   3. United States—Intellectual life—
19th century.   I. Title.   II. Title: Civil War awakening.
E459.G66 2011
973.7'11—dc22 2010051326

Vintage ISBN: 978-1-4000-3219-8

Author photograph © Barry Halvorson
Book design by Michael Collica

www.vintagebooks.com

Printed in the United States of America
10 9 8 7 6 5 4 3 2 1

For my family

and in memory of

Rose Sudman Goodheart
(Teleneshty, Russian Empire, 1905–Philadelphia, Pennsylvania, 1997),

who made America's history ours, too.

ARM'D year! year of the struggle!

No dainty rhymes or sentimental love verses for you, terrible
    year!

Not you as some pale poetling, seated at a desk, lisping cadenzas
    piano;

But as a strong man, erect, clothed in blue clothes, advancing,
    carrying a rifle on your shoulder,

With well-gristled body and sunburnt face and hands—with a
    knife in the belt at your side,

As I heard you shouting loud—your sonorous voice ringing
    across the continent;

Your masculine voice, O year, as rising amid the great cities,

Amid the men of Manhattan I saw you, as one of the workmen,
    the dwellers in Manhattan;

Or with large steps crossing the prairies out of Illinois and
    Indiana,

Rapidly crossing the West with springy gait, and descending the
    Alleghanies;

Or down from the great lakes, or in Pennsylvania, or on deck
    along the Ohio river;

Or southward along the Tennessee or Cumberland rivers, or at
    Chattanooga on the mountain top,

Saw I your gait and saw I your sinewy limbs, clothed in blue,
    bearing weapons, robust year;

Heard your determin'd voice, launch'd forth again and again;

Year that suddenly sang by the mouths of the round-lipp'd
    cannon,

I repeat you, hurrying, crashing, sad, distracted year.

—WALT WHITMAN, "1861"

It seems as if we were never alive till now; never had a country
till now.

—A YOUNG WOMAN IN NEW YORK WRITING
TO A FRIEND, MAY 1861

Contents

1·8·6·1

Storm flag of the United States garrison at Forts Moultrie and Sumter, 1860–61

A Banner at Daybreak

Then over all, (aye! aye!) my little and lengthen'd pennant
    shaped like a sword,
Runs swiftly up indicating war and defiance—and now the
    halyards have rais'd it,
Side of my banner broad and blue, side of my starry banner,
Discarding peace over all the sea and land.

—WALT WHITMAN,
"Song of the Banner at Day-Break" (1860–61)

Charleston Harbor, December 1860

NIGHT FELL AT LAST. Boats slipped off the beach, swift and almost silent, drawn by skilled oarsmen across the water. The rowers labored hatless and in shirtsleeves, breath visible in the chilly air, blue uniform coats draped over their muskets, concealing the glint of burnished iron. Somehow all three of their vessels eluded the patrolling steamers, crossing the broad belt of reflected moonlight at barely a hundred yards from the nearest one, then vanishing, undetected, into the gloom on the far side of the channel.

Only a few of their comrades had remained behind at the old citadel, working hour after hour in the darkness, attending to the final tasks. Last of all, they had been told, the towering flagstaff must come down. No easy task: it was well over a hundred feet tall and rooted deep in the earth, constructed to withstand shot and shell. As midnight passed and daybreak drew nearer, men toiled with saws at the rock-hard pitch pine, like woodsmen at the base of a great tree. They fastened ropes to guide its fall. The soldiers carefully arranged bags of gunpowder, placed the fuse, lit a match. With a splintering crack the staff snapped perfectly at the cut, toppled forward, and split again upon the parapet. It lay at the foot of the wall, irreparably broken.

The work was done. That morning, for the first time in half a century, the flag of the United States would not fly above Fort Moultrie.[1]

THE MAN WHO LED that dangerous transit had arrived in Charleston just five weeks earlier.

Major Robert Anderson had been sent to command the federal garrison at Moultrie, a stronghold at the tip of Sullivan's Island, just across the harbor from the city wharves. His official orders were to strengthen the harbor's defenses against the far-fetched possibility of an attack by Great Britain or France, but everybody knew this was a sham.[2] The real reason for his appointment had to do with the looming crisis threatening to split the country in half. Abraham Lincoln had been elected president just weeks earlier, and in response, the Southern states were moving quickly toward secession. It seemed certain that South Carolina would take the lead.

The three forts commanding Charleston Harbor—Fort Moultrie,

Fort Sumter, and Castle Pinckney—not only dominated the very hotbed of disloyalty but could also, if properly manned, instantly shut down the largest Southern port on the Atlantic seaboard. Most important, holding on to them would be a crucial symbolic statement to the nation and the world: the United States would not relinquish its grip on any federal property, nor on any of the states, without a fight. It would deal with secession as treason. If, however, it let the forts go peacefully, the national government would be sending quite a different message: that it was ready to negotiate with the aggrieved leaders of the slaveholding South, and perhaps even let the seceding states go peacefully as well. The new commander in Charleston Harbor had to be a dependable messenger—faithful and prompt—of either message, as circumstances might warrant.

The junior officers waiting to salute his arrival could have been forgiven if their first sight of Anderson, as he stepped gingerly from a small launch onto Moultrie's wharf, failed to inspire great confidence. Everything about their new commander seemed middling: he was a man in his fifties, of midlevel rank, medium height, and moderate demeanor; mild-mannered, nondescriptly handsome—the sort who left few vivid impressions even on those who had known him well. (None, surely, could have guessed that women would soon beg for locks of that meticulously combed gray hair; that woodcuts of that bland, impassive face would appear on the front pages of magazines on both sides of the Atlantic.) A scrupulous, methodical man, he was known in the service mainly for having translated certain French artillery textbooks into English. And yet here was the person to whom the United States government had just entrusted one of the most delicate military and political assignments in American history.[3]

Anderson was, moreover, a Southerner who had grown up with slavery, and whose family included strong partisans for the South. Nearly all of the staff officers at Moultrie happened to be from the North. They included men like Captain Abner Doubleday, a New Yorker and a radical by army standards. The mustachioed, barrel-chested Doubleday considered himself a thoroughly modern man, unencumbered by the cheap affectations of honor and chivalry with which so many officers still bedecked themselves. Not one to keep his opinions to himself, he unabashedly opposed slavery and had voted for Lincoln. (He was probably the only man within two hundred miles of the Charleston Battery who would admit aloud to having done so.) He relished being hissed in the streets as a "Black Republican" when his official duties took him over the water to downtown Charleston. The fort's other company captain was a lean, introspective Yankee named Truman Seymour, son of a Methodist minister from Vermont.

Anderson had no reputation as a fire-breathing secessionist. Nor were Doubleday and Seymour the kind of men to question the honor of a superior officer—at least openly. But would a man of his background and temperament be ready to wrestle the Southerners into submission, if it came to that?

Not that the federal force at Charleston appeared capable, as yet, of much coercion. Luckily for the founding fathers of the nascent Republic of South Carolina, Anderson's three federal citadels "guarded" the harbor in only the most figurative sense. Waiting on Moultrie's parade ground to welcome Anderson was a tiny detachment of soldiers that could scarcely be termed even a garrison: just two companies of barely thirty men each, not counting a small brass band. Sumter, in the harbor's mouth, lay unfinished after decades of start-and-stop construction, and housed just a few military engineers supervising some civilian workmen. Castle Pinckney, whose guns overlooked the town itself, was manned by a single ordnance sergeant.[4]

And even if Moultrie, the Charleston post's official headquarters, had been garrisoned with hundreds of men rather than a few dozen, it wouldn't have been much of a stronghold.

During the Revolution, the fort had been the site of a famous American victory. In the summer of 1776, just a few days before the passage of the Declaration of Independence, a single regiment of South Carolina troops held it against an entire fleet; British cannonballs sank harmlessly into its fibrous palmetto-log ramparts while the American artillerymen exacted a terrible toll on enemy officers and sailors. (South Carolinians adopted the palmetto tree as their state symbol shortly after the battered enemy turned tail.) That victory at Moultrie—a thousand miles south of the previous American triumphs at Boston—was celebrated throughout the newborn United States, and was seen by many Americans as a sign, perhaps even a heaven-sent portent, that the loose concatenation of former colonies could stand together as one nation.[5]

But by 1860, no foreign power had sent its fleets against America's coastline in almost two generations. Moultrie's defenses, built early in the century atop the old palmetto fort, were antiquated, its brick walls cracked and eroding. Sand drifts nearly buried its outer fortifications; stray cows from nearby farms could—and occasionally did—wander across the ramparts.[6] Moreover, the southern end of Sullivan's Island had become a fashionable beach resort in recent decades. Wealthy

Charlestonians had built summer cottages among the sand dunes overlooking the fort, and on pleasant evenings would saunter through its open gates to promenade on the parade ground with wives and sweethearts. It was clear to everyone, from Anderson down to his last private, that the place was about as defensible as a public park.[7]

Nonetheless, as November turned into December, it also became clearer and clearer that Moultrie might soon need to be defended—and from attackers based not in the mouth of Charleston Harbor, toward which the fort's gun platforms faced, but onshore. When the new commander arrived, South Carolina's legislature had just unanimously passed a resolution calling for a statewide convention to discuss secession, and local militia had placed the U.S. military arsenal in town under guard, ostensibly to defend it in case of a slave revolt.[8] On November 29, the *Charleston Mercury* published a draft ordinance of secession.[9] Visiting the city daily to procure fresh provisions, the men of the Moultrie garrison heard bands playing "La Marseillaise," and saw the streets draped with banners bearing slogans like "Good-bye, Yankee Doodle" and "Let Us Bury the Union's Dead Carcass."[10] The state's governor was whipping up excitement with talk of the glorious future that awaited an independent South Carolina—promising laws that would reopen the African slave trade, officially declare white men the ruling race, and punish "summarily and severely, if not with death" any person caught espousing abolitionist views.

Charleston was filling up with militiamen who drilled under the state flag—a white banner with a palmetto tree and single red star—and spoke openly of hauling down the Stars and Stripes, which flew above the harbor fortifications.[11] On December 1, a rumor reached the garrison that South Carolina was about to place artillery just across Sullivan's Island, pointing directly at Moultrie.[12]

In letters and telegrams to their superiors back at the War Department, Anderson and his staff described their increasingly desperate situation in the tones of cool appraisal befitting seasoned officers. If they were to hold on to Charleston Harbor, additional troops, ammunition, and supplies were needed immediately. Fort Moultrie must be reinforced, and the two other federal strongholds in the harbor—Fort Sumter and Castle Pinckney—garrisoned with soldiers loyal to the United States. The sand hills looming just yards from Moultrie's walls must be leveled, or they could quickly become nests of sharpshooters who could pick off the men inside, one by one, in a matter of hours.[13]

Replies from Washington were dilatory, vague, and ambivalent. More troops would be sent—at some point. The garrison's officers must prepare to defend Moultrie as best they could—but not touch the sand hills, which were believed to be private property. (They weren't, in fact.) Above all, they must not do anything that the hot-tempered South Carolinians might find provocative—a category that seemed to include almost any action whatsoever that the little band of men might take.[14]

The U.S. forts in Charleston Harbor were ground zero in the exploding secession crisis, yet no one at the War Department seemed to be taking their defense seriously. In fact, the garrison's only direct communication from the secretary of war lately had been a one-sentence telegram ordering them to return a few dozen muskets that Seymour had managed to extract from the federal arsenal in Charleston.[15]

Curiously enough, the only measure that the War Department fully supported was an all-out effort to buttress the fortifications themselves. Nearly a quarter of a million dollars was allocated to the building project, and throughout the autumn more than a hundred laborers, many of them Irish and German immigrants brought down from Baltimore, toiled busily at Sumter, rapidly completing the officers' quarters, raising the height of the walls, and readying the upper tiers of the fort to support cannons. Back at Moultrie, an even larger group dug ditches, built makeshift gun platforms, and cleared sand from the outer walls—discovering, in the process, quite a few cannonballs that had been casually mislaid over the years. Anderson sent a third detachment of the civilian workers over to Castle Pinckney to commence repairs, on the assumption that Washington would soon send enough troops to man all three forts.[16] This construction further infuriated many Charlestonians, who assumed that the Yankees were preparing to bombard their city. Bands of secessionists now patrolled day and night outside Moultrie, itching for any pretext to commence hostilities. The little garrison was stretched so thin that officers' wives were taking shifts on guard duty.[17] And still no reinforcements came.

What Anderson and his men didn't realize is that the secretary of war was playing a double game—or at least would shed no tears if their citadel fell to the rebels. John B. Floyd was a former governor of Virginia firmly aligned with states' rights and the South—within a few months, he would wear the uniform of a Confederate brigadier general. Since his appointment by President James Buchanan, the War Department had become a den of graft and peculation, his staff entangled in an under-the-table scheme funneling government money held in trust for Indians into the pocket of a crooked military contractor.[18]

Afterward, it would remain unclear if Floyd had been involved in the scheme himself, or if he had simply allowed it to happen out of innocent laziness and incompetence.

So, too, his response—or lack of response—to the Sumter crisis may have been rooted in treasonous tendencies, or may have been due to simple indifference. In the Charleston predicament, Secretary Floyd may have seen an opportunity: if no troops were sent to man the three harbor forts, no amount of sprucing up would prevent their tumbling into the laps of the South Carolinians. That way, the three citadels would be in tiptop shape, at the expense of the U.S. government, just in time to protect Charleston from any federal fleet that might come steaming down to crush the rebellion. (This was what Doubleday would later come to believe.)[19] Or he may simply have wished to passively let the situation drift along, sparing himself the mess, unpleasantness, and extra work that might come from more decisive action. Either way, the result would be the same.

In fact, the reason Floyd had dispatched Anderson to Moultrie in the first place was his expectation that the major would not raise any sort of fuss. Anderson, a Virginian by ancestry and a Kentuckian by birth, was known to sympathize with the grievances of Southern slaveholders. His wife, a more ardent Southerner, was the daughter of one of Georgia's wealthiest rice planters; she and the major had recently sold off most or all of her inherited slaves and their progeny, causing him once to quip that "the increase of her darkies" had made him rich.[20] Nor did the major appear to be the sort to attempt an inconvenient act of heroism. When Floyd plucked Anderson out of the middle ranks of the officer corps for the Charleston appointment, he was serving on a commission to revise the curriculum at West Point, where he had once been an instructor. Anderson's rigid deference to military duty was, as everyone in the service knew, exceeded only by his Christian piety.[21]

Even the junior officers at Moultrie were at times beginning to suspect their new commander of disloyalty to the Union or simple lack of backbone—not that it was clear what even a loyal stalwart could have done without more arms and men. Their best tactical move, Doubleday and Seymour knew, would be to occupy Castle Pinckney, where they could easily bring Charleston to heel by lobbing artillery shells into the city at close range. But, as Doubleday put it sardonically, "with only sixty-four soldiers and a brass band, we could not detach any force in that direction."[22] Pinckney lay more than three miles across the harbor from Moultrie, a stone's throw from the downtown promenade known as the Battery, with its high row of fine mansions that housed many of Charleston's wealthiest citizens—and its leading secessionists. Even under cover of darkness, there was no way that Anderson's men could make it there without being intercepted.

Their other option was Fort Sumter. Sumter sat on its own artificial island—a sturdy pedestal of granite boulders, hewn from the quarries of New England—just inside the narrowest part of the harbor's mouth, alongside the main ship channel. Though still unfinished after decades of fitful progress, because no one had expected that Charleston Harbor would ever again become a key strategic point, its 360-degree view of the surrounding water made it more or less impregnable to sneak attack, and its high brick walls, designed by the Army Corps of Engineers to withstand modern artillery fire, were much more formidable than Moultrie's. Its armaments included a fearsome array of heavy mortars and columbiads, the bulbous ten-ton cannons that could hurl a heavy projectile as far as three miles—though many of these guns still lay dismounted and inoperable beneath the unfinished gun platforms. Sumter's location in the port's tight entrance, with land close by in three directions, might make it vulnerable to shot and shell fired from batteries onshore: the fort's builders, like Moultrie's, had never anticipated the need to defend against an attack from "friendly" territory. But that position, however vulnerable, did command the shipping lane. Most critical of all, Fort Sumter lay barely a mile from Moultrie—just close enough that the garrison might, with a bit of luck, slip across under the secessionists' noses.

The junior officers, Doubleday most of all, pleaded with their commander to make that move. Anderson dug his heels in and refused. The War Department had assigned him to Fort Moultrie, he said, and he would not budge without an official order to do so. The officers pointed out that if the Carolinians themselves occupied Sumter—which they might do at any moment without so much as firing a shot—its columbiads turned against Moultrie could pound the old fort's walls into rubble. Still the major blandly demurred. His resistance seemed incredible. Any captain or lieutenant in the army was used to dealing with the stubbornness or even stupidity of his superiors, but Anderson's position defied common sense, as well as basic principles of military science that he had taught at West Point. Worse yet, in the event of forced surrender, the power and prestige of the entire army—perhaps even the entire national government—might be sacrificed to a few thuggish traitors.

In bewilderment, the staff officers returned to overseeing the ceaseless—and, it seemed, pointless—work of digging sand away from the walls, building picket fences, and moving cannons from one place to another.[23] Occasionally Captain Doubleday would relieve his frustration by loading a howitzer with double rounds of canister shot, pointing it out to sea, and blasting a furious volley against the insolent Southern waves. It was the only thing he could do.

Just before sundown on December 20, the rooftops and church steeples of Charleston lit up with flashes of red, as the reflected lights of bonfires and Roman candles flared amid the gathering darkness. From across the harbor, the soldiers at Moultrie could hear booming cannons and pealing bells. The city was celebrating. Delegates to the Convention of the People of South Carolina, meeting downtown in St. Andrew's Hall, had voted unanimously that afternoon to approve a resolution: "The Union now subsisting between South Carolina and other states, under the name of the 'United States of America,' is hereby dissolved."

Almost immediately afterward, the Convention took up another pressing matter: what should be done about "the property of the United States"—now considered a foreign nation—"in South Carolina." This referred especially, everyone knew, to the three harbor forts.

One of Moultrie's officers, Assistant Surgeon Samuel Wylie Crawford, was in the city on the historic day. He even made his way into the Convention itself, where he took note of a gavel on the Speaker's desk with the word SECESSION cut deep into it in black letters. In the streets he saw almost every hat sporting palmetto leaves or a blue secession cockade, and almost every shop and house flying a palmetto flag. There were also, as he would recall years later, "coarse representations on canvas" crudely allegorizing the politics of the moment: one portrayed the detestable old rail-splitter himself, Abraham Lincoln, wielding his axe ineffectually against a stout palmetto log, while another "showed the anticipated prosperity of Charleston, the wharves crowded with cotton bales and negroes."[24]

Still, Crawford discovered, very few of the patricians who had led the charge toward secession actually wanted all-out war. Rabble-rousing newspaper editors, upcountry militiamen, and assorted urban rowdies might clamor for the chance to shed Yankee blood, and even take a few potshots at Fort Moultrie, but most worldly men of good sense believed that the South should, and eventually would, be left to go in peace. There would be heated talk on both sides, negotiation, some gentle—or, if necessary, not so gentle—arm-twisting, but in the end, frock-coated dignitaries of the North and of the South would come to an understanding, and the federal garrison in Charleston Harbor would board a government steamer and vanish conveniently into the wide Atlantic. Indeed, some of the South's best statesmen were already in Washington, working discreetly toward just such a resolution.

Yet it was also obvious to Crawford that Charlestonians were doing a collective war dance. The city's streets were filled with men in militia uniforms, from young recruits performing their first musket drills to old colonels, buttoned laboriously into epauletted tunics they had last worn twenty years before. "Military organizations marched in every direction, the music of their bands lost amid the shouts of the people," Crawford later wrote.[25] There could not have been a greater contrast with the lassitude and bureaucratic foot-dragging of the "loyal" commanders back in Washington.

Across the water on Sullivan's Island, the noose seemed to be drawing tighter. Word came that the harbor pilots of Charleston were all made to swear an oath that they would not bring any U.S. government vessel into port, lest it be carrying reinforcements. Steamers manned by secessionist militia—each with more men aboard than were in the entire federal garrison—patrolled the harbor every night, their dark silhouettes visible from the parapets of Moultrie.

For each of the fort's officers, these days of anxiety and frustration were also tinged with melancholy. Trained to defend their nation against its foreign enemies, they now faced siege and possible attack by their own countrymen. Whatever might be the outcome of the present crisis, the nation they had grown up in already seemed irretrievably lost. Not long after the secession vote, an elderly South Carolina statesman, Judge James L. Petigru (born days after George Washington's inauguration), came across the harbor to bid a sad farewell to the garrison, and, by proxy, to the United States of America. Doubleday went down to the wharf to greet the old man. "The tears rolled down his cheeks," the Yankee captain later recalled, "as he deplored the folly and the madness of the times."[26*]

And all the while, just across the water—so close that you could almost touch it—loomed the commanding citadel of Sumter, seeming to represent all that Doubleday and his comrades longed for: Safety. Honor. Perhaps even, in the end, victory. The junior officers redoubled their pleas. Their commander, as ever, refused to budge.

What the junior officers didn't know is that beneath his inscrutable gray exterior, the major was as frustrated as any of his men. Since the

---

*Not long earlier, Petigru had been asked by a Charlestonian whether he intended to join the secession movement. "I should think not!" the judge replied. "South Carolina is too small for a republic, and too large for a lunatic-asylum."

third day after his arrival, Anderson had been barraging Washington with ever-more-urgent letters and telegrams, pleading with his superiors for orders to make just such a move. It was as obvious to him as to anyone that an attack on Moultrie could end only in a humiliating surrender or the wholesale slaughter of his force. The War Department sent cursory replies, blithely assuring him that no assault on Moultrie was imminent—this despite the shrill war cries in almost every newspaper of the South—but that if one were, he was, of course, to defend it "to the best of your ability." On December 23, an adjutant arrived with a two-paragraph letter from the secretary of war himself, the first time that Floyd had deigned to communicate directly with Anderson.

Writing on the morning after secession became official, the secretary wished to clarify—in strictest confidence—Anderson's previous instructions. While the major ought to defend himself if attacked, he must not take this to mean that he should sacrifice his men's lives "upon a mere point of honor." Indeed, it was neither wished nor expected in Washington that Anderson should undertake "a hopeless conflict in defense of these forts." Floyd continued: "If they are invested or attacked by a force so superior that resistance would, in your judgment, be a useless waste of life, it will be your duty to yield to necessity, and make the best terms [of surrender] in your power. This will be the conduct of an honorable, brave, and humane officer, and you will be fully justified in such action."[27]

Floyd's meaning was unmistakable. If Anderson were threatened directly by any military force stronger than his own contingent of sixty-four men and a brass band, he was free to surrender all of Charleston Harbor without firing a shot. Perhaps the letter even assumed that Anderson, a good Southerner, would be happy to do so. Between the lines, Floyd could almost be seen winking.

But the secretary of war had misjudged his man.

To the civilian Floyd, Anderson looked like a reliably obedient officer, and he was. But even more, he was a career soldier. The middle-aged bureaucrat had—although he rarely spoke of it—fought against Black Hawk and the Seminoles, and marched on Mexico City under General Scott, in that glorious advance from the shores of the Gulf to the Halls of Montezuma. At Molino del Rey, nearly at the gates of the enemy capital, he had charged the Mexican lines and taken a bullet in the shoulder, leading his outnumbered regiment through another two hours of battle before collapsing from loss of blood.[28] Such perils came all in the due course of military life, as they had also done for Anderson's father, a soldier of the American Revolution who had defended the old palmetto fort right here at Moultrie more than eighty years ago. Anderson had seen secretaries of war come and go—and he must certainly have known a good deal, mostly unflattering, about this particular one—but he also knew that acts of courage or cowardice on the battlefield echoed down through generations.

It would be one thing if President Buchanan had simply announced that he was withdrawing the troops from Charleston Harbor and turning the forts over to South Carolina, a decision that Anderson would certainly have obeyed, perhaps even welcomed. But he would be damned if he was to surrender—even worse, perform a shabby pantomime of surrender—before a rabble of whiskey-soaked militiamen and canting politicians. Still, an officer's orders were his orders. Anderson felt trapped.

But after poring untold hours over Floyd's infuriating letter, he suddenly saw a window—a narrow one, but perhaps a way out. One might say it was not Anderson the gallant soldier who noticed it but rather Anderson the meticulous academic and scrupulous translator. Floyd had told Anderson to mount no hopeless defense of the *forts*, plural. This was possibly just a slip of the pen: the secretary was not known for verbal precision. But it could also be construed to mean that Anderson and his men were responsible for defending all three of the forts, not just Moultrie. In that case, a move from one to another would be no violation of orders, merely a slight tactical shift, like wheeling a cannon to a different side of the battlements. Nowhere in the previous orders had Floyd or his adjutants directly commanded Anderson *not* to occupy Sumter. They had merely ignored his pleas to do so.

It must have been just after Anderson's small epiphany that the sharp-eyed Captain Doubleday noticed something odd. He was out on Moultrie's parapet with his commander, discussing the need to purchase some wire to make an entanglement at the base of the fort's walls. "Certainly; you shall have a mile of wire, if you require it," Anderson replied—but in such a peculiar, distracted way that it was clear the major was no longer thinking much about Moultrie at all.[29]

Anderson now sent his quartermaster over to the city to charter some boats, ostensibly to carry the fort's women and children out of harm's way. (Many of the men had their families living with them.) On Christmas Day, all hands at the fort were kept busy loading supplies aboard, on the pretext that these were only the families' effects and necessary supplies. A couple of local citizens showed up at the wharf to watch the preparations—incredibly enough, civilians were still permitted to wander freely into and out of the fort, perhaps because suddenly barring them would have put the secession forces on alert—and became suspicious when they saw a crate marked "1,000 ball cartridges" being stowed aboard. They were quickly assured that this had been just an error, and left after seeing the box off-loaded again.[30]

On the 26th, just as the sun was setting, Anderson gave his officers and men twenty minutes to gather up whatever personal possessions they could and board the boats. He ordered the guns of Moultrie to be aimed at the passage to Sumter, ready to sink any vessel that might attempt an interception. The major left a small rear guard, with instructions that once the rest of the garrison was safely across, it should spike the cannons (that is, hammer spikes into the touchholes so that they couldn't be fired), burn the gun carriages, and finally cut down the flagpole so that nothing but the Stars and Stripes could ever fly upon it. Then Anderson himself took the folded garrison flag and, tucking it snugly under his arm, stepped aboard.[31]

The next morning, astonished Charlestonians saw smoke from the smoldering gun carriages curling into the clear air above Moultrie. At Castle Pinckney, secessionist riflemen stormed the all-but-abandoned fort.[32] In Washington, Secretary Floyd was already dictating a furious telegram.

But by noon at Sumter, a flag—the one Anderson had carried with him from his father's old fort—was raised upon a new staff. It hung limp for a moment before the wind stirred life into its folds. Then it unfurled itself, the red stripes of war and white stars of union, a banner defiant.

IN THE SUMMER OF 2008, in a crumbling plantation house on the Eastern Shore of Maryland, my students and I discovered an attic full of family papers spanning thirteen generations of the owners' family—more than three hundred years of American history. There were land deeds in the spidery handwriting of the seventeenth century, from the earliest years of the colonial settlement. There was business correspondence about a slave purchase in Philadelphia during the American Revolution, transacted as the Continental Congress was meeting just a few blocks away in Independence Hall. But what fascinated me the most was a small bundle of old documents, wrapped in paper and bound up tightly with a faded yellow silk ribbon that clearly had not been untied in more than a century. On the outside of the wrapper was a date: 1861.

Carefully untying the ribbon and opening the wrapper's stiff folds, we found a series of private letters written in the spring of that year. They involved a member of the family, a career officer in the U.S. Army stationed at a remote fort in the Indian territory of the far West. Writing to his wife and brother back East, the major agonized over which side he should choose in the impending conflict. He was a Southerner and a slaveholder—yet in his heart of hearts he looked forward to the day when slavery would end. He was a close friend of Jefferson Davis's; had been at the Academy with Robert E. Lee—yet could he betray the flag under which he had served ever since that remote day when, at the age of fourteen, he had first donned the scratchy gray uniform of a West Point cadet?

In the end, the major chose to stand by his country. In the process of deciding on that course, though, he had to wrestle with many different questions—and not simply those of honor, patriotism, and politics. What would his choice of allegiance mean for his family, for his friendships, for his ancestral farm, for his career? Whichever side prevailed in the war, the nation was clearly about to change forever: what kind of country did he want to live in, what kind of country would he want for his children? "It is like a great game of chance," his wife wrote. The urgent exchange of letters brought out tensions among his loved ones, too, as the major tried to assimiliate conflicting reports and advice from two thousand miles away. His wife, a Northerner, had one set of ideas; his plantation-owning brother had another.[33]

Reading those letters, across the distance of almost a century and a half, gave me a new appreciation of how history is decided not just on battlefields and in cabinet meetings, but in individual hearts and minds. The Civil War had fascinated me since I was a teenager, but most of the books about it seemed to dwell on whose cavalry went charging over which hill. (One historian has described this approach as treating the war like "a great military Super Bowl contest between Blue and Gray heroes.")[34] Or else they treated American society as a collection of broadly defined groups—"the North," "the South," "the slaves"—each one mechanically obeying a set of sociological and ideological rules.

I realized I already knew from my own experience that this isn't the way history works. On September 11, 2001, I had observed how everyone I knew responded to the terrorist attacks in his or her own way. The responses didn't derive simply from whether someone was liberal or conservative, Republican or Democrat. They also depended on a whole complicated set of personal convictions, fears, character traits, religious beliefs. They depended on where people came from, where they lived, and where they had traveled. On how and where people had experienced the day of the attacks itself. And all these complications influenced not just ordinary people but also those I knew who worked in the media and in government. Presumably they influenced the nation's leaders, as well.

In fact, the startling events in New York and Washington hadn't simply changed the course of future history, they had shaken up old categories and assumptions. In a way, they had changed the past just as much as the future; rewritten not only our expectation of what was to come but also our sense of what had gone before. For a brief moment, in a most terrifying and thrilling way, anything seemed possible. The only certainty was the one expressed by a family member of mine phoning an hour or so after the first plane hit, one that no doubt occurred to countless others: "The world is never going to be the same again."

When, seven years later, I came across that bundle of old letters, I realized that this very sense was what was missing from my understanding of the Civil War. I wanted to learn more about how Americans—both ordinary citizens and national leaders— experienced and responded to a moment of sudden crisis and change as it unfolded. I especially wanted to understand how that moment ended up giving birth to a new and better nation. I wanted to know about the people who responded to that moment not just with anger and panic but with hope and determination, people who, amid the ruins of the country they had grown up in, saw an opportunity to change history.

LIKE SO MUCH ELSE about the beginning of the Civil War, Major Anderson's move from Fort Moultrie to Fort Sumter is largely forgotten today. At the time, however, the little garrison's mile-long journey was seen not just as a masterstroke of military cunning but as the opening scene of a great and terrible national drama. "War has begun," one correspondent telegraphed from South Carolina. "Major Robert Anderson," thundered the *Charleston Courier*, "has achieved the unenviable distinction of opening civil war between American citizens by a gross breach of faith."[35] Northerners, meanwhile, held enormous public banquets in Anderson's honor; cannons fired salutes in New York, Chicago, Boston, and dozens of other cities and towns.[36]

And considered in retrospect, Anderson's move seems freighted with even more symbolism. He lowered his flag on an old fortress, hallowed by the past, yet half ruined—and then raised it upon a new one, still unfinished, yet stronger, bedded in New England granite. That folded banner's crossing of Charleston Harbor foreshadowed another defiant journey ahead, longer and more perilous: from the old America to a new one.

Twenty years after the war, when officials at the War Department began preparing the *Official History of the War of the Rebellion*, a massive compilation of documents that would eventually grow to more than two hundred thousand pages,[37] the first of all the innumerable documents that they included was Anderson's brisk telegram announcing his arrival at Sumter. Nineteenth-century historians knew that without this event, the war might not have happened. A remarkable thing about Anderson's move, too, is that it was no calculated act of heroism or symbolism—much less the intentional commencement of a revolution. It was, indeed, motivated by the major's deep conservatism, by his desire to preserve his honor and his garrison. And yet its results were revolutionary; it ended up touching off a series of events whose repercussions would be incalculable.

When the saga of the Civil War is recounted now, it usually begins four months later, when the Confederate batteries at Charleston finally opened fire. That's the version that I, and probably most people, grew up with, and it's a good story, too. Yet it's also one that turns the Union side into simply the passive target of the Confederacy's aggression. It glorifies the "lost cause" at the expense of the one that would win. It elevates a moment when war was already a fait accompli, with Americans on both sides simply awaiting the opening guns.

The Civil War story told in this book begins with the raising of a Union flag, not the firing of a Confederate shot. The war described here was not just a Southern rebellion but a nationwide revolution—fought even from within the seceding states—for freedom. And while the South's rebellion failed, with the Confederacy fated to become a historical dead end, this revolution—our second as a people—reinvented America, and a century and a half later still defines much of our national character. It was a revolution that engaged both the nation's progressive impulses and, at the same time, some of its profoundly conservative tendencies: many Americans saw it as a struggle to create new freedoms, many others as an effort to preserve a cherished legacy.[38] But in the end, the outcome would be the same. Swept away forever would be the older America, a nation stranded halfway between its love of freedom and its accommodation of slavery, mired for decades in policies of appeasement and compromise.

· · ·

WALT WHITMAN FAMOUSLY WROTE that the "real war," by which he meant the squalor of hospitals and blood-drenched battlefields, would never make it into the history books. It was the heroism of the Union cause, he assumed, that would carry down through the generations.

Yet, if anything, the war's squalor is remembered today while its heroism, in the truest and most complicated sense of the term, has been gradually erased. Books and documentaries dwell on the blood and filth, the bloating bodies on the fields of Antietam, the sons and brothers lost. If heroism is to be measured by human suffering, surely both Northerners and Southerners were heroes in equal measure—indeed, by that measure, the South was probably more heroic. It is also intellectually fashionable to deprecate the Union cause, at least so far as it relates to slavery and race: to point out the casual racism of everyone from lowly infantrymen up to President Lincoln himself; to say that the Emancipation Proclamation was simply a convenient military stratagem; to repeat the truism that the Civil War began not as a war to abolish slavery but as a war to save the Union. It is also common for historians to say that soldiers went to war in the spring of 1861 "more or less on a lark," to quote one I recently spoke with. But people do not often go to war—much less against their own countrymen—on a lark.

Men and women at the time, on both sides of the conflict, did understand it as a war against slavery, even before it began. This is clear from what they said and wrote.

An important distinction must be drawn here: a war against slavery did not necessarily mean a war for abolition, at least not in 1861, or not for everybody. It did mean, though, that many white Northerners and even some white Southerners were ready to say *Enough*. Enough compromise of principles; enough betrayal of people and ideals; enough cruelty; enough gradual surrender of what had been won in 1776. The war represented the overdue effort to sort out the double legacy of America's founders: the uneasy marriage of the Declaration's inspired ideals with the Constitution's ingenious expedients.

Just as impressive, or more so, was the heroism of black men, women, and even children who were ready not just to be free but also to become citizens. They were partners, and sometimes leaders, in the project to reinvent their country—a project that was still incomplete at the end of the Civil War, but which had been even less complete at the close of the Revolution. The fact that these former slaves and children of slaves were ready to make it *their* project, to make it *their* country—almost from the moment that hostilities began—was perhaps the most strange and wonderful thing to come out of the war.

Americans today find it fairly easy to fathom the idea that there was a right side and a wrong side in World War II, a side that stood for freedom and a side that stood against it. It is possible to accept this even while acknowledging that both sides committed atrocities; that most Axis soldiers did not go to war in order to exterminate other races, nor most Allied soldiers to save them; and that in 1941, casual anti-Semitism was probably taken for granted among many GIs, as it also was in the clubby Anglo-Saxon milieu of Roosevelt and Churchill.

We find it harder, though—much harder than most people did in the 1860s—to accept that there was a right side and a wrong side in our own Civil War. It is difficult to fathom that millions of Americans could have fought as enemies of America. It is even harder to accept this when we come to realize that in some senses the Civil War really was, as some defiant Southerners still call it, a "War of Northern Aggression."

Most accounts of the months leading up to war focus tightly on the parallel dramas in Charleston and Washington, as the clocks ticked away the last opportunities for peace. This is indeed an important, even essential, part of the story. But to get the full story of that moment in American history, it is necessary to go much farther afield: to the slums of Manhattan and the drawing rooms of Boston, to Ohio villages and Virginia slave cabins, and even to the shores of the Pacific. It is also necessary to consider people and ideas that were migrating from the Old World to the New. It is only then that this defining national event can truly be understood as a revolution, and one whose heroes were not only the soldiers and politicians.

That revolution began years before the first guns opened, as a gradual change in the hearts and minds of men and women, until suddenly, in the months before the attack on Sumter, this transformation attained irresistible momentum. One person at a time, millions of Americans decided in 1861—as their grandparents had in 1776—that it was worth risking everything, their lives and fortunes, on their country. Not just on its present reality, either, not on something so solid; but on a vision of what its future could be and what its past had meant.

Eighteen sixty-one, like 1776, was—and still is—not just a year, but an idea.

*   •   •

WALT WHITMAN UNDERSTOOD THIS, probably even before the actual year 1861 began. Sometime in mid-1860, when the war clouds were gathering, still distant, on the horizon, he sat down to write a singularly prophetic poem.

"Song of the Banner at Day-Break" is a mystical, surreal vision, an American version of Ezekiel's wheel turning in the sky. Instead of a fiery wheel, though, floating in Whitman's sky is the American flag. What does it stand for? asks the poet. Is it simply a piece of fabric? Is it an emblem of America's prosperity, of the banks and merchant houses that make the nation "envied by all the earth"? Is it a banner of war? Then the truth is revealed as the poet looks up to see the flag become an apparition of things soon to come:

> I hear and see not strips of cloth alone,
> I hear the tramp of armies, I hear the challenging sentry,
> I hear the jubilant shouts of millions of men, I hear Liberty!
> I hear the drums beat and the trumpets blowing . . .
> O you up there! O pennant! where you undulate like a snake hissing so curious,
> Out of reach, an idea only, yet furiously fought for, risking bloody death, loved by me!
> So loved—O you banner leading the day, with stars brought from the night!
> Valueless, object of eyes, over all and demanding all—O banner and pennant!
> I too leave the rest—great as it is, it is nothing—houses, machines are nothing—I see them not;
> I see but you, O warlike pennant!—O banner so broad, with stripes, I sing you only,
> Flapping up there in the wind.

Though the poem is little read today, the poet himself cherished it almost from the moment he wrote it. Whitman originally intended to publish a book early in 1861 titled *The Banner at Day-Break*, with this strange prophecy leading off the volume. His publishers unexpectedly went bankrupt and the book never appeared. But Whitman, as was his custom, continued writing and rewriting the poem, at least until the country's centennial year of 1876.

Another flag raising, that at Sumter on a chill December morning, also embodies the second American Revolution. Before that day, the flag had served mostly as a military ensign or a convenient marking of American territory, flown from forts, embassies, and ships, and displayed on special occasions like the Fourth of July. But in the weeks after Major Anderson's surprising stand, it became something different. Suddenly the Stars and Stripes flew—as it does today, and especially as it did after September 11, 2001—from houses, from storefronts, from churches; above village greens and college quads. For the first time, American flags were mass-produced rather than individually stitched, and even so, manufacturers could not keep up with demand.[39]

As the long winter of 1861 turned into spring, that old flag meant something new. The abstraction of the Union cause was transfigured into a physical thing: strips of cloth that millions of people would fight for, and many thousands die for.[40]

This book, like Whitman's poem, tells a story foreshadowing things to come. It is not a Civil War saga of hallowed battlefields drenched in blood, much less of which general's cavalry came charging over which hill. It is a story, rather, of a moment in our country's history when almost everything hung in the balance.

It is a story of how some people clung to the past, while others sought the future; how a new generation of Americans arose to throw aside the cautious ways of its parents and embrace the revolutionary ideals of its grandparents. The battleground of that struggle was not one orchard or wheat field, but the quickly growing country itself.

CHAPTER ONE

Wide Awake

Enough, the Centenarian's story ends,
The two, the past and present, have interchanged . . .

—WALT WHITMAN,
"The Centenarian's Story" (1861)

Ralph Farnham, age 102, 1858   Lincoln Wide Awake, 1860

Boston, October 1860

ON A FINE AFTERNOON in the last autumn of the old republic, an ancient man stepped haltingly onto the platform of the Boston & Maine Railroad depot and peered about him with watery eyes. Ralph Farnham was 104 years old, but besides this extraordinary achievement, he had—at least since young manhood—led an unremarkable life. He had boarded the train that morning near the small farm in southern Maine from whose steep and stony fields he had eked out his subsistence for the past eighty years. Like thousands of other hardscrabble New England farmers, Old Uncle Farnham (as all his neighbors called him) woke every day before dawn, went to bed at dusk, and in the hours between lived a life that varied only according to the demands of the changing seasons. He had not been to Boston in many, many years.

Now, squinting into the shadowy dimness of the station, he could see figures moving all around him; feel them clasping his hands; hear them calling his name. "Give us your hat, sir," someone close by cried out, and as he uncertainly proffered it toward whoever had spoken, he felt it grow suddenly heavier in his grasp as coins were dropped in from all sides, weighting it with silver and even gold. As news of his arrival rippled through the crowd, the cheers grew louder, echoing up and down the length of the cavernous train shed and even from the sunlit square beyond: "Hurrah! Hurrah for the last hero of Bunker Hill!"

Old Uncle Farnham did not tell them—had he tried to, would any have listened?—that he had not actually *fought* at Bunker Hill, had not even fired a shot, having simply watched from a mile's distance, as a green eighteen-year-old recruit, while the smoke of the minutemen's volleys drifted across Charlestown Neck. Ever since a Boston paper had "discovered" his existence that summer—as if he were one of Mr. Barnum's rare beasts!—the writers had embellished his military career more and more, until, as they would tell it, he had practically fended off General Howe's grenadiers single-handed. And what of it? People wanted Revolutionary heroes, and Old Uncle Farnham would oblige them. He would even, at their insistence, get on the train and come to Boston. It seemed suddenly so important to everybody.[1]

Indeed, all across the country that autumn, Americans were almost desperate for heroes, old or new, and for a renewed connection to their glorious past. The quickly dwindling ranks of General Washington's comrades-in-arms seemed to herald a larger loss: it was as though the last faint rays of the nation's sunny youth were disappearing into the horizon. Over the past few decades, more and more Americans had come to share a sense that the nation's leaders, and even its common citizens, had declined shamefully since the founding era, a race of giants giving way to dwarfish petty politicians and shopkeepers. As early as 1822, nineteen-year-old Ralph Waldo Emerson, writing to his brother on the eve of Independence Day, quipped cynically that his countrymen had marched forward since the Revolution "to strength, to honor, and at last to ennui."[2] In the ensuing years, more and more would come to share such feelings. In 1855, one magazine writer lamented that "the chair of Washington and Jefferson has come to be occupied by a Tyler and a Pierce." He continued:

> The dream that this young land, fresh from the hands of its
> Creator, unpolluted by the stains of time, should be the home
> of freedom and the race of men so manly that they would lift
> the earth by the whole breadth of its orbit nearer heaven . . .
> has passed away from the most of us, as nothing but a dream.
> We yield ourselves, instead, to calculation, money-making, and
> moral indifference.[3]

In fact, the nation's antebellum political leaders were trimmers and compromisers by necessity. Men like Tyler and Pierce—and even those with more glowing names such as Daniel Webster, Henry Clay, and Stephen Douglas—struggled to keep the fragile union of states together at almost any price. "We can win no laurels in a war for independence," Webster once admitted. "Earlier and worthier hands have gathered them all. . . . But to us remains a great duty of defence and preservation." Charles Francis Adams put it more succinctly: "It is for us to *preserve*, and not to create."[4]

Some Americans—especially Southerners, it seemed—actually cheered the decline of the heroic spirit in America. "Happy the people whose annals are dull," a writer (styling himself "Procrustes, Junior") declared in the leading Southern literary magazine at the start of an 1860 essay titled "Great Men, a Misfortune."[5] Unfortunately for the South, many of the author's countrymen—especially Northerners, it seemed—did not share his feelings.

And despite the best efforts of the skillful preservationists, the country was changing fast. The land of Ralph Farnham's youth—and even that of his middle age, at the beginning of the current century—had been a very different America. In those days the tiny cabin that he had built with his own hands, of logs felled from the surrounding forest, stood in the middle of an almost virgin wilderness, country so rough that only the poorest and most desperate pioneers settled there. Books and newspapers never reached him; clocks and watches were virtually unknown; a man guessed the time of day by looking at the sun. Neighbors—that is, anyone within ten miles—were rarely seen. A journey of even a short distance meant hiking through the woods along tenuous pathways and old Indian trails. When General Washington first ran for president, Farnham had walked all day to reach the nearest town and cast a ballot for his former commander. Life had been hard in those days, but independence was something tangible and real.[6]

Now the little wooden farmhouse looked out not over endless waves of treetops but on a deforested valley of cornfields, orchards, and prosperous villages. The fast-flowing streams that fed the Great East Lake were lined with sawmills, gristmills, even a few large factories. In the nearby towns were ingenious devices that he would never have dreamed of even twenty years before. Not long before the Boston trip, a man had shown up at the farmhouse and asked to take his likeness with one of the new photographic machines. The old soldier assented, put on his best suit of clothes, and sat up very straight and dignified, holding his walking stick tight to steady himself as the big lens fixed his image forever on a sheet of glass.[7] Visits from strangers were no longer much of a surprise, anyway. His once remote hillside was now connected to the rest of the world; any day might bring news or callers. When Farnham had first settled his land, not a single newspaper was published in all of Maine; now there were almost seventy, copying the latest dispatches from across the nation and even from overseas. The railroad passed within a few miles of his front door; he could leave home in the morning and arrive in Boston just after lunch, or in Washington the following day. But such a journey still would have seemed to him nearly as fanciful as flying to the moon. He hadn't even been to Boston since he'd marched there with Captain Hubbard's militia back in the spring of '75.

America in 1860 was much like Old Uncle Farnham: making its way as best it could from the Revolutionary past into the revolutionary future, and facing the present sometimes with fuddled confusion, sometimes with unexpected grace. The contrasting realities of the old and new could be jolting. Although people now dashed cross-country at unheard-of speeds by rail, the rest of the time they could travel only as fast as horses could pull them or the winds push them. Innovative military engineers were designing high-powered cannons that could hit a target five miles away, while ordinary soldiers still trained for hand-to-hand combat with swords. Although St. Louis could contact New York almost instantaneously with a few taps at a telegraph key, getting a message to San Francisco still meant doing as the ancient Romans had done, enlisting relays of horsemen—in this case, the celebrated new Pony Express—galloping two thousand miles across mountains and deserts with mail pouches strapped to their saddles. A journey of even a few miles in 1860 could take you from bucolic isolation—and most Americans still lived on farms or in small villages—into a maelstrom of ceaseless news, advertisements, celebrities, and mass spectacle; the incessant hawking and haggling of commerce and the constant migrainous din of people pronouncing, preaching, debating, complaining, shouting one another down. In other words, America had all the ruthless drives of a developing nation. Its big cities were, in at least one sense, like third-world capitals today: you could check into a luxury high-rise hotel (by nineteenth-century standards) with elevators and the most modern plumbing—and then, around a corner, find yourself amid the clang of blacksmiths' hammers and stench of open sewers, next to shadowy doorways opening onto dens of child labor or prostitution.

After Farnham and his fellow passengers threaded their way among all the well-wishers, emerging at last from the Boston & Maine depot into Haymarket Square, they would have been instantly beset by another insatiable throng: newspaper urchins scurrying toward them from every direction, from behind every pillar and post, like so many hungry mice vying for a just-fallen crumb of cheese. "Get yer *Daily Advertiser* right here, gents!" squeaked one. Another: "*Boston Evening Transcript*, first edition, fresh off the press!" "*Boston Post*, the true-blue Democratic paper, only three cents!" "Get yer *Boston Herald*!" "Yer *Boston Traveller*!" "Yer *Daily Bee*!" "*Daily Journal*!" "*Morning Journal*!" "*Gazette*!" Shins were furtively kicked; smaller boys elbowed unceremoniously to the rear. The news business was cutthroat even in Boston, better known for the genteel literary lights who graced the monthly pages of *The Atlantic*.

Americans everywhere were ravenous for news. Just a few decades earlier, the major dailies had filled their drab columns mostly with ship departures, commodities prices, reprinted speeches, and a few reports on current events in the form of letters, haphazardly submitted by any self-motivated reader. Now all the cities and even smaller towns had competing broadsheets with teams of reporters fanning out widely in search not only of commercially useful information but of stories, opinions, personalities, and color. It wasn't just that people enjoyed gossip, controversy, and scandal, although they did. Ordinary Americans also felt connected in new ways to the world beyond their own rural villages or city neighborhoods. The phenomenon fed on itself: soon nearly everyone wanted to be the first to know the latest.

It still seemed like yesterday that Professor Morse had tapped his biblical four words into a wire he'd just strung between Washington and Baltimore. Now, less than fifteen years later, telegraph lines already crisscrossed the country. (That network spread much more quickly than the Internet would in more recent times.) For better or for worse, the loosely united states were now a union indeed, knit together, if not by bonds of affection, then at least by some fifty thousand miles of rubber-coated copper. When Massachusetts had something to say, South Carolina heard it, and vice versa, for better or for worse—usually the latter. A couple of years earlier, some entrepreneurs had even run a fragile cable across three thousand miles of Atlantic seabed between far eastern Newfoundland and far western Ireland. The thing had quickly failed after a few stately, half-garbled transmissions between Queen Victoria and President Buchanan, but everyone knew it was only a matter of time before New York was chatting easily with London. Already, fast "news boats" from the major New York papers raced one another to meet arriving steamers that carried foreign news across the Atlantic in less than two weeks. (Back in Ralph Farnham's youth, it had taken considerably more than a month for word of the first shot at Lexington to reach London, and then another six weeks—well into the summer of 1775—before Americans in the coastal ports, let alone elsewhere, started hearing their English cousins' first responses.) Action and reaction were now subject to a law of accelerated motion.

What other people did or thought in Paris or Calcutta—or Charleston or New Orleans, for that matter—suddenly mattered more than it ever had before. The world was beginning to seem, for the first time, like a single interconnected web, where a vibration at some distant point might set even solid Boston trembling.

The newspapers that the urchins were waving at Old Uncle Farnham on that long-ago afternoon of his arrival survive today mostly as microfilmed ghosts. Even so, their pages glow with life. The story getting the most attention that day was not, in fact, the impending presidential election in the United States. Rather, it was the triumphant march through southern Italy of General Giuseppe Garibaldi ("the Italian Washington," the *Daily Advertiser* called him) and his red-shirted comrades, an army of liberation and national unification. The reactionary regimes of popes and princes seemed to crumble before the youthful crusaders with hardly a shot fired. On the front page of the *Boston Evening Transcript*, a brand-new poem by William Cullen Bryant, America's most revered literary figure, hailed the newly unchained inhabitants of those medieval fiefdoms: "Slaves but yestereve were they, / Freemen with the dawning day."

Other noteworthy news came from even farther afield. The *Advertiser's* front page carried a dispatch just received from the sloop-of-war USS *Constellation*, on patrol along the coast of Angola. It reported the recent capture of several slave ships by vessels of the U.S. Navy's West African squadron. Commander LeRoy of the USS *Mystic* had just seized two slavers: the *Triton* out of New Orleans and the brig *Russell* of New York. Off the mouth of the Congo River, Commander Dornin of the USS *San Jacinto* had intercepted the brig *Storm King* of New York and, on boarding her, found 619 slaves, likely bound for the sugar plantations of Cuba. Another New York ship taken the same day had no fewer than a thousand unfortunate souls packed in her hold. The newly freed men, women, and children were sent on to Liberia. It might have seemed odd to some Boston readers that their national government was liberating slaves across the Atlantic while zealously protecting the property rights of slaveholders closer to home. Not long after Congress abolished slave importation in 1807, however, U.S. and British naval vessels had begun to roam the African coasts and the waters of the Caribbean, assiduously (or sometimes not so assiduously, depending on who was in charge back in Washington) suppressing the trade, occasionally even bringing the captains and crews back to stand trial under federal law. It was one of many such contradictions born of compromise that Americans took for granted, while foreign travelers viewed them, like so much else in this land, with astonishment.

All the Boston papers that day covered two related stories that had transfixed the nation: the travels of the first official Japanese delegation to visit America (now on its way home) and, even more exciting, the tour of these states by the Prince of Wales. The Japanese envoys had been cordially received at the White House and fêted at a grand ball in New York, but their enjoyment of the trip had been dampened somewhat by the fact that their "translator" spoke only broken English and not a single American citizen, as yet, spoke Japanese. Still, they had been impressed by how frequently Americans combed their hair and by the ingeniousness of Western bathroom facilities—though the envoys had caused a near scandal at their Washington hotel when several were found naked together in the same bathtub, a Japanese, though apparently not American, custom. (Some of the envoys, for their part, were shocked when they visited a Washington brothel and found multiple couples having sex in the same room—an American, though clearly not Japanese, custom.) Several of the diplomats kept diaries of their journey; one noted that in America, "anyone of good character except a negro may be elected president."[8]

Prince Albert Edward's tour, on the other hand, seemed so far to have been an unqualified success, and mostly unhampered by language barriers. (The public was unaware, however, that Queen Victoria's eldest son, later to become King Edward VII, was sometimes inwardly appalled at the jostling rudeness of American crowds. While paying his respects to a statue of Washington, for instance, he was greeted with jeers of "He socked it to you in the Revolution!" and "He gave you English squirts the colic!") Edward was the first British royal to visit America since the end of the Revolutionary War, and Americans—at least most of them—were eager to show their country in the best possible light.* The chubby-cheeked teenage prince and his retinue coasted through Washington, Baltimore, Philadelphia, and New York on a wave of democratic obsequiousness, each city trying to outdo the others with the splendor of its galas and receptions. (With Boston now awaiting its turn, the newspapers were full of ads for fine silks suitable to the occasion.) The distinguished guest had also, somewhat to the discomfort of many Northerners, made a brief foray into the South, a two-day visit to Virginia. Passing through the Fredericksburg depot, he glimpsed a large crowd of slaves gathered by the tracks, bowing low and crying out, "God bless massa!" His Royal Highness bowed gravely to them in reply.[9]

In all the papers, however, were abundant intimations of the crisis that was about to break over the country—and that would, within just a few years, make that scene in Fredericksburg seem like a relic of another age. Gubernatorial elections in several states were scheduled for the following day, and all eyes were on Pennsylvania. If that important bellwether—"the most conservative and distrustful of the middle states," according to the *Advertiser*—went to the Republicans,

---

*Edward's great-uncle Prince William Henry—later King William IV—had served in New York as a teenage Royal Navy midshipman during the Revolution, and eluded a plot by George Washington to kidnap him.

their victory in next month's national election seemed probable, if not almost certain. As to what this could mean for the nation, the firmly Democratic *Boston Post* had few doubts. In Ohio, it reported, a "Black Republican" judge named Brinckerhoff had just handed down a decision conferring voting rights on fourteen thousand free Negroes in the state. If the Republicans took the White House, it hinted grimly, the same thing might eventually be in store for the whole country.

If Ralph Farnham was nostalgic for the revolution he had participated in so many years before, he may have been encouraged by signs that his more youthful countrymen might be itching to start a new one of their own. In New York, the *Advertiser* reported, a Republican parade a few days earlier had included some twenty thousand young men dressed in military-style uniforms, singing and marching by torchlight down Fifth Avenue. One group of French émigrés—some of them refugees from the autocracy in their homeland—had composed for the occasion a special pro-Republican, antislavery version of "La Marseillaise": *"Aux urnes, citoyens! Portons nos bulletins!"* Even the *Advertiser*'s editors, loyal Republicans all, asked how long it might be before the streets of Manhattan—or, heaven forbid, Boston itself—rang with cries of *"À bas les aristocrats!"*

And just across the river in Charlestown—where General Putnam's men had stood fast against the redcoats' volleys—a "Great Republican Wide-Awake Demonstration" was scheduled for that very evening. Young men from Cambridge and East Boston, Medford and Lynn would be marching or riding horseback straight across Bunker Hill Green.[10]

It is unclear whether anybody even mentioned to Old Uncle Farnham what would be happening that night, on the very field where he was supposed to have so nobly fought. But it seems likely he would have approved. When someone asked the grizzled veteran if he planned to vote in the upcoming election, the old man replied stoutly that he would indeed be casting a ballot—"for the Rail-Splitter."[11]

THE MOST FEARED and most famous person in America was also, throughout that entire summer and fall, one of its least visible. Following the precedent set by nearly every presidential nominee since Washington, he did not go out on the stump himself, which would have been unseemly. The man who would become known as the nation's greatest communicator did not even offer a single public statement to the press. Instead, Abraham Lincoln sat in his office in Springfield, Illinois, as the political operatives, newspapermen, photographers, and portrait painters came and went. He attended to his law practice as best he could, going to court once to litigate for a client who claimed patent infringement on a plow he had invented. He didn't even show up to meet the Prince of Wales when His Royal Highness passed through Springfield in late September, lest this seem presumptuous. Curious members of the public arrived by the hundreds to shake hands with the Republican nominee, and he obliged them all. But whenever these visitors asked him for his position on one or another of the urgent issues facing the nation, he just smiled politely and suggested they refer to his published speeches, especially the series of debates he had held with Senator Douglas two years earlier. Then he might launch into an anecdote about his youthful days as a flatboatman on the Ohio River, or ask whether they'd ever heard that joke about the Kentucky hog farmer.[12]

Not all the presidential contenders that year were quite so coy. Lincoln's longtime rival—Senator Stephen Douglas, the Illinois Democrats' own Little Giant—was barnstorming the country. His tour had started almost surreptitiously, or so he had fancied: in July, after decorously avowing that he "would make no political speeches," he suddenly decided to visit his elderly mother in upstate New York. En route, it just so happened that crowds showed up at every railway station, begging him to make a speech, and he could not but oblige them. Somehow, the trip from New York City to Ontario County ended up taking two months and requiring a long detour through most of New England, then a swing down to Pennsylvania and Maryland. Before long, the candidate's journey "in search of his mother" became a national joke among Republicans. "That poor maternal relative of his must be hard to find," one newspaper quipped. "It is said that he will next visit Japan, Algiers, Liberia, South America, and Mexico in search of her." Then, once the long-awaited family reunion occurred, Douglas suddenly discovered that he had to take care of some urgent business in North Carolina regarding the estate of his late mother-in-law, which required an equally circuitous and loquacious pilgrimage through the South. Even worse than the public mockery was the inconsistency in what he said to audiences from region to region, as if he were oblivious to the fact that besides the thousands of locals who came out to hear him, millions of others would read his speeches in the national press, making him seem disingenuous or worse. When, several days before the election, a dock in Alabama collapsed under the weight of his supporters, tossing everyone—including Senator and Mrs. Douglas—into the water, it seemed to symbolize the collapse of the Little Giant's presidential ambitions. Millions admired his principles; few thought him electable.[13]

Lincoln, on the other hand, literally couldn't be dragged out to make a political speech. In August, thousands of supporters gathered in Springfield for a "monster meeting." An eight-mile-long parade marched past the candidate's house at Eighth and Jackson, and Lincoln, in a white summer suit, came out to greet them and be photographed. Finally they prevailed upon him at least to drive over in his carriage to the state fairgrounds, where thirty thousand of his followers awaited. When he arrived, the mob hauled him out of the carriage and carried him on their shoulders across the fairgrounds, landing him with a thump on the speakers' platform. The candidate spoke only a few awkward words of appreciation to the vast assembly before he managed to wriggle off the dais, squeeze his way through the crowd, jump onto the back of a horse, and gallop off homeward as fast as the beast could carry him.[14]

As that dragooning in Springfield suggests, Lincoln's candidacy was becoming a public sensation. Just a few months earlier, he had been but a former one-term congressman and failed Senate candidate from Illinois. It was more than a decade since he had even set foot in Washington. Now his bid for the presidency was riding a surge of emotion rarely seen in the annals of electoral politics. Whatever he was saying or not saying about his actual policies, millions saw him as the embodiment of their hopes and ideals.

It had all started that May, thanks largely to two weather-beaten pieces of wood. As Illinois Republicans prepared to gather for their state nominating convention, one of Lincoln's staunchest supporters, Judge Richard Oglesby, was talking with one of Lincoln's country cousins, a grizzled pioneer farmer named John Hanks. Hanks happened to mention that some thirty years earlier, he and Cousin Abe had split fence rails together when they were clearing some land about twelve miles west of Decatur. Sensing an opportunity, Oglesby drove out there in his buggy with Hanks in tow, and they managed to find what Hanks proclaimed the very fence: testing it with the blade of his penknife, he found that it was constructed of black walnut and honey locust, just as he recollected. The two men grabbed a couple of rails—whether they had asked the fence owner's permission is unclear—and loaded them into the buggy, later stashing them in Oglesby's barn.

On May 9, delegates gathered in the convention hall: an enormous tent, or "wigwam," erected for the occasion. Just before the first formal ballot, Oglesby arose and announced that a certain person wanted "to make a contribution to the Convention." This was Hanks's cue. He and another man came marching up the center aisle carrying the two old rails, which were freshly festooned with red, white, and blue streamers and large banners reading:

ABRAHAM LINCOLN
The Rail Candidate
FOR PRESIDENT IN 1860
Two rails from a lot of 3,000 made in 1830 by John Hanks and
Abe Lincoln, whose father was the first pioneer of Macon County.

The effect of this, a local newspaper reported, "was electrical." The wigwam's canvas rippled with the delegates' cheers as exuberant Republicans threw hats, canes, and books into the air. Soon the tenting started to tear free of its wooden framework—"the roof was literally cheered off the building," one observer wrote.[15] Lincoln was brought up to the speakers' platform and made to tell the story of how, in his early twenties, he had split rails, built a cabin, and cultivated a small farm down on the Sangamon River. He was unanimously nominated the next day. And when Republicans from across the country gathered four days later for the national convention, held in an even bigger wigwam in Chicago, even more rails found their way into the hall. (Oglesby and Hanks had gone back down to Decatur for a few more wagonloads and were raking in a tidy profit selling them for the exorbitant sum of a dollar apiece.) Lincoln won his party's nomination, knocking down the longtime favorite, Senator William Henry Seward of New York, considered the tribal leader of the national Republicans. Within weeks, "Rail-Splitter" and "Rail-Mauler" clubs were springing up throughout the Northern states—even in the bosom of Manhattan, leagues away from the nearest split-rail fence. Chicago had a short-lived pro-Lincoln newspaper called *The Rail-Splitter*.[16]

It is hard to imagine today how some lengths of old lumber could electrify a large tentful of jaded politicos—let alone much of the nation. But the split-rail fence, sometimes known as a "worm fence," was a powerful symbol in the nineteenth century, and a brilliant choice as an emblem for the Lincoln campaign, perhaps the most ingenious ever devised in more than two hundred years of presidential politics. For one thing, it was a distinctively American construction. (Visiting Europeans often mentioned such fences in their letters home, as an instance of local color.) For another, it was almost ubiquitous in Lincoln's time. Just after the Civil War, a government survey found that 86 percent of Ohio's fences were made of split rails; 75 percent of Maine's; 92 percent of Oregon's.[17] Split-rail fences required hard work to build. They represented individual independence and private ownership, and yet also a sense of community, since they were often constructed by groups of neighbors coming together to pitch in. They epitomized America's working class and its rural way of life. They were homely, yet strong—perhaps like Lincoln himself.[18] Perhaps most important, though, the split-rail fence was a symbol of the West (mainly what today we would call the Midwest), since it was often the first permanent structure that a pioneer would build after clearing the land. In 1860, regions that not long before had been remote frontier territories peopled mostly by Indians—places like Iowa, Minnesota, and Oregon—had suddenly become settled states with significant voting blocs. These were places where people still lived much as Ralph Farnham had in Maine at the end of the previous century, lives of hard work and fierce independence, secured with an axe in one hand and a rifle in the other. But the image, and the romance of the West, resonated back East, too: dime novels and illustrated monthlies had brought the frontier to every street-corner newsstand.

Cringing under the barrage of fence rails, Lincoln's rivals for the presidency tried to fire back in some fashion. Supporters of John Bell, who bore the standard of the Constitutional Union Party, carried little tinkling bells to their rallies and formed clubs called the Bell Ringers or the Clapperites. Douglas's followers organized themselves as the Little Dougs. But all emblems are not created equal, and these enticements did not noticeably boost either man's candidacy.[19]

Still, Lincoln's opponents seemed to have history on their side. The country may have been increasingly fractured along sectional lines, but in the spring and summer of 1860, two concerns united many Americans in both North and South: the fear of disunion and the desire for peace. For forty years, the precarious balance had been held through conciliation and compromise, with political bargains by which Southerners could feel secure that their "peculiar institution" would be tolerated and even protected by the government of the United States, while Northerners were assured that their own soil would never know the moral taint of slavery. In most Americans' minds as of 1860, the ideal of union and the ideal of universal freedom stood in direct antithesis, irreconcilable at present or anytime in the foreseeable future.

Events of the past decade had only proved the precariousness of the balance, and set blood boiling on both sides. Most white Southerners were furious over John Brown's attempted invasion of Virginia the previous year. They suspected it was part of a concerted Northern plot to realize the South's worst nightmare: a widespread and bloody slave revolt like that in Haiti seven decades before, when Negroes were alleged to have raped, tortured, and slaughtered whites by the thousands. Northern abolitionists, they believed, surreptitiously fanned the flames of "servile rebellion" by circulating abolitionist literature in the South, even slipping it into the hands of slaves whom they had perfidiously taught how to read. And they had robbed Southerners of property, constitutionally protected property, when Northern thieves helped slaves escape through the Underground Railroad. Northern propagandists who had barely set foot in the South fabricated outrageous slanders like *Uncle Tom's Cabin*, defaming their Southern brethren to the entire world. Even the Supreme Court's ruling in the *Dred Scott* case—which had declared eloquently and unequivocally that slave ownership was a basic constitutional right and that blacks could never, at least in a legal sense, be considered fully human—had not been enough to check their outrages. Some of the Northern extremists now even idolized Brown, the insane fanatic who had put weapons into the Negroes' hands and had himself once slaughtered five law-abiding Kansas settlers with a broadsword simply for being pro-slavery. Finally, many in the South feared that the North's burgeoning population, increasing economic power, and growing strength in national politics would only multiply the audacious encroachments on Southern liberties.

Increasing numbers of Northern voters, meanwhile, were coming to suspect a Southern scheme to establish a vast slave empire stretching from the Caribbean (where renegade Southern adventurers had recently tried to take Cuba and Nicaragua by force) to the Pacific coast. How else to understand their violations of the Missouri Compromise and attempts to expand slavery into Kansas and Nebraska, far north of the bounds Congress had set? Northerners had been forced to swallow the Fugitive Slave Act, making local courts complicit in the kidnapping of Negroes living peacefully among their white neighbors. They had seen antislavery settlers massacred in Missouri and Kansas, and, throughout the South, anyone expressing even the mildest antislavery sentiments had suffered imprisonment, flogging, tarring and feathering, and sometimes death. This violence had reached even the sacred halls of the Capitol when Preston Brooks, a South Carolina congressman, brutally beat Senator Charles Sumner of Massachusetts on the Senate floor. Slaveholders and their allies burned books, banned newspapers, and terrorized ministers of the gospel. They had, in fact, made a mockery of the entire idea of American democracy, turning the phrase "land of the free" into a sneer on European lips. And all this was over and above the crimes and outrages that Southerners perpetrated every day against four million helpless men, women, and children whom they kept in bondage, sold like cattle, and exploited for their sexual pleasure.

As with all politics, there was also a broad middle ground on which most white American males—which is also to say most voters—probably stood. Some Southerners, especially in states of the Upper South like Kentucky, Missouri, Maryland, and Virginia, saw slavery as an unfortunate arrangement and hoped it could gradually be done away with, perhaps by sending freed blacks to Liberia and compensating their owners, whose slaves often constituted most of their wealth. A larger share of Northerners, while wishing to limit the spread of slavery, felt it would be dangerous, as well as unfair to slaveholders, to impose a program of emancipation. They certainly did not identify themselves as abolitionists, a term reserved for members of a radical, crankish New England sect. Indeed, the vast majority of white Americans on both sides of the Mason-Dixon Line accepted without question the premise that blacks were inherently inferior and that the two races could never live together as equals. Some white Northerners even agreed with the common Southern sentiment that slavery was good for the Negro.

Each of the three major parties in the 1860 presidential election sought to capture as much of this middle ground as possible, promising some form of compromise that would keep the peace. Wasn't this, after all, the very essence of American democracy: balancing interests, reconciling contrary views, and protecting each community's right to make its own laws and follow its own conscience? Few were those, either abolitionists or slaveholders, who didn't maintain that even an uncomfortable truce was preferable to the horrors of civil war.

Some Northern and Southern moderates had banded together in February to form a new national party based on the simplest version of this logic. The platform of the Constitutional Union Party was little more than a slogan: "The Constitution of the Country, the Union of the States, and the Enforcement of the Laws." It nominated Bell, a Tennessee slaveholder who believed the Constitution protected the right to own slaves but opposed recent Southern expansionism, especially the effort to foist slavery upon Kansas. Bell was a colorless, even dour man with a hangdog face that seemed drawn into a permanent frown—indeed, he made ex-presidents like Tyler and Fillmore look dashing by comparison—but perhaps stolid, uncharismatic conservatism was just what the overexcited nation needed.

The Democrats fielded not one but two candidates in 1860. In June, the party had split into regional factions, one of them dominated by Southerners and the other by Northerners.[20] The Southern wing nominated Buchanan's vice president, a handsome, courtly thirty-nine-year-old Kentuckian named John Breckinridge. Breckinridge was, personally, no lover of the "peculiar institution"—he hoped that blacks could eventually be freed and resettled in Africa—yet considered himself a proud and loyal Southerner and believed the federal government had no right to interfere with any aspect of slavery, including its expansion into any state or territory. The right to hold slaves was protected, he said, wherever the Stars and Stripes waved. He had won credentials as a moderate in 1854 when he pronounced an eloquent eulogy over the body of his fellow Kentuckian Henry Clay, the Great Compromiser. Southerners of all persuasions rallied behind Breckinridge as the man most likely to protect the rights of slaveholders by following in the cautious footsteps of Pierce and Buchanan. Indeed, many declared that he was the only major candidate they were willing to accept as the next president.

By far the most renowned of the four presidential contenders was Douglas, nominee of the Northern Democrats. Douglas was a controversial figure: it was he who had fathered the Kansas-Nebraska Act, resulting in a Midwestern bloodbath. Still, he was widely admired as one of the greatest intellects in the U.S. Senate, perhaps even in all of America. His massive forehead seemed to bulge out over the rest of his face from the sheer volume of the throbbing brain inside; a *New York Times* correspondent called it "a head most difficult to describe, but one better worth description, in a phrenological aspect, than any other in the country." The famed orator's rhetorical style had "nothing of the cavalry slash in its impressiveness, rather resembling a charge of heavy infantry with fixed bayonet."[21] Relentlessly logical, Douglas argued that the Constitution clearly enshrined the right of each state to be governed by its own people. Each new territory should choose its policy on slavery by a fair majority vote—thus, he promised, "burying Northern Abolitionism and Southern Disunionism in a common grave."[22]

As for the Republicans, they, too, tacked toward the political center. Although founded six years earlier by antislavery hard-liners, the party had now broadened its platform to embrace popular causes such as protectionist tariffs and a transcontinental railroad. Delegates in 1860 chose Lincoln specifically—with all due respect to Judge Oglesby and his rails—as a man moderate enough to make mainstream voters comfortable. Some expected he could be an impartial broker who would soothe Northern and Southern tempers alike. Lincoln, one Republican speaker assured an audience in Ohio, was "a sound conservative man." A Republican editor promised readers that the party's nominee, if elected, would "follow a moderate, fair, constitutional course of policy."[23] Perhaps the Illinoisan's greatest asset as a candidate, actually, was that very few people outside his home state had any strong opinions about him, or even any idea who he was. Many newspaper editors couldn't even spell his name: he was "Abram" until election day.[24]

Yet, regardless of the party bosses' clear intentions, and regardless of their candidate's tightly closed lips, the Republican campaign of 1860 quickly began to spin out of control, to transform itself into something neither intended nor envisioned.

Perhaps, in retrospect, it did actually have something to do with those fence rails, which for many Americans began to assume proportions that old John Hanks and his cousin Abe never dreamt of as they cleared that farm along the Sangamon back in the spring of 1830. Most of the great sectional struggles and compromises of the 1850s had hinged on the fate of the new Western states and territories, such as Kansas and Nebraska: whether they would be slave or free, and how to decide the question. Symbols of the pioneer West spoke to the Republicans' commitment to block the westward spread of slavery. Split rails also powerfully evoked the party's "free labor" ideology: a belief in the dignity of the independent workingman, in contrast to the indolent Southern aristocrat whose livelihood depended on slaves.[25] The old pieces of walnut and locust, originally mere stylistic flourishes, became eloquent, while still discreet, antislavery symbols.

Even more potent was the image of Lincoln himself as a rail-splitter. Campaign posters bore crude woodcuts portraying the bookish attorney as—improbably enough—a mighty he-man, sleeves rolled up and muscles bulging as he wielded an enormous mallet. (Even most printers knew that you cut timber with an axe, but you didn't split rails with one.) For the past two decades, America had been governed mostly by the genteel but weak-spined alumni of the finest colleges in the East. The White House's current occupant, Buchanan—"Granny Buck" to his detractors—was openly derided as effeminate, not because of any physical mannerisms, but for his timid impotence in the face of the nation's looming crises. Lincoln would be a different kind of president. Perhaps some—both supporters and opponents—even hoped the

Rail-Splitter would drive a wedge that would split North and South forever, solving at a single stroke the conundrum of a nation half slave and half free.

Far from the banks of the Sangamon, far from the wigwams and fence rails and tobacco-spitting backcountry bosses, men and women lingered over white-linened breakfast tables, unfolded the morning's crisp copies of the *Boston Daily Advertiser*, and wondered what it all meant. The capital of New England—still in those days almost a separate principality within the union of states—was also the capital of the abolitionist movement. It was the holy see of something even more exalted, too: the American compulsion to make the world perfect.

The great-grandchildren of the Puritans may have given up the hellfire-and-brimstone sermons of earlier times, but they had never abandoned their forefathers' dream of building a city on a hill. A cynic might have quipped that they already possessed one, and a rather comfortable one at that: the elegant streets and squares of Beacon Hill, where Boston's patrician families had lived in redbrick gentility since the early part of the century. Walking alongside a row of discreet bow-fronted facades, their first-story windows lifted above the eyes of curious passersby, one might not have guessed at the purifying ardor that burned within. But behind the silk curtains lived the gentlemen and ladies whose patronage (and purses) advanced such worthy causes as the Boston Female Anti-Slavery Society, the Boston Society for the Prevention of Pauperism, the Boston Society for Propagating the Gospel Among the Indians, the Boston Infidel Relief Society, the Boston Temperance Association, the Boston Female Moral Reform Society, the Boston Total Abstinence Society, and the Boston Trustees of Donations for Education in Liberia—to name just a few.[26]

"There is a city in our world," the philosopher Bronson Alcott wrote, "upon which the light of the sun of righteousness has risen,— a sun which beams in its full meridian splendor there. . . . It is the source whence every pure stream of thought and purpose emanates. It is the city that is set on high; it cannot be hid. It is Boston." And if many of New England's great fortunes happened to derive from the sun-ripened cotton of Southern plantations, and the stream-powered mills that wove the cotton into cloth—well, all the more reason to put that money into more righteous hands. (Mr. Alcott himself wore only wool and linen.)[27]

Abolitionism, however, was more than simply a Sunday-afternoon hobby of meddlesome Brahmins, although Southerners sometimes portrayed it as such. Down the hill and across Boston Common, where the Revolutionary militiamen had once drilled, was a maze of narrow streets and shabby alleys little changed since colonial times. This was where the movement's real work got done. Here was the ink-soaked printshop of *The Liberator*, the nation's most influential abolitionist newspaper. (Lincoln's law partner in faraway Springfield was a subscriber.) Its famous editor, William Lloyd Garrison, may have looked like a primly bespectacled Yankee schoolmaster, but his sympathy with the downtrodden came from all-too-personal experience: he had grown up in a shack in Newburyport and been put to work at the age of six. Here, too, in a narrow little house next to a shoemaker's shop, lived Garrison's unlikely brother in arms: the handsome, sonorous-voiced Wendell Phillips.[28] Phillips, New England's greatest antislavery orator, was a Harvard-educated lawyer, born in one of the finest mansions on Beacon Street, but he and his wife now dwelt in an ascetic simplicity befitting the righteousness of their cause.

The ardor for abolition reached into farther-flung quarters, too. In 1854, when an escaped slave named Anthony Burns had been arrested under the Fugitive Slave Act, an urban mob—variously composed of free Negro laborers, radical Unitarian ministers, and others—gathered to free him. They stormed the federal courthouse, which was surrounded by police and wrapped in protective chains (an apt symbol, many people thought, for the current state of American justice). Amid the melee, one protester shot and killed a police deputy. Two weeks later, Burns was marched in shackles down State Street, guarded by hundreds of soldiers with loaded guns and an entire battery of artillery, toward the wharf, where a naval cutter waited to carry him back into bondage. Lampposts and storefronts along the route were draped in black mourning; crowds hissed at the soldiers as they passed, then surged forward into the street until cavalrymen beat them back with the flats of their sabers. It was Boston's most thrilling demonstration against tyranny since the Tea Party almost a century before. The city was—before the eyes of all the world, and to the satisfaction of many Bostonians—a battleground for freedom once more.[29]

Garrison and Phillips condemned the mob violence. Yet they, too, grew increasingly radical, and increasingly certain that the day of jubilee for American slaves would never arrive by legal means. Phillips gave up the practice of law entirely, saying he could never work within a system in thrall to slaveholders. Garrison went even further. A month after Anthony Burns was sent south, the Massachusetts Anti-Slavery Society held its annual Fourth of July picnic. One by one, orators addressed the assembly from a dais on which an American flag hung upside down and draped in mourning. Finally it was Garrison's turn. The abolitionists' chieftain, his spectacles flashing in the summer glare, spoke passionately of the document that had been signed on that very day in 1776, asserting the equality of all mankind—the document that had been a touchstone of the antislavery movement almost since its original publication. But then, as Garrison's speech reached its climax, he lit a candle on the table beside him and held up a copy of the United States Constitution: the document that had betrayed the promises of the Declaration, hardened the chains that held black men and women in servitude, and created a corrupt system by which slaveholders, almost since its ratification, had imposed their political will on the entire nation. Declaring it "the source and parent of all other atrocities—a covenant with death and an agreement with hell," Garrison touched the document to the flame.

As the paper blazed up and then flaked into ashes, he intoned: "So perish all compromises with tyranny! And let all the people say, Amen!"

"*Amen!*" roared the crowd in reply.[30]

Perhaps it is no surprise that men like these should have reacted skeptically, at best, to the Republicans' presidential nominee in 1860. To Garrison and Phillips, the unknown Midwesterner (born in Kentucky to Virginian parents, they must have noted with alarm) was simply one more mediocre politician to warm the presidential chair for another four years, while the nation drifted closer and closer toward despotism. Lincoln would "do nothing to offend the South," Garrison predicted after hearing of the nomination. But Phillips's outrage truly boiled over. Addressing an antislavery meeting just after the Republicans announced their nominee, he sneered: "Who is this huckster in politics? Who is this county court advocate? . . . What is his recommendation? It is that nobody knows anything good or bad of him. His recommendation is that out of the unknown things in his past life, journals may make for him what character they please. His recommendation is that his past is a blank." In an article he wrote for *The Liberator* a month later, Phillips went further still: he sent Garrison a manuscript headlined ABRAHAM LINCOLN, THE SLAVE-HOUND OF ILLINOIS.[31]

In Phillips's denunciations there was more than a trace of the Harvard man's disdain for an uneducated rail-splitter from backcountry.

Even more, though, he and Garrison had long since lost all trust in politics itself: its tidy backroom deals, its stump speakers and ward heelers, its party platforms all bombast and no substance, and, worst of all, its endless progression of sordid compromises. They, like most other Americans, assumed that this year's presidential race would bring simply more of the same. They had seen enough to expect nothing else.

Yet there were already signs that the 1860 election might prove them wrong. If some abolitionists believed the four nominees' platforms simply ran the gamut from bad to worse—all of them, to one degree or another, trying to appease "the slave power"—still, a careful reader would have noticed a signal difference. The Constitutional Unionists' platform and both the Democratic factions invoked the Constitution. The Republicans, however, quoted the famous passage of the Declaration proclaiming all men equal, endowed equally by God with certain inalienable rights. They spurned the backroom compromises of 1787 in favor of the original, radical American dream of 1776.

The Republicans had, to be sure, used the same language in their platform in 1856. This time, though, the more moderate wing had almost succeeded in taking it out until an impassioned speech at the national convention by Joshua Giddings, a party leader from Ohio, convinced the delegates to let Jefferson's words remain. Despite all the shadowy deals struck in Chicago, the Republicans still stood for a very new—and at the same time very old—idea in mainstream American politics. The critical difference from 1856 was that now, thanks to simple electoral math, they stood a very good chance of winning the presidency.

By midsummer, the full implications of this prospect were dawning on Americans in both the North and South. In fact, Democratic newspaper editors and stump speakers, far more than any Northern Republicans, began turning the election into a national referendum on slavery, race, and equality in the very broadest sense, often in the ugliest possible terms. A St. Louis newspaper charged flatly that the principle of "negro equality" lay behind the entire Republican ideology. A Texas paper referred to Lincoln as "the candidate of the niggers."[32] And almost every anti-Lincoln paper in the country consistently referred to the "Black Republicans," just in case any inattentive voter might somehow miss the point.

America's rough-and-tumble young democracy had always dealt its share of bruises to those who entered the arena. But technological innovations, along with political trends, were now making the game more merciless than ever. Cheap printing and the telegraph made it easier and easier for the shrillest ideologues to find audiences, even national ones. And each fresh blast of rhetoric from the enemy demanded an even harsher volley in return. If it were cleverly enough phrased, sympathetic editors around the country might pick it up. An upstart newspaper could make its reputation that way; so could an ambitious young congressman.

The intensity of racial invective in 1860 was shocking even by the standards of that time. Northern Democrats could be as offensive as their Southern counterparts. A Chicago Democratic paper warned its readers that if Lincoln's party won in November, the entire country would soon be overrun by "naked, greasy, bandy-shanked, blubber-lipped, monkey-headed, muskrat-scented cannibals from Congo and Guinea," who would live on terms of perfect equality with the proud descendants of "Washingtons [and] Lafayettes."[33] Probably the worst offender in the North, though, was the *New York Herald*. Its editor, the acid-tongued James Gordon Bennett, had captured the largest circulation of any daily in the country by serving up a patented blend of sarcasm and sensationalism. The *Herald*'s editorial page cracked wise almost every day about "the Eternal nigger," the "Almighty nigger," the "Irrepressible nigger," and the "nigger-loving black republicans."

Bennett's fellow New Yorkers, in fact, seemed especially virulent in their racism. Democrats paraded through the streets of Manhattan with banners reading "No Negro Equality." One showed a crudely caricatured black man embracing a white girl. Another banner bore a cartoon of an African-American above the words "The successor of Abraham Lincoln in 1864."[34] (Interestingly, the specter of a future black president cropped up repeatedly throughout the campaign as an anti-Republican scare tactic. "What will you do with these people?" one pro-Bell orator asked rhetorically. "Will you allow them to sit at your own table, marry your daughters, govern your states, sit in your halls of Congress and perhaps be President of the United States?")[35]

Many Democratic newspapers warned of possible horrors even worse than a Negro in the White House. "There can be no reasonable doubt that the direct result of Black Republicanism . . . is to ferment servile insurrections in the South, and provoke such horrible atrocities as marked the negro insurrection in St. Domingo and Hayti," one editor wrote. The implication was clear: loyalty to the Union demanded loyalty, first and foremost, to the white race.[36]

Only by standing faithfully at the side of their slaveholding white brethren, many Northerners believed, could they preserve the nation intact. At a rally in the Cooper Union—the same hall where Lincoln had delivered his great speech on slavery and the Constitution a few months earlier—a crowd of several thousand Democrats sang in unison:

> *We fight to save the Union, and God is on our side;*
> *We fight against a faction who would let the Union slide;*
> *To put down these rail-splitters, who would split it into two,*
> *They love the nigger better than the red, white, and blue.*

As the Democrats' drumbeats grew louder, though, so did some Republicans'. Boston's own Charles Sumner—the abolitionist martyr beaten almost to death on the floor of the Senate after one of his tirades against slavery—descended from the Olympian heights of Beacon Hill to stump for Lincoln just after Independence Day. "Prostrate the slave oligarchy," the Massachusetts senator commanded a large gathering of the party faithful:

> Prostrate the slave oligarchy and the North shall no longer be the vassal of the South. . . . Its final doom may be postponed, but it is certain. Languishing, it may live yet longer; but it will surely die. Yes, fellow-citizens, surely it will die. . . . It can no longer rule the republic as a plantation . . . can no longer fasten upon the Constitution an interpretation that makes merchandise of men, and gives a disgraceful immunity to the brokers of human flesh and the butchers of human hearts. . . . It must die, it may be, as a poisoned rat dies of rage in its hole.

For some Americans who would read the speech in the days to come, another of Sumner's exhortations may have been even more alarming: "If bad men conspire for slavery, good men must combine for freedom. Nor can the holy war be ended until the barbarism now dominant in the republic is overthrown, and the Pagan power is driven from our Jerusalem."[37]

As for the Republican candidate himself, he sat silent as ever in Springfield. The party's moderate leaders fanned out across New York and Pennsylvania, talking busily about tariffs, about railroads—about anything except slavery. In Boston, Garrison and Phillips poured forth their crystalline stream of prophecy, as ever untainted by the muck of politics. But across the North, almost imperceptibly at first, a grassroots army was banding together: one that would enter the presidential contest as though enlisting in Senator Sumner's holy war.

•   •   •

No one would ever know exactly how, where, or when the movement started. Some proslavery men claimed it was born that summer as part of a vast and sinister conspiracy in the West; even that the malign hand of John Brown had reached out of the grave and coaxed it to life. Northern Democrats believed devious political bosses were pulling strings from behind the scenes; Republicans denied this, saying they could trace its origins back to a similar organization in the campaign of '56.

Eventually, though, the explanation that gained the most currency was a tale about five young dry-goods clerks in Hartford, Connecticut. In February 1860, the story went, a noted Republican orator—an antislavery Kentuckian named Cassius M. Clay—visited the city. The young men, Republicans all, took on the duty of escorting the dignitary from the railway station to his hotel, and in order to make the little procession of shop assistants somewhat more impressive, they fashioned makeshift uniform capes out of some shiny oilcloth, and borrowed whale-oil torches from a local fire company. They marched through the streets in military formation with Clay tagging along behind, perhaps somewhat nonplussed.

Some onlookers scoffed at the odd spectacle, but other young Hartford men along the parade route—fellow shop assistants, counting-house clerks, insurance-company actuaries—found themselves oddly stirred. Within a week or two, some fifty of them met to organize themselves as a Republican marching club. By the end of the month, its ranks had swelled to more than two thousand. Somewhere along the way, they came up with a name for their group: the Wide Awakes. By the summer, similar groups were forming across the country, until eventually even Bennett's skeptical *New York Herald* was asking: "Who are these Wide Awakes?"[38]

Well might the *Herald* wonder. A first glimpse of a Wide Awake battalion on parade was a strange, even frightening, experience. Late at night, city dwellers would be startled from their sleep by the rhythmic crashing of a drum drawing closer and closer. Rushing to the window, they would see the darkened street below them suddenly blaze up with fire as a broad row of men with torches rounded the corner in marching formation, and more followed, rank upon rank, their boots striking the cobblestones in perfect cadence. The marchers wore military-style caps and were shrouded in full black capes of a shiny fabric that reflected the flames. Some carried rail-splitter axes strapped to their backs. Perhaps most chilling of all, they marched in complete silence, their eyes fixed straight ahead, the only sound the beating of drums and the tramp of boot heels. They were unlike anything ever seen in American politics, unlike the boisterous parades, rowdy songs, and brass bands of elections past. "Quiet men," the *Herald* warned its readers, "are dangerous."[39]

Details of the organization's inner workings began to trickle out. New members signed enlistment papers as if in an army. The groups were organized into companies and battalions, with their own sergeants, lieutenants, and captains, each wearing appropriately fancier versions of the Wide Awake uniform. These officers, many of them veterans of the Mexican War, taught enlistees formal military drill using official army handbooks. (In St. Louis, a shop assistant and former army lieutenant named Ulysses Grant often coached the local Wide Awakes.) The sinister symbol of the new organization, painted on its banners and printed on its membership certificates, was a single all-seeing, unblinking eye.[40]

What did that open eye mean? How exactly did these men consider themselves "wide awake"? Were they standing vigil against a rising danger? Were they spies, stalking the streets by night? Or had they somehow fully awakened to a new and clearer vision of the world, while the rest of their countrymen still drowsed?

In any case, the movement grew. From Hartford it spread across New England, down into Pennsylvania and New York, even to distant San Francisco. It seemed to catch fire especially among the new cities of the upper Midwest, towns where New Englanders had, like their English ancestors, borne their missionary fervor westward to a new frontier: Milwaukee, Madison, La Crosse, Kalamazoo. Many members were clerks, mechanics, or common laborers, but in Boston, even some Beacon Hill aristocrats were swept into the ranks, shouldering torches along with the rest.[41] Most of the "Rail-Splitter" clubs from back in the spring disbanded to join the more exciting organization. There were special clubs of German Wide Awakes and Irish Wide Awakes. In some places, women formed Wide Awake units and, wearing the same familiar hats and cloaks, rode on horseback alongside the marching men.[42] The one thing nearly all members had in common is that they were young—many were teenagers not even old enough to vote. ("Half of our Wide Awakes," one New York journalist scoffed, "are not too big for their mothers to spank.")[43] Finally, the movement grew so large that even the Republican Party's senior statesmen began taking notice. Senator Seward himself, gamely stumping for his onetime rival, addressed a huge gathering of Wide Awakes in Detroit, hailing them as a new generation of Americans, ready to throw off the "prejudices" that still encumbered their elders. "Today," Seward proclaimed to the wildly cheering throng, "the young men of the United States are for the first time on the side of freedom and against slavery."[44]

It was not only the North that had noticed the Wide Awakes. Some Southerners were watching as well, with growing disquiet. Was this, they wondered, the first stage of a Yankee invasion? Or had that invasion already begun? Flames began to spread across the South, perhaps kindled by the Wide Awakes' own torches.

The summer of 1860 was the South's hottest and driest in memory. Nowhere was it worse than in Texas. Crops shriveled; farmers sold off their herds lest the cattle die of thirst. And then the fires started. On the afternoon of July 8, a day of scorching heat, a general store in Dallas (then a village of fewer than seven hundred people) suddenly burst into flames, and before panicked residents could bring the blaze under control, nearly all of the little business district was reduced to ashes. The same day, a similar fire broke out in Denton, forty miles west. Before long, a dozen towns across the state were swept into what seemed to be a wave of spontaneous combustion.

At first locals blamed a lethal combination of the heat, drought, rickety wooden buildings, and a widespread new invention, phosphorous matches, which were chemically unstable and sometimes blazed up suddenly in high temperatures. Many, if not most, of the businesses where the fires began had held large stocks of these matches. But then one young newspaper editor began suggesting another explanation: an abolitionist plot. The fires, he wrote, were the first stage of "a general revolt of the slaves, aided by the white men of the North in our midst." The next step in the insurrection, he revealed, was for blacks to start poisoning all the wells with strychnine. Soon these rumors—and a thirst for revenge—were spreading across Texas even faster than the fires themselves.

Vigilantes banded together to hunt down the perpetrators. First, hundreds of slaves were rounded up and beaten until they provided the information that the interrogators were looking for. After a few began to "confess" under the lash and to implicate others—or, worse, were found in possession of strychnine, a common rat poison—the killings began. Across the state, black men were left dangling from fence posts and makeshift gallows, or tied to trees and used for target practice. A local Baptist newspaper urged that they be "shot like wolves or hung like dogs." The plot's supposed instigators were not spared, either. White men whose only crime was to be Northerners recently arrived in the state—an innkeeper, a laborer, a schoolteacher—were lynched alongside the blacks. Texans of all classes and ages zealously joined the purge. "Schoolboys have become so excited by the sport in hanging Abolitionists that the schools are completely deserted," one Texas paper reported. "They . . . will go 15 or 100 miles on horseback to participate in a single execution of the sentence of Judge Lynch's court." By the time the vigilantes finished their work, somewhere between thirty and one hundred blacks and whites had been killed and hundreds more tortured and terrorized—without a single person ever caught in any act of sabotage or insurrection. The memories would linger for a long time to come. After one white Methodist preacher was hanged (his crime was to have expressed mild doubts about slavery), his executioners stripped the flesh off his skeleton and brought it back to town to be preserved as a public trophy. More than seven decades later, an old man who had been a child in that town would still remember playing with "the abolitionist's bones."[45]

As news of the "Texas troubles" spread across the rest of the country, very few white Southerners doubted the vigilantes' version of events. After all, weren't the Northern abolitionists already drilling for an invasion of the slave states? The Wide Awakes, a Georgia paper charged, "may yet, should the signal be given, commence a drunken bacchanal, to end in wild orgies of blood, of carnage, lust and rapine. . . . These semi-military organizations, the sport of the hour, shall erect the guillotine, tear down the temples of justice, sack the city and the plain, and overturn society." And a Mississippi editor told his readers: "They parade at midnight, carry rails to break open our doors, torches to fire our dwellings, and beneath their long black capes the knife to cut our throats." In response, Southerners began forming—and arming—companies of "Minute Men" to resist the Northern onslaught.[46]

Perhaps there was indeed reason to fear the Wide Awakes. Some actually *had* begun carrying knives, and even revolvers, beneath their capes—and occasionally had needed to use them. Republican marchers were coming under attack, especially in the border states. Opponents threw stones and bricks at their processions, and sometimes mobs formed, screaming, "Kill the damn Wide Awakes." In Indiana, a local Democratic leader shot one marcher in the shoulder. Every so often it was the Wide Awakes themselves who started the brawls. In New York, one company attacked a firehouse at the corner of Fourth Avenue and Thirteenth Street, smashing the glass and woodwork with their "Lincoln" axes until the firemen emerged to charge at the young Republicans, clenching clubs and wrenches.[47]

Newspaper reports of such battles—the whiff of smoke and blood on the wind—only attracted more recruits. Young Republicans, it seemed, were not just ready but eager for a summons to combat. By October, many estimates put the organization's national membership at half a million men.[48] When a small earthquake shook New England that month, many Bostonians assumed it was just Wide Awakes drilling, as usual, on the Common.[49]

The earth was shaking in Boston in more ways than one. From *The Liberator*'s print shop to the mansions on Beacon Hill, the city seemed to be feeling the tremors of an impending convulsion—perhaps something like the day of judgment that the Puritan fathers had so often prophesied. At last even the august *Atlantic Monthly* deigned to take notice, with an essay in the October issue by the editor-in-chief himself, James Russell Lowell. Beginning with an apt classical allusion to "the new Timoleon in Sicily"—that is to say, Garibaldi—Lowell helpfully informed his readers that while they had all been paying attention to the thrilling news from the Italian states, an important election had been going on closer to home. Perhaps, indeed, it might turn out to be a revolution in its own right. "Whatever its result," he wrote, "it is to settle, for many years to come, the question whether the American idea is to govern this continent." For many years, he reminded his readers, the slave states had shackled the nation to a barbaric past—the recent lynchings in Texas, in fact, had been like nothing seen on the continent since witches were burned in Salem. Moreover, "the slaveholding interest has gone step by step, forcing concession after concession, till it needs but little to secure it in the political supremacy of the country. . . . The next Presidential Election is to say Yes or No."[50]

Three weeks before that final day of decision, a youthful army streamed into Boston from all over New England. Railroad cars wobbled and steamboats rocked precariously as men and boys arrived in groups of hundreds from county seats and market towns in upland Vermont and coastal Maine—the call of the Wide Awakes had reached even there. Those who could not fit into the boats or cars, or could not afford them, simply walked to the city, by the thousands. They carried bundles of oilskin cloth folded under their arms and torches waiting to be lit.

Boston would see many young men march through over the next five years: parades both ebullient and somber, strutting off toward glory or trudging homeward, shattered, from the fields of death. The Wide Awake rally of October 16, 1860—the last great parade of the peace—was an unwitting dress rehearsal for all that would follow. As dusk approached, the Common was alive with men, stooping to pull on their boots, adjusting one another's capes, shouldering unlit torches like muskets. Then, at exactly 7:45, with the firing of a signal shot, ten thousand torches sputtered and flared to life, and the entire Common was, as one spectator would write, "a sea of glass mingled with fire."[51]

Like a rivulet of lava spilling from a volcanic crater, the ranks of men erupted in a single thin stream out of the ragged old field. The rhythm of their tramping boots increased to double time as the procession swung onto Beacon Street. This was no silent midnight march but a vaudeville of devils. Fifes piped patriotic tunes; cornet bands blew brassy fanfares. The marchers carried not just torches but flags, split rails, flapping linen banners, and gaudy illuminated transparencies; they did not plod straight ahead this time but almost danced, zigzagging in formation from one side of the street to the other, imitating the crooked path of a split-rail fence. Rockets and Roman candles flared into the night sky. Most of the narrow streets were festooned with Chinese lanterns, and many of the houses were decorated, too, as the procession wended its way toward the point where the companies would disband, in Haymarket Square by the Boston & Maine Depot. On Hancock Street, up the slope of Beacon Hill, the austere brick mansion of Charles Sumner was ablaze with candles in every window, and rank upon rank of men cheered lustily as they passed.[52]

From a corner on Dover Street, William Lloyd Garrison was watching. Twenty-five years earlier, almost to the day, a mob had tied a rope around him and dragged him through the streets of Boston, howling for the blood of the Negro-loving abolitionist. Now he stood, bundled up against the autumn chill, while company after company swung into view. As the banners passed, he read them one by one: *Vigilance the Price of Liberty; No More Slave Territory; The Pilgrims Did Not Found an Empire for Slavery.* But the sight that made his heart leap was the company of West Boston Wide Awakes: two hundred black men marching proudly in uniform, keeping stride in perfect tempo with their white comrades, under a banner that read *God Never Made a Tyrant or a Slave.*

Garrison's twenty-two-year-old son was at his side that night. As he watched the torchlight gleam on row after passing row of youthful, joyous faces, he looked over at his father and saw reflected flames shining, too, on the pinched features of the old abolitionist. "Verily," the younger man murmured, "the world does move."[53]

ON TUESDAY, NOVEMBER 6, an uncanny calm fell over most of the country, although calm, in those days, was a relative thing. Americans went about the business of democracy—or, as some might have said, the business of revolution—in a fashion as orderly as any election day of the nineteenth century. By contrast with most such occasions, there were only scattered reports of street violence and voter beatings in the larger cities and towns, including, of course, in most of the rougher wards of Lower Manhattan. The most serious incident occurred in Washington, where, after the final results came in, a proslavery mob stormed a Wide Awake company's clubhouse a block or two from the Capitol. The attackers practically demolished the building with bricks and stones, and were only narrowly prevented from burning the ruin—along with several Wide Awakes trapped on the third floor—by the timely arrival of the District police.[54]

In his office in Springfield, the Republican candidate himself was thronged all morning by journalists and well-wishers, all of whom knew that Electoral College calculus made his victory almost a foregone conclusion. It was a brisk, glorious autumn day in Central Illinois, and most citizens were thrilled at the prospect of their neighbor becoming president, even if they hadn't voted for him. When someone asked Lincoln whether he was concerned about all the fear and anger that his campaign had seemed to evoke, the candidate replied optimistically, and with typical rough humor, that "elections in this country are like 'big boils'—they cause a great deal of pain before they come to a head, but after the trouble is over the body is in better health than before." In the afternoon, he put on his tall hat and walked over to the courthouse to cast his vote. Facing his fellow citizens, he held up the printed Republican ticket and snipped his own name and the names of his electors from the top: a gesture of modesty to show that he would not vote for himself.[55]

On a rainy Boston morning, meanwhile, "vote distributors," the men who handed out the ballots with each party's slate of candidates printed on them, patrolled outside the polling places in each ward. So did the Wide Awakes, dressed in their civilian clothes and without torches. (They had held their last big rallies throughout New England a few nights earlier; the young Henry Adams, freshly arrived from an encounter with Garibaldi in Europe, got home just in time to see the Quincy march.) Vote casting was more or less public business in those days—the rival parties' vote distributors, who usually happened to be on the burly side, hovered close to see whose ballot you dropped into the box—so it certainly made sense to have a few Republican reinforcements, just in case. Pickpockets were out in force, too, upholding another tradition of American election days as gold watches and rolls of banknotes vanished from the pockets of well-padded vests. In neighborhoods with many black voters, white politicians stood outside the polls shaking hands and addressing everyone as "Sir"—the only time until next election day, the *Post* hinted, that colored men would enjoy this extraordinary honor. (Massachusetts was one of five states, all of them in New England, that allowed free blacks to vote.[56]) A few African-Americans, however, chose to vote with brickbats instead of ballots, letting fly a hail of projectiles at a procession of John Bell's supporters passing them on Centre Street.

That night, anxious Bostonians of every party crowded telegraph stations and newspaper offices as results came in from across the country. Only a few years earlier, they would have had to wait days or weeks to know who would be the new president. Now there was round-the-clock coverage, with the *Transcript* publishing extra editions every half hour long past midnight, and as for the newsboys, the next morning's paper reported, "the little imps had no sleep last night." First Indiana went for Lincoln, followed by Wisconsin, Iowa, and Connecticut. Massachusetts itself, to no one's surprise, fell into the Republicans' column. When word came that even the conservative states of New York and Pennsylvania had chosen Lincoln, cheers rocked Faneuil Hall, the old Revolutionary shrine, where the city's Wide Awakes had gathered to celebrate their impending victory.[57]

The next morning, the only thing left for Boston to do—at least for the moment—was to sweep up the cigar stubs and crumpled ballots and wonder, once again, what it all meant. The *Transcript*'s editors hailed "a revolution so imposing and grand." "There is something better than being in a majority," they informed readers. "It is better to be in the right. And with that satisfaction Massachusetts has waited through dark nights in the national government, confident that to the darkest night there would be a dawn."

Only one man in the city, perhaps, felt even more confident that he understood the true purport of the Republicans' great victory. That night, a chastened Wendell Phillips strode onstage to address a large audience of abolitionists in the Tremont Temple, just off the Common. "Ladies and gentlemen," he intoned as the hall fell momentarily quiet, "if the telegraph speaks truth, for the first time in our history, the slave has chosen a President of the United States."

SEVEN WEEKS LATER, outside the Boston & Maine depot, the urchins again tugged at travelers' coattails with exciting news. The same story filled the front pages of the *Transcript* and the *Courier*, the *Herald* and the *Bee:* the day before, in Charleston Harbor, Major Anderson had moved his garrison from Fort Moultrie to Fort Sumter. The first blow of resistance to secession had been struck.

That day the newspapers carried another item, too, this one buried inside, and much shorter: Ralph Farnham, the last soldier of Bunker Hill, had died at his farm in Maine. The country would have to look to the future for its heroes.

United States Capitol, Washington, D.C., 1860

CHAPTER TWO

The Old Gentlemen

"Still men and nations reap as they have strawn" . . .
O'er what quenched grandeur must our shroud be drawn?

—JAMES RUSSELL LOWELL,
"The Washers of the Shroud" (1861)

Washington, January 1861

IT MIGHT HAVE SEEMED an unusual transaction, hardly in the common line of business for a big auction house like Green & Williams, with its commodious premises just off Pennsylvania Avenue, halfway between the White House and the Capitol. The partnership's stock-in-trade ran more to real estate, furniture, kitchenware. These were the sorts of valuables that the capital city's transient denizens often left behind, as the ever-revolving wheel of congressional elections and presidential administrations, the waxing and waning of political parties, regularly returned large numbers of inhabitants to the far-flung provinces from which they had so recently arrived.

Still, the potential commission on this sale was tempting, since it might well prove substantial. A Negro male just past the prime of life could fetch a thousand dollars—the price of a modest house and lot in the city—and the one now on offer was no common field hand, but a first-rate house servant. If a sharp-eyed speculator or two attended the sale, the price might go even higher. Shipped down to the New Orleans market, this fellow could bring as much as fifteen hundred, or at least close to it, even if his eventual master only intended to put him to work cutting sugarcane.

A newcomer to Washington that winter might have been surprised, even shocked, to see a slave put on the block here in broad daylight. This was, after all, 1861—hadn't the slave trade in the District of Columbia been abolished more than a decade earlier, as part of the Compromise of 1850? Indeed, it had been heralded at the time as the South's most important concession to the North. For decades, abolitionists had been wailing about the moral stain of human traffic here in the capital of the republic. Their propaganda broadsides had shown coffles of black men and women, shackled together, being marched past the dome of the Capitol itself. Visiting foreigners had written letters and books telling their own countrymen—in tones of outrage permeated with more than a hint of smug satisfaction—about the squalid slave pens at the heart of the Americans' supposed empire of liberty. Now all that was supposed to be a thing of the past.

Few people—at least outside of Washington—noticed that the 1850 law did not actually prohibit slave trading itself. It simply banned anyone from bringing Negroes into the District of Columbia for the purpose of selling them out of state. That took care of those embarrassing coffles: Washington would no longer be a major entrepôt for Negroes being shipped off to the slave-hungry Cotton Belt from the overstocked Chesapeake region. But it was still perfectly legal for a Washingtonian to put his house servant up for public auction, and even to advertise the offering, as Green & Williams did, in the pages of the *Daily National Intelligencer*, the city's leading newspaper and a semi official chronicle of congressional proceedings. If the unlucky slave happened to turn up the following week in one of the Alexandria slave pens right across the Potomac, ready to be packed onto a New Orleans–bound schooner—well, that too was perfectly within the law.[1]

The Negro coming up for sale on this particular occasion was a thirty-three-year-old man named Willis. Selling him might even be called a prestige transaction for Green & Williams, which, though large, was by no means known as one of the more genteel auction houses in the capital. For this slave had been, as the firm boasted in its advertisement, the valued property of "the late Hon. Judge George M. Bibb deceased," one of the District's most distinguished longtime residents.[2]

The courtly, white-haired Judge Bibb—known also, depending on whom you spoke to, as Chancellor Bibb, Senator Bibb, Secretary Bibb—had been a fixture of Washington politics and society ever since his arrival as a young senator from Kentucky during President Madison's first term.[3] As his respectful obituaries noted, he had been at various times United States attorney, secretary of the treasury under President Tyler, and—after retiring from government service and taking up practice as a leading Washington attorney—a habitué of the U.S. Supreme Court chamber. In his politics, the late judge had been admirably moderate: both a proslavery man and a Union man, in the hallowed tradition of his native Virginia. His most notable speech in the Senate had been back in 1833, when South Carolina had threatened to secede over tariffs, one of those almost ceaseless sectional crises and compromises that had preoccupied the federal government throughout recent decades. "My voice is still for peace," Bibb sonorously began, and then spent three and a half hours professing his belief in peace and the Union, the Union and peace. Making frequent allusions to the Founding Fathers, he spoke of states' rights and "the horrors of civil war," and of freedom-loving South Carolina "smarting under the rod of injustice and oppression"—a speech so worthy and so boring, one newspaper noted, that by the time it concluded, every living creature in the Senate chamber, with the exception of the satisfied orator himself, had either fallen asleep or fled.[4]

This is not to say that the late Judge Bibb had been a drab figure. Indeed, he was well known around town for his distinctive ways. Until the end of his life, he clung steadfastly to the fashions of Jefferson's day: silk stockings, buckled knee breeches, and a ruffled white cravat. People saw him, sighed sentimentally, and knew beyond all doubt that they were gazing upon a true gentleman of the old school. The judge was an accomplished musician; his Georgetown neighbors were used to strolling past his fine brick house on a warm evening and hearing the strains of his violin through the open study windows. Then one spring the violin was heard no more.

As for Willis, the Negro, he had been for some years the old gentleman's trusted body servant. It had been he who neatly laid out the silk stockings and knee breeches each morning; who put the violin away in its case; who shaved the grizzled jowls and attended faithfully by the bed during his master's final illness. On the afternoon of the funeral, it was he who prepared refreshments for the distinguished mourners gathered in the judge's parlor, including President Buchanan and most of his cabinet.[5]

Perhaps it was a bit unseemly for a fine family like the Bibbs to advertise their loyal household retainer for sale in the public prints—and then to make poor Willis stand on the block at that shabby auction house as Messrs. Green and Williams hovered assiduously, pointing out his finer qualities to whoever cared to look. As a man approaching middle age, Willis may well have had a wife and children, perhaps members of the District's large free-Negro community, who would be heartbroken if he were sold south. But then, what use had the widow Bibb for a gentleman's valet? Manumission was out of the question: had not the judge himself often declared his staunch opposition to the practice, calling free blacks "a nuisance to society"?[6] There were estate taxes to think of, too; the deceased had left no fewer than seventeen children, and how, pray tell, was a Negro to be divided seventeen ways? Wasn't the sale perfectly legal? Wouldn't the good people of Washington, in any event, forget the matter quickly, remembering the late Hon. George M. Bibb only as a selfless public servant, a kindly neighbor, an honest gentleman?

Money, in the end, was money. So the advertisement appeared in the *Intelligencer* for "One Negro man, named Willis, about thirty-three years of age, and a slave for life." Below that, a shorter line of type: "Also, one Gold Watch."

• • •

WASHINGTON IN THE YEARS before the Civil War often seemed like a city of slaves and old gentlemen.[7]

Black men and women were everywhere: their labor, to a large degree, made the engine of the city run. Northern newcomers in the capital, imagining that slavery meant Negroes toiling by hundreds in the cotton fields, were often surprised at what they saw. Washington's slaves shoveled coal and carried water; carved stone and split wood. Perched on the drivers' seats of hackney cabs, enslaved men solicited fares outside the main railway station; trudging alongside creaking wagons, enslaved women converged on the Central Market each day before dawn, bringing their masters' cabbages and country hams from Maryland farms. It was slaves who, to a considerable degree, were building the grand and gleaming new extensions of the Capitol, just as they had built the old Capitol and the White House more than half a century before. And it was slaves who hauled up Sixteenth Street the daily cartloads of human dung—patrician and plebeian waste all democratically commingled—to be dumped onto a stinking field ten blocks north of the presidential mansion.

Like today's Washington, the nineteenth-century capital attracted both foreign and American tourists. Visitors sometimes remarked that the big hotels—Willard's, Gadsby's, Brown's—seemed like intricate machines run wholly by the Negro servants, who tended fireplaces, waited at table, emptied chamber pots and spittoons, and slept on the bare hallway floors outside guests' rooms. In the city's barbershops, it was almost exclusively black men who shaved the whiskers of lowly and mighty Washingtonians alike: "The senator flops down in the seat," one traveler noted with amusement, "and has his noble nose seized by the same fingers which the moment before were occupied by the person and chin of an unmistakable rowdy." When customers dined at Absolom Shadd's National Eating House on Pennsylvania Avenue, one of the District's finest restaurants, slaves tucked napkins into their collars before serving up specialties of the house: steamed Chesapeake crabs, spit-roasted game birds, and a buttery green soup made with sea turtle meat freshly imported from the Bahamas. Three of those slaves belonged to the hospitable Mr. Shadd himself—who happened to be a free colored man.[8]

Indeed, the usual categories of slave and free, black and white—terms that seemed so simple and stark in the speeches of abolitionist preachers or proslavery politicians—were all mixed up here in the shadow of the Capitol. Census takers recorded only a few thousand slaves in Washington just before the Civil War, a figure that nearly all modern historians have accepted unquestioningly. But most of the District's slaves didn't belong to Washingtonians, and so they weren't counted in the census.⁹ Some were the property of Southern senators, congressmen, and even presidents, who brought them along as butlers, chefs, and body servants.¹⁰ Many more were owned by Maryland and Virginia planters who rented their Negroes out, often for years at a time, to work in the city. Other masters simply sent slaves off to seek employment on their own, demanding only a share of the earnings. The lives of such men and women, though often squalid and impoverished, could occasionally seem like freedom. The District's large population of free Negroes and mulattoes, on the other hand, lived in what sometimes seemed like slavery. In countless small ways each day, they were reminded that Washington was the capital of a country not their own. Any person of African descent was barred from entering the grounds of the Capitol—except, of course, for the servants and laborers whose work was in many respects more indispensible than that of the congressmen. Socializing publicly with whites was almost unthinkable: if Absolom Shadd had tried to sit down for a meal in his own restaurant, it might have sparked a riot. And each night at ten o'clock, when the bell of the Perseverance Fire Company at Eighth and Pennsylvania rang, all blacks—whether slave or free, ash haulers or restaurant owners—had to get off the streets or face arrest, followed sometimes by flogging.¹¹

Curious foreign travelers often found themselves at a loss to understand the intricacies of local racial codes, or even to guess who was a slave and who wasn't. Early in 1861, an English journalist was standing by the front window of Willard's Hotel when he saw a tall, handsome young black man, elegantly attired from head to toe, strolling proudly up the Avenue. The Englishman turned to a white American who stood nearby: "I wonder what he is?" he inquired. "Well," the stranger drawled, "that fellow is not a free nigger; he looks too respectable. I dare say you could get him for fifteen hundred dollars with his clothes off."¹²

What, then, were these Negro men and women? The Supreme Court had ruled that they could never be citizens, and that they had no rights whatsoever that whites were bound to respect. Were they therefore simply property, as anyone might conclude from reading the classified ads in the *Intelligencer* or the ponderous folios kept by the recorder of deeds, where sales of human beings were duly inscribed among the real estate transactions? Or was it possible that they were simply people? Was it even possible that they could, one day, be Americans?

Such were the questions that had for decades bedeviled the capital city's Old Gentlemen: the senators, congressmen, cabinet secretaries, justices, and presidents whose steady hands kept the ship of state on course. These matters had, indeed, bedeviled America's elder statesmen ever since the nation's founding, when a previous generation of wise men, sitting in a shuttered room in Philadelphia in the summer of 1787, had ruminated and decided that the new Constitution would reckon each slave as three-fifths of a human being for purposes of electoral math, and more or less ignore them otherwise. That had seemed to settle the issue—at least to the extent of freeing the new federal union to turn its attention to other things.

Perhaps, indeed, it would be more accurate to say that the Old Gentlemen of the antebellum period were preoccupied not with the question of what black men and women were or might ever be, but with how to avoid the question entirely. Toward that end, they, and much of the nation, had mastered the art of circumlocution. In the best of times, in the politest Washington circles, *slaves* were mentioned rarely; the relative abstraction of *slavery*, only slightly more often; while "our peculiar institution," "the domestic arrangements of the South," and "a certain species of property" were among the euphemisms of choice. And when they talked about "Union," it meant something very different from what it would come to mean a few years later. The word meant a nation united by compromise, preserved through the careful balancing of Southern interests and Northern ones, of slavery and freedom.

They were men of distinction, these Old Gentlemen—of nobility, even. One could see it immediately in their faces. Just down the avenue from Shadd's restaurant, a glass-topped case outside Mathew Brady's National Photographic Art Gallery displayed them in splendid array: "grave and reverent seignors," an admiring reporter for the *Daily National Intelligencer* called them.[13] Everyone came to sit for Mr. Brady in the prewar years. It was a political rite of passage no more optional than a new congressman's taking the oath to support and defend the Constitution. No more partisan, either: men of every party and principle climbed the three flights of wooden stairs—some more nimbly than others—to arrive in a skylighted room where a flock of assistants, and sometimes even the famous proprietor himself, welcomed them. Brady, foppish and ingratiating, made the whole experience so pleasant.

There was a little dressing room with a marble washstand where the client could mop his brow and arrange his hair—generally brushing the locks, scanty though they might be, forward in picturesque Caesarean fashion. When he emerged, a carved oak chair awaited, with a pedestal next to it ready to hold an appropriate prop: a thick gold-stamped volume of the *Annals of Congress*, for example. Occasionally the gentleman wrapped himself in a toga-like cloak, the better to hide a metal clamp that would keep his head from moving during the long exposure. (If he wished instead to rise and strike an oratorical pose—perhaps his recent speech on the tariff question had drawn favorable notice in the newspapers—a convenient metal armrest was also provided.) Then he drew his head back, knit his brows together, formed his mouth into a tight-lipped frown—and within thirty seconds, the Alabama cotton planter or Connecticut attorney was transformed into a veritable Cato the Elder, his visage suitable to be lithographed in a monthly magazine. Perhaps one day it might even be rendered in marble to adorn the state capitol back home.[14]

But anyone stopping by Brady's gallery on the eve of the Civil War would have noticed that the noblest visages, though still ensconced honorably in their glass case, were no longer to be seen in the halls of the Capitol. The statesmen of restraint and moderation, the tongues that spoke in careful euphemisms or cried out eloquently for *Union, Union*, above all else, were becoming scarce. Webster and Clay, twin titans among the compromisers, were dead; so was Thomas Hart Benton, the lion of Missouri. John Bell had gone back to Tennessee, Sam Houston to Texas. Even the ranks of lesser men whose cautious ways had kept the Union safe—men like old Judge Bibb—were dwindling fast.

Brady's studio now received a different sort of senator, in outlook and aspect: Ben Wade of Ohio, flinty eyed and obdurate, a Republican whose radicalism went beyond antislavery to embrace women's suffrage and trade unionism, and who was said to have carried a pair of horse pistols onto the Senate floor. Clement Clay of Alabama, lean and ascetic as an early Christian saint, who railed against Northern abolitionists for "seducing" gullible slaves away from their happy existence in the South, the better to satisfy a perverted appetite for interracial sex.[15] Zachariah Chandler, Republican of Michigan, on whose saturnine head a Democratic colleague broke a milk pitcher one afternoon in the dining room of the National Hotel, this by way of correcting the legislator on a point of political doctrine.[16] And Senator Davis of Mississippi, whom Brady shot standing in three-quarter profile: a figure unbending as ice, eyes distant and pale, like an astronomer gazing toward some far-off star.

A few men of the old cast remained in public life, however, keeping faith that the Union could be preserved through appeals to reason, history, and the rule of law. The scholarly chief justice of the United States, with encouragement from the president himself, had recently tried to resolve the slavery matter once and for all when the case of a Missouri slave named Dred Scott came before the high court. Judge Roger Taney, in fifty-four erudite and densely reasoned pages, had delved deep into English common law, colonial history, and constitutional precedent before reaching his elegantly simple conclusion: men and women of African descent could never, under any current or future circumstances, be considered Americans. Thanks to some quiet political pressure, two Northern justices had even concurred with Taney and his fellow Southerners on the court, lest the ruling seem simply a matter of sectional prejudices. And the result? Like every previous attempt to address slavery directly, this one had ended in disaster. "The Triumph of Slavery Complete," proclaimed newspaper headlines in the North. "Wherever our flag floats," cried William Cullen Bryant in his *Evening Post*, "it is the flag of slavery."[17] The delicate balance maintained for decades collapsed. The abolitionists grew shriller and more militant than ever. John Brown launched his bloody conspiracy. The Union pitched headlong toward dissolution, pushed over the brink by a ruthless paradox: the republic of liberty was also the single largest slaveholding nation in the world.[18]

Now, in the wake of Lincoln's election, the nation's only hope was to stitch together yet another new compromise, by which to continue sheltering both freedom and bondage beneath the same threadbare tent. A generation or two earlier, many Americans, Southerners and Northerners alike, had invested their hope in the gradual and peaceful elimination of slavery. Washington and Jefferson themselves had said this would be the only permanent solution. But by now it was impossible for the nation's leaders to propose such an eventuality, or even to hint that it might be desirable. Not if they wanted to preserve the Union, that is. Slaveholding was now woven so tightly into the South's culture and economy—indeed, into the whole nation's economy—as to be almost inextricable. Even its foes acknowledged this. In 1858, Lincoln himself noted in a speech that the region's four million slaves were valued at no less than two billion dollars. (Most recent historians have put the figure even higher.) This was an absolutely mind-boggling sum, greater than the value of all the nation's factories and railroads, North and South, combined.[19] Any scheme of compensated emancipation—like that adopted by Great Britain several decades earlier—would consume an impracticably huge portion of the federal budget (then about 75 million dollars annually) for at least thirty years, without even accounting for the disruption of Southern agriculture and Northern industry. Slaves, even more than land, were the Southern planters' most valuable and reliable capital asset: not only did they produce annual income (and increase in number over time); they also could be mortgaged, rented, or liquidated quite easily, at prices that were rising steadily each year. The more new territory was opened to slave agriculture, the greater the fresh demand for slave labor, and the higher the value of those human investments would soar.*

No wonder many Southerners, fully aware of these financial realities, so fiercely opposed any limit on slavery's expansion: their stake was not merely in their individual holdings but in the system and market as a whole. No wonder they had long since begun maintaining that slavery was not a tolerable evil but rather a positive good. No wonder, indeed, that many even made a well-reasoned case that white Americans' continued freedom depended on the blacks' continued enslavement. "Actual liberty and equality [for] our white population has been approached much nearer than in the free states," wrote one of the most extreme theorists, Virginia's George Fitzhugh. "Few of our whites ever work as day laborers . . . or in other menial capacities. One free citizen does not lord it over another; hence that feeling of independence and equality that distinguishes us." As for the Declaration of Independence, with its promise of universal equality, Fitzhugh professed disgust that a fellow Virginian and slaveholder could ever have written such a thing, calling the document "absurd and . . . dangerous. . . . Some were born with saddles on their backs," he concluded, "and others booted and spurred to ride them—and the riding does them good."[20]

In 1854, when Fitzhugh wrote those words, it had been easy enough for Northerners to dismiss him as a mere crank propagandist. But soon, even mainstream Southern politicians would be publicly espousing such views. In early 1861, ex-governor Richard Call of Florida—an old-line Unionist—wrote to a friend in Pennsylvania to explain why Northerners must accept slavery as a permanent feature of American life:

---

*As late as 1931, a Florida congressman named R. A. Green introduced a bill in the House that would have paid reparations to former slaveholders and their descendants for the loss of their human "property."

It should be considered as it is, an institution interwoven and inseparably connected with our social and political system, as a domestic institution of the States, and a national institution, created by the American people and protected by the Constitution of the United States. . . . The African seems designed by the Creator for a slave . . . with a mind incapable of a higher elevation than that which is required to direct the machinery of his limbs to useful action.[21]

By then, every American—whether Yankee or Southerner, abolitionist or slaveholder—knew that if the Union was to survive without bloodshed, it would have to remain a version of Washington, D.C., writ large. The squalid realities of slavery would continue their uneasy coexistence with the gleaming monuments of freedom or all would be lost. So, in the dark winter days when the states of the Deep South, one by one, lined up to follow South Carolina out of the Union, it was to the last surviving Old Gentlemen that the hopes of the nation turned.

THROUGH THE SLUSHY STREETS of Washington that January hurried a figure familiar to all the longtime residents of the capital: a white-haired man, his hollow cheeks and lantern jaw like a death's-head on a slate gravestone, his black overcoat flapping around him in the wind. This was the Union's unlikely guardian angel. Almost everyone in the city knew John J. Crittenden, and all who knew him were fond of him, whatever their political faction. He had the bluff good nature of a backcountry farmer: on meeting an acquaintance, the weather-beaten senator would, surprisingly, flush with pleasure like a boy, his thin lips breaking into a lopsided grin to reveal a mouthful of splayed teeth stained mahogany by a lifetime of tobacco chewing. (At one of Senator Seward's high-toned soirees, Crittenden once absentmindedly, though expertly, squirted an ample stream of brown juice onto the richly carpeted floor.)

Kentuckians had first sent Crittenden to the Senate more than forty years earlier. Throughout most of that long span, he had been content to remain in the shadow of his close friend and senior colleague, a man with whom he shared an appreciation for fast horses and fine bourbon: Henry Clay, the Great Compromiser. After Clay's death in 1852, Crittenden had, somewhat against his will, been anointed the moderates' new chieftain. Though he had never made a notably brilliant speech, he hated neither slaveholders nor Republicans, and loved his united country with the unfeigned earnestness of one who had come of age in the days of Jefferson, dined with Lafayette, and fought to defend his nation's sovereignty in 1812. While still a teenager, Crittenden had been a student and protégé of the late Judge Bibb, for whom he later named his eldest son. A Baltimore newspaperman once called him the Senate's "connecting link between the glorious past and the doubtful present."[22]

Now many people hoped Crittenden might be the connecting link that could hold together North and South. By the time the secession crisis broke, he was not only the Senate's leading moderate but also its most senior member. In the days after the presidential election, some Republican newspapers predicted that Lincoln, as a gesture of national unity, would appoint him secretary of state. Other rumors had it that the seventy-four-year-old statesman was on a confidential mission to South Carolina, working behind the scenes to restore calm. Meanwhile, dozens of Crittenden's influential friends—from former President Martin Van Buren to Winfield Scott, the army's highest-ranking general—barraged him with letters proposing various schemes for reconciliation. One envisioned splitting the Union into two perfectly equal parts, while another suggested a law that would emancipate all America's slaves by 1890, at a rate of precisely 3.3 percent each year. John B. Bibb, the brother of Crittenden's old mentor, wrote from his Kentucky plantation to recommend—as many other correspondents did—that the Missouri Compromise of 1820 be reinstated, drawing a line straight across the continent to separate slave territory from free. General Scott laid out a detailed plan that would amicably divide the entire country into four "new Unions," with their capitals at Albany, New York; Columbia, South Carolina; Alton, Illinois; and some unspecified point on the Pacific coast. (If Crittenden found this an odd suggestion from the man in charge of defending the nation's borders, he didn't say.)[23]

Ordinary citizens sent missives, too, offering dozens of different solutions, many of them even more elaborate and far-fetched than Scott's: surely the national puzzle could be solved with a bit of practical Yankee ingenuity, like a mantelpiece clock that had stopped and just needed some tinkering to set it aright. Many forwarded petitions, resolutions, sermons. Appeals came from the concerned citizens of Dubuque, Iowa, and from the inmates of an asylum for "deaf mutes" in Georgia. One New Jerseyan spoke for many when he vented his disgust at abolitionists and Southern extremists alike, proposing that the middle states should together form their own new country, "leaving all the New England states out, to burn witches . . . and affiliate with Niggers. After we get rid of them we shall have peace." There was one thing nearly all the letter writers had in common: they extolled Crittenden as the only person who could save the country. A Virginian addressed him as "one of the Fathers of the Republic." Another called him "the patriarch of the Union." A third man hailed "one of the last of our Country's noblest Patriots," adding, in parentheses, "Alas, for the old days!" An anonymous correspondent signing himself "A Southerner & Lover of His Country" could not restrain his passion: "I love you God knows I love you," his somewhat surprising letter to Crittenden began.[24] Never in his long life had the genial Kentuckian been the object of so much attention, let alone adoration.

It was as though these citizens believed that, by the sheer force of their hopes and prayers, they could somehow transform an elderly, mild-mannered legislator into some sort of reincarnation of George Washington, into a latter-day national saint. "The eyes of all good men in all sections are turned toward you," a minister in Baltimore wrote. "The prospect looks dark, but the God of our Fathers will I believe yet in some way bring deliverance. . . . Unless indeed our national sins are so great that God must punish us."[25]

Interestingly, few Americans pinned their hopes for compromise on either the outgoing president or the incoming one. Buchanan was a lame duck, while Lincoln remained at home in Springfield, still seemingly as mute about his plans and intentions as the inmates of that Georgia asylum.[26] ("We don't know *what Lincoln wants*," even a leading Republican congressman complained. "He communicates nothing even to his friends here & so we drift along.")[27] Anyhow, the federal government's executive branch in the antebellum period had usually been far less powerful than its legislative branch. In nearly all past crises, the compromises that preserved the Union had been forged in Congress.

Four years earlier, when Preston Brooks had bludgeoned Charles Sumner on the floor of the Senate, it was Crittenden who tried to step between the two men, crying out, "Don't kill him!"—only to have another Southern congressman brandish his cane to block the Kentuckian from intervening.[28] He had failed to stop the bloodshed that day. Now the nation seemed to depend on whether he could succeed—this time on a far larger scale.

So the old man made his sedulous way around the city, pushing his blueprint for national harmony on almost any colleague who would listen. It was not quite as intricate as General Scott's exercise in topographic geometry, but almost. The Crittenden Compromise, as it came to be known, proposed six amendments to the U.S. Constitution, all of them granting major concessions to the peculiar institution. The first of these amendments would reinstate the Missouri Compromise line, protecting slavery in all the states and territories south of it—including any territories that might be acquired in the future. The second would deny Congress the authority to abolish slavery anywhere under its jurisdiction within a slave state (a military base, for instance). The third specifically protected slavery's existence in the District of Columbia. The fourth barred Congress from interfering with the interstate slave trade (and thus abrogated the Commerce Clause, which since 1787 had been a cornerstone of the Constitution). The fifth promised that slaveholders who had been forcibly prevented from recovering escaped slaves—prevented by abolitionists, that is—would receive full restitution for their "property" from the federal government. Crittenden's sixth and final amendment would block all the other amendments from ever being altered, and deny Congress forever the power to abolish slavery.[29]

His mission was a lonely one. Since Congress had reconvened at the beginning of December—the first time since Lincoln's election—sarcasm, invective, and histrionics had prevailed.[30] Legislator reopened old wounds at any opportunity, called one another "the *honorable* Senator" in tones communicating quite the opposite, and turned disagreements over minor points of order into occasions for roiling tirades against the treason of secession or the perfidy of abolition. About ninety seconds into the session's first day, Senator Thomas Clingman of North Carolina, seizing the floor by responding to a routine motion about printing a document, swerved sharply into an hour-long attack on the president-elect as a "dangerous man" whose aim was "to make war on my section [of the country] until its social system is destroyed." As soon as Clingman sat down, Senator Crittenden rose to beg his colleagues to maintain a tone of "calm consideration" in the face of impending national disaster. His entreaties were futile. The next morning, Senator Alfred Iverson of Georgia arrived with a speech in hand that made Clingman's sound measured: "Sir, disguise the fact as you will, there is an enmity between the Southern people that is deep and enduring, and you can never eradicate it—never! . . . We are enemies as much as if we were hostile States." Southern politicians who opposed secession, Iverson intimated, should be assassinated if they did not submit. And he closed with a promise to "meet . . . all the myrmidons of Abolitionism and Black Republicanism everywhere, upon our own soil; and . . . we will 'welcome you with bloody hands to hospitable graves.'"[31]

Perhaps the feistiest Southerner of all was Louis T. Wigfall, a freshman senator from Texas. If Crittenden represented the past, this new man from a new state might represent the future—though there were many who devoutly hoped not. His very face was that of a man who, whatever his other endowments might be, found it unbearable to hear more than three or four words spoken consecutively by anyone else. His beetling eyebrows clenched and unclenched when he talked (which was almost incessantly), and his pugnacious black beard seemed to jut out perpendicular to his face. Even his nose, an English journalist wrote, was somehow "argumentative." But his eyes, the writer continued, were most dangerously transfixing: "of wonderful depth and light, such as I never saw before but in the head of a wild beast. If you look some day when the sun is not too bright into the eye of a Bengal tiger, in the Regent's Park, as the keeper is coming round, you will form some notion of the expression I mean."[32]

By the age of twenty-five, Wigfall had managed to squander his considerable inheritance, settle three affairs of honor on the dueling ground, fight in a ruthless military campaign against the Seminoles, consume a small lakeful of bourbon, win an enviable reputation in whorehouses throughout the South, and get hauled before a judge on charges of murder. Three years after that, he took the next logical step and went into Texas politics. Of all the Southern fire-eaters in the Senate, Wigfall was the most flamboyant—and inflexible. He scorned the very idea of compromise, openly relished the prospect of spilling Yankee blood, and crowed the war would end only after Southern troops had cut a swath of destruction across the North, with the final capitulation signed in Faneuil Hall.[33]

Just before Christmas, when Crittenden first unveiled his proposal before the full Senate, a respectful calm fell over the chamber for the first time in weeks. Everyone knew that he had been laboring over a plan. When the senior senator rose, he began neither a philippic against secession nor a sentimental paean to the Union. Instead, he set forth his series of amendments as dryly as if he were introducing a bill to adjust domestic postage rates. Then he turned to the widening chasm over slavery. In such controversies, he assured his colleagues philosophically, "all the wrong is never on one side, or all the right on the other. Right and wrong, in this world, and in all such controversies, are mingled together." Finally, he called on his countrymen, of every state and party, to set aside their differences in the name of the Constitution, of the flag, of the memory of Washington. Why consign all these to oblivion, he asked, when the alternative was "a comparative trifle": simply drawing across the national map a perpetual "line of division between slavery and freedom" that would ensure a lasting peace? Hearing Crittenden's peroration from the back of the chamber, one young Democratic congressman was deeply impressed. The old man spoke, he later wrote, "as if the muse of history were listening to him."[34]

Would anyone besides Clio listen, though? Crittenden had no sooner sat down than John P. Hale, Republican from New Hampshire, sprang to his feet to praise "the purity of his motive, the integrity, the disinterestedness, and the fervor of his patriotism." Surely Crittenden winced. After forty years in this chamber, he knew that such praise was only ever spoken as a kind of legislative eulogy. And in fact, Hale's next words were like the coffin lid slamming shut: "Everybody accords to him that [much], whatever may be thought of the value or the practicability of the remedy he proposes, and I do not propose to discuss it." The honorable body then fell back into bickering over the four-year-old *Dred Scott* case. Crittenden's six amendments were respectfully lowered into the deep, dark grave known as a special bipartisan committee. The next morning's newspapers confirmed his compromise dead and buried already. "There is no gleam of sunshine, no ray of hope," began a typical report, in the *New York Herald*. The newspaper went on to suggest that the only chance for peace was a well-timed smallpox epidemic to wipe official Washington off the map.[35]

Soon enough, though, despite the dismissive pronouncements of journalists and politicians, many Americans would be calling for a resurrection of the Crittenden Compromise. Two days after the bill had been declared dead, news came from Charleston that South Carolina had seceded. Six days after that, Major Anderson—Crittenden's friend and fellow Kentuckian[36]—moved his troops into Fort Sumter. Suddenly war felt like a much more imminent and real prospect than it had a week earlier, when it had seemed to many merely a phantasm of congressional bluster. The senator's "comparative trifle" of safeguarding slavery might indeed be a bargain price for peace. So while Crittenden's plan languished in the oblivion of the special bipartisan committee, his name became a rallying cry for people across the country. Each day, larger and larger bundles of mail arrived in the Capitol post office: sheaves of individual letters at first, and then parcels bound up in twine and brown paper, some of them quite bulky. The first of these mass petitions was from the citizens of Harrisburg and Carlisle, Pennsylvania, conservative towns in the southern part of the state. Before long, others were arriving from Philadelphia, from Illinois, even from New England. New York City's two petitions bore 63,000 names. The appeal from St. Louis filled ninety-five pages of foolscap paper and came wrapped, literally, in the American flag. The one from Massachusetts—hit hard by the first economic shocks of the crisis—was a scroll so massive that it had to be rolled like a cartwheel onto the floor of the House. One particular petition especially pleased Crittenden: it was signed by 14,000 women in states from Vermont to North Carolina. ("I hope their interposition may have some influence upon the sterner nature of man," he told the Senate.) So many entreaties eventually arrived that it required four pages of small type in the *Senate Journal* simply to list the names of all the towns and cities. Elsewhere massive outdoor rallies were held despite the January cold. On a snowy night in Philadelphia, six thousand "workingmen" gathered outside Independence Hall and unanimously endorsed Crittenden's plan with throaty cheers.[37]

Part of the reason for such an outpouring is that people were starting to grasp the potential costs—the literal costs—of war. The first warning came from the stock market, which began to falter and then plunge in the first weeks after Lincoln's election. Few ordinary citizens owned shares in those days, but when wealthy bankers like August Belmont began reporting that their investments were down as much as 30 percent, more democratic misery seemed certain to follow. Textile manufacturers and their shareholders panicked at the prospect of losing the South's cotton shipments; by January, their stocks had fallen 40 percent from what they were a year earlier. Western merchants and steamboat lines faced the possibility that the entire lower Mississippi might be closed to commercial shipping indefinitely. And would secession mean that all the debts owed by Southern planters—many of them mortgaged up to their eyebrows—would become uncollectable? Demand for new goods plummeted, and soon enough factories began laying off workers by the tens of thousands. "Boston streets to-day are full of discharged workmen," reported the *Boston Courier*. "Our laboring population have a dreary winter before them."[38] Ads that began appearing in the major New York newspapers did not exactly help matters:

In consequence of the
PANIC! PANIC! PANIC!
We are determined to offer our very large stock of fall importa-

tions for the balance of the season at such prices as will command an immediate sale.

E. WILLIAMS & CO.

Owing to the troublesome times into which our country has
    fallen we have made a
FURTHER REDUCTION
in our prices, in order to convert our goods into cash before the
UNION GOES TO PIECES!

W.J.F. Dailey & Co.[39]

One day in early January, when a rumor reached Wall Street that "the
compromise measures proposed by Mr. Crittenden had been agreed to
unanimously," stocks shot instantly back up, only to drop again when
the report proved erroneous. In the weeks that followed, as grassroots
support for the Crittenden plan surged, the market began gradually
rising once more. " 'It is said' and 'perhaps' are quite sufficient to give
stocks a lift," noted the editor of one commercial newspaper.[40]

It was a month of hearsay, anonymous leaks, and contradictions; a
month when everything seemed to be happening much too fast, and
when many of the strangest reports were the ones that turned out to
be true. In Washington, there was talk of an impending coup d'état
against the federal government, a popular uprising against the "official
imbecility" that was letting the nation drift toward the brink of catastrophe. Hastily formed militia units drilled by night in the remoter
reaches of the District, pledging that they would sooner reduce the
entire capital to ashes than permit the inauguration of a Black Republican president.[41] In New York, Mayor Fernando Wood declared his
support for secession: not just of the South but also of his own city,
which was to become an independent trading republic. (One presumes
that the mayor himself would have become its president.) Wood even
had a name for his imaginary nation: "Tri-Insula," since it would con-
sist of Manhattan, Staten Island, and Long Island. New York's city
council endorsed the idea, as did a number of leading businessmen. "I
would have New York a free city," one of them wrote, "not a free city
with respect to the liberty of the negro, but a free city in commerce
and trade."[42]

The national disaster seemed to have unleashed all manner of explo-
sive energies, sending the planets spinning out of their accustomed
orbits. Every day brought fresh astonishments. One morning in late
January, Northern readers opened their newspapers to discover sup-

port for Southern secession coming from the very last place they would have expected. At a Boston abolitionist meeting, Wendell Phillips had rejoiced at the slave states' departure and the Constitution's demise. "The Covenant with Death is annulled—the Agreement with Hell is broken to pieces," he cried. "The chain which has held the slave system since 1787 is parted." The closing words of his speech seemed calculated to provoke howls of rage—and did: "All hail, then, Disunion!"

Telegraphic dispatches brought Phillips's speech to readers across the North, most of whom—even those who spared no sympathy for slaveholders—branded him a traitor. ("THE UNHOLY ALLIANCE," screamed a typical headline in the usually staid and solidly Republican *New York Times.* "The Abolitionists Giving the Right Hand of Fellowship to the Disunionists.") Less than a week later, when Phillips again stepped onto a public stage at the annual meeting of the Massachusetts Anti-Slavery Society, several hundred rough-looking characters—clearly not dues-paying members—packed the balconies. As soon as he tried to speak, they drowned him out with hisses, jeers, foot-stomping, barnyard noises, cheers for Crittenden and the Union, and even a sarcastic chorus or two of "Dixie." Next, no less a luminary than Ralph Waldo Emerson stepped up warily with a sheaf of lecture notes in hand, only to be hooted and heckled off the speakers' platform. At last, after the mayor of Boston ordered the hall cleared to avert a full-on riot and abolitionists scattered in all directions, several hundred infuriated demonstrators chased Phillips back to his house on Essex Street, waving brickbats and howling "Carve him out!" as policemen struggled to restrain the mob. For weeks afterward Phillips was a virtual prisoner, with bodyguards standing vigil outside his front door and Boston toughs prowling nearby, vowing vengeance.[43]

Back in Washington, however, Crittenden's cause—despite such warm support in the North—was growing more and more desperate. Time and again he took to the Senate floor with his latest armload of petitions. He hosted a dinner party for thirty people at the National Hotel—hospitality that stretched the limits of his modest pocketbook—including such potential allies as General Scott and the justices of the Supreme Court, as well as influential senators and congressmen from both parties. When that availed him little, he made an unprecedented proposal: Congress, instead of voting on the compromise package, should submit it to a nationwide popular referendum. Finally, to render his legislative ideas yet more alluring to the South, he added two new constitutional amendments that had originally been suggested by Stephen Douglas. One would bar free blacks from voting in elections or holding public office, while the other guaranteed that if any state wished to eliminate its population of free blacks entirely, the federal government would pay to have them shipped off to Africa or South America. "Peace and harmony and union in a great nation were never purchased at so cheap a rate," Crittenden pleaded to his Northern colleagues, sounding more than ever like a rug merchant trying to unload the last odds and ends of his shopworn stock. A few weeks earlier, he had called the price a comparative trifle; now he compared it to "a barleycorn" and "a little atom."[44]

But fewer and fewer of Crittenden's fellow senators from the free states seemed much interested in his merchandise, no matter how low the price. The entire existence of the Republican Party was predicated on a commitment to containing slavery within its present bounds. Were its leaders to abrogate this fundamental principle, at the very hour of their electoral triumph? The cartloads of petitions in support of compromise must be weighed against the grassroots fervor of the recent campaign: nearly two million Americans in the North had voted for Lincoln, despite all the Southern warnings that his victory would mean disunion. Although it was true that the Republican candidate had carried the nation as a whole with fewer than 40 percent of the votes cast, all but three of the Northern states had given him solid majorities—in some cases, overwhelming ones. It was clear which way the wind was blowing above the Mason-Dixon Line; Major Anderson's move to Fort Sumter had made him a hero precisely because he had refused to yield to Southern threats.

Perhaps more important, the radical slave-state senators were making it clear that even the Crittenden plan would not satisfy them. Wigfall and others proclaimed a "Southern Manifesto": "The argument is exhausted. All hope of relief in the Union . . . is extinguished, and we trust the South will not be deceived by appearances or the pretense of new guarantees. . . . We are satisfied the honor, safety, and independence of the Southern people require the organization of a Southern Confederacy."[45]

Faced with such intransigence, and with news of the secession fever sweeping across the South, many Northerners began wondering what gain would come of abasing themselves yet again before the slave power. By mid-January, even such a moderate as George Templeton Strong, who had cheered the hanging of John Brown, and who since November had been hoping earnestly for a compromise, was ready to throw up his hands. All the slave states seemed now to be tilting toward secession, he noted in his diary. "But what can we do? What can *I* do? What could I do if I were Webster and Clay combined? Concession to these conspirators and the ignorant herd they have stimulated to treason would but postpone the inevitable crisis a year or two longer."[46]

One by one, the states of the Deep South were already withdrawing. As they joined the new Confederacy, one Southern senator after another rose in the chamber to declaim his valedictory address. Some left bitter recriminations as their last entries in the congressional annals, others gave unctuous and regretful farewells. On January 7, Senator Robert Toombs of Georgia used his departure speech to fire parting shots at "Black Republicans" and abolitionists: "We want no negro equality, no negro citizenship; we want no negro race to degrade our own; and as one man [we] would meet you upon the border with the sword in one hand and the torch in the other." On January 21, David Levy Yulee of Florida took his leave more genteelly, "acknowledging, with grateful emotions, my obligations for the many courtesies I have enjoyed [from] the gentlemen of this body, and with most cordial good wishes for their personal welfare." His fellow Floridian, Stephen Mallory, blasted the North with brimstone: "You cannot conquer us. Imbrue your hands in our blood and the rains of a century will not wipe from them the stain, while coming generations will weep for your wickedness and folly." Finally it was Jefferson Davis's turn. In a low, hoarse voice, weakened by recent illness and by the emotion of the moment, he offered a courtly godspeed to his longtime colleagues: "I carry with me no hostile remembrance. Whatever offence I have given which has not been redressed, or for which satisfaction has not been demanded, I have, Senators, in this hour of parting, to offer my apology. . . . Senators, having made the announcement which the occasion seemed to me to require, it only remains to me to bid you a final adieu."[47]

At these words, Davis and four of his fellow Southerners turned to make their way slowly up the aisle toward the door. It is said that spectators sobbed in the gallery, as stern legislators choked back tears. The Union seemed truly—perhaps irrevocably—dissolved. Democrats and a few moderate Republicans crowded around to shake the five men's hands and wish them well. The rest of the Northerners sat, hands folded, at their desks. Then the Senate returned to the rest of the day's business: Kansas statehood, the Crittenden amendments, sarcastic potshots, and occasional full-on broadsides of vilification and bombast.

The centrifuge was spinning faster and faster. Washington itself seemed to be coming apart. There was only one strange, surreal point of calm at the center of the tempest: the old gentleman in the White House.

NEW YEAR'S DAY in the nation's capital was, by tradition, a moment of partisan truce and the annual reenactment of a peculiar democratic ritual. On the first afternoon of each year, the doors of the White House were thrown open to any moderately respectable and decently washed citizens who wished to shake hands with their chief executive, wish him the compliments of the season, and partake liberally of federally funded punch and cake.[48]

The mansion had achieved unprecedented splendor during James Buchanan's administration. Shortly after the inauguration, Miss Harriet Lane, the bachelor president's niece and White House hostess, had undertaken a costly redecoration using funds generously appropriated by Congress. The austerely classical furnishings dating back to President Monroe's era were sent to auction, replaced by heavy draperies, fine carpets, and amply stuffed settees and divans in the latest rococo style. Moreover, Mr. Buchanan and Miss Lane entertained often and generously. Though the president had few, if any, close friends, he delighted in small talk, especially with the ladies, trading tidbits of gossip on the capital's latest social scandals. It was a golden age of female fashions, and the state rooms' gilded chandeliers shone on gowns of crimson velvet, gloves trimmed with antique lace, and wreaths of clematis crowning the glossy hair of senators' wives. The Democratic president was no snob, however. He opened his home to everyone from ambassadors to Indian chiefs, and held public levees quite frequently even when it did not happen to be New Year's Day. During a recent reception for the Japanese envoys, uninvited strangers had packed the East Room, some even clambering atop Miss Lane's precious pier tables for a glimpse of the exotic Orientals.[49]

But the last New Year's levee of the Buchanan administration was a sadly diminished affair. Four years of indiscriminate hospitality had taken their toll on the White House. Its wallpaper was greasy in places where visitors had brushed against it with sweaty hands or pomaded hair; its carpets were worn down by muddy boots and stained with tobacco juice. (In antebellum days, one senator later remembered, brown spittle flowed so freely that "you had to wear your overshoes into the best society of Washington.") Moreover, the crowd was sparse and the mood anything but cheerful. As the strains of the marine band sounded from a nearby vestibule, political enemies squared off warily on opposite sides of the East Room as if for some elaborate quadrille.

Some men and women wore ribboned cockades on their chests as tokens of political sympathies: red, white, and blue for the Union, solid blue for secession. More than a few from each faction had come for the punch and cake but disdained to shake their host's hand. The president and his niece were receiving guests in the (solid) Blue Room, surely just an unfortunate coincidence. As at all their levees, the slim, blond Miss Lane was dressed to perfection, and Mr. Buchanan's tall figure, at least from across the room, looked stately in its black frock coat and high collar. His head, as usual, was cocked quizzically to one side from some odd nervous tic, as though he had always just failed to catch the last thing that was said. It was only when guests drew closer that they noticed the president's customary aspect altered. His hair—which a female admirer had once found as silky and glistening as the tail feathers of the glass birds of paradise in Barnum's Museum—was now shockingly white. Buchanan's one good eye was dull and unfocused, his head more askew than ever. "It was his last New Year as President," the *New York World*'s correspondent mused afterward, "perhaps the last of our republic; and as he went through the hollow mockery of the occasion, he could not but feel how unreal it was."[50]

It should never have ended thus. James Buchanan had been one of the best-qualified men ever to win the presidency: so long and diligent had been his career in government that he liked to refer to himself deprecatingly as "the Old Public Functionary." Over the past half century, he had served his nation ably as representative to Congress, senator, and secretary of state. Though born the son of a country storekeeper, he had represented the United States with distinction at the courts of Czar Nicholas and Queen Victoria, returning home with all the subtle expertise in diplomatic graces to be learned in St. Petersburg and London. At the Court of St. James's, indeed, he had been so scrupulous as to agonize for weeks over what to wear when presenting his credentials to the Queen. Should he costume himself like George Washington in knee breeches and powdered wig? Carry the customary sword of a European envoy? In the end, he steered a prudent middle course, attiring himself in black like an ordinary American gentleman, but bringing the sword along, too. Some might have scoffed, but Buchanan's admirers saw this as just the kind of evenhandedness that the country needed in its leading statesmen.[51] His domestic positions, too, were always judicious. Though a Pennsylvanian, he loathed abolitionist rabble-rousers, never spoke a disparaging word about slavery, and appointed a carefully balanced cabinet of Northerners and Southerners.[52]

Disunion had long seemed to him such a far-fetched proposition as to be almost existentially impossible. Back in 1832, Buchanan had written in mild frustration to President Jackson about his first visit to the Russian court. The czarina, he said, would not stop talking about the difficulties between the Northern and Southern states—rumors of which had reached even as far as St. Petersburg. Was this not a serious threat to the young republic, she asked, perhaps worse even than the possibility of war with a European power? Buchanan told the president that his efforts to convince her otherwise had been in vain:

> I endeavored in a few words to explain this subject to her; but she still persisted in expressing the same opinion, and, of course, I would not argue with her. The truth is, that the people of Europe, and more especially those of this country, cannot be made to understand the operations of our Government. Upon hearing of any severe conflicts of opinion in the United States, they believe what they wish, that a revolution may be the consequence.[53]

Now it seemed that Her Imperial Highness, surveying American politics from that distant Baltic shore, had been shrewder than he.

Buchanan's inauguration in 1857 had come at a rare moment of relative concord, and was greeted with such pomp and fanfare that one observer said it resembled an imperial coronation. The swearing-in, another wrote, drew supporters "from every State and Territory in the Union; the pale-faced, sharp-set New England man jostled the thicker-skinned and darker-hued Southerner."[54] Then, just two days later, the Supreme Court—having received discreet encouragement from the president-elect—handed down its *Dred Scott* decision. So much for national unity. For the next four years, Buchanan buried himself in the minutiae of office, toiling sixteen-hour days at the White House; some called him the hardest-working president in history. He labored over multiple handwritten drafts of even the most mundane letter, and each routine official document—whether a land grant, a military commission, or a consular appointment—could not receive the president's signature without his careful perusal of every line. It surprised no one that he showed no desire to seek reelection in 1860. As Buchanan's term drew toward its close, the president would tell anyone who would listen that he couldn't wait to get out of the accursed White House and back to his Lancaster County estate. In any case, there was little danger he would have been asked to remain. By then, millions of Northerners detested him as an appeaser of the slave power, while Southerners distrusted him as a weak and vacillating ally at best. Both sides despised the corruption that had seeped into federal officialdom under his stewardship. Neither would have wished the secession crisis to happen on his watch.

Though Buchanan may already have proven a spectacularly ineffectual leader, he was neither a villain nor a coward, despite what his enemies said at the time and what his detractors have said since. When secession loomed in the weeks after Lincoln's election, he stepped into the breach with the mightiest weapon at his disposal: his pen. He had always been a man who trusted pieces of paper to solve things—witness his misplaced faith in *Dred Scott*—and so now he set out to compose a document that would freeze disunion in its tracks.

At the end of each year, it was the president's responsibility to issue an annual message to Congress, the precursor to today's State of the Union address. Buchanan began writing his just a day or two after Lincoln was elected, and for the next month he did little but work on the draft, anxious that the document should be ready to send to the lame-duck Congress when it opened its session on December 3. As chief executive of the nation, Buchanan felt it was his role to serve as high arbiter of the unfolding conflict, expressing judgments that all factions would have to concede were wise and fair.

Toward that end he revised and polished the composition numerous times, reading various sections aloud to his Northern and Southern cabinet members and asking for comments, which were naturally so contradictory of one another that the poor president found himself doing far more scribbling and crossing out than he could have anticipated. (The only point on which everyone concurred was how felicitously written it was.) Toward the end of November, he welcomed Senator Davis into his office to endure a full recitation. The Mississippian made many helpful suggestions—all of which Buchanan "very kindly accepted," Davis would recall much later—although by the time the document was complete, it had gone through so many further drafts that Davis could no longer find in it much to agree with. Still, the president dutifully toiled, though he was now feeling increasingly unwell and, instead of going into his office, would work in his private library, dressed in a silk robe and chewing on an unlit cigar. He at last finished his opus, now running to some fourteen thousand words, at the beginning of December. (To be fair, Buchanan expended some of those words addressing not merely the crisis of the Union but also such other pressing matters as crop failures in Kansas, Chinese-American diplomatic relations, and problems with mail delivery on the Pacific coast.) By this time, of course, South Carolina's leaders had set a date for their secession convention and were cheerfully making plans for their state's future as an independent republic, while the rest of the cotton states were preparing to follow suit.[55]

Unsurprisingly, Buchanan's message ended up satisfying no one, either within Congress or without it. The Southern states, he firmly declared, had no legal right to secede from the Union. If they elected to do so, he suggested, they really ought to call it "revolution" instead of "secession." And even if they did have a right to leave the Union, why do so simply because a man they didn't like had been elected president? And even if they did feel compelled to leave the Union because Lincoln had been elected president, why not wait until after he took office, to see whether he was truly as awful as they feared? The North, meanwhile, needed to realize that the slaveholders' only real wish was "to be let alone." So why not oblige them? As for the federal government's role in averting the disaster, Buchanan admitted regretfully that "it is beyond the power of any president, no matter what may be his own political proclivities, to restore peace and harmony among the states," since this would be a violation of state sovereignty. In other words, while the Constitution forbade secession, it also forbade the federal government to prevent it. Buchanan's final suggestion: What if the United States bought Cuba from Spain? That would help the South by adding a major new slave state, but it would also please the abolitionists. Under Spanish rule, the island imported thousands of slaves each year from Africa, but U.S. law would forbid this. Everybody (except perhaps the Cuban slavers) could be happy.

"Seldom," wrote the editors of the *Cincinnati Enquirer*, "have we known so strong an argument come to so lame and impotent a conclusion." *The Atlantic*'s James Russell Lowell was even harsher: President Buchanan's message, he wrote, was "the last juiceless squeeze of the orange."[56]

WHILE BUCHANAN HAD BEEN off squeezing his orange, members of his administration had been playing rather more influential roles in the developing crisis, and not necessarily in support of the government they were sworn to uphold.

At the center of the intrigue was an urbane Charlestonian named William Henry Trescot, who had been serving for the past six months as assistant secretary of state. During most of that time, he had more or less run the State Department. The venerable secretary himself, Lewis Cass, was a crumbling monument to another age whom Buchanan had appointed as a sop to the North, which considered Cass a hero for his gallantry in the Michigan Territory during the War of 1812. Trescot was the administration's only high-ranking South Carolinian; he was also perhaps its only truly industrious and enterprising member. Two days after the presidential results came in, he called on Secretary Floyd at the War Department, bearing a purchase order for ten thousand muskets to be sent to his native state, which Floyd was happy to execute. As the Fort Moultrie confrontation began to take shape, Trescot also took it upon himself to open a channel of private communication with South Carolina's governor, William Henry Gist, whom he kept apprised of the Buchanan administration's plans.

After Buchanan finished his message to Congress, still completely unaware of Trescot's machinations, he summoned the assistant secretary to carry a copy to Governor Gist. (Little did he know that Gist had been informed of its basic substance weeks earlier, possibly sooner than Buchanan knew it himself.) The president was confident that the message would prove persuasive. Trescot hinted gently that such optimism was unwarranted, but went to Columbia anyhow, taking the occasion to familiarize himself thoroughly with South Carolina's strategy for winning its independence without resistance or bloodshed. A crucial part of that strategy was making sure federal troops did not reinforce the forts in Charleston Harbor. Trescot assured Governor Gist that Floyd and his fellow Southerners in the Buchanan cabinet would never let this happen. (The fact that Trescot's family owned a summer cottage a hundred yards from Fort Moultrie on Sullivan's Island may have been further inducement to forestall an artillery barrage.)[57]

Floyd himself, while believing in the justice of slavery and loathing the Black Republicans, may not yet have been fully convinced that secession was in the South's best interests. Still, if hostilities did break out, he was in little doubt as to which side he would support. It was not difficult for the glib Trescot to maneuver him—and, through him, the president.[58]

Buchanan was now beset from several sides at once. A delegation of South Carolina congressmen, knowing that their days in Washington were numbered, visited the White House. They sought Buchanan's assurance that Major Anderson would stay where he was until an amicable settlement could be worked out, while the other two Charleston forts would be left unoccupied. In return, they said, they would try to ensure that no one attacked Moultrie—at least for the next ten days, until South Carolina could secede officially. Ever the courteous diplomat, Buchanan nodded, smiled gravely, and assured them that he was in complete sympathy with their views. "After all, this is a matter of honor among gentlemen," he told his visitors as they rose to depart. "We understand each other."

No doubt Buchanan was satisfied with himself: he had won at least an extra week and a half of peace with little more than a handshake and a few reassuring words. But what exactly had he promised in return? The Carolinians were certain that they understood the arrangement, but there is little evidence that Buchanan did.[59]

The tacitly arranged truce—unknown, of course, to Major Anderson and his officers at Charleston—did last the ten days until South Carolina's secession, and even a week after that. Then one morning at the end of the month, President Buchanan was upstairs in the White House when a servant brought him word that three gentlemen were calling unexpectedly: Assistant Secretary Trescot, Senator Davis, and another Southern senator, R. M. T. Hunter of Virginia. Buchanan found the visitors seated in his office. Anxious that something unpleasant was afoot, he began toying with his cigar, making nervous small talk about a certain thorny problem he had just been addressing, a vexing issue that concerned the American consul at Liverpool. Jefferson Davis cut him off. "Mr. President," he said, "we have called upon you about an infinitely greater matter than any consulate." "What is it?" Buchanan asked. Davis asked if he had heard any reports from Charleston in the past two or three hours. The president had not. "Then," said Davis, "I have a great calamity to announce to you."

As the president listened to Davis's news—that Major Anderson had transferred his force to Fort Sumter—he slumped against the marble mantelpiece, crumpling the cigar between his fingers. "My God," Buchanan said, "are misfortunes never to come singly? I call God to witness—you gentlemen better than anybody know—that this is not only without, but *against* my orders. It is against my policy."[60]

But the following days would show that all Buchanan's assurances and apologies were in vain. It was not long before the South Carolina congressmen complained publicly that the president had broken his solemn word. He had tried to be a friend to all, to settle things as a matter of honor among gentlemen. Now both sides called him not merely a weakling, but a traitor. There was not much left for James Buchanan to do but wait—like millions of other Americans—and see what other hands might arrange.

•   •   •

IN THOSE LAST ANTEBELLUM DAYS, the White House was over-shadowed in its role of governing the country by another institution, two blocks away. This was Willard's Hotel. The folds and ravels of its endless corridors sheltered more political intrigue than the presidential mansion, while on any given morning, far more business was legislated at its breakfast tables than in either chamber of Congress. A morning repast at Willard's might include oysters, roast pigeons, fresh shad, pigs' feet, and robins on toast—all washed down, perhaps, with official Washington's two favorite digestifs: strong cigars and stronger whiskey. The cocktail hour, guests noticed, began early and ended late—often, indeed, sometime after sunrise the following day.[61]

Since its beginnings in President Madison's time as a humble inn, the hotel had, through a characteristically American process of incessant self-aggrandizement, grown to encompass almost an entire block. Rather than demolish any buildings that stood in its path, Willard's strangled them like some relentless jungle vine, sending out shoots and tendrils of faux marble, carved oak, and polished brass until the unfortunate structures were wholly engulfed. In the winter of 1861, it had recently swallowed up God himself, in the form of a handsome little Greek Revival church that the Presbyterians hastily vacated, paying due reverence to the superior claims of America's nascent hospitality industry.[62]

During the first days of February, employees of Willard's could be seen fussing over the nave of that church, which had been reconsecrated as a conference room with the secular name of Willard's Hall. At the altar end they installed three portraits: George Washington, Andrew Jackson, and Henry Clay.[63] Soon afterward, a fourth figure from American history was installed beneath the other three: John Tyler. The former president appeared not as a lithographed engraving but in the actual—now fairly diminished—flesh. In most important respects, though, he had a great deal in common with those other heroes. Like Washington, Jackson, and Clay, he was a slaveholder. Like them, he was a border-state man—in his case, a Virginian, a scion of the Cavaliers, not one of those swaggering Gulf Coast parvenus who had lately made such mischief on the congressional floor. And like them, Tyler loved the Union, at least for the time being. On the basis of these claims, the last one especially, he was selected by unanimous acclamation president of the Peace Conference of 1861.

This meeting was Virginia's idea. The Old Dominion, after all, had once invested heavily in the concept of the United States as . . . well, *united states*. (Wizened Mr. Tyler, as a boy, had shaken the great Washington's hand.) In 1787, when the loose-jointed American confederation was tottering precariously, it had been the Virginians who stepped forward to steady things, orchestrating a new form of government that balanced North and South, states and nation, freedom and slavery. So the concept of a Virginia-led "solemn family council"—as the Charlottesville patriarch William Cabell Rives, once Thomas Jefferson's law student, put it—seemed, at least to its organizers, to be blessed by history itself. (Nor were such men as Rives unmindful of self-interest. They knew that in the event of all-out war, their state would be the battleground.) Virginia's state legislature issued the call to convene; her fellow border states and all but a few Northern ones answered it.

The delegates assembled in the winter of 1861 with the summer of 1787 foremost in mind, and with a grave self-consciousness born of the prospect that their names would be handed down to futurity. They were, indeed, the best that the old Union had to offer: not only the ex-president, but also senators, congressmen, former ambassadors, war heroes, and railroad owners. They were also, as many observers noted, disproportionately elderly, in some cases actually decrepit. (One man, seventy-seven-year-old John C. Wright of Ohio, was feeble and nearly blind—and, having vowed to sacrifice his life for the Union, made good that pledge by dying eight days into the convention.)

"Our godlike fathers created," President Tyler exhorted his fellow delegates as the first session opened, "we have to preserve. They built up, through their wisdom and patriotism, monuments which have eternized their names. You have before you, gentlemen, a task equally grand, equally sublime, quite as full of glory and immortality. . . . If you reach the height of this great occasion, your children's children will rise up and call you blessed."[64]

Not everyone in Washington shared such optimism. Twenty-two-year-old Henry Adams was in town serving as secretary to his father, a powerful congressman closely allied with Seward. In early February, he attended a ball hosted by Senator and Mrs. Douglas. Half the capital seemed to be there, packing the stifling parlors; Adams attempted to waltz with a female acquaintance, but finally was "obliged to drag her from the room in a suffocating condition, and administer ice to her." He surveyed the room with a jaundiced eye and afterward described the scene to his brother Charles:

> A crowd of admiring devotees surrounded the ancient buffer Tyler, another crowd surrounded that other ancient buffer Crittenden. Ye Gods, what are we, when mortals no bigger—no, damn it, not so big as—ourselves, are looked up to as though their thunder spoke from the real original Olympus. Here is an

old Virginia politician, of whom by good rights, no one ought ever to have heard, reappearing in the ancient cerements of his forgotten grave—political and social—and men look up to him as they would at Solomon, if he could be made the subject of a resurrection.

In another letter, Adams spoke for many Americans—especially those not on the Douglases' guest list—when he predicted of the Peace Conference, "I suppose they will potter ahead until no one feels any more interest in them, and then they may die."[65]

Out in the expanses of the Republic, beyond the Douglas mansion and Willard's Hotel, troubling omens could be perceived on all sides. The states of the far Northwest—Minnesota, Wisconsin, Michigan—refused even to send delegates to the Peace Conference. "We have fed the [Southern] whiners with sugar plums long enough," one Michigan newspaper declared. A paper in Minnesota framed its position in more alarming terms: "Before this rampant fever of disunion will abate, THERE MUST BE BLOOD-LETTING!"[66]

Public opinion was shifting throughout the North; newspapers that only weeks earlier had been frantic for compromise now mocked the Peace Conference as "the old gentlemen's convention." The *New-York Tribune*, for all its radical reputation, had been a staunch advocate of reaching an accord with the South. Now each morning's edition bore the motto NO COMPROMISE! NO CONCESSIONS TO TRAITORS! *The Constitution As It Is.*[67] Yet the idea that anything could remain "as it is" for very much longer seemed dubious at best. The familiar, if not quite comfortable, old Union was making way for something new—even if no one was at all sure what this would be.

In the White House, President Buchanan rarely even ventured downstairs anymore, let alone tried to intervene in the secession crisis; he was hard at work settling diplomatic issues with Venezuela and Paraguay regarding some valuable guano deposits, finalizing a treaty with the Delaware Indians, and resolving a disputed water boundary in the San Juan Islands. When a deputation of Peace Conference members paid him a courtesy visit—marching to the White House "with the solemnity of a funeral procession," one would later recall—they found the president "advanced in years, shaken in body, and uncertain in mind." To their embarrassment, he physically embraced each of the men, many of them complete strangers, as he begged them each to save the country from "bloody, fratricidal war."[68]

At the Capitol, meanwhile, Senator Wigfall was telling his colleagues: "It is the merest balderdash—that is what it is—it is the most unmitigated fudge for any one to get up here, and tell men who have any sense, who have brains, that there is any prospect of two-thirds of this Congress passing any amendment to the Constitution, that any man who is white, twenty-one years old, and whose hair is straight, living south of Mason and Dixon's line, will be content with."[69]

And just down Pennsylvania Avenue, as the Peace Conference of 1861 entered its second day, as Mr. Tyler was exhorting his colleagues to courageously take up "the great work of conciliation and adjustment," a Negro named Willis went to the auction block and was duly sold to an unknown bidder for an unrecorded sum.

CHAPTER THREE

Forces of Nature

The old forms rattle, and the new delay to appear.

—RALPH WALDO EMERSON,
"Natural Religion" (lecture, February 3, 1861)

James A. Garfield, circa 1858, and a page of his lecture notes on the
"Unity of the Human Race," Western Reserve Eclectic Institute, circa 1860

Central Ohio, February 1861

EASTWARD RAN THE TRAIN, through thawing fields where green seedlings of winter wheat were taking early root; past the felled brown ranks of last year's corn. Farmers' wives looked up and saw it in the distance, a solitary moving speck and drifting plume. All along the tracks curious folk gathered, massing at the little junctions with plain names: Milford, Loveland, Spring Valley. These were mere villages, most of them—scatterings of clapboard houses, thin and white as a child's paper cutouts—but they possessed a certain dignity and sense of purpose that made them pleasing to the eye of a passing traveler. A few of the larger ones had mustered brass bands to creak out patriotic airs along the sidings, or hauled old cannons out of who knows where to boom salutes. At one station, a stout county dignitary strode toward the train clutching a speech he had laboriously prepared: half a dozen close-scribed foolscap pages of patriotic allegory and sagacious reflection on the national crisis. But the hurried engine and its three cars barely slackened their pace; just enough for the crowd to admire its bunting draperies trimmed with boughs of evergreen, and to glimpse a black-clad figure taking his angular bow from the rear platform. Then it whistled, gathered steam again, and continued on. The would-be orator was left gaping after it, speech still in hand. He had come for a rendezvous with American history, and it had passed him by.[1]

In a few months' time, in spring, the cannons and brass bands would return to those little stations, as local men and boys departed to answer their country's call. In their own way, those little Ohio towns were Civil War battlegrounds as important as Manassas or Antietam. They formed the heartland of the North, the fields on which the contest for minds and souls would be won or lost, where ordinary Americans' commitment to the Union cause would be constantly tested during the next four years, weighed over and over against the war's ever-steeper price.

Ultimately, the Midwest would provide the brawn and brains that saved the nation: 300,000 Ohioans would serve in the Union armies, and Midwesterners overall would make up more than 40 percent of the North's forces, a far larger share than from any other region of the country.[2] The North's three greatest generals would all be Ohioans: Grant, Sherman, and Sheridan.[3] And of the next six men to be elected president of the United States—through 1900, that is—all but one would be Ohio-born Republicans who had fought for the Union.

All that lay in the future. Manassas and Antietam were still names as obscure as Loveland and Spring Valley. The men who would lay down their lives on those distant fields were as yet ordinary farmhands, shopkeepers, and schoolboys. The officers who would lead them off to war were still lawyers, merchants, and legislators. The soul of the North, the soul of Ohio—and even, for that matter, the hearts and souls of those future soldiers—were still contested and uncertain territory.

In COLUMBUS THAT MORNING, a young man—one of those future soldiers—was hurrying toward his own rendezvous with the president-elect. He splashed cold water on his face, buttoned himself into his best coat—the one with its torn coattail visibly mended, alas—and headed out toward the statehouse. This was a day for excitement and also for apprehension. For all that he had expatiated to his students about the grand forces of history, he had never personally experienced anything like it, not during his years as a college professor, not in his days as a circuit preacher, nor even in the months since taking his seat as junior member of the state legislature. James A. Garfield, twenty-nine years old—his friends still called him Jim, or Jemmy, or "Jag"—already wore the serious expression of middle age on his handsome face, while retaining the awkwardness and ardor of youth. To his pupils back at Hiram College he was a kind of surrogate older brother. To those who gathered for his Sunday sermons, he was a modern-day apostle. To the hard-nosed chieftains of the Ohio Republican Party, he was a rising man, an exemplar of a new generation in American politics.

Out in the brisk open air, crowds were already moving toward the railway station. Volunteer militia companies formed their jostling ranks along High Street, while cavalry horses (most likely just ordinary mounts pressed into reluctant service for the special occasion) stamped and snorted at all the commotion. Chain-gang prisoners hauled away wagonloads of mud that they had shoveled off the streets, lest the grand procession bog down in a sea of ooze. The sun was out, shining with unseasonable warmth: a perfect day for a parade. Garfield the young man would have liked to join the eager throng, but Garfield the state senator knew this would be unseemly. He would wait instead with his distinguished elder colleagues at the statehouse.[*]

All Columbus, it seemed, was turning out to see Mr. Lincoln, who would stop in the Ohio capital overnight. It, along with the rest of America, had been following his progress in the newspapers as he made his circuitous way from Springfield to Washington for the inauguration in a few weeks. No one had ever traveled from farther away to assume the presidency. Nor had anyone come to the White House out of deeper obscurity than the former one-term representative from the Seventh Congressional District of Illinois.

Lincoln had obliged the public's curiosity about him by planning a roundabout route through the Midwest, western Pennsylvania, and New York State, then down through New York City and Philadelphia. He would give speeches before thousands at the important stops, and many thousands more would have a chance to glimpse him as the train passed through their towns, perhaps even shake his hand as he stopped for a few minutes. Some came out to cheer the great Rail-Splitter, others just to inspect the notoriously homely face and form their own judgments on the beard that Old Abe had reportedly begun to cultivate. All of them wanted to see for themselves this man on whom the Union's fate depended.

Few Ohioans had been more ardently for Lincoln and his party than Garfield—at least during the heat of the campaign, six months earlier. Not that Lincoln had ever met, or even heard of, the junior state senator from Portage County. But for Garfield—and others of like mind—the Republican cause was a matter not merely of politics, not merely of the nation's destinies, but of something even more transcendent, a vision combining modern science with religious mysticism.

History, the young professor firmly believed, was a sublime process of Nature. Everything he had read so far convinced him that it was so, that it must be so: not just the annals of human civilization but also the heavy tomes of political science, the Greek and Roman classics, the Old and New Testaments, the latest theories of geology and paleontology. (He had eagerly purchased one of Ohio's first available copies of that controversial new book by the English naturalist, *On the Origin of Species*.) Great nations, as he envisioned them, arose like continents from the sea. Generations of men strode the earth like the mysterious behemoths of past ages, then sank into extinction, their fossilized bones forming strata of bedrock on which future generations would build. Avalanche, earthquake, and flood scoured again and again the surface of the world. All moved in accordance with the majestic and inexorable laws of nature's God. All brought mankind closer and closer to a state of perfect freedom. All was part of a divine plan.[5]

On July 4, 1860—a few months after he'd bought Darwin's book—Garfield's neighbors had asked him to give an oration before the annual Independence Day picnic at the county seat. If they expected the usual patriotic platitudes about the heroes of '76, they got far more than they bargained for. Their new state senator didn't even mention Washington and Jefferson. The true significance of the Revolution, he told them, was as the onset of a new era in the evolution of the human species, when for the first time a man's success depended solely on his own brains and brawn as he "went forth to fight for himself the battle of life." Then he began to speak of America's history in geological, even cosmological, terms. Over the course of more than an hour, shock waves of revolution could be heard shattering the rocky strata of past millennia; the arctic ice of aristocratic privilege broke apart and clouds of discord were dispelled by the waxing light of truth and virtue. (Meanwhile the picnickers' ice cream slowly melted in the July sun.) In this speech—one of the first addresses of his long political career—Garfield unveiled a mystical, radical vision that would obsess him for many years to come. America, he told his audience, was like a vast and restless sea, forever one and indivisible, yet composed of countless droplets of water, all in constant motion. A modern ear picks up echoes of Whitman as well as Darwin:

> That kind of instability which arises from a free movement and interchange of position among the members of society, which brings one drop up to glisten for a time upon the crest of the highest wave, and then give place to another while it goes down again to mingle with the millions below—such instability is the surest pledge of permanence. On such instability the eternal fixedness of the universe is based. . . . So the hope of our national perpetuity rests upon that perfect individual freedom which shall forever keep up the circuit of perpetual change.[6]

Freedom and dynamism, liberty and union: all could be forever one.

His listeners—plain Midwestern farmers though they might be—found themselves strangely moved by his peculiar revelation. So much so, in fact, that the address was printed as a pamphlet, and Garfield received dozens of invitations to speak before Republican meetings and Wide Awake rallies in the months before the presidential election. He bought a horse and buggy so that he could take to the campaign trail for Lincoln throughout his own legislative district and beyond. He even delivered a version of the speech when the Republicans held an important statewide rally in October at their very own wigwam in Columbus.[7]

James A. Garfield was not yet famous, of course—much less the grave Victorian statesman he would become, part of the bewhiskered blur of Gilded Age presidents. Although his sisters and cousins predicted fondly that he would someday reach the White House, this was no more than was fondly predicted of ten thousand other rising young men in a republic that rewarded youthful ambition. He might well have remained a state legislator, regulating toll roads and proposing new ordinances to prevent steamboat accidents; or a small-time college teacher, sometimes inspiring, often eccentric, beloved on campus and unknown beyond it.

Yet he turned out to be a man whom the coming age would favor extravagantly; upon whom the renewed nation would, briefly, confer the highest gift in its power. His life and his early thoughts, when viewed in retrospect, take on almost the aura of prophecy; all the more so since from the age of seventeen, Garfield had been documenting that life and those thoughts almost obsessively, hardly ever throwing away even the most insignificant scrap of paper. He kept daily diaries, saved receipts for trifling purchases, and squirreled away the notes to almost every lecture he delivered at Western Reserve Eclectic Institute (later known as Hiram College), the tiny institution where he taught before the Civil War. (Decades later, a journalist would visit the president-elect's house and describe rolls of documents stacked waist-high like cordwood throughout the house, even in the bathroom.) As with most men who ended up in the White House, every one of those surviving scraps would be hoarded for posterity. After a century and a half, the young professor's mind is still an open book—more so than almost anyone else's of his generation, place, and time.[8]

Very few Americans of Garfield's age were famous in the winter of 1861. The nation's great public figures were still the Douglases, the Sumners, the Crittendens. That was about to change, however. It was people like Garfield and his peers, in places far from the nation's capital, who would set the course of what was to come—far more than the gray eminences in Washington. Their rising generation would soon eclipse the old one. Their thoughts, beliefs, and ambitions already mattered more in many ways. They would win a war, and then lead their nation until the turn of the next century.

Not only did Garfield's life span the old America and the new one, it also spanned a vast social and economic gulf. Along with Lincoln—a full generation older than he—Garfield was considered in his time an exemplar of the self-made man. He was an intellectual, to be sure, but his ideas were deeply informed by his upbringing, his early surroundings, and his strenuous climb up the ladder. His native state was a place where struggles over abolitionism, national unity, and the Underground Railroad played themselves out as dramatically as they did anywhere else in the country. Garfield wrestled with those issues throughout his early life. And the conclusions he reached resonated profoundly with those Ohio farmers at the Fourth of July picnic; indeed, speeches like that one made his career. So, in a sense, to peek inside Garfield's mind is to peek inside theirs as well.

Individual responses to the impending conflict did not hinge merely on political principles or intellectual abstractions. Amid all the fears and uncertainties, many young Americans in 1861 spied the not-so-distant glimmer of personal opportunity. As preoccupied as they were with what a civil war might mean for their country, Garfield and his peers were no less intrigued by what it might mean for the course of their own lives. "What will be the influence of the times on individuals?" he asked a close friend and former student, Burke Hinsdale, before answering his own question: "I believe the times will be more favorable than calm ones for the formation of strong and forcible character." Just a week or so before Lincoln's visit, the mail brought Hinsdale's reply: "It is revolution that calls out the man. If it is true, as Horace says, that 'the tallest pines are broken oftenest by the wind,' it is no less true that the tallest grow when the winds oftenest blow." The hurricane of war might uproot the ancient giants of the forest, but in so doing, it would clear space for the upstart saplings.

Like young adults of every generation, Garfield and Hinsdale were plagued by a sense of indirection and self-doubt. However strong and confident he might have looked to others, Garfield privately lamented the "vacillation of purpose" that made him feel like "a frail man" while he longed to be "a strong steady man of purpose and decision." "Do you suppose that real strong men have such waverings?" he plaintively asked his wife. Perhaps the war might resolve the dilemma and make him into the man he wanted to be. Perhaps it might even make him into something more. "Future historians will mark 1861 as the beginning of Period II in our history," one of Garfield's older friends wrote him in early February. "At your age and with your abilities and popularity you owe it to yourself to prove satisfactorily that in you there is the stuff of which giants, intellectual and moral, are made. Most of the world's renowned were men who, when comparatively young men, by one significant stroke made themselves peers of men who had strove slowly and painfully to their positions."[9] The French Revolution, as everyone knew, had turned an obscure Corsican artilleryman into an emperor.

Indeed, the sense had been growing for some time that the nation—

perhaps even the world—might be entering a new epoch of history. During the last prewar years, one of Garfield's students would later recall, "the ferment of scientific research had opened up a thousand new fields of inquiry. The great conflict between old decays and new creations in the world of politics was at hand. . . . The very air seemed surcharged with the new life that already threatened storms and hurricanes."

History and science seemed to be moving in a dance whose choreography was only just beginning to reveal itself. The excitement could be felt even among young men and women on the campus of the obscure little Eclectic Institute, who believed that their generation would help lead the way into this brave new future. "The era is dawning when a broad and unsectarian mind shall be more influential than ever before, and I do believe we could make a strong mark for good upon our time," another of Garfield's students wrote to him. "The old race of leaders and lights, religious social and political are fast fossilizing and fast becoming extinct."[10]

Abraham Lincoln was somehow part of all this. The Republican candidate, so different from any other national leader in their lifetime, seemed to embody the gathering forces of change. A self-made man, he stood for the vision of a free and dynamic—an oceanic—democracy. A Westerner, he stood for a new frontier, a place where the epochal struggle between liberty and slavery would be won or lost. "The centre of national power is moving with the sun—and in the West will be the final arbitrament of the question," Garfield declared in one of his speeches. "When civilization has linked the seas and filled up the wilderness between, there will have been added to our own present union 40 states as large as Ohio—or 200 as large as Massachusetts. . . . Upon what system of labor shall these new states be erected? What shall be the genius and spirit of their institutions?" The victory of the Lincoln-Hamlin ticket in November seemed to provide a resounding answer. At midnight on election night, Garfield drove his buggy fifteen miles to the county seat to await the national results coming in via telegraph. "L. and H. were elected," he wrote in his diary. "God be praised!!"[11]

But three months later, as the president-elect's train drew toward the Columbus depot, much seemed to have changed. Seven states—the entire Deep South—had now left the Union. They had proclaimed themselves the Confederate States of America, elected a so-called president, and armed for war. Republicans had looked to Lincoln as a white knight—albeit a somewhat ungainly one—to ride in out of the West, sweep away the blunders and bad faith of the Buchanan years at a single stroke, and save the nation. The staunch antislavery wing of the party had expected him to brook no compromise with the South, to put down the rebellion by force of arms. His more moderate supporters, the "Republican emasculates," as Garfield scornfully called them, had hoped he would throw his weight behind the Crittenden plan or Tyler's Peace Conference, or forge a compromise of his own. (He was, after all, a native Kentuckian—perhaps he would prove another Henry Clay?)

Lincoln had so far done none of these things. Instead, he seemed to hide from the unfolding events, staying safe at home in Springfield and uttering nary a word in public about the crisis. Newspapers described this policy, with tongue firmly in cheek, as "masterly inactivity." Worse yet, they reported that the Rail-Splitter seemed not to grasp the magnitude of the disaster, continuing to spin his buffoonish yarns while the country fell to pieces around him. One cartoon in *Harper's Weekly* depicted a cretin-faced president-elect, empty whiskey glass in hand, cracking up at one of his own jokes as a funeral cortege passed behind his back, its crape-shrouded coffin inscribed CONSTITUTION AND UNION. (The caricature was unfair in at least one respect: Lincoln was a staunch teetotaler.)

Even rock-solid Republicans were beginning to lose faith. Garfield, disenchanted, wrote to a close friend: "Just at this time (have you observed the fact?) we have no man who has power to ride upon the storm and direct it. The hour has come but not the man."[12]

Still, there was reason to keep hoping. Certainly the plainspoken, rugged Illinoisan would be a vast change from Buchanan. The exuberance of the 1860 campaign had not entirely faded. And the public addresses that Lincoln had already given on his journey from Springfield had—according to newspaper reports—offered sustenance both to the conciliators and the war hawks in his party, even though their style was at times rather gauche, even indecent. (In the Indianapolis speech, he made an off-color joke—not universally appreciated—comparing the secessionists' idea of the Union to a "free-love arrangement" of short-term sexual convenience.)[13] Which Lincoln would present himself to the citizens of Columbus—and to the leaders of Ohio, at the very center of the loyal North?

BOTH HOUSES OF THE LEGISLATURE filled the floor of the representatives' chamber; the galleries above were packed with ladies, crinolines rustling as they fidgeted in their seats. That spring the statehouse had finally been completed, after more than two decades of planning and building, and it was the pride of Ohio: a symbol in granite and marble of the rising Midwest. The structure had cost the stupendous sum of a million and a half dollars and was said to be larger even than the Capitol at Washington. The painter Thomas Cole—famous for his imagined landscapes of imperial rise and decline—had taken part in its design, projecting a vaguely Grecian fantasy that looked, upon completion, like a lost temple of Atlantis somehow washed up on the banks of the Scioto River. Worked into the marble floor at its very center, beneath the dome of the immense rotunda, was a design evoking the idea of Union as elegantly as a Euclidean theorem: a sunburst of thirty-four rays, one for every state, encircled by a band of solid black, representing the Constitution.

Despite the building's architectural message of rock-solid American harmony, it concealed a fault line beneath its foundation that winter. Ohio, no less than the nation as a whole, seemed to be coming apart at the seams. As in most other states across the North, political leaders were locked in mortal combat over how—or even whether—to keep the South from leaving the Union. In Albany, New York's state legislators wrangled over a statement branding the South's seizure of federal forts and arsenals as "treasonable." In Springfield, Illinoisans traded volleys over a resolution to support the Crittenden Compromise. And in Columbus, Ohioans were arguing over almost everything.

The state was, in some respects, a microcosm of the nation. On its southern border, Cincinnati faced the slave plantations of Kentucky across the Ohio River. On the northern edge, Cleveland gave onto the Great Lakes and was the last stop for fugitive slaves on their way to Canada. And the upper and lower halves of Ohio viewed each other with suspicion. Many in southern Ohio—where large numbers of Virginians and Kentuckians had settled—thought northern Ohioans were all wild-eyed abolitionists. Many in the north—themselves pioneers or the children of pioneers from New England and the mid-Atlantic states—thought southern Ohioans were all lackeys of their slaveholding neighbors. Occasionally the two sides came together. In January 1860, the state legislature invited those of Kentucky and Tennessee to visit Columbus as a gesture of trust and goodwill between the free states and the slave states. A local newspaper rejoiced at the sight of Southerners, many of whom had brought their black body servants along for the trip, joining Northerners in champagne toasts "to the Union and the equality and fraternity of the States" with no fear that anyone would try to meddle with their slave property during the banquet. "Sambo has become an obsolete idea," another article exulted.[14]

A year later, no one was proposing champagne toasts or declaring

"Sambo" a dead letter. Rather, Democratic legislators were proposing a battery of laws that would make it illegal for Ohioans to aid fugitive slaves and even for free Negroes to immigrate into the state. "Are we to ruin our glorious Republic for an inferior race?" one supporter asked his colleagues. Republican hard-liners—Garfield was in the vanguard—answered with a bill to recruit and arm fifteen regiments of militia, ostensibly to defend against invasion: after all, in the event of war, a Southern force occupying Ohio could cut the Union in two. Democrats howled that this would just antagonize Southerners, who in any case would never invade the North. One quipped caustically that the only part of Ohio really in need of soldiers was the far northeast, where the troops could be employed to enforce fugitive slave laws.[15]

The Peace Conference, too, sparked a fierce debate. The more radical legislators opposed sending an Ohio delegation to Washington; most vocal among them was Garfield's Columbus roommate, Jacob Cox, another young Republican. "There *is* no *compromise* possible in the nature of things," Cox wrote in a private letter. "For us to do it after our [electoral] victory would be to confess ourselves dastards unworthy of the name of freemen."[16]

The Republicans' militia bill languished in legislative deadlock. So did the Democrats' fugitive-slave proposals. Meanwhile, Garfield bought handbooks of military science and began reading them by lamplight in his rented bedroom after each day's session ended. A week or two before Lincoln's visit, the professor and his roommate began staging their own two-man drills with light muskets on the east portico of the statehouse.[17]

FROM THE DIRECTION of the station, a mile or so off, cannon blasts rattled the windowpanes: a thirty-four-gun salute. Gradually, the blare of brass bands mingled with cheers grew closer. After what seemed an interminable wait, the carved oak doors of the chamber finally swung open, the clerk announced the arrival of the president-elect, and the legislators rose from their seats. Escorted by Governor William Dennison, Lincoln sloped up the aisle toward the speaker's stand, his deeply furrowed face and scraggly new beard unmistakable as he loomed above the crowd. The Rail-Splitter was less ugly than the papers had made him out to be, many spectators would later remark. Yet only three days out of Springfield—and three weeks before the start of his presidency—he already looked anxious and careworn. "His whole appearance indicates excessive weariness, listlessness, or indifference," wrote even the sympathetic *New York Times* correspondent.[18]

After a brief welcome from the senate president, Lincoln started to speak, his incongruously high, flat tenor unusually nasal, for the president-elect was suffering from a cold. He held no notes, and was clearly extemporizing. Lincoln started by observing portentously that the responsibilities facing him were even weightier than those George Washington had borne in the Revolution, an observation he had also made upon departing from Springfield, and for which he had been widely ridiculed. (How dare this political arriviste compare himself to the father of his country?) Next he tried to explain his passivity for so many months: "I have received from some a degree of credit for having kept silence, and from others some deprecation. I still think that I was right." (Not exactly a ringing self-vindication.) He continued: "In the varying and repeatedly shifting scenes of the present, and without a precedent which could enable me to judge by the past, it has seemed fitting that before speaking upon the difficulties of the country, I should have gathered a view of the whole field"—odd words from a man who had barely ventured out of his own front parlor for the past year!—"to be sure, after all, being at liberty to modify or change the course of policy as future events may make a change necessary. I have not maintained silence from any want of real anxiety." (All this seemed to be a fancy way of confessing that he had little confidence and no real plan.) Then the speech grew even more nonsensical: "It is a good thing that there is no more than anxiety, for there is nothing going wrong. It is a consoling circumstance that when we look out there is nothing that really hurts anybody. We entertain different views upon political questions, but nobody is suffering anything."[19]

This seemed idiotic at best, insane at worst. *Nobody suffering anything*, while the North was on the brink of financial catastrophe! *Nothing that really hurts anybody*, while a hostile army prepared for civil war! *Nothing going wrong*, while the Union itself was collapsing!

The president-elect's address in Columbus was mocked in Democratic newspapers all across the country. The *Baltimore Sun* called Lincoln a clown, observing that it was impossible to read his remarks aloud without succumbing to "irresistible bursts of laughter." "Old Abe is a failure as a President," declared the *Cincinnati Daily Enquirer*. "By the time he gets through his tour his friends will wish they had boxed him up and sent him home." Even the Republican papers found the speech hard to defend: it satisfied neither wing of the party. The *Philadelphia Press* explained lamely that when Lincoln said no one seemed to be suffering, he must have been thinking of the lush Ohio farm country that he had passed through that morning. The best that the *Cincinnati Daily Commercial* could manage was to laud his sincerity: "He is not guilty of any diplomacy, and does not understand why he should not in his own plain way tell the plain truth as it appears to him"—qualities that contrasted favorably with "the courtly graces and diplomacy of the whited sepulchre who is the present occupant of the White House." Even so, the president-elect's naïveté and lack of what we would call media savvy were astonishing: "Mr. Lincoln talks as if without the fear of the telegraph in front of his eyes."[20]

Garfield, pushing his way out of the statehouse through the densely packed rotunda, felt similar pangs of disappointment. Nearby, Lincoln was backed up awkwardly against the foot of a stone stairway as the throng surged around him. "The scene," a local paper reported, "presented all the animating features of a free fight." Pushing, pulling, and jostling, hundreds of ordinary Ohioans—who had not heard the speech, and in any case cared less about the niceties of political rhetoric than for accomplishing something to brag about back home—struggled to clasp for an instant the hand of the president-elect. Both of the Rail-Splitter's spindly arms were now flailing wildly left and right as he tried his best to satisfy one and all. "The physical exertion must have been tremendous," the newspaper continued:

> People plunged at his arms with frantic enthusiasm, and all the infinite variety of shakes from the wild and irrepressible pump-handled movement, to the dead grip, was executed upon the sinister and dexter of the President. Some glanced into his face as they grasped his hand; others invoked the blessings of heaven upon him; others affectionately gave him their last gasping assurance of devotion; others, bewildered and furious, with hats crushed over their eyes, seized his hand in a convulsive grasp, and passed on as if they had not the remotest idea who, what, or where they were, nor what anything at all was about.[21]

Could this amiable, guileless, well-intentioned man possibly measure up against the challenges ahead? Could his charisma hold even the North together? Could he save the Union? Could he—if it came to blows—win a war? And was he even remotely equipped to win the epochal, cosmic struggle that Garfield had described so glibly in his speeches last summer?

That evening, Governor Dennison hosted a private reception at his mansion near the statehouse. Gaslights flickered above richly set buffet tables; a butler guided visitors upstairs to deposit their hats and coats before coming back down to meet the guests of honor. In one of the two main parlors, Garfield was introduced to the future first lady, holding court in a dark silk gown. He was not impressed with Mrs. Lincoln: "a stocky, sallow, pugnosed plain lady," he wrote to his wife.[22]

In the room across the hall, with Governor Dennison hovering close by, stood Lincoln. Dressed for the occasion in full white tie, gloves, and a black tailcoat—giving him the appearance of a country bumpkin on his wedding day—he was cracking jokes with the men around him as though he'd known them for years. The governor introduced the young senator, and Garfield clasped Lincoln's white-gloved hand, which was surprisingly muscular and firm. Afterward, he would not recall much of their brief conversation—just social pleasantries, no mention of politics—but the president-elect's face made a profound impression on the younger man all the same. "Through all his awkward homeliness," Garfield wrote afterward, "there is a look of transparent, genuine goodness, which at once reaches your heart and makes you love and trust him." In a letter to a friend, he ventured further: "His remarkable good sense—simple and condensed style of expression—and evident marks of indomitable will—give me great hopes for the country."[23]

The next morning dawned dreary under gathering clouds. Lincoln passed on again eastward, toward Washington and his presidency. Rain began to fall, then came in torrents as the train rushed through more junctions, more villages: Newark, Frazeysburg, Dresden, Coshocton. Newcomerstown, Uhrichsville, Cadiz Junction. No bands to play now, no cannons to fire in salute, but at every station, small knots of people huddled beneath umbrellas to wave, to cheer, to watch—and to wonder what lay ahead.[24]

THE WESTERN RESERVE ECLECTIC INSTITUTE sat on the crest of a small hill in northeastern Ohio, one of so many colleges that had recently sprung up on so many Ohio hills. Professor Garfield was the lone instructor in classical languages, English literature, philosophy, natural sciences, American history, geography, geometry, and religion: such a disparate array of subjects semester after semester that they all became jumbled up inside his head in one glorious mess. A typical set of lecture notes, scribbled on a torn and blotted sheet of cheap notepaper: "Engine—Professions—Divinity. Bunker Hill. *Suspension Bridge.* Manners—Henry Clay. . . . To awaken—Conflict. Challenge the Soul."[25]

A jumble, perhaps. But the students, by and large, adored him.

When you enrolled in a class taught by James A. Garfield, one said, it was like making contact with "a vast elemental force." Even Professor Garfield's course in arithmetic had been brilliant, unforgettable. Campus legends proliferated: it was said he could simultaneously write Latin on the chalkboard with his left hand and Greek with his right while lecturing in English.* Yet the professor seemed less a wise adult than an elder brother. Still in his late twenties, he was only a few years his students' senior and, like many of those children of farmers or itinerant preachers, had come from hardscrabble fields into the grove of academe. He joined their snowball fights on the campus green, and in springtime led them on tramps along the creek bed at the foot of the hill, seeking out specimens of rocks or tadpoles. Rumpled, bearish, and warmhearted, he looked like an overgrown boy, and his tousle of dark-blond hair, luxuriant new beard, and startlingly blue eyes lent him particular appeal among the female students: "a Sir Galahad, our knight without stain and reproach," one sighed. Even more deeply important, the students felt, his voice was the voice of their own generation, and his life a model for theirs.[26]

Some might even have seen Garfield as a junior version of the famous Rail-Splitter himself. Indeed, Lincoln's attraction was based less on his exceptional qualities—as they might seem to us today—than on his ordinariness, his formative experiences resembling those of so many nineteenth-century Americans. Though a full generation younger than Lincoln, Garfield, too, had been born in a log cabin, the last American president who could claim that distinction.[27] His parents, Abram and Eliza, had crossed over from western New York in the 1820s, during the great migration from the seaboard states into the area known as the Western Reserve, the northeast corner of Ohio.[28]

Ohio . . . a name still resonant with romance in those distant days; a deep-drawn breath of open air.

Across the steep Alleghenies, the land flattened and spread, as though the hand of God had generously smoothed a hollow there, between the shores of the south-flowing river and Erie's inland sea. Revolutionary War veterans and their families drove in Conestoga wagons to claim their bounties: 160 acres for each man who had helped his country win its freedom. This was federal land, ceded to the national government by the states in the earliest years of union. It was free land:

---

*The myth of Garfield writing simultaneously in Greek and Latin persists into the present day as an old chestnut of presidential trivia. Its origin is that Garfield was ambidextrous, and sometimes showed off for students by signing his name on the chalkboard with both hands at the same time.

in 1787, Congress had outlawed slavery in perpetuity across the whole of the Northwest Territory, from the Virginia border to the uppermost reaches of Lake Superior. The Northwest was a fresh start. One early settler, a Virginia planter of distinction, journeyed there with all his slaves and, as they drifted together on a raft of flatboats down the Ohio River, gathered them to announce that they were in a new land now, and slaves no more.[29]

True, many Easterners mocked the emigrants as dupes, bound only for ruin, famine, and Indian massacres on what seemed then like a remote frontier. (One widely circulated woodcut showed a prosperous farmer on a sleek horse, with the caption "I am going to Ohio"—and, next to that, a skeletal man on a broken-down nag, with the caption "I have been to Ohio.") Many did suffer, including Abram and Eliza, who settled along a stagnant and malarial bend of the Cuyahoga River, not far from a village of six hundred souls called Cleveland. Unable to afford their own land to farm, the Garfields soon moved on and then moved again, with Abram working sometimes as a fieldhand, sometimes as a laborer helping to dig canals. Bad luck and failure seemed to follow the family.[30] James lost his father to disease while barely out of infancy, although this was not unusual enough to merit much comment, let alone sympathy. Fathers disappeared often: borne away by nameless fevers, crushed and broken in freak accidents, or simply absconding without a word, going off one day in pursuit of a business chance or a new woman or just the hope of a fresh and unencumbered start in a place still farther west.[31]

In the end, however, the hardships of those early years seemed only to confirm God's ultimate beneficence. The settlers—even, to a modest degree, the Garfields—eventually prospered. By the time James reached adulthood, the village of Cleveland was an exemplary New World metropolis: "the city of broad streets and stately avenues, of charming drives and romantic scenery, of rural taste and architectural beauty," wrote one local booster on the eve of the Civil War. Some visitors were still unimpressed with Ohio—or, perhaps worse, bored by it. A New Englander complained about its "soulless utilitarianism": "No visions here—no poetry here . . . all stern realities."[32]

He could not have been more wrong. Beneath the bland exteriors of middle-class Ohioans beat idealistic—even poetic—hearts. They scribbled diaries and romantic verses; painted watercolors; relentlessly sought self-improvement by reading books and attending public lectures on every subject.[33] The very barns that they built seemed almost Athenian in their noble proportions, diminutive Parthenons among the cow pastures. They schemed hard at making money, but they also schemed to remake the world—and turned to God for assistance.

The hard-living early settlers had spared little time for religion at first. Then, in the 1820s and 1830s, the Protestant revival sweeping much of the United States descended on Ohio with particular intensity. Such intensity, in fact, that one devout Methodist extolled the state as an "American Canaan" with "no red Sea in the way . . . & as for our Jordon (I mean the Ohio) it is easy to cross and (what's better) when once planted here our children are saved from the harmful practice of trading [in] their fellow creatures."

The Garfields and many of their neighbors in the Western Reserve joined a religious group known variously as the Campbellites, the Brethren, or the Disciples. Its adherents professed a radical, almost primitive version of Christianity. Unlike their New England Puritan ancestors, they turned away from the brutal majesty of the Old Testament toward what they esteemed the unadorned teachings of the Gospels: faith, repentance, and the imitation of Christ's virtues. Each member of the church was encouraged to study the Bible for himself or herself with the "fullest liberty of discourse and investigation," an extreme form of *sola scriptura*. Disciples renounced all hierarchies; church elders wore plain clothes and preached in simple wooden meetinghouses without steeple or pulpit; and followers addressed one another as Brother and Sister. Women played important roles in congregations, and at least a few integrated and all-black churches sprang up. The sect's founder, Alexander Campbell, was equivocal on the slavery question: he disapproved personally of human bondage, yet also felt that Christians had no business interfering in the relationship between master and servant and that politics had no place in the church. He wanted his religious message to attract both Northerners and Southerners (Brother Campbell and other elders preached under a huge canvas canopy known as the Big Tent. Later, during the Civil War, it was cut up into strips of cloth to make bandages for wounded Union soldiers.)[34]

So quickly did the movement spread across the Western Reserve that Brother Campbell and his fellow Disciples fully expected it just as quickly to convert the entire planet, sweeping aside old sects and heresies and bringing about the return of Christ in very short order. They were disappointed when the world continued going on, messiah-less, more or less as before. But they did not lose hope: Campbell began to prophesy that the year 1866 would usher in a new epoch in human and divine affairs.[35] After a time, these millenniarian dreams began hardening into militancy among some Disciples. In 1832, a group of Mormons—led by Prophet Joseph Smith himself—settled in Hiram and began converting townsfolk. Local Disciples hastened forth into battle. They seized the prophet from his bed in the middle of the night, stripped off his clothes, threatened to castrate him, and finally poured hot tar over his naked body, sending him fleeing into the darkness to seek a more hospitable haven farther west.[36]

James Garfield was born again into that austere faith at the age of eighteen, baptized one March morning in the bone-chilling waters of the Chagrin River.[37] Like millions of other Americans, especially in the North, swept up in the nation's Second Great Awakening, he embraced a form of Protestantism focused not just on the distant promise of Heaven but also on the obligations of the here and now. Conversion as a Disciple was not supposed to be an emotional or mystical experience but rather an intellectual one by which a man or woman became rationally convinced to accept Christ. (Perhaps Joseph Smith would have disputed this.) Brother Campbell and other elders held public debates on equal terms with prominent "nonbelievers," including the famous British socialist Robert Owen. Campbell also frequently preached a sermon called "The Progress of Revealed Thought," in which he traced the ever-growing human understanding of religion from pre-Mosaic times up through the "Modern age" or "Sunlight age" ushered in by Christ.[38]

Such intellectualism—and faith in progress—appealed to the scholarly young Garfield, so much so that he soon took to the circuit himself as a preacher. In Disciple meetinghouses throughout the Western Reserve, he gave sermons on Christian ethics and morality and on the relationship of science to religion. Reason and morality, he preached, "are alike the work of a perfect Creator who is himself the union of perfect intelligence and infinite goodness."

God's hand was visible in the scientific laws that governed nature—and also throughout the affairs of mankind. "In every nation," Garfield told his students in November 1860, "there is a political and a religious history. . . . Prophecy [is] the dim side of the tapestry—history the bright side." The discovery of the New World and the birth of "Republicanism" in America fulfilled God's promise to Isaiah: "For behold, I create new heavens and a new earth."

This history seemed to Garfield to be drawing toward some sort of grand culmination, one that could be fully reached only by a mighty human effort. "He was a firm believer in the swift-coming millennium," one of his students recalled. "He cited authorities to prove that it was surely coming; proved its desirability, and quoted some very good poetry; but wound up with, 'Let us, therefore, do all that we can to hasten the millennium.' "[39]

The Disciples were just one of dozens, even hundreds, of new religious creeds in antebellum America. Doctrine and practices varied enormously from place to place and church to church, running the gamut from cool rationalism to ecstatic mysticism; antislavery moralizing to justification of bondage. What those movements taught in common, though—even to those who remained outside them—was that individual men and women had the power to choose their own versions of Christian, or non-Christian, faith. Everyone was a free agent, and morally responsible for individual decisions. There was no obligation to blindly follow the beliefs of one's parents: each new generation of Americans had the power to, quite literally, rewrite the universe in its own terms.[40]

As the new sects jockeyed for power and for new converts, they became more aggressive. Many, moreover, shared the Disciple vision of an impending, apocalyptic battle between good and evil to precede a new golden era of godliness: a battle that only true Christian warriors could win. Garfield became popular among the Disciples not just for his intellectual gifts but also for his combative prowess. Theological debates on the Reserve were knockdown, drag-out, no-holds-barred brawls. In 1858, the young preacher went ten grueling rounds—two four-hour debates a day for five consecutive days—against a scientific theorist named William Denton, who claimed that life on earth had developed by "spontaneous generation." But rather than insisting on the literal truth of Genesis as his rebuttal, Garfield delved deep into the works of the greatest scientific thinkers of the time—Humboldt, Agassiz, Lyell, Comte—to show that nature's laws were themselves proof of God's role as Creator. As many as a thousand people attended each debate, and at the end, they hailed Garfield as the victor and showered him with invitations to give lectures on "Geology and Religion."[41]

Sometimes the combat was less rhetorical. Once, at a tent meeting, a "big two-fisted rowdy" tried to disrupt Garfield's sermon about the patience of Job. The powerfully built professor—as local lore maintained—stepped toward the bully and, remarking that even Job's patience would have worn thin under the circumstances, knocked off the man's cap and then "grasping him by the hair, hoisted him at arm's length from the ground, as easily as if he had been an infant." This was muscular Christianity at its best. The congregation loved it.[42]

At the same time that Garfield was being born again as a Christian warrior, he was awakening to another no less potent, no less muscular, if secular, faith—one drawing as many millions of young Northerners to its banner as the Gospel: the creed of the self-made man.

Many years later, a famous author who was almost Garfield's exact contemporary—they were born less than two months apart—would pen a highly embellished account of the late president's rise from obscurity to the White House. Horatio Alger titled his book *From Canal Boy to President*, and in it he turned Garfield into a version of one of his fictional heroes. (The biography's title page reminded readers, in capital letters, that Alger himself was already famous as the AUTHOR OF RAGGED DICK; LUCK AND PLUCK; TATTERED TOM, ETC.)[43] Even without embellishment, though, Garfield's swift rise in the world was indeed a novel-worthy tale of luck and pluck. Born into true poverty, he climbed up by dint of perseverance, intellectual accomplishment, and hard manual labor. He worked his way through a local academy, then the Eclectic Institute, and then Williams College, where he distinguished himself as a Greek and Latin scholar. On the strength of his Williams degree he was invited back to teach at the Eclectic, and ultimately to run the school. By the time he turned thirty, in November 1861, he could boast of having worked as a carpenter, canal boat driver, janitor, schoolteacher, farm laborer, preacher, college professor, college president, lawyer, state senator, and U.S. Army colonel. He was truly the author of his own destiny. "The world talks about self-made men," Garfield wrote to a friend in 1857. "Every man that is made at all is self made."[44]

The idea that every American was what he made of himself had already become a kind of civic religion in the antebellum North. Ralph Waldo Emerson's most famous lecture and essay, "Self-Reliance," seemed to capture the spirit of the age. "Trust thyself: every heart vibrates to that iron string," the sage proclaimed. And truly great men possessed a faith in themselves that transcended individuality: "To believe your own thought, to believe that what is true for you in your private heart is true for all men,—that is genius." Yet, Emerson said, men must also surrender themselves fully to the times in which they lived, and exist "not [as] cowards fleeing before a revolution, but guides, redeemers, and benefactors, obeying the Almighty effort, and advancing on Chaos and the Dark."

The Sage of Concord's message was complex, even cryptic—and, as even he admitted, seemingly self-contradictory—but this scarcely mattered to the millions of young Americans who heard or read his words and took from them the idea that they were independent spirits in a revolutionary age. To them, Emerson was as much performer as philosopher, more rhythmist than rhetorician; his public appearances were emotional events like the rock concerts of a later generation. Garfield first saw him lecture in 1854 and confided afterward to his diary: "He is the most startlingly original thinker I ever heard. The bolt which he hurls against error, like Goethe's cannonball goes 'fearful and straight shattering that it may reach and shattering what it reaches.' I could not sleep that night after hearing his thunderstorm of eloquent thoughts." Emersonian ideas became an important part of Garfield's own thought. In September 1860, he lectured his students at the Eclectic Institute: "We build our own character & make our own world." Each of us has innate "powers," and "our use of them decides our lives and destinies."[45]

This was an ideology particularly resonant in the fast-changing Midwest, a place of projected dreams—imaginary canals and railroads, conjectural towns, utopian communes—that might vanish in a puff or, more remarkably, take shape out of nothing, just as the glorious statehouse arose on what had recently been a manure-covered pasture. Such a world required every person in it to be nimble, ambitious, adaptable, and free.[46]

The only thing lacking, it often seemed, was the "Almighty effort" that Emerson also hailed, the revolutionary mission that would enlist Americans as "guides, redeemers, and benefactors . . . advancing on Chaos and the Dark." Where would it be found? For a while, almost nothing seemed too far-fetched. In 1852, the Hungarian revolutionary Louis Kossuth, whose independence movement had been routed by the forces of despotic Russia, visited Columbus on a tour through the United States. "My heart has always heaved with interest at the name of Ohio," he told the legislature at a special session. The governor vowed to lend him weapons and an army of young Buckeyes. Somehow, that local brigade never did end up marching off to liberate the distant Carpathians. But the heroic impulse remained.[47]

The idea of the brotherhood of man was more than an abstraction. Not only did Garfield and his friends address one another as "Brother" in the Disciple tradition, they also felt intense emotional—at times also physical—bonds with one another, clearly stronger than any James felt with his wife, Lucretia, to whom his letters were often brusque and businesslike. Young men in the mid–nineteenth century could be passionate in ways that some readers today find disorienting, driving modern scholars into endless—and probably irresolvable—debates over exactly where comradeship ended and sexuality began. They found nothing unorthodox in strolling arm in arm, addressing letters to "my dearest" or "lovely boy," and sharing fond embraces in a common bed. In 1858, when his old college friend Harry Rhodes was away from Hiram, Garfield wrote to him: "Harry Dear, do you know how much I miss you? In the school—the church, at home, in labor or leisure—sleeping or waking, the want of your presence is felt. I knew I loved you, but you have left a larger void than I ever knew you filled."

A few months later, he addressed the younger man even more passionately, quoting Longfellow: "I would that we might lie awake in each others arms for one long wakeful night and talk not in the thoughts or words 'Of the grand old masters / Nor from the Bards sublime,' but in that language 'whose tone gushes from the heart.'" Four years later, while Garfield was a general in the Union army, Rhodes would write wistfully to him, recalling the "real physical delight—an acute pleasure almost" when the two roughhoused together (presumably naked) in the creek at Hiram.[48]

Far from being disparaged as a sign of effeminacy, such attachments were prized as evidence of what the antebellum generation called "manliness": a quality that embraced strength, authenticity, independence, and a kind of romantic (or Romantic) intensity. To embody this quality fully was young men's highest ambition, they often professed to one another. Indeed, scarcely could Garfield lift his pen to address any topic, whether personal or political, without referring to manliness or manhood. An 1859 letter he wrote to a college senior is a good example:

> You are now about to conclude upon a profession in life and I hope you will take one in which your highest manhood will find scope, and I hope you will make it a rule that the rush of the world's work shall not crowd out those pursuits which enlarge and enrich the soul. We see too many instances of those who have degenerated into mints to coin money in, and the fine medallion work of whose souls was defaced. . . . I know that you will always keep a fresh strong heart quick to the touch of friendship, whose portals fly open at a friend's approach like the gates of Peter's prison at the angel's touch.[49]

When Garfield derided procompromise Republicans as "emasculates," he also averred that the proper mission of the party was to "sustain . . . independent and manly truth." Nor was he alone in this sentiment. Countless newspaper editorials from the period praised

Lincoln's (or other politicians') "manly independence and honest, sturdy firmness" and the "firm and manly tramp" of the Wide Awakes. At the height of the secession crisis, a Republican paper in Massachusetts assailed the compromisers: "We need, at the North, to inculcate the principle of manly, personal independence, a principle that will enable a man to avow his real sentiments, and maintain them too, by his vote, his acts and his voice."[50]

Like later generations, the men of the 1850s and 1860s expressed their ideals of masculinity through their physical appearance. Most noticeable, and revealing, was the astonishing profusion of facial hair that sprouted forth during those years, including on the previously smooth faces of Garfield and his friends. For a century and a half, American men (and most Europeans) had, nearly without exception, gone clean-shaven: it was a sign of gentility, civility, and restraint. (In the late eighteenth century, one Philadelphia woman considered it a matter of note that she had seen "an elephant and two bearded men" in the street that day.) This changed very suddenly. Most American historians, when they have considered the topic at all, have assumed it had to do with Civil War soldiers avoiding the inconvenience of shaving while in the field.

In fact, the phenomenon predated the war by a number of years—and was the subject of a great deal of contemporary comment and debate. As early as 1844, one physician began inveighing against "woman faced men" with their habit of "emasculating [the] face with a razor," even suggesting that shaving caused diseases of the throat. At the time, this was still an eccentric opinion. By the following decade, however, talk of a "beard movement" was sweeping the nation. In 1857, a conscientious journalist took a stroll through Boston's streets and conducted a statistical survey: of the 543 men he encountered, no fewer than 338 had full, bushy beards, "as God meant to have them," while nearly all the rest sported lesser facial hair of various sorts. Only four were "men of the old school, smooth shaven, with the exception of slight tufted promontories jutting down from either ear, as if designed as a compromise measure between the good old doctrine and modern radicalism."[51]

As that remark suggests, antebellum beards bristled with political connotations. American newspapers reported that in Europe, beards were seen as "dangerous" tokens of revolutionary nationalism, and claimed that the Austrian and Neapolitan monarchies even went so far as to ban them. In England, they were associated with the sudden burst of militarism at the time of the Crimean War. The phenomenon—like other European fashions—reached America slightly later, and the connotations of nationalism, militarism, and revolution traveled with it. They spanned the Mason-Dixon Line, too. It was no accident that Northerners who sympathized with slaveholders were called "dough-faces": in the American context, beards connoted a certain frank and uncompromising authenticity. Nor was it a coincidence that "Honest Abe" began cultivating his famous beard as he prepared to take over the presidency from "Granny Buck."[52]*

Such was the cultural soil in which the new Republican Party took root and then grew with astonishing speed: a world in which the values of individualism, manliness, and forthrightness were quickly supplanting the old ways of compromise and politesse.

Until midcentury, neither of the nation's two leading major political parties had taken either a straightforward proslavery or antislavery stance. In the interests of national harmony, the Whigs nominated presidential candidates like Zachary Taylor, a slave owning, though moderate, Virginian, while Democrats chose men like Franklin Pierce, a New Englander who believed in protecting slaveholders. But in 1854, as the fragile, timeworn truce over slavery suddenly came apart (and with it the Whig Party), the new Republicans raised the banner of "free labor and free soil." Proclaiming free labor as the natural and desirable state of all Americans, the party firmly opposed yielding another inch of national ground to the "slave power."

To be sure, this position was not the same thing as abolitionism, which remained a dirty word for many, if not most, Northerners. Even in those who hated slavery, this aversion was usually balanced to some degree against the desire to keep the South in the Union and a deference to white Southerners' right to keep their most valuable "assets" safe from confiscation. Most were quick to disavow, at least publicly, any wish to interfere with the peculiar institution. However, the Republicans' position did embrace a belief system in which freedom was good and slavery evil, and this was a position wholly unprecedented in America's political mainstream.[53] Ultimately, even some of the most radical abolitionists themselves came aboard, making large donations to the newborn party. Ordinary Northerners, too, flocked to the free-labor standard. By the late 1850s, Republicans held commanding majorities in both houses of Ohio's state legislature, as in various other Northern states.[54]

---

*The Republicans' first nominee, John C. Frémont, in 1856, had been the first bearded presidential candidate in American history.

The Republican Party also drew millions of formerly indifferent young Americans to participate with fervor in public life. In his late teens and early twenties, Garfield, for one, had been even more alienated from politics than most of his peers. He never bothered to vote, and one day when he happened accidentally to see a Whig candidate making a stump speech, he declared himself "perfectly disgusted." His religious faith, too, led him to believe that serious Christians should concentrate on self-betterment rather than meddling in the lives of others.[55]

Yet by 1856—the year of Bleeding Kansas, the Sumner beating, and the Republicans' first presidential bid—Garfield had made a complete about-face. One night, after attending a speech on the dire predicament of antislavery settlers in Kansas, he came home and wrote in his journal: "I have been instructed on the political condition of our country. . . . At such hours as this I feel like throwing the whole current of my life into the work of opposing this giant Evil. I don't know but the religion of Christ demands some such action." A few months later would find him at a Republican bonfire, leading college classmates and townsfolk in a chorus of hurrahs for Frémont.[56]

Three years after that night of the bonfire, Garfield was on his way to Columbus as the new senator from Portage County.[57] He had not plunged into public life without hesitation. Garfield knew that adding politics to his commitments as a preacher and professor might require moral and intellectual compromises. In the end he was swayed by his ambition, by his desire to realize, in terms that Emerson would surely have applauded, "the growth which my whole nature demands." Finally, too, there seemed to be a cause of sufficient grandeur: a party that stood for politics as a noble crusade, an Emersonian battle for liberty and human brotherhood.[58]

Yet the ideal of individual freedom still remained in uneasy truce with that of national unity. In the minds of nearly all Americans—even up to the moment the Civil War began—it was abolitionism, not slavery, that threatened to split the nation asunder. "Liberty *and* Union, now and for ever, one and inseparable," Daniel Webster had declaimed back in 1830—but in fact, the two seemed increasingly irreconcilable, stranded on opposite sides of a chasm growing wider with each passing year.

IN THE EARLY WEEKS OF 1861, not long before Lincoln's passage toward Washington, another train had crossed Ohio—without fanfare, but with the eyes of the state and the nation upon it. Aboard it was a young woman on a journey no less momentous: she and her unborn child were being conveyed back into bondage. It would be the last sad chapter of a history soon to be forgotten.

Three months earlier, Lucy Bagby, a twenty-four-year-old Virginia slave, had fled from her master in Wheeling, just across the Ohio River.[59] Her husband had already escaped and made his way to Canada; Bagby was pregnant with their child. She got as far as Cleveland, where, thanks to the city's extensive Underground Railroad network, she found work as a domestic servant, living quietly under an assumed name in the home of a sympathetic white family, the Bentons.

But just before dawn on January 19, a knock came at the front door, and when Bagby went to answer it, she found two U.S. marshals on the doorstep. Behind them was an all-too-familiar figure: her former master. Frantically, she fled upstairs into the bedroom where Mr. Benton was still sleeping, but the men cornered her, produced a judge's warrant for her arrest, and dragged her out of the house to the county jail. In full accordance with the Fugitive Slave Law, they had come to reclaim a slaveholder's stolen property.[60]

News of the arrest quickly spread across the city, then the entire state of Ohio; before long, it was drawing comment in newspapers throughout the country. It was deemed an outrage; a knife thrust by the slave power into the very heart of free territory. The Western Reserve was known nationwide as a stronghold of abolitionist sentiment, and Cleveland was its unofficial capital. By late morning on the day of Bagby's arrest, a journalist reported, large numbers of free blacks, many of them women, were gathering outside the jailhouse, vowing "that the girl should never go back to Virginia alive." Then a crowd of whites began to form, equally determined "to see the law enforced."[61]

For the next few days, as Bagby awaited her court hearing, the jailhouse was the scene of a tense standoff between whites and blacks, with club-wielding sheriff's deputies trying to keep the two sides from all-out street warfare. At one point, when a white man and a black man began to scuffle, a "colored barber" named J. D. Green charged in with a knife and slashed the white across the hand. Policemen immediately put Green under arrest, but before they could get him away, dozens of whites surged in, yelling, "Lynch him!" From somewhere in the crowd a rope appeared, passed eagerly forward from hand to hand. The officers managed to extricate the trembling Green and push him through the doors of the jail. Later that day, several more black men were clubbed to the ground by deputies and white civilians, while one "colored woman," provoked beyond endurance by the officers' taunts, threw a fistful of pepper into their faces and was manhandled into custody.[62]

Almost no white Clevelanders—not even the staunchest abolitionists—joined the black men and women at the courthouse. This was no time for heroism, they counseled. The same newspaper editions that reported Lucy Bagby's arrest also carried the news that Georgia had officially seceded, becoming the fifth state to join the Southern confederacy. The Upper South—Virginia, North Carolina, Tennessee, Kentucky, Missouri, Arkansas, Maryland—still hung in the balance, and the slightest breath might push them into secession. White Clevelanders were determined to prove that their city was not "disloyal to the Union" but rather "true and loyal to the Constitution"— in short, that it was ready to sacrifice its principles (and a woman's freedom) for what seemed the greater good. Even the *Cleveland Leader*, Ohio's most radical Republican daily, argued that if Lucy were sent back to her master without hindrance, it would send a message that "will be felt through all the country," helping unite slave states and free states once more under the same flag. The editors pleaded with blacks not to attempt any rescue: "No, colored citizens, do not undertake such a rash act, but show to the world that you are possessed of noble qualities which enable you to bear and forbear, even under such an unrighteous law."[63]

Meanwhile, Cleveland was also determined to show its most hospitable face to Bagby's master, the young Reverend William S. Goshorn, and to his wealthy father, John, who had joined him in the city. The two Goshorns lodged at the best hotel in town, the Weddell House, where Lincoln and his family would stay three weeks later, and when a Negro waiter refused to serve them breakfast one morning, the proprietor stepped in and fired the man on the spot, much to the Virginians' satisfaction.[64]

On the third morning after Bagby's arrest, the hearing opened and then quickly adjourned when her attorney, a leading white Republican named Rufus P. Spalding, asked for time to visit Wheeling and seek evidence that might disprove that she was truly the Goshorns' legal property. He returned two days later, on January 24, and ruefully informed the court that his mission had failed: "Nothing now remains that may impede the performance of your painful duty," he said. Yet, Spalding reflected, the "painful duty" might serve a larger purpose, as news of Ohio's appeasing gesture reached even the U.S. Capitol: "While we do this, in the City of Cleveland, in the . . . Western Reserve, and permit this poor piece of humanity to be taken peaceably, through our streets, and upon our railways, back to the land of bondage, will not the frantic South stay its parricidal arm? Will not our compromising legislators cry, 'Hold, enough!' "[65]

Well-meaning whites made a last-ditch effort to purchase Lucy's freedom from the Goshorns—even the chief marshal who had arrested her pledged $100 to the cause—but the Virginians declined all offers. They were determined to make a point. The elder Mr. Goshorn rose to have the last word in court, thanking the citizens of Cleveland for the "uniform kindness" they had shown during his sojourn with them. His mission, the Virginian said piously, had been only to pour soothing oil upon the troubled waters of the Union. "How pleasant it would be," he concluded, "if I could come among you with this same girl as my servant, and enjoy your hospitality as I have now."[66]

The "girl" in question was not invited to address the court. Hiding her face in a handkerchief, she was gently but firmly led from the room and out of the building by the marshals. The crowd on the courthouse steps was silent: Cleveland's colored citizens had decided to accede to the wisdom of their city fathers. At the railway station, Bagby, the marshals, and the Goshorns boarded a waiting train bound for Wheeling, followed by more than a hundred armed white men who had been deputized to make sure the dictates of justice were fully executed. Two years earlier, as every Ohioan remembered, a captured slave en route back to Kentucky had been successfully liberated by a determined group of abolitionist radicals from Oberlin—a mishap that must not be allowed to repeat itself.

This time, the journey proceeded peacefully until the train drew near the tiny village of Lima, just a few miles from the state border, where several dozen blacks and whites armed with muskets, clubs, and pistols lay in wait at the depot. But the engineer spotted the ambush just in time. Warning the deputies to draw their revolvers, he signaled as though he were going to stop—and then, at the last possible instant, gave the engine a full head of steam and tore on past the startled would-be attackers. The train and its young prisoner continued on their way south.[67]

LUCY BAGBY'S RETURN to Virginia seemed an allegory: not only of the doomed hopes of those last prewar months but of white Northerners' ambivalent loyalties. Rarely have the internal contradictions of

American attitudes toward race been starker than during the prelude to the Civil War. And nowhere were those contradictions starker than in Ohio.

As with many Northerners, James Garfield's feelings about slavery had evolved rapidly over the past ten years. In 1850, an African-American lecturer had visited his school at the invitation of the headmistress, herself an ardent abolitionist. Garfield had little to say afterward beyond noting laconically, "The Darkey had some funny remarks." Toward the middle of the decade, though, he found himself increasingly surrounded by a culture of antislavery activism: even his brother, a half-educated farmer, was writing letters proclaiming "Liberty or death" to the "southern deamons." By the fall of 1857, when Garfield encountered a fugitive slave passing through Hiram, he covertly slipped the man some money to aid him on his escape to Canada. And two years later, when John Brown was hanged for treason in Virginia, Garfield wrote in his diary:

> A dark day for our country. . . . I have no language to express the conflict of emotion in my heart. I do not justify his acts. By no means. But I do accord him, and I think every man must, honesty of purpose and sincerity of heart.
>
> When I reflect upon his devoted Christian character, his love of freedom drawn from God's Word, and from his Puritan ancestors . . . it seems as though God's warning angel would sound . . . the words of a patriot of other and better days [Thomas Jefferson], the words "I tremble for my country when I reflect that God is just, and that his Justice will not always slumber."
>
> Brave man, Old Hero, Farewell. Your death shall be the dawn of a better day.[68]

In a pocket notebook, he expressed himself even more firmly—in Latin, as befit the somber majesty of the occasion. "John Brown's Execution. *Servitium esto damnatum*," he wrote in thick black letters. *Slavery be damned.*

And yet . . . just months before, as president of the Eclectic Institute, Garfield had flatly forbidden local abolitionists from holding a rally at the college. "The school," he vowed in a private letter, "shall never be given over to an overheated and brainless faction." It was one thing to condemn slavery in the private confines of a diary, quite another in the open air, which would be reckless. Slavery might be damned, but it must be damned discreetly. It was a fine line, and Garfield found himself, as he put it, "between two fires": some of his friends criticized him as too moderate on slavery, others as too radical.[69]

The fire of radicalism was burning ever hotter in the Western Reserve. It was no coincidence that the martyred Brown himself had grown up in the town of Hudson, less than twenty miles from Hiram. Ohio's early settlers from New England (Brown's family included) had brought with them the moral ardor of their Puritan ancestors, combined with the toughness of pioneers, of men and women who kept rifles at their side to ward off heathen Indians. The second Great Awakening, together with the miraculous blessings that God's providence conferred upon their flourishing new state, made them confident in their own power to transform circumstances. Northeastern Ohio in the first half of the nineteenth century was a heap of dry kindling ready to be set ablaze.

Some said that the tinder was first lit in June of 1845, when the Ohio American Anti-Slavery Society—then a small and fairly sedate organization—held its annual meeting in a Disciple church in New Lisbon. The spark came in the form of a visitor from New England: Abby Kelley, a young woman on a mission into the West. Her gentle appearance—the blue eyes and rosy cheeks, the demure dress of Quaker gray—was misleading to many who did not know her, for here was an orator who could fling down brimstone from the pulpit for hours on end; a warrior who had been pelted with stones, rum bottles, eggs, and excrement; a politician who freely declared that she put Liberty before Union. She had been called a Jezebel, a nigger bitch, a "man woman," and worse, and none of it fazed her in the slightest. Her voice—starting low and quiet and then rising, rising, until it rang from every corner of the hall—was a fearsome and mighty weapon.

For three hot days in New Lisbon, Kelley preached to the crowd of sweat-soaked men and women who packed the little church and spilled out into the dusty street. Many had come unprepared for what they would hear. When she declared that "Washington and Jefferson were slaveholding thieves, living by the unpaid labor of robbed women and children," a male delegate rose to his feet, leapt onto the platform, and denounced her for this "slander" on the Founding Fathers, reminding the audience of Jefferson's famous remark about trembling for his country. "Ah," Kelley retorted, striding toward the intruder as if to shove him off the stage, "devils fear and tremble when the Almighty is thundering out his wrath upon them, but are they the less devils?" At this blasphemous attack, the hall erupted in gasps, shouts, denunciations. "She is proving it all," one man cried, "but it will lead to war and bloodshed!" Then a voice rose over the tumult—whether of man or woman has been forgotten—and began singing an abolitionist anthem:

> We have a weapon firmer set
> And better than the bayonet;
> A weapon that comes down as still
> As snow-flakes fall upon the sod,
> But executes a free-man's will
> As lightning does the will of God.

By the end of the three days in New Lisbon, nearly all of Kelley's beguiled listeners had been won over to her brand of warlike radicalism. The delegates adopted four resolutions, the last of which held that the federal Union, based on the Constitution, was nothing short of a "great bulwark of slavery, involving the North equally with the South in the guilt of slaveholding; and that it is the duty of every true friend of humanity, to give it no sanction of allegiance, but adopting the motto of 'no union with slaveholders,' to use every effort to bring about a peaceful dissolution of the Union."[70] Barely two weeks later—while Kelley was still barnstorming through the towns and villages of Columbiana County, preaching under a makeshift tent when no church would receive her—the Society launched a new weekly paper, the *Anti-Slavery Bugle*, its masthead bearing a quotation from Edmund Burke: "I love agitation when there is a cause for it."[71]

Within a year, the Society had changed its name: it would henceforth be known as the Western Anti-Slavery Society, in keeping with the geographical broadening of its ambitions. It moved its base northward, to the prosperous town of Salem in the heart of the Western Reserve. Kelley would return again and again in the years that followed, raising funds and—in the words of one unsympathetic newspaper editor—"ministering to the depraved appetites of her fanatical followers." In 1854, two Southerners were imprudent enough to pass through Salem on their way home to Tennessee with a recently purchased slave, a girl about twelve years old. Local abolitionists—led by a free black man—stormed the train and carried the little girl off in triumph. That night, at an impromptu rally in the town hall, they brought their liberated captive to the stage and bestowed on her a new name: Abby Kelley Salem.[72]

The girl's foolish owners should have known: Ohio meant freedom. Harriet Beecher Stowe had told all America as much—had told all the world, in fact—in her great novel. There was now scarcely a man, woman, or child who did not know the story of Eliza's flight from Kentucky, the most famous scene of the most famous book of the century. In the space of barely two paragraphs, the young slave woman crossed the frozen river, leaping from floe to floe, her bleeding feet staining the ice, "but she saw nothing, felt nothing, till dimly, as in a dream, she saw the Ohio side, and a man helping her up the bank."[73]

The truth was much more complicated than Stowe's fiction. The Ohio River was not a bright line between freedom and slavery but a muddy and disputed no-man's-land. The farmers and merchants of southern Ohio made their fortunes shipping corn, wheat, and salt pork downstream to feed the plantations' black field hands—whose sweat and toil, in the form of stacked cotton bales, came back up the river to feed the textile mills of the North. Many of these Ohioans would have been more than happy to return Eliza and her baby, or any other fugitive slaves for that matter, to their master. Few of Stowe's admirers cared to notice that she had made her villain, the sadistic slave master Simon Legree, a transplanted Yankee. Likewise, few heard Kelley when she said that North and South shared equally in the guilt of slavery.[74]

In fact, only a tiny portion of the millions of Northerners who read Stowe's novel even called themselves abolitionists. The term was still an ugly epithet for most people, connoting dubious patriotism and, perhaps worse, a most un-American tendency to trespass upon the affairs of one's fellow citizens. Abolitionists were attacked by mobs not just in the slave states but also in Boston and Philadelphia. The eminent Yankee intellectual Oliver Wendell Holmes, Sr., condemned them as traitors to the white race—as he sneeringly put it, "ultra melanophiles." Even the Western Reserve's congressman, Joshua Giddings, the most extreme antislavery politician in the national legislature, refused to wear the badge of outright abolitionism until after the war began.[75]

Among those few Americans who did fully embrace the cause, almost none accepted the idea that blacks and whites were equal intellectually, much less that they ought to be equal politically. At the antislavery meeting in New Lisbon, Kelley nearly lost her audience when she declared that black men and women were no different from whites under the skin. (Even James Garfield, despite eventually becoming an outspoken advocate of full civil rights for blacks, was never able to overcome an inward distaste for them as people.)[76] Indeed, many antislavery Republicans prided themselves on belonging to the true "white man's party," since the Democrats planned to "flood Kansas and the other

territories with Negro slaves." Keeping blacks out of white Northerners' midst was a good reason for opposing slavery's expansion.[77]

What did gain wide currency among Northerners—even many
who detested blacks and abolitionists in equal measure—was the
self-congratulatory conceit that the North was the land of liberty and
the South the land of slavery. On the eve of the war, the journalist
and future landscape architect Frederick Law Olmsted published a
widely read series of articles and books recounting his experiences as
a native New Englander traveling through the slave states. He came
home ready to admit that many blacks were happier and better provided for as slaves than they would be if free. What disturbed him
were the habits that slavery bred among whites, "habits which, at the
North, belong only to bullies and ruffians." In Charleston, he found
"police machinery, such as you never find in towns under free government: citadels, sentries, passports, grape-shotted cannon, and daily
public whippings." Southern whites, he said, ridiculed the very idea
of democracy. Their brutally hierarchical society, oppressive to poor
whites as well as blacks, made the ruling class not just arrogant and
backward but indolent, lacking all of the "practical industry and capac-
ity for personal observation and reflection" that many Northerners
cultivated. Even more disturbing, Olmsted asked whether Northerners, out of their fear of undermining national unity, had "so habituated
themselves to defend the South that they have become . . . blind to the
essential evils and dangers of despotism."[78]

Indeed, the fire-eating secessionists of Georgia and Alabama were
not the only ones who decided that Northerners and Southerners
were different nations. "We are not one people," said an editorial in
the *New-York Tribune* as early as 1855. "We are two peoples. We are a
people for Freedom and a people for Slavery. Between the two, conflict
is inevitable."[79]

Americans across the North were increasingly finding that they
could hate slavery without loving abolitionism. And they expected
their elected officials to hate slavery, too. Even Clement Vallandigham,
a congressman from southern Ohio who would become the nation's
most infamous "Copperhead" Democrat—second to none in his vit-
riolic racism and his hatred of the Lincoln administration—admitted
before the war that slavery was "a moral, social & political evil" that
he "deplored."[80]

Garfield, ever the professor, tried to make sense of the growing
chasm in scientific and historical terms: perhaps Northerners and
Southerners were even, in a sense, two separate races, diverging from
each other like different species of Darwin's finches. In lectures at the

Eclectic Institute, he told his students that God's natural laws were clearly at work. Variations in climate and other environmental factors had made the animals and plants of the earth's northern regions distinct from the southern: might those same variations have equally given rise to distinct types of human beings? "Which is superior?" he scribbled in his notes for one class. "In nature, South. In man, North. . . . Northern—Civilization—Temperate zones favorable to thought."[81]

If a less imaginative reading of Darwin suggested the unlikelihood of divergent evolution in the two short centuries since the Europeans' arrival, perhaps its roots lay further back in time, and in culture rather than nature. The settlers of the Northern and Southern colonies had always seemed to represent two different species of Englishman. "The South has never favored the democratic idea," one of Garfield's former students, Burke Hinsdale, wrote to him in February 1861. "We come from different parentage." There were, he explained, on the one hand, the virtuous, egalitarian Puritans who founded Plymouth in the North and, on the other, the haughty, autocratic Cavaliers who founded Jamestown in the South. "We did not agree in the beginning, we have never agreed yet, and I do not think we are likely to for some time." In reply Garfield concurred with Hinsdale: "I confess to the great weight of thought in your letter of the Plymouth and Jamestown ideas—and their vital and utter antagonism."[82]

For Garfield—as for a growing number of other Northerners who believed as he did—Southern secession had been felt as a sudden intellectual and political unstifling. The days of politics as equivocation and self-censorship were over, replaced by a new clarity and decisiveness, a sense that American history had finally aligned itself with the transcendental spirit of the age. "A stern, awful certainty is fastening itself upon the hearts of men," he wrote to Hinsdale in January 1861.

"I am inclined to believe that the sin of slavery is one of which it may be said that 'without the shedding of blood there may be no remission,'" he continued, quoting the Epistle to the Hebrews. "All that is left for us as a state or as a company of Northern States is to aim and prepare to defend ourselves and the Federal Government. I believe the doom of slavery is drawing near—let war come—and . . . a magazine will be lighted whose explosion must shake [the] whole fabric of slavery."[83] Whatever the character of human evolution and national history, this much was true. Since the days when he had ridiculed the "darkey" abolitionist, Garfield had now evolved to the point where there was very little to distinguish him from the most zealous followers of Garrison, Phillips, and Kelley.

The high priestess of abolition was in Ohio on the eve of the war.

She had trekked out to her old preaching grounds in the Western Reserve the previous autumn, as the Lincoln campaign neared its climax. In the fifteen years since her galvanizing first sermon, she had grown middle-aged and taken a husband, becoming Abby Kelley Foster. Despite chronic illness, she felt that she was needed in the Midwest to help hold the cause together at its moment of crisis, when the pressure to compromise principle for the sake of national harmony would be greater than ever before. In mid-March, she summoned enough strength to give a speech at the concert hall in Cleveland, not far from the courthouse where Lucy Bagby had met her fate six weeks before.

As soon as she stepped up to the lectern, the old fire rekindled. The fugitive's betrayal, she prophesied, would be slavery's last victory in the North. Now the time had come for "the ultimate triumph of God's truth." In years past, abolitionists had been a tiny band of persecuted martyrs: "Their bloody footprints track the prairies and plains of the North in their contest for the fundamental rights of man." But now, she cried hoarsely, "Governments founded on iniquity must perish. . . . And out of the present strife, will grow up a new Union in which the rights of all will be respected."[84]

But how many citizens of the North were ready for the impending cataclysm? And were the politicians—not just in the state capitals but in Washington, too—prepared to step off the safe ground of compromise and embark upon unfamiliar seas? Were they ready to fight—not for the old Union but for a new one?

Mr. Lincoln's eastbound train would reach its destination at last, though not in a fashion anyone had expected. From Pittsburgh to Cleveland it had continued on its appointed way; and from Cleveland to Albany, Buffalo, New York, Philadelphia. At daybreak on Washington's Birthday, the president-elect had stood at the flagstaff in front of Independence Hall and, coatless in the winter chill, hauled up a huge American banner toward the rays of the dawning sun.[85]

When he left Philadelphia that night for the final leg to Washington, though, he did not board the usual railway car draped with bunting and evergreen. Word had reached the president-elect's security detail that Maryland secessionists might be planning an assassination attempt: either the train would be blown up or derailed and rolled down a steep embankment, or, more likely, Lincoln might be ambushed and stabbed as he passed through Baltimore, where the cars were normally decoupled and drawn through the streets by horses to shuttle them from one depot to another—a perfect opportunity for an ambush. Accompanied by only two bodyguards, he therefore quietly boarded the regular late-night southbound train, stooping low to hide his face, and hurried into a private berth, drawing the curtains shut. Philadelphians thought that the president-elect was still in Harrisburg, where he and his entourage had been met with the usual fanfare that afternoon. Actually, he had doubled back. Telegraph lines out of the Pennsylvania capital had been cut lest word of the secret detour leak out. Reaching Baltimore at 3:30 a.m., Lincoln and his two companions made their stealthy way through the city, finally reaching Washington, disheveled and thoroughly exhausted, just before dawn.

Mrs. Lincoln and her young sons, meanwhile, following later that day, were welcomed to Baltimore with loud huzzas—for Jefferson Davis. As their car was drawn slowly through the streets by a team of horses, mobs of men and boys surrounded it, rocking it violently back and forth and forcing the windows open as they screamed threats and obscenities at the terrified family. Police rescued the Lincolns not a moment too soon and sent them on their way southward, toward the city that would be their home for the next four years.[86]

An anxious and dispirited capital awaited them. The celebration of Washington's Birthday the day before had been overshadowed by an unfortunate misstep. As the blue-coated cavalry, infantry, artillerymen, and marines—boots polished and dress uniforms crisply pressed—were forming ranks for their traditional parade down Pennsylvania Avenue, a courier arrived with orders from the White House: no troops were to march this year. John Tyler, still closeted with his fellow delegates at the Willard, had convinced President Buchanan that a display of military force was inadvisable at that particular moment. Later in the day, after cries of outrage from the city's Unionists, the president reversed himself in characteristic fashion, and a few of the dismissed soldiers were rounded up for a feeble second parade. Buchanan then sat down to write an apologetic note to his predecessor, begging pardon for having allowed U.S. troops to appear in broad daylight in the federal district.[87]

Rumors of secessionist plots circulated daily. It was said that the secessionists planned to kill Lincoln rather than let his inauguration proceed. An openly pro-Southern militia company drilled nightly in the streets, obliging the mayor—himself a Democrat who would eventually be jailed for sedition—to blandly reassure the public that these were merely members of a respectable political organization who enjoyed the cool air of February evenings. This did little to soothe

the District's jangled nerves. One morning when the sudden crash of cannon fire set windowpanes rattling, panicked Washingtonians ran into the streets to find out whether this was the opening volley of a secessionist uprising, or the first salvo in a federal invasion of the South. It was neither: just an artillery battery firing an imprudent thirty-four-gun salute, celebrating Kansas's admission to the Union.[88]

In Congress, the statesmen, too, were now firing blanks. From Americans in every corner of the North, petitions for peace and compromise continued to arrive—but now there were also more and more scrolls of signatures demanding that no compromise whatsoever be struck. These clamorous demands all converged upon a point of almost eerie inactivity. Daily debates in the House and Senate had become a tourist attraction and fodder for newspaper columns set in tiny agate type; little more. Politicians gave patriotic, long-winded, ineffectual speeches rebuking all the other politicians for doing likewise, while in the half-empty chamber their colleagues dozed, wrote letters, or picked their teeth with their penknives. The only other signs of life were the busy scratching of the stenographers' pencils and the scurrying of congressional pages bringing fresh glasses of water to cool the orators' overtaxed vocal cords. Senator Crittenden was now almost the only man with any faith in his compromise proposal, and even his was waning fast. He and his few allies—Stephen Douglas and a couple of other senators—could not even get the resolutions onto the floor for a vote. Most Northerners felt it went too far in appeasing the South, while Southerners, of course, felt it did not go far enough. A popular New England humorist offered Congress his own set of proposals to satisfy the seceded states: make the Republicans apologize for electing Lincoln; move the Missouri Compromise line north to the Canadian border; substitute a cotton bale for the stars on the U.S. flag and a Carolina turkey buzzard for the American eagle; slaughter all the free Negroes in the Northern states; and banish William Lloyd Garrison, Wendell Phillips, and Abby Kelley Foster, among others, to perpetual exile in Liberia. Crittenden's proposal had only slightly better odds of passage than this one.[89]

Americans were also quickly losing faith in the man they had elected president. Newspapers ridiculed Lincoln's undignified entry into Washington; cartoons showed him skulking off the train wrapped in an old blanket or even a woman's shawl and bonnet. The future president had arrived "like a thief in the night," sniffed a German diplomat. Even Mary Lincoln, it was said, went around telling everyone—discreetly, she thought—that her husband should never have compromised his honor to placate his cowardly bodyguards.[90]

Among the few who offered Lincoln any sympathy was Frederick Douglass, who noted, not so helpfully, the uncanny similarity between how the president-elect had reached the capital and how a fugitive slave would reach the North: "by the underground railroad . . . not during the sunlight, but crawling and dodging."[91]

The impression of cowardice fed expectations that Lincoln would prove to be simply another Buchanan: a puppet whose strings would be pulled by more decisive men in his party. Two days after his arrival, a journalist watched him tour the Capitol arm in arm with Senator Seward, his recently announced choice for secretary of state. So much shorter was the beak-nosed New Yorker than the lanky Illinoisan that he looked "very much like a dwarf waiting upon a giant" as he escorted Lincoln to their carriage. And yet, the reporter assured his readers, "Seward holds the Administration in the hollow of his hand."

Ever cryptic and calculating—the "wise macaw," Henry Adams, who knew Seward well, called him—the Republican sachem had spent the entire winter assiduously devising his own schemes to resolve the national crisis, barely taking into account the man who would soon occupy the White House. Seward, as Adams's brother Charles later recalled, "thought Lincoln a clown, a clod, and planned to steer him by . . . indirection, subtle maneuvering, astute wriggling and plotting, crooked paths." One of the senator's ideas was to provoke a war with England or France: if New York were attacked, he reasoned, "all the hills of South Carolina would pour forth their population for the rescue." Failing this, Seward advised, the federal government should simply refrain from doing anything that might enrage Southerners still further—allowing cooler heads to prevail below the Mason-Dixon Line. In any event, he concluded, "the negro question must be dropped," and the sooner the better.[92]

A new actor had stepped into the Washington limelight, too: an Ohioan with his own plan for banishing the Negro question. The beefy, genial Congressman Thomas Corwin was known fondly back home as "Tom Corwin the wagon boy," from when he'd been a supply train driver for General William Henry Harrison's campaign against the Indians in 1813. Even more widely, he was called "the king of the stump." During General Harrison's other famous campaign, when Old Tippecanoe led the Whigs to victory in 1840, Corwin boasted of having delivered more than a hundred tub-thumping orations to "at least seven hundred thousand people, men, women, children, dogs, negroes & Democrats inclusive." Though now nominally a Republican, the Kentucky-born Corwin had even less use for

Negroes and abolitionists than he did for dogs and Democrats. When a voter once asked him to commit to a clear position on slavery, he wisely "wrought out an elaborated nothing, a fogbank of words, as a reply."[93]

Now, though, Corwin had come up with a few words about slavery that he believed might just save the Union. And quite uncharacteristically, they were clear, simple, and far from a fog bank. The Ohioan proposed an amendment to the Constitution—the Thirteenth, if passed and ratified—that would not only bar Congress from ever interfering with slavery (delicately referred to as "domestic institutions") in any of the states, but also explicitly forbid the amendment's own repeal in perpetuity. In effect, it guaranteed slavery's constitutional protection forever. What more could the South want?[94]

The Thirty-sixth Congress would officially adjourn on inauguration morning, March 4. Its months of windy torpor ended with a spasm of activity. For weeks, Corwin's compromise had languished in the shadow of Crittenden's. But in the final days of the session, it began suddenly to gain ground. On February 28, it passed the House of Representatives, squeaking through by a single vote. As the old mahogany clock in the Capitol corridor ticked each minute away, the Senate wrangled on. At 7 p.m. on inauguration eve, a Sunday, the session was called to order one last time: Congress had never done business on the Lord's day, but the legislators reasoned that the Lord cared more about preserving the Union than about keeping the Sabbath. Senator Crittenden was to speak, offering a final entreaty on his plan's behalf. Visitors packed the galleries, pushing and shoving for seats and even spilling onto the sanctum of the Senate floor itself before the sergeant at arms stepped in. Some accounts say that Lincoln himself slipped into the chamber, as discreetly as he could, to join the spectators. Whether this happened or not, it has a certain poetic plausibility, since he was known to love the theater, and here was the last scene of play that had been by turns tragedy and farce.

Standing in the center aisle, his deathly head more haggard than ever, Crittenden spoke for an hour and a half. Some who had known the senator in his prime were saddened as he stumbled wearily and haltingly through the familiar patriotic formulae like an old man trying to recall some half-forgotten story from his youth. "We are about to adjourn," he rasped. "We have done nothing. Even the Senate of the United States, beholding this great ruin around them, beholding dismemberment and revolution going on, and civil war threatened as the result, have been able to do nothing; we have done absolutely nothing."

Debate continued. At midnight, the galleries were still full of spectators. Senators laid their heads on their desks; a lucky few claimed the sofas at the back of the chamber, where they sprawled, snoring, to be awakened by doomsday or the vote, whichever came first.

Somewhere in the small hours, Senator Wigfall of Texas—whose state had seceded a month before but who malingered in Washington, unwelcome as the last drunken guest after a dinner party—rose, wobbly with bourbon, and sarcastically offered some "few, little, conciliatory, peace-preserving remarks" about abolitionists, free blacks, New Englanders, rail-splitters, flatboat pilots, Plymouth Rock, and the American flag. This stream of vitriol dribbled out for more than an hour. Finally, at four o'clock in the morning, the Corwin proposal came up for a vote, and passed by the necessary two-thirds margin required for a constitutional amendment. "No amendment," it read, "shall ever be made to the Constitution which will authorize or give to Congress the power to abolish or interfere, within any State, with the domestic institutions thereof, including that of persons held to labor or service by the laws of said State." Having now passed both houses, the measure had only to be ratified by the states. Congress was ready to condemn itself, as well as the Negro, to a kind of perpetual bondage.[95]

This climax still did not cause the Senate to adjourn. As the windows began to glow with the pale gray light of dawn, the body turned to more routine matters: the incorporation of the Metropolitan Gas Company, the legal status of the Pacific guano islands, and a land grant to a small college in Kansas. Crittenden succeeded in one thing, at least—securing a $400 stipend to the widow of a laborer killed by a derrick falling from the Capitol's new dome—before Vice President Breckinridge banged his gavel and brought the Thirty-sixth Congress of the United States to a close. (By the end of the year, he would have his commission as a brigadier general in the Confederate service.) The senators staggered off to wash, shave, and change their linen for the swearing-in ceremony at noon.[96]

Several hours earlier, the president-elect had risen in his suite at the Willard and sat down to make a few last-minute changes to his inaugural address. Just before noon, President Buchanan's open barouche pulled up in front of the hotel to collect him. The two men had little to say to each other as the carriage rolled down Pennsylvania Avenue. The Old Public Functionary, for once, seemed at a loss for pleasantries; the Rail-Splitter gazed down contemplatively at the floorboards.

A short while later, as they waited inside the Capitol for the ceremony to begin, Buchanan finally drew Lincoln into a corner to offer a few parting words of wisdom. John Hay, who stood nearby, strained to listen. "I waited with boyish wonder and credulity," he later remembered, "to see what momentous counsels were to come from that gray and weatherbeaten head. Every word must have its value at such an instant. The ex-president said: 'I think you will find the water of the right-hand well at the White House better than that of the left.'"[97]

Lincoln's first inaugural address would be handed down to future generations as one of the greatest pieces of oratory in American history. It was inspired, tactful, perceptive, ageless in its eloquent final paragraph—and, at the time, almost entirely ineffectual. Seward had imposed many alterations and addenda, and although the president-elect made further revisions and polished up the language considerably, much of the New Yorker's equivocating spirit remained in the final version. Lincoln's final additions had been hastily scribbled on several scraps of lined paper and pasted on top of the printed text. By far the longest of these came nearly at the end of the speech. Even today, it is sometimes omitted from published versions. In this passage, Lincoln spoke of his willingness to rewrite parts of the Constitution to accommodate the South—and referred specifically to the amendment that the Senate had passed nine hours earlier. "I have no objection," he concluded, "to its being made express and irrevocable."[98]

The address very soon became—and remains—one of the most selectively quoted speeches ever given. Moderates liked Lincoln's assurance that he had neither the intention nor the desire "to interfere with the institution of slavery in the States where it exists," and that he was committed to enforcing the fugitive slave laws. Hard-liners applauded his pledge "to hold, occupy, and possess the property and places [in the South] belonging to the Government"—which must include Sumter. Temporizers like Seward appreciated his plea to both North and South that "nothing can be lost by taking time." There was also something in Lincoln's words for almost everyone to dislike. Frederick Douglass called it a "double-tongued document" offering little hope "for the cause of our heart-broken and down-trodden countrymen"—that is, the slaves. Lincoln, he observed sadly, "has avowed himself ready to catch them if they run away, to shoot them down if they rise against their oppressors, and to prohibit the federal government indefinitely from interfering for their deliverance." Wigfall, on the other hand, fuming and muttering among the dignitaries at the Capitol as he listened to Lincoln's remarks about federal property, hurried off to telegraph Charleston: "Inaugural means war . . . war to the knife and knife to the hilt."[99]

Oddly enough, hardly anyone at the time remarked on the passage that would become the most quoted of all—the only part of the speech that is still quoted much today. The original words were Seward's, to which Lincoln applied rhetorical gilding:

> We are not enemies, but friends. We must not be enemies. Though passion may have strained it must not break our bonds of affection. The mystic chords of memory, stretching from every battlefield and patriot grave to every living heart and hearthstone all over this broad land, will yet swell the chorus of the Union, when again touched, as surely they will be, by the better angels of our nature.

But even fewer would note or long remember the words that Crittenden had spoken, just yards away and hours earlier, in the Senate chamber—a room that would soon see half its desks vacant:

> Sir, if old Bunker Hill now had a voice, it would be, of course, as it should be, a voice like thunder, and what would she proclaim from her old and triumphant heights? No compromise with your brethren? No, sir, that would not be her voice; but I fancy to myself, if that venerated and honored old scene of American bravery, hallowed by the blood of the patriots who stood there, hand in hand, brethren of North and South, could but speak, it would be but one voice, a great and patriotic voice: Peace with thy brethren; be reconciled with thy brethren![100]

Few, too, throughout the years ahead, would remember much about the month that followed Lincoln's inauguration. Even at the time it seemed as though many Americans were in a trance, a fugue state, as they awaited whatever was to come. The president made hundreds of patronage appointments, adjudicated a hard-fought dispute over the postmastership of Bloomington, Illinois, and dutifully forwarded copies of the Corwin amendment to each state—including the seceded ones—for ratification.[101] His cabinet met for the first time and the subject of Fort Sumter did not come up. Crittenden packed up his few belongings at the National Hotel, announced his retirement from public life, and returned to his farm in Kentucky. John Tyler, having adjourned the Peace Conference, returned hastily to Richmond, where secession was still under debate. That very night he gave a speech on the steps of the Exchange Hotel, denouncing his own convention's final compromise plans as "poor, rickety, and disconnected" and exhorting Virginians to "act promptly and boldly in defense of the state sovereignty."[102] (In Montgomery several days later, Tyler's sixteen-year-old granddaughter was given the honor of raising the first Confederate flag over the rebel Capitol.) In Washington, in the same newspapers reporting Lincoln's inauguration, Mr. G. Mason Graham of Louisiana advertised that he was in town to purchase several dozen healthy Negroes, and that "any person having such to dispose of" might write to him care of the District of Columbia post office. From Charleston, Major Anderson wrote to tell the president that he and his men had only enough provisions left to last six weeks at most.[103]

Even far away from Washington, Richmond, and Charleston, those were strange and discordant days. In Ohio, an electrical charge seemed to hang in the air, a sense of possibility and impending revolution that expressed itself in unexpected ways. All bets were off; everything was subject to reinvention; anything could be proposed. Garfield introduced a bill in the senate to abolish the death penalty, and drafted a report arguing, with erudite references to practices among the ancient Greeks and Saxons, that the sovereign state of Ohio ought to adopt the metric system. The legislature received a petition to abolish any infringement of constitutional rights based on sex, and in an unprecedented gesture, women's rights activists—including Abby Kelley Foster—were allowed onto the floor of the senate to give speeches advocating their cause.[104]

Yet no matter how many or how various their preoccupations, the legislators could not help returning, time and again, to the one topic on everybody's mind. "A debate started on a bill to protect sheep from dogs," one newspaper complained, "would turn on the all-absorbing question of Slavery."[105] Democrats baited Republicans with a bill that would outlaw interracial marriage and sexual relations; Republicans responded with reminders that a Democratic vice president in the 1830s, Richard Mentor Johnson, had had a black common-law wife. That "amalgamation" bill passed; only Garfield and a handful of other senators dared vote against it at the risk of being thought to favor miscegenation. On almost everything else—the fugitive slave laws, the expansion of state militia, the stockpiling of arms—deadlock prevailed.

But in Columbus, like everywhere else in the country, each day's news brought fresh intimations that the momentary stasis could not last much longer. Headlines in the *Ohio State Journal* told of the worsening confrontation in Charleston Harbor, as well as another at Fort Pickens in Florida, also surrounded by Confederate troops. Which side would break the standoff—and would it concede peace or embrace war?

On April 13, a gray Saturday morning, the Ohio senate was in session as usual. A few spectators were in the gallery, including some women's rights advocates, still pressing their case. Today, however, the senate would be distracted from progressive aspirations and mundane matters alike. It had just managed to pass legislation authorizing the payment of bounties for killing blackbirds in Ottawa County— and was preparing, in desultory fashion, for the fortieth ballot on a bill locating a proposed state penitentiary—when a senator came rushing in from the lobby with a message for the chair. "Mr. President," he exclaimed, "the telegraph announces that the secessionists are bombarding Fort Sumter."

The legislators stood in stunned silence, absorbing the news. But the hush was shattered when, from the spectators' gallery, came a woman's fierce whoop of joy. The men looked up, startled—almost, one later remembered, as if the enemy themselves were in their midst.

It was Abby Kelley Foster. "Glory to God!" she cried.[106]

Fort Sumter under the Confederate flag, April 14, 1861

CHAPTER FOUR

A Shot in the Dark

World take good notice, silver stars have vanished;
Orbs now of scarlet—mortal coals, all aglow,
Dots of molten iron, wakeful and ominous,
On the blue bunting henceforth appear.

—WALT WHITMAN,
"Rise, Lurid Stars" (manuscript fragment, 1861)

Charleston Harbor, April 1861

AN HOUR BEFORE DAWN, a single shell announced the war's beginning.

Something flashed and boomed suddenly ashore. In the fort, men keeping watch saw the projectile coming toward them, arcing clean and high, like a small comet tracing its course among the scattered stars. The night was so still that they could hear—or so they would later tell—the hissing sound it made as it cut through the air. A spray of sparks trailed from the fuse, reflected on the rippled water below, so that not one but two streaks of orange fire seemed to race across the harbor, converging and converging. The ball burst at last above them, right over the ring of parapets, a hundred pounds of metal blown apart from within. Perfectly aimed. An instant of sudden clarity illuminated the bricks, stones, and panes of quivering glass; the silent iron guns; and the flag that hung, barely stirring, on its tall staff.[1]

Darkness and stillness again. That first shot had been one gun's signal to the others. Out across the water, all around the harbor, unseen cannons and mortars were being carefully adjusted and aimed. Then the full barrage began.

AFTER SO MANY MONTHS of waiting, the standoff at Sumter had been broken finally by an ancient law of siege warfare: the fort's defenders were being starved out. Major Anderson had been left with 128 mouths to feed—the officers and soldiers themselves, plus several dozen civilian laborers who had remained in the citadel—and precious little to give them. Over the past four weeks, the few remaining barrels of hardtack had dwindled away to mere crumbs, as had the flour, sugar, and coffee. Back in February, a singular piece of bad luck had befallen the fort's supply of rice: a cannon saluting Washington's Birthday smashed a window and sprayed the food store with splinters of glass. By early April, the men were sifting through that rice grain by grain. Each one represented another morsel of time.[2]

Grain by grain, that precious commodity, too, had been running out for the Union, and for peace.

Almost every morning throughout the four-month siege, a mail boat from Charleston had brought a bundle of newspapers out to the fort. These usually included the latest edition of the *Charleston Mercury*, with its banner headlines screaming blood and secession, as well as a grab bag of recent Northern papers forwarded by the men's families back home. Every day, Anderson and his officers pored over these papers, seeking clues to their own fate. For more than six weeks after their arrival at Sumter they had waited out the protracted, ever-feebler death twitches of the Buchanan administration. Then in late February, papers had started coming with reports on the president-elect and his journey to the capital. They had read Lincoln's speeches closely, noting how he seemed to change his mind at each new stop. Their naïve, inexperienced new commander-in-chief was obviously no more resolute a leader than Buchanan, and perhaps even less so.

"The truth is *we are the government* at present," lamented Dr. Crawford, the fort's surgeon. "It rests upon the points of our swords. Shall we use our position to deluge the country in blood?"[3]

The garrison was in a bizarre position of both power and powerlessness. On the one hand, as Crawford realized, they could at will, with a single cannon shot, change the course of American history. On the other hand, Fort Sumter, which had looked so commanding and impregnable from the sandy ramparts of Moultrie, was beginning to feel less and less so. On all sides of the harbor, they could see new artillery platforms under construction, cannons being wheeled into place, and in the distance bayonets glinting as if in Morse code, as recruits marched and countermarched on the beach. Each day, Captain Doubleday looked across the harbor at the hundreds of tiny figures moving busily over the dunes of Sullivan's Island: slaves whose Confederate masters had brought them from their plantations to assist in constructing earthworks. Anderson expressed it for most in the garrison when he wrote that he felt like "a sheep tied watching the butcher sharpening a knife to cut his throat."[4]

Worse even than the growing menace from Charleston was the uncanny silence from Washington.

Since its occupation of Sumter, the garrison had received no orders from the War Department except to stay firm, maintain a strictly defensive stance, and do nothing that might provoke bloodshed. As soon as President Lincoln was inaugurated, the men awaited a more decisive message. Would they be directed to abandon it, as many people, even old General Scott, were suggesting? Would reinforcements be sent to defend it, or at least provisions to sustain it as the still bloodless secession crisis continued to unfold?[5]

Days turned into weeks, and still no message came. Anderson

and his men speculated endlessly about which course of action Lincoln would choose. There was something to be said for—and against—each one.

Republican hard-liners in the North, they knew, wanted Lincoln to send more troops to Charleston Harbor. With the entire world watching, many Americans thought it insane to entrust the nation's military prestige, and perhaps even its destiny, to just a few dozen soldiers. Yet experienced tacticians like Anderson and his senior staff knew that with Southern troops massing by the thousands in Charleston, a foray by the North would likely end in bloody disaster. Several days before the inauguration, Anderson asked each of his officers to estimate, independently, how large an expeditionary force it would take to seize the rebel batteries and break the siege. Doubleday said ten thousand men, backed by a naval attack. Captain Seymour simply replied that he thought a large-scale reinforcement was "virtually impossible." The major himself concluded it would require at least twenty thousand soldiers—more than the number in the entire United States Army, which was then scattered among the frontier outposts of the West. In any event, a large-scale collision at Charleston was certain to bring on full civil war.[6]

An attempt to deliver fresh provisions to Anderson's men might well end likewise in failure and humiliation. In the months since the garrison's surprise move to Sumter, no ship under the U.S. flag had been permitted to approach, and the rebels had turned Charleston Harbor into a potentially deadly trap for any foolish enough to try. They had sunk hulks at the harbor's mouth, turning the already narrow channel into a tortuous maze navigable only by daylight with a local pilot's aid—certainly no sizable naval squadron could get through. Even if a supply ship did manage to slip in and anchor at Sumter, it would almost certainly be smashed to splinters by the enemy's heavy land-based artillery, assuming it was not first intercepted by the rebel patrol vessels, camouflaged black against the night, now prowling the harbor round the clock.[7]

The Southerners had made it clear that they would not hesitate to fire even at an unarmed vessel. Back in January, General Scott had chartered a private steamship, *Star of the West*, to bring a few fresh troops and supplies to the Sumter garrison, hoping that the enemy would take it for a harmless merchantman. Word of its true mission slipped out—in fact, it made headlines in Northern newspapers—and by the time it arrived at Charleston the rebels were ready at their guns, sending the *Star* fleeing ignominiously amid a badly aimed but still alarming barrage of iron balls. (Inside Sumter, an officer's wife almost set off the war three months early when she seized the lanyard of a loaded cannon, intending to fire back at the rebel battery, but a quick-thinking Doubleday stayed her hand.) And at the beginning of April, the clueless captain of a New England merchant schooner—he didn't read newspapers much and had only a vague idea of some sort of trouble between the North and South—came bobbing innocently into the harbor with his cargo of ice, the Stars and Stripes flapping from his masthead. It was only after a cannonball tore through the *Rhoda B. Shannon*'s mainsail that he swung her round rather hard and ran for the open sea. Anderson and his men watched with gritted teeth. It took every inch of their self-restraint to see their flag insulted with impunity, practically beneath the muzzles of their impotent guns. But they knew that if they responded to the rebels' provocation, this, too, would likely end in civil war.[8]

As a last resort, the Lincoln administration could simply let the rebels have Sumter, along with Fort Pickens, the only other significant stronghold in the South that remained in federal hands. Shameful as this might seem, it would be only the latest in a succession of bloodless Union surrenders. Since the fall of Pinckney and Moultrie at the end of December, forts, arsenals, navy yards, and other federal assets across the South had tumbled like pawns, one by one. In Florida, state troops had seized an arsenal that held almost a million rifle and musket cartridges and fifty thousand pounds of gunpowder. In Louisiana, U.S. officials meekly handed over the New Orleans mint and customs house, and with them $599,303 in gold and silver coin. In Texas, General David Twiggs, a native Georgian and stout veteran of both the 1812 and Mexican wars, made only a token demurral before bestowing all federal forts and armaments in the state upon a ragtag coterie of irregulars who had marched into San Antonio under the Lone Star flag. (Twiggs would be dismissed from the U.S. Army for treason—in absentia, since by then he had already joined that of the Confederate States.) Next to these rich prizes, Fort Sumter was of negligible value to the Confederacy—a small sacrifice, it would appear, in exchange for staving off "the horrors of a fratricidal war," as Major Anderson put it in one of his dispatches. More time might still buy a peaceful compromise with the South. More time might permit the Union to prepare itself for war as the Confederacy was doing, assembling munitions and volunteers.[9]

This last course of action, peaceful surrender, was the one that nearly all of Sumter's officers and men—and its commander—expected Lincoln ultimately to choose. Anderson felt that he had honorably held the fort throughout the worst of the secession mania. Now, he wrote to a friend, tempers in the seceding states would gradually cool, and, barring any rash federal action, "our errant sisters, thus leaving us as friends, may at some future time be won back by conciliation and justice." There would be no disgrace in lowering his flag to the forces of secession, now that the mob of local roughnecks shaking their fists at Moultrie in December had become a well-equipped army of seven thousand men, commanded by one of the ablest siege tacticians in America, General Pierre Gustave Toutant Beauregard. In fact, the dapper little Louisianan had studied artillery technique at West Point under no less an authority than Major Anderson himself, and the two men had remained warm friends.[10]

It was the most gentlemanly of sieges. Arriving in Charleston at the beginning of March, Beauregard had sent several cases of cigars and fine brandy over to Anderson as tokens of his undiminished esteem. (Anderson, mindful as ever of military etiquette, promptly returned them untouched.) When the two commanders had occasion to exchange messages, their notes were addressed "My dear General" and "My dear Major." A sympathetic lady of Charleston sent over a bouquet of early-blooming Carolina jasmine whose scent delighted the men, reminding them of "the woods and freedom," the surgeon Crawford wrote.[11]

South Carolina's governor, Francis Pickens, was not quite so courtly and obliging, but he did allow the garrison at Sumter to communicate with the outside world, with almost no interference. Visitors came and went, including one of Mathew Brady's photographers, who assembled Anderson and his officers for a group portrait. The daily mail boat from town brought confidential communiqués from the War Department inquiring about the military situation. It brought letters and small packages from home, and a large crate of prime-quality tobacco from an admiring merchant in New York. (Anderson did not send this back.) It brought requests from men and women all over the North for autographs, photos, and locks of hair, which the officers did their best to supply. It even brought emissaries from Washington: White House aides and War Department adjutants, interviewing, inspecting, inquiring, but offering no instructions. Beauregard and the Carolinians allowed these envoys to pass, believing that their reports would only hasten Lincoln's inevitable decision to surrender the fort peacefully.[12]

One day, the boat brought Mrs. Anderson. Worried by the lack of mail from her husband, the major's wife had traveled by train from

New York to see him, and received permission from the rebel authorities because, as Doubleday wryly put it, "she had many influential relatives among the Secessionists." She stayed only two hours, barely long enough to assure herself that her husband was safe and to take a meal together, but with her had come another visitor who would remain for three months. Peter Hart, a tough former sergeant, had accompanied the major as his orderly all through the Mexican War. Remembering her husband's fondness for him, the resourceful Eliza Clinch Anderson had decided to track him down. She found Hart serving as a New York City policeman in a remote district of Upper Manhattan—just above Twenty-sixth Street—and somehow persuaded him to join the defenders at Sumter. The rebels refused to let Hart stay, but Mrs. Anderson not being a lady to take no for an answer, they finally assented, on the condition of his word of honor not to fight as a soldier. This he gave, but he would still play an important role in the battle to come.[13]

Three essential things the boat from Charleston continually failed to bring: reinforcements, provisions, and orders from Washington.[14]

Back in December, as Doubleday's boat approached Sumter on its night voyage from Moultrie, he had thought the new fortress resembled a prison. Now it had become one in fact. On bright days, the men played at ball and leapfrog on the parade ground, but sunlight was a rare and fleeting thing. Dusk came early and dawn late within the gloomy walls of encircling brick. During those long hours of darkness, there was no light to read or write by; nothing to do but huddle beneath blankets and wait out the slowly passing hours. The damp, raw cold of late winter penetrated masonry and men's bones. Coal and firewood were running short along with the food and candles, and a guard was placed over the dwindling supply. The soldiers fished out passing driftwood to burn, before they began tearing down some of the fort's outbuildings for fuel. Still, they could barely keep themselves warm. Doubleday sacrificed a handsome mahogany table that he had carried with him from his well-appointed quarters at Moultrie.[15]

Amid this gloom and tedium, the men worked to shore up the fort's defenses. Sumter, created decades before to withstand an attack on Charleston by a foreign fleet, had been designed with its strongest bastions overlooking the main shipping channel and with the weakest flank, known as the gorge wall, directly facing the nearest land, Cummings Point, just twelve hundred yards distant. This rear flank was where, for safety's sake, the engineers had placed the main gate, hospital, and ordnance room. Now, with the enemy's guns on Cummings Point, Sumter's occupants must have wished they could lift up the entire fortress and rotate it 180 degrees. They had to make do instead with walling off the main gate with brick and stone, mounting howitzers above it, and constructing shrapnel-proof barriers in front of the fragile buildings. The Confederates, they expected, would try to storm the fort from this side. Captain Seymour, an inveterate tinkerer, devised makeshift weapons to drop on the attackers' heads: barrels, charged with gunpowder and loaded with paving stones, that would explode like giant grenades as they hit the ground. Every so often, the harbor echoed with booms as one side or the other tested its heavy guns, and one morning a live round, fired mistakenly by an onshore battery, crashed into the water just off Sumter's wharf. The Confederates hastily sent an officer over to apologize.[16]

While Sumter might have seemed at times like an island without a country—neither Northern nor Southern, Union nor Confederate—its occupants were nevertheless constantly reminded that they were situated in the middle of slave territory. The Union officers even had their own slave, a lively and bright teenager named James, whom they had rented from his master in Charleston to serve as their factotum around the fort and to run small errands in the city. James became a cause of contention—and of a rare breach of decorum between besiegers and besieged—when he failed to return from one of these errands. The officers soon learned that his master had seized him and was refusing to give him back, in violation of the rental agreement, because James, who was apparently literate, had exchanged letters with his mother about a possible slave uprising. In a letter to Major Anderson, a South Carolina official rudely suggested that the boy's "temper and principles" had clearly been corrupted by exposure to the Yankee degenerates at Sumter—an insult that brought Anderson nearly to the point of challenging the man to a duel.[17]

For the most part, though, quiet reigned. The excitement of December and January when Anderson's men had expected a Southern assault at any moment and were ready, even eager, to fight—had given way to a surreal calm, a stasis that seemed as if it might last forever, with the little band of soldiers fixed eternally on a point around which history's wheel would continue to turn, never touching them.

In some ways, the nine officers formed a microcosm of the Union itself, with men representing almost every region and every political orientation in the country, including one young Virginia lieutenant who later, when his state seceded, ended up switching sides, fighting—and dying in the Confederate service. They also included a wide range of personalities. The officer corps of the "Old Army," as the career military would be fondly remembered after the war, was a kind of men's club, a close-knit, sometimes affectionate, often rambunctious fraternity. You started at West Point before you could shave, and then worked your way through the ranks, flying hither and thither among states and territories at the mysterious whim of the War Department, until you were a grizzled pensioner—unless, of course, a Mexican bullet or a Comanche arrow found you first. Everybody seemed to know everybody else, and a single moment of glory or disgrace—whether on the battlefield or the dueling ground, in the barroom or the brothel—could seal an officer's reputation, and his fate. In many respects, though, a spirit of tolerant worldliness prevailed. The Old Army was one of antebellum America's few truly national institutions, and certainly the only one that required the sons of Georgia planters to bunk alongside those of New England schoolteachers, not to mention do daily business (peaceably or not, as circumstances might require) with Mormon emigrants and Sonoran bandits. "I have in my pilgrimage thus far found mankind nearly the same in every region," Major Anderson once reflected. There was room for many kinds of men around the officers' mess table—and Sumter's was no exception.[18]

Abner Doubleday, the garrison's blunt-spoken second in command, hailed from Auburn, New York, the antislavery Republican heartland, where his fellow townsfolk included William H. Seward and Harriet Tubman. The bulldoggish captain was used to being regarded as slightly eccentric, both for his radical politics and for his metaphysical turn of mind—neither of these being quite standard issue at West Point. He pored over Spanish poetry, theories of the afterlife, and transcendentalist essays—years earlier, in fact, as a freshly minted lieutenant, he had written Emerson a swoony fan letter, inviting the philosopher, whom he had never met, to come and stay for a visit at the fort where he was stationed off the coast of Maine, "my quarters being large for a bachelor."[19] But Doubleday could also be entertaining company. He had a boyish love of practical jokes and coarse anecdotes that could relieve the often dreary life of an army outpost—it took little prodding for him to regale his messmates with the story of General Kearney, General Sumner, the Irish cook, and the watermelon; or the one about Secretary Floyd's encounter with the Sioux Indian chief; or of how Lieutenant Tom Jackson—not yet known as Stonewall—got fleeced by a horse trader back at Fort Hamilton.[20]

The captain's connection to Cooperstown and the legend that he invented baseball are equally specious, alas. Versions of the game existed long before his birth, and Doubleday himself would mention baseball just once in any of his surviving writings: in 1871, while in command of a fort in Texas, he would ask the War Department for permission to purchase bats and balls for the members of a colored infantry regiment at the post. (This request was apparently denied.)[21] In a certain respect, however, it made sense for a later generation of Americans to associate the sport with a famously tenacious Union officer. Baseball was just coming into its own as the Civil War began—the first reference to it as a national pastime dates from 1856—and Americans associated it with some of the same ideas that were percolating through the political culture of the era, ideas that they would also come to associate strongly with the Northern cause. (Indeed, one political cartoon in 1860 showed Lincoln preparing to hit a home run, with a fence rail inscribed *Equal Rights and Free Territory* as his bat, and the words *Wide Awake* on his belt.) Writers praised it as a "manly" game, one that inculcated principles of self-reliance and free competition perfectly suited to "our go-ahead people." They promoted it as a "national institution" that could unite Americans in every region. In New York, where the baseball craze truly took off, an 1857 *Herald* article exhorted: "Let us have base ball clubs organized . . . all over the country, rivaling in their beneficent effects the games of Roman and Grecian republics." Perhaps the enlisted men at Sumter did play baseball—Crawford's diary records them as "playing ball," without further specifics—but even so, a career officer like Doubleday would almost certainly have considered it inappropriate to join them.[22]

Doubleday may have been the garrison's champion raconteur, but it was Crawford, the surgeon, who would eventually provide the most detailed account of life inside Sumter. As a medical man, Crawford had attended not West Point but rather the University of Pennsylvania, in his native state. After nearly a decade in the army, he still brought the eye of an outsider, and of a scientist, to bear on things around him. From the beginning of the crisis he had been taking meticulous daily notes—with an eye toward not only history but also the literary marketplace. "It will be a book eagerly sought after, I think, and would certainly pay," he wrote to his brother more than a month before the Confederate attack. "Two different firms have applied." An accomplished draftsman, the surgeon (like Captain Seymour) also made sketches of the fort and sold them by mail to *Harper's Weekly* for the handsome sum of $25 apiece. Crawford was ambitious, self-assured, and rather vain, sporting a pair of magnificent side-whiskers that hung down over his epaulettes like Spanish moss on a stately oak. Moreover, he craved fame not just as a litterateur, but also as a warrior, making no secret of the fact that he would happily trade his scalpel for a saber.[23] Like Doubleday, he was also quite open about his politics—though unlike his fellow officer, his time in the South had made him sympathetic to the slaveholders, and he blamed the Union's current predicament on the sentimental foolishness of Northern abolitionists.[24]

Truman Seymour, a Vermont preacher's son, was a man of a very different stamp. Dark-eyed and ruminative, with thick hair swept back from his forehead in Byronic fashion, he seemed at first more like an artist or poet than a warrior. Indeed, Captain Seymour was a fine watercolorist—a painter of precise, delicately hued landscapes—had taught draftsmanship for several years at West Point, and had recently taken a year's leave from the army to roam across Europe and commune with the works of Titian, Rubens, and Veronese. During his rare sojourns at home in New England, he loved to hike the Green Mountains with his sketchpad and brushes, fascinated not just by the misty peaks but by the complicated geology beneath them, which he had begun studying seriously as a teenager. Like them, Seymour concealed a stony core beneath a luxuriant exterior: while still a boy lieutenant, he had been brevetted twice for gallantry in Mexico, and later fought in Florida during the army's ruthless final campaign against the Seminoles. With little of the bellicose swagger affected by Doubleday and even Crawford, he was perhaps a better soldier than either: the kind who viewed the garrison's predicament at Sumter not as a hopeless cause, nor as a chance at patriotic glory, but as a logistical puzzle to be solved with cool ingenuity.[25]

Ultimately, however, Sumter's fate would depend on the man whose inmost thoughts were the most illegible.

For months after Major Anderson's arrival at Charleston, the skeptical Doubleday had done his best to get inside the new commander's head. He had observed the pious Kentuckian intently, tried to draw out his opinions, and even baited him on the subject of slavery. Anderson confessed he was disgusted by the North's refusal to enforce the Fugitive Slave Act, and quoted the Bible to demonstrate that God himself had ordained human bondage. Doubleday, in turn, wheeled the Bible around like a swivel gun and fired it straight back at Anderson, pointing out that since the slaves in the Old Testament were white, he saw no reason why some pious Southern master should not enslave the major himself, "and read texts of Scripture to him to keep him quiet." Anderson, he later boasted, was unable to counter his merciless logical volley. (A less tolerant superior might have clapped the captain in irons.)[26] Had Doubleday been slightly more sensitive, he might have realized that Anderson's reliance on revealed truth was no mere rhetorical strategy. Rather, it bespoke a profound discomfort with earthly affairs, a preference to render unto Caesar.

There was a brittleness to Anderson, Doubleday noticed—almost, it sometimes seemed, a kind of fragility. The strain and uncertainty were clearly taking a mental and physical toll on the major: soon there were a pallor to the man's skin and a dullness to his eyes and, abandoning his long-accustomed reticence, he began sharing his private opinions almost recklessly. In conversations around the officers' mess table, he blamed secession on the North, and confessed that if he were in charge in Washington, he would promptly surrender all the Southern forts. He could never take up arms against the Stars and Stripes, he said, but if his native state of Kentucky left the Union, he would be sorely tempted to do likewise—that is, resign his commission and move to some quiet corner of Europe.[27]

Was this a man to be trusted with the most delicate military assignment in American history? Certainly not, Doubleday had thought at first. In an act of plain insubordination, he had even managed to convey his misgivings directly to the new commander-in-chief. The previous autumn, Doubleday had begun sending frank letters about the situation at Charleston, written in a private code, to his brother Ulysses. Ulysses, a Republican campaign operative in New York City, then decoded them and sent them on to the candidate Lincoln and other "leaders of public opinion" across the North. Some of the early dispatches went so far as to hint that Anderson might soon show his true colors as a secessionist traitor.[28]

Yet there were facets to the new commander that Doubleday did not immediately appreciate. One of these was Anderson's deeply felt sense of honor and duty—a quality apparent in the move from Moultrie to Sumter.

Another, which revealed itself more slowly, was Anderson's hatred of war itself. Carnage sickened him, and he had already witnessed far too much in the course of his career. As a young officer in the struggle against Chief Black Hawk in Illinois, he had watched helplessly as the local settler militia, berserk for Indian blood, massacred unarmed civilians; had seen and smelled the emaciated bodies of women and children left rotting by the road under an August sun. He had rescued a four-year-old Indian girl, maimed by a musket ball, from beneath the corpse of her dead mother. He had beheld senseless misery, he wrote then to his brother, "exceeding any I ever expected to see in our happy land."[29] He had prayed God to spare his country from enduring the like ever again.

It was to peace that Anderson was most loyal, Doubleday began to realize. The major's experiences of war, his piety, and his staunch conservatism all committed him to preserving the Union—and not in name alone, but the Union as only a politically innocent man could conceive it: a Union without sectional strife, without secessionists, without abolitionists. Without even North and South, perhaps. Civil war, disunion, radicalism: these were anathema to every fiber of Anderson's being. Eventually Doubleday began to feel sympathy, verging on admiration, for his commander. "I feel deeply for him," he wrote in February. "I consider him an honorable and brave man [and] as much as we differ in the propriety of some of his acts, I have a high respect for him as a man and as an officer."[30]

All those in the fort had come to detest what they called the secessionist "madmen." But most had little more love, if any, for the incoming Republican administration. On March 4, a few hours after Lincoln had taken the oath of office, Dr. Crawford wrote to his brother back home in Pennsylvania: "A vulgar, third rate politician, a man without anything to entitle him to the position he holds, an uncouth Western Hoosier is now our President. . . . How any party could have . . . elected [such] a character as the present rail splitter is more than a mystery to me. He is however under the control of Mr. Seward almost entirely and from that single circumstance I permit myself to hope for the best."[31]

From the Northern newspapers that came on the daily mail boat, the men at Sumter knew that they had become famous. On distant Broadway, P. T. Barnum's "Museum" was staging "Union Drama, Anderson and Patriots at Sumter in '61," which spectacle filled the house twice daily at twenty-five cents a ticket. (A tall, handsome actor named J. H. Clark played Doubleday, who was portrayed—not without some justice—as the most warlike among the "Patriots," itching to unleash the fury of Sumter's cannons upon the rebels.) During the long hours of standing watch or supervising work on the fortifications, the junior officers whiled away their time in idle speculation about how their grateful country would eventually reward their heroism—heroism that, of course, had not yet included firing or withstanding a single shot. Crawford thought that the War Department should confer on each of them a brevet promotion in rank and pay grade. Doubleday actually designed a medal for Congress to bestow upon the garrison's members, depicting the evacuation of Fort Moultrie on one side and the word *Fidelity* on the other.[32]

Fidelity was a virtue all too rare in America that winter. Newspapers from the North also brought reports of a steady exodus of career military men resigning from the army to join the Confederate forces. These defections came as personal blows to the men at Sumter. "We cannot repress the sadness that comes over us when we see one by one of our old comrades dropping away, men with whom we have [shared] many a bivouac in the far distant frontier," Crawford wrote in his diary. "How are we to regard them as our enemies now?"[33]

On that same day, March 6, came word of Lincoln's inaugural speech, with its pledge to "hold, occupy, and possess" the Southern forts. Across Charleston Harbor, a new flag unfurled above the city, alongside the familiar palmetto banner. From Sumter's ramparts, it looked at first, confusingly, like the defenders' own flag, "the one flag we longed to see," as Doubleday called it. But as they took turns with the spyglass, they got their first good look: three broad red and white stripes and a circle of seven stars—the banner of the new Confederate nation.[34] From that moment on, the garrison's position felt even less tenable than before.

The officers and men at Sumter put little stock in Lincoln's rhetoric—let alone in the bluster of Republicans across the North who said the fort must be defended. Its ultimate fate could hardly be in doubt. Anderson had shared with the War Department the estimates of how many troops would be required to hold or resupply his post, and neither the major nor his subordinates could believe that elder statesmen like Secretary Seward and General Scott would approve a doomed mission that would lead inexorably to internecine war. Fort Sumter, Crawford wrote to his brother, "must be given up and the sooner the administration appreciate this the better. All this talk of 'occupying, holding, and possessing' the forts is nonsense. There is neither Army enough to do it, nor is it likely there soon will be." If it were up to him, he said bitterly, he would simply blow up the fort and leave the accursed harbor forever—and then, like Anderson, depart for Europe rather than remain in the "rump" of his former country. Yet even at the same time Crawford pined for escape, he expressed, paradoxically, an oddly sentimental attachment to the place, as if Sumter itself were the last remaining shred of the nation that he had loved and served: "I cannot tell you how grieved I am at the thought of leaving this fort, where every stone and surrounding is so impressed upon my heart." By the middle of March, both Northern and Southern newspapers were reporting confidently that evacuation was imminent, with some even announcing that the orders had been signed by the president and were on their way to Anderson. Meanwhile, the surgeon attended to his routine tasks, dutifully dispensing medicines and filing sick reports. As March drew to a close, he was treating one case of asthma, three of bronchitis, one of syphilis. Dysentery was spreading quickly, to no one's surprise.[35]

By the first days of April, the men were packing up their belongings for what they assumed was their impending departure. Crawford stowed away most of his medical supplies. Captain John G. Foster, the fort's chief engineer, even wrote to a friend serving with the Confederate forces across the harbor, telling him ("strictly entre nous") that he regretted having to leave without saying good-bye, and making arrangements to return a borrowed mustard spoon. Major Anderson had larger concerns. He agonized ceaselessly about the lack of orders from Washington. Within a week, he knew, the last crumbs of food would be utterly exhausted. At any time, he might simply send a polite request to Beauregard, and the officers and men under his command would be escorted to safety, rescued from the pointless siege. Yet he was ever conscious of his honor. In a letter to the War Department on April 5, he pleaded not to be "left without instructions," adding bitterly: "After thirty odd years of service I do not wish it to be said that I have treasonably abandoned a post and turned over to unauthorized persons public property entrusted to my charge. I am entitled to this act of justice at the hands of my Government."

In his heart, though, Anderson was no longer certain he could expect even this. Not from the new commander-in-chief, the dangerous fanatic who had brought the country to such a terrible pass. If only the nation had a soldier at its head once more: a General Jackson, a General Harrison, a General Taylor, even a General Pierce! Instead, it had a party hack whose only armed service had been as a militiaman in the Black Hawk War, at the head of one of those bumpkin companies that Anderson had so despised. (Anderson probably did not recall that on May 29, 1832, he had personally mustered the future president into temporary U.S. Army service as a rank private.)[36]

Spring should have arrived, but still the winter lingered. On April 8, the men awoke to a damp chill. Wind and rain swept the bleak waters of the harbor. Yet on all sides of the fort, things seemed suddenly different. The familiar patrol boats that had passed continuously at a distance now hovered nearby hour after hour. Other vessels were landing men and matériel near the rebels' newly constructed artillery battery on Cummings Point. Toward midmorning, a sudden boom came from the opposite side of the harbor, at the tip of Sullivan's Island, near Moultrie, and Sumter's startled sentries looked through their spyglasses to see a large wooden house explode into splinters. As the cloud of dust drifted into the misty air, they could make out something glinting beyond it, brutal and metallic: the blunt-nosed muzzles of four heavy cannons. The Confederates had unmasked yet another battery, one that they had been constructing in secret. It was brilliantly placed, allowing them to rake the fort's principal bastions from both sides, to dominate the only spot where a friendly ship might have anchored, and to fire directly into Sumter's uppermost tier, where Anderson had placed his heaviest artillery, the only weapons that might pose a serious threat to the enemy's fortifications. Now any men who attempted to work those guns would be cut to pieces by flying metal within minutes. General Beauregard had checkmated his old professor.[37]

The most marked change to be observed on that dispiriting morning was in the major himself. The officers were not privy to his official correspondence with Washington, but for days they had noticed Anderson's usual stoicism sinking into depression. He seemed even grayer and more melancholy than ever, as if oppressed by some new and secret care.

The following day brought a sudden change in the weather, a strange new portent—and an explanation. The ninth of April dawned fine and clear. Against the rooftops of the city, three miles distant, a fresh skyline seemed to blossom as hundreds of sails unfurled along Charleston's wharves. Not long afterward, the men at Sumter watched the departing armada pass them: more than forty merchant ships running free before the northwest breeze toward open water, their sails like so many white petals, each curled edge sharp against the blue. Charleston Harbor was left almost empty. "It was a beautiful sight I assure you," wrote Crawford in his last letter to his brother, a letter that would never be delivered.[38]

It was not many hours after this that Anderson gathered his officers and shared his private burden of almost two full days. He had received the long-awaited orders from Washington, in the form of a terse six-sentence communiqué from Simon Cameron, the new secretary of war. A relief expedition was already on its way with provisions and reinforcements. The garrison was to hold out, if at all possible, until its arrival. And Cameron conveyed a message from Lincoln himself: "It is not, however, the intention of the President to subject your command to any danger or hardship beyond what, in your judgment, would be usual in military life; and he has entire confidence that you will act as becomes a patriot and soldier, under all circumstances."[39]

At long last, the Kentuckian in the White House had made his wishes known to the Kentuckian in Fort Sumter. What unfolded in the coming days would depend, more than anything else, on these two men.

As Anderson's men were counting their crumbs one night during the last week of March, President and Mrs. Lincoln were hosting their first official dinner at the White House. Anxious about Washington protocol, they had sought the discreet coaching of Secretary Seward and his able staff—and by all accounts this initial Republican foray into formal entertaining was competent enough, if not exactly splendid. The gaslight and candles had been artfully arranged to conceal the State Dining Room's shabbiness, and the air was perfumed by fresh spring blossoms in gilt-silver vases, a refreshing change from the artificial flowers preferred by the previous administration. Mrs. Lincoln appeared, arrayed in garish silk, her plump hand clutching a fan that she fluttered energetically—coquettishly, she seemed to think. William Howard Russell, the acerbic correspondent for the *London Times*, peered at her through his wire-rimmed spectacles, taking mental notes on every detail of this frontier queen's curious mannerisms. (They were, he would tell his readers, "stiffened . . . by the consciousness that her position requires her to be something more than plain Mrs. Lincoln, the wife of the Illinois lawyer.")

With the exception of Russell, the guest list was, as might have been expected, an unadventurous one: the entire cabinet was in attendance, seated stiffly in their drab frock coats like a conclave of Methodist parsons, their ranks enlivened only by twenty-one-year-old Kate Chase, the treasury secretary's captivating daughter. The menu, too, was conservative: imported wines accompanied fish prepared *à la française*. In the end, it was the president himself who set his guests at ease, resting his bony elbows on the table and treating everyone to a comical yarn about a drunken Irish coachman he'd met in his days as a young lawyer riding the circuit.[40]

Only one of the administration's senior counselors was conspicuously absent: General Scott, the hero of 1812 and 1848, and typically a fixture at such occasions, his monumental bulk, gold-braided and brass-buttoned, making an impressive centerpiece at any Washington function. (Nor had Scott, whose appetite for good food and fine wine was almost as legendary as his martial exploits, ever been known to decline a dinner invitation.) The other guests awaited his appearance at table for some time—several of them had glimpsed him in the reception room as they came in—until finally word came that the general was indisposed. He had indeed come to the White House, everyone was told, but one of his myriad physical ills—known to include gout, rheumatism, and dropsy—had compelled him to retire to a guest bedroom upstairs for the remainder of the evening.[41]

This was untrue. Scott was, in fact, nowhere in the mansion. Nor was his decrepitude causing him more torment than usual. The general-in-chief's indisposition was of a political nature.

Scott had come early, summoned by an urgent note from the president. Lincoln's brief missive had not specifed the matter at hand, but Scott knew it must involve Forts Sumter and Pickens. Indeed, he assumed that the president was finally ready to discuss evacuation plans, a conversation the general had been awaiting with growing impatience. The day after the inauguration, he had informed Lincoln bluntly that any opportunity to reinforce Sumter had long passed, and that the only question was whether its garrison could be withdrawn before the rebels attacked. A few days later, Scott even took it upon himself to draft orders for the evacuation and forward them to the War Department pending the president's final approval. Major Anderson and his men, he said, should leave Sumter literally as soon as they could find a boat to carry them.[42]

Moreover, Scott knew that almost all of Lincoln's other top advisors, as well as the heads of both major political parties in the North, shared his opinions. Stephen Douglas, the Democratic leader, had publicly endorsed evacuating Sumter. (He was also pushing a scheme to replace the old Union, at least temporarily, with a kind of North American free-trade zone stretching from Upper Canada to the Isthmus of Panama.) Seward, still considered chieftain of the Republican Party, was working more actively—and at times covertly—toward the same end. The secretary of state still believed that the Deep South might be coaxed and petted back into the Union, and, communicating through Southern intermediaries, he had continually assured Confederate authorities that Sumter would soon be in their hands, once even asking them to inform President Davis that the fort would be evacuated within three days. At cabinet meetings, nearly everyone sided with Seward: only Montgomery Blair, Lincoln's postmaster general, consistently argued for reinforcement. Even as uncompromising a radical as Senator Sumner made it known he was ready to yield to the inevitable.[43]

It was with much self-confidence, then—and not a little condescension—that General Scott met Lincoln before the first White House dinner. At six foot five and more than three hundred pounds, Scott was one of the few men in Washington who towered physically over the president. His opinion of his new commander-in-chief had never been especially high; back in November, he'd snorted that if he'd ever laid eyes on the former Illinois congressman during his brief stint in Washington, he certainly couldn't recall it. Presidents might come and go—he had served eight of them in his years as general-in-chief—but the hero of Lundy's Lane and Veracruz remained. Scott took it for granted, naturally, that he would steer the administration's military policies himself. Now he barely gave Lincoln a chance to speak before he began lecturing the president about the Southern forts, and unfolded a memorandum on the subject he had penned earlier that day. Not only must Sumter obviously be evacuated, he said, but Fort Pickens as well. Such a gesture of magnanimity toward "our Southern friends," Scott opined, would unquestionably keep the Upper South in the Union, and might even bring South Carolina and Florida back in. (Actually, the general was far from certain about this last part: in private letters and conversations with others, including Seward, he suggested that the loyal states would ultimately have to let their wayward sisters depart in peace.) He had, he added helpfully, asked his secretary to draw up detailed instructions for the withdrawals of troops. These he offered for the president's approval.[44]

But the president, far from thanking Scott for his wisdom and diligence, was turning pale with anger. The general's plan, Lincoln told a confidant the next day, had given him "a cold shock." Abandon Sumter *and* Pickens to the Confederates? Moreover, how dare he instruct the president on matters of statecraft? The old soldier had overstepped his bounds, blundering off the military path into the thickets of politics, an area that had never been his strong suit, to put it mildly. (Scott had run for president in 1852 on the Whig ticket; his prodigious ineptitude on the campaign trail had helped seal the party's demise.)[45]

In fact, Lincoln had summoned Scott to the White House to talk not about evacuating Sumter but about reinforcing it—and to tell the general to be ready to implement plans for sending in food and supplies. Anderson had "played us false," the president snapped: the major, for reasons of his own, had been misleading his superiors about the true feasibility of holding on to the fort.[46] If Scott was not prepared to carry out his orders, Lincoln concluded coldly, he would find some other person who might do so.[47]

The general, crimson-faced, stuffed his memorandum back into his tunic and hastily departed, stomping out of the White House just as the first guests were arriving for dinner. It had taken as great an insult as this to make Winfield Scott pass up a meal.

The president played the genial host to perfection that evening. But William H. Russell, the canny journalist, noticed how his homespun stories always seemed to serve some deeper purpose, how he camouflaged himself in the "cloud of merriment" like a magician slipping away in a puff of smoke.[48] At the end of the meal, the cabinet officers were startled when Lincoln, with an unaccustomed sharpness in his voice, asked them to linger for a few minutes after the other guests had departed. He revealed the truth about General Scott's absence and told them to return in the morning for an important meeting.

The president could not sleep that night. He lay in bed, his mind racing as it turned over, again and again, the problem of the forts.[49]

But after months of vacillation and evasion, Lincoln had finally begun showing his mettle—an early sign of the decisiveness that would eventually come to characterize his leadership. Unlike most around him, he was thinking of Sumter in terms of its symbolism not just for the South (as the secessionists had defined it) but for the North. For almost six months, Union forces had been in retreat as the rebels pressed relentlessly forward. Beyond the corridors of power in Washington, in towns and cities throughout the loyal states, Americans were sinking into despair at their leaders' apparent impotence.

"The bird of our country is a debilitated chicken, disguised in eagle feathers," wrote George Templeton Strong, who had voted for Lincoln. "We are a weak, divided, disgraced people, unable to maintain our national existence." Indeed, after all the failed attempts at compromise, it was becoming clear to millions of Americans that nothing less than this—America's very existence as a nation—was now at stake. Acquiescence to secession would bring disgrace before the eyes of the world, proving that the republic had carried within itself, ever since its birth, the seeds of its own destruction. Submission to the South's demands would be tantamount to the same thing, making a travesty of majority rule.

Newspapers of both parties savaged the new administration. It was beginning to seem, one Republican editor in Wisconsin wrote, that "the North must get down on its knees and ask Jeff Davis for the 'privilege to breathe.'" A Pennsylvania paper quoted a Democratic congressman as calling Lincoln "vain, weak, puerile, hypocritical," "the weakest man who has ever been elected," and "a cross between a sandhill crane and Andalusian jackass." The exact nature of that last hybrid may not have been altogether evident, but it was clearly not meant to be complimentary.[50]

Since the very beginning of the secession crisis, the only glimmer of national pride had come with the surprise occupation of Fort Sumter back in December, the moment greeted with cheers and cannon salutes throughout the North. Whatever Major Anderson's true feelings and motives, he and his small band of men were as yet the Union's only heroes: the "Patriots at Sumter in '61," as P. T. Barnum had dubbed them. Could it be that Barnum had his finger on the North's pulse, more than Secretary Seward and all the wise heads in Washington?

The move to Sumter had been a declaration that the nation would fight rather than surrender its integrity; the fort had become the Unionists' sole emblem of defiance and steadfastness rather than compromise and withdrawal. Surrendering now would mean more than just giving up two acres of militarily worthless federal property, more than just throwing an easy sop to the South. To many people, it would mean nothing less than abrogating American history, abandoning the heroic struggle that—within living memory—had transformed thirteen small colonies into a vast and mighty empire. As one elderly citizen of Illinois, remembering his father's service under General Washington in the Revolution, asked plaintively, "Shall all this be thrown away to please a few villains and Traitors[?]"[51]

Lincoln had in any case come to doubt that the South could be appeased. Moreover, as he suggested to Scott, he had come to doubt that the military situation in Charleston Harbor was as hopeless as Anderson claimed. Two weeks earlier, Lincoln had met with an obscure former navy captain named Gustavus V. Fox. Since January, Fox had been peddling a complicated scheme he had devised to get troops, food, and supplies to Sumter. Balding, diminutive, and pear-shaped, Captain Fox had never commanded a vessel larger than a mail steamer, and since his retirement five years earlier had occupied himself chiefly in the woolens industry. The main reason his plan even got a hearing is that he happened to be married to Postmaster General Blair's sister-in-law. Instead of trying to get a heavily armed naval squadron into Charleston Harbor, Fox proposed keeping the warships out in deep water and sending in two shallow-draft tugboats that could slip over the sandbars and sunken hulks under cover of darkness. They would have to be civilian vessels, but their steam engines could be protected from incoming fire with bales of cotton or hay. Anyhow, Fox doubted that the rebels' heavy cannons would be able to hit small, speedy craft half a mile away, and enemy boats could be kept at bay with barrages from Sumter's own guns.

The president was intrigued by this improbable proposal—so much so that he ordered Fox to set out for Charleston and, taking advantage of the Confederates' lax visitation policies, inspect Sumter for himself to ascertain whether the plan was practicable. Fox would spend barely an hour talking with Major Anderson, who found the scheme—or as much of it as Fox hazarded to reveal—utterly harebrained. By that point, however, the ex-captain was so besotted with his own idea that probably nothing could have dissuaded him. Returning directly to Washington, Fox assured the president that his tugboat-and-hay-bale strategy was foolproof. Anderson, meanwhile, dashed off a quick but pointed memo to the War Department, neatly demolishing the plan in three sentences—or so he thought.[52]

On Friday, March 29, the day after Lincoln's sleepless night, he convened his cabinet again at the White House. They met in his upstairs office, around a scuffed walnut table stacked high with papers.

For the past three weeks, the president had largely deferred to these men on matters of policy. Before his arrival in Washington, he had met almost none of them, and appointed them mostly according to the need to balance patronage among key states and political factions. "Neither, on the other hand, did they know him," his secretaries Nicolay and Hay would later recall. "He recognized them as governors, senators, and statesmen, while they yet looked upon him as a simple frontier lawyer at most, and a rival to whom chance had transferred the honor they felt due to themselves. . . . Perhaps the first real question of the Lincoln Cabinet was, 'Who is the greatest man?' It is pretty safe to assert that no one—not even he himself—believed it was Abraham Lincoln."[53]

But now Lincoln revealed the momentous decision he had just made without consulting any of these respected statesmen: he had ordered Captain Fox to be ready to depart for Charleston Harbor in little more than a week's time if ordered to do so. It doubtless interested the president to note that his cabinet members' opinions, too, had begun to shift. Treasury Secretary Salmon P. Chase, considered the group's staunchest Republican partisan, had previously been wavering on the Sumter question. Now he came out firmly in favor of reinforcement. So did Gideon Welles, the sober-sided secretary of the navy. Still, the president did not commit himself. Perhaps Anderson was right after all. While Fox prepared his tugboats to launch, Lincoln could continue to ponder.[54]

Whom was the president to trust: Anderson, whose loyalty might be doubted but whose military expertise was unquestioned; or Fox, whose loyalty was indubitable but whose grasp of naval strategy seemed tenuous at best?[55]

The starkness of this decision, and the magnitude of the stakes, seemed too much for Lincoln to bear. The past few weeks had already taken a physical toll; those who knew him well had been astonished at how drawn and haggard he seemed. Not long after the cabinet meeting broke up, the president collapsed into bed again, incapacitated by a migraine "sick headache" such as he hadn't had in years. For the next three days, he plunged into one of the spells of profound depression that had plagued him periodically his entire life.[56]

But, as in previous such moments, Lincoln's acute mental pain seems to have culminated in a flash of clarity.[57] Sometime during that awful weekend, the president had an epiphany: he needed to trust neither Fox nor Anderson—only himself. If the tugboat mission succeeded, it would be a blow to secession, a victory for the new administration, and a rallying point for Unionists (and Republicans) everywhere. Even if it failed—if the rebel guns succeeded in driving off his fleet—it would at least be proof of the administration's resolve. Moreover, it would bring war. And this, Lincoln had come to believe, was no longer a result to be dreaded. At least not if the rebels fired the first shot.

Peaceful reunification with the wayward states now seemed clearly impossible. No offer, however generous, had been good enough for the Deep South. Crittenden had failed; Corwin had failed; the Peace Conference had failed; Douglas and Seward both appeared to be failing. The real issue now was whether the Upper South could be kept from casting its lot with the rebellion. The border states still wavered, with strong pro-Union factions active in all of them. A Northern show of strength—or a Southern display of intemperate aggression—might give those Unionists a rallying point. And a demonstration that secession would inevitably mean bloodshed might scare disunionists back into the fold. Marylanders, Virginians, Kentuckians, and Tennesseeans, especially, knew that their states would become battlegrounds in the event of full-scale war—and this consideration was not to be taken lightly.

Lincoln's decision was probably also influenced by what he had heard at the cabinet meeting. Blair must have reiterated, as he had for months, that Southerners who doubted "the manhood of Northern men," who mistakenly thought Yankees a pusillanimous race of "factory people and shop keepers" instead of warriors, needed to be taught a lesson.[58] Welles pointed out that armed resistance by the secessionists would "justify the government in using all the power at its command" to hold Sumter. But it was Salmon Chase, who just two weeks earlier had argued against provoking war, who now made the subtlest and most persuasive case for the other side. If war was now inevitable, the treasury secretary suggested, "I perceive no reason why it may not be best begun in consequence of military resistance to the efforts of the administration to sustain troops of the Union stationed, under the authority of the Government[,] in a Fort of the Union, in the ordinary course of service."[59]

The last phrase of Chase's argument was key. The administration must contrive to make the Sumter expedition seem not some covert raid, but a routine, peaceable delivery of supplies as would be made to any federal garrison. Indeed, Captain Fox, with his background delivering mail rather than cannonballs, was the perfect man to lead it.

Now Secretary Seward, who had dominated the Republicans' response to the crisis ever since the November election, suddenly found himself left in the intolerable, impossible position of advocating what had become a minority view. This threatened not only to unravel all the webs of statecraft he had woven over the past five months but also to discredit all the public and private assurances he had given. Even worse: to make a mockery of his assumption—shared by many others—that he would be president in all but name.

On Easter Sunday, March 31, as a last-ditch effort to resurrect his hopes, Seward sat down and composed an extraordinary memo to Lincoln. "We are at the end of a month's administration and yet without a policy either domestic or foreign," he lectured the commander-in-chief. Any aggressive act against the South by the federal government, he wrote, would confirm the public's belief, in both the loyal and rebel states, that the current national conflict was one "upon Slavery, or about Slavery." Keeping the garrison at Sumter would seem like the bellicose act of a hard-line abolitionist regime. Instead, the president must continue to buy time, until the slavery issue could be buried once and for all. The crisis must be framed as a question simply of "*Union* or *Disunion*." The best way to reunite the nation, Seward advised, was to declare war not against the South but against Spain and France, forming a grand North American and Central American alliance that would drive European colonizers permanently out of the hemisphere. (Maybe while they were at it, he ruminated, they should attack the British and the Russians, too.) No doubt Seward's sources in the White House had informed him of the president's sudden and mysterious illness, raising hopes that an even more astonishing proposal would be accepted, perhaps even welcomed: Seward suggested that perhaps Lincoln was not feeling up to the job of orchestrating all this complicated policy, in which case he, as secretary of state, might be willing to step in—modestly and reluctantly, of course—and take the administration's helm.[60]

As Seward put the finishing touches on his memo, he was so pleased with its contents, and so confident of its success, that he sent an urgent message summoning his friend Henry J. Raymond, editor-in-chief of *The New York Times*, to Washington. Raymond arrived after midnight, ready to telegraph the scoop that Seward had been named premier of the new administration. First thing the next morning, Seward's son

Frederick hand delivered the memo to the White House, while Raymond stood by, with his editors in New York holding the front page open in expectation of the breaking news.[61]

Lincoln's terse, stinging reply arrived within hours. In fact, he informed Seward, his administration *did* have a policy—it just happened not to be the one advocated by the secretary of state. Whatever needed to be done, he said, "*I* must do it," though of course he would always be glad to seek his cabinet members' advice. The president signed his letter—surely not without irony?—"Your Obedient Servant, A. Lincoln."[62]

The telegram Raymond sent to the *Times* was briefer than anticipated. "Nothing more," it read.[63]

Seward's memo, insulting as it was, steeled Lincoln's nerves, rousing him fully from the funk of the past several days. He, the upstart lawyer from Illinois, had now bid defiance to both the nation's most powerful soldier and to its most powerful politician. The path ahead would be his alone. He also realized now that he could no longer rely solely on the wise old men of his cabinet for information and advice. Recalling the candid letters he had received the prior autumn from one of the artillery captains at Fort Sumter, the president contacted Mary Doubleday, asking if she would mind sharing any of her husband's correspondence that might shed unbiased light on the circumstances in Charleston Harbor. Mrs. Doubleday, after busying herself with a pair of scissors to excise the purely personal passages of Abner's recent letters, gave several excerpts to Lincoln. "If Government delays many days longer," one read, "it will be difficult to relieve us in time, for the men's provisions are going fast."[64]

Letting the garrison be starved out would be equivalent to surrender. War must not only come but come soon.

As Fox hurriedly readied his expedition to embark from New York, Lincoln took stock of the Union's military preparedness. On the same day Seward received his presidential rebuke, a White House courier arrived at the War Department with one for the general-in-chief. "Would it impose too much labor on General Scott," the president's note asked tartly, "to make short, comprehensive, daily reports to me of what occurs in his department, including movements by himself, and under his orders, and the receipt of intelligence? If not, I will thank him to do so."

What Lincoln learned was not encouraging. In the entire country east of the Mississippi, the United States Army numbered fewer than four thousand men—several thousand fewer than the rebel forces at

Charleston alone. Only a few hundred men defended such places as New York, St. Louis, Baltimore, the mouth of the Chesapeake Bay, and even Washington itself. Most of the national military was stationed in forts along the trails of the Far West and the Pacific coast. In all, the troops totaled just over seventeen thousand enlisted men and officers, many of whom could be expected to defect to the South once hostilities began. Even the military bureaucracy was almost laughably undermanned. The entire War Department had only ninety-three employees, from Secretary Simon Cameron down to the file clerks. No wonder Scott and Seward, poring over the columns of these statistics in the most recent departmental annual reports, were so anxious to avoid the clash of arms, or at least delay it.[65]

Yet Lincoln, the Sangamon County militiaman, would step decisively into his role as commander-in-chief. This new assertiveness, too, would require him to look beyond War Department memos and official chains of command in Washington. Outside the purview of General Scott, Secretary Cameron, and their assorted file clerks, American citizens in the loyal states were arming themselves—in fact, had been doing so for months. Companies of Wide Awakes that had marched with lit torches to celebrate the Republican victory in November were now drilling with muskets. And amid the excitement that followed the occupation of Sumter, men throughout the North had formed new militia companies, "putting on their war paint to fight for the Union," as one newspaper had reported back in January. By the end of that month, according to one estimate, nearly half a million had pledged to take up arms against secessionist treason.[66]

The White House mail bags bulged with more and more letters like the one that arrived in mid-March from an old Springfield acquaintance, James L. Hill. Addressing his letter to "Dear Old Abe," Hill wrote:

We hear with pain and regret that you are debating about evacuating Sumter lowring our Glorious old Flag that Washington through so many trials and Privations unfurled and sustained to be trampled on by traitors and to be made the hiss and scoff of the World. Do you know that Genl Washington or Jackson never said "*I cant*"[?] . . . Say the word By the Eternal Fort Sumter *shall* be reinforced and that glorious old Flag sustained and my word for it 100,000 good and true men with Jim Hill amongst them will at once respond to the call. . . . You are now the head of this nation and of course know more and better than we the reasons that are leading to this result but for Gods sake for Humanity and for your own honor dont let that word *Cant* form any part of the reasons.[67]

Perhaps Lincoln was remembering Hill's letter the following month when—just after the Sumter attack—leaders of the Young Men's Christian Association visited the White House to make one last plea for compromise. "You gentlemen, come here to me and ask for peace on any terms," Lincoln told them. "You would have me break my oath and surrender the government without a blow. There is no Washington in that—no Jackson in that—there is no honor or manhood in that."[68]

On April 6, Lincoln met at the White House with the governors of Indiana, Maine, Illinois, Wisconsin, Michigan, and Ohio, whom the ardently Republican editor Horace Greeley had marshaled to deliver a hard-line message to the president. All were ready to proffer troops. From Pennsylvania came news that the state legislature had appropriated half a million dollars to arm its militia, readying it to march southward at a moment's notice in defense of the nation's capital.[69]

That same evening, Lincoln also made a decision that perhaps no career military officer would have made: he gave the enemy advance notice of Captain Fox's arrival. In a message to Governor Pickens of South Carolina, Lincoln announced that vessels were on their way with provisions—but not arms or reinforcements—for Anderson's men. Furthermore, barring an attack by the Confederates, Lincoln pledged no future military reinforcement of Sumter. He had, in fact, completely changed the purpose of the mission. It was now not merely destined to fail—as perhaps Lincoln had known all along it would be—but *designed* to do so. He would force the Confederates' hands: either they would bow to federal authority, or they would unleash their artillery on tugboats that had come to relieve starving men, becoming aggressors in the eyes of the entire world.[70]

Three days later, on the gray morning of April 9, the little flotilla under Fox's command steamed past Sandy Hook and out into the open Atlantic amid heavy seas.[71]

O N T H E L A S T D A Y O F P E A C E , Abner Doubleday found a potato. It had been kicked into a corner and stepped on but was not too badly squashed, so he dusted it off as best he could and stowed it away for safekeeping. In a few days' time, he knew, he might be glad he'd done so. The officers were down to half-rancid pork and a bit of the rice; the privates were issued one hardtack biscuit each as rations for the entire day.[72]

The morning was clear and bright; full southern spring had come at long last. All around the fort, Charleston Harbor stirred with activity. Small steamers ferrying men and supplies among the various Confederate outposts passed insolently right beneath the guns of Sumter. Sometime before dawn, an odd boxlike structure, like a large floating coffin, had been towed out to the point of Sullivan's Island and left inside the breakwater, its four square gun ports staring across the water like the eye sockets of a skull. This odd contraption clad in iron boilerplate—presaging later inventions that this war would inspire—the federal troops recognized as the Floating Battery, which the rebels had designed to be moved wherever they needed extra firepower. The now familiar Confederate flag flew from its gabled end. As Crawford noted, its new position, reinforcing the battery that the enemy had unmasked a few days earlier, made it utterly impossible for Fox's tugboats to reach Sumter without being blown to splinters. (Across the harbor, on Cummings Point—just over half a mile from Sumter's vulnerable gorge wall—the Carolinians had built a similar structure on land, the Iron Battery, with a metal roof angled to deflect cannonballs.) Perhaps most ominous of all, the rebels towed three wooden hulks out and moored them not far from the fort. At dusk they could be set afire and, lighting up Sumter's brick walls with their reflected flames, let the enemy gunners take aim by night.[73]

Late that afternoon, a small boat came creaking and splashing toward the fort's wharf, a white flag of truce fluttering at its stern. There were nine men aboard: three white and six black. The three white men wore rebel officers. Two of them, trusted aides to General Beauregard, had come to offer terms of surrender. The third had joined them as a representative of Governor Pickens—and also because, as he later explained, he was fortunate enough to be "the owner of a large six-oared boat and six superior oarsmen," property that he had brought to Charleston from his family plantation in case it might prove useful during the siege. Those "superior" slaves brought the Confederate envoys to Sumter.[74]

Beauregard's offer was a generous one. He would send vessels to carry Anderson and all of his men to safety. They would be allowed to take their personal possessions and any of their companies' arms and property and be granted passage to any port in the United States that they wished. And before departing, they would be permitted to salute "the flag which you have upheld so long and with so much fortitude, under the most trying circumstances"—before, of course, lowering it.

The rebels clearly wanted the battle to begin before Fox's arrival. They had no idea what sort of naval force might be accompanying his tugboats, and it made little sense to hold fire until they found out. At this moment, they sought the fort, and nothing more; certainly not a major clash of arms. Anderson courteously asked Beauregard's aides to wait while he conferred with his staff.[75]

The eight officers gathered in the major's quarters, standing around him in expectant silence. They had a decision before them, he said, that involved not only their military position but perhaps also their lives. He did not mention their honor. He did not mention their country. He read Beauregard's missive to them aloud.

"Shall we accede?" Anderson asked his officers.[76]

But before they could reply, their commander unfolded another piece of paper, this one dog-eared and creased. It was the letter he had received almost four months earlier and shared with no one until now: his final, secret orders from Secretary Floyd, addressed to him at Fort Moultrie, where they had reached him two days before Christmas:

> It is neither expected nor desired that you should expose your own life or that of your men in a hopeless conflict in defense of these forts. If they are invested or attacked by a force so superior that resistance would, in your judgment, be a useless waste of life, it will be your duty to yield to necessity, and make the best terms in your power. This will be the conduct of an honorable, brave, and humane officer.[77]

The words rang strangely in the small room. They seemed to come from another eon of history. Floyd was long gone now, under congressional investigation in absentia on charges of treason and peculation in office. Buchanan was back on his farm in Pennsylvania, reviled and already half forgotten. Moultrie's ramparts, manned now by Confederate gunners, seemed more distant and unreachable across the harbor than Sumter had ever been. How strange that Anderson should share those orders at this moment, after so many months—rather than, for that matter, reminding them about the dispatch that had come from Secretary Cameron just three days earlier, and which could be interpreted as giving him similar latitude to capitulate when necessary. And

weren't those orders from December the ones that he had already dis-
obeyed, in spirit if not in letter?

But Floyd's words burned as if they somehow formed the throbbing
center of the anguish that Anderson had barely concealed almost since
his arrival in Charleston Harbor. They were the ones he had gone over
in his mind again and again, poking and probing them like a wound:
What was the *honorable* thing to do, not just for his own sake but for
his country's? Could honor permit opening his guns upon his own
countrymen, upon the fort his father had defended long ago? Was the
honorable course the same as the *brave* one, or might it be braver to
save the nation from civil war, even at the expense of his own reputation? And what would a truly *humane* man, a devout man, do? How
best to avoid the senseless carnage that had so horrified him along the
Indian trails of Illinois and among the villages of Mexico?

The thought of Fox's expedition turned his stomach: that foolish
little man and his pathetic tugboats pounded to pieces in the harbor,
along with the soldiers and sailors unlucky enough to come under his
command. Just a few days before, after receiving the news, Anderson
had written to the War Department: "I frankly say that my heart is not
in the war which I see is to be thus commenced." He had sent that letter via his friend in Cameron's office, then asked him not to deliver it.
Still, his officers all knew his heart, for they had all been there on the
morning of the move to Sumter, when a rebel envoy came to demand
an explanation and Anderson told the man ruefully, "In this controversy between the North and the South, my sympathies are entirely
with the South. These gentlemen"—here he turned to the group of
blue-coated officers—"know it well."[78]

And yet those men knew other things about their commander, too.
Most of them had been to West Point and had read—had suffered
bravely through—Anderson's manual of field artillery instruction, a
book of such intricately crafted dullness that even a few paragraphs
made the unfortunate cadet's head spin and his eyeballs ache:

> At the first command the cannoneers run to their respective
> places, and stand facing the boxes upon which they are to mount.
> The gunner and No. 5 in rear of the gun limber, No. 6 on the
> right of the gunner. Nos. 1 and 2 in rear of the caisson limber,
> No. 7 on the left of No. 1, Nos. 3 and 4 in front of the centre
> box of the caisson, No. 8 on the right of No. 3. The gunner and
> Nos. 2 and 3 seize the handles with the right hand, and step
> upon the stocks with the left foot, and Nos. 5, 1, and 4 seize the

handles with the left hand, and step upon the stocks with the right foot.

At the second command, the gunner and Nos. 1, 2, 3, 4, and 5 spring into their seats, the gunners and Nos. 5, 1, and 2 with their backs to the front.

No. 8 then springs into his seat in the same manner as No. 3, and Nos. 6 and 7 step in rear of their boxes, place their hands upon the knees of the men already mounted, step upon the stocks with their nearest feet, and springing up, step over the boxes and take their seats. The gunner and Nos. 5, 1, and 2 then face about to the front by throwing their legs outward over the handles. . . .

. . . and so on, and on, and on, through 214 different maneuvers, each of them, and no others whatsoever, approved by the secretary of war, "with a view to insure uniformity throughout the army." These maneuvers were illustrated by neat copperplate diagrams just as devoid of human volition, with every gun drawn as a little cross, each man as a squarish dot.[79]

Could the author of such a treatise—whatever his personal feelings, whatever his inner pain—possibly strike his colors without returning fire? One might as well ask cannoneers Nos. 5, 1, and 4 to seize the handles of the gun carriage with their right hands instead of their left ones, or tell the squarish dots to abandon their little crosses and scamper off the margins of the page!

"The red tape of military duty," John Hay would later sneer, "was all that bound his heart from its traitorous impulses."[80] Though it may also have reflected Lincoln's private views, this was unfair. For, as Anderson stood before his officers, the men who had lived with him at close quarters for the past five months, none doubted that in the end he would fight.

Reemerging from his quarters, Sumter's commander addressed the Confederate officers. "I shall await the first shot," he told them calmly—and then added: "If you do not batter us to pieces we shall be starved out in a few days."

The envoys returned to their boat. Just before they departed, Anderson called after them with a final question: "Will General Beauregard open his batteries without further notice to me?"

One of the three men, Colonel James Chesnut of the provisional Confederate Army—until recently, the Hon. James Chesnut of the United States Senate—hesitated a moment before replying. "I think not," he finally said. "No, I can say to you that he will not, without giving you further notice."

Then Chesnut and the others stepped aboard and the slave oarsmen pushed off, carrying word to General Beauregard of his old professor's intransigence.

NOTICE CAME IN THE SMALL HOURS of the night. It can be found today among Anderson's papers in the Library of Congress: a single elegant sheet of lavender-blue notepaper, neatly creased where it was once folded between the gloved fingers of a Confederate adjutant. It reads:

April 12, 1861. 3:20 a.m.

Sir—By the authority of Brigadier-General Beauregard, commanding the provisional forces of the Confederate States, we have the honor to notify you that he will open the fire of his batteries on Fort Sumter in one hour from this time.

> We have the honor to be, very respectfully,
> your obedient servants,
> James Chesnut, Jr., Aide de Camp
> Stephen D. Lee, Captain, C.S. Army, Aide de Camp [81]

After receiving this missive, Anderson went to tell his officers and men—who had been anxiously awaiting news—that all except the sentries should return to their beds and try to get some sleep. It was clear that Sumter's defenders could accomplish little until sunrise, since the garrison had no lights; the fort's lamp oil and candles had long since run out. After breakfast, such as it might be, they would begin to return fire. The only other order he gave was to raise the fort's flag, which was duly run up its staff into the blackness above. But most of the officers and soldiers waited quietly on the ramparts to see the war begin. [82]

Beauregard's first shot, the signal shot, arrived ten minutes after its appointed time. Private John Thompson was one of the men who stayed on the parapet to watch it explode overhead like a Roman candle on the Fourth of July. Later, his clearest memory of the moment was glimpsing his comrades' faces in that quick flash of light: no one seemed afraid, Thompson wrote, but "something like an expression of awe crept over the features of everyone."

In the minutes that followed, one battery after another opened up around the harbor, until nineteen of them were hammering away at the fort, sending solid rounds and mortar shells flying in from all sides. The Confederate artillerymen were mostly shooting high, as inexperienced gunners usually did: "Shot and shell went screaming over Sumter," said Sergeant James Chester, "as if an army of devils were swooping around it." But they would eventually find their range.[83]

Abner Doubleday was among the few men to choose safety over scenery, no matter how awe-inspiring. He stayed in bed, in the makeshift but protected quarters he had improvised within one of the fort's deep powder magazines.[84]

The second shot of the Civil War crashed into the masonry at what seemed a foot away from Doubleday's head—"in very unpleasant proximity to my right ear," he recalled much later. Big patches of plaster cracked off the ceiling and fell in clouds of dust. The chamber shuddered again as another shell struck near the ventilation shaft, sending a burst of hot smoke roiling in, and Doubleday looked with some alarm at the crates of gunpowder stacked along one wall. He noticed, too, that some of the black powder had been carelessly spilled on the floor, where any stray spark might ignite it. The captain prudently dressed and went down early to breakfast, which consisted of tepid water and a little of the half-rancid pork.[85]

Clouds hung low in the gray sky, and mist over the water, dimming the faint rays of dawn. At long last, enough light shone through for Sumter's defenders to return fire. To Doubleday fell the honor, if honor it was, of firing the Union's first shot. After breakfast, Anderson had divided the soldiers into three combat details, whereupon Doubleday marched his squad promptly to the cannons that pointed toward the Iron Battery at Cummings Point, whose heavy columbiad guns had been pelting Sumter steadily with solid shot for three hours. Now the captain would try to lob a thirty-two-pound ball inside one of its narrow embrasures. "In aiming the first gun fired against the rebellion I had no feeling of self-reproach," he later recalled, "for I fully believed that the contest was inevitable, and was not of our seeking. The United States was called upon not only to defend its sovereignty, but its right to exist as a nation. The only alternative was to submit to a powerful oligarchy who were determined to make freedom forever subordinate to slavery. To me it was simply a contest, politically speaking, as to whether virtue or vice should rule."[86]

Perhaps the captain should have been less mindful of these political reflections, apropos as they were, and more attentive to his aim: his cannonball missed its mark by just a few yards, bounced harmlessly off the Iron Battery's slanting roof, and landed with a splash in the nearby swamp. For the next two hours Doubleday's men kept up a slow but steady fire, while from the other side of the fort—where the surgeon Crawford, having successfully pestered Anderson to let him join the fray, was commanding one of the gunnery details—they could hear round after round launched in the direction of rebel-held Fort Moultrie.[87]

Sumter was now clenched within a ring of fire and smoke. From all sides, metal tore through the sky. Solid iron balls smashed against masonry; huge mortar shells buried themselves in the earthen parade ground and then exploded, the entire fort shuddering deep within itself like some wounded beast struggling to keep its footing. Men at their posts reeled as streams of dust and debris poured down onto their heads. Most terrifying of all were the wickedly pointed projectiles that occasionally came hurtling toward them, as straight and accurate as the shots of a dueling pistol, from the direction of Cummings Point, apparently discharged by some diabolical weapon none of the enlisted men had seen before. (This was a rifled cannon known as a Blakely gun, recently developed in England, that had arrived direct from London just three days earlier, a gift from some South Carolina expatriates there.) Its shots tore into the vulnerable gorge wall or sometimes, with ruthless accuracy, pierced the gun embrasures, the narrow openings through which the Union artillerymen fired.[88]

PRIVATE THOMPSON WAS HELPING man one of Sumter's cannons from behind one embrasure, inside a narrow brick box known as a casemate. Like almost all the enlisted men, he had never been on the receiving end of an artillery barrage. Thompson was an Irishman, and he would vividly describe the battle later in a letter to his father back in the old country. "The hissing shot came plowing along leaving wreck and ruin in their path," he said. Soon the cannoneers were black with smoke and soot, and several men's faces, cut by broken chunks of masonry knocked loose from the casemate walls, were covered with blood.

In contrast to the garrison's officers, almost nothing is known of its ordinary soldiers. Only a few of their letters survive, and even those may well have been written on their behalf by more literate superiors.[89] A recent immigrant who listed his civilian occupation as "laborer,"

John Thompson, was not atypical. As many as two-thirds of the men in the U.S. army in the 1850s were foreigners, mostly German and Irish. Officers often complained of soldiers who could not understand commands in English, and a significant share of recruits were unable to sign their own names to the enlistment form, let alone pen a letter. Sumter's garrison was even more heavily foreign-born than average: of the seventy-three enlisted men whose birthplaces are known, only thirteen were born in the United States. The roster of privates reads like the roll call in an old World War II movie: Murphy, Schmidt, Onorato, Klein, Wishnowski.[90]

At those rare moments when the entire nation went to war—1775, 1812, 1846—soldiering suddenly became a proud calling for patriotic Americans of every class and condition. The peacetime "regular army" was a different matter. Service in its ranks was considered a last resort for men who couldn't get by otherwise in the merciless economy of nineteenth-century America—or the first resort of immigrants with no resources or connections. "Uncle Sam" (a figure known even to those newcomers) provided a roof over their heads (it was often one made of canvas), shoddy woolen uniforms, and food consisting mainly of bread and coffee, with occasional salt pork. Enlisted men existed in a different world than officers, even in such unusually close confines as Sumter's: the officers' letters and memoirs almost never mention soldiers as individuals, much less by name, and everyone took it for granted that officers would get the last of the rice and pork, while privates enjoyed their one daily biscuit apiece.[91]

It might seem inevitable that in the months of tension and uncertainty, crowded and makeshift quarters, and sparse rations, this heterogeneous cohort of enlisted men would have been driven to quarrels, brawls, or worse. Throughout the winter of 1861, newspapers in both North and South buzzed with rumors of soldiers at Sumter being shot for mutiny. Yet the reports from inside the fort show quite the opposite case: the longer the siege lasted, the more tightly the group knit itself together. Even the snobbish Crawford wrote often of the men's high spirits, and said that when the final battle loomed, "it increased their enthusiasm to the highest pitch." If anything, the common soldiers' morale was higher than their officers'. Although it is often said today that half the U.S. Army resigned in 1861 to join the Confederacy, this is untrue. Very few enlisted men in peacetime came from the South. Only twenty-six privates out of all sixteen thousand ended up defecting to the rebels—compared to more than three hundred out of the thousand or so men in the officer corps.[92]

The Sumter privates' sense that they were actors in an important moment of history seems to have intensified their sense of being Americans—even among those who, technically speaking, weren't. Thompson, though looking forward to the end of his enlistment in a few months so he could go back home to his family in County Derry, spoke of the pride and defiance he shared with his comrades when they "hoisted our colors the glorious 'Stars and Stripes,'" and of their scorn for the "rash folly" of the rebels: "They no doubt expected that we would surrender without a blow, but they were never more mistaken in their lives." [93]

Nineteenth-century cannon warfare required not just a brave heart but also a strong back. Artillery was thought the least glamorous branch of the service, with none of the élan of the cavalry or even the occasional chance at heroism offered by the infantry. Its men were considered mules; its officers technicians. In fact, artillery combat took considerable skill and coordination. Four cannoneers plus a crew chief, or gunner—usually a noncommissioned officer— fired each of Sumter's big casemate guns. After each shot, the men used iron handspikes and a roller to heave the gun back onto its wheeled carriage, no small feat considering that the barrel of one cannon might be more than ten feet long and weigh over four tons. Two men sponged out its still-hot chamber with a wet swab, lest the next charge ignite prematurely. To load the gun, they rammed in the cartridge (a woolen bag of gunpowder) and a cannonball weighing anywhere from twenty-four to forty-two pounds. Then they heaved the cannon forward again, and the gunner, with help from one of the cannoneers, used a handspike to aim the barrel left or right and an elevating screw to move it up or down. A cannoneer pushed a friction primer down into the vent hole at the back of the barrel, with a long lanyard attached that would set the primer aflame as it was pulled out. When the gunner gave the order to fire, the cannoneer yanked the lanyard, the charge exploded in the barrel, and the cannonball hurtled toward its target.[94]

The crash of an enormous cannon firing within a confined casemate could be literally deafening; the concussion that shook the massive brick walls forced the breath out of men's lungs, and left them gulping black smoke. Sumter's soldiers were, moreover, already dizzy from lack of food and sleep. It was only the adrenaline of combat that kept them, though barely, on their feet. They worked the guns in three shifts, and when a crew's turn ended, they collapsed into whatever seemed a protected spot, their heads spinning and stomachs tight with hunger.

As for the officers, they kept up their esprit de corps as best they could, even to the point of trading wisecracks. When Seymour came to relieve Doubleday at the end of a three-hour shift, he facetiously asked his friend, "Doubleday, what in the world is the matter here, and what is all this uproar about?"

"There is a trifling difference of opinion between us and our neighbors opposite," Doubleday replied, "and we are trying to settle it."

"Very well," said Seymour, "do you wish me to take a hand?"

"Yes, I would like to have you go in."

"All right, what is your elevation and range?"

"Five degrees, and twelve hundred yards."

"Well," said Seymour, "here goes!" And his gun crews stepped to their places.[95]

DISPIRITINGLY, THOUGH, all this labor was having almost no effect on the enemy. Sumter's casemate guns were designed to smash the hulls of wooden warships entering the nearby channel, not shore fortifications that lay at the very limit of their range. The fort's cannonballs glanced off the Iron Battery, one Confederate observer said, like marbles tossed at a turtle's back; Doubleday himself compared them to peas thrown on a plate. (One lucky hit did bring down its rebel flag, though, to cheers from Sumter's gun crews.) Shots aimed at Moultrie and the other rebel batteries had, if anything, even less effect, burrowing harmlessly into the sandbags and cotton bales that the Confederates had piled against the ramparts. This is to say nothing of the limits of manpower: Sumter's gun crews were so severely shorthanded that only a few cannons could be fired at a time. And Major Anderson refused even to let his gunners near the fort's heaviest artillery, its mortars and columbiads on the upper tier of the fort, for fear of exposing the men to undue harm.[96]

For their part, the Confederate cannons had as yet inflicted no more than minor injuries on any of Sumter's defenders. A muzzle-loading artillery piece could fire twelve times an hour at most without risk of exploding, so even at the height of the attack, the rebel shots were coming in at an average of just a few per minute, and could be spotted well before impact. Ex-sergeant Peter Hart, Anderson's old Mexican War aide, took the hazardous duty of stationing himself on the fort's parapet. "Now fire away, boys," he told his comrades, "I can't fight without breaking a soldier's word, but I'll tell you where your shots strike, and where to look for danger." Every time Hart spied an incoming round, he called out "Shot!" or "Shell!" and the men ducked into a protected corner of the casemates, as if playing some deadly version of dodgeball.[97]

Union and Confederate gunsmoke drifted, commingling, across the harbor. At midday, the clouds and mist gave way to sheets of rain. At last, through the downpour, Anderson and his officers spotted three vessels steaming toward the mouth of the harbor: the first detachment of Captain Fox's relief expedition. Briefly, the men's morale lifted. But then the friendly ships stopped and anchored outside the bar, to remain there, stolidly immobile, for the rest of the battle. (Fox would later blame his inaction on a combination of the weather and lack of firepower.)[98]

Gradually, the ceaseless Confederate volleys were taking their toll on the fort. The place that had been the men's little world for more than three months—whose every stone, Crawford had written, had impressed itself on his heart—was being obliterated. Cannonballs smashed through the brick walls of the officers' quarters and knocked down its chimney; exploding shells blew off large chunks of the parapet. And the constant battering was gnawing away, bit by bit, at Sumter's massive outer defenses. By the end of the afternoon, a gaping hole had opened in one corner of the gorge wall.[99]

Even more surreal, though, was the sight of Charleston—an American city, where a few months earlier, the men had strolled with their wives and sweethearts along the Battery or picnicked on the beach at Sullivan's Island—become enemy territory. Fort Moultrie, where some of the men had lived for years, was now a target of their guns.

As evening fell and the rebel gunfire gradually slackened, Sumter's defenders faced new worries. Chester later wrote: "The fleet might send reinforcements; the enemy might attempt an assault. Both would come in boats; both would answer in English. It would be horrible to fire upon friends; it would be fatal not to fire upon enemies." Meanwhile, Sumter's supply of cartridges was running low. The men cut up extra clothing and bedsheets to sew into bags for the gunpowder, and Major Anderson contributed several dozen pairs of his socks.[100]

The rain, meanwhile, had become a full-blown storm. Amid the rumble of thunder and the occasional crash of enemy fire, the crews loaded their guns with grapeshot and canister, aimed them toward the most vulnerable points in the outer wall, and at last, after midnight, bedded down next to them as comfortably as they could. "The enemy kept up a slow but steady fire on us during the entire night, to prevent us from getting any rest," Thompson recalled, "but they failed in their object for I for one slept all night as sound as I ever did in my life."[101]

By daybreak the storm lifted, and the morning of April 13 shone bright and clear. No rebels had stormed the fort by night—but no help had come, either. Fox's three ships lay outside the harbor, exactly where the men had last seen them.

Enemy fire rained down on Sumter more briskly than ever—and, thanks to the better weather, more accurately. As the soldiers struggled to work their guns, several were badly cut up by flying pieces of masonry; a shell bursting just outside one of the casemates sent metal fragments tearing into a man's legs. Soon the defenders could see the enemy firing red-hot cannonballs, heated in furnaces ashore. The rebel gunners were now truly shooting to kill. A mortar round plowed through the roof of the half-ruined officers' quarters, and the large building soon became a roaring tower of flame. The iron water tanks inside burst, and a scalding cloud of steam and smoke, acrid from the slow burning of damp pine floorboards and rafters, poured into the casemates as the artillerymen fell, blinded and choking, to the ground, masking their faces with wet handkerchiefs. Most of the garrison would have suffocated to death, Doubleday said later, had not the wind mercifully shifted and begun blowing the smoke in the opposite direction. But the men soon confronted an even more terrifying threat as the blaze that had begun in the officers' quarters began closing in on the cannoneers' gunpowder stores. The men heaved barrel after barrel out of the embrasures.[102]

Doubleday ordered his cannoneers to shoot off a few rounds, just to show the enemy "that we were not all dead yet." But everyone knew that they could not keep even this going for much longer. Only the casemates' fifteen-foot-thick walls sheltered the spent fighters from the inferno around them, and it was unclear how long even these could withstand the attack. "The roaring and crackling of the flames, the dense masses of whirling smoke, the bursting of the enemy's shells, and our own which were exploding in the burning rooms, the crashing of the shot, and the sound of masonry falling in every direction, made the fort a pandemonium," Doubleday later remembered.[103]

Across the harbor, meanwhile, the sun still shone. Thousands of Charlestonians—"male and female, white and black, young and old," one observer wrote—were watching the battle from wharves, rooftops, and church steeples. By midday, disappointingly little of the fort was visible: it was as if a volcano had risen from the sea at the center of the harbor, vomiting smoke. All that the spectators could make out through the thick clouds was Sumter's flag on its tall staff.[104]

The smoke hid even that flag for a while. When it drifted away once more, the enemy banner—the familiar Stars and Stripes—had disappeared. Cheers rang from the rooftops. All around the harbor, the rebel gunners held their fire. Fort Sumter, they congratulated themselves, had finally struck its colors.

ON THE ISLAND, the air began clearing enough for the battered garrison to continue its fight. Several guns boomed forth defiant once more. But just as Private Thompson and the rest of his gun crew were loading their cannon, they heard a commotion from the adjacent casemate. Cannoneers were seizing muskets and pointing at something, or someone, on the beach just outside the fort. And then—astonishing and absurd—a man's face appeared, right in the embrasure through which Thompson was about to fire his cannon.

It was the face of a middle-aged gentleman, a bit thick in the jowls, with a black beard that seemed to bristle angrily in all directions and black eyes that flashed with righteous indignation. He was dressed not in a military uniform but in a frock coat and top hat. Gasping with exertion, cursing and swearing, he was now struggling unsuccessfully to pull himself over the sill with one arm, while his other hand awkwardly grasped a sword, a white handkerchief tied to its point. The soldiers, crowding around, held the stranger at bay with their muskets. Was this some sort of rebel trick? The advance guard of an amphibious attack on the fort? No. The bizarre apparition was—though none of the men recognized him—the Honorable Mr. Louis T. Wigfall, lately United States senator from the now seceded state of Texas.[105]

Fort Sumter had not, in fact, surrendered: a stray shot from the rebels had toppled the flagstaff. Ex-Sergeant Hart and two comrades, at great risk to life and limb, had ventured forth to raise the banner again on a makeshift pole—for which valiant feat they would soon be celebrated by journalists, lithographers, and political orators throughout the Union. But during the brief silencing of the Confederate batteries, Senator Wigfall, smelling glory in the air, had taken it upon himself to set forth from Moultrie in a small rowboat with the goal of personally securing Anderson's formal capitulation. An unlucky Confederate private and three slaves, whom he had dragooned into service at the oars, accompanied him. By the time Moultrie's commanding officers noticed what Wigfall was up to and began yelling for him to stop, the boat was already out of earshot. They fired a warning shot across his bow, but still the senator—much to the consternation of his oarsmen—would not turn back. By the time they reached the middle of the channel, the Confederate batteries around the harbor had begun opening fire once more, as had Anderson's cannons, and the colonel in charge at Moultrie ordered his gunners to sink that "damned politician."

The politician in question, despite his extensive youthful experience with dueling pistols, found incoming artillery rounds a bit harder to face. Wigfall tied his handkerchief to his sword and stood up in the bow, hoping the gunners would honor his makeshift flag of truce, but managing only to nearly swamp the boat. With shots splashing around them, he and his crew somehow made it safely to the shore, with Sumter under a full-on Confederate barrage. Showers of bricks fell from above as the portly senator clambered over rocks and debris toward the embrasures, sword and handkerchief in hand. No one in the fort had noticed his boat coming.[106]

"We stubbornly refused him admittance for a while," wrote Thompson, "but he begged so hard, exhibited the flag he carried and even surrendered his sword"—handing it to Thompson—"that at last we helped him in." Now, to the artillerymen's astonishment, the bearded gentleman ordered them to stop firing, a command that they naturally ignored.[107]

At last someone called for Major Anderson, who tried to mask his own surprise as he stepped into the casemate and saw the stranger. "To what am I indebted for this visit?" he asked dryly.

"I am Colonel Wigfall, of General Beauregard's staff," the ex-senator rasped in as official a voice as he could muster. "For God's sake, Major, let this thing stop. There has been enough bloodshed already." He had come, he said, to offer terms of surrender. Under the present circumstances, in fact, the shell-shocked envoy appeared ready to accept any terms whatsoever that would make the shooting go away.

But Wigfall's little speech, plain enough on its face, was a bit specious at best. For one thing, the "bloodshed" so far consisted of a single Confederate horse. More important, although implying that he came on Beauregard's authority, Wigfall had not even seen the Confederate commander in several days, much less received any instructions from him. The men at Sumter could not have known this, of course.

Anderson pointed out that there had been no bloodshed, at least on his own side—"and besides, your batteries are still firing at me."

"I'll soon stop that," Wigfall replied briskly. He turned to Thompson, who held the sword and handkerchief under one arm, pointed to the embrasure, and told the astonished private, "Wave that out there."

"Wave it yourself," Thompson retorted in his thick brogue, handing the Confederate his sword back.

Wigfall leapt boldly into the opening, somehow believing that the gunners half a mile away would glimpse his handkerchief through the smoke and recognize it as a flag of truce. Presently a shot from Moultrie slammed into the nearby wall, disabusing him swiftly of this notion.

"If you desire that to be seen," Anderson said gently, "you had better send it to the parapet."

Several minutes later, Charlestonians on their distant rooftops spotted something waving on a pole above Sumter's bomb-scarred ramparts, alongside the Stars and Stripes. This was not Senator Wigfall's handkerchief but a full-size white flag. It signaled a cease-fire while Major Anderson negotiated—"or rather dictated," as Thompson later said—his terms of surrender.[108]

"Nothing of military importance has reached me today," scribbled Winfield Scott in a note to the president that evening, more or less precisely as Fort Sumter was falling into Confederate hands. "Except," the general added, "thro' the newspaper."[109]

If General Scott had been known for his drolleries, this might have come off as a rather clever one. (He was not, so it didn't.) For in fact, the headlines of every single paper throughout the Union blazed with the most astonishing military news since Cornwallis's surrender at Yorktown. Editors dug deep in their bins of lead type for the largest fonts available, nor did they stint on exclamation points. The *Milwaukee Sentinel*'s front page was typical: *"Hostilities Commenced!* FORT SUMTER BOMBARDED! *The Rebels Strike the First Blow!* MOULTRIE OPENS ON MAJ. ANDERSON! SEVEN OF THEIR BATTERIES FOLLOW! *Prompt Response from Sumter!"* (And so on, through nine more lines of boldface and italic type and another five exclamation points.)[110]

It had taken almost an entire day for most Americans to learn about the first shots at Sumter, since telegraphic communication between North and South had been erratic since secession. On the night of Friday the 12th, Walt Whitman went to the opera in New York. The Fourteenth Street Academy of Music was presenting Verdi's latest, *Un ballo in maschera*, which had been censored in Europe for its undertones of liberal nationalism but was now touring the United States to great acclaim. After the show, the poet was strolling back toward Brooklyn when he heard the shrill cries of newsboys ahead—a rare sound indeed at midnight. The lads came tearing down Broadway, "rushing from side to side even more furiously than usual," singing out "Extry! Got the bombardment of *Fort Sumter*!!!" Soon every gaslight on the street had its own little huddle of New Yorkers poring over dispatches from Charleston.[111]

The news, Whitman would later remember, "ran through the Land, as if by electric nerves." Many people didn't believe it at first: surely, they said, this was rebel propaganda. Perhaps someone had tampered with the telegraph lines. Contradictory reports began coming in: Major Anderson had shelled downtown Charleston, incinerating the city and sending thousands of civilians fleeing for their lives. No, he had gone over to the Confederate side, was blowing up his fort piece by piece, and planned to escape by sea in a small boat. Captain Doubleday, resisting surrender, had been clapped in irons by Anderson and then promptly went insane. And perhaps most prevalent: Sumter had been reinforced by Fox's fleet. (Saturday night's performance at the Academy of Music was interrupted during Act 4, when the house manager stepped onstage to announce this last piece of splendid news, inspiring the soprano to launch immediately into "The Star-Spangled Banner.")

In any event, wrote the skeptical George Templeton Strong, no man of sense could believe that the rebels "have been so foolish and thoughtless as to take the initiative in civil war."[112]

But when later reports confirmed the initial headlines, disbelief gave way to shock. Throughout the country—even in the heart of busy Manhattan, even on Wall Street—business came to a halt as men and women left their shops and offices to crowd into barrooms, hotel lobbies, and public squares, anywhere that they might hear the very latest facts and rumors. Crowds formed around newsstands, too, pushing and shoving to press pennies upon the beleaguered vendors. From Fort Kearny in the Nebraska Territory—the westernmost point of the telegraph lines—a Pony Express rider galloped off toward California with the news. In Washington, when a man in the lobby of Willard's ventured to express his sympathy with the rebels, police had to come break up the ensuing fracas.[113]

Perhaps the calmest place in the country was, oddly enough, just down Pennsylvania Avenue from Willard's.

"There was little variation in the business of the Executive Mansion on that eventful Saturday," Hay and Nicolay would remember. The president signed official papers, read his mail, and met patiently with the usual parade of dubiously qualified patronage seekers, who insisted on a hearing even at this moment of historic crisis. When a delegation of congressmen came bustling into Lincoln's office, pressing him for his reaction to the momentous news, he replied dryly, "I do not like it," and changed the subject. The only visitors who left the White House with something more substantial were three Virginians, members of the statewide convention considering secession. He reassured them that he would hold fast to the policy of nonaggression promised in his inaugural address. But, he now added almost matter-of-factly, "in every event, I shall, to the extent of my ability, repel force by force." This was, as the Virginians would soon learn, an all-important clarification.[114]

Although there is no record of exactly when or how Lincoln got the news of Sumter's surrender, initial reports probably reached him Saturday evening, not many hours after the event itself. Incredibly, the White House and War Department had no official intelligence or communications system of any kind, but at least two citizens in the South—one of them a prominent Charleston secessionist, the other an obscure Savannah accountant—were considerate enough to send Lincoln telegrams that night.[115]

Just six months earlier, very few Americans had ever even heard of Fort Sumter. But now the loss of this two-acre island—the lowering of one flag and the raising of another over a useless piece of federal real estate—was suddenly a national calamity. For many, it was also a summons to vengeance. In Philadelphia, one block from Independence Hall, a mob of young men wrecked the offices of a small pro-Southern newspaper imprudently named *The Palmetto Flag*, then marched up Market Street waving American flags and brandishing nooses, on the hunt for other secessionists. In a bucolic little Indiana village, schoolchildren hanged Jeff Davis in effigy.[116]

For others, though, that eventful weekend inspired more complicated thoughts and feelings.

Saturday afternoon found James Garfield sitting alone in the nearly deserted chamber of the Ohio senate. The legislators had adjourned early; rain beat monotonously against the windows; and only a small knot of men remained on the other side of the room, discussing the news and poring over a large map of Charleston Harbor. The militia bill that Garfield had championed vainly all winter had swept to passage immediately at the first word of the attack. But he took no pleasure in this belated victory. Struggling privately with a tangle of emotions—anxiety, excitement, melancholy, anger, mental exhaustion—Garfield began a letter to his old friend Harry Rhodes.

He felt almost as if he could see the battle at Sumter happening before his own eyes, he said. It enraged him to think of how his government had left Major Anderson on the island "with his hands tied" for three months while the rebels armed for the attack—so that now "he will almost certainly surrender to the traitors or perish." Here he set the letter down, unable to continue. By the time he picked it up again the next morning, word had come that Anderson had, indeed, struck his colors. Yet Garfield's spirits had lifted. He and Jacob Cox, his room-mate and fellow senator, had just been to see the governor—who, flat-teringly, had wished to confer with the two young men about Ohio's response to the crisis. With Sumter still burning, ruined, on its far-off island, Garfield felt a sudden rush of clarity about the future, which Rhodes doubtless recognized:

> The war has now fully begun. I am glad we are defeated at Sumter. It will rouse the people. I can see no possible end to the war, till the South is subjugated. I hope we will never stop short of complete subjugation. Better to lose a million men in battle than allow the government to be overthrown. The war will soon assume the shape of Slavery & Freedom—the world will so understand it—& I believe the final outcome will redound to the good of humanity.

He and Cox, he added, had been talking not just about "the prospects of the country [but] the future of our own lives." They had decided, Garfield reported, to leave politics behind. They would go into the army.[117]

In Boston, too, many were thinking about Slavery & Freedom. On Sunday afternoon, twelve-year-old Franky Garrison sprinted home from the Common, where he had just heard about Anderson's surren-der, to tell his father the news. A few days later, when he helped proof-read the galleys of that week's *Liberator*, the boy must have realized what a sea change was occurring. "The North United at Last," one headline ran. For thirty years, the elder Garrison had fought not just to defeat Southern slaveholders but also to win over the divided heart of his own region. He had hung the star-spangled banner upside down, as an emblem of the despicable Constitution. But now Franky and his father watched with pride as a huge American flag was raised right in front of the *Liberator* office, on a staff 140 feet tall. The more that slave drivers trampled on that banner, Garrison confessed, the handsomer it seemed. His comrade Wendell Phillips went even further. A week after Anderson's surrender, he stood amid red, white, and blue bunting before a cheering crowd of Boston abolitionists. "For the first time in my anti-slavery life," he told them, "I speak beneath the stars and stripes. . . . To-day the slave asks God for a sight of this banner, and counts it the pledge of his redemption."[118]

Indeed, the response to Sumter seemed to manifest itself, among Northerners of every political and cultural hue, as a kind of flag mania. Along the thoroughfares of major cities, each shop and office "successively ran up its colors like a fleet of ships on the eve of the action." On village greens and town squares—places where it had never previously occurred to anyone that the national emblem belonged—citizens gathered for solemn ceremonies around hastily erected poles. (And from that day to this, there would scarcely be a single American hamlet, no matter how tiny, that did *not* display the Stars and Stripes in its most conspicuous available spot.) Artists and intellectuals were swept up in the moment as well. The painter Frederic Church, previously known for producing landscapes of exquisite delicacy, now daubed a canvas with a garish piece of patriotic kitsch: a sunrise scene in which the clouds formed red and white stripes, with a square patch of stars twinkling against blue sky in the upper left. (This was quickly transformed into a best-selling lithograph.)[119]

For a century and a half, historians have struggled to explain exactly why the attack at Charleston struck such a transformative chord. Even Bruce Catton, one of the Civil War's greatest twentieth-century chroniclers, was left scratching his head: "In the strangely revealing light of the exploding shell," he wrote, Americans "saw something that was to carry them through four years of war. It is hard to say just what it was, for no one bothered to be explicit about it and time has dimmed it anyway." George Bancroft, America's most revered historian in the 1860s, did try to be explicit, and came up with a tortured explanation involving navigation rights on the Chesapeake and Mississippi. But in any case, he remembered of that April, "I witnessed the sublimest spectacle I ever saw."[120]

Perhaps there was an explanatory power in the flags themselves. Two weeks after Sumter's surrender, Henry Ward Beecher gave a sermon at his Brooklyn church to bless the colors that two local volunteer companies were carrying with them to war. With characteristic theatricality, the great preacher eulogized the flag in Christlike terms:

> It was upon these streaming bars and upon these bright stars that every one of that immense concentric range of guns was aimed, when Sumter was lifted up in the midst, almost like another witnessing Calvary. . . . And do you know that when it was fallen, in

the streets of a Southern city, it was trailed, hooted at, pierced with swords? Men that have sat in the Senate of the United States ran out to trample upon it; it was fired on and slashed by the mob; it was dragged through the mud; it was hissed at and spit upon; and so it was carried through Southern cities! That our flag . . . should, in our own nation, and by our own people, be spit upon, and trampled under foot, is more than the heart of man can bear! . . . It is not a painted rag. It is a whole national history. It is the Constitution. It is the government. It is the free people that stand in the government on the Constitution.[121]

Whitman expressed the same idea in plainer language—although the simple words masked deeper complexities—when he wrote: "The negro was not the chief thing: the chief thing was to stick together."

The attack on Sumter forced Americans everywhere to pick sides: to stand either with the flag or against it—and overwhelmingly, perhaps for a multitude of individual reasons, Northerners chose to stand with it. And that expression of national unity, in turn, became the strongest possible argument for the Union itself: for the idea that the flag could shelter beneath its folds Americans of many opinions and temperaments, and that disagreement need not mean disunion. The pure wordless symbolism of a piece of cloth could represent both the deepest traditions of American radicalism and those of American conservatism. For people like Garrison and Phillips, it had become a pledge to stand firm against the slave power and uphold what they saw as the purest distillation of America's commitment to liberty, as embodied in the Declaration. To more orthodox minds, it was a summons to defend the nation and the Constitution.

Even Emerson, the great apostle of individualism, found himself beholding with astonished admiration the "whirlwind of patriotism, not believed to exist, but now magnetizing all discordant masses under its terrific unity." He was then in the midst of a lecture series in Boston on the relationship between "Life" and "Literature." Amid his abstract ruminations, he had taken note of the national crisis; a few days before Sumter he had spoken of "the facility with which a great political fabric can be broken." But the following week, he threw aside his prepared text and spoke instead from a sheaf of hastily scribbled notes. The sage went so far as to admit he had been wrong:

It is an affair of instincts; we did not know we had them; we valued ourselves as cool calculators; we were very fine with our learning and culture, with our science that was of no country, and our religion of peace;—and now a sentiment mightier than logic, wide as light, strong as gravity, reaches into the college, the bank, the farm-house, and the church. It is the day of the populace; they are wiser than their teachers. . . . The interlocutions from quiet-looking citizens are of an energy of which I had no knowledge. How long men can keep a secret! I will never again speak lightly of a crowd. We are wafted into a revolution which, though at first sight a calamity of the human race, finds all men in good heart, in courage, in a generosity of mutual and patriotic support. We have been very homeless, some of us, for some years past,—say since 1850; but now we have a country again. . . . This affronting of the common sense of mankind, this defiance and cursing of friends as well as foes, has hurled us, willing or unwilling, into opposition; and the nation which the Secessionists hoped to shatter has to thank them for a more sudden and hearty union than the history of parties ever showed.[122]

Ironically, the Confederates' attack on, and swift victory at, Fort Sumter turned out to be their worst strategic blunder of the war, a blunder, indeed, that may have cost the South its independence. It is difficult to see what the rebels would have lost if they had allowed Major Anderson and his tiny force to be provisioned and remain indefinitely. Indeed, they could have couched their forbearance as a humanitarian gesture, a token of their peaceful intentions, that might have won them allies not just in the North but also—all-importantly—among the nations of Europe. Certainly leaving Sumter alone would have bought them more time: time to more fully organize and equip the South's armies; time to establish all the ordinary apparatus—a postal service, a stable national currency, a judicial system—that serve to make government a stable fact rather than a speculative figment. Both to its own citizens and to the rest of the world, the Confederate States of America might have come to seem like a fait accompli.[123] Instead, Davis, his cabinet, and his generals had only a perfunctory discussion before deciding to shell the fort.

As Lincoln told a confidant: "They attacked Sumter—it fell, and thus, did more service than it otherwise could."

To be sure, some Americans in the North continued decrying what they saw as a misbegotten war against slavery. "A servile insurrection and the wholesale slaughter of the whites will alone satisfy the murderous designs of the Abolitionists," wrote the editor of one New York paper in mid-April. "The Administration, egged on by the halloo of the Black Republican journals of this city, has sent on its mercenary forces to pick a quarrel and initiate the work of devastation and ruin."[124]

A few still held out hope for a bloodless reunion. One pro-Union meeting in New York began with extravagant toasts, not to Anderson or Lincoln but to John J. Crittenden. When the venerable senator had announced his retirement when Congress adjourned in March, he made clear to his friends that he wished never to see Washington again. He then hurried home, exhausted and demoralized, to his Kentucky farm. Just after the fall of Sumter, however, with his state teetering on the brink of secession, the old politician took to the stump once more, begging his fellow Kentuckians to steer a neutral course: remain loyal to their country but take up arms against neither North nor South. The state did not secede. In the coming months, however, Crittenden would see three of his own sons march off to war: two to fight for the Union, one for the Confederacy.[125]

A few abolitionists, too, could not bring themselves to join in the war fever. The farthest that Lydia Maria Child could go was to hope that someday the Stars and Stripes might be worthy of the adoration it was receiving. "Meanwhile," she wrote to a friend, "I wait to see how the United States will deport itself. When it treats the colored people with justice and humanity, I will mount its flag in my great elm-tree, and I will thank you to present me with a flag for a breast-pin; but until then, I would as soon wear the rattlesnake upon my bosom as the eagle."[126]

Child was not the only one to speculate on what war might mean for the slaves. On the morning he heard about Sumter's fall, William Russell, the *London Times'* urbane correspondent, was already in Baltimore on his way to catch a steamer bound for Charleston. Stopping for a quick shave, he asked the black barber what he made of the news. "Well, sare," the man replied, "'spose colored men will be as good as white men." [127]

Russell later offered this tidbit to his readers in a tone of mildly sympathetic amusement. The poor deluded Negro!

SHORTLY AFTER ANDERSON'S SURRENDER to the intrepid Wigfall, General Beauregard's authorized aides arrived at the fort. In the end, they decided to honor the agreement that the major and the ex-senator had reached. Only Doubleday seemed irked that the battle was over: he continued to believe that it might have ended differently if his commander had worried less about avoiding bloodshed and more about defeating the enemy, maybe by trying to shell Charleston itself. Anderson, for his part, was quick to assure the Confederate envoys that he had always aimed his cannons at fortifications rather than at men, and when told that none of the secessionists had been wounded by Sumter's fire, he lifted up his hands and exclaimed, "Thank God for that!" (Doubleday listened, fuming: "As the object of our fighting was to do as much damage as possible, I could see no propriety in thanking Heaven for the small amount of injury we had inflicted.")[128]

The only term of surrender at which the Confederates initially balked was Anderson's request to salute his flag a final time before lowering it. But in the end they allowed him to do so.

On Sunday afternoon—a day of splendid sunshine—the tattered national ensign rose again on its repaired flagpole and unfurled into a strong breeze. Anderson was determined to honor it with no fewer than a hundred cannon blasts. This was not to be. His salute, like the Union, was cloven in half. With the fiftieth shot came disaster and a terrible omen: a gun crew, exhausted by the recent ordeal, reloaded its weapon too hastily, neglecting to cool the muzzle with a thorough sponging before ramming in the powder. In the ensuing explosion, one soldier—a young Irish immigrant named Daniel Hough, well liked among the men of the garrison—was killed almost instantly, his body torn apart. Several others were badly wounded.

But there was no time to mourn the dead or care for the injured. Daniel Hough's remains were left behind to be buried by the enemy, as so many other men's would be in the years ahead. Still in shock, his comrades formed ranks behind Captain Doubleday and marched through Sumter's main gate toward a waiting transport. Behind them they could hear wild cheering as the Stars and Stripes came down and a Confederate banner went up.

Early the next day—Monday, April 15—the U.S. steamer *Baltic*, with Major Anderson and all his men aboard, cleared the bar of Charleston Harbor and set out into open water.[129]

CHAPTER FIVE

The Volunteer

Senior wisdom suits not now,
The light is on the youthful brow.

—HERMAN MELVILLE,
"The Conflict of Convictions" (1860–61)

Rally at Union Square, New York, April 20, 1861

Lower Manhattan, April 1861

IT WAS A DAY UNLIKE ANY the city had known before. Half a million people, or so the newspapers would report, crowded the streets between Battery Park and Fourteenth Street. If you were there among them that day, the thing that you would never forget—not even if you lived to see the next century—was the flags. The Stars and Stripes flew above the doors of department stores and town houses, from Bowery taverns and from the spire of Trinity Church, while Broadway, the *New York Herald* reported, "was almost hidden in a cloud of flaggery." P. T. Barnum, not to be outdone, especially when he sensed an opportunity for attention, had strung an entire panoply of oversize banners across the thoroughfare. The national ensign even fluttered, in miniature, on the heads of the horses straining to pull overloaded omnibuses through the throngs on Fifth Avenue. The one flag that everyone wanted to see—*needed* to see—was in Union Square itself, the unattainable point toward which all the shoving and sweating and jostling bodies strove. No fewer than five separate speakers' platforms had been hastily erected there, and every so often, above the ceaseless din, you could catch a phrase or two: *"that handful of loyal men . . . their gallant commander . . . the honor of their country . . ."*

If you managed somehow to clamber up onto the base of a beleaguered lamppost and emerge for a moment above the hats and bonnets of the multitude, you might glimpse what was propped up on the monument in the center of the square: cradled in General Washington's bronze arms, a torn and soot-stained flag on a splintered staff. (One hundred forty years later, in an eerie echo of that long-forgotten day, a later generation would gather around the same statue with candles and flowers in the aftermath of another attack on the nation.) Nearby, waving a bit stiffly to acknowledge the cheers, was a lean, gray-haired officer.[1] But then you lost your tenuous foothold, the gray-haired officer and his flag vanished from sight, and you were down off the lamppost again, buffeted this way and that by the odorous masses of New Yorkers, ripened by exertion and by the sunny spring day: Wall Street bankers in black broadcloth; pale, flushed shopgirls; grimy men from the Fulton docks, more pungent than anyone else, smelling of fish.

It was hard to imagine anybody swaggering through such a crowd, but here came someone doing just that—and not just one man but three abreast, nonchalant young toughs all dressed in identical, baggy red shirts. One had a fat plug of tobacco in his cheek and looked ready to spit where he pleased; another fellow none too surreptitiously pinched the prettiest of the shopgirls as he passed. Somehow, by common consent, the pressing throngs parted to let them through. They all knew exactly who these superior beings were: the fire b'hoys. And as of today, no longer simply that, either—for these b'hoys had signed their enlistment papers yesterday, and were very shortly to be sworn in as soldiers of the First New York Fire Zouaves.

On the way home after the great Union rally, you might have seen many more of them, over a thousand red-shirted recruits, crowding a park just off Fourteenth Street, arrayed in rough military formation. Uncharacteristically quiet, even subdued, they raised their brawny right arms as their colonel, the man they had just unanimously elected to lead them into war—for such was the custom still, in those early months of 1861—administered the oath.

The young colonel—he seemed, from a distance, barely more than a boy—was, unlike all his thousand-odd comrades, not a New York City fireman. He was not even a New Yorker, unless one counted his childhood far upstate. He was different in almost every way from the strapping men of his regiment, with their loose limbs and salty tongues: a small man, neat and self-contained, who never drank, or smoked, or swore. He thrilled to poetry as much as to the tattoo of drums; he had dined at the White House more often than in taverns or mess halls; and he had come not from the teeming wards of Brooklyn but from the West.

He was also one of those occasional American figures whose death, even more than his life, seemed to mark the passing away of one era and the beginning of another. He would be, briefly, the war's most famous man. And for that moment, the entire conflict, the irreconcilable forces that set state against state and brother against brother, would seem distilled into—as one who knew him well would write—"the dark mystery of how Ellsworth died."[2]

LIKE SO MANY AMERICANS of his generation, Elmer Ellsworth seemed to emerge out of nowhere. This wasn't quite true, but almost. In later years, some would swear they had roomed with him in a cheap boardinghouse in Washington, long before he was famous; or been his classmate at a high school in Kenosha before he suddenly dropped out and disappeared; or known him living up among the Ottawa Indians near Muskegon, where the tribe had adopted him as its chief. But no one was ever quite sure.[3]

Odd remnants of his diaries would eventually turn up. And his parents, at least, who would long outlive him, eventually shared everything they could recall of his boyhood. He had left home early, though. There were few enough opportunities for him there.

Ellsworth was born in the year of the country's first great financial depression, 1837, in the small village of Malta in Saratoga County, New York. His ancestors had settled nearby before the Revolution, but the family was poor. Ephraim Ellsworth, the boy's father, had struggled as a tailor until the Panic ruined him, forcing him to eke out a living doing odd jobs, netting wild passenger pigeons to sell for their meat, and peddling kegs of pickled oysters door-to-door on commission. His son, serious-minded and small for his age, was sent off at the age of nine to work for a man who owned a general store and saloon. Scrupulously, the boy refused to handle liquor or even—as his master expected—to rinse out the customers' whiskey glasses.[4] In a world where drunkenness was common (among children, too), he had already resolved to be different.

His early life, Ellsworth would write as an adult, seemed to him nothing but "a jumble of strange incidents." He was a child who seemed to live half in the gritty reality of his physical surroundings, half in a dream world of his own creation. Sometimes he cadged paint from a wagon shop in the village and daubed scenes onto a scrap of board or an old window shade. One of these has survived; it shows a forest-fringed river that might have been the nearby Hudson but for the turrets and spires of Arthurian castles rising along its banks. In summer, he wandered among the "green old hills" above the actual river, and in winter, he skated on the Champlain Canal, perhaps developing there the ease of movement that would later mature into a kind of balletic grace.[5] His schooling must have been intermittent, and when he did attend, he was often teased; the other children nicknamed him "Oyster Keg," on account of both his size and his father's ignominious occupation. The boy learned to defend his honor with his fists.

Occasionally, though, the larger world offered glimpses of a reality nearly as glamorous as his painted fantasies. Malta lay astride the road to Saratoga Springs, a watering place popular with the officers and cadets of West Point, and in summer, the sprucely uniformed soldiers (with fine young women at their sides) must have passed through the village in hired carriages on their way to the nearby resort. For the watchful boy, the sight must have seemed a visitation from an imagined country. Many years later, Ellsworth's aunt would recall him making forts out of loose bricks and shaping mud into breastworks; wooden blocks represented American soldiers and enemy redcoats.

His grandfather, George Ellsworth, had been a teenage militiaman in the Revolution, and although George's pension application from the 1830s reveals that he was illiterate—he signed the document with a quavering *X*—it also shows that in old age he could still recount vivid tales of battling Tories and Indians along the Hudson Valley.[6] Elmer's grandfather died when the boy was not yet three, but the old veteran's widow survived him by many years, and probably shared the stories she knew. The rocky slopes and tidy Dutch towns above the Hudson seemed themselves to tell tales of the many famous deeds they had witnessed. A boy with Ellsworth's active imagination, looking out over the placid landscape of fields and pastures, must sometimes have felt as if the cannons were still booming and the tomahawks still flying in the forests, somewhere over the next line of hills.

When the boy was about eleven, his family moved to Mechanicville, a larger town with its own railroad station. Peddling the New York papers through the aisles of the crowded passenger cars, he must have scanned reports of the Mexican War and its aftermath, and of the liberal, nationalist revolutions in Europe, some of them sparked by student agitators not much older than he.[7]

Perhaps because of these colorful stories in the penny papers, or perhaps from his boyhood sightings of West Point cadets, Ellsworth's dreams had early on taken a military cast. He organized the local boys into a militia company and somewhat grandiosely dubbed it the Black-Plumed Riflemen of Stillwater, the name stolen from a pulp novel he'd read about the Revolutionary War.[8]

Soon he was absent from home with increasing frequency, until finally, latching onto a prosperous-looking elderly gentleman who'd taken an interest in him one day on the train, he followed the stranger off to New York City to work in his linen shop. This is where the biographical record suddenly stops.

But we do know that he turned up eventually—as perhaps he was bound to—in Chicago. That town was in its restless adolescence in the 1850s, a half-wild place where patches of prairie still showed like blank canvas among the two- and three-story office buildings, and the occasional wolf still strayed in from the forested shores along Lake Michigan, to prowl the muddy streets and plank sidewalks.[9]

Restless, too, were the young men who roamed lean and hungry along those avenues of flimsy buildings. From villages in Ohio and western Pennsylvania, from New York and the stony farms of New England, from Germany and Ireland and Sweden, they crowded into the rising metropolis of the great West. Some found work in the sawmills that ran incessantly, gnawing virgin timber into clapboard and railroad ties; others amid the stench of the stockyards. Sometimes the tideless river ran viscous with the blood of slaughtered beasts.[10]

A year or two before the outbreak of the war, Elmer Ellsworth was one of these thousands of young men, clerking and copying papers in a law office for meager pay, living on dry biscuits and water, sleeping on the bare wooden floor. It was a life so spartan that when he could get a pound or two of salted crackers to vary his diet, the occasion was worthy of note in his diary: "Am living like a King."[11] It was a statement of characteristic, wildly unrealistic, optimism. Through all the years of roving, wherever they had taken him, he had never lost his boyhood dreams of glory. In his free time, Ellsworth pored over volumes on military tactics and drill formations until he knew some of them by heart.[12] Not long after his arrival in Chicago, he also joined a local militia, the Cadets of the National Guard, one of many such groups that drew in young men far from home and family, worn thin from hard work and striving, looking for anything solid to which they could fasten themselves.[13]

Today, in an era of full-time, highly professionalized national armed forces, it is hard to appreciate the vastly different culture of the nineteenth century, when for most Americans, volunteering for military service was more like joining a weekend bowling league than enlisting in the army as we know it. The colonial militia companies, which had provided the rank and file during the Revolution, had faded away in the succeeding decades, especially after the War of 1812 had proven them no match for the British army's hardened veterans of the Napoleonic campaigns. But the Founding Fathers' old vision of a United States without standing armies, in which citizen-soldiers were the first line of defense, still beckoned. In both cities and towns, men formed military companies that stood ready—at least in theory—to answer their country's call in case of emergency. In practice, most of these units were scarcely trained and haphazardly equipped; some marched with sticks or cornstalks instead of muskets. Members paraded on the village green every Fourth of July, unfurling tattered banners that had been stitched by local maidens who were now wrinkled grandmothers. The last serious mobilization had been the one back in 1812. Each month or two throughout the year, the boys gathered for "drills" that were often simply excuses to get away from home and do some hard drinking.[14] Larger towns and cities had rival companies: one militia for the Democrats and another for the Whigs; one for the Methodists and another for the Presbyterians; one for the Irishmen and another for the Germans. New York City even had several all-Jewish units.[15]

In the 1850s, however, Americans started becoming a bit more serious about their militias, marching in drills and parades with fresh ardor, and even making sporadic attempts at professionalism. The Mexican War, the nation's most dramatic military victory since the Revolution, had just been fought and won. From Europe came reports of the glorious charges and sieges of the Crimean War, and of the nationalist struggles for independence. And closer to home, some Americans were sensing the approach of civil war and beginning to sharpen their swords—in both the North and the South.

Elmer Ellsworth does not appear to have been one of these. None of his surviving writings suggests much thought about slavery and abolitionism, about the bloody struggles in Kansas or the wild-eyed prophecies of John Brown. He seems, rather, to have approached military drills with the enthusiasm and relentless discipline of an athlete pushing himself toward the big leagues.

And, like a basketball genius from the mean streets of the Bronx, or a home-run hitter sprouting amid the cornfields of Iowa, the oyster peddler's son from upstate New York turned out to be a natural. Quite soon—by the time he was nineteen, if not earlier—the Cadets had elected him their major. What was more, he quickly found himself in demand to serve as drillmaster for regiments throughout Chicago's environs. A photograph probably dating to around this time shows him in the resplendent but queerly antiquated garb of a militia officer, a remnant of the previous century: plumed cocked hat, tight breeches, and swallowtail coat with white facings.[16]

It is easy to picture this confident young man putting the even younger privates through their paces, lifting his sword to bark the commands: *Attention! Squad forward! Double quick—march!*[17] More difficult is imagining the splendid major returning each night to his hard lodgings and meager supper. Ellsworth hid his poverty from all but his closest friends; he would later tell of sitting in a restaurant with acquaintances and watching them feast on oyster stew, as he pretended that he had just dined so he could avoid buying a meal.[18] Such reticence fed the aura of mystery around him. His Hudson Valley origins and military prowess fueled whispers that he had attended West Point and been expelled for some mysterious infraction, rumors that Ellsworth may or may not have disclaimed.[19]

Sometime in the late 1850s, however, Ellsworth had an encounter that rivaled any romantic tale he might have dreamt up. It happened, improbably enough, in a Chicago gymnasium. There he met one Charles DeVilliers, a French fencing instructor recently arrived in the city. Back in Europe, DeVilliers had served as an officer in the Zouaves, an elite fighting force named for a band of Algerian tribesmen renowned for their ferocity in battle. The French Zouaves copied the North Africans' uniform—fez, baggy pants, and a loose jacket, "suited to rapid movement and fierce daring"—and developed a reputation both for their dashing appearance and for their fearsome use of the bayonet.[20] Newspapers and illustrated magazines worldwide, America included, covered the Zouaves' exploits in the Crimea (where DeVilliers had served) and in Italy's war of unification.[21] How a French Zouave ended up in Chicago is still a mystery, except that all sorts of people ended up in Chicago in those days. In any event, it is no surprise that the young militiaman gravitated toward the older officer and insisted on learning the Zouaves' distinctive tactics. Somehow, over the course of just months—in a miraculous transformation that Hollywood, had it existed yet, might have invented—the threadbare clerk became an expert fencer, gymnast, and drill instructor.

Before long, he was teaching those skills to others. The cadets' regiment was a militia unit "of the old school," one member recalled many years later, composed of young men who drilled in old-fashioned uniforms and bearskin hats, "ponderous, slow, and heavy."[22] It was also on the verge of bankruptcy; membership had been dwindling, perhaps due to competition from newer and more glamorous organizations. Ellsworth saw an opportunity. When he showed the militiamen the Zouave moves he had learned from DeVilliers, they were fascinated. Within a month or two, he was drilling them six nights a week, for hours at a time, and the unit had renamed itself the U.S. Zouave Cadets.[23]

The cadets' devotion to their new commandant was all the more remarkable in light of the strictures he imposed. The new company, he told them, was to be not merely a military organization but "a source of improvement morally as well as physically."[24] No member was allowed to enter any drinking saloon, gambling hall, or "house of ill-fame," on pain of immediate expulsion. Even playing billiards was off-limits, on the grounds that it might "naturally lead to drinking." The preamble to these rules explained that while many militia groups existed "with no higher object than the mere pursuit of pleasure," this one would be different.[25] And remarkably, the more rigid Ellsworth's strictures became, the more the men seemed to thrive under them. "The clerk from behind the counter, the law student from the books, the young man of leisure from his loiterings around town—all have lived under strict military discipline, self-imposed," wrote one impressed visitor to the regimental armory.[26]

And so it was that on July Fourth of the following year, Chicagoans lined the shore of Lake Michigan to observe a wholly unanticipated spectacle. Some forty cadets in the traditional blue-and-buff uniforms of the eighteenth-century militias—Algerian Zouave–style attire had been ordered but didn't arrive in time—gave a performance that was more like a gymnastics event (or a nineteenth-century version of Cirque du Soleil) than any military drill the onlookers had ever seen. Instead of forming neat lines, shouldering their guns, and marching straight ahead, these militiamen leapt and rolled and yelled, loaded muskets while lying on their backs, jumped up to fire them and then fell again, thrust and twirled their bayonets like drum majors' batons—all with a beautiful and precise synchrony. "The cadets are not large in stature, but athletes in agility and strength, moving at the word of command with the quickness and precision of steam men," one newspaper editor marveled.[27]

On the day before the Zouaves' first performance, on the far side of the Appalachians—and unknown but to a few others—John Brown arrived, incognito, at Harper's Ferry. His deeds in the months to come would electrify the country and the world. But so, too, would the sensation born that Independence Day beside Lake Michigan and soon to be sweeping beyond Chicago, across the Midwestern prairies and then past them, throughout an unquiet land.

AMERICA HAD ALWAYS HARBORED a deep ambivalence about war, going back at least as far as the Revolution. General Washington had won the nation's freedom on the battlefield, inspiring his men to many deeds of valor that would ring down through the ages, but after the final victory, when he resigned his commission and Congress disbanded the national army entirely, most citizens cheered. They associated standing armies with European monarchies, with troops of mercenaries and conscripts—"hirelings and slaves," as Francis Scott Key called British redcoats in his famous anthem—maintained in support of tyranny. What could be less democratic, after all, than the use of force to sustain power and impose policy? In 1847, as American troops fought a war of aggression and conquest in Mexico, one young Midwestern congressman had warned against "the exceeding brightness of military glory, that attractive rainbow that rises in showers of blood—that serpent's eye, that charms to destroy."[28]

Yet just a few months later, the same politician who had spoken those words took to the stump for Zachary Taylor—a leading general in the Mexican War whose only qualification for high office was "military glory," since he had never held a civilian post of any kind. (Pro-Taylor campaign lithographs showed him gallantly leading the charge at Buena Vista; an anti-Taylor cartoon showed him perched atop a gigantic heap of skulls, clutching a bloody sword in his hand.) As for the Midwestern congressman himself, he would go on to be America's greatest war president. That young legislator was, of course, Abraham Lincoln.[29]

Lincoln's metaphor of the "rainbow that rises in showers of blood" perfectly captured his countrymen's mixed feelings. Between the 1840s and the outbreak of the Civil War, however, more and more Americans, in the North as well as the South, were increasingly drawn to the gleam of that rainbow. The change was especially noticeable among antislavery advocates and other reformers. Theodore Parker, the famed Boston abolitionist, had once condemned war unequivocally as "an utter violation of Christianity." But by the late 1850s, referring to the Garibaldian struggle in Italy, but also thinking of the growing conflict closer to home, he reflected: "All the great charters of humanity have been *writ in blood*, and must continue to be for some countries. I should let the Italians fight for their liberty till the twenty-eight millions were only fourteen million."

In 1838, a dovish Emerson wrote in his journal: "a company of soldiers is an offensive spectacle." By 1859, in the aftermath of the Harper's Ferry raid, he was publicly calling John Brown "that new saint, than whom none purer or more brave was ever led by love of men into conflict and death." By 1863, Emerson had accepted an appointment to the West Point military academy's Board of Visitors.[30]

The 1850s saw an increasing spirit of militancy enter American politics and culture. The Wide Awakes who marched by the thousands for Lincoln in 1860 were simply the culmination of a trend, the logical outcome of the new republican ideology that prized manliness and unyielding idealism. It was a short step from such militancy to outright militarism. In retrospect, its seeds were clearly present even in the early work of avowed pacifists like Emerson: at the same time that he called for the outright abolition of war, he hailed Napoleon Bonaparte, the century's most famous general, as the hero of "young, ardent, and active men, everywhere," who had nobly transformed "old, iron-bound feudal France" into "a young Ohio or New York." The sage failed to mention, of course, that in the laudable process of turning France into Ohio, the late emperor had also brought about hundreds of thousands of deaths.[31]

Indeed, despite the new republic's professed aversion to war, military feeling often seemed more intense in the United States than it did among the European nations where Napoleon and Wellington had fought. Americans could lionize their military heroes as citizen volunteers, men who had freely chosen to lay down their lives for the nation. What higher expression of democratic values was there than willingly dying for the sake of one's country and countrymen? It was the ultimate pledge of allegiance, an extreme subjection of individual interests to the greater good of the majority. Americans celebrated the volunteer military tradition for the same reason that they shunned their own nation's peacetime standing army, a force whose ranks were filled by hirelings, if not quite by slaves. An Englishwoman, visiting Detroit in 1854 during the Michigan State Fair, was surprised at the martial tone of the festivities:

> Military bands playing "The Star-Spangled Banner" and "Hail, Columbia," were constantly passing and re-passing, and the whole population seemed on the *qui vive*. Squadrons of cavalry continually passed my window, the men in gorgeous uniforms, with high waving plumes. . . . Two regiments of foot followed the cavalry. . . . The privates had a more independent air than our own regulars, and were principally the sons of respectable citizens. They appeared to have been well drilled, and were superior in appearance to our militia.[32]

As foreign visitors also noted, many Americans of all social classes often seemed simply to enjoy a good brawl. The rough-hewn Westerner bristling with six-shooters and bowie knives and the aristocratic Southerner with his brace of dueling pistols became stock characters in European depictions of the young republic. Yankees—though perhaps not quite so bellicose—were not entirely excluded from this culture of violence. The most spectacular gang combat of the antebellum years took place in Northern cities, such as the storied street battle between New York's Roach Guards and Dead Rabbits, fought on Independence Day in 1857, which left eight men dead. Such fights often broke out between Democrats and Whigs, or Know Nothings and immigrants: decades before the Civil War began, some Americans were accustomed to battling other Americans over political differences. And Yankees filled the ranks of the nation's peacetime officer corps. Of the active duty officers in 1860, almost 60 percent came from the free states; the only branch the Southerners dominated was the cavalry.[33]

Both before and after the war, Southerners loved to glamorize themselves at the North's expense: their own region was redolent of magnolias, romantic chivalry, and Sir Walter Scott, while Yankeedom was a land of naught but cold-eyed profiteering. Later generations on both sides have largely accepted this Southern myth, like so many others. But the reality was much more ambiguous, and in many ways the two regions were more alike than different. The South's economy was as ruthlessly profit-driven as the North's; each plantation was, in a sense, a cog in a vast industrial machine, and many of the great cotton planters had actually come from above the Mason-Dixon Line. So too, young Northerners thrilled to chivalric fantasies just as much as their Southern counterparts.

Walter Scott was hardly the exclusive property of Southern cavaliers: Harriet Beecher Stowe remembered that as a girl, she read *Ivanhoe* no fewer than seven times in a single summer, until she was able to recite many of its scenes from memory. This was the era of Romanticism's exuberant flowering, when nary a middle-class parlor, even in the backwaters of New England or the Midwest, was without its thick, gilt-edged volumes of Byron and Tennyson, laid reverently alongside the family Bible. Such books were not just displayed but read and memorized. Like the rock lyrics of a later generation, their verses stirred millions of young Americans who heard in them the language of their own souls, and a kind of prophetic authority. As an adult, Ellsworth would cite a passage from Tennyson's *Idylls of the King* as his favorite lines of poetry. Something in the Arthurian legend, with its gallant young knights riding off to sacrifice their lives for their king, spoke powerfully to his heart.[34]

American authors of the 1840s and 1850s, especially in the North, developed home-grown versions of such heroic fantasies. One of the best sellers of the period, Richard Henry Dana's *Two Years Before the Mast*, is the true story of a privileged young Bostonian who makes his way as a merchant seaman aboard a vessel bound for California, via the perilous waters of Cape Horn. Dana returns to Boston no longer a sickly Harvard undergraduate but a tough and seasoned adventurer, a comrade of salty old mariners and California ranch hands, who has proven his manhood with brawn as well as brains. That book probably inspired the young Herman Melville to sign aboard a whaling ship the year after its publication, thus spawning still more magnificent tales of young men setting sail upon the high seas. (And it definitely inspired the teenage James Garfield to run away "to sea"—which in his case consisted of six weeks on a mule-drawn canal boat.)

Indeed, as the nineteenth century reached its midpoint, it seemed that youth was ascendant as it had never been before. A new generation scoffed at the values of its parents, proclaiming its devotion to deeper and truer things than mere getting and spending. A political movement called Young America swore eternal enmity to "old fogyism" in all its forms. Farm boys and apprentices, laboring at their drudge work in fields and shops, dreamed of greater things.[35]

Most young Americans, of course, never crossed the Pacific aboard a whaler. But hundreds of thousands embraced other opportunities to test their mettle in a world wider than their fathers had known—whether in America's booming cities or along her expanding frontiers. In places like rural New England and the Hudson Valley, where generations of the same families had farmed the same lands, and children often lived under strict parental authority well into adulthood, it was a bold and radical act for a young man to pull up stakes and seek his fortune in the gold fields of California or the bare-fisted markets of Chicago. Moreover, when the adventurers arrived at their destination, the competition—for jobs or gold, for the attention of would-be patrons or would-be wives—could be ruthless. The newcomers, nearly all in their teens and twenties, formed their own rough-and-tumble communities in mining camps and boardinghouses. Postadolescent tempers ran high, flaring into brawls with fists, knives, and sometimes pistols. Yet at the same time, ardent feelings of brotherhood, like those Garfield knew in rural Ohio, were quick to kindle, as solitary adventurers banded together against an unforgiving world. They joined militias, volunteer fire companies, "young men's societies," and gymnasiums. (The first true college fraternities began to flourish in the 1840s and 1850s, too.)[36]

So the culture of Ellsworth's generation of young urbanites, the generation of 1861, was a culture of toughness and comradeship, of tender yearnings and ruthless ambition. It was an American culture largely new. It was the world that Walt Whitman sang.[37]

It was also a world rife with pitfalls and temptations. Countless self-help books warned of the dangers that lay in wait for young men on their own, away from the watchful eyes of parents and clergymen. Brothels and billiard halls, saloons and gambling dens, all lured the unwary. Many, if not most, young men sampled these pleasures to some degree. (The immense quantities of alcohol they consumed are especially impressive.)[38] But the sinful pleasures of urban life often came with a heavy price of remorse, especially for the sons of traditionally devout families. Alongside low dens of iniquity, temperance societies and self-improvement associations also flourished. Antebellum cities became not only battlefields of economic competition but also, as the sea was for Dana and Melville, proving grounds of discipline, morality, and self-worth.[39] It is easy to see why Ellsworth's strict rules for his Zouaves, along with the all-consuming drill regimen and the promise of soldierly comradeship, appealed so strongly to certain rootless youth of Chicago, and to many who would answer their country's call a few years later.

For these men, too, the chief apostle of American youth was not Whitman, whose poems had found only a few thousand readers as of 1860, but Emerson. Unlike previous generations of Protestant sermonizers, who had equated age with authority, and treated the young merely as unformed minds in need of guidance and discipline, Emerson extolled youth for its own sake. America itself was a young country, and young men and women had a special role to play in its destiny. In his 1844 lecture "The Young American," first delivered at the Boston Mercantile Library, he exhorted, in ringing words:

> I call upon you, young men, to obey your heart, and be the nobility of this land. In every age of the world, there has been a leading nation, one of a more generous sentiment, whose eminent citizens were willing to stand for the interests of general justice and humanity, at the risk of being called, by the men of the moment, chimerical and fantastic. Which should be that nation but these States? Which should lead that movement, if not New England? Who should lead the leaders, but the Young American?[40]

Some years later—just about the time Ellsworth was learning to fence in a Chicago gymnasium—Abraham Lincoln took to the Illinois lecture circuit with his own variation on the Emersonian message, a talk that he called "Discoveries and Inventions." Speaking before audiences at colleges and young men's associations, he paid these listeners a characteristically wry, even sarcastic, tribute. "We have all heard of Young America," Lincoln said. "He is the most current youth of the age. Some think him conceited, and arrogant; but has he not reason to entertain a rather extensive opinion of himself? . . . Men, and things, everywhere, are ministering unto him." Thanks to global trade and modern inventions, he noted, any American youth of decent means lived like a virtual king, with the whole world catering to his every whim: he wore fabrics from England and France, drank tea and coffee from China and South America, smoked Cuban cigars and lit his home with oil from South Sea whales. "He owns," Lincoln said, "a large part of the world."

It was not just spoken words that summoned young men onto the global stage. Ellsworth's generation was the first to grow up in the thrall of mass popular media: news sheets carrying the latest telegraphic dispatches, cheaply printed books about the heroic exploits of 1776 and 1812, illustrated weeklies chockablock with wood engravings of cavalry clashes, political rallies, and militia parades. By bringing the wide world and its pageantry into young Americans' lives with such unprecedented immediacy, the new media of the 1840s and 1850s made once-distant adventures and opportunities seem achievable. They regaled readers with tales of far-off, yet newly accessible, California—an entire state of ambitious young entrepreneurs, drawn into the Gold Rush boom from every nation of the world, sometimes to gain fortunes and sometimes to lose their lives.

New horizons of possibility seemed to open on all sides in those final prewar years. The American press was also filled with even more outré tales of what were then known as "filibusters," men whose exploits are nearly forgotten today. The filibusters were gangs of young freelance military adventurers who set out to invade, in the name of Manifest Destiny, various soft parts of Latin America: Cuba, Nicaragua, Honduras, northern Mexico. These soldiers of fortune sailed from American ports under fanciful flags of nonexistent republics, of which they imagined themselves the founding fathers.

Though nearly all these expeditions flamed out like so many cheap firecrackers—with the occasional timely assistance of a Latin American firing squad—the dream of foreign conquest kept its hold on the American imagination right up to the eve of Fort Sumter. Ellsworth himself, even as a penniless clerk, kept a map of Mexico pinned to his wall and sketched out plans of empire somewhere below the Rio Grande. But his rendezvous with destiny, manifest or otherwise, would happen closer to home.

THE LAST SUMMER OF THE DECADE, the last summer of peace, was the summer of the Chicago Zouaves. The men—a corps of sixty handpicked by Ellsworth himself, plus a small regimental band—left home at the start of July, and by midmonth they were a national sensation.

From town to town they traveled, riding the railways across the Upper Midwest, through New York and New England, down the Eastern seaboard. Their performances dazzled nearly all who saw them, and the trip quickly became a thousand-mile triumphal procession. After their drill in Cleveland, they marched to the city's train station flanked by uniformed firemen, as torches flared and Roman candles arced across the dusk, with young girls running out into the street proffering bouquets of flowers to the cadets.[41] At Albany, New York, little more than a week into the tour, twenty-five thousand people turned out to watch. One of the town's most worldly—or, one suspects, just imaginative—local journalists claimed that he had "seen Lord Wellington review his veterans in Hyde Park; Napoleon, his Guards on Champ de Mars; and the Emperor of Russia, an Austrian army in Vienna," but this "simple corps of citizen soldiers" from the edge of the prairies excelled them all.[42]

Just past daybreak the following morning, when the lads from Chicago arrived by Hudson River steamboat at the Cortland Street pier in Lower Manhattan, a cheering crowd already lined the wharf to greet them, as artillery pieces boomed official welcome to the greatest city on the continent. Local papers were already using words like "mania" to describe the public's response to the Zouaves.[43] The *New York Atlas* satirized the media frenzy:

> They have come!
>   Who?
>   Again every man, woman, and child echoes the cry.
>   They have come!
>   Who?
>   Upon lightning wings the words reach the uttermost bowels of the Union, and millions reiterate them:
>   They have come!
>   Who?
>
>   . . .
>   The far-famed military organization, the Tan Bark Sheiks from Little Egypt, is in town.[44]

It would be more than a century before New Yorkers would swoon like this for a few out-of-town boys newly arriving in the metropolis. After breakfast at the city's finest hotel, the Astor House, the cadets shouldered their muskets and marched up Broadway to Union Square, then down the Bowery to Grand Street. Packed masses of spectators awaited them in front of City Hall, sweltering in the mid-July sun as policemen swung billy clubs left and right to make way for Ellsworth's troop. The windows of City Hall were crowded with Tammany grandees, and lesser mortals scrambled precariously along the roof for a better view, while the surrounding trees, one spectator wrote, "bent under the load of unripe boys they bore."[45] To Ellsworth, whose last experience of New York City had been his brief stint as a teenage shopboy, this triumphant return must have seemed like a waking dream.

Oddly, few of the watching thousands could describe afterward exactly what was so enthralling about Ellsworth and his men. For all the ink that was spilled on the subject of the Zouaves that summer, it is still hard to find any satisfactorily visual account, though some give us quick, glancing snapshots of the action: the young soldiers running in tight formation behind their commander; turning exuberant somersaults and handstands; crouching all together in a tight pyramid of men, bayonets bristling out on every side like the spines of a porcupine.[46] Newspapermen excused themselves by explaining that words could not fully capture the cadets' rapid maneuvers as they formed squares, triangles, crosses, and revolving circles, shifting from one shape to the next with the dizzying fluidity of a kaleidoscope.[47] "Now that the parade is over, my single impressions of the scene are indistinct," one of them confessed just a few hours later, recalling only a sense of "geometrical precision," of "action," of "runnings, hoppings, bayonet-guardings, and thrustings."[48] Many commented on the Zouaves' jauntily elegant uniforms, on their youthfulness and muscularity, on their air of high spirits with a dash of ferocity. Each man, one journalist wrote, was "as wiry, athletic, and agile as a squirrel"; others compared them to tigers, steam engines, and electric clocks.[49]

To convey the full splendor of the Zouaves' prowess, some scribes were driven to satirical exaggeration. One New York paper assured its readers that when he met an enemy soldier, a Zouave could drive the bayonet, musket and all, through the foe's body, turn a somersault over his head, and draw the weapon out the other side in a single flourish. When he had to cross a river, a Zouave would nonchalantly throw a rope across it and tightrope-walk to the other side. And if his commanders needed someone to reconnoiter the enemy's lines, a Zouave would climb into a skyrocket, blast a thousand feet into the air, and have a complete set of photographs and hand-drawn maps ready by the time he alighted on the ground.[50]

America's Zouave fever even caught the attention of Charles Dickens, who was following the Chicago cadets' exploits from across the Atlantic. "The individual action, the free agency of the Zouave drill, which is almost acrobatic, delight the Americans," he commented.[51] Dickens, who had toured the States twenty years before, was onto something important. What the Zouave drill demonstrated was how personal freedom could exist even amid military regimentation: a truly democratic way of soldiering.

The boys from Chicago caused Americans' chests to swell with national pride. Over the past decade, they had sat on the sidelines while European armies clashed gallantly on the fields of Sevastopol and Solferino. Now, it seemed, their own republic was ready to take its part in that panoply. One spectator at the Zouaves' performance in New York was inspired to write a poem. Its final stanza reads:

> Your Zouave corps, O haughty France!
> We looked on as a wild romance,
> And many a voice was heard to scoff
> At Algiers and at Malakoff;
> Nor did we Yankees credit quite
> Their evolutions in the fight.
> But now we're very sure what they
> Have done can here be done to-day,
> When thus before our sight deploys
> The gallant corps from Illinois,—
> American Zouaves![52]

Many observers' accounts betray an almost erotic excitement at the pure physicality of those men. In the early Victorian age, the idea that the human body could be simply that—a human body, strong and unconstrained—was radical and new in a way almost unimaginable in our own era obsessed with fitness and exercise. Here was a group of ordinary young Americans—law clerks and shop assistants, not circus acrobats, blacksmiths, or stevedores—who had decided to make their own bodies into beautiful and powerful machines, and not because they needed to hammer iron or lift barrels, or even defeat foes in battle, but for something like the sheer pleasure of it, simply, as one newspaper account put it, "to gain excellence in a certain direction for its own sake." And through the good old Puritan virtues of discipline and self-restraint, through all those months of cold water, hard floors, and endless hours in the gym, they had succeeded. These young men, the newspaper declared, were the harbingers of a new American phenomenon: "muscle mania."[53]

As for their captain, the penniless young striver from Mechanicville became, almost overnight, a sex symbol. That term wasn't used at the time, of course, but it is no exaggeration. Never before had any American become famous and adored not for any particular accomplishments—not for being a poet or an actor or a war hero—but simply for his charisma.

Looking at the surviving photographs of him, it is difficult to discern just what all the swooning was about. A short man even by the standards of his time, Ellsworth seems almost dwarfed by his own elaborate uniforms, blooming profusions of plumed hats, sashes, epaulettes, and medals. Add his hippie-length hair and droopy mustache, and he might almost be a member of a 1970s rock band. His face still has an unformed quality, a postadolescent doughiness. The dry-goods store clerk lurks not far beneath the surface of the martinet.

Yet throughout that prewar summer, the nation's eyes were on him. "His pictures sold like wildfire in every city of the land," John Hay later remembered. "School-girls dreamed over the graceful wave of his curls, and shop-boys tried to reproduce the *Grand Seigneur* air of his attitude." His body, too, attracted the camera's ravenous gaze: Hay described one photograph—now apparently lost—that showed only the hero's muscular arm: "The knotted coil of thews and sinews looks like the magnificent exaggerations of antique sculpture."[54] Just a few years earlier, an English inventor had created the first photographs that could be reproduced in large numbers from single negatives. Now Ellsworth became the first male pinup in America's—perhaps even the world's—history.

Other times, other tastes. Ellsworth's strict moralism, too, what seems to us his teetotaling Victorian priggishness, drew nearly as many plaudits as his curls. The press extolled him and his men as new moral exemplars of American youth. In a front-page article, *Frank Leslie's Illustrated Newspaper* declared that "the scope of the Zouave Cadet is to raise the standard of American freemen" and predicted confidently that if the movement caught on, "it would almost change the aspect of our great cities, and . . . vice, rowdyism, and bloodshed would disappear."[55] And indeed, though vice was not permanently banished from America, the movement did catch on. As Ellsworth crossed the country, new Zouave corps, brilliant in crimson and gold, blazed up like phosphorescence in the wake of a passing ship.[56]

Oddly, for all the talk of a "nationwide" tour, there was a large portion of the country—about half—that the Zouaves seem never to have even considered touring. On August 4, a steamboat carried them down the Potomac, past the sleepy port town of Alexandria, Virginia, whose citizens crowded down along the waterside to cheer as the vessel passed without stopping. It moored downriver, at the foot of the high bluff of Mount Vernon, where the Chicagoans disembarked for an hour or two to perform a tribute drill in front of George Washington's tomb. That brief veneration of the patron saint of liberty and union was the only time they somersaulted on the soil of the South. They shortly steamed past Alexandria again on their way to the national capital, where President Buchanan greeted them in the East Room of the White House and then hosted a Zouave drill on the South Lawn, as photographers crowded in to capture the scene.[57] Standing under the mansion's portico, Buchanan delivered a polite speech of welcome, observing blandly that the cadets' military prowess would come in handy in case the United States ever found herself at war against a foreign country.[58]

But the most important man to see the Zouaves that summer was a less obtrusive spectator, who came out to watch when they were almost home.

Just before its triumphal return to Chicago, the troupe made one final stop at the Illinois state capital, Springfield. Ellsworth's men were met at the station by a local militia company, the Springfield Grays, who escorted them through the streets to the music of a marching band, as several thousand curious locals followed on foot and in carriages. Gentlemen in top hats and young ladies in crinolines crowded around a large empty lot on South Sixth Street, near the State Armory, to watch the Zou-Zous—as the American public had fondly begun to call them—perform the famous drill. The excited crowd had to be pushed back as the young cadets pantomimed bloodless gestures of war: aiming harmless rifles, dodging and parrying invisible foes, slashing the thin air savagely with their bayonets.[59]

Watching over the heads of the crowd was a tall, solitary man, who had strolled over from his law office five blocks away.[60] Abraham Lincoln was, like Ellsworth, one of the most famous men in America that summer, but no one seems to have paid him much attention as he stood quietly beneath the shade of a cottonwood tree. This was Ellsworth's hour. Lincoln must have watched intently as the spruce, boyish colonel, leaner now and suntanned after six weeks' travel, stood at the head of his corps, his sword flashing in the midday glare as he led the cadets through their drill for the last time.[61]

Lincoln and Ellsworth knew each other already. Sometime the previous winter or spring, before Ellsworth's ascent to national fame and before Lincoln had been spoken of for the presidency, the two had met in Springfield, probably through John Cook, a local militia commander who had befriended the youth from Chicago. The young man made an immediate impression upon the elder. In March, a letter came to Ellsworth from Cook: "You ask me if I have seen our friend Lincoln. I answer, Yes, repeatedly, and never without the conversation turning upon you and his expressing an earnest desire that you should make [Springfield] your home, and his office your headquarters. He has taken in you a greater interest than I have ever seen him manifest in anyone before." [62] At another point, Ellsworth wrote to his fiancée, "Mr Cook told me that Mr L—— *especially desired him to leave no means unturned* to induce me to come to Springfield."[63]

Ellsworth seems to have perceived in Lincoln, twenty-eight years his senior, a potential role model and father figure who had likewise risen from humble birth. "I believe that the influence of Mr L—— would do me great service," he told his fiancée. "I mean the influence of his early example. He earned his subsistence, while studying law, by splitting rails."[64] On May 18, the night Lincoln was nominated for the presidency in Chicago, Ellsworth and some of his Zouaves celebrated by climbing onto the roof of the Tremont Hotel—adjoining the famous wigwam, where the Republicans had gathered—and hauling a howitzer up after them to fire off a salute. So exuberant was the little colonel that night, one cadet later remembered, that he nearly slipped off the hotel's roof and broke his neck.[65]

As to the causes of Lincoln's sudden, schoolboyish crush on Ellsworth, these are less immediately obvious. He was not one to develop intimacies easily, much less quickly. There is no surviving correspondence between them, and the only time Lincoln seems to have committed to paper his feelings for the younger man was in a single letter to Ellsworth's parents, written almost a year later. Just as Ellsworth looked up to the self-made Lincoln, Lincoln must have seen something of himself in the struggling law clerk turned national hero, and in the Westerner challenging the silk-stockinged traditions of the East. Yet their differences probably drew him as much as or more than their similarities. It is difficult to imagine two specimens of American manhood more physically different than the long-limbed, stoop-shouldered, middle-aged lawyer and the trim soldier-athlete. Each man had his own charisma, to be sure, and each inspired intense devotion among the cadre of young men surrounding him, though in entirely different ways. In the end, Lincoln seems to have felt that

Ellsworth complemented him, or perhaps even made up for parts of himself that were lacking.

In any event, something during the Zouaves' short visit to Springfield in August apparently cemented the relationship between the two men. The following night, Ellsworth and his cadets returned to Chicago to find the entire city illuminated with torches, bonfires, and the flashes of rockets and Roman candles. They were escorted to the great wigwam itself, fêted and banqueted and lauded, with typical Victorian excess, until even their adulation-hungry leader must have had more than his fill. A few weeks later, Ellsworth resigned his command of the Zouaves. The cadets disbanded. Within a month, the erstwhile colonel had moved to Springfield and was a clerk once more—this time for the most famous lawyer in the country.

In the law office, Ellsworth found himself in the company of a lively group of ambitious young men surrounding the Republican presidential nominee, including the pair who would become Lincoln's private secretaries, John Hay and John Nicolay. He quickly managed to win the confidence of both of these very different personalities: the urbane, satirical Hay and the dour, Germanic Nicolay. Hay—a doctor's son who had learned Latin and Greek as a boy before heading to college at Brown University—might have been expected to sneer at the oyster peddler's son. But the two struck up an intense friendship that would last the rest of Ellsworth's life. "His parents were plain people, without culture or means," Hay wrote many years later. "One cannot guess how this eaglet came into so lowly a nest." Ellsworth also attracted the interest of numerous young women in Springfield, including Mary Todd Lincoln's much younger half sister, Kitty.[66]

"Ellsworth read very little law that autumn," Hay would recall.[67] Instead, he almost immediately took to the campaign trail, firing up crowds in the barns and country schoolhouses of central Illinois, organizing the Republican cohorts just as he had organized the Zouaves.[68] Lincoln is supposed to have called Ellsworth "the worst law clerk that ever lived, and the best executive to handle young men that I ever saw."[69] Still, it is clear that their relationship was based more on personal esteem than on Ellsworth's political services; Lincoln, Hay wrote, "loved him like a younger brother."[70] The Zouave cadets' drummer boy remembered half a century later: "Often I had seen Mr. Lincoln place his hand on Ellsworth's shoulder or take hold of his arm in such a way as to show not merely liking, but sincere affection."[71]

Scarcely any evidence survives of the two men's specific interactions during this period, or in the months that followed. In contrast to the

Zouave tour, when the press had chronicled almost his every move, Ellsworth was now out of the spotlight and in Lincoln's shadow. One of the few detailed accounts has Ellsworth, shortly after his arrival in Springfield, sitting in the law office while Lincoln read poetry to him.[72] It was one of Lincoln's favorites, a composition by the obscure Scottish poet William Knox:

> Oh! why should the spirit of mortal be proud?
> Like a swift-fleeting meteor, a fast-flying cloud,
> A flash of the lightning, a break of the wave,
> Man passeth from life to his rest in the grave.
> The leaves of the oak and the willow shall fade,
> Be scattered around, and together be laid;
> And the young and the old, and the low and the high
> Shall molder to dust and together shall lie.

Four months later, when the president-elect bade farewell to Springfield—a parting that he did not know would be his last— Ellsworth was with him on the train.

THE FALL OF SUMTER must have seemed to Ellsworth like the last in a series of providential strokes, bearing him more swiftly toward glory than he could ever have dreamed. His meeting with the French officer in Chicago had made him a Zouave. His lucky meeting with the lawyer in Springfield had made him confidant to a president. And now, he thought, the shots in Charleston Harbor were about to make him a hero.

The question was not whether he would take to the field, but where. The day after the inauguration, Lincoln had already started working to get his young protégé an important—and well-compensated—post in the War Department, possibly even with the authority to over- see all of the nation's local militias. But once the conflict with the seceding states broke out in earnest, and war fever swept across the North, there was little chance that Ellsworth would be satisfied with a desk job.

His rapid rise as the new president's favorite had begun to make him enemies, however. The same press that had lionized him the summer before began to sneer at the pompous little "show business" drillmas- ter who thought he could vault over the army's chain of command to become one of the most powerful officers in the country. And perhaps they were right. In the cold gray light of imminent war, there was some-thing more than slightly ridiculous about the gamecock Midwesterner. The gaudy Zouave displays of the previous summer seemed frivolous, even silly. A leading Northern paper, the *Philadelphia Inquirer*, which not long ago had poured forth rapturous column-inches about the Chicago cadets at Independence Hall, now suggested sarcastically that the self-anointed colonel might simply be packed back off to Illinois "to promulgate, privately, his peculiar gymnastic drill."[73] This criti-cism depressed and infuriated Ellsworth, and gave him more reason than ever to seek a test on the battlefield.[74]

Luckily for him, the country needed even "show business" offi-cers now. Immediately after the fall of Sumter, Lincoln called upon the state governors to mobilize their militias and organize new state regiments to meet the crisis. His proclamation of April 15 asked for seventy-five thousand troops "to maintain the honor, the integrity, and the existence of our National Union, and the perpetuity of popu-lar government."

He need hardly have asked, given the national mood at that moment. Volunteers were coming, whether the president and his cabinet were ready for them or not. "All the world wants to march," wrote one of Lincoln's confidants.[75]

In New York, the first soldiers to depart for Washington were members of the high-society Seventh Regiment, who sashayed down Broadway in their fine gray uniforms, with heavy dirks and bowie knives tucked into each belt for hand-to-hand fighting, and cigars in each hatband for the more leisurely hours of soldiering.[76] (At least a few fashion-conscious militiamen, it was said, had stashed white kid gloves in their knapsacks, thoughtfully preparing to dress appropriately for the victory balls in Washington in just a few weeks' time.)

The sudden flash of national solidarity dazzled even Lincoln's most outspoken critics in the metropolis. The *New York Herald*'s editor, the feistily idiosyncratic James Gordon Bennett, had quite recently favored avoiding war at any cost, and at one point even suggested that the mid-Atlantic states should join the Southern Confederacy, leaving New England to fend for itself as an independent republic. The day after Major Anderson's surrender, the paper had taken almost comical pains to ignore the subject entirely, relegating the outbreak of civil war to its back pages, after reports on the new April fashions, harness races in Paris, and some interesting correspondence just received from Constantinople. But now even the perfidious *Herald*'s offices were duly adorned in red, white, and blue. This might have had something to do with a mob of warlike toughs that had hooted its editor down Fulton Street, then stormed the building and nearly destroyed it. Finally reemerging before the crowd to a chorus of jeers, Bennett had promised not just to raise the Stars and Stripes without further delay but also to reverse his previous stance on the secession crisis. He hoisted one flag on a staff, draped another from a front window, and hastily penned an editorial invoking Lexington and Yorktown, the Fourth of July and the Ship of State, the Potomac River and the Rocky Mountains, before declaring: "The North is consolidated as one man . . . we can no longer treat or temporize—we must fight." The *Herald*'s offices, and its editor, were allowed to remain intact.[77]

Back in Chicago, crowds jammed the Wigwam, where a judge stood up and administered a solemn oath of allegiance: ten thousand hats came off and ten thousand right hands went up, in a pledge to the Union and Constitution.[78] Recruiting stations were jammed; the crowd in front of the Zouaves' old armory was so dense that a group of students from Northwestern University, who had come into the city from campus in the hopes of enlisting, couldn't even get near it.[79] As for the former cadets themselves, they were soon scattered among a dozen different regiments, as most were given officers' commissions on the merit of their military prowess—"show business" fame notwithstanding.[80]

In Washington, in the telegraph office at the War Department, the overheated machine tapped for hours on end with messages from every corner of the Union. Since Lincoln had requested only seventy-five thousand volunteers, governors in the North worried not about whether they could fill their quotas but about how they could deal with the onrush of eager patriots. Governor Denison of Ohio begged Secretary Cameron to take as many militiamen from his state as humanly possible. From New York came a promise that the city by itself could meet two-thirds of Lincoln's requirement.[81] In a small town in Maine, thirty-odd veterans of the War of 1812 proclaimed themselves a military company and pledged to totter off southward into the thick of the fighting.[82] In Buffalo, former president Millard Fillmore put on the uniform of a militiaman. An Indian chief named Pug-o-na-ke-shick, or Hole-in-the-Day, and an ex-major of the Ottoman Army, as well as several groups of bellicose Canadians, all offered their services, and were politely turned down.[83] Hundreds of free blacks in Philadelphia rallied near Independence Hall, offered two regiments of colored troops "in whose hearts burns the love of country," and were ignored.[84]

Amid all this glorious confusion, Ellsworth went up to New York, just three days after Sumter's surrender, with a plan already formed in his mind. He arrived at 3 a.m., and as soon as the city began to stir, he began scouting the men who could help make his scheme a reality. One of the first places he called was in Printing House Square, at the office of Horace Greeley, the most important newspaperman not just in the city but in the country. Greeley was an unlikely power broker. With his round, bespectacled face above a fringe of long white whiskers drooping from the underside of his chin—more than a bit outré even in that era of exuberant facial hair—he looked like a cross between a Presbyterian Sunday school teacher and a superannuated gibbon. During his long editorial career, Greeley had espoused, with equal fervor, causes as disparate as vegetarianism, spiritualism, and human-manure farming. Yet he also possessed a curious sense for the pulse of his times. Many said he had made Lincoln president. His *New-York Tribune* had banged its drum unceasingly for Honest Old Abe, while behind the scenes, Greeley brokered votes at the Chicago convention and personally helped draft the Republican platform.[85] When the Southern states seceded, he was among the first to call for war without compromise. "Imagine Greeley booted & spurred with Epaulets on his shoulders and with a whetted blade in his hands," scoffed one politician. "The idea . . . is too ridiculous to be thought of."[86] However improbable Greeley was as a warrior, though, his pen was as mighty as any sword in the Union.

Ellsworth struck Greeley as possessing an "unusually fine physique," "frank and attractive manners," and "great intelligence." The editor must also have been impressed by a letter of introduction from the president that Ellsworth showed him. It was dated two days after Sumter's fall, and expressed Lincoln's great esteem for his protégé as both a military man and a personal friend.[87]

Still, the young officer's proposal may at first have startled even the idiosyncratic Greeley. He wanted to raise his own regiment. But its members, this time, would not be law clerks and shop assistants. Instead, he said firmly, "I want the New York firemen." In Washington, Ellsworth explained, the military authorities were "sleeping on a volcano," and while they dithered about organizing and training the various state militias, the forces of rebellion might blow them sky-high at any moment. "I want men who can go into a fight now."[88] Despite any skepticism Greeley may have harbored, he put an article detailing Ellsworth's plan into the next morning's *Tribune*.

Whatever else they may have been, the firemen of New York were certainly just what Ellsworth hoped for: ready for a fight. In fact, locals often remarked that they seemed less interested in battling fires than in battling one another. The city on the eve of the Civil War was not merely a rough-and-tumble place but "a huge semi-barbarous metropolis . . . not well-governed or ill-governed, but simply not governed at all."[89] As for the city's firemen, they were not merely ungoverned, they were almost completely, and famously, ungovernable.

Since colonial times, New York had relied for its fire protection on volunteer companies, much as the nation relied for its defense on volunteer militias. It was a marvelously democratic system that became an utterly impossible mess—though admittedly a colorful and entertaining one, so long as your own house was not the one going up in flames. As the city grew, its warehouses and tenements spreading ever northward up the island, so did the number of hose, hydrant, and hook-and-ladder companies, ever dividing and proliferating. Their official names formed a kind of prose poem of American grandeur: Mohawk, Valley Forge, Eagle, Excelsior, Niagara, Pioneer, Empire, Lady Washington.

But the unofficial nicknames by which New Yorkers actually knew them told a different story: Screamer, Black Joke, Hounds, Old Nick, Shad-Belly, Bucky-Boys, Dry Bones, Old Turk, Mankiller.[90]

The contests between these companies were epic, hard fought, and often bloody: thirty years' wars whose battlefields were the nighttime streets of Brooklyn and the Bowery, Greenwich Village and Five Points. The ringing of a fire alarm wasn't so much a signal of emergency as the starting bell of a no-holds-barred decathlon. Companies raced one another to the scene of the fire, hurtling through the muddy, unlit thoroughfares, young runners sprinting alongside with torches as brawny firemen pulled hand-drawn engines weighing up to a ton each—and woe betide any unfortunate gentleman, groping his way homeward from late revels at a tavern or bawdy house, who might stumble into their path.[91]

As the engines pulled up in front of the blaze, another competitive event began, as companies vied to see who could pump the fastest; the volunteers stripped to the waist and worked until their breath came in choking gasps; the foremen stood atop the engines bawling orders through brass trumpets above the din. Sometimes they drove the wooden pump handles into such a frenzy that the flailing shafts might crush a man's fingers or even break his arms if he momentarily lost his grip. Often, different engines had to connect their leather hoses to relay water from a hydrant or cistern, which meant that if one group pumped faster than the next one down the line, the water would burst out the sides of the rival company's engine, spilling out over the ornate woodwork and polished brass in a spectacularly humiliating torrent known as a "washing." Whether or not this calamity might interfere with the task of actually putting out a fire was wholly inconsequential: every company's fondest hope was to "wash" its enemies.[92]

Not surprisingly, these rivalries often degenerated into all-out brawls. The Black Joke men once rolled out a howitzer loaded with bolts and chain links to defend their firehouse from a rival company's attack, while Old Nick's main engine was known to other companies as the Arsenal, for it was rumored to hold a cache of loaded revolvers. In their impatience to avenge defeats, the firefighters themselves sometimes set buildings aflame so as to hasten the opportunity for a rematch.[93] For decades after the invention of horse-drawn, steam-pumped engines that carried their own water supply, New York firefighters refused to give up their inefficient machines, little changed since colonial times, since this would have taken all the sporting fun out of it.[94]

More genteel New Yorkers shuddered at press reports of nocturnal rampages, and agitated for reform, with little result. Not only were the companies an essential voting bloc for the city's Democratic political machine, they had become folk heroes. Ordinary workingmen coined the fond nickname "b'hoys"—based on Irish immigrants' pronunciation of "boys." Down in the taverns of Five Points, people swapped tall tales of the ultimate b'hoy, a semilegendary figure called Mose the Fireboy, an urban Paul Bunyan who stood eight feet tall, could swim across the Hudson in two strokes, carried streetcars on his back, smoked a two-foot cigar, and drank wagonloads of beer at a sitting. When a brawl broke out against a rival fire company, Mose uprooted lampposts with his bare hands to smite his enemies. The character of Mose may have been a slight exaggeration, but the actual b'hoys were still impressive figures. Their fame spread throughout the nation thanks to a series of plays about Mose that began touring to great popular acclaim in the 1840s.[95]

The b'hoys became emblems not just of sheer physical strength but also of the workingman and the immigrant—of America's rambunctious grassroots democracy, in all its vital, and sometimes brutal, force. Back in the 1830s, when Tocqueville toured the United States, he had celebrated it as a nation of "voluntary associations" (a category that might, indeed, have seemed to include the prewar Union itself). The post-Revolutionary era had been a time of few official decrees from on high, a time when federal authority and national politics were distant abstractions for most people—what mattered more were local loyalties and associations, the rough bands of tradesmen and farmers who paraded in the streets on Election Day or the Fourth of July. By 1861, the volunteer companies, each with its own storied victories and affectionate nickname, and their old engines, each meticulously hand-painted with elaborate historical and allegorical scenes—Jefferson penning the Declaration, Jupiter hurling his thunderbolts from Olympus—already seemed like quaint relics of a vanishing America. Like the colorful, ragtag local militia units to which the country had entrusted its defense, New York's volunteer fire companies would be swept away on the war's tide of modernization and consolidation. In 1865, two weeks before the surrender at Appomattox, a bill was passed creating a new Metropolitan Fire Department of paid and trained firefighters, using steam-powered engines, and under a set of strict regulations enforced by a citywide commissioner. The b'hoys were unceremoniously cashiered, along with Black Joke and Old Nick, Jupiter and Jefferson.[96]

In the first spring of the war, though, the old ways and the new still hung in fragile equipoise. So Ellsworth came to New York prepared to form a regiment after the model of the fire companies themselves: a free association of noble volunteers lending themselves to the Union cause. Moreover, he confidently assured Greeley, he could turn the recruits into proper Zouaves in as little as five days—after all, the b'hoys were the finest raw material the city or even the nation had to offer, combining Mose-like strength with the agility of those skilled at catwalking along rain gutters and swinging from ropes, the hardiness of those used to braving disaster at a moment's notice, the esprit de corps of those accustomed to rallying around the standard of their firehouse and upholding its honor with blood if necessary.[97] "The firemen of New York are renowned the continent over for their great qualities of endurance, hardihood, activity, and restless daring," enthused a correspondent of the *Chicago Tribune*. "Every man is a gymnast, and can run, jump, and climb like a catamount. There is no better material for Zouave soldiers in the world. We predict that Col. Ellsworth's regiment will reap glory or find a grave."[98]

IN LITTLE MORE THAN twenty-four hours after Ellsworth's late-night arrival, posters appeared on walls and fences throughout the city, bearing a screaming American eagle across the top and the legend DOWN WITH SECESSION! THE UNION MUST AND SHALL BE PRESERVED! In smaller type, an appeal signed by Ellsworth called on members of the fire department to enlist at recruiting offices hastily organized at fire-houses, meeting halls, and Republican Party clubhouses throughout Manhattan and Brooklyn.[99] Ellsworth set up his regimental headquarters in the elegant Fifth Avenue Hotel on Madison Square—perhaps not coincidentally, the same place where Lincoln had stayed the year before when he visited New York to give his Cooper Union address.[100]

Volunteers were offered pay of thirteen dollars per month, plus food and equipment. Their uniforms, Ellsworth promised, would be of the most dashing Zouave cut, with a special flourish: bright red firemen's shirts. The firemen answered his call; perhaps many of them had been in the crowd for his performance at City Hall the summer before. He asked for a thousand men, and by nightfall he had that many and more. Long lines formed at all of the recruiting offices. Engine Company 14 (Columbian), one of the finest organizations in the city, was rumored to have enlisted en masse, and made Ellsworth an honorary member while they were at it. Three hundred firemen from Brooklyn alone volunteered on the first day. Donations for uniforms and supplies poured in as well, including a handsome gift of one hundred dollars from Boss Tweed himself; less well-heeled citizens were invited to contribute fresh socks, towels, and underwear.[101]

On the day of departure for Washington and the battles soon to come, the Zouaves marched down Fifth Avenue to the cheers of thousands of spectators—chambermaids waving handkerchiefs from the sidewalks and tycoons leaning out the open windows of their brownstones. Mrs. Augusta Astor appeared in person to present a pair of silk regimental flags; the famous actress Laura Keene presented another. The most unusual fixtures in the military parade were the fire engines that rolled down Broadway alongside the ranks of marching men, gleaming with fresh paint and polished brass.[102]

Colonel Ellsworth and his men were already eagerly expected in the national capital. Just after their swearing-in, on the afternoon of the Union Square rally, he had telegraphed the War Department to let them know that the Zouaves were on the way. The news quickly reached the president and his staff. Before going to bed that night, John Hay jotted a note in his diary: "Much is hoped from the gallant Colonel's Bloodtubs."[103]

"The First Telegraphic Message from California," *Harper's Weekly*, 1861

CHAPTER SIX

Gateways to the West

But these and all, and the brown and spreading land, and
the mines below, are ours,
And the shores of the sea are ours, and the rivers great and
small . . .

—WALT WHITMAN,
"Song of the Banner at Day-Break" (1860–61)

Lower Carson River, Nevada Territory, May 1861

THEY MUST HAVE GLIMPSED one another sometime during that week, at some unrecorded point along the Central Overland Trail. Perhaps it was here, at a bend in the sluggish stream. Perhaps the mule drivers paused in their labor and watched the thing coming toward them: a shimmer against the dull, flat sky that resolved itself, quickly, into a horseman. A *horseman*, truly; for what approached them seemed no ordinary rider and mount but a compound creature, a man-beast out of some bygone millennium. It rushed on in a clatter of hooves, nimbly dodging among stray boulders, headlong and heedless. In the instant it took to pass them, they could see the hunched man-shoulders and the rippling horse-shoulders, the two faces straining forward, nostrils flared, ghost-white with alkali dust from the flats farther east. And then the apparition was gone.[1]

The rider, for his own part, barely saw the sunburnt men, the straining mules, or their strange burden: pale, stripped carcasses of aspen and pine, hauled from some distant wooded place into this tree-less desert. Mules, men, and tree trunks were obstructions, no more. For him there was only the trail ahead and the animal that strained and swerved between his clenching thighs, thighs that gripped a flat pouch of mail against the saddle as his mind gripped only one thought: *westward.*

That is how they may have met, two eras brushing past, never touching: the Pony Express and the Western Union Telegraph Company.

Never touching, at least, until a few miles farther on, at Fort Churchill. Here the rider slackened his pace, reining in as he passed the sentry and cantered through the main gate. This was a fresh built fort, its adobe bricks barely dry. The army had constructed it the summer before, after an ugly clash between the white men and the Paiutes: a lonely outcrop of federal power in a lawless land. For the past few months, Fort Churchill had enjoyed another distinction: it was the Pacific Coast telegraph's easternmost terminus, though it would not remain so for much longer.[2]

Now, at least, it was where the horseman handed his flat leather pouch to the operator, who quickly extracted its most precious contents and began tapping the key with his expert finger. In San Francisco, the next day's headlines would begin with words familiar to every reader: BY MAGNETIC TELEGRAPH. BY PONY EXPRESS. LATEST EASTERN INTELLIGENCE. And then a terse summary of that leather pouch's most important contents: Thirty-one thousand troops are now in Washington, ultimate destinations still unknown. All work on public buildings at the capital is suspended. In Baltimore, prorebel militia have seized six thousand muskets from the state armory. In St. Louis, an inquest convenes to examine the bodies of those killed in recent clashes.[3]

Without ceremony, the telegraphist handed back the pouch, the rider threw it across the saddle of a fresh mount, swung himself on top and was off again still westward, his precious cargo clutched again between his thighs: terse business letters from New York and Baltimore, minutely penned political dispatches from Washington, reports on the latest Eastern prices of California bonds and California bullion. There was little room for anecdote or sentiment in a Pony Express pouch; each half ounce of mail cost its sender a five-dollar gold piece plus surcharges, and each rider could carry only ten pounds. Recipients slit open envelopes with a surgeon's care and extracted leaves as thin as tissue paper, still smelling of sweat and dust and leather.[4]

Back up the trail at the river bend, the men and mules, too, had resumed their labor. Like the passing horseman, they had little time to spare. They carried with them, eastward, the promise of a future without ponies, without pouches, without onionskin paper. Only electrical impulses: weightless, instantaneous, smelling of nothing.

Congress had opened the way the previous summer, by enacting the Pacific Telegraph Act. This was guided discreetly to passage by a certain private gentleman from the East, Mr. Hiram Sibley of New York, who proved quite expert at ducking and running amid the legislative fusillades of sectional conflict, emerging safely downfield with the only major legislation of that entire miserable year.[5] He had strong incentives to succeed. The final version of the act offered a federal subsidy of up to $40,000, along with other valuable considerations, to any company completing a transcontinental line within two years. Competing bids were invited; rival consortia formed. When the deadline for bids arrived in September, however, it appeared that all except one had been unexpectedly withdrawn at the last minute. That lone bid—asking the maximum subsidy, of course—happened to be in the name of Mr. Hiram Sibley of New York.[6]

Why all the competition withdrew was a mystery perhaps known only to Mr. Sibley and his business partners. These were not men who felt particularly constrained by the rules of gentlemanly fair play. Indeed, they were exactly the type of hard-fisted Yankees that Southerners were always complaining about. Several years earlier, for instance, they had set their eye on the New Orleans & Ohio line, the most profitable in the South. One of Mr. Sibley's associates had shown up in Louisville, the northern terminus, and word quickly spread among the N.O.&O.'s owners that this Yankee interloper was scouting out the terrain, pricing poles, wiring coded messages to New York—in other words, clearly laying the groundwork for a rival line. In a cold panic, the Southerners signed a contract with Sibley for a relative pittance, effectively ceding him control of their company. It emerged later that the coded messages to New York had been mere gibberish; the whole "rival line" a ruse. And thus the N.O.&O. network had, like so many others, tumbled into the omnivorous maw of the Western Union.[7]

Still, whatever else you might say about Hiram Sibley and his ilk, they certainly knew how to get things done. Within weeks of receiving the Pacific telegraph contract, he had agents fanning out across the West. Lincoln had been elected; the South had seceded; Sibley barely noticed, except insofar as these developments might aid or impede his business plans. Via stagecoach and mule, his envoys set out to secure the friendship of useful men along the planned route: Brigham Young, Chief Sho-kup of the Shoshones, the governor of California. (These agents offered the Mormons lucrative contracts for supplying poles, along with a generous personal loan to Brother Brigham; they offered the Shoshones gifts of food and clothing. What they offered the governor of California, if anything, is unclear.)[8]

The new line would follow an established route, the Central Overland Trail. It was the exact route, in fact, of the Pony Express, across the desert wastes and mountain passes of Utah and Nevada and over the Sierra Nevada into California. Not many years earlier, this country had been considered impassable wilderness. In the winter of 1844, the great Pathfinder himself, John C. Frémont, was hailed as the first white man to cross the Sierra when he and his band of explorers turned up, famished and half naked, on the western side. Two years later, the Donner party met its gruesome fate trying to follow in his tracks, and for a decade after, few others dared to try. But at the very end of the 1850s, private entrepreneurs and military engineers laid out and graded a new trail. By 1861, it had become a busy highway, the quickest and shortest overland route to California. Where frontiersmen had died in a trackless desert, fast stagecoaches now rumbled to and fro, carrying passengers, mail, and even a few tourists. Emigrant wagons passed by the thousands, their occupants pleasantly surprised to find the route lined with trading posts, grog shops, army hospitals, post offices, even hotels. Bridges and ferry crossings spanned the newly tamed rivers.[9]

That was how things were in the West as the Civil War began. Everywhere, it seemed, the Hiram Sibleys and their money were rushing in, along with throngs of lesser entrepreneurs—all those sutlers, tavern keepers, stagecoach owners, and ferrymen. Together, these ruthless and ambitious seekers were changing the continent, connecting city to city and town to town, drawing lines across the blankness of the country.

Indeed, Sibley's own ambitions went beyond the continent, beyond even the hemisphere. His transcontinental telegraph was only the beginning. Soon, he hoped, he would continue the line up the Pacific coast, through Russian Alaska, and across Bering's Strait, where he would connect with the czar's engineers running their own line east from Moscow. Beyond Moscow: Berlin, Paris, London. Hiram Sibley was going to wire the world.[10]

And so it was that on May 27, 1861, a train of more than two hundred oxen, twenty-six wagons, and fifty men set out from Sacramento, onto the Central Overland Trail and across the Sierra, laden with coils of high-grade copper wire and crates of glass insulators shipped from back East. Hundreds of contractors had preceded them—those mule drivers along the Carson, for instance—to scour remote valleys for pole material. The route itself was mostly treeless, but they dragged trunks dozens or even hundreds of miles to it: the mighty Western Union bringing Birnam Wood to Dunsinane.[11]

A few weeks later, at Fort Churchill, they raised the first pole, to the top of which they had nailed an American flag. Tossing hats into the air, the men hailed this moment with a chorus of huzzas: three cheers for the telegraph and three cheers for the Union.[12]

"THERE ARE GRAVE DOUBTS at the hugeness of the land and whether one government can comprehend the whole."[13]

So wrote Henry Adams in 1861, fretting over whether the sundered Union could—or even should—be restored. But young Adams, though he may have been to Naples and dined with Garibaldi, had never seen Nevada or supped with the likes of Hiram Sibley, let alone with sutlers and stagecoach drivers. (He had rarely been west of Cambridge, Massachusetts, actually.) He and many other Easterners knew little, really, of what the Union was—of what it had become. It had grown and changed too quickly. And a large share of that growth and change was happening beyond the Mississippi.

The West was also the chessboard in the Great Game between North and South. For decades, each new expansion of the country had set off a flurry of tactical moves: advances, flanking maneuvers, sometimes grudging withdrawals. Each new line across the map—whether territorial boundary, national road, railway, or telegraph route—threatened to redraw the entire board, or so it often seemed. Sometimes the slave-state interests advanced; sometimes the free-state. More often, as with so much in the antebellum years, each set of moves ended in a carefully negotiated stalemate.

Recently, however, the game had seemed to tilt decisively toward the North. Eighteen sixty was a federal census year, and the results had begun coming in early that autumn—with exquisitely poor timing, as far as Southern paranoia and Northern presumptuousness was concerned.[14] Preliminary figures confirmed what many suspected: that immigration and westward expansion were shifting the country's centers of population and balance of power. Since the last count, in 1850, the North's population had increased an astonishing 41 percent, while the South's had grown only 27 percent. States like Michigan, Wisconsin, Iowa, and Illinois would each be gaining multiple seats in Congress; Virginia, South Carolina, and Tennessee would be losing some. Tellingly, the statistical center of national population had shifted for the first time not only west of the original thirteen states but also from slave territory into free: from Virginia to Ohio. (The *New York Herald* did find at least one source of comfort for the South: the paper's statistician declared it "very certain" that the nation's slave population would reach nearly fifty million by the year 1969.)[15]

Southern leaders did not lack for an expansionist strategy of their own in the years before the war. The more radical among them spoke of spreading American dominion through Latin America and the Caribbean, forming dozens of new slave states. The filibusters, as we have seen, even took matters into their own hands. In fact, there were occasional successes—and splendid ones—as when Southern planters moved into the Mexican state of Texas, eventually to take it over and annex it to the United States. The ensuing war added vast new territory to the southern half of the country, and many assumed that slavery would be legal there.

Nor did the South lack its own Hiram Sibleys, its own tough and resourceful breed of capitalists. But its Sibleys, by and large, did not invest in building railroads and telegraph lines: instead, they bought slaves and cleared new land for cotton.

All too often, the most visionary schemes for the West ended up stalled endlessly in Congress, victims of sectional infighting. Such was the case with the transcontinental railroad, an idea that had been under discussion for twenty years. Each time it came up for debate, Northerners refused to approve a Southern route and Southerners refused to approve a Northern route. When Congress did finally vote to fund a survey, it reached a compromise by sending out five separate expeditions to find suitable pathways at five different latitudes. Not surprisingly, the man who supervised this entire process—Secretary of War Jefferson Davis—was able to recommend the southernmost one, fudging a bit of data to support his argument. (Davis had already managed to orchestrate a major U.S. land acquisition from Mexico—the Gadsden Purchase—to serve as a southern corridor.)* Not surprisingly, Northern congressmen balked at this, and by the end of the 1850s, the rail line to the Pacific was still nothing more than a figment of the American imagination.[16]

As anxious as Southerners were to extend slavery through the Union's new states and territories, Northerners were anxious to contain it. The Hiram Sibleys may not have cared much about the plight of the poor downtrodden Negroes, but their own financial interests did demand a West that was free, open, modern, untrammeled—a place, in short, where Yankees could do business. They were damned if they were going to let the Southern oligarchs, with their canting talk of chivalry and their pretensions to aristocratic grandeur, stand in their way.

Now, in early 1861, the game had suddenly changed. It would be played in Congress no longer: the Southerners had called forfeit and gone home in a huff. Already, in the first few months of that year, Kansas had been admitted as a free state and Colorado, Dakota, and Nevada as free territories. An Illinois railroad lawyer was in the White House, and everyone expected that the long-blocked pathway to the Pacific would soon be open for business.

As the Civil War began, a new game opened on the chessboard of the West. There were two key places where it might be won or lost: one on the shores of the Pacific, the other on the banks of the Mis-

*Expedition leaders named an especially prickly new species of hedgehog cactus *Opuntia davisii* in honor of the secretary of war.

sissippi. It would be decided in one of these places with words; in the
other, with guns.

FROM HER VERANDA, the Pathfinder's wife watched the sun vanish between the two great western headlands, leaving America behind
until next dawn. She loved this place more than any other that she had
ever known, either on this continent or in her wide travels abroad. Her
quaint Gothic cottage commanded all of Black Point, the finest spot
on the whole bay, with dark thickets of scrub oak and laurel covering
steep hillsides that sloped down to a sandy beach. She had recently
built the porch around three sides of the house, laid out gardens and
gravel paths, and planted climbing rosebushes and trellised vines. She
took joy even in the tolling of the fog bells on oceanbound vessels, and
in the night beacon that flashed on the harbor fort: "my night light,"
she called it. When the wind was off the bay, she claimed, she could
hear the flapping of sails on the schooners as they rounded the point,
and the swearing of captains pacing their decks.[17]

But Jessie Benton Frémont could also look out at this wide,
God-given landscape and almost believe that she and her family had
brought it all into being, had conjured the ships and the fort and the
bay—and a prospering American city whose growth was the marvel
of the entire world—as surely as she had planted the clambering roses.

Her father, the legendary Senator Thomas Hart Benton of Missouri, had fought for three decades in Congress to advance his vision
of a transcontinental American empire, the grand historical culmination that Providence and nature had foreordained. As long ago as 1818,
he had written:

> Europe discharges her inhabitants upon America; America
> pours her population from east to west. . . . All obey the same
> impulse—*that of going to the West*, which, from the beginning of
> time, has been the course of the heavenly bodies, of the human
> race, and of science, civilization, and national power following in
> their train. Soon the Rocky Mountains will be passed, and the
> "children of Adam" will have completed their circumnavigation
> of the globe.[18]

After the American imperium had extended itself to the shores of the
Pacific, he said, it would reach farther yet, to East Asia, as "science,
liberal principles in government, and the true religion . . . cast their

lights across the intervening sea," while the newly liberated masses of China and Japan poured forth eastward, in turn, to settle the valley of the Columbia River. This empire, Benton said, would advance not by military conquest but by peaceful commerce, bringing in train universal principles of enlightenment. The senator championed his cause with all the tenacity and toughness to be expected of a man who had once gotten into a gunfight with Andrew Jackson, and had slain another opponent in a duel with pistols at three yards.[19]

Jessie's husband, Colonel John C. Frémont, had—in the eyes of many Americans—made her father's dream a reality. From the upper Mississippi to the southwestern deserts, he had mapped a quarter of the North American continent, gathering a wealth of geographical and scientific knowledge that made Lewis and Clark's contributions look meager in comparison. He had opened highways to the Pacific, and planted the Stars and Stripes on the highest peak in the Rockies.[20] He had led United States forces into California and captured the state for the Union. He had reached the wild shore of this bay, looked out at those very headlands that his wife now gazed at from her porch, and given the rocky portal a name: the Golden Gate.

Jessie Frémont took perhaps even greater pride in being the human link between the dream and the land; the senator and the soldier. In many respects, she was more remarkable than either of the two men. Jessie had inherited all of her father's toughness or even more: President Buchanan once called her, admiringly or not, "the square root of Tom Benton." She had a cooler head and sharper wits than the old senator, though—and was a more brilliant politician, philosopher, and strategist than her soldier husband. A better writer, too: she had taken the dry data of the colonel's expeditions and crafted them into literary epics of the American West, official government reports that became best sellers and made her husband a national hero.* (Some even went so far as to say that Jessie Frémont had made her husband what he was.) Her own vision of the West—unlike her father's baroque fantasies—was clean, compelling, and modern. "How can I tell all that

---

*Joaquin Miller, later a great Western poet, was then a boy on an Ohio farm; he would later remember his father reading him Frémont's reports aloud: "I never was so fascinated. I never grew so fast in my life. . . . I fancied I could see Frémont's men, hauling cannon up the savage battlements of the Rocky Mountains, flags in the air, Frémont at the head, waving his sword, his horse neighing wildly in the mountain wind. . . . Now I began to be inflamed with a love for action, adventure, glory, and great deeds away out yonder under the path of the setting sun." Leonard L. Richards, *The California Gold Rush and the Coming of the Civil War* (New York, 2007), p. 47.

the name, California, represents?" she once wrote, reflecting on her time there before the war. "If our East has a life of yesterday, and the [Midwest] of to-day, then here *to-morrow* had come. . . . What a dream of daring young energy—of possibility—of certainties—of burdens dropped and visions realized!"[21]

Burdens dropped and visions realized. Senator Benton and the two Frémonts were all Southerners, from slaveholding families, who had reinvented themselves as Westerners and in the process had become foes of slavery. How could human bondage coexist with the Western dream? The old man, though he owned slaves until the day he died, had made no secret of his distaste for the "peculiar institution," and ultimately sacrificed his political career to his conscience.[22] His daughter went considerably further. In 1849, California's new territorial legislature debated whether to allow slavery; some settlers from the South had brought their slaves with them, while many others had visions of gold mines worked by black and Indian bondmen. Jessie Frémont made her home the command center for the opposition, presiding at the dinner table—in the absence of her husband, usually—plotting strategy with the men.

Once she even invited fifteen proslavery lawmakers to her house to debate them single-handedly. Having received a piece of her mind, one of them replied dismissively, "Fine sentiment, Mrs. Frémont, but the aristocracy will always have slaves."

"But why not an aristocracy of emancipators?" she retorted. "It isn't a pretty sight in a free country for a child to see and hear chain gangs clanking through the streets."

The legislature voted to keep California free. A few months later, the debate was carried to Washington, when Congress considered statehood for the fast-growing territory. Jefferson Davis argued in the Senate that slavery was part of California's natural destiny: "It was to work the gold mines on this continent that the Spaniards first brought Africans to the country. The European races now engaged in working the mines of California sink under the burning heat and sudden changes of climate, to which the African race are altogether better adapted." In the end, though, Washington ratified the verdict already reached in Sacramento.[23]

In 1856, the Frémonts carried their antislavery ideals into the national arena. When the new Republican Party sought its first presidential nominee, it was John C. Frémont who—with considerable prodding from his wife—agreed to run, under the slogan "Free Speech, Free Soil, Free Men, Frémont." Unlike any previous candidate's wife in American history, Jessie figured prominently in the campaign (more than her soft-spoken husband, some critics would snipe). Republican marchers waved banners reading FRÉMONT AND JESSIE, and women, shockingly, joined these political demonstrations, wearing violets—Mrs. Frémont's favorite flower—pinned to their bosoms. When the colonel addressed his supporters, they often insisted that his wife step forward to wave and smile as well. Despite his loss to Buchanan, many staunch Republicans still thought him a better man than Lincoln, a more steadfast foe of the slave power.[24]

But here in California, slavery's supporters—though thwarted since Congress had declared it a free state—had never conceded defeat.

In early 1861, as Jessie Frémont looked out from her veranda over San Francisco Bay, her dream of the West, of a free American empire stretching from ocean to ocean, seemed to be in peril. Texas had already been lost to the Confederacy despite the valiant efforts of Governor Sam Houston, her father's old friend, who had been evicted from office after refusing to betray his country. The immense territory of New Mexico, then also encompassing what is now Arizona and part of Nevada, was leaning the same way. Much closer to Black Point, in the city just east of the sand dunes, men were plotting to detach California from the Union, too. Some reports had it that the island fort just opposite the Frémonts' cottage—the walled citadel of Alcatraz—might fall at any moment into enemy hands. Rumblings of disloyalty, and of secret plots, were being felt throughout the state.

Though California may officially have been free territory, its political leadership was still dominated by Southern sympathizers—voters called them the Chivalry faction, or the Chivs. No Northern state had more draconian laws restricting the lives and rights of its black inhabitants.[25] Moreover, it seemed to many citizens, even those with little fondness for the South, that only the most tenuous threads bound their state to the Union. California lay as far from the old Eastern states as could be; the quickest route from one American coast to the other was via a perilous sea voyage of four thousand nautical miles aboard a cramped steamer, with an overland trek across the Isthmus of Panama midway. (And this was affordable only for relatively well-heeled travelers; ordinary emigrants had to try their luck on the overland trails.) Many of the Gold Rush settlers were rootless adventurers who felt no particular loyalty to any piece of land except those on which they'd staked their mining claims up in the hills. Thousands upon thousands of foreigners had been drawn to the region, too: Europeans, East Asians, and Latin Americans, many of whom had simply come to scoop up Yankee dollars before heading home, and whose allegiances were still with Prussia, or China, or Chile. Two other significant populations, the Mormons and the Mexicans, had every reason to hate the United States, a nation that had quite recently defeated them on the battlefield.[26]

As Jessie Frémont herself recognized, California felt like a place wholly new. Why, then—a great many Californians reasoned—should it not be its own nation? Let the old states fight their old battles; this distant shore would turn its face away, toward its own destiny. The dream of a Pacific Republic had flickered for decades; now—with the word *pacific* taking on a newly ironic double meaning—the moment seemed more opportune than ever.[27]

In fact, most of the state's political leaders had already endorsed the idea of lowering the Stars and Stripes and running up the Bear Flag in the event that the United States split apart. Back in early 1860, then-governor John B. Weller predicted to the legislature that Californians "will not go with the North or the South, but here on the shores of the Pacific found a mighty republic, which may in the end prove the greatest of all." All of the state's senators and representatives had voiced similar ideas in Congress at one time or another, though they often retreated coyly when it seemed politically convenient. In the wake of Lincoln's election, Congressman John Burch declared that if war came, Californians should "raise aloft the flag of the 'Bear,' surrounded with the 'hydra' pointed cactus of the Western wilds, and call upon the enlightened nations of the earth to acknowledge our independence . . . [as] the youthful but vigorous *Caesarian* Republic of the Pacific."[28]

Burch hailed from slaveholding Missouri, but Governor Weller was a native Ohioan. In fact, not all Californians who desired independence sympathized with the South. Some—with eyes accustomed to picking out flecks of ore amid the gravel—saw opportunities glittering in the wreckage of the old republic. The *San Francisco Herald*, the city's Democratic newspaper, conjured alluring visions of a vast new transpacific trading empire. Detachment from the Eastern states, it suggested, would inspire Californians to reach out westward, toward China, Japan, Australia, and the South Sea islands. A neutral California's merchant ships would—unlike those of the Union and Confederacy—be immune to blockades and privateers, and thus capture the older states' overseas trade. Countless refugees from the war-torn East would move westward, bringing with them not only a new era of prosperity, but perhaps also the once-cherished ideals that had been trampled upon and broken in the United States. As the American republic had been for Europe, so the California republic would be for America. "Let California," the editor enthused, "become the home of the oppressed, the temple of liberty; the resting place of those who seek the blessings of peace rather than the questionable glories of war."[29]

Other Californians, less grandiose of temperament, simply didn't want to be bothered with the East Coast politicians and their incessant wrangling. "We don't care a straw whether you dissolve the Union or not," a settler from Maine named Frank Buck wrote to his sister back home. "We just wish that the Republicans and Democrats in the Capital would get into a fight and kill each other all off like the Kilkenny cats. Perhaps that would settle the hash."[30]

Buck lived up in Weaverville, a gold-mining settlement in the mountains of far-Northern California. Hundreds of miles away, among the cattle ranches and roughneck towns in the southern part of the state, people had somewhat less dismissive feelings about the unpleasantness back East. "Our emigration comes from the South; our population are of the South, and sympathize with her," wrote the editor of the *Los Angeles Star.* "Why, then, should we turn our backs on our friends, and join her enemies?" Militia companies of dubious allegiance sprang up among the pueblos; rusty sabers and muskets disappeared mysteriously from the state arsenals to resurface a few weeks later in private hands, gleaming beyond all recognition. In San Bernardino—a village of a thousand or so Mormons and Southerners—people openly cursed the Stars and Stripes.[31]

And throughout the state that winter and spring, certain ambitious men began to plot a masterstroke that would sever California from the Union with a single blow.

One of these men was a handsome young Kentuckian with a name out of comic opera: Asbury Harpending. He had come west through a series of picaresque adventures, running away from school at the age of fifteen to join William Walker's ill-fated filibustering expedition in Nicaragua. Failing to get as far as New Orleans before the federal authorities thwarted his plans, Harpending set out for California with nothing but a revolver and a five-dollar gold piece. Like so many enterprising youths, he went on to make a fortune in mining. But he never entirely gave up his dreams of derring-do. The approach of civil war seemed to bring with it an opportunity for another filibustering expedition of sorts—this one against his own country.[32]

One evening, Harpending was summoned to a meeting at the home of a wealthy San Franciscan. The house was in an isolated spot, he later recalled, and its owner "lived alone, with only Asiatic attendants, who understood little English and cared less for what was going on." One of these "soft-footed" servants ushered Harpending into a large room where about thirty young gentlemen—most of them wealthy, all of them Southern—awaited. That night, they swore a secret oath. Each man would assemble a small fighting force, an easy enough task, as Harpending later recalled, since "California at that period abounded with reckless human material—ex-veterans of the Mexican War, ex-filibusters, ex–Indian fighters, all eager to engage in any undertaking that promised adventure and profit." The freebooter units would then converge on Alcatraz, seizing the island, the arsenal at Benicia with its 30,000 stand of arms, and other key points. With that accomplished, they would proclaim a Pacific Republic and organize "an army of Southern sympathizers, sufficient in number to beat down any armed resistance." One particular fact made the plotters especially confident of success: the highest-ranking officer of the U.S. Army at San Francisco—in fact, the commander of the entire Department of the Pacific—was General Albert Sidney Johnston, a known Southern sympathizer and veteran of the Texas Revolution.[33]

Harpending wrote his version of the story as an old man, more than half a century later, and some of its details—those soft-footed Asiatics, for instance—seem rather more cinematic than perfectly true. Still, there is no question that in 1861, California was rife with secret pro-Southern groups, organizations with names like the Knights of the Columbian Star and the Knights of the Golden Circle. (The latter referred to the filibusters' long-held dream of ruling a slaveholding empire encircling the Gulf of Mexico, and including the American South and Southwest, the Caribbean, and much of Latin America.) Police detectives' reports revealed elaborate codes, rituals, signs, and countersigns—enough to leave loyal Californians badly spooked. Thus, a few hundred Knights multiplied, at least in the popular imagination, into a hundred thousand.[34]

Nothing seemed safe that spring, not even the rock-solid fortress at the center of San Francisco Bay. "We felt as though we were upon a volcano of social disruption," one Unionist later remembered, "and . . . that the guns of Alcatraz might signal us at any moment to throw up our hands."[35]

But even as the would-be founders of the Pacific Republic conspired among themselves, a counterplot of sorts was being hatched—this one in Mrs. Frémont's front garden.

THOUSANDS OF MILES from San Francisco Bay, at the West's opposite gateway—St. Louis, Missouri—two civilians sat disconsolately at the sidelines of the war.

One had recently taken a desk job running St. Louis's horse-drawn trolley line. He spent most of his days pushing papers, trying his hardest to concentrate on the minutiae of fare revenues and fodder costs, in an office permeated with pungent aromas from the company's adjacent stables. The other man was a visitor to town, a down-at-the-heels shop clerk from Illinois, who had come in search of an officer's commission. He camped out at his in-laws' house, trudging around the city each day, fruitlessly trying to attract the attention of the local military authorities.[36]

The trolley-car executive was named William Tecumseh Sherman. The luckless clerk was Ulysses S. Grant.

Of all the places where these two men could have found themselves, St. Louis was perhaps the one where war loomed largest. The leading city in one of the nation's most populous slaveholding states, St. Louis was a military prize like no other. Not only the largest settlement beyond the Appalachians, it was also the country's second-largest port, commanding the Mississippi as well as the Missouri River, the great waterway to the Rockies, then navigable as far upstream as what is now the state of Montana. It was also the eastern gateway of the overland trails to California, Oregon, and the Southwest. Last but far from least, the city was home to the Jefferson Barracks, the largest military installation in the entire United States, and to the St. Louis Arsenal, the biggest cache of federal arms in the South.[37]

Whoever held St. Louis truly held the key to the whole American West. And, in contrast to what was brewing in California, the struggle for the West in Missouri was in the open, it was armed, and it was about to explode into full-blown violence.

But it was not yet Grant's or Sherman's Civil War in the spring of 1861. During this opening act, the two future titans were fated to watch from offstage. It was not yet time for the clashes of great armies, for columns of conscripts trudging across the ruined landscape of the South. Instead, the struggle for Missouri was a civil war in the truest and rawest sense, resembling those fought in our own time in such places as Beirut and Baghdad: gun battles in the streets, long-simmering ethnic hatreds boiling over, and wailing mothers cradling slain children in their arms. It was also quite literally a revolution—but with the Union side, not the Confederates, as the rebels.

The Union revolutionaries who would soon fight the battle for Missouri were drilling clandestinely by night in beer halls, factories, and gymnasiums, barricading the windows and spreading sawdust on the floor to muffle the sound of their stomping boots. Young brewery

workers and trolley drivers, middle-aged tavern keepers and wholesale merchants, were learning to bear and aim guns, to wheel squads
left and right in the proper American fashion. Most of the younger
men handled the weapons awkwardly, but quite a few of the older
ones swung them with the ease of having been soldiers once before,
in another country, long ago. Sometimes, when their movements hit
a perfect synchrony, when their muffled tread beat a single cadence,
they threw caution aside and sang out. Just a few of the older men
would begin, more and more men joining in until dozens swelled the
chorus, half singing, half shouting verses they had carried with them
from across the sea:

> *Die wilde Jagd, und die Deutsche Jagd,*
> *Auf Henkersblut und Tyrannen!*
> *Drum, die ihr uns liebt, nicht geweint und geklagt;*
> *Das Land ist ja frei, und der Morgen tagt,*
> *Wenn wir's auch nur sterbend gewannen!**

There were two distinct Missouris in 1861: an old and a new.

The old flourished in the central counties of the state, in the rich
alluvial lands between the Mississippi and the Missouri rivers. Here,
in the early decades of the century, had come settlers from the seaboard South: enterprising young Marylanders and Virginians who had
forsaken the exhausted acreage of their ancestral plantations, rounded
up the able-bodied field hands, and marched them in shackled droves
through the Cumberland Gap. Others made the journey from Kentucky and Tennessee, moving southwestward with the frontier, as
their mothers and fathers had done before. Land could be had for
twenty-five cents an acre, and, after the slaves had cleared it, there
were abundant yields of cotton, tobacco, and hemp. These earliest set-

---

*The wild hunt, the German hunt,/For hangmen's blood and for tyrants!/O dear-
est ones, weep not for us:/The land is free, the morning dawns,/Even though we
won it in dying!

This song, "*Lützows wilde Jagd,*" dated from the German struggle against Napoleon in 1812–13 and had also been popular during the revolutions of 1848. Baron
von Lützow was the dashing commander of a German cavalry corps. The description of the St. Louis volunteers singing "Lützows wilde Jagd" is in Heinrich Börnstein (Henry Boernstein), *Memoirs of a Nobody: The Missouri Years of an Austrian
Radical*, ed. and trans. by Steven Rowan (St. Louis, 1997), pp. 284–85. The German
lyrics are from Lisa Feurzeig, ed., *Deutsche Lieder für Jung und Alt* (Middleton,
Wisc., 2002), p. 96.

tlers had agitated for Missouri's admission as a slave state, and after the Compromise of 1820 settled the matter, more followed. Although there were few large plantations, the region became known as Little Dixie.[38] Planters and small farmers sent their crops to market in nearby St. Louis, a frontier town of wood-frame houses that the early French colonists had built.[39]

As the Civil War began, Little Dixie still flourished as it had for the past half century. But St. Louis, in that time, had changed beyond all recognition. Here and there, a quaint French colonial house still tottered picturesquely, but most had given way to block after block of redbrick monotony: warehouses, manufacturing plants, and office buildings, stretching for miles along the bluffs above the river. Each year, more than four thousand steamboats shouldered up to the wharves, vessels with names like *War Eagle, Champion, Belle of Memphis,* and *Big St. Louis.* The smoke from their coal-fired furnaces mingled with the thick black clouds belching from factory smokestacks, so that on windless days the sun shone feebly through a dark canopy that hung above the entire city.[40]

More and more Northerners were coming to this new Missouri, attracted by the opportunities of booming industry—both wealthy businessmen and poor but hopeful laborers. So alarmed were the "old" Missourians by the influx that one Virginia-born judge suggested, only half in jest, that the state legislature pass a law barring Yankees from crossing the Mississippi. When asked how the ban could be enforced, he suggested that ferrymen require all their passengers to pronounce the word *cow*—anyone replying "keow" would be banished forever to the Illinois side of the river.[41]

But it was a wave of newcomers from even farther afield that was truly transforming the face of St. Louis. Beginning in the 1840s, German and other central European immigrants poured into the city, attracted at first by a pioneer propagandist named Gottfried Duden, who described the Mississippi Valley as a kind of American Rhineland: just as romantic, but with lusher vegetation and a milder climate, both politically and meteorologically. This may not have been quite accurate, but by the time Duden's countrymen made the trek and realized as much, the migration had taken on a momentum of its own. By 1861, a visitor to many parts of the city might indeed have thought he was somewhere east of Aachen. "Here we hear the German tongue, or rather the German *dialect*, everywhere," one Landsmann enthused. Certainly you would hear it in places like Tony Niederwiesser's Tivoli beer garden on Third Street, where Sunday-afternoon regulars quaffed lager while Sauter's or Vogel's orchestra played waltzes and sentimental tunes from the old country. You would hear it in Henry Boernstein's St. Louis Opera House on Market Street, where the house company celebrated Friedrich Schiller's centennial in 1859 by performing the master's theatrical works for a solid week. You would hear it in the newspaper offices of the competing dailies *Anzeiger des Westens* and *Westliche Post*, as well as the weekly *Mississippi Blätter*. You would hear it even in public school classrooms, where the children of immigrants received instruction in the mother tongue.[42]

St. Louis was still officially slave territory, of course. Indeed, it was here that Dred Scott—"the best known colored person in the world," locals liked to boast—had sued for his freedom; here that his widow and daughters still lived in an alleyway just off Franklin Avenue.* Mrs. Scott and her children were free, though—as were most black St. Louisans. The number of slaves in the city had dwindled to fewer than two thousand, or less than 1 percent of the population. Local politicians—even some who owned a few slaves themselves—were calling for the state to enact gradual emancipation. It would be good for business, they said; it would lure even more Yankee capital to town.[43]

No wonder that when cotton growers from Little Dixie came into the city they sometimes felt as though they were in an alien country. Yet Missouri as a whole still lay firmly in the political grasp of such men: the Southern planters, the slaveholders, the aristocratic scions of old French colonial families. As a bloc, they and their supporters far outnumbered the German newcomers, and in the early months of 1861, as their sister states seceded one by one around them, these men naturally assumed that it was they who would decide Missouri's fate.

In January, the state had sworn in a new governor. Claiborne Fox Jackson was a poker playing, horse trading, Little Dixie planter who had once led armed Border Ruffians into neighboring Kansas to keep it from becoming a free state. Better just to let the Indian savages keep Kansas forever, Jackson had once said, since "they are better neighbors than the abolitionists, *by a damn sight.*"[44]

---

*Dred Scott and his family had been freed just after their case ended; their master had become embarrassed by all the publicity. Scott took a position at Barnum's Hotel (owned by the circus impresario's cousin), where his job was simply to welcome arriving guests, as a kind of celebrity greeter. He enjoyed his freedom for barely a year: he died in 1858 and was buried in an unmarked grave in the city's Wesleyan Cemetery. His widow, Harriet, remained in St. Louis and supported herself as a laundress, living until 1876.

Officially, Jackson was neutral on secession, reassuring everyone that the ultimate decision would be up to the citizens of Missouri. But in his inaugural address, he made his leanings clear enough. "The weight of Kentucky or Missouri, thrown into the scale," could tip the balance nationally from the Union to the Confederacy, the governor said. And should the federal government try to coerce the seceding states, he warned, "Missouri will not be found to shrink from the duty which her position upon the border imposes: her honor, her interests, and her sympathies point alike in one direction, and determine her *to stand by the South*." (Judging by the printed sources, Jackson seems to have been a man who spoke frequently in italics.) One of the governor's first acts in office was to secure legislative approval for a statewide convention to determine where Missouri would pledge her loyalties and her considerable resources. To leave the Union would require a statewide referendum. But neither the Governor nor the legislature seemed to have the slightest doubt about which way the convention—or Missouri's citizenry—would vote. The delegates certainly seemed like a reliable enough group: some four-fifths of them were slaveholders. They gathered first in Jefferson City, the state's tiny capital, and then, seeking better hotel accommodations, moved to St. Louis.[45]

The gentlemen did indeed find the creature comforts of the metropolis far more satisfactory. In every other respect, however, the move to St. Louis was the worst strategic blunder that the hard-core Jacksonites could have ventured. For they arrived in a city that was tense, frightened, and divided—and whose inhabitants were arming themselves not just for secession, not just to preserve the Union, but for an all-out ethnic war.

Almost since their first arrival, the Germans of St. Louis had been a class apart politically as well as culturally. Many had left their native land to escape not only poverty but also the reactionary regimes that ruled Germany's claustrophobic labyrinth of tiny duchies and principalities. Arriving in the United States, they rejoiced in the expansive landscape, in the freedom of expression, and in the spirit of a nation whose watchword, they had been told, was liberty.

And they almost immediately fell afoul of their new American neighbors. In 1836, when a black St. Louis man was accused of murdering a police officer, a group of whites seized the prisoner from the city jail, manacled him to a tree at the corner of Seventh and Locust, and burned him alive before a large crowd of spectators. The next day, the shocked editor of the city's recently established German-language newspaper, the *Anzeiger des Westens*, denounced the atrocity. "Citizens of St. Louis!" he wrote. "The stain with which your city was defiled last night can never be erased."

Citizens of St. Louis promptly taught him a lesson. Several hundred of them gathered as an angry mob outside the *Anzeiger*'s office, and only with difficulty were restrained from committing another lynching. The next morning's issue of the St. Louis *Commercial Bulletin*, a leading English-language newspaper, chastised the editor for insulting in an "unjust manner the whole community."[46]

But the newcomers were not to be intimidated so easily. Over the succeeding years, as their ranks swelled, they grew ever bolder and more outspoken. In 1848 and 1849, the steady flow of arrivals became a flood as Germans, Austrians, Czechs, Poles, and Hungarians fled the aftermath of the failed liberal revolutions across Europe. Among those it swept into St. Louis was Franz Sigel, the daring military commander of insurgent forces in the Baden uprising, comrade of Louis Kossuth and Giuseppe Mazzini; in his new homeland, Sigel became a teacher of German and school superintendent. Another political refugee was Isidor Bush, a Prague-born Jew and publisher of revolutionary tracts in Vienna, who settled down in St. Louis as a respected wine merchant, railroad executive, and city councilman—as well as, somewhat more discreetly, a leader of the local abolitionists.*

Most prominent among all the *Achtundvierziger*—the Forty-Eighters, as they styled themselves—was a colorful Austrian émigré named Heinrich Börnstein. Whether Börnstein was a hero or a scoundrel depended on whom you asked. In Europe he had been a soldier in the imperial army, an actor, a director—and, most notably, an editor. During a sojourn in Paris, he launched a weekly journal called *Vorwärts!*, which published antireligious screeds, poetry by Heine, and some of the first "scientific socialist" writings of Karl Marx and Friedrich Engels. When Börnstein helped organize a German Legion to aid the 1848 revolution, things became a bit hot for him with the Parisian authorities, and he prudently decamped. In America he became Henry Boernstein: homeopathic physician, saloonkeeper, brewer, pharmacist, theatrical impresario, hotel owner, novelist—and, naturally, political agitator. After purchasing the ever more influential *Anzeiger des Westens* in 1850, he swung the paper even harder to the left. Though he may have cut a somewhat eccentric figure around town, with his flam-

---

*Bush tried at first to continue his publishing career in America by launching a Jewish literary and philosophical journal, *Israels Herold*, but this quickly proved unprofitable, since St. Louis in the 1840s had only about a hundred Jews.

boyant clothing and a pair of Mitteleuropean side-whiskers that would have put Emperor Franz Josef to shame, Boernstein was a force to be reckoned with in St. Louis, a man both admired and hated.[47]

For such men, and even for their less radical compatriots, Missouri's slaveholding class represented exactly what they had detested in the old country, exactly what they had come here to escape: a swaggering clique of landed oligarchs, boorish aristocrats obstructing the forces of modernity and progress. By contrast, the Germans prided themselves on being, as an *Anzeiger* editorial rather smugly put it, "filled with more intensive concepts of freedom, with more expansive notions of humanity, than most peoples of the earth"—more imbued with true democratic spirit, indeed more American, than the Americans themselves. Such presumption did not exactly endear them to longtime St. Louisans. The city's leading Democratic newspaper excoriated the Forty-Eighters as infidels, anarchists, fanatics, socialists— "all Robespierres, Dantons, and Saint-Justs, red down to their very kidneys." Clearly these Germans were godless, too: one need only walk downtown on a Sunday afternoon to see them drinking beer, dancing, and flocking to immoral plays in their theaters—flagrantly violating not just the commandments of God but the city ordinances of St. Louis.[48]

Few if any of the city fathers were prepared, however, to risk enforcing the blue laws. Those beer drinkers and theatergoers had become a powerful voting bloc. Many Missouri Germans cast their first votes for Thomas Hart Benton, when the old maverick—not unmindful of demographic shifts in his home state—steered toward populism. Then they rallied to the new Republican Party. Their special hero in 1856 was John C. Frémont. Here was a leader in the true style of the Forty-Eighters: no dough-faced politician but a dashing idealist, a man of action, a bearded paladin. (That Colonel Frémont happened to be the illegitimate son of a French mural painter only enhanced his Romantic cachet.) It was with somewhat less enthusiasm that they would unite behind Lincoln four years later—split rails held little charm for the acolytes of Goethe and Hegel. But support from intellectuals like Boernstein encouraged them: the editor, who was fast becoming one of Missouri's top Republican power brokers, hailed his party's nominee, in proper *Achtundvierzigerisch* terms, as "the man who will see his way through a great struggle yet to come, the struggle with the most dangerous and ruthless enemy of freedom."[49]

A few months later, the Wide Awake craze reached St. Louis. Capes! Torches! Secret meetings! It was just like the good old days back in

Dresden and Heidelberg. Before long, Germans by the thousands were joining up, and relishing the opportunity to get back into fighting trim. One of the local movement's leaders (discreetly writing in the third person) later recalled:

> From their headquarters . . . the *Wide Awakes* marched in procession to the places of appointed political gatherings, and while the meeting continued, (if at night,) each man, with a lighted lamp placed securely on the end of a heavy stick, stationed himself on the outside of the assembled crowd, thus depriving ruffianly opponents of their hiding-places in the dark. At the first two meetings which the *Wide Awakes* thus attended, the enemy, not understanding the *purposes* of the club, began their usual serenade of yells and cheers, but they were speedily initiated into the mysteries of the new order; which initiation consisted in being besmeared with burning camphene, and vigorously beaten with leaded sticks. The least sign of disorderly conduct was the signal for an assault upon the offender, and if he escaped unmaimed he was lucky indeed.[50]

The national Republican establishment was quick to exploit this touching display of pro-Lincoln sentiment in the heart of a slave state. William Seward hastened to the city and, from the balcony of his hotel room, addressed a crowd of Wide Awakes who had come to serenade him by torchlight. The master politician—forearmed, as usual, with flattery specific to his audience—exulted: "Missouri is Germanizing herself to make herself free." (Frederick Douglass had already expressed similar enthusiasm: "A German only has to be a German to be utterly opposed to slavery," he wrote.)[51]

Of all those attempting to harness the unruly energy of St. Louis's Wide Awake Germans, none was more assiduous or effective than Francis Preston Blair, Jr. The younger brother of Montgomery Blair—Lincoln's postmaster general, and his cabinet's strongest proponent of defending Fort Sumter—thirty-nine-year-old Frank Blair, a former protégé of Senator Benton, had won a seat in Congress as a Missouri Republican. Although publicly opposed to slavery (he favored resettling the nation's blacks as a new American colony somewhere in Central America), Blair was first and foremost a narrow-eyed opportunist, a tireless strategist for his own sake and for that of his vast web of kin by blood and marriage, a network whose nerve center was the family's Washington mansion, which faced the White House across

Pennsylvania Avenue. His canny instincts told him early on that secession and civil war were inevitable. In the Wide Awakes of St. Louis, he saw not a constituency of any national electoral importance—there was no way that Lincoln could carry Missouri anyhow—but rather a personal power base, a legion of Republican centurions who might march at his back through the chaotic days to come.[52]

Blair made sure that the Wide Awake clubs did not disband after the election. By Christmas, in fact, rumor had it—correctly, for once—that he was starting to arm them with Sharps rifles provided by certain unofficial sources in the East. (Some of the Germans' new weaponry arrived hidden, appropriately enough, in empty beer barrels shipped to Tony Niederwiesser's saloon and others.) Under the supervision of General Sigel, and with veterans of the Prussian officer corps acting as instructors, they began their clandestine drills, practicing with wooden muskets when they lacked real ones. St. Louis, however, was not a place where such things could be kept secret for long. By early March, Democratic papers carried reports of a terrifying new battalion known as the Black Jaegers (it sounded even more horrible in German, the *Unabhängige Schwarzer Jägerkorps*), allegedly so named because they would fight under a black flag, signifying no quarter to their foes.[53]

The Jaegers' foes, for their part, were not sitting idly by. The secessionists formed their own force of armed Minute Men—"the grimmest of German-haters," Boernstein called them—establishing a headquarters in the old Berthold mansion at the corner of Fifth and Pine. Many of the city's old-line militia groups affiliated themselves with the new organization. Unlike Blair's forces, the Minute Men had little need for secrecy. On February 13, in fact, they were officially mustered en masse into the Missouri State Guard—a clear signal of Governor Jackson's intentions, in case anyone was still in doubt.[54]

Democratic newspapers fanned the flames more vigorously than ever against "the Red Republicans or Infidel Germans," the " 'fugitives from justice' of foreign lands, who by some trickery have become citizens of our country." Abolitionist fanatics were concocting some dark plot, one editor warned, and "the German population of our city are to be used as the means for carrying out the objects of the dastard enterprise." Ordinary Missourians used more direct language: along with the usual racial epithets, "Damn Dutch," a corruption of *Deutsch*, became a term of abuse throughout the state.[55]

Such was the atmosphere in which the statewide convention assembled in St. Louis to determine Missouri's fate.

· · ·

ONE DAY TOWARD THE END OF 1860, Jessie Frémont tripped
over a board that had come loose on one of San Francisco's rickety
plank sidewalks, hurting her leg so badly that for the next six months
she was largely confined to the cottage at Black Point. But Mrs. Frémont hardly needed to go down into the city anyhow: San Francisco,
as usual, came up to see Mrs. Frémont.[56]

In her aerie above the Bay, she presided over a salon—almost all
male—of the quickest wits and keenest minds on the Pacific Coast.
The lure of a golden land had already drawn to California a remarkable array of thinkers, dreamers, talkers, and schemers, all of whom
rejoiced to discover a distant shore where the social proprieties and
cultural pieties of Boston and Philadelphia did not apply. At Jessie
Frémont's gatherings, silver-haired politicians chatted with youthful poets; famous novelists collected sea yarns from the captains of
China-trade clippers. The house itself suggested a kind of newfan-
gled cultural mélange unlike anything seen in the East: silk hangings
and damask-shrouded furniture in the latest Paris taste intermingled
with American Indian baskets and photographs of Western landscapes,
along with a splendid Albert Bierstadt painting of the Golden Gate.
On the walls of her young sons' room Mrs. Frémont pasted cutout
pictures of ships and horses.

Guests lingered for hours over luncheon on the veranda, or strolled
together through the gardens, enjoying the perfume of flowers mix-
ing with the smell of the sea. They relished, too, the charisma of their
famous hostess, who enthralled them with her tales of a girlhood spent
dandled on the knees of presidents. She had never been a conventional
beauty, and was growing stout and matronly as middle age approached,
but she still retained all the charm that had won her, at the age of seventeen, the handsomest man in Washington as husband.[57]

When Herman Melville, in the gloomy eclipse of his literary fame,
passed through San Francisco, he naturally called at Black Point,
where a lively afternoon of conversation cheered him considerably. A
much more frequent visitor was a shy, intense young writer named Bret
Harte, whom Jessie Frémont had discovered while he was working as
a typesetter and living in a tiny apartment above a restaurant. Harte's
comic poems and tales of life in the mining camps enchanted her, as
did his newspaper columns, signed The Bohemian, which evoked a
particularly Californian kind of cultural life in which writers and artists lived as rugged free spirits. Each Sunday afternoon, he would come

to dinner and read aloud from his latest manuscript for her to critique. "Sometimes her comments cut like a lash, but her praise is sincere and freely given," Harte told a friend. "To know her is a liberal education." Mrs. Frémont soon shared her "pet," as she called him, with the Eastern literary establishment, helping him land a short story in *The Atlantic Monthly*—and thus introduced a new, distinctively Western voice into American letters.[58]

As for the famous Pathfinder, when he was there at all he was usually just a taciturn presence hovering at the margins of his wife's sparkling soirees. More often, Colonel Frémont was away from San Francisco attending to his troubled gold-mining enterprises and other personal affairs.

Even when the former presidential candidate was absent, though, politics was very much in the air at Black Point. Senator Edward D. Baker, the West Coast's most prominent Republican—indeed, one of the national party's rising stars—was a habitué. A handsome, hot-tempered, powerfully built Midwesterner, the Gray Eagle probably reminded Mrs. Frémont of her father. Like old Tom Benton, Baker was one of the most captivating orators in Congress. His skills had been honed back in Illinois, where he had joined the Disciple sect to become, like James Garfield, a youthful sensation on the preaching circuit.[59] Only after migrating to the West Coast, however, did he develop his own distinctive brand of Republicanism.

In October 1860, shortly before she injured her leg, Jessie Frémont brought several friends along to the American Theatre on Sansome Street to see Baker give a campaign speech for Lincoln. The senator had arrived in town by steamer the week before, met at the wharf by a phalanx of Wide Awakes, his ever-present "bodyguard" for the duration of his stay. Thousands of San Franciscans turned out to hear his address at the theater; Baker's friendship with Lincoln went back more than twenty years, to a time when they had both been young lawyers in Springfield, and no doubt many of his listeners hoped to hear personal anecdotes of the Rail-Splitter. It turned out, however, that Baker had very little to say about his party's nominee. He addressed larger themes, in words that spoke directly to an audience of Western pioneers:

The normal condition of the Territories is freedom. Stand on the edge of the Sierra Nevadas, or upon the brow of any eminence looking down upon the Territories beyond, and what do you behold? You find there the savage, the wild beast, and the wilderness; but you do not find slavery. . . . The Western man goes into the Territory with his family, his horses, his oxen, his ax and other implements of labor. The Southern man goes with his slave.

A savvy politician, the senator reassured everyone that a vote for the Republicans was simply a vote for free white labor, not a vote for black emancipation: the party was committed not to interfere with slavery wherever it was already legal. Yet, at the climax of his speech, Colonel Baker, as he was often called, seemed to advocate nothing less than an American revolution:

Everywhere abroad, the great ideas of personal liberty spread, increase, fructify. Here—ours is the exception! In this home of the exile, in this land of constitutional liberty, it is left for us to teach the world that slavery marches in solemn procession! that under the American stars slavery has protection, and the name of freedom must be faintly breathed—the songs of freedom be faintly sung! Garibaldi, Victor Emanuel, hosts of good men are praying, fighting, dying on scaffolds, in dungeons, oftener yet on battle fields for freedom: and yet while this great procession marches under the arches of liberty, we alone shrink back trembling and afraid when freedom is but mentioned!

At this, one newspaper reported, the entire hall broke out into "terrific cheers." And that was not all: "While the people were cheering, Mr. Harte, who sat on the platform, apparently carried away with enthusiasm, rushed to the footlights, and with extended arms, excessive vehemence and loud voice, declared: 'It is true! it is true, gentlemen! We are slaves, compared with the rest of the world. The colonel is right!'—then, pale as a ghost, staggered back to his seat, the people cheering vociferously."[60]

It was, to say the least, out of character for the shy young poet. People said afterward that his patroness must have put him up to it. More than a few said that but for being a lady, and a famous man's wife, Mrs. Frémont would have liked to be shouting from the footlights herself.[61]

But the voice that would carry farthest and loudest across California in the months to come was neither the distinguished senator's nor the mercurial poet's. It was another of Jessie Frémont's protégés who accompanied her to the American Theatre that evening. He was perhaps the most unlikely-looking hero in the entire hall. But in years to come, people would call him "the man who saved California for the Union."[62]

Mrs. Frémont had become acquainted with the young Reverend Thomas Starr King one evening in the spring of 1860, when he and his wife had come to dinner at Black Point—an obligation of all interesting newcomers to San Francisco. The hostess, possessing as she did a keen eye for masculine beauty, cannot have been particularly impressed as she clasped King's frail white hand in welcome. The clergyman stood barely over five feet tall, with greasy hair that hung lankly over the collar of his ill-fitting coat. His eyes, large and luminous, bulged slightly from their sockets like a sickly child's; indeed, he seemed somehow not fully adult, a sexless boy-man in the garb of a preacher.

Yet behind those strange eyes flashed a wit as keen as Mrs. Frémont's own. Almost as soon as they began conversing, both felt a marriage of true minds: a sense of communication as free, electric, and unimpeded as a telegraphic transmission. "An enchanted evening," she would call it. The Gray Eagle was at the dinner table that night, too, as was the Great Pathfinder, but these political giants could only sit and watch as the bons mots flew back and forth between the mistress of Black Point and this odd little creature. Mr. King's conversation was extraordinary: an incessant running commentary on life's perplexities, spiced with literary references, antic puns, self-deprecating jokes, mimicry, and even some slightly risqué allusions. Only Jessie Frémont, perhaps, could have kept up with him. King was no less charmed by his new friend—not least because of her responsiveness to his performance. "She *is* a superb woman," he wrote. "She is my one admirer in the universe." Before long he was a regular at the cottage, coming and going almost as if it were his own home and talking with Mrs. Frémont for hours on the veranda.[63]

They were the same age, thirty-five, but in most respects their lives could hardly have been more different. Unlike the pampered senator's daughter, the little clergyman had grown up in a modest house in Charlestown, Massachusetts, beside Boston Harbor—"under the shadow of Bunker Hill," he liked to say—and, being unable to afford the tuition at Harvard, had scrounged an education in lecture halls and free libraries, where he picked up French, Spanish, Italian, Latin, Greek, Hebrew, and a bit of German by the time he was nineteen.[64] While propriety forbade Mrs. Frémont, as the wife of a public man, from speaking before an audience or publishing under her own name, Mr. King had built a public career entirely out of words. He wrote, but—much more surprising—he also *spoke*, in a "manly, sonorous" voice, by turns pas-

sionate and playful, that was all the more impressive because it ema-
nated from such a tadpole-like body. Called to the ministry, he had his
own pulpit by the age of twenty-four, at a Unitarian church in Hollis
Street, Boston. By his early thirties, King was hobnobbing with Emerson, Phillips, Beecher, and the Adamses; he was earning fifty dollars
each time he lectured at a college or lyceum; and, inspired by Thoreau,
he had just published a little book (half ode and half travel guide) about
his rambles in the White Mountains. It was he who would bring Melville to see Mrs. Frémont.[65]

And then, in April 1860, he suddenly gave it all up—Hollis Street,
Bunker Hill, tea with the Adamses—and went to California.[66]

He did not come to convert the Golden State, Sodom though it may
have seemed. Rather, King came to *be* healed and converted himself.
As he wrote to a friend not long before departure: "I do think we are
unfaithful in huddling so closely around the cosy stove of civilization
in this blessed Boston, and I, for one, am ready to go out into the cold
and see if I am good for anything." In fact, Boston was "cosy" for him
only to a point. Emerson might compliment his work; Mr. and Mrs.
Adams might enjoy his tea-table chitchat; but their Brahmin circle
could never accept the man from Charlestown as its moral and intellectual preceptor.[67]

Now, just a few weeks later, here he was, taking his tea not in some
stuffy Beacon Street parlor but on an airy hilltop above the Pacific,
as this brilliant and world-renowned woman spoke with him as few
people in Boston ever had: with neither condescension nor deference
but frankly, directly, as between equals.

There was so much for them to talk about! He loved California, and
hated it. San Francisco appalled him, at first: its swaybacked wooden
shanties, its fleas and bedbugs, its streets "bilious with Chinamen." But
the Golden Gate, carpeted with spring flowers in colors more vibrant
than any he had seen in a New Hampshire autumn, delighted him.[68]
Even the occasional earthquakes, he said, made him want to stand
up and shout "Encore!" King made a midsummer jaunt to the Sierra
Nevada—no doubt at the Frémonts' urging—and sent an ebullient
series of articles about it to the *Boston Evening Transcript*, the paper of
record for the Beacon Hill set. One dispatch included, amid the scenic
sublimities, an equally extravagant appraisal of the colonel's real estate
holdings, currently on the market for investment: "perhaps the most
valuable mining property in the world," King called it. (Clearly, the
author was already getting the hang of California, a place where high
art and hucksterism bunked contentedly together.)

But it was the garden at Black Point that truly opened King's eyes to the wonderful possibilities of the West. Life and landscape were integrated there. Nature was not something you traveled to on the Boston & Maine Railroad. The wild heart of the American continent lay just beyond the edge of the luncheon table. "Yesterday I dined with Mrs. Frémont," King told an old friend back East, "& walked bareheaded among roses, geraniums, vines & fuchsias in profuse bloom." Here was a place where even a Boston Unitarian could take his hat off outdoors![69]

Another afternoon, King came unannounced, asking simply whether he could sit alone in the garden, on a small rug that he spread beneath a laurel tree: the view of sea and mountains, he told Mrs. Frémont afterward, helped him to "regain" himself. After this she set up a study in a secluded corner of the grounds where he could come each morning to work undisturbed on his articles and sermons. At noon, she would send over a servant with lunch, and at teatime he would emerge to share with her what he had written.[70]

The West was transforming him. In his Boston sermons, King had trod somewhat cautiously down the pathways of transcendentalism, offering palatable versions of Emersonian abstractions. In his White Mountains book, he had rhapsodized over the scenery but had also taken care to advise readers on local hotels. Here in California, however, he made the very crags and valleys resound with divine reproach, with glory and terror: "So many of us there are who have no majestic landscapes for the *heart*—no grandeurs of the inner life! We live on the flats. We live in a moral country, which is dry, droughty, barren. We have no great hopes. We have no sense of Infinite guard and care. We have no sacred and cleansing fears. We have no consciousness of Divine, All-enfolding Love. We may make an outward visit to the Sierras, but there are *no Yosemites in the soul*."[71]

He had always hated slavery, of course, but from his pulpit on Hollis Street he had rarely even uttered the offensive word, let alone tried to preach politics. His denunciations were almost always couched in biblical allegories. (The week that Anthony Burns was marched down State Street between ranks of soldiers, King had preached a sermon that he was rather proud of, on the trial of Christ before Pilate.) Indeed, he had made quite clear that he disdained "radical eloquence" and "abstract principles": Boston already had more than enough Sunday-morning legislators.[72]

In San Francisco, though, his resolve began to waver. He accompanied Mrs. Frémont and Mr. Harte to the American Theatre on the night of Senator Baker's great speech and was overwhelmed with several strong emotions, not least of them envy. "That is the true way to reach men!" he said, pacing around the Frémonts' private box in his excitement. His own preaching was a paltry thing by comparison, he told Jessie: it could never have the seismic effect of Baker's. Later that night, she set out to convince him otherwise. She told him he was destined for politics; she even claimed, King said in wonder, to be "distressed that I have not lived longer in the state, so that she could have me elected *Senator* this winter." In this pasty-skinned clergyman, she saw not only wit and intellect but also something that less perceptive eyes missed: a kind of soldierly strength. Indeed, something there had often reminded her of her husband's old frontier guide, Kit Carson: the gunfighter, the sunburnt trailblazer, the hero of pulp fiction.[73]

Needless to say, Mrs. Frémont's protégé did not get a Senate seat that winter. But at a San Francisco theater on the evening of February 22, 1861—at the very hour when, three thousand miles away, President-Elect Lincoln was pulling a shawl over his face and slipping aboard the night train to Baltimore—the Reverend Mr. King stepped up to a lectern draped with an American flag.

It was Washington's Birthday, and San Francisco was celebrating the holiday as never before: schools and businesses were closed, people filled the streets, and, as the *Bulletin* reported, "there were as many stars aloft as a cloudless night displays—as many stripes as the traitors who plot to despoil the country of its unity and glory are entitled to." In the afternoon, more than ten thousand had gathered for a mass meeting and adopted, by acclamation, a series of resolutions professing their loyalty to the Union—as well as their willingness to "cheerfully acquiesce" in any honorable compromise that might keep the South in the fold. King's oration, before an overflow crowd at the Music Academy, was to be the climax of the day, the crowning expression of unconditional love for the united country.[74]

But his message was one his listeners were unprepared for. What would George Washington do today if he were in the White House, he asked? And then with a ferocity such as the audience had never seen in him, came the surprising answer: "Nothing. He would have acted four months ago. He would have purged his Cabinet of treason. He would have awed out of it conspirators and thieves. He would not have been a lump of shilly-shally incarnate."

Then he tore into the would-be compromisers—into the very ideas that San Francisco's Unionists had unanimously embraced earlier that day: "Change the Constitution in order to save it!" This was not politics but suicide. And King spoke powerfully of the American continent's geography, how it bound together East and West, North and South:

> [Washington] believed that God created this country to be one. The Creator placed no Mason and Dixon's line upon it; that was the work of foolish men. He marked no boundaries for rival civilizations in the immense basins of the West. . . . The Mississippi, like a great national tree, has its root in the hot Gulf, and spreads its top in the far icy North, a glorious tree, with boughs in different latitudes, and branches binding the Rocky Mountains and the lakes together, its great trunk the central artery of a national unity.[75]

Afterward, in a letter to a close friend (a black New Yorker named Randolph Ryer), King exulted like a warrior returning from the field of victory. "I pitched into Secession, Concession, and Calhoun, right and left," he wrote, "and made [even] Southerners applaud. I pledged California to a Northern Republic and to 'a flag that should have no treacherous threads of cotton in its warp,' and the audience came down with thunder." When the oration was all over, Mrs. Frémont made her way to King through the pressing throng, and told him, he said, that "she would like to hear it forty nights in succession. . . . [I] am urged to give it all over the State, and help kill the Pacific-Republic folly. It was *the* occasion, thus far, of my existence."[76]

He did not offer it for quite forty solid nights. But in the weeks ahead, King gave that speech again and again, to one packed house of Californians after another—not just in San Francisco, but in Marysville, Stockton, Sacramento. He spoke in gold-mining camps, and standing on saloon porches or tree stumps in towns with names like Deadwood, Rough and Ready, and Mad Mule—places where Southerners hissed him, or worse. He had never known the true exhilaration of public speaking, he told Mrs. Frémont, until he had to encounter a front row bristling with revolvers and bowie knives. Far better to face these, somehow, than the supercilious front pews of the Hollis Street church.[77]

When not traveling and speaking he was writing, usually in Mrs. Frémont's garden. He composed a new oration on Daniel Webster—conveniently glossing over the Compromise of 1850, he admitted privately, but taking the occasion to remember the senator's words when California achieved statehood: "At last we have seen our country stretch from sea to sea, and a new highway opened across the continent from us to our fellow-citizens on the shore of the Pacific. Far as they have gone, they are yet within the protection of the Union, and ready, I doubt it not, to join us all in its defence and support." On April 19, he spoke on the anniversary of the Battle of Lexington—another opportunity to turn American history to the uses of the present.

Even the Eastern press was taking notice now. "The ghost of old Sam Adams abides with Mr. King," wrote the *New York Times'* West Coast correspondent. "While he charms his hearers with eloquence, he charges them with the very spirit that filled the air about Bunker Hill in 1774 and '75. . . . He has brought every element of power that his popularity gives him to bear in all our cities in favor of liberty and human rights."[78]

To be sure, the "Pacific-Republic folly" lingered, but now its would-be founding fathers were in full retreat. Asbury Harpending's Alcatraz plot was foiled when one of his own coconspirators—a failed Senate candidate who had publicly called for Lincoln's assassination—approached General Johnston to enlist him in the scheme. General Johnston may have been a Southerner, but he was a man of honor first. His response was to fortify all the federal outposts at risk, especially Alcatraz, and to transfer weapons from the Benicia arsenal to the less vulnerable island fortress. A few months later, the general would resign his commission and cross a thousand miles of the West on foot to take command of a Confederate army—but until then, as he promised the governor of California, he would defend the property of the United States, "and not a cartridge or a percussion cap belonging to her shall pass to any enemy while I am here as her representative." The Alcatraz plot was dead, and Harpending and his friends slunk off into other, more promising, pursuits.[79]

Thomas Starr King, the awakened Christian warrior, relished the sense of combat. "I do not measure enough inches around the chest to go for a soldier," he told Jessie Frémont, "but I see the way to make this fight." What a remarkable war, to enlist even him as a hero!

And he considered her a soldier, too—if anything, a more potent force than he. "Have you met Mrs. Frémont?" he would later ask a friend. "Her husband I am very little acquainted with, but she is sublime, and carries guns enough to be formidable to a whole Cabinet—a she-Merrimack, thoroughly sheathed, and carrying fire in the genuine Benton furnaces."[80]

Indeed, he had spent precious little time with Colonel Frémont. The Pathfinder was off on an extended trip through Europe in pursuit of capital for his mining ventures—accompanied by his mistress, a certain Mrs. Corbett of San Francisco.[81] Mrs. King, for her own part, hardly appeared at Black Point. Irritable and chronically unwell, she missed Boston and despised their new home—"an ardent hater of this city, coast, and slope," King called her.[82] Whether he and Jessie Frémont ever took the opportunity to advance their mutual admiration past friendship is doubtful, however. Both seem to have remained devoutly observant of Victorian sexual proprieties, despite long hours alone together, including at least one overnight trip spent strolling in the meadows of San Mateo, skipping rocks on a stream, and lodging at a country inn.[83] But they were ecstatic comrades-in-arms all the same: they shared in the giddy exhilaration of wartime, and thrilled at the events unfolding around them. "What a year to live in!" he exulted. "Worth all other times ever known in our history or in any other."

Mrs. Frémont observed, with somewhat more restraint but greater penetration: "All over our country now we are being called to lay aside self." To be selfless, perhaps; but perhaps also to shed old selves and create new ones.

Several days after King's speech on Washington, Jessie Frémont dared step into the public limelight as she had never done before: she published an article in a newspaper. The Frémonts' former coachman, Albert Lea, a Negro, had been sentenced to death for murder, and although he was clearly guilty, she felt the sentence was unjust, motivated by the judge's racism and pro-Southern leanings. Her open letter of protest in the daily *Alta California*, signed *J.B.F.*, shocked the city: a lady of national prominence airing a political grievance in the press, and defending a Negro murderer to boot!

Lea would go to the gallows in the end, but in Mrs. Frémont's life it was a turning point. Never again was she content merely to be one famous man's daughter and another's wife.[84]

Did Mr. King and Mrs. Frémont's rhetorical campaign—in which she was the chief strategist, he the field marshal—actually save California for the Union? She would never stop believing that it had. Many others thought likewise; Ralph Waldo Emerson would write King the following year to say that "the salvation and future of California are mainly in your hands."[85]

This was almost certainly an exaggeration. The shock of actual secession, and of the news from Fort Sumter, were surely more influential in making most Californians realize that no middle ground, no neutrality, was possible. Their state could not stand outside American history, any more than any other part of the country. California—and each of its citizens—would have to stand with the new Union, with the warlike Union, or be classed among its enemies. This realization awoke in many people an idealism they had not known they possessed. "The noble and beautiful side of the nation is now apparent," Mrs. Frémont wrote to a friend back East.[86]

Yet there is no denying that King's words, reaching millions in person and in print, articulated a rationale for linking California's destiny to that of the beleaguered East. Speaking as if he were the voice of history itself, he reconnected what seemed the land of the past to the land of the future. In his Lexington speech—first delivered while news of Sumter's surrender was crossing the plains in a Pony Express pouch—he asked the audience to imagine the sun rising on that first morning of the Revolution: shining first on the Maine coast and his beloved New England mountains, then sweeping over the Alleghenies and turning the Hudson into a thread of gold, crossing the Mississippi, flooding the prairies with light, climbing the far slope of the Rockies, then gleaming upon the highest peaks of the Sierras before dawn rolled at last over the western ocean—this heavenly path confirming the rightness of the continent's unity.[87]

The men, women, and children in the room listened in silence. It was the kind of journey that almost every one of them had also taken. And it was a time when gorgeous words could move spirits in a way that they rarely can today.

King brought Eastern culture with him to the West, even into the mining camps. Curious people came just to see this expatriate Bostonian, this friend of Beecher and Emerson: names that all literate Americans knew. Another message that King carried with him wherever he spoke: *This is yours, too.*

In June 1861, Frank Buck—the man who had told his sister that he didn't "give a straw" if the Union perished—went to hear King's speech on Washington in the raw wooden meetinghouse up in Weaverville. As soon as he came home, still electrified by the experience, he sat down to write her another letter:

> Who do you think we had to preach? 'T. Starr King.' . . . It was beautiful beyond description. Language just flows from his mouth so easily. Everybody was in ecstasies. He held the audience spell bound for two hours. It was a great treat for us I assure you. Even the men from Virginia and Texas admired him although he lashed the Secessionists without mercy.
>
> I had intended to write you at some length on politics but there are no longer any political parties. We are all either for this Gov-

ernment or against it. . . . You may set us down as loyal to the Union. No matter whether this rebellion was caused by Northern Abolitionists or Southern Fire Eaters we won't discuss the matter but put it down at any sacrifice.[88]

Back in San Francisco three weeks later, King accompanied Mrs. Frémont and her children to the wharf where the Vanderbilt Line steamship *North Star* awaited them. The Pony Express had brought a letter from Colonel Frémont in London: he was returning at once to the United States, and wanted her to close up the cottage at Black Point and meet him in New York. King escorted his friend to the door of her stateroom. Their parting was difficult; both were overcome not just with emotion but with the exhaustion of the past few months. At last he pressed into her hands a bouquet of long-stemmed violets and a volume of Emerson's essays. "Smell, read, and rest," he said.[89]

Neither she nor he would rest much in the months and years ahead. Each would continue separately the campaign they had begun together.

THE CONVENTION TO DETERMINE Missouri's course in the national crisis assembled in St. Louis on March 4. Although this was also, by chance, the day of Lincoln's inauguration, it dawned unpropitiously for the local Unionists. They awoke to find two secessionist flags flying above their city. One floated from the staff atop the courthouse dome; unguarded, it was easily removed. The other would be a good deal trickier to deal with. It wasn't much to look at: a dark blue cloth hastily stitched with a crude patchwork of secession emblems, from the palmetto and star to the Southern cross to the state arms of Missouri. But it hung from the front porch of the Berthold Mansion, which was very well guarded indeed.[90]

Before long, a large and angry crowd—mostly Germans—was filling the streets for several blocks in each direction, shouting for the flag to be taken down. Each window of the mansion bristled with loaded muskets: clearly the Minute Men were prepared to defend their banner at all costs. (The protesters didn't know it, but the defenders also had a swivel gun, loaded with musket balls and tenpenny nails, aimed from the inside at the front door.) Soon, drumbeats were heard approaching through the streets: the Wide Awakes were coming, and they too were armed.[91]

The two sides faced each other across the narrow porch. A thousand miles away, the Black Republican president was taking his oath of office. Everyone knew that this standoff on Fifth Street might erupt at any moment into a bloodbath—and they knew what such a bloodbath could mean, not just for their state but for their country.

Somehow violence was averted that morning. One eyewitness account says vaguely that "after many entreaties by the thoughtful and intelligent of the Unionists, the rank and file accorded obedience." Another, more specific, describes a civic elder who climbed atop an Italian fruit vendor's small donkey cart—a convenient platform accidentally stranded there—to address the crowd. The donkey, "suddenly taking fright either at the eloquence of the orator or at the shouts of the crowd," bolted and sent the gentleman tumbling, to the spectators' amusement. Perhaps credit is due to that donkey—whose name, if he had one, is lost to history—for breaking the tension and preventing a clash of arms that might have touched off the Civil War six weeks early.[92]

In any event, the rebel flag still flew unmolested from the Berthold Mansion the next day. Thanks to it, however, the Missouri leaders meeting to decide their state's allegiance had just caught a glimpse of the future. The consequences of secession, which had seemed like remote abstractions in bucolic Jefferson City, were now all too vividly manifest. Isidor Bush, the only Forty-Eighter among the delegates, rose to admonish his colleagues: "While you . . . only imagine the horrors of war and fancy the evils of revolution, I know them. My eyes have seen what you cannot imagine, what I cannot describe." The next day, to Governor Jackson's chagrin, the convention almost unanimously endorsed a resolution that "*at present* there was no adequate cause to impel Missouri to dissolve her connection with the federal Union."[93]

Still, every Missourian knew that in the event of federal aggression toward a Southern state—say, a battle at Charleston or elsewhere—the "adequate cause" might very suddenly present itself.

What only a few knew was that the raising of the two rebel flags had not been some rash act of a few young hotheads. It had been a coolly plotted provocation. The Minute Men had actually hoped to spark an explosion of violence throughout the city. Amid the chaos, they thought, they could seize the choicest prize of the Mississippi Valley, indeed, one of the choicest in the entire country: the United States Arsenal at St. Louis.[94]

The Arsenal was a central munitions depot for federal forts throughout the West. Its present stores could equip an entire Confederate army: 60,000 muskets, 90,000 pounds of gunpowder, 1.5 million cartridges, and several dozen cannon—in addition to machinery for arms manufacture, of which the South had woefully little. The Buchanan administration, displaying its usual strategic acumen, had initially left only forty soldiers guarding this bounty, the largest single arms cache in all the slave states. Thanks to some urgent string pulling by Frank Blair, the force was increased to some five hundred federal troops, still hardly enough, given the thousands of secessionist volunteers now arming themselves in St. Louis and throughout Missouri. But as winter turned into spring and the plots and counterplots multiplied, the Arsenal's greatest asset would turn out to be one very strange little man.[95]

Captain Nathaniel Lyon of the United States Army could hardly have seemed a less imposing warrior. A slight, red-bearded Yankee, he was constantly sucking on hard candies, which clicked wetly against his ill-fitting dentures. Yet Lyon embodied, in his five-foot-five frame, nearly everything that Southerners loathed and feared. He was a man of fervent, almost fanatical, Republican antislavery beliefs, which he never hesitated to vocalize in his harsh, nasal Connecticut bray. It was not, he made clear, that he gave a damn about the slaves—in fact, he publicly professed himself "not concerned with improving the black race, nor the breed of dogs and reptiles." No, it was mostly just that he hated the South, detested its authoritarian institutions, and tasted bile at the very thought of secessionist treason. Many tales about him circulated in the army. Perhaps the most famous was of the time at Fort Riley when the captain came upon one of his privates beating a dog: after knocking the soldier to the ground and kicking him in the stomach a few times, he made him get on his knees and beg the animal for forgiveness. To know that story was to know Nathaniel Lyon.[96]

People called him "mentally unbalanced"; no doubt present-day psychiatry has a term for his condition. When an underling committed some trifling infraction, Lyon would inflict an ingeniously sadistic punishment—one favorite involved honey and stinging flies—then seek out his victim a few hours later and abjectly apologize. On meeting someone, Lyon would coax out of him some mild expression of political or religious opinion (the captain himself was an avowed atheist), so that he might reply with a scalding shower of profanities. And yet somehow he also managed to inspire loyalty, even trust. A brother officer wrote:

> If he had lived four hundred years ago he would have been burned at the stake as a pestilent and altogether incorrigible person, whose removal was demanded in the interests of the peace

of society. . . . There was no middle ground with him in any matter that engaged his attention, and he conceived that it was his
duty to enforce his doctrines or ideas upon all with whom he
came in contact, even to the point of being offensive. At the same
time he was possessed of as tender a heart as ever beat in a man's
breast. . . . He had in him an indomitable spirit that was always
awake, a fixity of purpose that never faltered, and a courage that
was never for an instant met by the slightest feeling of fear. He
did not know what fear was.[97]

In this man's hands rested the fate of the St. Louis Arsenal.

He had arrived in February at the head of a company of reinforcements, just eighty soldiers, and reported to his superior officer at the
Arsenal, a certain Major Hagner, who seemed not quite combat-ready,
to put it mildly. (When a squad started moving howitzers across the
yard, the major admonished them sharply "not to spoil his lawn.")[98]
But within days of his arrival, Lyon met Frank Blair and immediately
recognized a kindred spirit: one as hard-nosed and ruthless as himself.
Blair had thousands of men at his command, but few weapons; Lyon
commanded just a few dozen men but had access to enough weapons
to arm half of St. Louis. No wonder they found each other.

There was another very important respect in which the well-
connected Blair could be useful: he had the ear of the Lincoln administration. Within a week of the inauguration, he dropped a quick note
to Secretary of War Cameron, and almost immediately, new orders
went out to St. Louis, assigning command of the Arsenal's troops and
defenses to Captain Nathaniel Lyon, relieving the feckless Hagner.[99]

The armed standoff—between the Minute Men and heavily secessionist state militia on one side, and the Arsenal troops and former
Wide Awakes on the other—lasted through early April. (Blair had now
renamed his forces the Home Guards.) Then came the momentous
news from Charleston Harbor. Now it was the governor's turn to act.

On the very day that word of Sumter's surrender arrived in St.
Louis—Sunday, April 14—Jackson struck the lowest and most das-
tardly blow he could inflict on the German community: he orches-
trated a police raid to enforce the blue laws. Squads of officers fanned
out across the city, storming into saloons and beer gardens and driving
the clientele into the streets. (Drinking establishments popular among
"Americans," such as the bar at the Planter's House hotel, famous for
its mint juleps and sherry cobblers, were not disturbed. Afterward,
one report had it that misdirected police came to break up a saloon

where Governor Jackson himself happened to be drinking with some cronies, but this seems too good to be true.) Forty armed policemen appeared at Henry Boernstein's Opera House just before the evening performance and shut down the theater; it never reopened. This was, however, only the opening salvo of a larger campaign to oppress the city's Unionists by the arbitrary exercise of government authority. It was quickly announced that English would henceforth be the only official language of state business, and that funds for St. Louis's public schools were being reallocated to arm Governor Jackson's militia. Citizens were forbidden from gathering in large groups in the streets. All assemblies of "negroes or mulattoes," including church services, were summarily banned unless a police officer was present, and hundreds of free blacks, terrified that reenslavement might be next, flocked to the courthouse seeking official certificates of freedom.[100]

"Not One Word More—Now Arms Will Decide," the *Anzeiger*'s headline announced grimly. "Every question, every doubt has been swept away," the article continued. "The Fatherland calls us—we stand at its disposal."[101]

The Fatherland's first official call to the state of Missouri, however, failed to elicit the desired effect. When Governor Jackson received Lincoln's April 15 order for state troops to be mustered into federal service, he replied in no uncertain terms:

> Sir, . . . your requisition in my judgment, is illegal, unconstitutional and revolutionary in its object, inhuman and diabolical, and cannot be complied with. Not one man will the state of Missouri furnish to carry on such an unholy crusade.

Even many moderate Missourians who would have disowned their governor's harsh rhetoric agreed in wanting no part of Lincoln's call to arms. One man spoke for many when he wrote to a pro-Union acquaintance: "We ask nothing of the gov't at Washington but to be left alone." Publicly, Jackson announced a policy of "armed neutrality" for the state. Privately, he sent envoys to Montgomery to ask Jefferson Davis for siege guns and mortars to be used against the Arsenal.[102]

On village squares, county fairgrounds, and fallow fields across Missouri, young men were forming militia companies to defend their state against the Yankees. They armed themselves with hunting rifles and shotguns, sharpened homemade bowie knives to a razor's edge, and buckled on old swords cadged from neighbors who had fought in Mexico. Many years later one of these Missouri volunteers would pen a wry account—a parody of the Civil War memoir genre—of his company from the town of Hannibal. In his telling, the unit was little more than a dozen or so boys playing at war, fighting hand-to-paw combats against barnyard dogs and "retreating" headlong through the night from nonexistent Union patrols. But ex-Lieutenant Sam Clemens was viewing the past through the sentimental haze of a quarter century, not to mention through the satirical lens of Mark Twain. In the spring of 1861, the secessionist militias were in deadly earnest.

A different volunteer, making his way from the far west of the state to join the rebel forces, stopped with his comrades at a wayside inn, where the landlord's pretty daughter entertained them with "Dixie" on the piano. "I made a promise to her that I would kill two 'duchmen,'" the young man recorded.[103]

Across the country, in fact, many people framed the conflict in ethnic as well as racial terms—an aspect of the war that has been largely forgotten. Many white immigrants embraced the opportunity to prove their identity as true Americans, and as they watched their adopted homeland fall unexpectedly to pieces, they looked to their own traditions for guidance. In New York, the Irish Brigade marched down Broadway behind a banner reading "Remember Fontenoy," referring to a 1745 battle where Irish Jacobites fought British troops. (Although Irish soldiers have often been stereotyped as racists and unwilling conscripts, one immigrant, writing in February 1861, compared enslaved blacks to his own oppressed nation and said of the impending war: "this is Just the only effectual Speedy way of setting the Coulered population at liberty.") In Kansas, a young Jewish immigrant had a final conversation with his parents before riding off to join the Union cavalry: "My mother said that as a Jehudi [Jew] I had the duty to perform, to defend the institutions which gave equal rights to all beliefs."[104]

And in St. Louis, a group of German women made a flag. They stitched it together out of heavy silk, with stars of silver thread. Across its red and white stripes they painted an inscription in gold letters: "III. Regiment MISSOURI VOLUNTEERS. *Lyons Fahnenwacht*."[105] "Lyon's Color Guard" was a new unit under Sigel's command. The ladies presented their handiwork at an impressive ceremony with both Sigel and Lyon in attendance, as well as the entire regiment. Miss Josephine Weigel stepped forward and addressed the commander in their native tongue:

Herr Oberst Sigel! It is a great honor for us to present you with this flag, made by German women and maidens, for your regiment. . . .

In keeping with old German custom, we women do not wish to remain mere onlookers when our men have dedicated themselves with joyful courage to the service of the Fatherland; so far as it is in our power, we too wish to take part in the struggle for freedom and fan the fire of enthusiasm into bright flames.[106]

Nor was this the only female contribution to the cause—far from it. Throughout the city, one St. Louisan reported, women and girls were wrapping gunpowder and musket balls into cartridges "as fast as their fingers could fly."[107]

The resourceful Lyon and Blair had managed to take Jackson's rebuff of Lincoln's orders and turn it to their advantage. In a long letter to Secretary Cameron on April 18, Blair officiously instructed the administration on how to win the war within a few months, laying out an elaborate strategy that began with mustering his Home Guards into the U.S. Army and putting him and Lyon in charge of them.

In other words, if Jackson would not supply his militia, their motley bands of Germans would step in to fill the gap. Cameron passed this request along to General Scott, who approved the order with a shrug, scribbling, "It is revolutionary times, and therefore I do not object to the irregularity of this," before Lincoln signed off as well. Thus, Lyon, still officially a mere company captain, now found himself briefly commanding the entire Department of the West—in other words, almost everything between the Mississippi and the far side of the Rockies. April 1861 was a time when such things could happen.[108]

Within days, four regiments of loyal Home Guards were mustered into federal service: Sigel's *Lyons Fahnenwacht*, plus one regiment under Blair, one under the versatile Boernstein (who dusted off the skills he had acquired in the Imperial Austrian Army), and one under Nicholas Schuettner, another local Forty-Eighter and leader of an anti-secessionist street gang. Of these forty-two hundred troops, all but one hundred were Germans. Several more regiments started forming as reserves. Lyon, without any official promotion, began styling himself "General." Forests of white tents sprouted on the Arsenal grounds, as thousands of muddy boots dealt their coup de grâce to Major Hagner's beloved lawn. Bands played; companies marched; some of the soldiers, according to a reporter, even tried "running and leaping in the Zouave practice." At dusk the light of cooking fires flickered among the encampments, while "all nooks and crannies sounded with German war songs and soldiers' choirs," Boernstein recalled after the war. Ever upbeat, he claimed that even those officers with the most refined

European palates pronounced the camp food excellent. "The general happiness, the humorous mood, the awareness of doing a good deed and the physical exertions served as seasoning to stimulate the appetite," he wrote. "I cannot recall days so cheerful, exciting or invigorating as those first few days at the arsenal when we were forming our volunteer regiments." The main thing, one recruit wrote, was that each man was "eager to teach the German-haters a never-to-be-forgotten lesson."[109]

Less visible maneuvers were also taking place at the Arsenal. Having issued his troops all the weapons and ammunition they would need, Lyon determined to send much of what remained out of harm's way, to the Union troops mustering in Illinois. As a handpicked crew of men worked secretly to pack up the weaponry, Lyon had spread a rumor, via local barrooms, that a shipment of weapons from the Arsenal would be sent across the city in streetcars that night. Sure enough, at 9:00 p.m., a trolley convoy loaded with wooden crates rolled slowly up Fifth Street. Minute Men instantly rushed out of ambush, halted the trolleys, pried open the containers, and pulled out the guns: a few rusty old flintlocks from the Arsenal's junk room. Meanwhile, down on the river, the steamboat *City of Alton*, her lamps doused and paddle-wheels barely turning, slipped quietly from the Arsenal quay and up the Mississippi with 25,000 well-oiled muskets and carbines aboard.[110]

Over the next couple of weeks, the opposing forces in St. Louis performed an uncanny pantomime. Across the city from the Arsenal, secessionists set up an armed camp of their own in an area called Lindell's Grove, formerly a park and picnic ground. They dubbed it Camp Jackson in honor of the governor, laid out rows of tents grandiosely dubbed Beauregard Street and Davis Street, and before long, more than a thousand state troops had arrived, under Missouri's militia commander, General Daniel Frost. These soldiers, William T. Sherman later recalled, included many "young men from the first and best families of St. Louis." Ostensibly, Jackson and Frost had assembled them for a regular militia encampment, just as might be done in peacetime. As at a typical antebellum militia gathering, a festive, even indolent atmosphere prevailed; young ladies came and went to visit their beaux, and mothers brought hampers of food to their sons. But in fact, the commanders were expecting more troops to assemble, and they were awaiting a much-anticipated gift from Jefferson Davis.[111]

Late on the night of May 8, another mysterious steamboat docked in St. Louis—this one unloading cargo rather than taking it aboard. Perplexed longshoremen were summoned to the levee to help move some enormously heavy crates marked "Tamaroa marble": material for an upcoming art exhibition, they were told. Actually, the crates contained two howitzers and two siege cannons, five hundred muskets, and a large supply of ammunition, all recently confiscated by Confederate authorities from the U.S. arsenal down in Baton Rouge. As far as arms caches went, this wasn't much, but it was a start.[112]

Unlike Lyon's ingenious trolley-car trick, though, the midnight shipment of "art supplies" was a lame ruse indeed. By midmorning, several longshoremen, who happened to be Germans, had reported the suspicious activity to the Arsenal commander.

Instead of being alarmed, Lyon seemed elated. For weeks he had thirsted for a chance to humiliate the rebels. But the state militia and Minute Men had not given him an opportunity. Jackson, though hungry for the Arsenal and its stores, could not attack while so badly outgunned and outnumbered. Without such provocation, Lyon and Blair had felt constrained from moving against Camp Jackson. After all, the officers and men there were officially state troops, and the state had not yet gone over to the Confederacy; indeed, the Stars and Stripes still flew above the camp. So while the arrival of Jeff Davis's cannons and muskets may not have given Jackson and Frost much additional firepower, it gave Lyon and Blair exactly what they needed: a pretext.

IN THE EARLY AFTERNOON of May 9, a handsome barouche with a black coachman in the driver's seat pulled up to the front gate of Camp Jackson. Inside it rode a genteel old lady dressed in a shawl, a heavy veil, and an enormous sunbonnet. In her lap she held a small wicker basket. The sentries waved her through; clearly this was just a widow paying a visit to her militiaman son. The basket must be full of sandwiches she had lovingly prepared for her dear boy.

In fact, the wicker basket held two loaded Colt revolvers. And if the sentries had peered under the old lady's veil, they would have glimpsed something even more surprising: a bushy red beard.

Surely there must have been a hundred simpler ways to reconnoiter the rebels' picnic ground. Nathaniel Lyon, however, was not one to pass up an opportunity for intrigue, and apparently thought his escapade would seem picturesque rather than ridiculous. He had borrowed the dress, shawl, veil, and sunbonnet from Frank Blair's mother-in-law. Anyhow, his leisurely drive through Camp Jackson showed him exactly what he wanted to see: the mysterious crates from the steamer, still unopened.[113]

Early the next morning, a horseman was seen galloping south-ward down Carondelet Road, on his way to the U.S. troops' outlying encampments. By midday, columns of soldiers were marching through the streets of the city, converging on Camp Jackson. Boernstein, in a splendid plumed Alpine hat, rode astride a horse at the head of his regiment. *Herr Oberst* Sigel, on the other hand, rolled along in car-riage behind his men: the first casualty of the day, he had fallen off his horse onto the cobblestones and hurt his leg. Tony Niederwiesser, the saloonkeeper, strutted at the head of a company.[114]

For weeks, the city's German press had throbbed with ever-purpler prose. "The North has awakened from its slumber; the earth shakes under the tread of its legions, and the South trembles," exulted the *Westliche Post.* "Suddenly a new race arises like a phoenix from the general conflagration, and our workaday politicians sink into the oblivion they deserve. . . . The great goal of mankind—the demand for freedom—will rise ever more glorious and flow like gold in the heat from the fire of battle." Two days before the advance on Camp Jack-son, the editors had hailed "the uprising of the people in the Northern states"—that is, the tremendous surge of patriotic feeling and military enlistment after Sumter—as one of the greatest events in world history since the defeat of Napoleon. "This period will be called the *second American Revolution*," they predicted. "It will . . . be able to turn the great principles enunciated in the first revolution into reality." And, thanks to the quick dissemination of news by steamboat and telegraph, this revolution would also spread across the Atlantic, so that "soon the cry of jubilation of the liberated nations of Europe will echo across the ocean, greeting us as saviors and brothers."[115]

Yet the German volunteers themselves, after all their excitement during the previous months, seemed strangely subdued on the morn-ing of the attack. As they marched through the streets of St. Louis, no one sang; no bands played. Dressed in their civilian clothes, they seemed to trudge like cattle, one observer said. Perhaps, like Isidor Bush (himself now a private in one of the Home Guard regiments), too many had already seen firsthand the unpredictable calamities of war.[116]

Ulysses Grant stood across from the Arsenal's main gate, in front of the Anheuser-Busch brewery, watching the troops file out. (Still eager to make acquaintances that might lead to a commission, he took the opportunity to introduce himself to Blair, who was on horseback marshaling the companies, and wish him luck.) William T. Sherman, on his way to the streetcar company office, heard people on every cor-ner saying excitedly that the "Dutch" were moving on Camp Jackson.

The streets were filling with people hurrying after the troops, swept along almost involuntarily, "anxious spectators of every political proclivity," one witness wrote, "never doubting for a moment that if a fight should occur they could stand by unharmed and witness it all." One big, bearded man, distraught at Lyon's surprise attack, shouted, "He's gone out to kill all the boys,—to kill all the boys!" Although a couple of Sherman's friends urged him to come and "see the fun," he hurried in the opposite direction, walking quickly home to make sure his seven-year-old son, Willie, had not joined the packs of schoolboys scampering toward the excitement.[117]

With soldierly precision that impressed the onlookers, Lyon's regiments surrounded Camp Jackson on all sides. In the grove itself, there seemed to be little commotion and no sign of resistance. General Frost's militiamen were outnumbered at least eight to one. Lyon, on horseback, surveying the scene with satisfaction, sent in an adjutant with a curtly worded note:

> SIR—Your command is regarded as evidently hostile to the Government of the United States.
>
> It is for the most part made up of those secessionists who have openly avowed their hostility to the Government, and have been plotting at the seizure of its property and the overthrow of its authority. You are openly in communication with the so-called Southern Confederacy, which is now at war with the United States; and you are receiving at your camp, from the said Confederacy and under its flag, large supplies of the material of war. . . .
>
> In view of these considerations . . . it is my duty to demand, and I do hereby demand of you, an immediate surrender.

Frost had little choice. He sent the adjutant back with a note acquiescing, under strong protest, to the demand.[118]

At this point the second casualty of the day was suffered. Dismounting with the note in hand, Lyon was promptly kicked in the stomach by the overexcited horse of one of his aides. Doubling over in pain, he collapsed senseless on the ground. A doctor from one of the German regiments hurried over to him, and Lyon gradually began regaining consciousness, but apparently he was still incapacitated when the evacuation of Camp Jackson began.[119]

Blair's and Boernstein's regiments drew up in formation on each side as Frost's men began to file out through an opening in the fence. All around them, crowds of civilians pressed in. Many were friends and relatives of the captured soldiers, anxious to see that their loved ones were all right; others had come to hail the Union triumph; most were probably just gawkers. Even Sherman, hearing that Frost had surrendered peacefully, now came to watch, holding young Willie by the hand. These spectators were amazed at the sight: militiamen in the splendid uniforms of Missouri's most elite dragoon regiments; the flower of the old families—Longuemares, Ladues, Gareschés; the cream of St. Louis in "the beauty of youth, aristocratic breeding, clannish pride"—now captives, every one of them, stacking their arms in submission, trudging sullenly down Pine Street between the ranks of their drab "Dutch" captors. Two black women in the crowd, exultant, began laughing and yelling taunts at the humiliated militia. Soon other bystanders began hurling insults at the victorious Germans: "Damn Dutch!" "Hessians!" "Infidels!" One man cheered for Jeff Davis; another for Abe Lincoln. Lyon's officers, trying to drown out the cacophony, ordered a brass band at the head of the column to start playing. Still the obscenities flew; women spat on the Union volunteers; others started scooping up rocks and dirt to throw at them. A few men brandished revolvers and knives.[120]

Afterward, no one could agree on how the shooting started. One teenager recalled seeing a boy his own age pitch a clod of dirt at a mounted officer. Other witnesses described an unarmed man stepping out of the row of onlookers and being savagely bayoneted by one of the "Dutchmen." The most credible accounts corroborate what Sherman would remember. As he and Willie watched, a drunken man in the crowd tried to push his way through the ranks of Sigel's troops to reach the other side. When a sergeant blocked him with his musket, shoving him roughly down a steep embankment, the drunkard staggered to his feet, pulled a small pistol from his pocket, and fired. An officer on horseback screamed as the bullet tore a gaping wound in his leg. (The captain, an exiled Polish nobleman named Constantin Blandowski, would die of his injury a few weeks later.) And so it was that the panicking soldiers turned their muskets on the crowd. Somewhere up at the head of the column, surreally, the German band kept playing.[121]

Sherman ran back toward the grove, pulling Willie into a ditch and covering the boy with his body as they heard bullets cutting through the leaves and branches overhead. Around them people stampeded in all directions, some of them wounded. A few bold civilians stood their ground and fired back at the soldiers. Captain Lyon, one of the few professional soldiers on hand and perhaps the only one capable of bringing his raw recruits under control, was still woozy from the kick he had received. By the time the shooting stopped, bodies lay everywhere: a middle-aged street vendor, a teenage girl, a young German laborer in his work clothes, and several soldiers from both Frost's and Lyon's commands. A wounded woman sat keening on the ground, clasping the body of her dead child in her arms. In all, more than two dozen people had been killed or mortally hurt.

Lyon, dazed, stood looking around him, murmuring in a strange, soft voice: "Poor creatures . . . poor creatures . . ."[122]

Others stared amazed at the sight of buildings pockmarked with bullet holes, like wounds torn in the city itself. Much commented on afterward was the remarkable power of the new Minié rifle balls, how such small lumps of lead could make such big craters in brickwork and stone.

A twelve-year-old boy, returning home with his father to Pine Street, saw something that would still haunt him more than six decades later:

> Two bullets had struck our house, and just outside a German soldier was sitting on the side-walk with his back to the wall. Coming closer we could distinguish where the Minié bullet had penetrated his temple. He was dead. Close by a servant with a pail of water was washing a stream of blood off the side-walk where someone had been killed, and the sight to me was indescribably horrible. My father said this was civil war.[123]

The retaliation began that night. Crowds of secessionists gathered in front of the Planter's House as impromptu orators railed against the Black Republicans and Hessian mercenaries. At last the mob decided to wreck the *Anzeiger* print shop; storming down Main Street, they smashed the window of Dimick's gun store and began grabbing shotguns and rifles. Fortunately for Boernstein's paper, some quick-thinking Home Guards blocked the street and fended off the attack with fixed bayonets. For the next twenty-four hours, though, Germans foolish enough to appear in public were chased down and beaten, stoned, sometimes lynched. One of the reserve regiments was ambushed by secessionists firing from behind the pillars of a Presbyterian church; in the ensuing confusion, several soldiers unlucky enough to become separated from their comrades were seized and executed with shots fired point-blank to the head. Rumors began reaching the city of similar reprisals across the state; in towns too small to have any Germans, Republicans were slain or "abolitionist" churches burned.[124]

Meanwhile, in the wealthier neighborhoods of St. Louis, it was said that the "Dutch" were about to sack and burn the city. "The 'upper ten,' the rich, proud slaveholders," as Boernstein called them, loaded up draymen's wagons with mahogany furniture and chests of linen and evacuated by the thousands, crowding aboard ferryboats, seeking the safety of the Illinois shore.[125]

But Captain Lyon's sights were now set beyond St. Louis. He had accomplished everything he needed to do there.

Within a matter of weeks, Lyon, Blair, Sigel, and their German volunteers were marching toward central Missouri in hot pursuit of Governor Jackson, who by this point had unilaterally declared war on the United States and called for 50,000 volunteers to defend against Yankee invasion. (Boernstein and his men stayed behind to guard St. Louis.) Jackson evacuated Jefferson City at the troops' approach, accompanied by most of the prosecession legislature and the Missouri state troops. Lyon caught up with them fifty miles away, at Boonville, where he dealt them a quick but decisive defeat. After just a few casualties on each side, the state troops broke ranks and fled, hotly pursued by the German regiments, into the far southwestern corner of the state. Missouri would never again be in serious danger of falling into rebel hands.[126]

While Thomas Starr King and Jessie Frémont may not have saved California for the Union, it is reasonable to say that Nathaniel Lyon, Frank Blair, and the Germans did save Missouri. Somehow, the strange, almost accidental alliance of two outsize egotists (one of them possibly psychotic) and several thousand idealists had carried the day.

Grant himself would believe for the rest of his life that but for them, the Arsenal—and with it St. Louis—would have been taken by the Confederacy. Some historians have argued that the militia at Camp Jackson, even if reinforced, could never have posed any serious threat by itself, which is perhaps true. But by seizing the initiative, by transforming the Wide Awakes into soldiers and moving against the secessionists before they could properly organize, the "damn Dutchmen" had sent their enemies reeling, never to regain balance. In effect, a small band of German revolutionaries accomplished in St. Louis what they had failed to do in Vienna and Heidelberg: overthrow a reactionary state government. And they had done it in a matter of weeks, while in the East the armies were stumbling toward a war of attrition that would last almost four years. If the Union in 1861 had just had a few more Lyons and Blairs in charge of its troops, its conquest of the South might have played out very differently.[127]

But even swift victory did not come without a price. For the rest of those four years, Missouri would be the scene of atrocities unlike any seen elsewhere: ceaseless guerrilla warfare that erased distinctions between soldier and civilian almost entirely; violence with no greater strategic purpose than avenging the violence that had come before; in a few notorious instances, hundreds lined up and executed in cold blood. There would be many more shattered buildings, dead children and dead mothers, gutters awash in blood.

O n J u l y 4 , 1 8 6 1, a thousand miles from Fort Churchill—at Julesburg in the newly organized Colorado Territory—a crew of workmen raised the first pole at the eastern end of the transcontinental telegraph. On the same day, too, news went out that President Lincoln had just appointed John C. Frémont, newly returned from Europe, to command the Department of the West. He and his wife would set out as soon as possible for St. Louis.

Throughout that summer, two telegraph lines converged over the deserts and plains. As the termini drew closer, the route of the Pony Express grew shorter and shorter, until at last the swift horsemen were carrying messages across only the little distance between the wires. The connection was made in October at Salt Lake City; the indomitable Hiram Sibley and his partners had beaten Congress's seemingly impossible deadline by more than a year. Within days, communications traffic was so heavy that operators began talking of the need for a second wire and even a third. "When once the Yankees get started," an Ohio newspaper editor marveled, "it is hard for them to stop."[128]

The honor of sending one of San Francisco's first messages across the continent was accorded to the Reverend Thomas Starr King. His words raced eastward as dots and dashes, arriving thus at the office of the *Boston Evening Transcript:*

> All hail! A new bond of union between Pacific and Atlantic! The lightning now goeth out of the west and shineth even in the east! Heaven preserve the republic, and bless old Boston from hub to rim!

The arc of the sun he had once so powerfully traced was now reinforced by a strand of copper filament.

Over the four years to come, as the war raged east of the Mississippi, more and more lines would be drawn across the West.

In 1862, Congress—suddenly liberated from sectional gridlock in its half-empty chamber—would pass the Homestead Act, promising 160 acres of federal land to any man or woman willing to settle it. In the autumn of the following year, the first lengths of the transcontinental railway were laid at Sacramento. Lines of new counties, farm boundaries, townships, and streets spread across the map, mere pencil markings that soon took shape on the landscape itself. Miles of rail fences followed, and the twin ruts of new wagon roads.

And across all of it, the wire—busier and busier, its indifferent electrons carrying speeches and sermons, grain prices and casualty lists, through mountain passes that the Pathfinder once had crossed.

CHAPTER SEVEN

The Crossing

Who here forecasteth the event?

—HERMAN MELVILLE,
"The March into Virginia" (1861)

The Marshall House, Alexandria, Virginia, circa 1862

Washington, May 1861

DURING THE FIRST DAYS OF MAY, an unusual sight greeted visitors to the Capitol. In the great Rotunda, beneath the interrupted dome, young men in gray-and-red uniforms and fezzes swung like merry acrobats from ropes and shimmied up pillars. They capered over the muddy grounds, one observer wrote, "leaping fences, knocking down sentinels, turning aside indignant bayonets, hanging like monkeys from the outer ledges of the dome, some two hundred feet above the firm-set earth."[1]

Those staid classical halls had witnessed some strange things already that year. The rancorous scenes to which they had long since become accustomed—Northerners thundering against Southerners, slaveholders denouncing abolitionists, torrents of baroque invective relieved only by occasional fistfights—had yielded suddenly to an unprecedented calm. But now, just weeks later, there was neither tranquility or rancor here. Rather, it might have seemed at first glance that a flying circus had invaded the Capitol.

Like the nation itself, the Capitol Building was a work in progress that spring. Several years earlier, a forward-thinking Southern statesman had directed an ambitious expansion project, spreading the marble wings across their hilltop, ready to encompass all the delegations and committees, offices and bureaus, that the rapidly growing federal union might require. To maintain proper scale, an architect was engaged to remove the old low-rise curve of the roof and replace it with a soaring new dome of cast iron, as serenely presumptuous in its grandiosity as a Natchez cotton planter's mansion or a Newport railroad baron's "cottage." Then lawmakers busied themselves with deciding what kind of statue should crown the new structure. Taking a break from their debates over Kansas and slavery, they found a rare moment of bipartisan accord: the nation's temple of democracy must be topped with a heroic statue of Freedom, that amiable and versatile goddess. But when the sculptor presented his plaster model, sectional strife erupted again. On her head, the figure wore a pileus, the Roman cap of liberty, a conventional bit of allegory. But the Southern politician who had taken such interest in the work, a man with a fine classical education, knew that the pileus had been used in ancient times to denote a slave who had been freed by his master. The gentleman—Jefferson Davis, then serving as secretary of war—protested lest such a blatant symbol of abolitionism crown the very pinnacle of the Republic.[2]

Now the statue, her objectionable liberty cap replaced by a politically innocuous, if allegorically dubious, Roman helmet, lay in pieces, yet to be assembled, at a Maryland bronze foundry. (*Freedom*'s casting was being overseen there by an expert metalworker, a slave named Philip Reid.) The Capitol dome itself rose half finished, wooden scaffolding and an enormous crane jutting up above its open shell, which seemed to hang in the balance between creation and destruction. Sage minds reflected that it symbolized the incomplete—and imperiled—Union itself. The metaphor, if not the building, was satisfyingly perfect. Walt Whitman, though he had little use for the statue of Freedom, deriding it as "an extensive female, cast in bronze, with much drapery, especially ruffles," loved the incomplete Capitol and suggested it be left perpetually as it was, with the derrick crane a more "poetical" emblem of the republic than Davis's statue.[3]

What, though, was the meaning of the sight—to say nothing of the sounds and smells—that greeted visitors in May? No poetical explanations came immediately to mind. In corridors off the rotunda, statues of lawmakers and patriots trembled precariously on their pedestals as hordes of young rowdies raced past. The building reeked of urine (and worse) as men, tired of lining up for the overcrowded privies, availed themselves of any corner they could find. When a sentry tried to block one group from entering an off-limits area, they rolled him down the Capitol steps. In the House of Representatives, they playacted a session of Congress, in the course of which they "elected a Speaker, Clerk, and other officers, went into full session, dissolved the Union and reconstructed it and then wound up the joke by going into executive session."[4] Others put their feet up, enjoying penny-ante card games on the desk of one South Carolina legislator, a fire-breathing states' rights man, who had decamped when his state seceded.

In the Senate, the invaders quickly found the desk that until recently had been occupied by Senator Davis, still bearing a placard with his name neatly inked. A distraught custodian arrived to find the young men hacking it to pieces with their bayonets, and feebly protested that it was the property not of the Confederate traitor but of the federal government that they had just pledged their lives to defend. Ignoring him, the soldiers divvied up the wooden fragments as souvenirs.[5]

These were the thousand soldiers of the First New York Fire Zouaves, who, through the infinite wisdom of military authorities, had been bivouacked in the Capitol upon their arrival in Washington, two days before.

They had landed in a city already teeming with soldiers—so many, one newspaperman reflected, that its customarily drab streets at last resembled, in at least one respect, the imperial capitals of Paris, Vienna, and St. Petersburg: every third man you passed wore some sort of gaudy uniform. Everywhere, too, particularly in the grandest public buildings, in fact, was the stench of unwashed bodies and fresh piss. Troops bunked on makeshift cots among filing cabinets and display cases in the Patent Office; in the courtyard of the Treasury on Pennsylvania Avenue; even in the East Room of the White House, twenty feet directly below the president's desk.[6]

Several different regiments quartered in the Capitol. Soldiers slept under congressmen's desks by night; by day drilled hourly before the east front; in the intervening hours stretched out on the young grass beneath horse chestnut trees heavy with pink-white blossoms in the burgeoning spring. Sometimes they played baseball on the lawn where, weeks earlier, a crowd had gathered to see Mr. Lincoln give his inaugural address. (How distant that seemed now!) At night, recalled one New York private, the crimson-and-gold House chamber reverberated with the rhythmic breathing of a thousand sleepers, until the drums beat reveille at dawn, when the din of rambunctious voices began again, unceasing until dusk. The irony of his location was not lost on this thoughtful recruit, Theodore Winthrop, a poet and travel writer of some repute who had joined up with the New York Seventh, and who was now hunched over a lamp in one corner of the hall, penning a dispatch to *The Atlantic Monthly*. "Our presence here was the inevitable sequel of past events," he wrote. "We appeared with bayonets and bullets because of the bosh uttered on this floor; because of the bills—with treasonable stump-speeches in their bellies—passed here; because of the cowardice of the poltroons, the imbecility of the dodgers, and the arrogance of the bullies, who had here cooperated to blind and corrupt the minds of the people. Talk had made a miserable mess of it." He scoffed at the departed congressmen as belonging already to "that bygone epoch of our country when men shaved the moustache, dressed like parsons, said 'Sir,' and chewed tobacco"—supplanted now in their own inner sanctum by a bolder and more colorful generation.[7]

NO CROWDS HAD GREETED the Zouaves' entry into the capital. The troop train from Annapolis rattled slowly and unceremoniously through the fields of Maryland amid the gathering dusk, through cow pastures and then past the garbage dumps, drainage pipes, and heaps of abandoned bricks that lined the approach to the city. At last the dome of the Capitol loomed up from out of nowhere, moments before it was blotted from sight by the low roof of the soot-blackened central depot.[8] No one but the president himself seemed to have been notified of the regiment's arrival—and in any case Washington was, by this point, jaded by the coming of troops—so only a few passersby were there to give the disembarking men handshakes and wan cheers.[9] Even the military authorities seemed less pleased to see them than irritated at the task of having to find somewhere to put them, before shrugging their shoulders and deciding to quarter the Zouaves in the Capitol.

None of this was exactly what Ellsworth had planned for his triumphant return at the head of his regiment. So, before letting his weary and hungry men find rest and food in their makeshift barracks, he insisted on marching them up Pennsylvania Avenue in the opposite direction, toward the White House. Though it was now fully dark, an overcast and almost moonless night, he was still set on making the grand entrance he had lovingly envisioned. By the time the regiment reached the presidential mansion, he could see a familiar stooping figure silhouetted against the north portico. The president, his family, and a few aides had gathered on the gravel drive to watch as the companies passed by for their impromptu nighttime review, and hundreds of throaty voices boomed, "Three cheers for Abraham Lincoln!" or "Hooray for Old Abe!"

As the marchers strode abreast past the streetlamps, circles of gaslight revealed their whiskered faces, flattened noses, and shining scalps. The firemen had, nearly to a man, shaved their heads in preparation for battle. "A jolly gay set of blackguards," John Hay called them.[10] These Zouaves were not the lithe gymnasts Ellsworth had paraded here for President Buchanan the summer before, a summer that already seemed a century ago. Their uniforms may have been just as splendid—red caps and shirts, gray jackets, baggy pantaloons in authentic Franco-Algerian style—but from their belts hung unromantic implements of killing: large and wicked-looking bowie knives, omens of fraternal bloodshed not merely imminent but brutal and close range.

In New York, the war had seemed a somewhat remote adventure, a fanfare in the middle distance. Here in Washington, it was palpable in the ever-present drumbeat of men drilling for war, the measured tramp of boots, and the urgent click of telegraph keys transmitting mostly bad news. Virginia's legislature had cast its lot with the Confederacy three weeks earlier; Arkansas and Tennessee were teetering on the brink. Resignations still arrived daily at the War Department from many of the most seasoned officers of the regular army. Amid the panic and disorder after Sumter's fall, many residents had fled the city—Union sympathizers jammed Seventeenth Street in carriages, wagons, and loaded carts, pressing northward toward the Maryland line, while Southerners slipped one by one across the Potomac.[11]

There had been good reason for those Unionists to panic. Washington was encircled by slave territory, and it looked as though Marylanders might be following the Virginians into rebellion. Baltimore secessionists, who controlled the city's telegraph office, severed communications between the nation's capital and the rest of the loyal states. Railroad travel was interrupted; mail stopped. Just a handful of troops defended the District, and when the Sixth Massachusetts tried to relieve the capital, it was attacked by a mob on its way through Baltimore. In the confused melee, four soldiers and twelve civilians were killed. These were the first combat deaths of the war; a Northern lithographer issued a print showing apelike street toughs hurling bricks at the stalwart boys in blue, and titled it *The Lexington of 1861.*[12]

Southerners were calling for an immediate attack on the capital. "There is one wild shout of fierce resolve to capture Washington City, at all and every human hazard," wrote the editors of the *Richmond Examiner.* "The filthy cage of unclean birds must and will be purified by fire. . . . Many indeed will be the carcasses of dogs and caitiffs that will blacken the air upon the gallows, before the great work is accomplished."[13]

But the birds, dogs, and caitiffs had managed to squeak through, at least for the time being. The Sixth Massachusetts, the Seventh New York, and other regiments eventually arrived, and soon more troops were pouring into Washington daily. They represented, if not a cross section of the North, then at least a vivid assortment of citizen-soldiers. Later in the war, Union enlisted men would nearly all be clad in identical navy blue tunics, factory made by the tens of thousands—indeed, the concept of standard sizes in men's clothing, eventually picked up for civilian attire, began with that wartime mass production. But there was nothing mass-produced about the war in early 1861. The volunteers who had converged upon the capital sported scarlet plumes and gold lace, turbans and tyroleans. (That is, those who had any uniforms at all: quite a few, awaiting shipments from home, were still in civilian garb.) Some belonged to prewar militias, but there were many newly formed regiments. As with the Fire Zouaves, these had customarily been organized in local communities by individual men of sufficient wealth or charisma to rally the troops together, arm them, and lead them off toward the front. Each of these colonels was a grandee of some sort—whether a metropolitan police commissioner or a country squire—and often the regiment bore his name.[14]

These fresh volunteers, with their spotless clothing and jaunty self-confidence, had done much to relieve the feeling of siege, and some Washington citizens were returning home, a bit sheepishly. Still, no one could forget that the enemy forces were massing just on the other side of the river. In Alexandria—until recently part of the District of Columbia—a hotelkeeper had raised an enormous secession banner atop his establishment, so large that on the clear spring afternoons it could be seen in downtown Washington. From the windows of the White House, Hay, Nicolay, and even the president and first lady stole glances at it through a spyglass.

For the New York fire boys, many of whom had never ventured farther from home than certain out-of-the-way sections of Brooklyn, the national capital was a disappointment. Even in wartime, the city seemed sleepy in comparison to Gotham, almost rustic. With the exception of a few gleaming federal temples, the buildings were mostly ramshackle wooden affairs set amid sprawling yards, where black men and women—the first slaves that most of the Yankees had ever actually seen—looked up from their chores to watch with wary eyes the passing troops. Pigs and goats foraged for scraps in the avenues laid out optimistically by L'Enfant at the end of the previous century: broad, empty thoroughfares that dead-ended suddenly in cornfields, and whose mud was so deep in springtime that you often had to walk several blocks before finding a safe place to cross the street. Not many years earlier, the Great Compromiser himself, Senator Henry Clay, had found himself attacked by a large billy goat in the middle of Pennsylvania Avenue, much to the delight of the newsboys and bootblacks who gathered to watch the contest between quadruped and statesman.[15]

"Everything worth looking at seemed unfinished," said one acerbic visitor. "Everything finished looked as if it should have been destroyed generations before." Indeed, the Washington of 1861 seemed in itself a kind of tacit argument against the very idea of a national government, or at least as evidence of that government's incapability to maintain its own existence. The few offices of the executive branch had an almost makeshift feel: even the State Department possessed the atmosphere of a county courthouse, with a posted notice in the front hall listing the weekly hours that Secretary Seward received callers. "The government had an air of social instability and incompleteness that went far to support the right of secession in theory as in fact; but right or wrong, secession was likely to be easy where there was so little to secede from," Henry Adams later wrote. "The Union was a sentiment, but not much more."[16]

The local civilians' sole professional activity seemed to be the leisurely task of waiting: waiting for a bill to wend its way through the slow peristalsis of congressional committees; waiting in the lobby of Willard's for an elusive cabinet patron to make his appearance; waiting in the shabby White House anteroom to ask a favor of the president. The archetypal Washingtonian had his feet propped on the end table, a wad of tobacco in his cheek, and a newspaper in his hand.[17]

Waiting may have been the locals' favorite pastime, but the New York firemen did not share their taste. After four days en route to the capital, cooped up on the steamer and then the train, they had expected and hoped to disembark straight into the thick of battle. (You could hardly blame them—it had been weeks since their last chance for even a good street brawl.) As they tumbled out of their train, a newspaperman had heard one Zouave ask, "Can you tell us where Jeff Davis is? We're lookin' for him." A comrade chimed in: "We're bound to hang his scalp in the White House before we go back." Others squinted in perplexity, looking around for secession flags to capture but failing to discover any.[18]

On the morning after their arrival, ten-year-old Willie Lincoln, whose parents had allowed him to stay up late and watch the grand procession the evening before, wrote excitedly to a former playmate in Illinois, eking out the letters in a laborious schoolboy hand: "I suppose that you did not learn that Colonel, E.E. Ellsworth had gone up to New York and organized a regiment,—divided in to companys, and brought them here, & to be sworn in—I dont know when. Some people call them the B'hoys, & others call them, the firemen." It wasn't long before Willie and his younger brother, Tad, had asked their indulgent father for their own pint-size Zouave uniforms, in which they paraded, chests out and heads high, around the White House grounds. Their parents solemnly reviewed the two-man regiment (which the boys had named Mrs. Lincoln's Zouaves) and presented it with a flag; a photograph of Tad in his uniform survives to this day.[19]

Willie and Tad Lincoln were not alone in having gone a bit b'hoy crazy. "Every zouave is surrounded by a group of eager listeners," a *New York Herald* writer reported, amused at how these ordinary Bowery roughnecks had become exotic novelties. Washington was not without its own, homegrown rowdy element, to be sure: "Riot and bloodshed are of daily occurrence," reported a Senate committee in 1858, exaggerating perhaps just a little. But it is safe to say that few locals had ever observed at close range such a colorful troupe of ruffians as the b'hoys. Their salty New York dialect won particular admiration.[20]

Local newspapermen delighted in regaling readers with tales of the Zouave exploits—many at least slightly exaggerated in the telling—and these stories were picked by newspapers throughout the Union, even in the odd corner of the Confederacy. One gang of b'hoys was said to have strolled nonchalantly into a restaurant, ordered themselves a fine meal, knocked over the tables, and smashed the crockery, at the end of their romp cheerfully telling the proprietor that he should charge the whole bill to Jeff Davis. Another group swaggered over to the National Hotel, treated the barroom to a few rounds of drinks, "and tendered three cheers for the Union as payment in full." Still others raided cigar shops and liquor stores, bowling over any unfortunate policeman who tried to interpose himself. Wild rumors of sexual outrages circulated, "terrifying all the maiden antiques of the city for several days," as Hay dryly put it.[21] Even some of the b'hoys' Union comrades kept their distance: "I fear we shall stand a poorer chance with these fellows than with the Southerners," a Massachusetts soldier wrote home.[22]

Barely twenty-four hours after his triumphant arrival, Ellsworth found himself compelled to place an apology in the newspapers, explaining that the "Regiment of Zouaves were recruited in great haste," and promising that although a few miscreants had found their way into the ranks, they would be sternly dealt with.[23] It could not have pleased him that his gallant b'hoys had already acquired the sarcastic new moniker "Ellsworth's pet lambs."

Within the week, however, the pet lambs were given a fortuitous oportunity to redeem themselves. In the early-morning hours of May 9, a liquor store on Pennsylvania Avenue caught fire. Before long, the flames had spread to a second building and were licking against the walls of a third—one of the many lesser offshoots of the Willard Hotel. A couple local fire companies arrived and tried fecklessly to quench the flames. At last the cry went up for the Fire Zouaves. Within minutes, the red-shirted b'hoys had leapt out the windows of the Capitol and were rushing pell-mell down the avenue, pausing only to break into an unattended firehouse and make off with its engine. When they reached the Willard, it was filling rapidly with smoke, and the tarred roof was in imminent danger of catching fire. The New Yorkers called for ladders and, discovering that there were none, promptly formed a human pyramid and clambered six stories to the top of the hotel. Some hauled up a hose, while others grabbed washbasins, tubs, and chamber pots from the guest rooms and filled them with water to soak the roof. One particularly agile and fearless Zouave hung upside down from the cornice, as a comrade held him by the ankles, to hose the burning liquor store from the best possible angle. In no time, the fire was quenched, the hotel was saved, and hundreds of onlookers and evacuated guests cheered lustily for the boys from New York.

As the last flames flickered out, an upstairs window opened and a gray-haired man peered out curiously. The crowd redoubled its cheers—for the man was none other than Major Robert Anderson, who had arrived in the capital several days earlier to meet with General Scott, Secretary Cameron, and the president (who had rewarded his heroism by offering a lengthy leave of absence from active duty). After Sumter, apparently, he would let no mere hotel fire disturb his rest. After a quick wave to the crowd and salute to the Zouaves, Anderson closed the window again and returned to bed.

The next day's newspapers were, of course, full of the story, and *Harper's Weekly*, the leading national magazine, soon blazoned its cover with a full-page woodcut of the brave fire b'hoys silhouetted against a sheet of flame, while the Stars and Stripes waved implausibly above them, unscathed. In the highly charged atmosphere of wartime, unnamed rebel arsonists were believed to be behind the conflagration—a reasonable conjecture, *The New York Times* opined, since the hotel "has so often sheltered good and loyal Republicans."[24]

Further enhancing their new dignity, Ellsworth's New York recruits were now no longer mere volunteer militiamen but sworn soldiers of the United States. The day before the hotel fire, the entire regiment had gathered to take the oath of national service. Those witnessing this ceremony would not soon forget it. Late that afternoon, on the east side of the Capitol, the thousand men formed a square around the marble statue of Washington. At a signal, they straightened to attention and their colonel stepped forward to address them. He began with a stern denunciation of those whose conduct had disgraced the regiment, and vowed that any doing likewise would be sent home in irons forthwith. Then Ellsworth's tone changed. Here is how Hay, writing later that same night, recorded his words:

> You are now about to be mustered into the service of the United States, and are the first regiment who will pledge yourselves

not for thirty days or sixty days, but *for the war!* (Tremendous applause, and nine loud, long, and hearty cheers.) Now if any man of you has the desire to back out, wants to leave this glorious war and go home, now is the time. Let him sneak away like a hound, and crawl over the fence and be off! (Cries of "No!" "No!" "Not one!" and three cheers for Colonel Ellsworth.)

Then, facing the Capitol, the men lined up in two rows across the entire width of the grounds. As the roll was called and each answered, a carriage drew up with the president, leading by the hand his younger son, Tad. Lincoln walked slowly along the row of soldiers, father and son inspecting each man as they passed.[25]

At last, two officers of the regular army stepped forward to administer the oath. One was the craggy, white-haired General Lorenzo Thomas, still dressed in the uniform of a colonel, having received his brigadier's star only that morning. The other was a tall officer, stately and perhaps somewhat pompous-looking, with an out-thrust chest and lovingly tended Napoleon beard. This was Major Irvin McDowell, then commanding the troops guarding the Capitol. (In two months' time, occupying a more exalted rank, he would be forever linked with this regiment in front of him, and with a catastrophic summer afternoon at Bull Run.)

There was another, humbler detail that Hay recorded that night. As he stood near the regimental flags, the proud standards that Mrs. Astor and Laura Keene had bestowed on the troop, he saw one of the Zouave color guards wrap his arm affectionately around a flagpole, as if he were embracing an old friend.

"The red, white, and blue! God bless them!" the man told Hay. "We boys is going to fight for these pieces of cloth till we die!"

Another added, "We're going to have one more flag when we come back. It'll be the flag of secession, nailed on the bottom o' this flag staff."[26]

DAYS OF WAITING FOLLOWED: not the languid expectancy that was the local specialty but an atmosphere of preparatory tension. Ellsworth seemed to be everywhere around the city, incessantly pestering officials for better arms and equipment. He was thin as a greyhound, his voice hoarse from the incessant shouting of drill commands. A curious civilian spotted the little colonel bounding into the lobby of the Willard with an enormous revolver flapping at his belt. Indeed,

Ellsworth seemed to go everywhere armed as if ready at any moment to engage in single-handed combat against a grizzly bear. In addition to the revolver, he wore both an elaborately gilded officer's sword and a more businesslike bowie knife, its blade more than a foot long, the kind jocularly known as an "Arkansas toothpick." An amused Hay remarked that it looked as though it might easily "go through a man's head from crown to chin as you would split an apple."[27]

No task was too trivial for him. One newspaper correspondent wrote that at one moment, he would be seen marching at the head of his troops, and the next, "assisting a colored servant to carry a box of muskets across the room," or showing a raw recruit how to fasten his knapsack. One fine Sunday afternoon, he was even spotted, in his billowy red Zouave shirt, playing a game of baseball with his men.[28] Although barely twenty-four years old (he had celebrated his birthday the eve of the attack on Sumter), the colonel was already winning the affection and respect of the hardened New York firemen, who seemed willing to overlook that he had never bloodied his knuckles in a Bowery brawl, nor ever heard a gunshot fired in anger.

Much of Ellsworth's boyishness remained, not just in his romantic approach to soldiering but in his quickness of affection and his longing for family. His parents still lived in their village in upstate New York; he had hardly seen them in years. The day before the regiment had left from New York, his mother had made her way down to the city and come to the Astor House, amid the bustle and fanfare of departure, to bid her only son farewell. Elmer's much-loved brother, Charley, had died in Chicago the previous summer, just before the cadets set out on their tour.[29]

The Lincolns had become, in a sense, surrogate parents. Any free moment usually found Ellsworth at the White House. When the president and Mrs. Lincoln were unavailable, he would be romping through the corridors with Willie and Tad, or horsing around with Hay, Nicolay, and Lincoln's other young aides.* One afternoon, he was in the office at the Executive Mansion, spiritedly showing a presidential secretary, William Stoddard, how to handle a carbine Zouave-style, when he twirled the gun too close to a window. The two young men made up a far-fetched story to explain the broken glass: an assassin had been lurking in the shrubbery outside, they said, and, mistaking Ellsworth for the president, had fired a bullet through the windowpane.[30]

---

*Earlier that spring, in the weeks before the firing on Sumter, Ellsworth was put temporarily out of commission after contracting measles from the Lincoln boys.

On other occasions, Ellsworth would join the Lincolns in peering curiously across the river at the large rebel banner that had mocked them for a month from the skyline of Alexandria. Afterward, some would say that Mrs. Lincoln had begged him to tear it down as soon as he and his troops reached Virginia, although others disputed this.[31] For some anxious Unionists, that flag was becoming a symbol of the administration's slowness to move against the gathering forces of the Confederacy. When one visitor to the White House, the radical abolitionist Senator Benjamin Wade of Ohio, pointedly complained to the president about the banner still waving there after so many weeks, Lincoln replied that he should not expect to see it waving much longer.[32]

Finally, the awaited order came. For days, Northern newspapers had been full of reports that a federal advance into Virginia was imminent. ("Secret Military Moves on Foot!" announced a headline in the irrepressible *New York Herald*.) Union and Confederate forces faced off across the Potomac, with opposing sentries posted just a few hundred yards apart, at the ends of the two bridges that spanned the river. Alexandria, the railway hub of northern Virginia—and a secessionist stronghold within sight of the capital—was the logical point of attack. And there was no overlooking its port as a potential haven for Confederate smugglers or privateers. Since early May, the federal gunboat *Pawnee* had lain just off Alexandria's wharves, its full broadside of nine-inch cannons aimed at the town.[33]

On May 23, Virginians voted in a special referendum to ratify the state's secession—the final step in leaving the Union. That night, before the last votes had been counted, federal troops gathered on the banks of the Potomac, and the first major Northern incursion into rebel-held territory was under way.

SHORTLY AFTER MIDNIGHT, the planks of the Long Bridge, four miles above Alexandria, resounded with the rhythmic tramp of crossing infantry. Several miles upstream, Union cavalrymen were riding across the Chain Bridge. The plan was for these troops to approach the town overland from the north, while a smaller amphibious force crossed the river by steamer to land directly at the waterfront. Men from New York, New Jersey, Michigan, and Massachusetts were making their way into Virginia.

It was a balmy, summer-like night: "mild, dewy, refulgent," wrote Theodore Winthrop, whose kid-glove New York regiment was among the advancing infantry. The pale light of a full moon glinted off newly burnished bayonets and sabers. Scarcely a whisper was heard among the troops, only occasionally the muffled command of an officer. So silent was this crossing of thousands that on the shore behind them, the darkened capital slept; only William Seward, intent as ever on seeing and knowing as much as he could, had come down to survey the operations intently from the Washington end of Long Bridge.[34]

Ellsworth and his Zouaves were still in camp, on a rise just beyond the southeastern edge of the city. Despite the late hour and the hard work to come, the men went about their battle preparations quickly and almost gleefully, breaking out every so often into snatches of patriotic song. At last, the b'hoys were going to get the fine bare-knuckle fight they had been itching for. They checked and cleaned their new rifles, which had been fitted with saber bayonets: broadly curving steel blades that could, in an instant, turn a gun into a spear. When all was ready, the colonel gathered them for a few words of exhortation—no doubt the kind of night-before-the-battle speech he had been rehearsing in his mind since his boyhood in Mechanicville—and then told them to retire to their tents for a couple of hours' rest. Ellsworth himself sat up writing at his camp table, scribbling orders to his company commanders before turning to a more solemn task: composing letters to his parents and his fiancée, to be opened in the event of his death. Then he buttoned up the coat of his dress uniform, and at the last moment pinned to his chest a gold medal that had been given him the year before, during the Chicago cadets' summer tour. *Non solum nobis, sed pro Patria*, the Latin inscription read: "Not for ourselves alone, but for our Country."[35]

The Fire Zouaves had been chosen to carry out the amphibious part of the attack—and, as seemed likely, to be the first troops that would encounter enemy forces. At two o'clock in the morning, a navy captain arrived to tell Ellsworth that three vessels—the steamers *James Guy, Baltimore*, and *Mount Vernon*—were ready to carry them across, accompanied by a couple of launches from the USS *Pawnee*, which awaited them at anchor off Alexandria. The moon was now shining at its fullest: "bright and handsome as a twenty-dollar gold piece," one soldier thought, while another would later recall that you could write a letter by its light. Many of the Zouaves, following their commander's example, were doing just this, penning hasty notes to loved ones, which they tucked into knapsacks as they made their way down to the river.[36]

Another man present was busy scribbling as well: Ned House, a newspaper correspondent for the *New-York Tribune*. Though barely older than Ellsworth, House was one of the most ambitious and intrepid of Greeley's protégés: eighteen months earlier, at John Brown's execution, he had (at least by his own account) disguised himself as an army surgeon and managed to get a place standing on the scaffold just a few feet from the condemned man. His firsthand report in the *Tribune*—including all the ghastly details of Brown's body jerking at the end of the rope—had shocked Northern readers.[37] Now, getting wind of the impending attack on Alexandria, House had tried to talk his way past Northern sentries on the Long Bridge, and, failing this, hastened to the Zouave camp, attaching himself to Ellsworth's regiment. It was a decision he would not regret. Watching the soldiers leave for battle, he found himself stirred by the sight: "the vivid costumes of the men—some being wrapt from head to foot in their great red blankets, but most of them clad in their gray jackets and trowsers and embroidered caps; the peaks of the tents, regularly distributed, all glowing like huge lanterns from the fires within them; the glittering rows of rifles and sabres; the woods and hills, and the placid river . . . and all these suffused with the broad moonlight."[38]

Even some of the b'hoys themselves were moved, not just by the beauty of the night but by the sense that they were about to participate in history. "We believe it to have been the most impressive and beautiful scene we ever witnessed," one of them wrote a few days later. "No length of years can wipe it from our memory—it is daguerreotyped on our mind forever."[39]

By the time the steamers neared Alexandria, the moon was sinking, and the glassy surface of the river had begun to gleam red with the rising sun. Crowding along the rails, the Zouaves scanned the waterfront for the enemy and, as they drew closer, spotted a thin line of Confederate sentinels, who fired their muskets into the air in warning. A few of Ellsworth's men, thinking that these were the opening shots of the battle, let fly a volley in return. But the rebels were already scattering up the hillside, running "as if the Devil himself had been after them with a particularly sharp stick," one Zouave thought. What the Union forces didn't know is that those sentinels were simply rejoining their compatriots, who were withdrawing en masse from the town. The canny rebel commanders knew that they couldn't hold Alexandria, and that the best strategy was to lure the enemy deeper into Virginia, and into the morass of war. The only risk was that some men might be captured by the advancing federals.[40]

Meanwhile, aboard his steamer, Ellsworth discovered that his troops would not, after all, be the first to reach Alexandria. A small landing party of marines from the *Pawnee* was already rowing toward shore in a cutter, flying a white flag of truce. The junior naval officer in charge, a certain Lieutenant Lowry, quickly found the Confederate colonel and offered to let his entire rebel force evacuate unmolested in exchange for the surrender of the town. By the time Ellsworth leapt ashore at the wharf, Lowry was waiting to inform him that the deal—an incomprehensible one, to the Zouave colonel's mind—had just been sealed. The Stars and Stripes already flew from the town flagpole. The Battle of Alexandria was won before it could be fought.[41]

But it was not in Ellsworth's nature to remain dejected for long. There was still work to be done, and laurels for his bold Zouaves to win. There were arms and matériel to be captured, railroads to be seized, telegraph lines to be cut. And in any event, he knew, this landing was only the initial stage of a glorious Union sweep across Virginia toward victory. It was the first morning of his war.

His disembarking Zouaves must have felt equally let down by their first steps on enemy soil. Before them now was not the alien citadel that had menaced them from across the river but an ordinary American town, with white-steepled churches, rows of old-fashioned brick houses, and wide, muddy streets. An air of patrician dowdiness hung about the place, a sense that its best days were fifty years in the past. The wharves should have been starting to bustle with activity at this early hour, but the complete silence of night still reigned. Shutters were closed or curtains drawn in most of the windows. Wherever the townsfolk might be, they were not to be seen or heard. Only the long, high whistle of a steam engine in the middle distance broke the stillness, as a train pulled away from Alexandria's station carrying the last of the Confederate garrison.[42]

Even before everyone was ashore, Ellsworth ordered Company E of his regiment to march at all speed to the railway line and, albeit somewhat belatedly, tear up the tracks leading to Richmond. The other companies were to remain at the wharf and await further orders. The colonel himself would lead a small force into town and take control of the telegraph office. He chose an unusual group for this mission: there were Ned House of the *Tribune;* Henry J. Winser, the regimental secretary, who did double duty as an occasional correspondent for the *New York Times;* and the Zouaves' chaplain, the Reverend E. W. Dodge. At first, Ellsworth planned to set out without any other men—Alexandria was officially under truce now, after all—but at the last moment, on Winser's suggestion, he turned and called for a single squad of soldiers to follow.[43]

The men jogged quickly up Cameron Street toward the center of town. But as soon as they rounded the corner toward King Street, Alexandria's main thoroughfare, they halted. In front of them was a tall brick building, and hanging from the large pole atop it, stirring only slightly in the morning air, was the rebel banner that had taunted Washington for weeks, the one President Lincoln could see from his window.

The Marshall House was an old hotel, really just a tavern with guest rooms upstairs, known among locals as a second-rate lodging for travelers. It was also known as a center of prosecession activity; the innkeeper, James W. Jackson, was one of the area's most ardent secessionists. Jackson had a powerful six-foot build and a temperament always spoiling for a fight—once, when a Catholic priest made the mistake of offending him, Jackson beat the cleric senseless. Anyone foolish enough to utter antislavery remarks in his presence received similar treatment. Two years earlier, Jackson had been one of the first local militiamen to rush off to Harper's Ferry in pursuit of John Brown. He returned having missed the fight, but bringing as a trophy one of the captured pikes with which Brown had planned to arm the slaves, as well as a wizened bit of flesh that he boasted came off the ear of Brown's son, who had died defending his father. As soon as the other Southern states began leaving the Union, Jackson and a friend had commissioned a couple of local seamstresses to stitch up a banner some eighteen feet wide, blazoned with the clustered stars and three broad stripes of the first Confederate flag. Each time another state joined the rebellion, Jackson had the women add another star. On the afternoon of April 17, the day Virginia's legislature voted for secession, a single large star was added to the center, and the banner hoisted on the forty-foot staff above his hotel.[44]

On the night of May 23, just as Union troops were massing on the opposite shore to attack Alexandria, the Marshall House hosted a raucous party, complete with a brass band and carousing militiamen, to celebrate the statewide secession referendum. But the fun broke up before midnight and the militiamen dispersed. Jackson had gone to bed, and the hotel was now quiet.[45]

Spotting the flag, Ellsworth ordered a sergeant back to the landing for another company of infantry as reinforcements, and then started trotting off quickly again toward the telegraph office. But suddenly, on some impulse, he stopped and turned back toward the steps of the Marshall House. His boyish pride, and perhaps a desire to impress the two journalists, had trumped military prudence. If he was going to have this trophy, he would cut it down with his own hands.[46]

Ellsworth entered the hotel accompanied by seven men: House, Winser, Dodge, and four Zouave corporals. Immediately inside the front door, they encountered a disheveled-looking man, only half dressed, who had apparently just gotten out of bed. Regardless of who this person was, he was the first real, live Confederate that the New Yorkers had encountered up close. So Ellsworth demanded to know what the rebel flag was doing atop the hotel. The man replied that he had no idea—he was only a boarder. All the other guests seemed to be still asleep. Without further delay, the Union men hastened upstairs. Ellsworth stationed one soldier at the front door, another on the first floor, a third at the foot of the stairs. Revolver in hand, he bounded up the final flights toward the roof's trapdoor, followed by the two newspaper correspondents, the chaplain, and a single Zouave armed with a rifle, Corporal Frank Brownell. Climbing a short ladder to the hatch cover, Ellsworth pushed it open and handed Winser his revolver before sawing away with a bowie knife at the halyards tethering the huge flag to its staff.[47]

Finally the ropes gave way and the banner drooped, then collapsed almost onto the men's heads, its defiant stripes suddenly a slack heap of red-and-white cloth. Ellsworth started pulling it through the open trapdoor, but it was so large he needed Winser's help to get the whole thing inside. As the little group made its way back downstairs, the colonel still had most of the flag draped around his shoulders, while Winser followed behind, clumsily trying to roll it up over one arm as they descended.

What happened next was too fast for any of the men to fully comprehend. Quickly rounding the turn between the third and second stories, Brownell, House, and Ellsworth saw a figure step out onto the landing and level a double-barreled shotgun at point-blank range. Winser, struggling with his end of the flag, had barely heard the blast of the gun before he felt the cloth go suddenly taut as Ellsworth, still wrapped in its folds, pitched forward. Almost instantly there was a second, louder explosion, and Jackson—the assailant, the man they had seen downstairs—lurched back, his face torn away in a mess of gore, as Brownell thrust his saber bayonet again and again into the innkeeper's body. Moments later, two men—one Northern, one Southern—lay dead on the staircase, their blood pooling across the dusty boards, soaking the shabby floorcloth, seeping into the folds of the fallen flag.[48]

ACROSS THE RIVER, five miles away, the capital avidly awaited news. President Lincoln had hastened early to the War Department telegraph office for the first dispatches from the front lines. Ordinary

Washingtonians, too, were waking up and learning that the invasion of the Confederacy had commenced—an invasion that, according to the *Tribune*'s editorial page, was sure to cut a victorious swath from Richmond to the Gulf of Mexico in a matter of months. District residents, peering from their bedroom windows, were disappointed not to see the smoke of musket fire rising above the Virginia shoreline or hear the deep rumble of artillery.[49]

By morning's end, however, a different sound echoed over the city's rooftops, as dozens of bells tolled in mourning from church steeples and firehouse belfries. The steamer *James Guy* was pulling slowly into the Navy Yard with a body aboard, and everyone in Washington already knew who the dead man was.

Ellsworth's companions had brought his corpse into a room at the hotel and covered it with the Confederate flag. When reinforcements finally arrived, the body was wrapped tenderly in a red Zouave blanket. Six men formed a stretcher with their muskets to carry their dead colonel through the streets that he had jogged up just minutes before. The sun had only half risen over Alexandria, and eight hundred men at the wharf were still awaiting their colonel's orders. Many of the fire b'hoys wept when they heard the awful news; others raged against the Alexandrian traitors and talked of burning the town. But the murder had been avenged in the instant of its commission. There was no battle to fight; no enemy to vanquish. There was only the blind, stupid fact of death.

As reports flashed by telegraph across the Union, flags dipped to half-mast in cities, towns, and villages throughout the North. By early afternoon, in newspaper offices from Maine to Nebraska, editors were composing eulogies, reporters compiling obituaries, and poets penning elegiac verses that would crowd the next day's newspaper columns.[50] By the following evening, public gatherings in New York and other major cities offered grandiloquent testimonials and took up collections for the support of Ellsworth's parents, left destitute by the death of their only child. Army recruiting offices were mobbed as they had not been since the first week of the war. At the beginning of May, Lincoln had asked for 42,000 more volunteers to supplement the militiamen called up in April. Within four weeks after Ellsworth's death, some five times that number would enlist.[51]

A torrent of emotion had been released, pouring out for a dead hero who had never fought a battle but rather, as one newspaper put it, had been "shot down like a dog."[52] There was more to the response than just nineteenth-century sentimentality, more than just patriotic fervor. Sumter's fall had loosed a flood of patriotic feeling. Now, across America, Ellsworth's death released a tide of hatred, of enmity and counterenmity, of sectional bloodlust that had hitherto been dammed up, if only barely, amid the flag waving and anthem singing.

Indeed, it was Ellsworth's death that made Northerners ready not just to take up arms but actually to kill. For the first month of the war, some had assumed that the war would play out more or less as a show of force: Union troops would march across the South, and the rebels would capitulate. Yankees talked big about sending Jeff Davis and other secessionist leaders to the gallows but almost never about shooting enemy soldiers. They preferred to think of Southerners in the terms that Lincoln would use throughout the war: as estranged brethren, misled by a few demagogues, who needed to be brought back into the national fold. Many Confederates, however, openly relished the prospect of slaughtering their former countrymen. "Well, let them come, those minions of the North," wrote one Virginian in a letter to the *Richmond Dispatch* on May 18. "We'll meet them in a way they least expect; we will glut our carrion crows with their beastly carcasses. Yes, from the peaks of the Blue Ridge to tide-water will we strew our plains, and leave their bleaching bones to enrich our soil."[53]

After the tragic morning in Alexandria, it suddenly dawned on the North that such talk had not been mere bluster. Newspapers dwelled on every lurid detail of the awful death scene, especially the "pool of blood clot, I should think three feet in diameter and an inch and one half deep at the center," as one correspondent described it. The point-blank shotgun blast had torn open Ellsworth's heart.

On the Southern side, editorialists rejoiced at the slaying of Ellsworth, boasting that he would be only the first dead Yankee of thousands. "Virginians, arise in strength and welcome the invader with bloody hands to hospitable graves," exhorted the next day's *Richmond Enquirer*. "Meet the invader at the threshold. Welcome him with bayonet and bullet. Swear eternal hatred to a treacherous foe." The *Richmond Whig* proclaimed, "Down with the tyrants! Let their accursed blood manure our fields."[54]

Although the Union rhetoric would never quite reach such levels, many in the North now began demanding blood for blood. The Zouaves, Hay wrote with solemn approbation, had pledged to avenge Ellsworth's death with many more: "They have sworn, with the grim earnestness that never trifles, to have a life for every hair of the dead colonel's head. But even that will not repay." In the *Tribune*, Greeley demanded that the entire neighborhood surrounding the Marshall House be leveled. With the deaths of just two men, the unthinkable—Americans killing their own countrymen—became the imperative.[55]

In Washington, Ellsworth's body was brought to lie in state in the East Room of the White House, his chest heaped with white lilies. On the second morning after his death, long lines of mourners, many in uniform, filed through to pay their respects; so many thronged into the presidential mansion that the funeral was delayed for many hours. In the afternoon, the cortege finally moved down Pennsylvania Avenue, between rows of American flags bound in swaths of black crape, toward the depot where the Fire Zouaves had disembarked a few weeks earlier. Rank after rank of infantry and cavalry preceded the hearse, which was drawn by four white horses and followed by Ellsworth's own riderless mount. Behind came companies of Zouaves, then a carriage with the president and members of his cabinet. But the figure that drew the most attention was Corporal Brownell, who walked alone behind the hearse with the bloodstained flag, the accursed trophy for which Ellsworth had died, crumpled up and speared upon the end of his bayonet.[56]

At the depot near the Capitol, a black-shrouded funeral train waited to carry the iron coffin to New York, where tens of thousands lined the streets from Union Square to City Hall to view the cortege. As Brownell passed with the now famous Confederate banner, crowds overwhelmed the human barriers of straining policemen, breaking through and rushing into the street to clasp the young Zouave's hand or touch a corner of the flag.[57]

Even after Ellsworth's body had, at last, been laid to rest on a hillside behind his boyhood home in Mechanicville, the nationwide fervor scarcely waned. Photographs, lithographs, and pocket-size biographies paying tribute to the fallen hero poured forth by the tens of thousands. Music shops sold scores for such tunes as "Col. Ellsworth's Funeral March," "Ellsworth's Requiem," "Col. Ellsworth Gallopade," "Brave Men, Behold Your Fallen Chief!," "Ellsworth's Avengers," "He Has Fallen," "Sadly the Bells Toll the Death of the Hero," and "Our Noble Laddie's Dead, Jim," the last referring to a remark that one sorrowing Zouave was supposed to have made to another on the morning of the killing. For years afterward, enlisted men wrote letters home on stationery stamped with crude woodcuts of the colonel teetering on the steps of the Marshall House, clutching his wounded breast with one hand and the captured flag in the other—and invariably, a motto pledging vengeance to traitors. One regiment, the 11th New York, even rechristened itself "Ellsworth Avengers." At least twenty thousand Northern babies born during the war years were named after him.[58]

The young colonel seemed to have been transfigured by death into a kind of national saint. Within hours of his killing, a *New York World* editor wrote of his "halo of martyrdom." Significantly, Ellsworth became the first notable American whose body was treated with the newly discovered practice of chemical embalming. As he lay in state, mourners peering into his coffin were amazed to see that the boyish face looked, as one man wrote, "natural as though he were sleeping a brief and pleasant sleep"—or as though modern technology had sanctified his flesh, rendering it incorruptible.[59]

As with a medieval saint, too, relics of his martyrdom became objects of veneration. In Alexandria, soldiers vied for pieces of the sacred flag within hours of the killing; it would have quickly been reduced to shreds had the Zouave officers not placed it under round-the-clock guard and threatened any man who approached it with thirty days' imprisonment. By evening, the few pieces that some Zouaves had managed to obtain were being traded literally for more than their weight in gold. One man enclosed a bit of red cloth in a letter he sent to his family the next day, entreating his mother to "keep it under lock and key" and "let no one have even one thread." "I tried hard to get a piece with his blood on it," he added, "but could not."[60]

Relic-hungry soldiers unable to obtain any of the flag took their knives and sliced up the oilcloth floor covering on the Marshall House staircase, which was drenched with even more blood than the flag. Once all the oilcloth was gone, they started in on the floorboards. During the next year, thousands of Union troops, passing through Alexandria on their way to the front, would make pilgrimages to the Marshall House, their relic-hunting encroaching upon the planks of the stairs, the banisters, the nearby doors and door frames, and the wallpaper, all whittled away one sliver at a time. When Nathaniel Hawthorne visited in the spring of 1862, so much of the hotel's interior was gone that, he wrote in *The Atlantic Monthly*, "it becomes something like a metaphysical question whether the place of the murder actually exists."[61]

Ellsworth's death was different from all those that followed over the next four years: most Northern writers referred to it as a "murder" or "assassination," an act not of war but of individual malice and shocking brutality. By the time Hawthorne's article appeared, however, many other American places had been soaked in blood. Thousands of Northerners and Southerners, in almost equal numbers, had been cut down amid the peach orchards and cotton fields at Shiloh. On the hillsides of southern Virginia, over seven murderous days, whole regiments had uselessly sacrificed themselves to McClellan's pointless slog toward Richmond. And at Bull Run, just eight weeks after Ellsworth's death, his gallant b'hoys had been in the forefront of the war's first disastrous Union defeat. At first the Zouaves advanced boldly toward the Confederate lines, crying "Ellsworth! Remember Ellsworth!" Then the rebel infantry and cavalry counterattacked. The New York firemen got off only a single volley before they broke ranks and ran. The Zouaves had more men killed, wounded, or captured at Bull Run than any other Union regiment.[62]

As the war's inexorable toll rose and rose, touching almost every family throughout the nation, Americans would lose their taste for collective mourning. Death became so commonplace that the demise of any one soldier, whether a fresh-faced recruit or battle-scarred hero, was drowned in the larger grief. Not until the war's final month—when another body would lie in state in the East Room, and another black-draped train make its slow way north—would Americans again shed common tears for a single martyr.

Ellsworth's memory never faded for those who knew him well. Hay, Nicolay, and Stoddard, who all lived to see the twentieth century, would reflect for decades on the meaning of his death. Stoddard always remembered how, as the crowds of mourners filed through the White House, he glanced over at the windowpane Ellsworth had broken a few days earlier and saw that the new glass was still smudged with the glazier's fingerprints. "I am not afraid to say that it was a little too much for me then," he wrote. "We had not become so hardened as we grew to be under the swift calamities that afterward trod so rapidly upon each other's heels." Nicolay, in his panoramic history of the war, wrote that the response to Ellsworth's death "opened an unlooked-for depth of individual hatred, into which the political animosities of years . . . had finally ripened." Hay, throughout his own long career as a statesman, never stopped pondering what might have been. Thirty-five years after Ellsworth's killing, he wrote: "The world can never compute, can hardly even guess, what was lost in his untimely end. . . . Only a few men, now growing old, knew what he was and what he might have been if life had been spared him."[63]

As for Lincoln, his young friend's death affected him like no other soldier's in the four years that followed. On the morning that the news reached the president, Senator Henry Wilson of Massachusetts and a companion, not yet aware of Ellsworth's death, called at the White House on a matter of urgent business and found Lincoln standing alone beside a window in the library, looking out toward the Potomac.

He seemed unaware of the visitors' presence until they were standing close behind him. Lincoln turned away from the window and extended his hand. "Excuse me," he said. "I cannot talk." Then suddenly, to the men's astonishment, the president burst into tears. Burying his face in a handkerchief, he walked up and down the room for some moments before at last finding his voice:

> After composing himself somewhat, the President took his seat, and desired us to approach. "I will make no apology, gentlemen," said the President, "for my weakness; but I knew poor Ellsworth well, and held him in great regard. Just as you entered the room, Capt. Fox left me, after giving me the painful details of Ellsworth's unfortunate death. The event was so unexpected, and the recital so touching, that it quite unmanned me." The President here made a violent effort to restrain his emotion, and after a pause he proceeded, with tremulous voice, to give us the incidents of the tragedy as they had occurred. "Poor fellow," repeated the President, as he closed his relation, "it was undoubtedly an act of rashness, but it only shows the heroic spirit that animates our soldiers, from high to low, in this righteous cause of ours. Yet who can restrain their grief to see them fall in such a way as this, not by the fortunes of war, but by the hand of an assassin?"[64]

Almost alone among the millions of mourners, perhaps, Lincoln could admit that Ellsworth's death had not been glorious. Others might talk of his gallantry, might hail him as a modern knight cut down in the flower of youth. But for the president, preparing to send armies into battle against their brothers, the double homicide in a cheap hotel represented something else: the squalid brutality of civil war.[65]

Even close friends of the Lincoln family were afraid, for a long time afterward, to talk about Ellsworth in front of the president, who sometimes wept at the mention of his name. On the morning of the funeral, the East Room was crowded with dignitaries: generals, cabinet secretaries, ambassadors. At the end of the service, all rose to file past the open casket. Then the line suddenly stopped. Lincoln and his wife stood at length, looking down on the face of their dead friend. Those standing nearest could hear the president lament: "My boy! My boy! Was it necessary this sacrifice should be made?"[66]

MORE THAN A DECADE LATER, a reporter named Eli Perkins of the *New York Commercial Advertiser* happened to be passing through

Mechanicville, New York, and decided to stop and take a look. Perkins had known Ellsworth slightly in former days, and recalled that his old acquaintance's boyhood home was in the village. Perkins found the dead soldier's elderly parents still living alone in the little wooden cottage. The front parlor was a kind of shrine to their son, its walls lined with the many lithographs and *cartes de visite* that had been published shortly after his death. But when Perkins walked up the hill behind the house in search of the fallen colonel's tombstone, he was surprised to find that there was none.

"When Elmer fell," old Mr. Ellsworth explained, "so many people and societies were going to put up a monument that I suppose they got it all mixed up. First the Chicago people were going to do it—then the regiment, and then the State. Then the citizens around here made an attempt, but still it remains undone." The late war's first great hero—the man whose name, one New York newspaper had proclaimed, "will not be blurred so long as the record of our war of liberty survives"—still lay in an unmarked grave.[67]

The Marshall House in Alexandria has long since disappeared. On that corner today stands a Hotel Monaco. A bronze plaque on an outside wall, installed sometime in the last century, reads:

> The Marshall House stood upon this site, and within the building on the early morning of May 24, 1861, James W. Jackson was killed by federal soldiers while defending his property and personal rights, as stated in the verdict of the coroners jury. He was the first Martyr to the cause of Southern Independence. The Justice of History does not allow his name to be forgotten.

On a recent morning in Washington, I made an appointment with a curator at the Smithsonian's National Museum of American History to see something that had not been on display for a long time. I waited as she went to a metal filing cabinet and retrieved a small box, which she placed on the table in front of me. Inside were two artifacts: a scrap of red bunting and a small piece of nondescript oilcloth, its corner stained with faded blood.

CHAPTER EIGHT

Freedom's Fortress

O a new song, a free song,
Flapping, flapping, flapping, flapping, by sounds, by voices
   clearer,
By the wind's voice and that of the drum,
By the banner's voice and child's voice and sea's voice and
   father's voice,
Low on the ground and high in the air . . .

—WALT WHITMAN,
"Song of the Banner at Day-Break" (1860–61)

Fugitives fording the Rappahannock, Virginia, 1862

Hampton Roads, Virginia, May 1861

THIS WAS WHERE IT HAD ALL BEGUN.

Here, where the river washed into the great bay: a place as freighted with the heavy past as anywhere in the still-young country; a place of Indian bones and deep-cellared manor houses and the armor of King James's men rusting away beneath the dark soil.

Time itself seemed to move here like that tidal river, its ambivalent currents stirred first upstream, then down. By night, from the water, the sharp-edged silhouette of the federal fort might seem to soften and sink, becoming again the low palisades that the first colonists had raised on the same spot two and a half centuries ago. The navy steamship, moored in the fort's lee, might raise its black hull into the form of a bygone man-of-war.

History recorded that late in the summer of 1619, a Dutch corsair under an English captain had come in from the south and anchored at Point Comfort. On this promontory at the mouth of the James, thirty miles downstream from their fledgling capital, the Virginia colonists had built a lookout point and trading post that they called Fort Algernourne. John Rolfe, Pocahontas's widower, recounted the ship's arrival in a letter. The corsair, he wrote, "brought not any thing but 20. and odd Negroes." These it had captured from a Portuguese slaver, bound to Veracruz from the coast of Angola. A strange and circuitous voyage, a strange cargo, and yet exactly what the colonists needed. A single pound of tobacco would fetch three shillings in London, but here in Virginia there were never enough hands to tend and harvest the crop. English men and women were lured across the ocean with false promises; stray boys were kidnapped on London streets and shipped off to be auctioned like calves at the Jamestown wharf. They worked the fields for a few months and then died, regretted but unmourned. These Negroes, cheaply bought, would be put to work in the tobacco fields, too.[1]

Two and a half centuries later, there were four million descendants of Africans held in slavery.

But now, on a spring night in 1861, three of them were making their way across those same waters, toward the fort at Point Comfort—and, this time, to freedom.

．　　　．　　　．

THIS IS HOW IT WOULD ALL END.

The three men who crossed the James River to the fort that night—Frank Baker, Shepard Mallory, and James Townsend—had been enslaved field hands on a farm outside Hampton, a quiet county seat on the north bank of the river. Then the war came. Like so many other Americans at that moment, the men unexpectedly faced a new set of challenges and decisions.

The tranquil rural landscape they had known suddenly blazed with activity. Seemingly overnight, it emerged as one of the most strategically important regions in the entire Confederacy—especially since its shoreline bordered the expanse of water at the mouth of the James known as Hampton Roads. One of the greatest natural harbors on earth, this estuary commanded direct water routes to the capitals of both belligerents: the James, highway to Richmond; and the Chesapeake Bay, highway to Washington. It would be repeatedly contested in the years to come, most famously in the 1862 naval battle between the *Monitor* and the *Merrimack*.

As the war opened, Hampton Roads and its surroundings were dominated by one of the few military strongholds in the South that the federal government had managed to keep: Fortress Monroe, which sat at the tip of Point Comfort, a mile or so from the town of Hampton.[2] The small peninsula had been occupied as a strategic point not just by the Jamestown colonists but also by both British and French forces in turn during the Revolution. Construction of the massive stone citadel, designed to hold heavy armament and a large garrison, had begun after the War of 1812—during which the British had secured Hampton Roads with embarrassing ease and spent the next two years raiding and burning towns and cities up and down the Chesapeake, including the nation's capital. The federal government was not about to let that happen again. Unlike such haphazardly designed coastal defenses as Fort Sumter, Fortress Monroe had received punctilious attention from the nation's best military engineers, among them a talented young lieutenant named Robert E. Lee.[3] Once complete, it became America's most impregnable military installation. At the start of the secession crisis, the War Department quickly sent additional artillery pieces and hundreds of extra troops to the fort. Thousands more Union reinforcements arrived in the weeks after Sumter. Fortress Monroe was now poised to become a major base of operations in the heart of enemy territory.[4]

The Confederates, too, were hurriedly marshaling forces in the area. And one of their leaders happened to be Colonel Charles King Mallory: county judge, commander of the local militia, and master of the three nocturnal fugitives, Frank Baker, Shepard Mallory, and James Townsend.

On May 13, the Union commander of Fortress Monroe sent a small squad of men across the narrow creek separating the fort from the mainland. Their job was to secure a well that lay on the far side, since the fort's limited cisterns could not support all the new troops arriving continually by steamer. Although the federal soldiers had advanced merely a few yards into Virginia, and although the state had not yet officially ratified its secession, the vigilant Colonel Mallory perceived nothing less than a Yankee invasion of the Old Dominion's sacred soil. He immediately called up his troop, the 115th Virginia Militia.[5]

Gallant as they may have been, these defenders of Southern rights and Southern homes were not exactly ready for a full-scale engagement with the enemy. (The militiamen's previous duties had consisted largely of standing guard on local pilot boats to prevent fugitive Negroes from escaping.) Instead, they joined the several thousand other Virginia troops already dispersed throughout the area, busily setting up camps, digging entrenchments, and building gun platforms.

Or rather: the Virginia militiamen were *supervising* the construction of entrenchments and gun platforms. The actual hard labor was being done by local slaves, pressed into service from surrounding plantations. Soon, indeed, Confederate authorities required every slaveholder in the three nearest counties to offer at least half his able-bodied hands for military use. "Our negroes will do the shovelling while our brave cavaliers will do the fighting," a Richmond newspaper said.[6]

Baker, Mallory, and Townsend had accompanied their master across the James to Sewell's Point, where, directly opposite Fortress Monroe, the Confederates were constructing an artillery emplacement amid the dunes. The three men labored with picks and shovels beneath the regimental banner of the 115th Virginia, a blue flag bearing a motto in golden letters, GIVE ME LIBERTY OR GIVE ME DEATH.[7]

After a week or so of this, however, they learned some deeply unsettling news: their master was planning to send them even farther from home, to help build Confederate fortifications in North Carolina. They were bidding farewell to the area where they had spent most, if not all, of their lives. Moreover, two of them—probably Baker and Townsend, the elder members of the trio—had wives and children on the opposite side of the river. If they went south, away from their master's immediate supervision, into the hands of unknown military authorities, and in the direction that all slaves dreaded most, would they ever see their families again?[8]

Just four miles across the water, in the direction of their home and their families, sat Fortress Monroe. It must have been a familiar sight to them, especially since Colonel Mallory had a house not far from its ramparts, on the outskirts of Hampton. Indeed, it is quite possible that they had been inside the fort already, in peacetime; relations between the townsfolk and the soldiers had always been neighborly, so any number of errands for their master might have taken them there. Now, of course, their master, along with all the other loyal Confederates, considered it enemy territory. . . .

That was when the three slaves decided to choose their own allegiance. And they joined the Union.

All it took was one small boat. With Confederate officers frequently coming and going across the James, there must have been plenty such vessels at Sewell's Point. On the night of May 23, Baker, Mallory, and Townsend slipped down to the beach and rowed stealthily away. As they drew nearer to Hampton, they must have heard distant shouts and commotion. It was the day Virginians had voted to ratify the ordinance of secession, and here, as in distant Alexandria, citizens of the newly independent state were celebrating. (Only six townsfolk had cast votes for the Union.) The fugitives' timing may have been no coincidence, either. Colonel Mallory had served as his county's delegate to the secession convention; it is hard to believe that on the big night he would have stayed to swat sand flies by the campfire at Sewell's Point. Perhaps he was in town, rejoicing at his state's self-liberation, when his three slaves spied a chance to liberate themselves, too.[9]

Still, it cannot have been an easy decision for the men. What kind of treatment would they meet with at the fort? If the federal officers sent them back, would they be punished as runaways—perhaps even as traitors? Even if they were allowed to remain inside, might this leave their families exposed to Colonel Mallory's retribution? How, and when, would they ever reunite with their loved ones?

But the choice was theirs to make, and they made it. Approaching the high stone walls, they hailed a picket guard, and were admitted within the gates of Fortress Monroe.

Next morning they were summoned to see the fort's commanding general himself. The three fugitives could not have taken this as an encouraging sign. And however familiar Monroe's peacetime garrison may have been to them, at least by sight, the officer who now awaited them behind a cluttered desk was someone whose face they had never seen in their lives.

Worse still, as far as faces went, his was not a pleasant one. It was the face of a man whom many people, in the years ahead, would call a brute, a beast, a cold-blooded murderer. It was a face that could easily make you believe such things: low, balding forehead; slack jowls; and a tight, mean little mouth beneath a drooping mustache. It would have seemed a face of almost animal-like stupidity, had it not been for the eyes. These glittered shrewdly, almost hidden amid crinkled folds of flesh, like dark little jewels in a nest of tissue paper. One of them had an odd sideways cast, as though its owner were always considering something else besides the thing in front of him.

These were the eyes that now surveyed Baker, Mallory, and Townsend. The general began asking them questions: Who was their master? (This was not an auspicious start.) Was he a rebel or a Union man? Were they field Negroes or house Negroes? Did they have families? Why had they run away? What had they been doing at Sewell's Point? Could they tell him anything about the fortifications they had worked on there? Their response to this last question—that the battery was still far from completion, with only two cannons, although the rebels planned to install many more—seemed to please him. Next, to be sure there had been no collusion to deceive him, he carefully interrogated each man privately, making sure that their stories did not conflict with one another. At last he dismissed the three brusquely, offering no indication of their fate. But as terrifying as the general had initially appeared, something in his manner may have reassured them. Was there a hint of compassion, even, in that gruff Yankee voice?[10]

Major General Benjamin Franklin Butler had arrived at the fort only a day ahead of the three fugitive slaves—although unlike them, of course, he had been greeted at the esplanade by a thirteen-cannon salute and a squad of soldiers at parade attention. His new command was one of the most significant in the army: the Department of Virginia and North Carolina. Admittedly, that entire department now comprised, in practical terms, little more than the sixty-three acres within Fortress Monroe's stout walls, but it might soon become the staging point for a major Union assault on Richmond. That morning, before the slaves were brought to his office, Butler had sat down to compose an all-important initial report to General Winfield Scott, detailing the garrison's troop strength, supplies, and fighting readiness. Yet when an adjutant interrupted to inform him about the fugitive slaves, Butler immediately set down his pen. General Scott could wait. The three ragged Negroes waiting outside were a matter of even more pressing urgency.[11]

To many Union commanders in the spring of 1861, the runaways would have presented no dilemma whatsoever. The laws of the United States, of course, were perfectly clear: all fugitives must be returned to their masters. The Founding Fathers had enshrined this principle in Article Four of the Constitution; Congress had fortified it in 1850 with the Fugitive Slave Act; and it was still the law of the land throughout the nation, including, as far as the federal government was concerned, within the so-called Confederate states. The war had done nothing to change it.

In fact, federal forces had already found occasions to prove as much. Back in March at Fort Sumter, a sentry standing watch one night had heard a splashing sound alongside the wharf, and looked down to see a slim, dark figure disappearing among the pilings. Finally the soldier persuaded the fugitive to come out. He was a young man who claimed to have been beaten almost to death by his master but had managed to escape and paddle across the harbor in a canoe, trusting the Northern "gem'men" of Sumter to shelter and protect him. Those Northern gentlemen promptly sent him back to his lawful owner.[12] At Fort Pickens, meanwhile, the Union commander had sent back eight fugitives. And Butler himself, at his previous post in Maryland, had seemed as ready as anyone to do his constitutional duty. When rumors of "an insurrection of the negro population" began spreading around Annapolis in late April, he wrote immediately to the state's governor to assure him of his readiness to put it down by force of arms.[13]

Most important, noninterference with slavery was the very cornerstone of the Union's war policy, as every sentient American knew. President Lincoln had begun his inaugural address by making this clear, pointedly and repeatedly. "I have no purpose, directly or indirectly, to interfere with the institution of slavery in the States where it exists," the president said, quoting one of his own speeches from 1858. "I believe I have no lawful right to do so, and I have no inclination to do so." The same pledge had been reiterated in countless other Republican speeches, countless newspaper editorials.

Yet, to Fortress Monroe's new commander, these three Negroes who had turned up at his own front gate seemed like a novel case, in several important respects. The fugitives had just offered him some highly useful military intelligence. The enemy had been deploying them for offensive purposes—to construct a battery aimed directly at his fort, no less—and no doubt would put them straight back to work if recaptured, with time off only for a good sound beating. And circumstances had changed. The renditions at Sumter and Pickens had occurred before war was declared, Maryland, where he had so gamely offered to help enforce the law, was still loyal to the Union. But Virginia, as of twelve or so hours ago, was officially in rebellion against the federal government, marshaling all her resources to wage fratricidal war. (Indeed, on the far side of the state, at this very hour—though Butler was unaware —the Fire Zouaves were carrying their dead colonel's body back across the Potomac.) Here were Butler's men on their sixty-three acres, a tiny oasis of safety amid vast hostile territory. They needed all the help they could get, and they certainly could not afford to do anything that might help their opponents. He knew this much about military strategy, at least.

Despite his exalted rank, Major General Butler had been a professional soldier barely five weeks. In private life back in Massachusetts, he was a lawyer, and a very successful one, though he had grown up poor, the swamp-Yankee son of a widow who kept a boardinghouse for female factory workers in Lowell, the famous textile-mill town. Unlike Boston's white-shoe attorneys, the self-made Butler could not attract clients through social connections or charm, so he became a grind, a man who knew every loose thread in the great tangled skein of common law, and who could unravel an opponent's entire case with the gentlest tug. (At his bar examination, he liked to boast, he had corrected the presiding judge on a subtle but important legal point, causing the distinguished jurist to hurriedly reverse one of his recent verdicts.) By his early forties, at the beginning of the Civil War, Butler had offices in both Lowell and Boston and was earning the princely sum of eighteen thousand dollars a year. He had also built quite a successful political career, becoming a prominent state legislator, one of the leaders of the state Democratic Party, and its candidate for governor in 1860. Though he had lost, many people (not least Butler himself) remained convinced that he had bright prospects.[14]

This, indeed, was the reason behind his military apotheosis. Lincoln, fearful of having his contest with the South branded a "Republican war," had elevated a number of reliably Unionist Democrats to high rank. Benjamin Butler's long service as a leader of the volunteer militia was the least of his dubious qualifications; much more important, he was the last man anyone could accuse of being an abolitionist zealot. Race-baiting was red meat to many of his working-class Lowell constituents, and he had always been glad to toss healthy morsels of it in their direction. He had publicly endorsed the *Dred Scott* decision, and a central plank of his gubernatorial campaign was his fiercely sarcastic opposition to enlisting blacks in the state militia. (He also reminded his fellow citizens that "we buy and sell the products of slave labor"—no doubt with his hometown textile mills in mind.) In fact, when representing his district at the 1860 Democratic National Convention, Butler had cast his vote for Jefferson Davis as the party's nominee—not once but on fifty-seven successive ballots, an extravagant blunder that would dog his political career for decades to come.[15]

A fellow officer once said that Butler was "less like a major general than like a politician who is coaxing for votes." And after barely twenty-four hours at Fortress Monroe, the new commander had already sized up his new constituency. The garrison was made up predominantly of eager volunteers from New England, men who had flocked to the recruiting stations while the smoke of battle still hung over Fort Sumter. These were no Lowell mill hands, either. The Third Massachusetts hailed mainly from the starchy old Puritan settlements around Boston; there were many college men in its ranks—one entire company had formed at Cambridge. The soldiers of the First Vermont had marched off to war with evergreen sprigs pinned to their lapels, under the leadership of Colonel John W. Phelps, a West Pointer and Mexican War veteran and, as it happened, an abolitionist of the deepest dye. (The London *Times'* ubiquitous William H. Russell, visiting the fort in July, would call him "an excellent type of the chief of a Puritan regiment"—and, on a later occasion, "one who places John Brown on a level with the great martyrs of the Christian world.") The sentry who had brought Baker, Mallory, and Townsend into the fort belonged to the First Vermont; the tale of their plucky escape from the rebels was no doubt spreading quickly through the regiment, if not the entire garrison. Finally, closest at hand among the bleeding hearts, there was Butler's new military secretary, Theodore Winthrop, the poet-turned-private (elevated now to the rank of major) who had sent correspondence to *The Atlantic* from his makeshift bivouac in the Capitol. When Winthrop left for the war, he had written to his family: "I go to put an end to slavery."[16]

How was Butler to win the confidence—or even obedience—of such men if his first act as their commander was to send three poor Negroes back into bondage?

And it was not only a matter of calculation. The general was a more complicated person than he at first appeared. His features were brutish, his manners coarse, but inwardly, he nursed the outsize vanity of certain physically ugly men—vanity often manifest in a craving for approval and adulation. He also possessed a sympathetic, even occasionally sentimental, heart. He had fought hard in the state legislature to win shorter workdays for the Lowell mill hands, a crusade informed to some degree by political self-interest, no doubt, but also by memories of the wan and sickly young women in his mother's boardinghouse. Once, after the death in battle of a beloved junior officer, Butler wrote to the young man's mother: "Although a stranger, my tears will flow with yours." This was no mere formula—one hundred fifty years later, the rough draft of that letter, written in a tremulous hand, still bears the splash marks of his lachrymosity.[17]

Still . . . sentiment was a fine thing; so was the admiration of one's subordinates. Ultimately, though, his duty was to his commander-in-chief. With a few strokes of his pen, Lincoln had made Butler a major general; the president could just as easily unmake him, sending him back to Lowell as a mere civilian—and with another stroke, for that matter, send the Negroes back to Hampton as slaves.

Whatever Butler's decision on the three fugitives' fate, he would have to reach it quickly. He had barely picked up his pen to finally begin that report to General Scott before an adjutant interrupted with another message: a rebel officer, under flag of truce, had approached the causeway of Fortress Monroe. The Virginians wanted their slaves back.

FROM THE FORT'S PARAPET, the black men could see the world they had left behind.[18]

This was not the South of cotton fields and column-swagged mansions, of slaves toiling by the hundreds under the overseer's lash. The land beyond the moat and the creek spread out low and flat, lagoons and marshes rising almost imperceptibly into a patchwork of small farms, each with its plain old-fashioned farmhouse, its orchard and vegetable patch, its woodlands and its field of wheat, now ripening from green into gold for the early-summer harvest. A few roads, paved with oyster shells, crisscrossed the landscape like wavering lines of white chalk.

A mile or so off lay the town of Hampton, venerable survivor of an earlier Virginia. Along the waterfront, shaded by stands of slender cypresses, stood high-fronted brick mansions from colonial times, nearly all with neatly fenced gardens behind, bowers of peach trees, blueberry bushes, grapevines, and rambling roses. Owners of those houses were summoned to prayer each Sunday morning by the ancient bell of St. John's Church, reputedly Virginia's oldest place of worship, where the pious lips of eight generations had brushed the silver rim of the communion chalice, a treasured relic of the first King James's day. Hampton was a place not just of inherited privileges but of inherited civilities; a place of wax-dimmed mahogany and dusty volumes of *The Spectator*, the legacies of one's great-grandparents.

The old families, like all aristocrats, had been *nouveaux riches* once upon a time, back in the days when the James River was the British Empire's far West—when an inspector of His Majesty's Customs presided over the busy port of Hampton, recording outbound cargoes of tobacco and wheat; rum and slaves and Old World luxuries coming in. The Revolution, although many local patriots took up arms on its behalf, had left little lasting mark. No one bothered to suggest renaming King and Queen Streets, Hampton's two main thoroughfares. County and town continued to be governed by the same rules and same families as before—even as the latter grew both less *nouveaux* and less *riches* with every passing year. By 1861, it had been an age since a ship called at Hampton from Lisbon or Antigua. The harbor, half silted in, now saw few vessels larger than an oyster boat or a bay schooner. Hampton's more venturesome sons and daughters went westward to seek their fortunes, while their conservative brothers and sisters stayed behind to prune the rosebushes and polish the mahogany. Values passed from one generation to the next at the Hampton Military Academy, whose principal—one John Baytop Cary, possessed of the most desirable surname in the county—schooled his young gentlemen beneath a painted sign: "Order is heaven's first law."[19]

Colonel Charles King Mallory, who held ownership rights to the three Negro fugitives at Fortress Monroe, was also a sprig on one of tidewater Virginia's loftiest family trees, just the slightest gradation beneath that of the Carys themselves. His ancestors had prospered here since the seventeenth century. A previous Colonel Mallory, his grandfather, had fallen in combat against the invading redcoats in 1781, beside a nearby church known as Big Bethel. The family still reverently preserved this martyred ancestor's buff waistcoat, pierced by British bayonets in no fewer than eleven places. (Over the years—thanks, perhaps, to the depredations of sacrilegious moths—the purported number of bayonet slashes would eventually grow to nineteen.)[20]

Slaves, too, were part of the ancestral legacy. Among the tattered folios in the county courthouse could be found a deed, dated at Hampton on the 18th of December, 1696, by which a certain William Mallory—the present colonel's great great-great-grandfather—granted unto his son Francis "one negro Lad nam'd Will and one Gray Mare & their Increse to him & his heirs for ever."[21]

All through the pre-Revolutionary decades, slave ships called frequently at Hampton—sometimes dozens in a single year—almost all of them direct from the West Indies, often bringing just three or four Africans for sale, but now and then forty or fifty at a time. There had been occasional annoyances over the years—during the two wars against Great Britain, local slaves had showed a disconcerting eagerness to flock to the enemy, who had promised freedom to any cooperative bondsman. But the British departed, the overseas slave trade ceased, and by the eve of the Civil War, the county's population remained more or less the same year after year: half black and half white; and, it so happened, half slave and half free, including a small community of free Negroes, some of whom had even won a degree of prosperity. Each of the town's handsome old mansions had behind it a little lean-to shanty where the slaves lived and where they did their masters' cooking and washing.[22]

Slavery wore a more human face here than among the industrial-scale cotton and sugar plantations of the Gulf Coast, where each Negro man, woman, and child might be little more than an anonymous line in the absentee owner's ledger book. Around Hampton, people knew one another. Even the largest planters rarely owned more than a couple of dozen slaves—Colonel Mallory possessed thirteen. The county had its old black families as well as old white ones. Indeed, these were quite often intertwined. Outsiders noticed what the locals seemed not to: very few of the area's so-called blacks were anything approaching black in color, and the physical resemblances to their white neighbors (and masters) could be striking. Occasionally, relationships emerged into the open; forty years before the Civil War, a local white man left half his estate to the daughter he had conceived with a black woman, the slave of a close friend of his. Much more often, things went unspoken. "Well, ah ain't white an' ah ain't black, leastwise not so fur as ah know," an octogenarian farmer named Moble Hopson would tell an interviewer in the 1930s. "Fo' de war dere warn't no question come up 'bout et."[23]

At least one of Colonel Mallory's three fugitives was an instance of such ambiguity. Shepard Mallory was the only one described consistently as a mulatto; he was also the only one who claimed the colonel's surname as his own, as he would continue doing for the rest of his long life. (It is unclear whether he used the Mallory name while still in slavery.) Shepard Mallory was born when Charles King Mallory was in his early twenties, either not long before the colonel's marriage or not long after it.[24] Such facts hint at the possibility—intriguing even if speculative—that in leaving his master, Shepard Mallory might also have been leaving his cousin, his uncle, or maybe even his father.*

In years to come, philanthropic Northerners would be surprised (perhaps in a few cases secretly disappointed) to learn that not all Hampton slaves were lashed daily—and, moreover, that quite a few spoke of their masters as decent, even kindly, people. Some slaves here, as in other places, were left to lead more or less independent lives, working aboard oyster boats on the Bay or practicing trades in town, and simply remitting most of their earnings to their masters. The town's location also offered them unusual access to information about the outside world. In the decades before the war, a summer resort called the Hygeia Hotel turned Hampton into a popular watering place for wealthy visitors, including men of national prominence. John Tyler, Winfield Scott, and Roger Taney, among others, became familiar faces. Indeed, Tyler and his family purchased a beachfront villa right next door to the Mallory estate; when they arrived each summer they would erect a temporary cabin behind the house to accommodate their retinue of slaves. As these visiting blacks mingled with Hampton's local Negroes, they must have confided a good deal of inside political news and high-class gossip that James Gordon Bennett and Horace Greeley would have given their eyeteeth to acquire.[25]

And yet Hampton's picturesque, shabby-genteel exterior hid far shabbier, and far less picturesque, realities under its surface. One visiting Northerner, asking an elderly slave if she had a "good" master, was assured that the man was "a kind—a *werry* kind massa!" And then she added: "Why, bless de Lor' . . . he nebber put wires in his cowhides in all his life!" The woman, of course, was making a larger point: a whip without metal wires woven into it is still a whip. There was no such thing as a "good" slaveholder; no such thing as a gentle version of bondage.[26]

In July 1850, an article titled "New Way of Raising Pigs" appeared in a magazine called *The American Agriculturalist.* "Dr. Mallory, of Hampton," it began, "has a new way of keeping both pigs and negroes out of mischief." It went on to explain that the esteemed doctor—he was the colonel's elder brother, Francis—made a practice of giving each of his slaves one or two piglets every spring to tend and feed throughout the rest of the year. Then, at slaughtering time, half the

---

*Contrary to popular belief, most freedmen did not automatically adopt the surnames of their masters, preferring to distance themselves from the bonds of slavery, and more often choosing the last name of a local family they admired, a famous name (Washington, Jefferson, Lincoln), a name that they simply liked—or, sometimes, the name of a family to which they claimed kinship.

butchered hog would go to the master, the other half to the slave. It was an efficient way to fatten swine, the article noted—"and besides, it is contrary to negro nature to run away and leave a fat pig."[27]

That was how slavery worked in Hampton. As beneficent as a master might be, he ultimately had to treat his Negroes as a type of livestock—a type, moreover, that could be damnably hard to keep from straying off. This was no small matter, as Virginia's slaves were growing more and more valuable over time. With the Old Dominion's best soil long since exhausted, its farmers could only gaze enviously southward at the bountiful fields of the Cotton Kingdom. Yet the good fortunes of the Gulf States did not bypass Virginia entirely. The Chesapeake became America's own Congo River, its new slave coast.[28] The higher the price of cotton in New Orleans (and in Lowell and Liverpool, for that matter), the higher the price of Negroes in Richmond. Indeed, it was often said that black folk were Virginia's only worthwhile cash crop.

The old fortunes of the tidewater stretched thinner and thinner with each new generation. Heirs multiplied; debts multiplied; a gentleman from even one of the finest bloodlines might easily find himself in financial embarrassment. Meanwhile his Negroes had multiplied, too—more mouths to feed; more backs to clothe; more hands to do the same amount of work. *Their Increse to him & his heirs for ever.* Then one heard about the most remarkable prices being fetched: two thousand dollars for a prime male! It was beyond exorbitant—it was insane; it couldn't last. It was also, by coincidence, the exact amount of the note of hand that one had imprudently signed two years ago, back when it had seemed, briefly, that grain prices must rise—the note of hand that would fall due next quarter, and nary a cent of cash to pay it with. The slaves' rations had already been cut to bare subsistence; their annual clothing allowance postponed; but still one's balance sheet showed an appalling deficit. Perhaps, indeed, they would be better off with a master who could afford to feed and clothe them properly. Surely it would be no sin to sell just one or two, sparing at least the faithful house servants. And come to think, there *was* that strapping young fellow Billy, on Uncle Jack's old farm . . . the one with the unpleasantly truculent look in his eye, as if he were daring you, his master, to show him who was boss. . . .

And so came the discreet trip upriver, to shamefacedly answer one of those vulgar ads inside the Richmond papers: CASH FOR SLAVES! CASH FOR SLAVES! CASH FOR SLAVES! Well, better that, anyhow, than having one's ancestral house on King Street—its roof a bit leaky these days, to be sure, but still a handsome old place—seized and auctioned by the sheriff at the courthouse door.

This was how it might have gone with a slaveholder of the very best intentions. There were many whose intentions were a good deal worse.

Back at the turn of the century, no less a Virginian than Thomas Jefferson had recognized the strong financial incentives for a planter to increase his yield of Negro children. The author of the Declaration was always half idealist, half scientist—the two halves often at war with each other. The idealist dreamt of universal emancipation (someday), while the scientist could not help calculating that the offspring of a "breeding woman" at Monticello were worth substantially more than her labor. "I consider a woman who brings a child every two years as more profitable than the best man of the farm," Jefferson wrote to his son-in-law—since, as he explained, "what she produces is an addition to capital." (A few lines later, he went back to discussing his lofty schemes for the University of Virginia.) By the 1850s, this calculus had given rise to an industry that each year converted tens of thousands of black Virginians into hard cash before sending them south. The Richmond firm of D. M. Pulliam & Co.—one of many competing dealers in the state capital—went so far as to classify its wares into twenty separate categories, from "No. 1 MEN, Extra" down to "Scrubs," a term for the elderly, the sickly, or the crippled.[29]

Rare was the black family in Hampton that had not lost one of its members—a sister, a husband, a daughter, a father—to this ever-burgeoning trade. On local farms where slaves were expressly raised for sale, the common practice was to send children to market when they reached the age of eight: old enough to have survived the common diseases of infancy and to be useful in the fields.[30]

For those not sold, enslavement still often meant a life of sudden disruptions and separations. Hampton was neither quite as placid nor quite as stable as it appeared. The antebellum South had invested heavily in its self-image as a place of changeless order, but in truth, it could sometimes be almost as ruthlessly dynamic as a California gold field or a New England factory town. When the more ambitious scions of the old families decided to seek their fortunes in Arkansas or Texas—or even just in another county—the slaves must be equitably divided according to their cash value. Many tidewater field hands, too, were "hired out" annually: slaveholders who possessed more Negroes than they needed rented them to planters short of labor. In Hampton, as in many other places, January 1 was when old rental contracts expired and slaves' services were auctioned off for the year ahead, sending them to different, often far-flung, plantations. One former slave would recall how each New Year's Day, "the cries and tears of brothers, sisters, wives, and husbands were heard in [Hampton's] streets" as black families were separated—at least for twelve months, but possibly forever.[31]

In short, enslaved Negroes bore witness to, and suffered, all the unbridled energy and restless change of entrepreneurial America, without ever reaping its benefits. Occasionally, perhaps, a slave might put aside a fistful of seeds at harvest time and plant a little garden behind the kitchen shed, tending and watering it each evening after her long day's toil in the master's fields, hoping to raise a few gourds and melons that she could send to town—if she were permitted—on market days. Some pennies here, a silver dime or quarter there, and perhaps one day she might hoard enough to purchase her own freedom or her children's. But then one morning the arbitrary hand of fate would intervene, dispatching her suddenly to another farm or to another state, leaving the young shoots to wither.

No wonder that so many dreamt of running away, of at last seizing command over their own destinies. Some succeeded; the kindly captain of a Providence schooner might sneak a stowaway aboard on the homeward voyage. But the price of failure could be steep. One June 23, 1859, the clerk of Hampton's county court—a panel comprising a dozen leading citizens—penned a chilling entry in his minute-book:

> It appearing to the Court from satisfactory evidence adduced before it, that certain slaves, the property of the estate of Sarah A. Twine deceased—to wit, Sam Watts, Mary Watts & child Louisa; Ann Riddick, John Riddick, Mariah Becket & her child Georgeanna; Frank Williams and Purdah—are making preparation to abscond to a free State & thereby become a loss to said Estate—It is ordered that Jacob K. Wray personal representative of the estate of Sarah A. Twine dec'd do sell the said slaves in Richmond at a public slave auction for cash.[32]

Thus the hand of justice dealt with Negroes in antebellum Virginia—Negroes who had not even committed a crime but were simply believed to be considering one.

More surprising is another entry dated five months later, this one an indictment against a white man:

> On the 1st of November 1859, Severn Knottingham (or Nottingham) did seditiously speak & utter the following, to wit: He believed that Brown done perfectly right in doing as he did at Harper's Ferry.

In making this statement, the court continued, Knottingham (or Nottingham) was implicitly "maintaining that owners have not the right of property in their slaves, to the manifest injury of the institution of slavery."[33]

Sedition against the institution of slavery. A heinous offense in Virginia—or, indeed, anywhere in the South—just two weeks after John Brown had come on his mission of divine retribution.

And yet Severn Knottingham—whose ultimate sentence, if there was one, is unrecorded—was not alone. Two other white men in the county faced similar criminal charges that day. Jefferson Craven had been overheard saying "that he wished or would be glad if the insurrection would happen to-night." Most shocking of all, a certain Henry Hawkins had allegedly declared that "he wished all the slaves would rise & kill the whites, & damn Henry A. Wise [the governor of Virginia] & Harper's Ferry."[34]

Nor were Knottingham, Craven, and Hawkins the only white Virginians to feel this seemingly perverse sympathy with the fanatic who had invaded their state and tried to destroy the world they knew. Even Governor Wise himself, along with other Southern political leaders, had come to see Brown immediately after his capture and sat almost mesmerized for three hours as the old man, bleeding from a serious head wound, held forth about human rights, the curse of slavery, and the inexorable judgment of eternity. Wise said afterward: "They are mistaken who take him to be a madman. . . . He is a man of clear head, of courage, fortitude, and simple ingenuousness. He is cool, collected, and indomitable, and it is but just to say [that] . . . he inspired me with great trust in his integrity, as a man of truth." Certainly Wise did not agree with Brown's position on slavery, to say the least; he yielded to no one in his defense of the peculiar institution. And yet some part of him seems to have responded not just to Brown's courage but also to the stark grandeur of his moral message. "Black slaves make white slaves," Wise had once confessed. This lament spoke for many of his fellow Virginians.[35]

The old Jeffersonian ambivalence about slavery had never disappeared: it had simply gone underground. Within their most private selves, many Southerners—even those with large investments in the institution—had secret thoughts that they would never have spoken aloud; thoughts that, if spoken, would have been crimes. Even in South Carolina; even in the very heart of the rebellion. Mary Chesnut, the most penetrating gazer into the Southern soul, was married to a former United States senator and ardent Confederate, heir apparent to more than five hundred family slaves. (Indeed, James Chesnut was one of the two adjutants who delivered Beauregard's surrender demand to Fort Sumter.) Publicly, Mary supported her husband when, for instance, he declared on the Senate floor that "commerce, civilization, and Christianity" all went hand in hand to sanctify Negro servitude. Privately, she wrote in her diary in March 1861: "I wonder if it be a sin to think slavery a curse to any land. [Charles] Sumner said not one word of this hated institution which is not true." A few months later she confessed her belief that two-thirds of the slaveholders in the Confederate army inwardly "dislike slavery as much as Mrs. Stowe or Greeley." And yet, she also recognized, they had just gone off to lay down their lives for it.[36]

The last time any significant misgivings about slavery had been aired publicly in Virginia was thirty years earlier, in the wake of the terrifying 1831 Negro uprising led by Nat Turner. A month after Turner's execution—he was flayed, quartered, and beheaded—legislators gathered in Richmond to consider various plans that would have emancipated the state's slaves and resettled them somewhere beyond the Old Dominion's borders. The governor, John Floyd (father of the Buchanan administration's notorious secretary of war), went so far as to write in his diary: "I will not rest until slavery is abolished in Virginia." But it soon evolved into the same classic debate that would reemerge, in different shapes and colors, at other moments in American history: when threatened from within, should the state reform itself, or clamp down on dissent? In the end, Virginians chose to clamp down. And so sedition laws and slave patrols became indispensible elements of Southern life. Northern publications expressing unorthodox sentiments on the peculiar institution were seized and destroyed by local postmasters. By 1861, the patrols around Hampton paid surprise visits at least weekly to every slave quarter in the county, making sure that no Negroes would "stroll from one plantation to another" or hold "unlawful assemblies," among other misdeeds. Colonel Mallory's militiamen checked outbound vessels for fugitives. Order must be heaven's first law.[37]

Memories of the Turner rebellion stayed fresh in Hampton. The calamity and its backlash had unfolded just across the James River in Southampton County—formerly just another quiet old corner of the tidewater, another place of small farms and "kind" slaveholders.[38] There, in a matter of hours, the time-hallowed relationship between the races had devolved into a nightmare: white children with their brains dashed out, black men's heads skewered on stakes along the road to deter other would-be conspirators. After that, who was to say that such horrors might not occur without warning elsewhere in the Virginia tidewater—or, indeed, in any town or county of the slave states? This never-ending threat of black violence must be met with a never-ending, and even more forceful, threat of white violence in return. Pieces of Turner's body were distributed as talismans among the whites; one Southampton man made a change purse from its skin. Eternal vigilance would be the price of Southern liberties. Whites must learn, and must teach their children—as blacks had been doing for centuries—to bear a constant burden of fear. Perhaps even more difficult, they must learn to pretend that this fear did not exist. "There is something suspicious," noted the sharp-eyed William H. Russell, reporting this time from a South Carolina plantation, "in the constant never-ending statement that 'we are not afraid of our slaves.'"[39]

Thus, even if on some deep level slavery was, as Mary Chesnut said, a hated institution, it must be defended unequivocally, unambivalently. (All the more so, in fact, since the slightest crack in the façade, whites feared, might become an invitation to rebellion, to rape, and to murder.) Defended illogically, too: slaveholders must learn to insist that their slaves were happy and affectionate, while insisting in the same breath that even the mildest abolition propaganda might spark a bloody massacre. Yankee voices must be silenced in the South. Negro voices, too, needless to say. Southern voices, meanwhile, became ever more stridently defensive, rising in an awful crescendo with secession.

Little wonder, then, that Mrs. Chesnut, by 1861, would come to call slavery the "black incubus."

Little wonder, too, that in the front yard of Hampton's quaint colonial courthouse stood the naked, wizened trunk of an old locust tree: a whipping post.[40]

WAITING ON THE CAUSEWAY before the front gate of Fortress Monroe was a man on horseback. He wore the blue-and-green uniform coat of the 115th Virginia Militia and the white-plumed hat of an officer.[41]

He was Major John Baytop Cary—in civilian life, the principal of Hampton Academy and promulgator of heavenly order among the local youth, but now commander of the Virginia Artillery company of the 115th. Colonel Mallory, he explained, was "absent," and had sent Cary to represent him. In truth, Mallory himself probably could have found his way there if he had wished. After all, those three prime field hands represented as much as 10 percent of his net worth.[42] But it would have been humiliating, going to beg these Yankees for something you knew was yours by law and by right. And the balding, purse-lipped Mallory would have looked more or less like what he was: a lawyer on horseback. The splendid Cary, on the other hand—silver-gray whiskers, erect bearing, haughty tilt of chin—appeared every inch the Southern cavalier.[43]

Major Cary, moreover, knew General Butler slightly from before the war. Barely a year earlier, both had been delegates to the Democratic National Convention in Charleston, that ill-fated assembly where men like Butler had supported Jefferson Davis in the interests of national unity, but where, in the end, North and South had still failed to reach an understanding. Even so, the Virginian could address the Massachusetts man—painful though this might be—as one gentleman to another.[44]

Butler, also on horseback and accompanied by two mounted adjutants, went out to meet Cary at the midpoint of the sandy causeway. The men rode, side by side, to the far bank of the creek—off federal property and into rebel Virginia.

After an exchange of pleasantries and a recollection of their previous acquaintance, Cary got down to business. "I have sought to see you for the purpose of ascertaining upon what principles you intend to conduct the war in this neighborhood," he began stiffly.

First the major wished to know whether the Union fleet in Hampton Roads would allow Virginia civilians safe passage from the area. General Butler replied that the naval blockade would hardly be much of one if it let any Southern ships through. Cary asked if they could go by land. Certainly, Butler replied—since all but a few square miles of Virginia were rebel territory anyhow, who was to stop them?

The two men had turned their horses and were riding together along a country road, with woodlands on one hand and fields on the other, sloping gently down to the creek. They must have seemed an odd pair: the dumpy Yankee, unaccustomed to the saddle, slouching along like a sack of potatoes; the trim, upright Virginian, in perfect control of himself and his mount.

Now Cary reached the third and most delicate question he had come to address.

"I am informed," he said, "that three negroes belonging to Colonel Mallory have escaped within your lines. I am Colonel Mallory's agent and have charge of his property. What do you mean to do with those negroes?"

"I intend to hold them," Butler said.

Here Cary reminded the general about the Fugitive Slave Act: "Do you mean, then, to set aside your constitutional obligation to return them?"

Butler, dour though he usually seemed, must have found it hard to suppress a smile. This was, of course, a question he had expected. And he had prepared what he thought was a fairly clever—even a rather witty—answer.

"I mean to take Virginia at her word, as declared in the ordinance of secession passed yesterday," he said. "I am under no constitutional obligations to a foreign country, which Virginia now claims to be."

"But you say we cannot secede," Cary retorted, "and so you cannot consistently detain the negroes."

"But you say you have seceded," Butler said, "so you cannot consistently claim them. I shall hold these negroes as contraband of war, since they are engaged in the construction of your battery and are claimed as your property."

Ever the diligent scholar of jurisprudence, Butler had been reading up on his military law. In time of war, he knew, a commander had a right to seize and hold any enemy property that was being used for belligerent purposes. The three fugitive slaves, before their escape, had been helping build a Confederate gun emplacement. Very well, then—if the Southerners insisted on treating blacks as property, this Yankee lawyer would treat them as property, too. In that case, he had as much justification in confiscating Baker, Mallory, and Townsend as he would in intercepting a shipment of muskets or swords. Legally speaking, Butler's position was unassailable.

There was, he admitted to Cary, one loophole: "If Colonel Mallory will come into the fort and take the oath of allegiance to the United States, he shall have his negroes." The rebel officer was, to say the least, unlikely to do so.

If anything could have flustered the courtly headmaster-major, surely this conversation must have. Cary rode back to the Confederate lines having accomplished none of the aims of his errand. Butler, for his part, returned to Fortress Monroe feeling rather pleased with himself. Still, he knew that vanquishing the rebel officer with case law was only a minor victory, and perhaps a momentary one if his superiors in Washington frowned on what he had done.

The following day, a Saturday, Butler picked up his pen and resumed his twice-interrupted dispatch to General Scott. Certain questions had arisen, he began, "of very considerable importance both in a military and political aspect, and which I beg leave to hereby submit."

But before this missive could even reach the general-in-chief's desk up in Washington, matters at Fortress Monroe would become even more complicated. On Sunday morning, eight more fugitives turned up at Union lines outside the fort. On Monday, there were forty-seven, and not just young men now but women, old people, entire families. There was a mother with a three-month-old infant in her arms. There was an ancient Negro who had been born in the year of America's independence.[45]

By Wednesday, a Massachusetts soldier would write home: "Slaves are brought in here hourly."[46]

"WHAT'S TO BE DONE WITH THE BLACKS?" asked a headline in the *Chicago Tribune*. It was a question that more and more white Americans—in both the North and the South—were starting to pose.[47]

Before the attack on Sumter, the answer had seemed clear to many. The *Tribune*'s rival paper, the *Chicago Times*, expounded it in no uncertain terms:

> Let the South have her negroes to her heart's content, and in her own way—and let us go on getting rich and powerful by feeding and clothing them. Let the negroes *alone!*—let them ALONE! . . . ABOLITION IS DISUNION. It is the "vile cause and the most cursed effect." It is the Alpha and Omega of our National woes. STRANGLE IT![48]

For many Northerners, the outbreak of armed hostilities did little to change this—at least initially. In early May, the *New York Herald* praised Lincoln's "humane war policy"—by which it meant "his respect . . . for the rights of 'property'" as opposed to the "lawless disorganizers" within his own party who urged "a war policy of extermination and confiscation against the South." The paper's position, in effect, conceded the premises on which the Confederates themselves had gone to war: Law and slavery were on the same side. So were slavery and union. Liberation of the slaves would be a confiscation of Southerners' rightful property—and would mean the extermination of Southern society, perhaps even quite literally. The North's struggle was simply one against a treasonous conspiracy, and for "the integrity of the Union." In other words, Unionism was still a purely conservative cause.[49]

Even some of the Northerners who were considered radicals had deferred to what seemed the necessity of disavowing any abolitionist intentions. "Some people ask if this is to be a crusade of emancipation," Henry Ward Beecher told his congregation. "No, it is not. I hate slavery intensely. . . . Liberty is the birthright of every man, yet ours is not an army of liberation. Why? Because the fifteen States of the South are guaranteed security in their property, and we have no right by force to dispossess them of that property."[50]

For America's small community of black intellectuals, the spring of 1861 was a disorienting time. "I have never spent days so restless and anxious," Frederick Douglass confessed two weeks after Sumter. "Our mornings and evenings have continually oscillated between the dim light of hope, and the gloomy shadow of despair."[51]

The past few years had been dispiriting and exhausting ones for Douglass, who had never ceased fighting for emancipation since his own escape from slavery in Maryland more than two decades earlier. In 1855, he closed the second edition of his autobiography with a ringing prophecy:

> Old as the everlasting hills; immovable as the throne of God; and certain as the purposes of eternal power, against all hindrances, and against all delays, and despite all the mutations of human instrumentalities, it is the faith of my soul, that this anti-slavery cause will triumph.[52]

Of all the Negro abolitionists, Douglass had always been the one to insist, often to the derision of other black leaders, that Africans might one day also fully be Americans, that the promise of freedom embedded in the Declaration might one day apply to them, too. He remembered when, as a boy clandestinely teaching himself to read, he had pored over a book of political oratory from the Revolution, deciphering the stirring words one letter at a time. He spurned those who sought an independent black republic in Africa or the Caribbean.

By 1861, however—after Bleeding Kansas, *Dred Scott*, and John Brown—even Douglass's solid faith had been badly shaken. The final blow for him was the inauguration of the new Republican president. Douglass had campaigned for Lincoln. But the "double-tongued document" of the inaugural address, as he had called it, came as a shocking betrayal. If even such a leader as Lincoln would sacrifice four million Negroes to appease the South, then clearly all hope was lost. Blacks had no future in America. At the end of March, he booked passage to Haiti, planning to set sail from New Haven on April 25 and arrive in

Port-au-Prince by May 1. If the island nation lived up to its promise—as a sun-kissed "city set on a hill" for former slaves—Douglass would move down there for good, and he would urge other black Americans to do the same.[53]

But at the last minute, ten days after the attack on Sumter and in the midst of his oscillations between hope and despair, Douglass changed his travel plans, staying behind in the chilly dampness of western New York State. On April 27, as the ship steamed toward Port-au-Prince without him, he gave a lecture at a church in Syracuse. It was one of only a few speeches that Douglass, usually a tireless orator, would deliver in the year ahead. At the most tumultuous moment of the national crisis, he seemed briefly to find the voice, by turns soaringly prophetic and frankly personal, that had moved audiences ever since his first public address in a Nantucket meetinghouse, many years before. Instead of trying to hide his doubts and uncertainties about the future, Douglass embraced them. "We cannot see the end from the beginning," he confessed. "Our profoundest calculations may prove erroneous, our best hopes disappointed, and our worst fears confirmed." He continued:

And yet we read the face of the sky, and may discern the signs of the times. We know that clouds and darkness, and the sounds of distant thunder, mean rain. So, too, we may observe the fleecy drapery of the moral sky, and draw conclusions as to what may come upon us. There is a general feeling amongst us, that the control of events has been taken out of our hands, that we have fallen into the mighty current of eternal principles—invisible forces—which are shaping and fashioning events as they wish, using us only as instruments to work out their own results in our national destiny.[54]

"At any rate," Douglass also wrote that week, "this is no time for us to leave the country."[55]

WITHIN DAYS AFTER FRANK BAKER, Shepard Mallory, and James Townsend crossed the James River in a stolen boat, their exploit—and their fate—were being discussed at the White House. Indeed, they were a topic of conversation throughout the entire nation.

Word of Butler's decision on the three fugitive slaves hit the Northern press on Monday morning, May 27, not long after Scott received his dispatch; almost certainly Butler himself, never one to shy away from publicity, had leaked it to a correspondent. At first the news-papers played it more or less as a joke. "General Butler appears to be turning his legal education to good account," a five-line report in *The New York Times* began. "We think the people of [Virginia] will find the General a match for them in more ways than one." It was like a comic sketch in a minstrel show: a Yankee shyster outwits a drawling "F.F.V.," as the *Times* described Major Cary. (This was short for First Families of Virginia, a term of blueblooded pride in the Old Dominion that had become the butt of widespread ridicule in the North.) In fairness, the paper's readers badly needed something light that day, on the heels of a mournful weekend: the Butler item was wedged among long columns of type describing every detail of Colonel Ellsworth's funeral cortege and its passage through the streets of Manhattan.[56]

Winfield Scott was also inclined at first to take the whole thing as a joke—for he, too, was in dire need of comic relief. The general-in-chief's gout had flared up even worse than usual, forcing the Hero of Lundy's Lane to spend his days prostrated on a sofa, his swollen feet propped up on a stack of pillows, as he gestured with a stick at a large wall map, barking commands at his scurrying bevies of secretaries and aides. (This scene of military grandeur, a correspondent wrote, "was one on which the pencil of a Leutze would dwell lovingly"—the acclaimed painter of *Washington Crossing the Delaware* had just been commis-sioned to paint a new mural at the Capitol.) On Wednesday morning, Lincoln met with Scott and found the old man chortling delightedly at what he called "Butler's fugitive slave law." Afterward, the president told Montgomery Blair that "he had not seen old Lundy as merry since he had known him."

Of course, Scott also expected that Lincoln would instruct him to overrule Butler. And perhaps it was this prospect, even more than the joke itself, that cheered him: this greenhorn president had just been shown what could happen when you slapped a major general's epau-lettes onto the undeserving shoulders of a politician.[57]

But Lincoln was not so certain. "The President seemed to think it a very important subject," Blair wrote after their conversation, "and one requiring some thought in view of the numbers of negroes we were likely to have on hand in virtue of this new doctrine." Lincoln made it known that he would address the matter with his cabinet the following morning.[58]

By all appearances, nothing in the administration's slavery policy had changed in the past three months. Lincoln had continued to avow, both publicly and privately, that he had no desire to interfere with the peculiar institution in either the rebellious or the loyal states. And yet one or two of those closest to him—closer, certainly, than the members of his own cabinet—had begun to notice that his position was slightly less absolute than his inaugural address would have it. They may even have known that the news from Fortress Monroe did not catch him entirely off guard.

On May 7, John Hay had gone into Lincoln's office to brief him on some of the recent White House mail. He found the president contorted into a most unusual position: scrunched up in a chair with his boots braced against the windowsill and a large telescope balanced on the tips of his toes. He was apparently surveying some naval steamboats passing on the Potomac.[59]

Hay told the chief executive that several correspondents were suggesting the administration could quickly kill secession, present and future, by attacking the taproot of the South's economy: slavery. Orville Browning, a leading Illinois Republican and a close friend of Lincoln's for the past thirty years, had sent the most extraordinary letter urging him to "crush all rebel forces" without mercy, and let the Negroes, after having "avenge[d] the wrongs of ages," turn the confiscated Cotton Belt into a republic of their own. Perhaps Hay even read some of the letter aloud:

> Our armies must march into the rebel states, and the negroes will flock to our standard. What is to be done with them? We cant avoid considering and dealing with this question. . . . There is no escaping it. We must meet it, and solve it, and we had better do it in advance—before the emergency is upon us. When they come we cannot repulse them—we cannot butcher them, we cannot send them back to bondage. Heaven would blast us with its wrath if we did. We cannot incorporate them into our population in the free states. We cannot drive them into the sea—We cannot precipitate them upon any other country. What are we to do with them?[60]

Lincoln chuckled at this. Yes, he told Hay, some of his Northern friends seemed a bit "bewildered and dazzled by the excitement of the hour." Some of them appeared to think that the war—still less than a month old and practically bloodless—was going to result in the total abolition of slavery. One gentleman had even proposed—in earnest, it seemed—that he should enlist blacks in the army!

The young secretary persisted. Quite a few people were saying such things, he told Lincoln. Not just politicians, either, judging by the White House mailbag, but ordinary citizens, too.

Behind his boss's back, Hay had recently given Lincoln a nickname: "the Tycoon." This word had entered American slang within just the past year or so, as part of the fad for all things Japanese. *Taikun* was the title of the chief shogun, and suggested—at least to the Western mind—not just a wise and powerful ruler but a figure of deep oriental inscrutability. The Tycoon now made a reply worthy of his name. It impressed Hay so much that he copied it word for word that night into his diary; thirty years later, he would also copy it verbatim into his biography of Lincoln.

"For my own part," the president began, "I consider the central idea pervading this struggle is the necessity that is upon us, of proving that popular government is not an absurdity. We must settle this question now, whether in a free government the minority have the right to break up the government whenever they choose. If we fail it will go far to prove the incapability of the people to govern themselves."

So far this was clear enough. In fact it was classic, lambent Lincoln: in three simple sentences he had explained why secession represented not just the failure of democracy but the triumph of anarchy. Those sentences have been quoted in innumerable Civil War histories and Lincoln biographies. But it was also part of his genius with language to deploy words as camouflage, to reveal and mask himself at the same time, like a *taikun* behind a rice-paper screen—or like an Illinois lawyer in front of a jury. It was this Lincoln who spoke next, in oblique phraseology that would be quoted by very few historians or biographers besides Hay:

> There may be one consideration used in stay of such final judgment, but that is not for us to use in advance. That is, that there exists in our case, an instance of a vast and far reaching disturbing element, which the history of no other free nation will probably ever present. That however is not for us to say at present. Taking the government as we found it we will see if the majority can preserve it.[61]

One consideration. Disturbing element. Where Browning had conjured images of fire and blood, the president declined even to breathe the words *slavery* or *slave*. In speaking of a "stay of . . . final judgment," however, he was using legalese—Lincoln the attorney talking to Hay the law clerk in unmistakable terms. Hay understood the startling import of what he was hearing: Lincoln had just admitted, for the very first time, that a decree of emancipation might become necessary in the course of the war. It would be the Union's last appeal, to the universe's highest court, for a stay of execution. (This was not the last time Lincoln would conjure a vision of Providence as supreme tribunal: in his second inaugural address, he described more explicitly a God who sat in impartial judgment of North and South, master and slave.) Lincoln's choice of language revealed something else, besides: when the day of jubilee did come, judgment would not be hurled down from Sinai amid wrathful blasts of brimstone, as Browning would have had it. Rather, the slaves would have to be released from bondage by mundane legalese—perhaps even allowed to slip out through a legal loophole. Legalese, Lincoln knew, was the language of democracy itself: the rule of law, whether civil or military, came down to the power of words to compel. Had not the Founding Fathers framed their declaration of independence as a last-ditch political "necessity" to which they must reluctantly "acquiesce" in the face of tyranny? Decrees by fire and brimstone were a version of anarchy, just like secession.[62]

It is somewhat ironic: anarchy was what both Lincoln and the South feared most.

In his conversation with Hay, the president had characterized slavery as a "vast and far reaching disturbing element": a great structural crack in the edifice of the old Union. Here Lincoln reiterated what many other Americans—notably Jefferson—had been saying ever since the nation's founding. (He was also echoing his own famous "House Divided" speech.) Meanwhile the edifice of the new Confederacy had been, in the words of its vice president, Alexander H. Stephens, "founded upon exactly the opposite" of Jefferson's idea: "Its foundations are laid, its corner-stone rests, upon the great truth that the negro is not equal to the white man; that slavery—subordination to the superior race—is his natural and normal condition." By using this metaphor, Stephens was not simply saying that he and other Confederate founding fathers believed profoundly in the rightness of slavery and white supremacy. He was also confessing that their new Southern republic would stand or fall depending on the solidity of its peculiar institution. In this perverse way, the very architecture of the Confederacy relied on blacks, no less than Colonel Mallory's gun platforms at Sewell's Point.

But by late May of 1861, some Southerners were already starting to realize that their war to defend the institution of slavery was actually *undermining* the foundations of slavery—in all sorts of alarming and unexpected ways—before even a single federal regiment had marched onto rebel territory.

In the first months of the war, Southern newspapers often boasted of slaves' loyalty to the Confederate cause. The *Richmond Dispatch*, under the headline "Negro Heroism," told its readers about some black men in North Carolina who—under the direction of local whites—had collected a thousand pounds or so of scrap iron to be molded into cannonballs. The Negroes, according to the editors, "express themselves highly pleased with the preparations that are being made to kill up the Black Republicans. Wonder what Greeley will say to that?" Another report spoke of fifteen hundred "patriotic yellow men" in New Orleans—members of the free mulatto community—who had offered to defend their city if necessary.[63]

Yet the slaveholders' confident public declarations were belied, as usual, by their private confessions.

It is true that some Confederate officers had enough faith in certain trusted slaves to bring them along to war and even put guns in their hands. This occurred especially at the beginning of the war, in tight-knit local militia units, including those around Hampton. It is also true that a handful of free blacks, especially those of mixed race, voluntarily—perhaps, in a few cases, even enthusiastically—joined up. Human nature is a complicated thing. Later history would show, moreover, that such support of their oppressors was not entirely irrational. Moble Hopson, a very light-skinned mixed-race man near Hampton, would recall that when he was a boy before the war, no one mentioned his race, and local authorities even looked the other way when he attended a tiny church school with the white children. But as soon as the war ended, he was summarily thrown out of that school. He and his family would henceforth be classed as Negroes and lumped together with the masses of destitute (and now dangerous) black freedmen, their past privileges revoked.[64]

The "black Confederates"—a misleading term, since the Confederacy never accepted Negro enlistments—have received a great deal of attention from present-day apologists for the Lost Cause. Far more widespread throughout the South in early 1861, though, were signs of white fear and black rebellion.

On April 13, as her Charleston mansion trembled with the shock waves of bombs falling on Sumter, and with her husband away at the Confederate fortifications, Mary Chesnut had found herself studying the faces of her black house servants. James Chesnut's valet, Laurence, sat by the door, apparently "as sleepy and as respectful and as profoundly indifferent" as ever. The other Negroes wore similar expressions. But, the canny Mrs. Chesnut observed, "they carry it too far. You could not tell that they hear even the awful row that is going on in the bay, even though it is dinning in their ears night and day. And people talk before them as if they were chairs and tables. And they make no sign. Are they stolidly stupid or wiser than we are, silent and strong, biding their time?"[65]

For her, as for many slaveholders, that question answered itself. As early as November, towns and counties across the South had begun stepping up slave patrols, worried that Lincoln's election would inspire Negroes to rebel. One unsettling story told of a Georgia slave who suddenly refused to chop wood for his master and mistress, telling them that "Lincoln was elected now, and he was free." The black man, according to a newspaper, "after being sent to the whipping-post, gained new light on the subject of Lincoln and Slavery, and returned to his duty." Many of the first Southern militia companies that formed that winter, the reporter added, "had quite as much to do with fighting niggers as with repelling Abolitionists."[66]

When war became inevitable, Mary Chesnut herself predicted that Southerners would have to deal "with Yankees in front and negroes in the rear."[67] Many whites shared this expectation. On May 4, a farmer in Alabama named William H. Lee wrote to warn Jefferson Davis: "the Negroes is very Hiley Hope up that they will soon Be free so i think that you Had Better order out All the Negroe felers from 17 years oald up Ether fort them up or put them in the army and Make them fite like good fells for wee ar in danger of our lives hear among them."[68]

Southerners tried in vain to keep their slaves from learning any information that might put the wrong sorts of ideas into their heads. William Henry Trescot, the wealthy Charlestonian who had acted more or less as a double agent within Buchanan's State Department, took to speaking about current affairs only in French when a Negro was present. This was not a widely applicable precaution, however. (It would likely not have worked in William Lee's case, for instance.)[69]

Jefferson Davis was prepared neither to "fort up" all the Negroes nor to put them in the Confederate army. He simply let whites like Lee continue fearing for their lives, which dampened military enlistment, since many men were unwilling to leave their wives and children unguarded with the slaves. (The following year the Confederate Congress would reluctantly vote to exempt owners of twenty or more slaves from conscription, exacerbating Southern complaints that

the conflict was "a rich man's war and a poor man's fight.") Some
state governments even refused to turn over their arms stockpiles
or dispatch all their troops to the Confederate authorities, afraid of
being left helpless when the Negroes rose up to butcher their masters. They cited "local defense" as their justification, and the authorities in Richmond—committed as they were to the doctrine of states'
rights—found it difficult to overrule.[70]

And in many places, rebel troops quickly found themselves facing
exactly the kind of two-front battle that Mary Chesnut had predicted.
The heavenly order of slave society—enforced for so long by the constant threat of white Southern violence—began to crumble as soon as
white Southern violence needed to be directed externally, against the
North, instead of just internally, against the slaves. Colonel Mallory's
militiamen were no longer chasing fugitives; they were aiming cannons at the Yankees. Or at least that was how it was supposed to work.

On May 8, Brigadier General Daniel Ruggles, commanding Confederate forces at Fredericksburg, Virginia, reported to General Lee's
headquarters that he had sent his cavalry off in pursuit of Negroes.
The day before, he wrote, a local planter named John T. Washington—
great-great-nephew of the late president, as it happened—had noticed
that five of his slaves seemed to have disappeared. Hastening off to
nearby plantations in search of them, Washington discovered that
almost all of his neighbors were missing some Negroes as well, and
they alerted the military authorities. General Ruggles told headquarters that he had immediately dispatched mounted troops "to intercept
and recover the slaves supposed to have escaped, but thus far without
satisfactory results."[71]

In other words, the Confederates were fighting Negroes on Virginia soil weeks before they fought even a single Yankee.

Northerners, of course, delighted in such tales. Even those who
loathed the thought of abolition loved the idea of traitorous rebels
scurrying helter-skelter across the countryside in pursuit of mischie-
vous blacks. The *New York Herald*, certainly no friend of the slave,
welcomed Butler's "contraband of war" decision, noting that the ruling "meets with universal approbation of the supporters of the Union
cause throughout the country"—as a clever military tactic, it meant.
(The *Herald* was also glad to praise a good solid Democrat like Butler; no radical, he.) The *Springfield Republican* reported: "The entire
country laughed at the exquisite humor of the transaction." A cartoon
captioned "The (Fort) Monroe Doctrine" began circulating widely.
It showed a grinning Negro standing outside the citadel, poised to

flee, as a Southern planter (broad-brimmed hat, stringy goatee) brandishes a whip, yelling, "Come back you black rascal." The black man points toward the fort with one hand and thumbs his nose with the other. "Can't come back nohow massa," he says. "Dis chile's contraban." Meanwhile, behind the planter's back, dozens more fieldhands dash toward the walls of Monroe.[72]

There was, however, a serious undertone to such humor. By the end of May, Northerners were starting to accept the idea of Southerners not just as opponents—let alone as the wayward brethren they had been just a few months earlier—but as enemies. The cold-blooded slaying of Ellsworth had given the nation a glimpse of the horrors to come. Many loyal Americans started asking themselves whether it was worth making such sacrifices simply to restore a Union that would still be committed to respecting slaveholders' "rights," and to fight an all-out war against the South while still trying to handle slavery with kid gloves. The old arguments against abolitionist troublemaking were already ringing hollow.

Two days after Ellsworth's death—just as the second group of fugitives was arriving at Fortress Monroe—a Baptist minister in Albany, New York, gave a sermon about the young colonel's slaying before an audience of Union volunteers. The Reverend J. D. Fulton began with a passage from the Old Testament about David's lament over the death of Jonathan: "Thy love to me was wonderful—passing the love of woman." Lincoln, the minister said, was like David, and Ellsworth was his Jonathan. When David spoke those words, Fulton noted, the Kingdom of Israel was riven by civil war. King Saul had anointed David as his successor but had then suddenly turned on him and had heaped up obstacles "in the path of the choice of the people and the favorite of Heaven." Jonathan's death, terrible as it was, had signaled the moment when David the former shepherd boy became King David, the monarch who reunited his kingdom and brought the Tablets of the Law to Jerusalem. Perhaps the death of Ellsworth would mark a similar rebirth for Lincoln, and for America. However, the preacher continued:

> If it be the business of the North to squander her millions, and to give up her sons, simply that we can place the old flag-staff again in the hands of those who ask protection to slavery, then . . . you will see an inglorious termination to the campaign. But, if we are to fight for freedom; if we are to wipe out the curse that infects our borders; if we are to establish justice, teach mercy,

and proclaim righteousness, then will our soldiers be animated by a heroic purpose that will build them up in courage, in faith, in honor, and they will come back to us respected and beloved.[73]

Lincoln and his cabinet convened on Thursday, May 30—a week after the first three Hampton fugitives' escape—to address Butler's decision. Unfortunately, no detailed account of their deliberations survives. But a letter that Blair wrote to the general later that day suggests that they may have been fairly perfunctory. Previously the postmaster general had advised that he planned to argue for leaving the treatment of fugitive slaves up to Butler's discretion—reminding him, however, that "the business you are sent upon . . . is war, not emancipation." Needless to say, Fortress Monroe should not harbor any slaves belonging to pro-Union masters, or those not useful for military purposes. After the meeting Blair gloated, "I so far carried my point this morning about the negroes that no instructions will be given you for the present and I consider that I have in fact carried out my programme of leaving it to your discretion. I think this conclusion was arrived at by most from a desire to escape responsibility for acting at all at this time"—a common enough desire in Washington, then as now. (Another account suggests that Seward's deft hand may have helped coax his colleagues toward this nonresolution.)[74]

By that point, the administration had already received a second dispatch from Butler, describing the influx of women and children into the fort. With this in mind, Blair suggested one pragmatic "modification" to Butler's policy: "I am inclined to think you might impose the code by restricting its operations to working people, leaving the Secessionists to take care of the non working classes of these people. . . . You can . . . take your pick of the lot and let the rest go so as not to be required to feed unproductive laborers or indeed any that you do not require." As to the slaves' eventual fate, Blair wrote, of course no one was suggesting that all the Negroes be set free. Perhaps at the end of the war, those who belonged to men convicted of treason could be legally confiscated and sent off to Haiti or Central America—in fact, he was enclosing a speech that his brother Frank had once given in Congress about just such a plan. (The Blairs may have been rabid Unionists, but they had no more love of Negroes than the *Herald*—which, by the way, proposed that all the confiscated slaves should be held by the federal government and then eventually sold back to their owners, at half price, to finance the cost of the war.)[75]

A week or so later, Blair wrote Butler again, somewhat more urgently:

he had learned that even more fugitives had come into the fort, and thought the general really ought to start following up on that Haiti idea sooner rather than later. Maybe Butler could have a chat with "some of the most intelligent [Negroes], and see how they would like to go with their families to so congenial a clime"?[76]

Perhaps Lincoln realized what Blair did not: developments were unfolding far too quickly for any of that. The president left no record of his own thoughts on the news from Fortress Monroe. But he might have agreed with Frederick Douglass's recent words, had he known of them: *The control of events has been taken out of our hands . . . we have fallen into the mighty current of eternal principles—invisible forces—which are shaping and fashioning events as they wish, using us only as instruments to work out their own results in our national destiny.*

At least one person grasped the full import of Butler's little joke. Back at the fort, Theodore Winthrop, the general's belletristic secretary, wrote a Latin tag from Horace in his notebook: *Solvuntur risu tabulae.** Then he added, in English: "An epigram abolished slavery in the United States."[77]

IN PEACETIME, the interior of Fortress Monroe was, and still is today, a serene enclosure. Winthrop might have called it a *hortus conclusus;* another visitor from the North thought it looked like a better-armed version of the Boston Common. Along its well-graveled paths, live oaks and magnolias spread themselves with aristocratic negligence, the tips of their lowest branches nearly brushing the clipped lawn. The officers' quarters were less like barracks than summer cottages, each with a flower garden and double veranda. A happy posting, in the days of the Old Army; indeed, one end of the citadel's moat was literally filled with oyster shells, tossed insouciantly from the casemate windows by several generations of military gourmands. General Scott himself paid loving tribute to those local mollusks almost every time someone brought up the subject of Fortress Monroe—which was quite often, of late.[78]

The Chesapeake seafood still abounded, and demand for it had never been higher, but serenity was in short supply at Fortress Monroe in the spring and summer of 1861. Teams of workmen busied themselves everywhere. (One of General Butler's first orders had been to clear those oyster shells from the moat.) War correspondents in search

*"The tablets of law are erased with a laugh."

of the war arrived by the dozens. Draymen's wagons rumbled incessantly to and fro, hauling barrels and bundles of supplies, provisions,
and donations from well-meaning civilians back home, including far
more pocket handkerchiefs than the Third Massachusetts knew what
to do with. A self-appointed "aeronaut" named Professor La Mountain did mysterious things with silk bags and hydrogen before finally
making the first successful balloon reconnaissance in American history,
discovering a secret camp concealed behind the Confederate batteries
at Sewell's Point. Deputations of clergymen from various denominations bustled about, anxious to ascertain that the Union's defenders
were marching off to face death untainted by profane thoughts or
spiritous liquors. Perspiring squads of soldiers hauled giant columbiad
cannons from the fort's wharf up to its parapets, like colonies of ants
with the gleaming black corpses of enormous beetles. Scouts were dispatched to advance posts and returned the next day, usually "covered
with wounds inflicted, not by the Secessionists, but by their allies the
misquitoes, who swarm in the woods, and whom nothing can induce
to secede."[79]

The Union's foothold on Virginia soil had spread itself beyond
the immediate vicinity of the fort; white tents by the thousands blos-
somed across the wheat fields, and U.S. flags flew triumphantly from
President Tyler's villa, from the cupola of Colonel Mallory's house
next door, and from Major Cary's academy. Fresh regiments seemed
to arrive daily. One morning in late May, the steam tug *Yankee* spilled
forth the gaudy soldiers of the Fifth New York, Colonel Abram Duryee's Zouaves, resplendent in white turbans and baggy red calico pants.
Close on their heels came an all-German unit, the Turner Rifles,
marching under both the Stars and Stripes and the black, red, and yellow banner of their homeland. Their picturesque colonel, Max Weber,
his aggressively martial mustaches waxed needle-sharp, was one of
Franz Sigel's comrades-in-arms from Baden in '48. (Weber ensconced
himself in Tyler's former study, delighted to find busts of Goethe and
Schiller already there.) Each new regiment was like a troupe of cos-
tumed actors arriving in the wings of a theater: anxious and excited
supernumeraries waiting for their cue to go onstage.[80]

And then there were the Virginia Union Volunteers: less resplendent, perhaps, but equally picturesque.

That was the unofficial name—or one of them—given to the fugitive slaves who had taken refuge at the fort. "I wish you could see
some of their clothes," a New England soldier wrote home. "They
are all patches, sewed together, and patches on that, sewed with cot-

ton strings, and a hat that would be too poor for a hen's nest." Soon this was supplemented with bits and bobs of Union uniforms: cast-off caps, shirts, and trousers, and even the odd scrap of Confederate attire plucked nimbly from a master's knapsack before departure. Almost all the Negroes came barefoot, and most remained that way. Yet each morning, dozens of the aptly named Volunteers lined up to pitch in with manual labor around the fort. Moreover, as the garrison's medical chief remarked, "they are the pleasantest faces to be seen at the post." A Northern visitor wrote:

> I have watched them with deep interest, as they filed off to their work, or labored steadily through the long, hot day; a quiet, respectable, industrious . . . folk, with far more agreeable expressions than one could ever see in a low white laboring class. Somehow there was to my eye a weird, solemn aspect to them, as they walked slowly along, as if they, the victims, had become the judges in this awful contest, or as if they were the black *Parcae* disguised among us, and spinning, unknown to all, the destinies of the great Republic. I think every one likes them.[81]

There was another nickname that caught on much more widely, one that evolved out of General Butler's renowned legalism. Journalists across the country quipped relentlessly about the Negro "shipments of contraband goods" or, in the words of *The New York Times*, "contraband property having legs to run away with, and intelligence to guide its flight"—until, within a week or two, the fugitives had a new name: *contrabands*. It was a perfectly crafted bit of slang, a minor triumph of Yankee ingenuity. Were these blacks people, or property? Free, or slave? Such questions were, as yet, unanswerable, for answering them would have raised a whole host of other questions that few white Americans were ready to address. *Contrabands* let the speaker or writer off the hook, by allowing the escaped Negroes to be all of those things at once. "Never was a word so speedily adopted by so many people in so short a time," one Union officer wrote. Within a few weeks, the average Northern newspaper reader could scan, without blinking, a sentence like this one: *Several contrabands came into the camp of the First Connecticut Regiment to-day.* As routine as the usage soon became, however, a hint of Butler's joke remained, a slight edge of nervous laughter. A touch of racist derision as well, perhaps: William Lloyd Garrison's *Liberator* carped, justly enough, that it was offensive to speak of human beings that way. Yet in its very absurdity, reflecting the Alice-in-Wonderland legal reasoning behind Butler's decision, the term also mocked the absurdity of slavery—and the willful stupidity of federal laws that, for nearly a century, had refused to concede any meaningful difference between a bushel of corn and a human being with black skin. Eventually, even many Negro leaders adopted it.[82]

To a few people, the strange inscrutability of the word suggested somehow the uncertainty of the moment. "*Where* we are drifting, I cannot see," wrote the abolitionist Lydia Maria Child, "but we are drifting *some*where; and our fate, whatever it may be, is bound up with these . . . 'contrabands.' "[83]

In all events, the contrabands kept coming to Fortress Monroe, their numbers multiplying as the perimeter of the Union lines expanded. Only a couple of days after the first three fugitives' flight, nearly all of Hampton's white residents fled in turn as federal troops occupied the town. Some slaveholders simply left their Negroes behind, especially those too elderly or infirm to be of much use or value. Most tried to coax them to follow; some warned that the Yankees would eat them, or send them north to be processed into fertilizer, or sell them to a Cuban sugar plantation. But the blacks, not surprisingly, made themselves scarce, slipping off into the woods and fields until their masters were safely away. For some whites, who had considered their house servants almost (there was always an *almost*) like family, that day was a rude awakening. One white Hamptonian would later recall how his aunt and uncle "were particularly fond of a boy now perhaps 16 or 18 who had been in the house since he was a little child. He was a bright boy and very fond and considerate of them. This mulatto, though he had been raised almost like a son, was so ungrateful as not long after to break into the house with others and take all the money that this old couple had. The young rascal went off, and neither I nor anyone about here ever knew what became of him."[84]

By early June, some four or five hundred such "rascals" were within the Union lines. STAMPEDE AMONG THE NEGROES IN VIRGINIA, proclaimed *Frank Leslie's Illustrated Newspaper*, with a double-page spread of dramatic woodcuts showing black men, women, and children crossing a creek under a full moon, then being welcomed heartily into the fort by General Butler himself (or rather, by the artist's trimmer, handsomer version of him). One correspondent estimated that "this species of property under Gen. Butler's protection [is] worth $500,000, at a fair average of $1,000 apiece in the Southern human flesh market."[85]

Despite the stern counsels of the postmaster general, Butler was not turning away the "non working classes" of fugitives. Perhaps stretch ing the strict definition of militarily valuable contraband, he wrote to Blair, "If I take the able bodied only, the young must die. If I take the mother must I not take the child?" In a letter to General Scott, he added: "Of the humanitarian aspect I have no doubt. Of the political one, I have no right to judge." Scott, judging both, let this enlargement of the original doctrine stand.[86]

Abolitionists among the Union troops watched these developments with delight. Major Winthrop was at his desk in Butler's office one evening when a local civilian, perhaps unaware of the latest permutations in contraband law, arrived seeking an audience with the general. He was an elderly, grave, pious-looking Virginian who, until extremely recently, had been the master of some forty slaves. He came bearing a tale of woe. By good fortune, he had managed to get half his slaves away to be sold in Alabama before they could run off to the Yankees. But then he had come home from church that Sunday to find that nearly all of the rest were gone. "Now, Colonel," the man addressed General Butler, "I'm an invalid, and you have got two of my boys, young boys, sir, not over twelve—no use to you except perhaps to black a gentleman's boots. I would like them very much, sir, if you would spare them. In fact, Colonel, sir, I ought to have my property back."

The supplicant seemed so consumed with honest self-pity that Butler, Winthrop, and the other officers burst into uncontrollable guffaws. They sent him away empty-handed. Winthrop exulted that night in a letter to his sister. "By Liberty! but it is worth something to be here at this moment, in the center of the center! Here we scheme the schemes! Here we take the secession flags, the arms, the prisoners! Here we liberate the slaves—virtually."[87]

Winthrop, like most men at Fortress Monroe, had been a soldier for hardly over a month. (And the only secession flag captured so far had been one sad piece of flannel needlework that Colonel Duryee's Zouaves had found at ex-President Tyler's house.) In ordinary life, the slight, fair-haired thirty-two-year-old was a rising author with two travel books to his name—*The Canoe and the Saddle* and *Life in the Open Air*—and a drawerful of unpublished poems and novels. His two closest friends were the writer George W. Curtis and the painter Frederic Church, who was also a hiking companion on rambles through the Adirondacks and along the coast of Maine (where the two had gone, improbably enough, to drum up votes for Frémont in the summer of 1856). Fresh out of Yale, Winthrop had been a tourist in Europe in 1848, and the revolutions there had left a lasting impression, a determination to find a life that would combine poetics and politics. Just after Sumter's surrender, he marched down Broadway in the ranks of the dandyfied Seventh Regiment, whose members had pledged themselves to the defense of Washington for a not terribly generous thirty-day enlistment term. But Winthrop was under no illusion that the war would be a frolic. "I see no present end of this business," he wrote Curtis shortly after his arrival in the capital. "We must conquer the South. Afterward we must be prepared to do its polic[ing] in its own behalf, and in behalf of its black population, whom this war must, without precipitation, emancipate. We must hold the South as the metropolitan police holds New York. All this is inevitable. Now I wish to enroll myself at once in the 'Police of the Nation,' and for life, if the nation will take me."[88]

At the close of a brief and wholly bloodless campaign, the men of the Seventh had dispersed, leaving behind as their only casualties a thousand velvet-covered camp stools that had somehow gotten misplaced in transit. Winthrop remained, joining Butler's staff. At Fortress Monroe, he was already witnessing the emancipation of the blacks, a bit more precipitately than he had envisioned. Appalled at the ragged condition of the fugitives, he began sending urgent appeals for decent clothing to his friends in the North.[89]

He was also determined to write down what he saw happening around him. Back in New York, on the Sunday that news came of Sumter's surrender, he and Curtis had sat together late into the night on the porch of Curtis's house on Staten Island, talking about the present and the future. Winthrop told his friend that he thought someone should keep a careful record of the quickly unspooling events: "for we are making our history hand over hand."

While in Washington with the Seventh, he had written those brilliant accounts for *The Atlantic*—full of sly wit and vivid detail—of the troops bunking in the House chamber and the army's march by moonlight over the Long Bridge into Virginia. Now, at Fortress Monroe, Winthrop began a new essay: "Voices of the Contraband," he would call it.[90]

Indeed, there were new voices, and new stories, to be heard every day at the fort. Some of the contrabands had led extraordinary lives.

One of the first fugitives to arrive was George Scott. He had originally been the field hand of a man in Hampton, but then through a complicated family transaction became the property of his original owner's son-in-law, who planned to take him to his plantation in a different county, on the far side of the James. Worse yet, the new master, one A. M. Graves, was widely known as a brute who abused both his wife and his Negroes. Before Graves could gain possession of him, Scott slipped off into the woods outside town. For about two years he hid out in a cave, where a sympathetic and courageous young girl regularly brought him food. Many of the local whites sympathized, in fact, to the extent that they paid him to help with farmwork, even while he was on the lam: they, too, knew what Graves was made of. Still, Scott had plenty of tales about hairsbreadth escapes from the slave patrols. Once Graves himself had managed to corner him, brandishing a pistol and bowie knife. The agile, powerfully built Scott wrenched both weapons out of his hands before disappearing again into the woods. Now he was well armed, and his master, as well as the constables, became perceptibly less zealous in their attempts to recover him.

Scott came out of hiding almost as soon as the Union troops arrived. He quickly attached himself to the Zouave regiment. After two years as a fugitive, he knew every inch of the marshes, fields, and country lanes around Hampton, and became a valuable scout for the commanders at Fortress Monroe.[91]

In fact, rare was the group of contrabands that did not include at least one person with useful military intelligence, and it became standard practice to debrief them upon arrival at the Union lines. Montgomery Blair, who had grown up in a slaveholding Maryland family, advised Butler early on: "I have no doubt you will get your best spies from among them, because they are accustomed to travel in the night time and can go where no one not accustomed to the sly tricks they practice from infancy to old age could penetrate." His prediction was already coming true.[92]

Just after dawn on May 31, a young black man named Waddy Smith showed up at the Zouaves' camp, having risked his life to get there and bringing some highly detailed information. Smith told the officers that he had escaped two days before from a Confederate camp near Yorktown, where he and 150 other slaves had been put to work building fortifications. He was ready to offer the Northerners a precise account of the enemy forces: how many men and cannons they had, where their camps were located, and what he had overheard the Southern commander telling another officer about plans for an attack. Smith's owner had suspected that he might try to slip away; the officer who debriefed him wrote that "his master . . . told him 'you're mine and I'll keep you or kill you' and [Smith] said he thinks he would do so if he had a chance." Colonel Duryee forwarded this report immediately to General Butler.[93]

Even the contrabands with less dramatic stories than Scott's and

Smith's shared tales that fascinated—and in some cases shocked—the Union soldiers. Many of the Northerners had never really spoken with a Negro before; some of the Vermont farm boys had perhaps never even seen one before leaving home, unless you counted the blackface performers in a traveling minstrel show.

Now they were conversing with actual men and women who had been (and perhaps still were) slaves: people who had previously figured only as an abstraction in speeches on Election Day. Mothers told of trying somehow to care for their children while laboring in the fields from sunup to sundown—and at harvesttime, sometimes even longer, husking corn well past midnight so that it could go early to market. They spoke of being left to forage somehow for themselves and their families, at times living on whatever roots and berries they could find. Some Negroes had been so ill supplied with clothing that they worked in the fields almost naked—and as for the children, certain masters routinely did not provide a stitch of clothing until they were old enough to work. Relatively few reported having been whipped, but those who did had some horrific accounts; one man described "bucking," a practice in which a slave, before being beaten, had his wrists and ankles tied and slipped over a wooden stake. Most stories, though, were of the sorts of routine cruelties born of masters' stinginess or carelessness, hardship or avarice. Almost all the Hampton fugitives spoke of loved ones sold away; indeed, the most chilling thing was that they said it matter-of-factly, as though their wives or children had simply died of some natural cause.

Perhaps most impressive of all—for Northerners accustomed to Southern tales of contentedly dependent slaves—was this, in the words of one soldier: "There is a universal desire of the slaves to be free. . . . Even old men and women, with crooked backs, who could hardly walk or see, shared the same feeling." They all wanted to learn to read, too (a few had been taught on the sly, as children, by their elders or white playmates), and before long, part of the Tyler villa was converted into a schoolroom for black youths.[94]

Although no detailed account written by a black person of those early days at Fortress Monroe survives, the reports of white soldiers and journalists—and freedmen's stories from later in the war—allow us to imagine both the exhilaration and the disorientation of the fugitives. The world that they had known their entire lives had vanished almost literally overnight. Their masters' houses stood eerily empty; most of Hampton, one Northern visitor wrote in June, resembled "an above-ground Pompeii." Nearly all the town's whites had disappeared.

In their place were seemingly boundless fields full of strangers, more and more of them each day: white men with harsh, uncouth accents (some did not even speak English), who stared at you curiously, often rudely, breaking into snorting guffaws at the oddest things. Some were kind; others, bored and restless after weeks in camp, tried to turn blacks into pets and playthings, making children scramble for pennies in the dust or playing practical jokes, sometimes cruel ones—and occasionally worse, as when one "particular favorite" Negro companion of a Zouave captain was beaten up when he imprudently ventured into the camp of the rival First New York.[95]

They made you feel self-conscious in ways that Southern whites did not. And yet the most ordinary gestures became revolutionary: you could look these white men straight in the eye; you could shake their hand. ("Attended a prayer meeting," a New York private wrote in his diary one day in July. "Got a good many heart[y] shake of the hand by the colored brothers.") Even the obnoxious ones were often curious to learn your life story, whereas the Virginia whites never were; in fact, they seemed actively to avoid realizing that you had one. But now every visiting dignitary, every Northern newspaperman, wanted to meet General Butler's famous contrabands. Whatever else they did, these Yankees never looked through you as if you were a table or a chair.[96]

Far more important: you were *free*. Not officially, of course. But you were free of the past—and perhaps even free, more startlingly, of what had been your future. Free to decide when to come and go, and where; when to work; when to sleep; when to be with your family; when to be alone. Some of the contrabands chose not to remain in the fort, preferring to live more independently, despite the risk, in encampments of their own just beyond the Union lines. At least one tried to enlist as a Union soldier: an intrepid young man named Harry Jarvis, who had come from the Chesapeake's Eastern Shore, crossing thirty-five miles of open water alone in a canoe to reach Monroe. "I went to [Butler] an' asked him to let me enlist, but he said it warn't a black man's war," he later remembered. "I tol' him it would be a black man's war 'fore dey got fru." Jarvis and many others stayed on to work as manual laborers for the garrison; they got army rations for themselves and their families in return. (Two years later he would get his wish, joining one of the Union's first black regiments, the Fifty-fifth Massachusetts—and would lose a leg in the Battle of Folly Island.)[97]

Back in April, as the military transport of the Third Massachusetts had lain at anchor off Boston, a small boat had unexpectedly come alongside, and a well-dressed young man, perched in its bow, hailed the officer on watch. Did the Third have room for one more volunteer? The Third did, and the stranger hopped aboard, satchel in hand. He was Edward L. Pierce, a thirty-two-year-old attorney with degrees from Brown and Harvard, highly placed connections in the Republican Party, and strong abolitionist convictions—who, by his own admission, had not handled a gun since he was a boy hunting squirrels in the woods near Milton. This was the man whom Butler appointed to superintend the black laborers at Fortress Monroe.[98]

Each morning, Pierce rang the bell of the old courthouse, and several dozen of the Virginia Union Volunteers gathered in the front yard to be issued picks and shovels and sent off for a day's work on the federal entrenchments. Soon these men felt almost like members of the garrison. A *New York Times* correspondent wrote:

> Their shovels and their other implements of labor, they handle and carry as soldiers do their guns—the result of the native talent of imitation peculiar to the race. Going to and from their work, they do not straggle along in promiscuous crowds, but fall into regular files and columns, and with a step and regularity that would do credit to enlisted men, march with clearly defined pride, and sometimes to the tune whistled by one of their number who, while he has caught a chance-sight of the morning parade, has at the same time learned the music of the band. I have no doubt they would make fair or even excellent soldiers.[99]

Pierce was a man of scholarly bent, and in his free time he sometimes wandered curiously among the empty streets of Hampton or paged through the records in the courthouse, which dated back deep into the seventeenth century. He explored the overgrown gardens and abandoned mansions—coming across, in one vacant house, a fine early edition of *Paradise Lost*. But it was the contrabands themselves, he felt, who best repaid his attention and study. "Broken as their language is, and limited as is their knowledge, they reason abstractly on their right to freedom as well as any white man," Pierce wrote. "Indeed, Locke or Channing might have strengthened the argument for universal liberty by studying their simple talk."[100]

Locke and Channing aside, some of the black fugitives were working more directly to secure their people's freedom. About two weeks after his arrival at Fortress Monroe, George Scott went on a dangerous mission to reconnoitre the enemy positions north of Hampton.

"I can smell a rebel furderer dan I ken a skunk," he promised before departing. He was right: near Big Bethel Church, about eight miles from town, Scott discovered several Confederate companies, defended by an artillery battery. He concealed himself in the bushes for a full twenty-four hours, observing what he could. A sentry finally caught sight of Scott, but he managed to escape, a rebel bullet grazing the sleeve of his jacket as he scrambled away, and reported to Butler's staff on what he had seen.

Butler and Winthrop sat down almost immediately to draw up a plan of attack: "part made up from the General's notes, part from my own fancies," the major boasted that night in a letter to his mother. But Scott's information was, a newspaper reported afterward, "the main spring of the operation." It would be the garrison's first significant advance against the enemy—indeed, the first real land battle anywhere in America between Union and Confederate troops. In the orders that Butler approved was a line of nearly as much historic significance: "George Scott is to have a revolver." This was almost certainly the first time in the war that a federal officer put a gun into the hands of a black man. And in the ensuing combat, according to one witness, Scott would be "in the thickest of the . . . fight."[101]

The Union force of some five thousand New York, Vermont, and Massachusetts men left on its mission at midnight, with Butler staying behind at the fort as Winthrop rode off near the head of the column, Scott riding at his side. Part of the attack's objective was to drive off roving bands of Confederates that had been terrorizing some of the Negroes who were making their way toward the fort, rounding up the able-bodied men for hard labor in the trenches and in some cases sending the rest to the Richmond slave market.[102]

As the soldiers left Fortress Monroe, contrabands thronged around to wish them well. "Oh," one woman said, as tears streamed down her cheeks, "I hope and pray de Lord for dese sojers, and dat dey may go on from conquer to conquer!"[103]

The Union troops did not conquer at Big Bethel. The Confederates, forewarned by a watchful civilian, were dug in behind their sturdy earthworks with cannons and rifles loaded and aimed. One of their officers was Colonel Mallory—posted, by coincidence, near the very spot where his Revolutionary forebear had fallen with the eleven (or was it nineteen?) bayonet wounds. The colonel fared better than his grandfather: the entire rebel force lost only one man, a teenage private from North Carolina. The Union troops were not so lucky. Panicking under fire, they never got near the first line of Confederate earthworks; the debacle became worse when one New York regiment mistakenly fired at another, whose men happened to be wearing gray militia uniforms. (Duryee's brightly plumed Zouaves, meanwhile, proved easy targets for the rebel guns.) Eighteen were killed and dozens more wounded before the Yankees retreated through the woods in confusion back toward Fortress Monroe.[104]

Among the fallen was Theodore Winthrop, killed while trying vainly to rally the New England troops. A Carolina rifleman had put a bullet through his chest. Back in his quarters at the fort, the young soldier-author had left a half-filled sheet of manuscript: the first few sentences of "Voices of the Contraband."*

FOR THE REST OF THE SUMMER, Butler's men would fight only occasional small skirmishes with the enemy. But the most significant victory at Fortress Monroe had already been won, back in May, when three black men crossed the James River in the darkness. On the night the Union troops marched on Big Bethel, the soldiers would encounter another group of fugitives, who asked them for directions to "the freedom fort."[105]

The general from Massachusetts grew ever more steadfast in the defense of "his" contrabands, to a degree that must have shocked his old political associates. In July, when the Lincoln administration asked General Irvin McDowell to issue orders barring all fugitive Negroes from the Union lines in northern Virginia, Butler immediately fired off a letter to Washington, making it known that he planned to enforce no such rule around Hampton Roads. (By now there were a thousand contrabands in the fortress.) In a long missive to the secretary of war, Simon Cameron, Butler also took the opportunity to argue that the contrabands were not really contraband: that they had become free. Indeed, that they were—in a legal sense—no longer things, but people. He wrote:

Have they not by their master's acts, and the state of war, assumed the condition, which we hold to be the normal one, of those made in

---

*The following month, Confederate general D. H. Hill returned Winthrop's gold pocket watch, taken from his corpse, to Butler, so that the Union commander could forward it to the dead man's mother. The Confederate's accompanying note read: "Sir, I have the honor herewith to send the Watch of Young Winthrop, who fell while gallantly leading a party in the vain attempt to subjugate a free people." (D. H. Hill to Butler, July 5, 1861, Butler Papers.)

God's image? Is not every constitutional, legal, and moral requirement, [both] to the runaway master [and to his] relinquished slaves,
thus answered? I confess that my own mind is compelled by this
reasoning to look upon them as men and women.

In a loyal state, I would put down a servile insurrection. In
a state of rebellion I would confiscate that which was used to
oppose my arms . . . and if, in so doing, it should be objected that
human beings were brought to the free enjoyment of life, liberty,
and the pursuit of happiness, such objection might not require
much consideration.[106]

This time, however, Butler's lawyerly arguments proved less effective. It would take another fourteen months, and tens of thousands
more Union casualties, before the Lincoln administration was ready
to espouse such a view.*

"Shall we now end the war and not eradicate the cause?" the general wrote to Edward Pierce in August. "Will not God demand this
of us now [that] he has taken away all excuse for not pursuing the
right[?] . . . All these matters run through my head as I see the negro."[107]

True, Butler's newfound zeal was not entirely selfless. Since the
arrival of those first three contrabands, a steady stream of mail had
come in—from old friends and total strangers—extolling him for having struck the first blow to free the Negro of his shackles. Butler had
quickly warmed to this train of thought, especially now that he was no
longer a state legislator from cotton-addicted Lowell. Emancipator of
an entire race . . . why not?[108]

Pierce, his three-month enlistment expired, left Fortress Monroe in
mid-July. On his last evening, he assembled the Virginia Union Volunteers at the courthouse yard in Hampton to bid them good-bye. As
the men and women gathered around him, he thanked them for their
work and complimented them on their "industry and morals." Then
something further occurred to him: never before in American history had a Northern abolitionist found himself in a situation where he
could speak freely before an audience of Southern slaves.

I said to them that there was one more word for me to add, and
that was, that every one of them was as much entitled to his free-

---

*George Scott pressed this case as well. He accompanied Colonel Duryee to
Washington in July, saying that he "was going to plead with Pres. Lincoln for his
liberties." It is unclear if he was given a hearing. (Lewis C. Lockwood to "Dear
Brethren," April 17, 1862, AMA Papers, Fisk University.)

dom as I was to mine, and I hoped they would all now secure it. "Believe you, boss," was the general response, and each one with his rough gravelly hand clasped mine, and with tearful eyes and broken utterances said, "God bless you!" "May we meet in Heaven!" "My name is Jack Allen, don't forget me!" "Remember me, Kent Anderson!" and so on.

"No," Pierce wrote afterward, "I may forget the playfellows of my childhood, my college classmates, my professional associates, my comrades in arms, but I will remember you and your benedictions until I cease to breathe! Farewell, honest hearts, longing to be free!"[109]

ON THE EVENING OF November 9, 1989, a tumultuous throng of East Germans pressed against the Berlin Wall at Checkpoint Charlie. They had come to cross over into freedom. But this epochal moment had begun with a bureaucratic snafu: that afternoon, a spokesman for the Communist regime, assigned to read a press release describing a gradual, orderly process by which the government planned to ease travel restrictions, misread the document and accidentally announced that the ban on travel to the West would be lifted immediately.

An American reporter at the checkpoint that night watched as befuddled East German border guards surveyed the vast crowd from their command post. The captain in charge dialed and redialed his telephone, trying to find some higher-up who could give him definitive orders. None could. Then he put the phone down and stood still for a moment, pondering. "Perhaps he came to his own decision," the journalist would write. "Maybe he was simply fed up. Whatever the case, at 11:17 p.m. precisely, he shrugged his shoulders, as if to say, 'Why not?' . . . 'Alles auf!' he ordered. 'Open up,' and the gates swung wide."[110]

The Iron Curtain did not unravel at that moment, with the breach of a small segment of border in a single city. Many more walls would have to come down in the weeks and months ahead; there would be setbacks as well as advances in the years to come. But that night, watched by the world, was the moment when the possibility of cautious, incremental change in the old Soviet bloc—perestroika, glasnost, a slow and partial transition toward democracy—ceased to exist, if it had ever really existed at all. The Wall fell that night because of those thousands of pressing bodies, and because of that border guard's shrug.

In the very first months of the Civil War—after Frank Baker, Shepard

Mallory, and James Townsend had breached their own wall, and Benjamin Butler shrugged—slavery's iron curtain began falling, all across the South. John Hay and John Nicolay, in their biography of Lincoln, would say of the three slaves' escape and Butler's decision: "Out of this incident seems to have grown one of the most sudden and important revolutions in popular thought which took place during the whole war."[111]

Within weeks after the first contrabands' arrival at Fortress Monroe, slaves were reported flocking to the Union lines just about anywhere there *were* Union lines: in northern Virginia, along the James, on the Mississippi, in Florida. A veritable "exodus" even from loyal slave states such as Maryland was said to be taking place. In southern Pennsylvania, until recently an area that fugitives had traversed with great caution, a couple of obvious runaways were observed strolling up Harrisburg's Market Street at twilight, and according to a local newspaper, "they trudged along with their heavy bundles unmolested, and, in fact, almost unnoticed." It is unclear how many of these escapees knew of Butler's decision, but probably quite a few did. Edward Pierce marveled at "the mysterious spiritual telegraph which runs through the slave population," though he was probably exaggerating just a bit when he continued: "Proclaim an edict of emancipation in the hearing of a single slave on the Potomac, and in a few days it will be heard by his brethren on the Gulf."[112]

Union officers in all these areas wrote to Washington, asking for instructions. The administration, punting once again, told them that decisions about sheltering runaways should be based on military necessity, but that they were left entirely to their own discretion how to determine this. (Congress endorsed this position in August in the Confiscation Act.) The result was that each commander ended up with his own policy. General George McClellan, entering western Virginia, proclaimed that his troops would interfere with slavery in no way whatsoever. Meanwhile, Colonel Harvey Brown, the new commandant at Fort Pickens, announced flatly, "I shall not send the negroes back as I will never be voluntarily instrumental in returning a poor wretch to slavery."[113]

The confusion was compounded by the fact that no matter what the individual commander's decree, his junior officers and enlisted men, having ideas of their own, might be unwilling to enforce it. In July 1861, a New York soldier wrote from northern Virginia:

> A slight case of rebellion occurred in one of our camps a few evenings ago, when a young man on guard was ordered to arrest

any slaves who undertook to pass. He promptly answered: "I can obey no such order; it was not to put down [Negro] insurrection that I enlisted but to defend my country's flag! I am ready to bear the consequences, but never to have a hand in arresting slaves."

The man's superior decided to back off; "it was deemed politic not to try the temper of the men too hard."

Sometimes the refusals were even more peremptory. In Missouri—where, since it was Union territory, *all* fugitives were supposed to be returned to their masters—a brigadier wrote to his commanding general, who had just ordered him to send back some runaways: "In answer to your note of this day I have this to say that I don't give a fig about rank. . . . The institution of slavery must take care of itself." And he added, even more sharply: "I had a man cowardly shot in the woods to-day within sight of camp by the very men I have no doubt whose property you are so anxious to protect."[114]

In August, Secretary Cameron tried to bring some clarity to the chaos by asking that Butler and other commanders collect detailed information on each fugitive: not just name and physical description but "the name and character, whether loyal or disloyal, of the master," since, this, of course, was essential to determining whether the particular Negro counted as legitimate contraband. Such a system, Cameron said, would let the federal government assure that slaveholders' "rights" were protected, and possibly return the slaves to their proper owners once the rebel states had rejoined the Union. But how were officers supposed to tell whether a master whom they had never laid eyes on was loyal or disloyal—even assuming that the slave was telling the truth in identifying him? Besides, didn't the military have more pressing business at the moment, such as fighting the war?

Butler's contraband doctrine was utterly impossible almost from the moment it was devised, but it became hugely influential precisely *because* it was so impossible: it did not open the floodgates in theory, but it did so in practice, and with very little political risk to the Lincoln administration. Indeed, preposterous as the contraband doctrine was as a piece of law, it was also, albeit inadvertently, a political masterstroke; it satisfied nearly every potential theoretical and political objection at the same time as being completely unworkable in real life. "There is often great virtue in such technical phrases in shaping public opinion," Pierce noted. "The venerable gentleman, who wears gold spectacles and reads a conservative daily, prefers confiscation to emancipation. He is reluctant to have slaves declared freemen, but has no objection to their being declared contrabands."[115]

Though an impractical way to adjudicate the fate of fugitives per se, the system was eminently practical in other terms. Not all the Union troops who harbored runaways were doing so out of the kindness of their hearts—probably most were not. Regiments needed labor: extra hands to cook meals, wash clothes, and dig latrines. ("Half the Federal officers now have negro servants," a journalist reported from Monroe on June 12.) When Negro men and women were willing to do these things, whites were happy not to ask any inconvenient questions—not the first or the last time that the allure of cheap labor would trump political principles in America.[116]

Blacks were contributing to the Union cause in larger ways. Not just at Fortress Monroe but throughout the South, it was they who provided the Northerners with valuable intelligence and expert guidance. When Lincoln's master spy, Allan Pinkerton, traveled undercover through the Confederacy, he wrote, "in many . . . places, I found that my best source of information was the colored men. . . . I mingled freely with them, and found them ever ready to answer questions and to furnish me with every fact which I desired to possess." In a broader sense, they were often the only friends—indeed, the only Unionists—that the Yankees encountered as they groped their way anxiously through hostile territory. "No where did we find any sign of kindly recognition," one Northern soldier wrote from Virginia in August 1861, "except from the poor slaves, who are rapidly learning, through the insane hatred of their masters, to look upon our troops as [their] great Army of Deliverance."[117]

The "enemy of my enemy" principle operated on whites, too, and not only on those at the front lines. Barely six weeks after Sumter, the Democratic *New York World* reported: "Whether it be deemed a good thing or not, the fact is unmistakable that the northern people are fast learning to hate slavery in a way unfelt before. . . . It comes home to every loyal man, with a force not to be resisted, that the sole cause of this most wicked treason the world ever saw, is SLAVERY; and, just in proportion as the treason itself is abhorred, in just that proportion do hatred and detestation attach to its cause."[118]

Slaves were coming to seem not just players in the drama of the war but also, in a way, heroes. In July, New York's Winter Garden theater staged a "new drama of the times," a production laden with special effects, called "America's Dream; or, the Rebellion of '61." The show opened with Sumter burning, the flames reportedly so realistic it seemed the theater might catch fire. There was a thrilling battle between the Baltimore street toughs and the brave boys of the Sixth Massachusetts—while poor Colonel Ellsworth was being vividly murdered at the other end of the stage. But the most unexpected and certainly most fanciful scene was a tableau in which, while "real bomb-shells" burst around them, a "small but resolute band of Northern contrabands" helpfully launched provisions out of a mortar into a besieged Union fort.[119]

Meanwhile, within the rebel South, the erosion of the peculiar institution was becoming harder and harder to control—even hundreds of miles away from where slaves were becoming contrabands. Union and Confederate newspapers alike reported an astonishing number of alleged insurrections. They were mostly very small scale. In Louisiana, Negroes were supposed to have torched a Confederate general's house the night after Sumter was attacked. In Arkansas, a black preacher was hanged after using threatening language to his mistress. In Tennessee, at least five alarms were sounded in April and May alone. Whether these had any basis in fact almost does not matter; the panic was real. As Pinkerton observed after one of his reconnaissance missions, "The very institution for which these misguided men were periling their lives, and sacrificing their fortunes, was threatened with demolition; and the slaves who had so long and so often felt the lash of their masters, were now becoming a source of fear to the very men who had heretofore held them in such utter subjection."[120]

A telling fact: the price of slaves was already dropping precipitously. Numerous reports attest that by mid-1861 it had fallen to half or even a third of what it had been the year before. The "property" that slaveholders were fighting for was now not only less reliable (you never knew when it might run off in the night) but less valuable—perhaps, in a sense, less worth fighting for.[121]

Just as important was what did *not* happen: the long-expected and long-feared Negro uprising—the apocalypse when slaves would rise up, rape their mistresses, and slaughter their masters—never occurred. Indeed, even now it is remarkable to consider, given what the slaves had suffered and the turmoil in the South over the next four years, that they ended up committing so little violence against their masters. It soon became apparent from the behavior of the contrabands that the vast majority of blacks did not want vengeance; they simply wanted to be free, and to enjoy the same rights and opportunities as other Americans. Many were even ready to share in the hardships and dangers of the war.

This realization had enormous repercussions, not just in the South but in the North. For decades, abolitionist "agitators" had been vilified as traitors to their race and nation for trying to bring about "another St. Domingo." As the Democrats had sung in the 1860 presidential campaign: *They love the nigger better than the red, white, and blue.* Even as stalwart a Unionist as Jessie Frémont sometimes felt torn between her loyalty to her country and her loyalty to her race and her sex. A few weeks after the attack on Sumter, she wrote to a friend, "When I think of the hideous [danger] the Southern states hold in themselves, I don't know to which women the most sympathy belongs. Our side is great & noble & to die for it . . . is a great duty. But they have no such comfort & at their hearths is the black slave *Sepoy* element."[122] When it turned out that the South's Negroes were not like St. Domingo's revolutionaries or India's Sepoy mutineers, Jessie Frémont's dilemma vanished. She and millions of other white Americans realized they did not actually have to fear a bloodbath if the slaves were suddenly set free.

This awareness in itself was a revolution in Northern politics. Moreover, why worry about abolitionism splitting apart the Union, when the Union had already split? And why defend the "property" of people who were now sworn adversaries in a terrible war?

Most important, though, was the revolution in the minds of the enslaved Negroes themselves. Though they may not have known about the production at the Winter Garden, they knew that they had become actors on the stage of American history in a way that they had never been before. The bolder the blacks grew, the more fearful the whites grew—and when the whites grew more fearful, the blacks grew bolder yet. At first this typically took the form of blacks simply refusing to work as hard as they had before—easy enough with so many masters and overseers away in the rebel armies. But in time this would amount to a significant act of sabotage against the Confederate cause, especially after Southern troops began experiencing shortages of food, which happened as early as the autumn of 1861. And soon more and more Negroes were taking the boldest step of all, from slavery into freedom. Even before Lincoln finally unveiled the Emancipation Proclamation, in the fall of 1862, the stream of a few hundred contrabands at Fortress Monroe had become a river of many thousands. "The Negroes," a Union chaplain wrote, "flocked in vast numbers—an army in themselves—to the camps of the Yankees. . . . The arrival among us of these hordes was like the oncoming of cities."[123]*

---

*Exact estimates of the numbers of contrabands are rare. As of early January 1863, a Northern newspaper estimated that 120,000 fugitives had been received into the Union lines. (*Utica Morning Herald*, Jan. 6, 1863.) However, the means of arriving at this figure are unclear, and it does not account for the large numbers of fugitives who remained outside the Union encampments or continued north to the free states. Certainly by that point there were a number of Union bases (including Port Royal, South Carolina, and Fortress Monroe) that each had at least 5,000 or 10,000 contrabands.

On the September day of Lincoln's proclamation, a Union colonel ran into William Seward on the street in Washington and took the opportunity to congratulate him on the administration's epochal act.

Seward snorted. "Yes," he said, "we have let off a puff of wind over an established fact."

"What do you mean, Mr. Seward?" the puzzled officer asked.

"I mean," the secretary of state replied, "that the Emancipation Proclamation was uttered in the first gun fired at Sumter, and we have been the last to hear it."[124]

ON AUGUST 6, 1861, Brigadier General John Bankhead Magruder, commander of Confederate forces in southeastern Virginia, received intelligence—unfounded, as it would turn out—that enemy troops, having withdrawn from Hampton some weeks earlier, were about to reoccupy the town. And not only that: the Yankee Butler planned to house Negroes there. "As their masters had deserted their homes and slaves," Magruder reported back to headquarters in Richmond, "he [would] consider the latter free, and would colonize them at Hampton, the home of most of their owners." This could not be countenanced.

Although many of the rebel general's troops had been busy on a mission to "scour the [surrounding] country" for fugitive blacks, Magruder immediately summoned his officers to a council of war. Steps must be taken at once to prevent the empty town from becoming once again a "harbor of runaway slaves and traitors." The other Confederates, most of them residents of Hampton and its surrounding farms, agreed. And there was another motivation, too. It was time, some felt, for a grand and splendid gesture of renunciation. It was time to show the Yankees—to show the world—what Southern men would forfeit for their freedom. "A sacrifice," one soldier said, "to the grim god of war."[125]

The following night, Union pickets from Colonel Weber's regiment, who were standing watch just across the inlet, were surprised by noises from the direction of the darkened town. First there were shouts of alarm from some of the few civilians, black and white, who had remained in their homes. And then they heard the slow, deliberate tramp of marching feet. Two snakelike lines of yellow flame threaded their way among the houses, then broke apart, balls of light dancing wildly in every direction as hundreds of Confederates fanned out with torches through the streets. They knew the way; this was their town.

"Many a young man set fire to his own father's house," one Hamptonite would remember.

From their posts across the bridge, the Yankees watched in astonishment as first one building, then another, was engulfed. "The loud roar of the flames, the cries of the terrified negroes as they were being driven from their huts by the enemy and marched off under guard to their lines, all combined to make up a wild scene," a soldier said.

Major Cary's columned academy was the last building to catch fire. At first the federals thought it was being deliberately spared. But finally the youths of Hampton fell with a vengeance upon their former schoolhouse, soaking the desks and chairs with turpentine and camphene, hacking holes in the floors and ceilings so the flames could rise. It lit up, window by window, from within.

And so the old town burned. The ancient church; the Negro shanties; the courthouse with its whipping post and bell; the fathers' mansions—separate fires at first, then all consumed into one, an inferno reflected in the black waters of the James.

The Great Comet of 1861, from *Bilderatlas der Sternenwelt* (1888)

CHAPTER NINE

Independence Day

And is this the ground Washington trod?

—WALT WHITMAN,
"The Centenarian's Story" (1861)

ONE SUNDAY NIGHT in early summer, James Ferguson, assistant astronomer of the United States Naval Observatory, was making a routine survey of the skies above Washington when he noticed an unusual ray of light pulsating just above the northern horizon. As the night was somewhat overcast, he was unable to determine the exact nature of this phenomenon, and decided that it was probably just a stray beam of the aurora borealis.[1]

The following evening, the first night of July, a rainstorm swept the capital. Afterward, when Ferguson returned to the Observatory dome, he saw the same pale streak flickering in a slightly different place, once again half hidden amid drifting banks of heavy cloud. At last, just past midnight, the sky cleared and the mysterious object swam free into his view. Indeed, it soon glowed so bright that Ferguson pushed the telescope aside and simply stared in astonishment at the ball of luminescence that swelled and became more brilliant by the minute, soon outshining every star and planet. A pale brushstroke of light trailed behind, streaming higher and higher above the horizon, waxing like the flame of a lamp newly lit.

Millions of people across the country saw the comet—indeed, half the world did. By the next night, its head looked as large as a three-quarters moon, and the tail traversed more than half the sky, seeming to one observer as if it were made of "infinitesimal specks of fire" that swayed from side to side. It cast a faint shadow, and reflected on the surface of the sea. Some even claimed they could see it by day.

Scientists were as dazzled as the general public. They were accustomed to watching comets approach earth gradually, from a great distance; none had imagined that such a spectacular celestial body could loom up so unexpectedly. One overstimulated astronomer in Pittsburgh, confessing that the first glimpse made his hair "fairly [stand] up with wonder and excitement," announced to the press: "I think by the cut of her jib she will probably be remembered, and also recorded, as one of the most extraordinary craft that has floated into our horizon in hundreds of years."

At Fortress Monroe, Edward Pierce observed the comet as it burst into full splendor just past dusk on July 2, its tail sweeping across the zenith of the sky like a second Milky Way. Thomas Starr King saw it in San Francisco and was reminded of the fiery dragon in the Book of Revelation. In Manhattan on the night of the 3rd, according to the *New York Herald*, one enterprising citizen set up a large telescope at the corner of Broadway and Warren Street, the usually jaded city lining up to pay for a quick peep. Perhaps inevitably, the *Herald*, not fully satisfied with the news value of a mere cosmic event, dubbed the celestial apparition the "War Comet of 1861."

On the following night, the Fourth of July, the New York Fire Zouaves watched it from their camp in Alexandria. "While a grand pyrotechnic display was taking place throughout the loyal States," one observer there wrote, "a still grander and more beautiful one took place in the heavens."

INDEPENDENCE DAY WAS CELEBRATED throughout the rebellious states as well as the loyal ones, it so happened. Early that morning, as the garrison at Fortress Monroe was busy preparing for its festivities—which were to include a speech by General Butler, a reading of the Declaration (postponed indefinitely, it would turn out, when no one could locate a copy), and then an opportunity for officers and men to get blind drunk—the Yankees were startled to hear artillery booming on the far side of the James, volley after volley in stately cadence. For a moment everyone thought it might be some sort of surprise attack. But it was only the enemy's salute to the holiday.[2]

In the latter years of the Civil War, most of the Confederacy would let the day go unobserved, or even openly scorn it. In 1861, however, the Fourth of July was one of the few things that the two halves of the sundered nation still kept in common—more or less, anyway.

Across the South, editors and orators proclaimed their own region the true heir to the Revolutionary legacy. After all, what had the thirteen colonies done but secede from the mother country? Indeed, the Founding Fathers—led by Virginia's immortal Washington, Jefferson, and Henry, slaveholders all—had established the very principles on which the Confederate states based their own claim to independence. Governments, the leaders of 1776 had said, derive their just power from the consent of the governed, and the subjects of a despotic regime have not only the right but a sacred duty to take up arms against it. "The people of the Confederate States of the South," wrote the editor of the *New Orleans Daily Picayune*, "alone remain loyal to the principles of the Revolution.... To them now belongs of right the custody of all the hopes of human progress, of which the

Fourth of July is the symbol in history, and it is by their swords that it is to be saved for mankind."[3]

True, there was ambivalence in many Confederate quarters about certain aspects of the past. Jefferson, in particular, was a problem. Some of the fiercer secessionists called him a traitor to his state and to his race; Vice President Stephens, in his "cornerstone" speech a few months earlier, had stated flatly that the author of the Declaration had been "fundamentally wrong" when he wrote that all men were created equal. President Davis, more tactfully, had ignored Jefferson's later statements against slavery and argued, in his farewell speech to the U.S. Senate, that the doctrine of universal equality applied only to "the men of the political community."[4]

The North had long harbored its own mixed feelings. Only the previous summer, Lincoln's Republican Party had argued bitterly over whether to include the Declaration's principles in its national platform, conservatives deeming this too inflammatory. Meanwhile, Frederick Douglass spoke for many black Americans and white abolitionists when in 1852 he extolled the Founding Fathers' "sublime faith in the great principles of justice and freedom"—but railed in almost the same breath that American hypocrisy never seemed more "hideous and revolting" than it did each Fourth of July.

Northerners' response to the holiday in 1861 reflected new internal divisions, too. The editors of the *Philadelphia Inquirer*, in their office just down Chestnut Street from Independence Hall, exulted: "This day inaugurates a second war of Independence. . . . We shall look forward to the United States of the Future as a still closer approximation than the United States of the Past to that bright ideal of Government, the vision of which has ever haunted the Seers and Thinkers of mankind." Other Americans, though, found little to celebrate. Some considered it a mockery that President Lincoln had chosen Independence Day, of all moments, to convene the national legislature for its emergency session in Washington. "What a melancholy contrast between the Congress of 1776 and the Congress of 1861," a Democratic editor in Ohio wrote. "One was the Star of Bethlehem, the other the darkness which rent the [veil] of the Temple. The Christ and the Crucifixion."[5]

This was more than slightly melodramatic. Still, as the Congress of 1861 prepared to convene, no cosmic portents—with the possible exception of the comet—were yet evident, and no one visiting Washington would have mistaken it for Bethlehem. The charms of the capital in summertime, an acquired taste in the best of circumstances, had not been enhanced much by the presence of a hundred thousand troops, unless one's tastes ran to ladies of pleasure. "Beauty and sin done up in silk, with the accompaniment of lustrous eyes and luxurious hair, on every thoroughfare offer themselves for Treasury notes," a Union officer wrote in his diary. Sin did not come in such uniformly luxurious guise, though: just after the national holiday, Private Thomas Curry of the Fire Zouaves was found knifed to death in front of one particularly "low" brothel.

And prostitutes were not the only ones making heavy use of L'Enfant's stately boulevards; the constant passage of army wagons had deepened Pennsylvania Avenue's ruts and morasses to the point that unwary pedestrians almost risked sinking out of sight, never to reemerge, while Second Street had gotten so bad that one poor gentleman's carriage toppled off the eroding curbside and into the adjacent Tiber Creek canal, drowning him in the miasmal waters. (The capital's sanitation system, if the term can be applied to a crude network of drainage ditches, was so overtaxed that official government reports used phrases like *accumulated filth . . . hotbed of putrefaction . . . immense mass of fetid and corrupt matter.*)[6]

Things had improved considerably at the Capitol itself, however. Arriving regiments were now shunted off to less stately campsites, as workmen readied the building for the legislators' return, expunging every visible trace of the Fire Zouaves and their comrades-in-arms. Furniture was refinished; carpets replaced; graffiti scrubbed from the frescoes. The Senate chamber was painstakingly deloused. The paneling in the House chamber, formerly blazing red, was repainted a quiet "dove color," perhaps in a belated attempt to tranquilize the distinguished members, perhaps to address the aesthetic concerns of critics like Theodore Winthrop, whose posthumously published essay in the July *Atlantic* suggested that the Capitol's décor had "a slight flavor of the Southwestern steamboat saloon." A less pleasant job was scooping up and hauling off what the building's shell-shocked chief architect described to his wife as "cart loads of ---- in the dark corners," apparently deposited there by certain members of the soldiery. (To be fair, one might argue that this particular commodity, then as now, was even more abundantly produced by Congress itself.) President Buchanan's portrait had been removed to a private office to protect it "from threatened indignity," while Tyler's was exiled to deep storage. (It now hangs in the Blue Room of the White House.)[7]

In another respect, too, the Capitol was returning to normal, not counting a few important absences. On the morning of July 4, the two chambers began filling up again with senators and congressmen—mostly the same men who "dressed like parsons, said Sir, and chewed tobacco" whom Winthrop had mocked as belonging to a bygone epoch. Clearly their epoch was not wholly bygone just yet. But they were lonelier, and it did not take an especially sharp eye to discern that their desks and chairs had been artfully rearranged, a bit more widely spaced than before, to conceal the thinning of ranks. One significant absence was not the result of secession—or at least not quite as directly as the others. Stephen A. Douglas, Lincoln's old rival, the man whose popular sovereignty doctrine had promised Americans the freedom to commit a state to slavery, had died a month earlier at the age of forty-eight, after a grueling lecture tour on which he rallied Northern Democrats "to protect this government and [our] flag from every assailant."[8]

For form's sake, the clerk of the House called on each of the seceded states' delegations when he took roll, pausing just a moment as if by some remote possibility they would come creeping back, all past sins forgiven and troubles forgotten. Before this, however—perhaps more fruitfully, perhaps not—a Methodist chaplain addressed the Almighty at considerable length, in terms that made it clear he thought God was a Republican.[9]

Lincoln's summons to Congress had coincided with his demand for seventy-five thousand troops, on April 15, perhaps suggesting his belief that the decision for war would have to be ratified first by the people themselves, in the form of the volunteer militia, even before their elected representatives considered it. In the same vein, he had resisted calls to convene the national legislature immediately, deferring the special session almost three months. There were good political reasons for him to do this. The president feared, justly, that Congress would try to take the conduct of the war into its own hands—or worse, that it might try to broker a dishonorable peace, offering terms that coddled slavery even more than the Crittenden, Corwin, and Peace Conference plans had done. Clearly he intended to make his own decisions first and seek congressional blessing later.[10]

But the unusual timing of July 4 for the special session's opening day also signaled that in Lincoln's mind, the business before the nation's representatives in 1861 was somehow related to the business of their predecessors in 1776. The president made it known that he would issue a written communiqué to Congress on the session's first day. Perhaps it would clarify the connection more fully.

Almost from the moment of the April announcement, Lincoln threw himself tirelessly into drafting his message. This in itself was remarkable, even astonishing. Most chief executives, faced with the war's multitudinous and urgent demands, would probably have let military undertakings trump literary ones. In fact, Lincoln's Confederate counterpart, Jefferson Davis, had not even begun work on his own unmemorable inaugural address until the day before the ceremony.[11]

As early as May 7, however, John Hay recorded in his diary that Lincoln was "engaged in constant thought upon his Message: It will be an exhaustive review of the questions of the hour & of the future." That was the same day that the Tycoon had made his intriguing statements to Hay about the philosophical underpinnings of the Union cause, while dropping a hint about the future of slavery; he was clearly rehearsing the ideas he planned to air publicly on the Fourth of July.[12] (Elmer Ellsworth and John Nicolay had both been at the White House that morning, too; Nicolay was definitely present during Lincoln's conversation with Hay and Ellsworth may well have been also.)

Curiously, Lincoln tried his ideas on a second audience on that same day in May, a most unlikely one: the "regent captains" of the minuscule European nation of San Marino. He had recently received by letter a conferral of honorary citizenship from them, and it was now his duty to acknowledge their gracious gesture. He could easily have asked one of his secretaries to dash off a pro forma response. But the president knew that San Marino was more than just a five-mile-wide enclave of Italian-speaking sheep farmers. It was also the longest-lived constitutional republic in the world, claiming origins in the fourth century A.D. So, when Lincoln picked up his pen and addressed the regent captains, he did so as the leader of a young and immense democratic nation speaking to the leaders of an old and tiny one:

> Although your dominion is small, your State is nevertheless one of the most honored, in all history. It has by its experience demonstrated the truth, so full of encouragement to the friends of Humanity, that Government founded on Republican principles is capable of being so administered as to be secure and enduring.
>
> You have kindly adverted to the trial through which this Republic is now passing. It is one of deep import. It involves the question whether a Representative republic, extended and aggrandized so much as to be safe against foreign enemies can save itself from the dangers of domestic faction. I have faith in a good result.[13]

In choosing to share these ideas with the Sammarinesi rather than with political associates closer at hand, Lincoln was being characteristically discreet; he was not yet ready to address the American public, and the regent captains were unlikely to be in regular communication with James Gordon Bennett or Horace Greeley. Yet he also revealed a deep belief that the conflict in America was one of critical significance to the rest of the world, and that in his July Fourth message he needed to speak not only to Congress, not only to the American people, but perhaps, in a sense, to all of humanity. Perhaps posterity, too. In 1861, republics were still rarities: tiny San Marino was one of only two in Europe. Since they were so few, the American Civil War would matter not so much in terms of preserving existing democracies (clearly the Sammarinesi were doing just fine) as in stimulating or inhibiting the birth of future ones. Like the Forty-Eighters in St. Louis, Lincoln was well aware of the impact that the Union's ultimate victory or defeat might have among the restless nations of Europe and even beyond.

By mid-June, Lincoln was "engaged almost constantly in writing his message," Nicolay recorded. On the 19th, with two weeks left, the president took the extraordinary step of announcing publicly that he would receive no visitors until after submitting it to Congress.[14] (Indeed, Lincoln worked far harder on his July Fourth document than Jefferson had done on his own, more famous one; the Declaration of Independence was written and revised over the course of seventeen days at most.) By this point, Lincoln had developed a keener appreciation of the potential damage of ill-considered remarks. "Nobody hurt," a quotation from one of Lincoln's ill-considered speeches during his train trip through Ohio, was still a national catchphrase, a barbed joke that grew sharper-edged with each fresh report of war casualties. He would not allow himself a second such rhetorical disaster.

Even so, many Americans shook their heads in disbelief at how much time the president was spending on his message. Would this end up like the last presidential epistle to Congress, Buchanan's fourteen thousand words of ineffectual wind? No less a literary craftsman than Emerson himself wrote reproachfully in his journal that Lincoln "writes his own message instead of borrowing the largest understanding as he so easily might." The apostle of self-reliance was arguing in favor of crowdsourcing, or at least the time-honored American habit of plagiarism.[15]

As the momentous date grew near, Lincoln shared a rough draft with a few select counselors. One, predictably, was Seward, who did not stint in offering suggestions, although he would play a far smaller role than he had in drafting the inaugural address: the secretary of state prevailed upon the president to tone down several passages, substituting more tactful language in places. But the president's other sources of advice were somewhat surprising. Among them was Charles Sumner, to whom he read his draft aloud in late June; the two men were hardly close, and in fact their few face-to-face encounters had left each somewhat put off by the other. Another of Lincoln's chosen confidants was a man he had never even met before, the eminent historian John Lothrop Motley, who was visiting the capital and dropped by the White House to call on the president; Lincoln not only broke his vow of seclusion but impulsively scooped up the scattered sheets of manuscript on his desk and read Motley nearly the entire draft. Finally, the night before sending off the message, still engrossed in last-minute revisions, he shared it with Orville H. Browning, the old Illinois friend who had written him that fierce letter about emancipating the slaves.[16]

One cannot help looking to Lincoln's choices to find clues to his thoughts and preoccupations at the time. Sumner and Browning, of course, were both ardent antislavery men. Sumner and Lothrop, meanwhile, shared an expertise in European affairs, an area of weakness for Lincoln: the former had recently become chairman of the Senate's committee on foreign relations, while the latter had spent much of his adult life on the Continent and was best known for his widely acclaimed history of the defunct Dutch Republic. Yet none of Lincoln's various drafts of the July Fourth message mentioned slavery directly at all, nor did any address foreign relations in anything but the most brief and perfunctory fashion. (Sumner, for this reason, was disappointed by the document; Lothrop was impressed by the "untaught grace and power" of Lincoln's writing; Browning did not record his own response.) Could it be, however, that by selecting these three men, Lincoln was sounding out—more for himself than for them—the unspoken but implicit parts of what he wanted to communicate to Congress, the nation, and the world?

At last the document was complete, and Lincoln put it into Nicolay's hands to deliver it to the Capitol. In keeping with the tradition of that time, it would be read aloud not by the president himself but rather by the clerks of the respective chambers. (The Senate clerk performed his duty in a nearly inaudible monotone.)[17]

In a sense, Nicolay's simple trip down Pennsylvania Avenue was an eloquent statement of its own. This ritual of the democracy reaffirmed the chief executive's accountability to Congress and to the American people. And the grueling labor that Lincoln had put into his message attested to his faith in the power and necessity of words, of arguments, of explanations, in a democratic system. By contrast, the lackluster, shopworn rhetoric of the new Southern republic's leading statesmen was not merely a failure of aesthetics, but proof of the intellectual poverty and moral laziness undergirding their entire enterprise. The Confederacy was never truly much of a cause—lost or otherwise. In fact, it might better be called an effect; a reactive stratagem tarted up with ex post facto justifications. This was borne out in the practices of the two national legislatures. Over the next four years, the Confederate Congress would transact nearly all its important business in secret, and even some of the most fervent secessionists would decry its lack of true accountability to the Southern public. (Indeed, Robert Barnwell Rhett, a leading fire-eater in 1860 and 1861, ultimately blamed the South's loss on the absence of any informed public debate within the Confederacy that might have held the Davis administration's policies up to scrutiny.) By contrast, the Congress of the United States—notwithstanding all the bitter infighting that lay ahead—would never once go into closed session during the course of the war.[18] President Davis opened his executive messages (like his inaugural address) with the words "Gentlemen of the Congress of the Confederate States of America." President Lincoln began his with "Fellow-citizens."

The first half of the July Fourth message was a historical narrative. Lincoln recapitulated the events that had transpired since the start of his presidency, exactly four months earlier. He made clear, to begin with, that he had held firm to the pledge of his inaugural address: not to fire the war's first shot. Indeed, he deftly turned the Union's relative military unpreparedness into evidence of its honorable intentions: while the rebels had been arming for war, the North's citizens had continued striving for peace, keeping faith in the instruments of democracy—"time, discussion, and the ballot-box"—to resolve the national crisis. Lincoln described the letter from Major Anderson that had arrived on his first full day in office, presenting him with the stark choice of surrendering the fort or trying to supply it with fresh provisions. (In a very early draft, the president had even mentioned General Scott's support for evacuating Sumter, heedless, it seems, of how this revelation would publicly humiliate the general-in-chief; clearly he was still working through the last remnants of his political naïveté.)[19] He spoke of Captain Fox's relief expedition and the advance notice he had given the rebels, casting their bombardment of Sumter as an act of deadly aggression provoked merely by "the [attempted] giving of bread to the few brave and hungry men of the garrison."

As conciliatory as Lincoln made his military policies sound, he was unwilling to concede a single inch of rhetorical ground to the enemy.

From his experience as a lawyer, he knew the fatal effect of allowing one's opponent to define the terms of an argument. Whereas the Northern press and public had more or less automatically begun referring to "the Confederate States," Lincoln pointedly referred to "this illegal organization in the character of confederate States." The lowercase spelling and lack of a definite article made clear that he was using the word *confederate* as it might apply to a member of a gang of highway robbers.

In fact, this idea lay at the core of Lincoln's argument: that the very existence of the Southern Confederacy (or confederacy) was not merely a threat but a crime. And not a victimless crime, either—not, as the rebel leaders would have it, a benign act of withdrawal from a voluntary political compact. It was a crime against their fellow citizens, collectively and individually. It was an act of theft: the rebels had appropriated federal property paid for by loyal taxpayers, while defaulting on their own share of the federal debt and leaving their former countrymen holding the bag. More important, though, secession was an act of vandalism—terrorism even—against the very foundation of democratic government: the concept of obedience to majority rule. "If we now recognize this doctrine, by allowing the seceders to go in peace," Lincoln wrote, "it is difficult to see what we can do, if others choose to go, or to extort terms upon which they will promise to remain." (Such an act of extortion, this Congress knew well, had come quite close to success.)

Indeed, secession would render democracy's survival impossible, not just in the Northern states but, ironically, in the Southern ones, too: what besides force could keep Virginia or Louisiana in the Confederacy as soon as they found themselves in the minority on some important national issue?

Here was the difference between the American colonies' revolution and the Southern states' rebellion. The colonists had been subjects, not citizens; they were parties to no formal political compact with the mother country; they were not voters in parliamentary elections even to the limited extent allowed to their English cousins, suffering taxation without representation among other tyrannies of government without consent of the governed. Their withdrawal from the British Empire may have hurt that empire economically, but it did not threaten it existentially. Lincoln directly refuted the Southerners' claim to be Jefferson's legitimate heirs. Referring to the various state ordinances of secession, he wrote:

Our adversaries have adopted some Declarations of Independence; in which, unlike the good old one, penned by Jefferson, they omit the words "all men are created equal." Why? They have adopted a temporary national constitution, in the preamble of which, unlike our good old one, signed by Washington, they omit "We, the People," and substitute "We, the deputies of the sovereign and independent States." Why? Why this deliberate pressing out of view, the rights of men, and the authority of the people?

Lincoln returned again and again to the idea of "the people." He was determined to prove that the Union was not fighting against the cause of freedom, as the Confederates maintained, but actively for it—and according to a very different understanding of the word. To the secessionists, freedom meant the ability to elude authority. To Lincoln, freedom was in itself a form of authority—indeed, the only legitimate form of authority, as the only alternative was authoritarianism. "And this issue embraces more than the fate of these United States," he wrote.

> It presents to the whole family of man, the question, whether a constitutional republic, or a democracy—a government of the people, by the same people—can, or cannot, maintain its territorial integrity, against its own domestic foes. It presents the question, whether discontented individuals, too few in numbers to control administration, according to organic law, in any case, can always, upon the pretences made in this case, or on any other pretences, or arbitrarily, without any pretence, break up their Government, and thus practically put an end to free government upon the earth. It forces us to ask: "Is there, in all republics, this inherent, and fatal weakness?" "Must a government, of necessity, be too strong for the liberties of its own people, or too weak to maintain its own existence?"

Here Lincoln was not merely echoing, more eloquently, what he had told the regent captains of San Marino two months earlier. He was also foreshadowing what he would tell a crowd of Americans at Gettysburg two years hence. *A government of the people, by the same people.* That superfluous word *same*, like a lead weight, tethers the phrase to earth, keeping Lincoln's prose from rising into poetry; the reader longs to cut it loose. But Lincoln's thought is the same, and would remain a lodestar for him throughout the stormy years to come. Although he might not have scribbled his 1863 address on the back of an envelope, as legend would have it, it should be no surprise that he wrote it fairly quickly. Lincoln had already done the hard work of the Gettysburg Address, the heavy intellectual lifting, in 1861. The two intervening years would go to pare away the nonessentials, to sculpt 6,256 words of prose into 246 words of poetry.

When people like Emerson had criticized Lincoln for spending so long toiling over the Independence Day message, they did not understand that the president, in doing so, had in a very real sense been fighting the war. Through his lonely Emersonian struggle, all those torturous hours alone with his thoughts and his half-filled pages, he had been arming himself for the terrible conflict ahead.

Again and again over the next four years, those who knew Lincoln would express their amazement at his lack of self-doubt, his tenacity in staying the course—so different from the early weeks of his presidency. But once he had written his address to Congress, Lincoln never again needed to ask himself whether he should be fighting or what he was fighting for. With these large questions settled, the smaller ones of *how* to fight often answered themselves. The proper resolution of the Sumter crisis, which had tortured Lincoln in March and early April, seemed almost obvious in retrospect. Reasoning backward from the principles he articulated on July Fourth, he could not possibly have behaved any differently. Reasoning forward, much of his course ahead was clear.

This is not to say by any means that Lincoln's thinking remained static after 1861—far from it. The difference between the July Fourth message and the Gettysburg Address is not simply a matter of elegance or conciseness; it also reflects what had happened in the meantime. The story that Lincoln would tell America in 1863, like his earlier one, began in 1776: four score and seven years ago. But the importance of the additional time accounts perhaps for his chronological precision. The later document is suffused with a sense of national tragedy, understandably enough—hundreds of thousands of Americans had died in the war by that point—and is deeply informed by a tragic understanding of world history, as well as by very ancient ideas about redemption through sacrifice. The political compact that Lincoln had described earlier had now been sanctified by death. The other immense fact of the last two years, along with all the deaths, was the Emancipation Proclamation. Thus the soaring final line of the Gettysburg Address contains not just a rearticulation of the 1861 idea, *government of the people, by the people, for the people*, but also something wholly novel: *a new birth of freedom*.

Yet were these two things entirely missing from the earlier document? By July 4, 1861, Lincoln, along with millions of other Americans, had already caught a glimpse of emancipation: those bold contrabands escaping slavery, hailing Lincoln and his armies as liberators. With Ellsworth's death, he had also already suffered the agony of personal loss, in a way that few of his countrymen yet had done. And in fact, his message to Congress carries in itself hints of the inevitable sacrifices ahead—both the price to be paid by ordinary Americans and what they would gain by paying it:

> This is essentially a People's contest. On the side of the Union, it is a struggle for maintaining in the world, that form, and substance of government, whose leading object is, to elevate the condition of men—to lift artificial weights from all shoulders—to clear the paths of laudable pursuit for all—to afford all, an unfettered start, and a fair chance, in the race of life. Yielding to partial, and temporary departures, from necessity, this is the leading object of the government for whose existence we contend.

After publication, Lincoln's message would be roundly criticized by abolitionists, who accused him of skirting—in fact, entirely omitting—the very issue that had sparked the war. "Any one reading that document, with no previous knowledge of the United States, would never dream from any thing there written that we have a slaveholders war waged upon the Government," Frederick Douglass lamented.[20]

But it may have been the proslavery forces, this time, who inferred a subtler understanding of Lincoln's words. The editors of the *Baltimore Sun*, unbending in its defense of slaveholders' rights, described the document as "strikingly at variance with all our preconceived ideas of the principles of [American] government." They pointed specifically to the "People's contest" passage:

> This paragraph has been understood to signify, in somewhat ambiguous terms, the amplest doctrines of the abolitionists. "To elevate the condition of men, to lift artificial weights from all shoulders," &c., is scarcely susceptible of any other practical application than to the colored race, slave and free. It seems to mean the abolition of slavery, and the social, civil, and political equality of the Ethiopian, Mongolian, Caucasian, and all other races.

Lincoln, the newspaper complained, was claiming to find ideas and intentions embodied in the Constitution that its framers had never intended to put there: "The President might [as well] assert that it is one particular design of the Union to regulate the tail of the comet, the cut of a coat, or the size of a lady's hoops."[21]

The *Sun* was right: when Lincoln wrote of "an unfettered start," he chose his words deliberately. An earlier draft had used the phrase "an even start," an image that fit much more neatly with the "race of life" metaphor.[22] But when the president crossed out the word *even* and wrote *unfettered* above it, he sacrificed metaphorical coherence for an unmistakable evocation of the plight of the slaves. The *Sun* was also correct in discerning another new idea: the government as guarantor of "a fair chance, in the race of life," something that might well have left the nation's founders scratching their heads. Lincoln was speaking not in the voice of the eighteenth century but that of the nineteenth, a voice informed by new ideas in science—*the race of Life*—as well as in politics.

This came as no small shock to some of Lincoln's longtime doubters: those members of the nation's intellectual establishment who had seen him as a half-educated Midwestern rube, a man unequal to the times. George W. Curtis, the journalist and Republican activist, had originally dismissed him as a cipher, believing that William Seward was the man who must save the Union. But now, still reeling from the death of his friend Winthrop at Big Bethel, Curtis wrote privately:

> I envy no other age. I believe with all my heart in the cause, and in Abe Lincoln. His message is the most truly American message ever delivered. Think upon what a millennial year we have fallen when the President of the United States declares officially that this government is founded upon the rights of man! . . . I can forgive the jokes and the big hands, and the inability to make bows. Some of us who doubted were wrong.[23]

Indeed, Lincoln's 1861 message to Congress stands as a milestone not just in the development of his thought but also in the evolution of his reputation. The Rail-Splitter had crafted a subtle and brilliant work of political science, and at the same time had succeeded, as one man present at the Capitol wrote, in narrating "the whole story of our troubles so that every man woman & child who can read it can understand." Henceforth he might be—would be—reviled, but he would never be underestimated. Some would denounce him as a tyrant, but after July 4, fewer and fewer would mock him as an "ape" or a rube. His eloquence and intellect were in themselves powerful arguments for why *all* Americans, even an unschooled backwoodsman from Kentucky, even a slave, deserved a fair chance in the race of life.

"In this hour of its trial," one Philadelphian wrote, "the country seems to have found in Mr. Lincoln a great man."[24]

NOT LONG BEFORE JULY 4, the author Nathaniel Parker Willis visited the nation's capital. While there, he crossed the Potomac to the Virginia side in order to see Arlington House, the splendid mansion recently evacuated by Robert E. Lee and his wife, Mary Custis Lee, great-granddaughter of Martha Washington. Federal troops had occupied the property, setting up a telegraph station in the dining room and digging entrenchments in the surrounding fields. Exploring the garden behind the house, the writer came upon an elderly Negro hard at work weeding a bed of strawberries, as if all the military commotion around him did not exist, and as if his master and mistress might return at any moment to check on their plantings. "Well, uncle, what do you think of the war?" Willis asked him.

The old man hesitated for a moment. "Well, massa," he said, *"it's all about things we've been so long a puttin up with."* And then, Willis wrote, he went diligently back to work.[25]

Other visitors' accounts from the summer of 1861 describe curious encounters with a white-haired Negro at Arlington House whom they came upon faithfully tending the grounds—he must have been the same man. (One report gives his name as Daniel.) John Nicolay and Robert Lincoln had a conversation with him one afternoon when they took a ride on horseback into Union-occupied Virginia. On that occasion, the philosophical old man—who was delighted to meet the president's son—shared a piece of information that none of the other accounts mention: he had been born at Mount Vernon, back before the turn of the century. He had been Mrs. Washington's slave.[26]

This particular kind of Revolutionary connection was not much on people's minds as the nation's capital celebrated the first Independence Day of the war. At dawn's first light, the deep boom of a columbiad sounded from the Arsenal grounds, and before its echoes could fade they were answered by other cannons among the far-flung encampments, the fields of tents whose occupants were just stirring themselves to dress and shave. Soon, a witness reported, "for ten miles along the whole line of entrenchments on the Virginia side, there was a continuous sheet of flame, volumes of smoke, and thunders of artillery that must have shaken the earth even under the feet of the rebels at Manassas Junction." In the streets of the federal city itself, schoolboys by the thousand, roused from their beds with greater alacrity than on any other morning of the year, applied themselves gravely to the task of setting squibs alight at every curbside, adding their small detonations to the overall din.[27]

Flags lined the thoroughfares, of course. The most conscientious patriots had stitched on one extra star before raising them: as of that day, the national banner officially bore thirty-four, the final acknowledgment of Kansas's entry into the Union.[28]

By eight o'clock, a crowd was gathering on Pennsylvania Avenue in front of the White House, where a reviewing stand had been set up for the president and other dignitaries to watch the military parade from beneath a large canopy. They were fortunate; the broiling sun soon began taking its toll on the waiting soldiers, buttoned up smartly in their woolen dress uniforms. "That was the hardest Fourth I ever saw," an infantryman in the Thirty-second New York wrote to his brother afterward. "All N. York regiments were reviewed that day by Old Abe and Gen Scott. The day was very warm and some of the boys dropped down, overcome by the heat and fatigue."[29]

Old Abe and the general, accompanied by Seward and the other cabinet secretaries, emerged together from the White House a moment before nine and took their places just as a brass band strode up the avenue playing "Hail to the Chief," and struggling a bit to manage the tune as the throngs pressed in from all sides. But then the way was cleared, and the parade began to pass. At its head strode the First German Rifles under Colonel Max Blenker, an old Forty-Eighter from Bavaria turned prosperous Manhattan merchant. Next was the Twelfth New York, from out near Elmira, with a fine regimental band. The Cameron Highlanders made a colorful impression with their skirling bagpipes and kilted officers; as a peacetime militia regiment, they had made a similarly jaunty showing the year before, parading for the Japanese ambassadors and the Prince of Wales.

The day's great sensation was the Thirty-ninth New York, a regiment known as the Garibaldi Guard. Its ranks included not just Italians but Germans, Frenchmen, Hungarians, Spaniards, and Swiss, along with a smattering of Russian Cossacks and Indian Sepoys. The men wore green-plumed *bersaglieri* hats and red shirts, just like their namesakes, and marched behind three different flags: the Stars and Stripes, the Hungarian ensign, and, most honored of all, the very same red, green, and white tricolor that General Garibaldi had planted on Rome's Capitoline Hill in 1848, a gift to the New York regiment from an emigré Italian officer. (Garibaldi fever would reach its climax in America later that month, when William Seward tried unsuccessfully to entice the "distinguished Soldier of Freedom" to leave his Mediterranean homeland and accept a major-generalship in the Union army.) The soldiers had already delighted Washington with their habit of singing "La Marseillaise" as they marched along with baguettes speared on their bayonets, the way French troops were supposed to carry their field rations. Now each of the dashing warriors sported a sprig of evergreen or a small bouquet of flowers tucked into his hatband. As they passed, the men flung these botanical offerings onto the reviewing stand with Continental panache. Most seemed aimed at Winfield Scott—whether in tribute to him as head of the army or because he presented such a large target—and before long, the nonplussed general-in-chief resembled nothing so much as a mountainside in springtime.[30]

But then came the drabber, blue-uniformed ranks of plain American soldiers: Manhattan shop clerks, upstate farm boys, Buffalo flatboatmen. They had no storied tricolors to wave, no bouquets to throw, so that the next day's newspapers simply listed their regimental numbers, one after another, with very little comment.

One regiment, the Twenty-sixth New York, was apparently so ordinary that the journalists could report only one distinctive thing: as it swung up Pennsylvania Avenue toward the White House, a young Negro contraband marched alongside. He saluted Lincoln smartly as he passed.[31]

EVENTUALLY, ASTRONOMERS WOULD LEARN a good deal about the mysterious comet—still known today as the Great Comet of 1861—which happened to arrive at a moment in history when scientists' ability to gauge, measure, and predict the natural world was improving at an astonishing rate. They quickly ascertained its size, velocity, trajectory, and distance from Earth. Comparing their measurements to historical data, they decided initially that it was the same comet that had last passed by in 1556, alarming Charles V to the point of abdicating the throne of the Holy Roman Empire; upon further consideration, however, they decided that the new comet was in fact previously unknown, an uncharted traveler of the heavens. It turned out to have been first spotted on May 13 by a sheep farmer and amateur stargazer in New South Wales. Not long after this, it appeared in the skies above Cape Town, and Dr. Livingstone, the explorer, saw it from his campsite in deepest Africa.

Telegraphic communications in the Southern Hemisphere were still a few years away from the point when scientists there would have been able to alert their colleagues in London, Berlin, and Washington. So by the time the comet blazed into view of the top half of the globe, in late June, it was already extremely close by the standards of astronomy—about twelve million miles away. One reason it had been so hard to spot at first is that it was headed almost straight for Earth (but, luckily, not quite). Astronomers calculated—correctly, it seems—that on the comet's closest approach, Earth actually passed through its tail, which was believed to explain why certain vicars in rural England reported a strange greenish haze in the air that night, requiring them to light their altar candles unusually early.

Yet, for all the closely printed columns of explanatory data in all the major newspapers, many Americans were still not really sure what to make of the wandering star.

For some, the magnificent nocturnal spectacle was simply a pleasant distraction from the political troubles around them. Eighteen sixty-one was a time just before electric light would pollute the skies above the world's cities and towns—a time when the heavens were, at least for the moment, still visible. Mary Chesnut, who had followed the Confederate government to Richmond, described how gentlemen enticed ladies out under the stars during those humid Southern nights: "Heavens above, what philandering there was, done in the name of the comet! When you stumbled on a couple in the piazza they lifted their eyes—and 'comet' was the only word you heard."[32]

Others gazed at it a bit more searchingly. Like grizzled Ralph Farnham on the train to Boston, they were uncertain travelers between an old world and a new one, between an age of faith and an age of reason. They laughed about how astronomy had debunked the ancient superstition that comets were omens from Heaven, portending war and the death of kings—and then they proceeded to speculate on what it might foretell.

So much had changed in the past few years—even in the past few months. Fixed truths seemed to be casting themselves adrift; familiar stars departing from their orbits. *Revolution*, in the sense that astronomers at Washington's Naval Observatory used the term, meant something stately and predictable, an orbit tethered by the gravity of the sun. Elsewhere in the capital city, of course, the word meant something quite different; elsewhere in the nation, different things still. Until recently, America's own revolution had come to seem like a fact moored safely to the ever-more-distant year 1776. That was now no longer the case. It blazed again across the sky, a thing of wonder and terror, still uncertain in its import.

Groping for words adequate to express their thoughts, some yoked the language of science to that of prophecy. "History is like the progress of a comet, moving slowly, at a snail's pace, for hundreds of years, far away in the unfathomable abysses of space, then pitching down headlong on the sun," one essayist wrote. "We are now, as a nation, in our perihelion of light and heat. We are in our blossoming period. . . . [These] are times in which a whole people or a community are filled with a common conviction, united in the same faith, inspired by the same purpose, are of one heart and one soul."[33]

This announcement of universal harmony seems to have been premature, in light of other responses to the comet. Americans may all have looked up at the same starry wanderer, but each saw something different.

Yankees, flattered that it graced the northern part of the sky, hailed it as an augury of triumph for the Union, though several also expressed the fond hope that it would change course and hit Richmond. Meanwhile, a Southerner noticed on closer inspection that "the tail of the comet sweeps directly over the north star, which is the fixed representation of northern power, and bans it with its baleful influence, while its light gleams as a pillar of flame to the south, beckoning her armies on to victory." Abolitionists, naturally, said it heralded the liberation of the slaves, like the ancient Hebrews' pillar of fire. One artist drew a cartoon that showed the comet with the head of Lincoln, trailing red stripes across a starry blue sky; he captioned this "Star of the North, or the Comet of 1861." Another artist copied this drawing, but gave the comet the unmistakable jowly head of Winfield Scott, while an editorial writer, for reasons not fully explained, compared it to Colonel Frank Blair. A Richmond newspaper proposed that the comet be dubbed "the Southern Confederacy" in tribute to the new nation, to which one in Providence retorted: "The name might be appropriate to that body, which has the least conceivable head with the largest conceivable tail, and is running away as fast as possible."

The president saw the comet, too.

Seventy years later, a woman who had played often as a girl with the Lincoln children, until Willie's death from typhoid fever in 1862, wrote down her recollections of that long-ago spring and summer. The memoirist, Julia Taft Bayne, remembered how the Negroes of Washington "cowered under the great war comet blazing in the sky." There was, she said, one particular slave named Oola, a woman so old she was said to have been born in Africa, and to possess the gift of prophecy. "You see dat big fire sword blazin' in the sky?" she supposedly said. "De handle's to'rd de Norf and de point to'rd de Souf and de Norf's gwine take dat sword and cut de Souf's heart out. But dat Linkum man, chilluns, if he takes de sword, he's gwine perish by it." Mrs. Bayne described how she had gone and told Tad and Willie of this prediction, leaving out the part about their father, and how they, in turn, ran immediately to tell him.

"I noticed him, a few evenings later, looking out of the window intently at the comet and I wondered if he was thinking of the old Negro woman's prophecy," Mrs. Bayne wrote in 1931. But she was very old herself by then, grasping at a few frayed strands of memory, and if there had ever been any truth to the story, it may have been lost somewhere along her passage from one century into the next.[34]

Perhaps it was James Gordon Bennett's *New York Herald* that, for once, came closest to the truth—closest, even, to prophecy. On Independence Day, 1861, a remarkable article appeared on the paper's editorial page. It was headlined "Annus Mirabilis":

The present is a year productive of strange and surprising events. It is one prolific of revolution and abounding in great and startling novelties. Our own country is resounding with war's alarms, and half a million of Northern and Southern men are preparing to engage in a deadly conflict. And meanwhile all Europe is threatened with one tremendous revolution, growing out of our own, which will shake thrones to their foundations. The premonitory symptoms of change are already observable here and there. Even Russia will not escape; for the troubles in Poland and the emancipation of the serfs have already made her empire ripe for revolt. In China and Japan, too, the hand of revolution is also busy. This is indeed a wonderful year; for while all the world is more or less filled with apprehension and commotion, a luminous messenger makes its appearance in the heavens, to the consternation of astronomers. . . . That we are entering, to say the least, upon a new and important epoch in the history of the world, all these wars and rumors of wars, these miracles on earth and marvels in the sky, would seem to indicate.[35]

In any event, the comet began to fade as quickly as it had appeared. By the Fourth of July, it had already peaked; over the next few days, it would rapidly dwindle. Late that month, as the shattered Union army retreated from the field of Bull Run, it could still be discerned with the naked eye, a fast-receding pinpoint among the night stars.

In April of the following year, an astronomer at the Imperial Russian Observatory near St. Petersburg glimpsed it one last time through the lens of his telescope. And then it was gone, continuing on its own mysterious errand toward some incalculable future rendezvous, beyond human sight.

Fort Sumter, April 14, 1865

Postscripts

Word over all, beautiful as the sky,
Beautiful that war and all its deeds of carnage must in time
    be utterly lost,
That the hands of the sisters Death and Night incessantly
    softly wash again,
and ever again, this soil'd world . . .

—Walt Whitman,
"Reconciliation" (1865)

DESPITE HEAVY NAVAL BOMBARDMENTS of the citadel throughout 1863 and 1864, *Fort Sumter* did not fall into Union hands again until the surrender of Charleston at the end of the Civil War.

On April 14, 1865—the fourth anniversary of the original Union garrison's evacuation—a ceremony was held at Sumter to celebrate the war's end. Some three thousand people attended, both civilians and soldiers, black and white. The Fifty-fourth Massachusetts, the famous "Glory" regiment, served as a color guard; Abner Doubleday, Charles Sumner, and William Lloyd Garrison were among the guests of honor. Charleston Harbor was full of flag-bedecked gunboats, steamers, and ironclads, firing salutes throughout the morning.

Just before the ceremony, according to *The New York Times*, a large steamship arrived "loaded down with between 2,000 and 3,000 of the emancipated race, of all ages and sizes. Their appearance was warmly welcomed."

After a brief prayer, Major—now General—Robert Anderson stepped to the fort's flagpole and slowly raised the same tattered banner that he had lowered there four years before.

Memories of the ceremony were overshadowed by the assassination that night of President Abraham Lincoln.[1]

.

James Buchanan never returned to Washington, D.C. He spent the rest of his life trying to clear his name, and supported the Lincoln administration throughout the war as a pro-Union Democrat. He died in 1868.[2]

.

Eight months after the close of his Peace Conference, *John Tyler* was elected a congressman of the Confederate States of America. He died of a stroke in January 1862, before he was able to take his seat. His villa just outside Hampton, Virginia, remained a Freedmen's Bureau school for black children until his widow finally regained possession in 1869. Hampton University is currently building a new dining hall on the site where it once stood.[3]

.

Notwithstanding *John J. Crittenden*'s intention to retire from public life at the beginning of the Civil War, his friends pressured him to return to Washington as a congressman and continue striving to peacefully reconcile North and South. This he did until his death in July 1863, three weeks after the Battle of Gettysburg.[4]

•

Abby Kelley Foster remained an outspoken critic of Lincoln throughout the war, maintaining that he was not aggressive enough in his policies on slavery and race. After emancipation, she joined Frederick Douglass in arguing that the American Anti-Slavery Society should not disband but should continue fighting for black civil rights. The society held its last meeting in April 1870. Foster gave one of the final speeches, in which she rejoiced at all the changes that she had seen over the course of her life: "Have we not moral as well as physical rail-roads and tele-graphs? I feel as if I had lived a thousand years."[5]

•

Lucy Bagby liberated herself a second time from slavery in June 1861, becoming a contraband when Union forces entered Wheeling, Virginia. Her master, a leading secessionist, was imprisoned by federal troops in the same jail where he had once placed her.

On her return to Cleveland as a free woman in 1863, she was greeted with an enthusiastic welcome; the city's black community held a "Grand Jubilee" in her honor. She later remarried, to a Union Army veteran, and died in Cleveland in 1906.[6]

•

In the late summer of 1861, *James A. Garfield* received his commission as colonel of the new Forty-second Regiment of Ohio Volunteers. In its ranks were many of his old pupils from Hiram College. The regiment would play a key role in securing Kentucky for the Union, and its early victories made Garfield a brigadier general, bringing him national acclaim. He later commanded troops at Shiloh and Chicka-mauga. Garfield resigned from the army in 1863, at Lincoln's behest, to take a seat in the House of Representatives. In 1865, he was one of Congress's most committed advocates of the Thirteenth Amendment, which abolished slavery throughout the United States.[7]

Garfield fought staunchly not just for emancipation, but also for black civil rights. On Independence Day, 1865, he returned to the site of his Fourth of July oration five years earlier and gave a passionate speech rebutting those who believed that "the Negro" did not deserve the right to vote:

He was intelligent enough to understand from the beginning of the war that the destiny of his race was involved in it. He was intelligent enough to be true to that Union which his educated and traitorous master was endeavoring to destroy. He came to us in the hour of our sorest need, and by his aid, under God, the Republic was saved. Shall we now be guilty of the unutterable meanness, not only of thrusting him beyond the pale of its blessings, but of committing his destiny to the tender mercies of those pardoned rebels who have been so reluctantly compelled to take their feet from his neck and their hands from his throat? But some one says it is dangerous at this time to make new experiments. I answer, it is always safe to do justice. However, to grant suffrage to the black man in this country is not innovation, but restoration. It is a return to the ancient principles and practices of the fathers.

Garfield's nomination and election to the presidency came about unexpectedly. After several candidates ended up in a deadlock at the 1880 Republican National Convention, delegates began stampeding toward the relatively obscure Ohioan. The party placed him at the head of its ticket ("I don't know whether I am glad or not," the somewhat dazed nominee said), and he went on to win by a slim plurality in November.

The new president's inaugural address, almost wholly forgotten today, is a remarkable document, a clarion call for the nation to fulfill its promises to the former slaves. Indeed, over the course of more than two centuries, no other chief executive has begun his term with such a bold, firm, specific statement on the dangerous subject of civil rights, to which Garfield devoted more than half his speech. The emancipation of the Negro, he said, was the most important event in the nation's history since the signing of the Constitution:

> It has freed us from the perpetual danger of war and dissolution. It has added immensely to the moral and industrial forces of our people. It has liberated the master as well as the slave from a relation which wronged and enfeebled both. It has surrendered to their own guardianship the manhood of more than five million people, and has opened to each one of them a career of freedom and usefulness.

Yet, Garfield continued, this epochal transformation would not be complete until blacks were granted their full privileges as Americans: voting rights, educational parity, and equal access to economic opportunities. All of these, his listeners knew, had been largely abrogated four years earlier when the previous Republican administration decreed the abrupt end of Reconstruction.

"There can be no permanent disfranchised peasantry in the United States," Garfield now warned. "Freedom can never yield its fullness of blessings so long as the law or its administration places the smallest obstacle in the pathway of any virtuous citizen."

In the end, he offered a hopeful vision, in words eerily foreshadowing others that would be spoken, eighty-two years later, at the opposite end of the National Mall. Garfield said:

> Let our people find a new meaning in the divine oracle which declares that "a little child shall lead them," for our own little children will soon control the destinies of the Republic.
>
> My countrymen, we do not now differ in our judgment concerning the controversies of past generations, and fifty years hence our children will not be divided in their opinions concerning our controversies. They will surely bless their fathers and their fathers' God that the Union was preserved, that slavery was overthrown, and that both races were made equal before the law. We may hasten or we may retard, but we can not prevent, the final reconciliation.

Garfield would continue espousing such views throughout his short presidency, notably in a speech at the Hampton Institute on June 4, 1881.

But that occasion at Hampton, almost exactly twenty years after the first contrabands' liberation, would be his last public address. Less than a month later, as he walked through Washington's train station on his way to a summer holiday with his family, Garfield was shot by a mentally deranged man, Charles Guiteau. The president lingered throughout the summer in great pain—as much from the inept medical care he received as from the wounds themselves—before dying on September 19.

He was succeeded by Chester Arthur, who showed little of his predecessor's interest in achieving racial justice. James Garfield's inaugural prophecy would wait much longer than fifty years to be fulfilled.

•

Exhausted mentally and physically by his ordeal at Fort Sumter, *Robert Anderson* was never able to file an official report on the bombardment and surrender. He was appointed brigadier general in May 1861 and briefly commanded Union forces in his native Kentucky, but for reasons of health was relieved from active duty that October. He died at Nice, France, in 1871.

.

After being spurned by Jefferson Davis in his attempts to win a high post in the rebel government, *Louis T. Wigfall* joined the Confederate Congress and became Davis's fiercest political foe. In March 1865, he strongly opposed the Confederates' last-ditch attempt to stem the tide of defeat by conscripting blacks into military service. He fled to Texas in May of that year, hoping to continue the struggle by leading Southern troops across the Rio Grande into Mexico.

When this plan failed to materialize, Wigfall left for England, where he spent the next five years attempting to restart the war by first provoking hostilities between the United States and Great Britain. He finally returned to Texas and died of apoplexy in 1874.[8]

.

The dead at First Bull Run included Noah Farnham, Elmer Ellsworth's successor as commander of the *New York Fire Zouaves*. Already sick with typhoid, Farnham was wounded by a Confederate bullet and died several days later. After the battle, the Zouaves were scapegoated in the press for the Union defeat and ridiculed as cowards; the flashy uniforms of the firemen soldiers became (and for some historians, remain) symbols of the early pride and folly of the Northern side. A few weeks after the battle, when the Zouaves' regimental flags—the same ones they had paraded so proudly down Broadway that spring—were found abandoned on a trash heap in Alexandria, it was the unit's final humiliation. By autumn, more than half the men had deserted, and a few months later, the regiment officially disbanded.

The following year, an attempt was made to reconstitute it under the command of a new colonel, Henry O'Brien. Not long after O'Brien began enlisting fresh Zouave recruits from among the fire b'hoys, the New York draft riots broke out, and he was among those murdered by the mob, tortured and hanged from a lamppost. Ellsworth's unlucky regiment was never resurrected again.

.

In September 1861, *Jessie Benton Frémont* traveled alone by train from St. Louis to Washington to meet with President Lincoln. Ten days earlier, her husband, as the Union military commander in Missouri, had issued an edict summarily liberating all slaves in the state belonging to masters who aided the rebel cause. When news reached the president, he had immediately asked General Frémont to rescind the order.

Mrs. Frémont, hoping she could stay Lincoln's hand, went immediately to the White House. She found the president adamant in his position; he annoyed her still further when he said condescendingly, "You are quite a female politician." Lincoln told John Hay afterward that Mrs. Frémont had pressed him so hard that it was all he could do to avoid having an open quarrel with her.

(Mrs. Frémont, hearing of this many years later, wrote: "Strange, isn't it, that when a man expresses a conviction fearlessly, he is reported as having made a trenchant and forceful statement, but when a woman speaks thus earnestly, she is reported as a lady who has lost her temper.")

His emancipation order revoked, *John C. Frémont*'s career in public life abruptly ended soon after, but Jessie Frémont was just beginning a prolific and successful career of her own as a writer. Her first work, an account of the early months of the Civil War in Missouri, appeared in 1863. It included a passage in which Mrs. Frémont said she hoped readers would not think it "unwomanly" of her to publish a book, but, she added, "the restraints of ordinary times do not apply now."

During the financial crisis of the 1870s, the Frémonts lost what remained of their once vast fortune. Throughout the next two decades, as they struggled on the edge of poverty, Jessie kept them afloat with the income from her many books and magazine articles. After John's death in 1891, newspapers ran articles about the Great Pathfinder's widow, now living in destitution.

Embarrassed, the California legislature voted her a pension, and some Los Angeles women raised money to build a house for her in their city. Jessie Frémont died there on December 27, 1902, her death mourned as the passing of a vanished West.[9]

•

The house and gardens at *Black Point* were seized by the federal government during the Civil War and demolished to build earthworks and an artillery battery. The Frémonts, still on the East Coast, were not informed, and Jessie learned only when a Union officer she met at a party happened to mention it in casual conversation. ("Your boys' room was so pretty I hated to put soldiers in it," he said, "still more to tear down the walls, where you had pasted pictures of ships and horses and written verses.") Throughout the rest of her life she tried unsuccessfully to recover the property, which became part of Fort Mason. For more than a century, no trace of her gardens was thought to survive, but in 2010, horticultural experts identified a rosebush that is believed to date from the Frémonts' occupancy.[10]

.

The "Gray Eagle," Senator *Edward D. Baker*, was killed at Ball's Bluff, Virginia, in October 1861, at the head of the First California Regiment.

.

Thomas Starr King continued working tirelessly for the Union cause in California. Beginning in the autumn of 1861, he became a leading organizer and fund-raiser for the United States Sanitary Commission, a government agency that organized citizen volunteers, especially women, in aiding wounded and sick Union soldiers. (It later inspired the founding of the American Red Cross.) King spent nearly all his time on the lecture circuit giving patriotic speeches and soliciting money for the commission; he is said to have been personally responsible for more than one and a half million dollars in contributions from the West Coast. Exhausted by these labors, he died of diphtheria in San Francisco on March 4, 1864, at the age of thirty-nine.

He and Jessie Frémont had never seen each other again. At her request, telegraphed from New York, a small bouquet of violets was placed on his chest at the funeral.

In 1931, the state of California placed a statue of King in the U.S. Capitol, thus honoring him as one of the two heroes permitted to be enshrined there by each of the fifty states. In 2009, his statue was removed and replaced with one of Ronald Reagan.[11]

.

Nathaniel Lyon was killed on August 10, 1861, at the Battle of Wilson's Creek in southwestern Missouri, the first Union general to die in the Civil War.

.

In 1862, *Benjamin Butler*, then commanding Union forces in occupied New Orleans, became one of the first Union commanders to enlist Negro troops, which he did without authorization from the Lincoln administration. He fought unsuccessfully to secure equal treatment, including equal pay, for black soldiers, as well as to protect them from the Confederate policy of reenslaving them when captured as prisoners of war. When his colored troops fought with conspicuous gallantry in the assault on Richmond, he personally designed medals for the men, to be struck in silver at his own expense. These bore the Latin inscription *Ferro iis libertas perveniet:* "Their freedom will be won by the sword."

Butler's harshness in maintaining order and quashing pro-Confederate sentiment in New Orleans—along with his unbending support for black civil rights—made him hated throughout most of the South. The general's enemies nicknamed him "Beast Butler" and "Spoons Butler," the latter because of a false rumor that he had stolen silver spoons from the house of a rebel commander.

After the war, Butler reentered politics as a radical Republican and was instrumental in passing the federal Civil Rights Act of 1875, which mandated equal treatment for blacks in all public accommodations, including restaurants, hotels, and trains. The law was never enforced in the South, and the U.S. Supreme Court ruled it unconstitutional in 1883. Its provisions did not become part of federal law again until the civil rights legislation of the 1960s.[12]

·

Over the course of the war, *Hampton, Virginia,* became home to thousands of black contrabands, who officially became freedmen and freedwomen when the Emancipation Proclamation took effect on New Year's Day, 1863. The liberated slaves built houses and makeshift shelters among the burned-out ruins of the old town, and turned the brick shell of the former courthouse into a school and church. The classes taught by Northern abolitionists and missionaries under General Butler's auspices eventually evolved into Hampton University, one of the leading historically black institutions in the country.[13]

·

Charles King Mallory remained in Confederate service until 1865. His eldest son, an eighteen-year-old midshipman in the rebel navy, was killed in the war. Mallory died in 1875; an account of his funeral in a local newspaper described it thus: "The procession, nearly three-quarters of a mile long, proceeded to the old family burying ground . . . eight miles from Hampton. The fact that a very large number of the colored citizens of Hampton and the county walked the entire distance shows how much the deceased was loved and respected by all classes." The site of Colonel Mallory's house, long since demolished, is part of the Hampton University campus.[14]

•

At the end of the war, *Mary Chesnut*, a refugee from her plantation and from her family's ruined fortunes, greeted the demise of slavery with an emotion she described in her diary as "an unholy joy."[15]

•

After serving almost continuously as the site of a military base for more than four hundred years, *Fortress Monroe* is slated to be decommissioned in September 2011. As of this writing, its future is uncertain. The governor of Virginia has endorsed a "mixed-use" development of residential and commercial space combined with "historic preservation." Some Hampton locals, led by African-Americans, including descendants of the contrabands, are calling on the National Park Service to acquire the site.[16]

At the end of the Civil War, *Jefferson Davis* was imprisoned in Fortress Monroe for two years before being released on bail; he was never brought to trial.

Today, the fort contains a Jefferson Davis Memorial Park. There is no memorial or monument to Benjamin Butler or the contrabands.

•

The three original contrabands all remained in the Hampton Roads area after the war. *Frank Baker* and *James Townsend* raised families and worked as day laborers; neither ever learned to read or write.

•

Shepard Mallory was the last survivor among the significant characters in this book. He learned to read and write and became a prominent figure in Hampton's black community. The former contraband apparently mended fences with his former master, who attended one of his weddings. (Mallory would marry at least four times; his last two wives were approximately forty and thirty years younger, respectively, than he was.) In the early twentieth century he was working as a carpenter and school janitor and living in the house at 260 Lincoln Street that he owned, free and clear, for the last four decades of his life. Shepard Mallory last appears in the census records in 1920, aged about eighty and still working, self-employed.[17]

The American Declaration of Independence Illustrated, 1861

N O T E S

Prologue: A Banner at Daybreak

1. Abner Doubleday, *Reminiscences of Forts Sumter and Moultrie* (New York, 1876), pp. 63–7; Samuel W. Crawford, *The History of the Fall of Fort Sumter, and the Genesis of the Civil War* (New York, 1887), pp. 104–112; J. G. Foster to J. H. B. Latrobe, Jan. 10, 1861, in Frank F. White, Jr., ed., "The Evacuation of Fort Moultrie in 1860," *The South Carolina Historical Magazine*, vol. 53, no. 1 (Jan. 1952), pp. 1–5; John Thompson to "Dear Father," Feb. 14, 1861, in "A Union Soldier at Fort Sumter, 1860–1861," *The South Carolina Historical Magazine*, vol. 67, no. 2 (Apr. 1966), pp. 99–104; J. G. Foster to R. E. De Russy, Dec. 27, 1860, in *Official Records [of the War of the Rebellion]*, series I (hereafter *OR* I), vol. 1, pp. 108–9; James P. Jones, ed., "Charleston Harbor, 1860–1861: A Memoir from the Union Garrison," *The South Carolina Historical Magazine*, vol. 62, no. 3 (July 1961), pp. 148–50; *Frank Leslie's Illustrated Newspaper*, Jan. 5 and Jan. 19, 1861. There are a few discrepancies among firsthand accounts of the departure from Fort Moultrie. Original texts can be found on the website for this book, www.1861book.com.

2. Abner Doubleday, "From Moultrie to Sumter," in *Battles and Leaders of the Civil War* (New York, 1887), vol. 1, p. 41; Doubleday, *Reminiscences*, chap. 1.

3. *Dictionary of American Biography* (hereafter *DAB*) (New York, 1944), vol. 1, 274; George W. Cullum, *Biographical Register of the Officers and Graduates of the U.S. Military Academy at West Point, N.Y.* (Boston, 1891), vol. 1, pp. 347–52.

4. Fitz John Porter to Cooper, Nov. 11, 1860, *OR* I, vol. 1, p. 71.

5. Terry W. Lipscomb, *South Carolina Revolutionary War Battles: The Carolina Low Country, April 1775–June 1776, and the Battle of Fort Moultrie* (Columbia, S.C., 1994); Edwin C. Bearss, *The Battle of Sullivan's Island and the Capture of Fort Moultrie: A Documented Narrative and Troop Movement Maps, Fort Sum-

ter National Monument, South Carolina (Washington, D.C., National Park Service, 1968).

6. Doubleday, "From Moultrie to Sumter," pp. 40–41.

7. James Chester, "Inside Sumter in '61," in *Battles and Leaders of the Civil War*, vol. 1, pp. 50–51.

8. David Detzer, *Allegiance: Fort Sumter, Charleston, and the Beginning of the Civil War* (New York, 2001), p. 53.

9. Charles H. Lesser, *Relic of the Lost Cause: The Story of South Carolina's Ordinance of Secession*, 2nd ed. (Columbia, S.C., 1996), pp. 2–3.

10. W. A. Swanberg, *First Blood: The Story of Fort Sumter* (New York, 1957), p. 25.

11. Roy Meredith, *Storm over Sumter: The Opening Engagement of the Civil War* (New York, 1957), p. 37.

12. Anderson to Cooper, Dec. 1, 1860, *OR* I, vol. 1, p. 81; Detzer, *Allegiance*, p. 63.

13. Anderson to Cooper, Nov. 28, 1860, *OR* I, vol. 1, pp. 78–79.

14. Cooper to Anderson, Dec. 14, 1860, *OR* I, vol. 1, pp. 92–93.

15. Floyd to Anderson, Dec. 19, 1860, *OR* I, vol. 1, p. 98.

16. Doubleday, *Reminiscences*, ch. 3; Doubleday, "From Moultrie to Sumter," p. 41; Crawford, *History*, p. 66.

17. Doubleday, "From Moultrie to Sumter," p. 43.

18. Detzer, *Allegiance*, pp. 71–72.

19. Doubleday, "From Moultrie to Sumter," p. 41.

20. Detzer, *Allegiance*, pp. 23–24.

21. *DAB*, I, p. 274; Cullum, *Biographical Register*, pp. 347–52.

22. Doubleday, "From Moultrie to Sumter," pp. 42–43.

23. Crawford, *History*, p. 95.

24. Ibid., pp. 50–51.

25. Ibid., p. 55.

26. Doubleday, *Reminiscences*, p. 56.

27. Floyd to Anderson, Dec. 21, 1860, *OR* I, vol. 1, p. 103.

28. *DAB*, Cullum, *Biographical Register*, pp. 347–52; Eba Anderson Lawton, ed., *An Artillery Officer in the Mexican War, 1846–7: Letters of Robert Anderson, Captain 3rd Artillery, U.S.A.* (New York and London, 1911), pp. 311–13.

29. Doubleday, *Reminiscences*, pp. 60–61.

30. Crawford, *History*, pp. 102–03.

31. Doubleday, *Reminiscences*, pp. 61–67; Crawford, *History*, pp. 103–07.

32. *Charleston Mercury*, Dec. 28, 1860.

33. The family correspondence of Major (later Colonel) William Hemsley Emory is now part of the James Wood Poplar Grove Papers in the Maryland State Archives.

34. David Brion Davis, *Inhuman Bondage: The Rise and Fall of Slavery in the New World* (New York, 2006), p. 10.

35. *Charleston Courier*, Dec. 28, 1860; *Baltimore Sun*, Dec. 28, 1860.

36. Swanberg, *First Blood*, p. 145.

37. This figure includes supplements that were published in the twentieth century. The original series totals 138,000 pages.

38. For an illuminating discussion of Lincoln as both progressive and conservative, see Richard Striner, *Lincoln's Way: How Six Great Presidents Created American Power* (Lanham, Md., 2010).

39. Scot M. Guenter, *The American Flag, 1777–1924: Cultural Shifts from Creation to Codification* (Rutherford, N.J., 1990), pp. 57–87; Michael Corcoran, *For Which It Stands: An Anecdotal Biography of the American Flag* (New York, 2002), pp. 78ff. Even though flags were now printed rather than individually stitched, that spring the cost of red, white, and blue bunting increased from $4.75 to $28 per yard.

40. Congress created the Medal of Honor in 1862. Of the more than 1,500 that would be awarded for acts of heroism in the Civil War, more than half involved a rescue of the American colors, or a capture of the enemy's.

Chapter One: Wide Awake

1. C. W. Clarence, *A Biographical Sketch of the Life of Ralph Farnham, of Acton, Maine, Now in the One Hundred and Fifth Year of His Age, and the Sole Survivor of the Glorious Battle of Bunker Hill* (Boston, 1860); *Daily National Intelligencer,* July 18, 1860; *Boston Bee,* Oct. 9, 1860; *Boston Post,* Oct. 9, 1860.

2. Quoted in James Elliot Cabot, *A Memoir of Ralph Waldo Emerson* (Boston, 1887–88), vol. 1, p. 91.

3. "The Kansas Question," *Putnam's Monthly* [*Magazine of American Literature, Science and Art*], vol. 6, no. 34 (Oct. 1855).

4. Webster and Adams both quoted in George B. Forgie, *Patricide in the House Divided: A Psychological Interpretation of Lincoln and His Age* (New York, 1979), pp. 67–68.

5. "Procrustes, Junior" [pseud.], "Great Men, A Misfortune," *Southern Literary Messenger,* April 1860, p. 308.

6. Clarence, *A Biographical Sketch;* Alan Taylor, *Liberty Men and Great Proprietors: The Revolutionary Settlement on the Maine Frontier, 1765–1820* (Chapel Hill, N.C., 1990).

7. Massachusetts Historical Society, Ambrotype Collection, photo 2.16.

8. Masao Miyoshi, *As We Saw Them: The First Japanese Embassy to the United States (1860)* (Berkeley, 1979), pp. 10–15; [Masayiko Kanesaboro Yanagawa], *The First Japanese Mission to the United States* (Kobe, 1937), pp. 48–50, 69. Since Dutch traders had been going to Japan for centuries, a number of educated Japanese spoke that language. Communications with English speakers usually required two translators: one of them Japanese to Dutch, the other Dutch to English.

9. Robert Cellem, *Visit of His Royal Highness the Prince of Wales to the British North American Provinces and United States, in the Year 1860* (Toronto, 1861), p. 372. When Ralph Farnham was told that the prince was about to arrive

in Boston, he responded, "I don't want to see him." Finally, however, he grudgingly deigned to call on the royal personage, who had taken a suite on another floor in the same hotel. After a cordial exchange of pleasantries, the old revolutionary remarked slyly that in light of the enthusiastic reception given to George III's great-grandson, he was worried his countrymen might be turning royalists again. The prince chose to laugh this off. (*Philadelphia Inquirer*, Oct. 12, 1860; *New York Herald*, Oct. 19, 1860.)

10. *Boston Daily Advertiser*, Oct. 9, 1860.

11. *New York Herald*, Dec. 31, 1860.

12. Reinhard H. Luthin, *The First Lincoln Campaign* (Gloucester, Mass., 1964), pp. 169–70; Earl Schenck Miers, ed., *Lincoln Day by Day: A Chronology, 1809–1865* (Washington, 1960), vol. 2, pp. 282–84. No less a sage than William Cullen Bryant advised Lincoln: "Make no speeches, write no letters as a candidate, enter into no pledges, make no promises." Bryant to Lincoln, June 16, 1860, quoted in Gil Troy, *See How They Ran: The Changing Role of the Presidential Candidate* (Cambridge, Mass., 1996), pp. 61–62; Michael Burlingame, *Abraham Lincoln: A Life* (Baltimore, 2008), vol. 1, p. 656.

13. Troy, *See How They Ran*, pp. 64–66; *The Ripley* [Ohio] *Bee*, Aug. 16, 1860; *Freedom's Champion* [Atchison, Kansas], Sept. 1, 1860; Wayne C. Williams, *A Rail Splitter for President* (Denver, 1951), pp. 36–37.

14. Lincoln remained very disconcerted by the experience. "I was afraid of being caught and crushed in that crowd," he wrote afterward. "The American people remind me of a flock of sheep." Burlingame, *Abraham Lincoln*, vol. 1, p. 651; Williams, *A Rail Splitter*, pp. 109–110; *New York Herald*, Aug. 14, 1860.

15. Joshua Wolf Shenk, *Lincoln's Melancholy: How Depression Challenged a President and Fueled His Greatness* (Boston, 2005), p. 3.

16. Wayne C. Temple, "Lincoln's Fence Rails," *Journal of the Illinois State Historical Society*, vol. 47 (1954), pp. 21–28; Mark A. Plummer, *Lincoln's Rail-Splitter: Governor Richard J. Oglesby* (Urbana, Ill., 2001), pp. 44–45.

17. Williams, *A Rail Splitter*, p. 50.

18. Gary Kulik, "The Worm Fence" in *Between Fences*, ed. Gregory K. Dreicer (Princeton, N.J., 1996), pp. 20–22; John Stilgoe, *Common Landscape of America, 1580 to 1845* (New Haven, 1982), pp. 321–23. Interestingly, many friends and family members who had known Lincoln in his youth said he'd hated physical labor. "Abe was awful lazy," one farmer who'd employed him told an interviewer in 1865. John Hanks's own brother Charles said publicly during the 1860 campaign that "jumping and wrestling were his only accomplishments. His laziness was the source of many mortifications to me; for as I was an older boy than either Abe or John, I often had to do Abe's work at uncle's, when the family were sick . . . and Abe would be rollicking about the country neglecting them." (Burlingame, *Abraham Lincoln*, vol. 1, pp. 77, 667.)

19. Williams, *A Rail Splitter*, pp. 158–59; *New York Herald*, Sept. 29, 1860.

20. Contrary to what some have assumed, the Democrats' split did not directly bring about Lincoln's victory. Even if the party, and the Constitutional Unionists, for that matter, had united behind a single candidate, Lincoln would still have won enough electoral votes to give him the presidency.

21. Quoted in the *Daily Ohio Statesman*, Jan. 28, 1860.

22. Troy, *See How They Ran*, p. 65.

23. Eric Foner, *Free Soil, Free Labor, Free Men: The Ideology of the Republican Party Before the Civil War*, 2nd ed. (New York, 1995), pp. 216–19; Burlingame, *Abraham Lincoln*, vol. 1, p. 669.

24. See, e.g., *New-York Tribune*, Oct. 28, 1860.

25. See Foner, *Free Soil*, esp. chaps. 1–2.

26. James M. Volo and Dorothy Denneen Volo, *The Antebellum Period* (Westport, Conn., 2004), p. 68.

27. F. H. Sangborn and William Harris, eds., *A. Bronson Alcott: His Life and Philosophy* (Boston, 1893), vol. 1, pp. 145–46; Geraldine Brooks, "Orpheus at the Plough," *The New Yorker*, Jan. 10, 2005, p. 58.

28. William Carlos Martyn, *Wendell Phillips: The Agitator* (Boston, 1890), p. 149; *Boston City Directory for 1855* (Boston, 1855); *Boston City Directory for 1865* (Boston, 1865).

29. Oscar Sherwin, *Apostle of Liberty: The Life and Times of Wendell Phillips* (New York, 1958), pp. 323–33; Henry Mayer, *All on Fire: William Lloyd Garrison and the Abolition of Slavery* (New York, 1998), pp. 440–42.

30. Mayer, *All on Fire*, pp. 443–45; Ralph Korngold, *Two Friends of Man: The Story of William Lloyd Garrison and Wendell Phillips and Their Relationship with Abraham Lincoln* (Boston, 1950), p. 249.

31. Mayer, *All on Fire*, p. 510; Korngold, *Two Friends of Man*, pp. 269–70.

32. Burlingame, *Abraham Lincoln*, vol. 1, p. 664; *San Antonio Ledger and Texan*, July 28, 1860.

33. Burlingame, *Abraham Lincoln*, vol. 1, p. 664. The newspaper's editors were perhaps unaware that Washington had died childless and that Lafayette's descendants all lived in France.

34. Ibid. p. 665; *New York Herald*, Oct. 24, 1860.

35. *New York Herald*, Oct. 5, 1860.

36. *Council Bluffs* [Iowa] *Bugle*, Oct. 31, 1860.

37. *New York Herald*, July 12, 1860.

38. Osborn H. Oldroyd, *Lincoln's Campaign: Or the Political Revolution of 1860* (Chicago, 1896), pp. 104–05; *New York Herald*, Sept. 10 and 19, 1860; *The Mississippian* [Jackson], Sept. 28, 1860; Jon Grinspan, "'Young Men for War': The Wide Awakes and Lincoln's 1860 Campaign," *Journal of American History*, vol. 96, no. 2 (Sept. 2009), pp. 357–78. Grinspan's recent article is the only in-depth account of the Wide Awakes that has ever been published.

One variation on the Hartford story had it that the five shop clerks were attacked en route to the hotel by a burly Democrat who tried to throw one of them to the ground. He was laid low by a swing of the young clerk's torch. (*Frank Leslie's Illustrated Weekly*, Oct. 13, 1860.)

39. *New York Herald*, Sept. 19 and 26, 1860.

40. Grinspan, "'Young Men for War'"; Ulysses S. Grant, *Personal Memoirs of U. S. Grant* (New York, 1999), p. 114.

41. *Milwaukee Daily Sentinel*, Aug. 1, 1860; Grinspan, " 'Young Men for War.' " One enlistee in Boston was the young Charles Francis Adams, Jr.

42. *Daily Cleveland Herald*, Sept. 17, 1860; *New York Herald*, Oct. 4, 1860.

43. *New York Herald*, Sept. 26, 1860.

44. *Milwaukee Daily Sentinel*, Sept. 10, 1860.

45. My account of the "Texas troubles" of 1860 is drawn largely from the only scholarly book on the subject, Donald E. Reynolds's carefully researched *Texas Terror: The Slave Insurrection Panic of 1860 and the Secession of the Lower South* (Baton Rouge, 2007). It is difficult to estimate the number of lynchings, since most of the period sources are anecdotal, and some killings doubtless went unreported. The range I have given is from Reynolds's book.

46. *Georgia Chronicle*, n.d., reprinted in the *Daily Cleveland Herald*, Oct. 23, 1860; *Semi-Weekly Mississippian* [Jackson], Oct. 16, 1860.

47. Grinspan, "'Young Men for War'"; *New York Herald*, Nov. 5, 1860.

48. Grinspan, "'Young Men for War,'" thinks the real total was probably closer to 100,000, but notes that even this figure "would be the equivalent of about 1 million Wide Awakes in the current population of the United States."

49. Ibid.

50. James Russell Lowell, "The Election in November," *Atlantic Monthly*, Oct. 1860.

51. *Bangor Daily Whig and Courier* [Maine], Oct. 20, 1860.

52. *Boston Evening Transcript, Boston Post, Boston Evening Traveler*; all Oct. 17, 1860.

53. *The Liberator*, Oct. 19, 1860; Mayer, *All on Fire*, p. 513.

54. Walter C. Clephane, "The Local Aspect of Slavery in the District of Columbia," *Records of the Columbia Historical Society*, vol. 3 (1900), pp. 253–54.

55. Burlingame, *Abraham Lincoln*, vol. 1, pp. 676–771; Harold Holzer, *Lincoln President-Elect: Abraham Lincoln and the Great Secession Winter 1860–1861* (New York, 2008), pp. 22–31.

56. James M. McPherson, *The Struggle for Equality: Abolitionists and the Negro in Civil War and Reconstruction* (Princeton, 1964), p. 223. Blacks could also vote in New York if they owned $250 in property.

57. *Boston Evening Transcript, Boston Post, Boston Evening Traveler, Boston Daily Advertiser*; all Nov. 7, 1860.

Chapter Two: The Old Gentlemen

1. Mary Beth Corrigan, "Imaginary Cruelties? A History of the Slave Trade in Washington, D.C.," *Washington History*, vol. 13, no. 2 (Fall/Winter, 2001–2), p. 6.

2. *Daily National Intelligencer,* Jan. 11, 1861. The description of Green & Williams's auction house is based on contemporary newspaper advertisements.

3. My account of George Mortimer Bibb (1776–1859) is drawn from the following: *DAB*, vol. I, p. 235; John S. Goff, "The Last Leaf: George Mortimer Bibb," *The Register of the Kentucky Historical Society*, vol. 59, no. 4 (Autumn 1959), pp. 331–42; *Biographical Encyclopaedia of Kentucky* (Cincinnati, 1878), p. 394; John E. Kleber, ed., *The Kentucky Encyclopedia* (Lexington, Ky., 1992), p. 75; *The Constitution* [Washington, D.C.], Apr. 15 and 28, 1859; *Charleston Mercury,* Apr. 19, 1859; *New-York Tribune,* Apr. 28, 1859; *Baltimore Sun,* Apr. 19, 1859; *Daily Confederation* [Montgomery, Ala.], Apr. 20, 1859. Judge Bibb's house, 1404 Thirty-fifth Street, N.W. (formerly 55 Fayette Street), still stands in Washington.

4. *Register of Debates in Congress,* 22nd Congress, 2nd Session, pp. 264–312; *Georgia Telegraph,* Feb. 13, 1833.

5. My description of Willis is in part conjectural, based on the Green & Williams newspaper advertisement and on information about Judge Bibb's own life and habits. The ad describes Willis as thirty-three years old, the late judge's "body servant" and "a good cook and dining room servant, etc." The duties I describe were those typical of an antebellum body servant, especially in an urban setting where the family kept only a few slaves. (The U.S. Census Slave Schedules for 1850 recorded Bibb as owning three slaves in Washington: a twenty-four-year-old woman, a twenty-four-year-old man, and a twenty-three-year-old man. Based on the ages, it is quite possible that one of the two men was Willis.) Bibb's final illness was pneumonia; President Buchanan and cabinet members did attend the funeral at his house on the afternoon of April 17, 1859.

6. George M. Bibb to John B. Bibb, Feb. 24, 1839, quoted in Goff, "The Last Leaf," p. 342.

7. An English visitor in the 1850s, Laurence Oliphant, sniffed that the capital was "a howling wilderness of deserted streets running out into the country and ending nowhere, its population consisting chiefly of politicians and negroes." Alice Oliphant, *Memoir of the Life of Laurence Oliphant and of Alice Oliphant, His Wife* (1892), vol. 1, p. 109, quoted in Mrs. Roger Pryor, *Reminiscences of Peace and War* (New York, 1908), p. 3.

8. Josephine F. Pacheco, *The Pearl: A Failed Slave Rescue Attempt on the Potomac* (Chapel Hill, 2005), pp. 15–18, 23; Frederick Law Olmsted, *A Journey in the Seaboard Slave States, with Remarks on Their Economy* (London, 1856), pp. 12–13; Felicia Bell, " 'The Negroes Alone Work': Enslaved Craftsmen, the Building Trades, and the Construction of the United States Capitol, 1790–1800" (PhD dissertation, Howard University, 2009), p. 235; Margaret Leech, *Reveille in Washington 1860–1865* (New York, 1941), p. 10; William H. Russell, *My Diary North and South* (London, 1863), vol. 1, pp. 32, 50; Randall M. Miller and John David Smith, eds., *Dictionary of Afro-American Slavery,* 2nd ed., (Westport, Conn., 1997), p. 192; *Daily National Intelligencer,* Aug. 29, 1849; June 21, 1850; July 8, 1852.

9. Pacheco, *The Pearl*, p. 20.

10. Ten of the first fifteen U.S. presidents were or had been slaveholders: Washington, Jefferson, Madison, Monroe, Jackson, Van Buren, Harrison, Tyler, Polk, and Taylor. However, Washington never lived in Washington, D.C., and Van Buren and Harrison both freed their slaves long before taking office.

11. Constance McLaughlin Green, *The Secret City: A History of Race Relations in the Nation's Capital* (Princeton, 1967), pp. 41–42; Pacheco, *The Pearl*, pp. 18–24. In fact, Shadd's predecessor at the restaurant, a free black man named Beverly Snow, did spark a riot in 1835 when rumors spread that he had made disrespectful remarks about white women. A mob destroyed the restaurant and almost lynched him; Snow sold the business to Shadd and moved to Canada.

12. Russell, *My Diary*, vol. 1, p. 46.

13. *Daily National Intelligencer*, June 21, 1858.

14. Description based on Josephine Cobb, "Mathew B. Brady's Photographic Gallery in Washington," *Records of the Columbia Historical Society*, vols. 53/56 (1953/56), pp. 28–69.

15. Leech, *Reveille*, p. 19; *Speech of Mr. Clement C. Clay, Jr., of Alabama, on the Contest in Kansas and the Plan and Purpose of Black Republicanism: Delivered in the Senate of the United States on Monday, 21st April, 1856* (Washington, 1856). "The time may not be remote," Clay prophesied, "when one of [Massachusetts's] senators may offer to introduce at one of the levees of the President his sable spouse."

16. Wilmer Carlyle Harris, *Public Life of Zachariah Chandler, 1851–1875* (Chicago, 1917), p. 77.

17. Allan Nevins, *The Ordeal of the Union*, vol. 2: *A House Dividing, 1852–1857*, part I (New York, 1947), pp. 92, 96.

18. James M. McPherson, "The Civil War and the Transformation of America," in William J. Cooper and John M. McCardell, eds., *In the Cause of Liberty: How the Civil War Redefined American Ideals* (Baton Rouge, 2009), p. 5.

19. See, e.g., Claudia Dale Goldin, "The Economics of Emancipation," *The Journal of Economic History*, vol. 33, no. 1 (Mar. 1973), pp. 66–85. Goldin, in her much-cited study, calculates the total value of slaves in 1860 at $2.7 billion. Lincoln, like almost all antislavery politicians, believed strongly before the war (and even, to a diminishing degree, during it) that any emancipation plan must fully compensate slaveholders. Furthermore, he and many other white Americans believed that any such plan ought to provide for the newly emancipated slaves' resettlement in Africa, which would have added (by Goldin's calculations) almost another $400 million to the total cost. Goldin suggests that the ultimate direct and indirect economic costs of the Civil War (let alone its human toll) were higher than compensated emancipation's would have been. This was, of course, impossible to predict in 1860–61. For

Lincoln's estimate, see William Lee Miller, *Arguing About Slavery: The Great Battle in the United States Congress* (New York, 1996), p. 10. See also David Brion Davis, "The Central Fact of American History," *American Heritage*, vol. 56, no. 1 (Feb./Mar. 2005). Davis notes that a single prime fieldhand in 1860 "would sell for the equivalent of a Mercedes-Benz today."

20. George Fitzhugh, *Sociology for the South; Or, the Failure of Free Society* (Richmond, 1854), p. 255; Fitzhugh, "Southern Thought," *DeBow's Review*, vol. 23 (1857), reprinted in Drew Gilpin Faust, ed., *The Ideology of Slavery: Proslavery Thought in the Antebellum South, 1830 to 1860* (Baton Rouge, 1981), p. 279.

21. R. K. Call to J. S. Littell, Feb. 12, 1861, in Frank Moore, ed., *The Rebellion Record; A Diary of American Events* (New York, 1864), vol. 1, pp. 416–20.

22. Mrs. Chapman Coleman, *The Life of John J. Crittenden, with Selections from His Correspondence and Speeches* (Philadelphia, 1871), vol. 2, pp. 362–63; Albert D. Kirwan, *John J. Crittenden: The Struggle for the Union* (Lexington, Ky., 1962), pp. 15, 42, 102, 322–23; Glyndon G. Van Deusen, *William Henry Seward* (New York, 1967), p. 265. See also *New Hampshire Sentinel*, July 8, 1847; "Death of the Hon. J. J. Crittenden," *Proceedings of the Massachusetts Historical Society*, vol. 7 (1863), pp. 139–42. Crittenden, who was not wealthy and had made his career as a lawyer rather than a planter, owned nine slaves in 1860, but never championed the institution. As a state legislator in the 1830s he opposed the importation of slaves into Kentucky. U.S. Census for 1860, Slave Schedules, Franklin County, Ky.; Maury Klein, *Days of Defiance: Sumter, Secession, and the Coming of the Civil War* (New York, 1997), p. 124.

23. Kirwan, *John J. Crittenden*, p. 373; John B. Bibb to JJC, Dec. 16, 1860, in John J. Crittenden Papers, Library of Congress; Winfield Scott to JJC, Oct. 29, 1860, in Crittenden Papers, LC.

24. A. F. Ball to JJC, Jan. 2, 1861; John Grame to JJC, Dec. 8, 1860; F. R. Farrars to JJC, Dec. 31, 1860; Robert H. Looker to JJC, Dec. 24, 1860; "A Southerner & Lover of His Country" to JJC, Dec. 19, 1860; all in Crittenden Papers, LC.

25. F. Burton to JJC, Dec. 1860; Crittenden Papers, LC.

26. Buchanan's papers (archived at the Historical Society of Pennsylvania) contain only one letter from a concerned citizen during this period, although it is possible that others have not survived.

27. John Sherman to Frank Blair, February 9, 1861, quoted in Kenneth Stampp, *And the War Came: The North and the Secession Crisis, 1860–1861* (Baton Rouge, 1950), p. 111.

28. David M. Potter, *The Impending Crisis, 1848–1861* (New York, 1976), p. 522; William W. Freehling, *The Road to Disunion: Secessionists Triumphant, 1854–1861* (New York, 2007), p. 82.

29. Kenneth M. Stampp, *And the War Came: The North and the Secession Crisis, 1860–1861* (Baton Rouge, 1950), pp. 129–30.

30. This was, admittedly, not too different from the tone of Congress during the entire 1859–61 session. When the Japanese envoys sat in the spectators'

gallery in the summer of 1860, they understood little if anything of the debates, but were impressed by all the shouting and gesticulation. One of them compared it in his diary to the Edo fish market.

31. Klein, *Days of Defiance*, p. 127; *Congressional Globe*, 36th Congress, 2nd Session (hereafter *CG*), pp. 3–5; 11–12. Referring to Texas Governor Sam Houston, an outspoken foe of secession, Iverson threatened that "if he does not yield to public sentiment, perhaps some Texan Brutus will arise to rid his country of the hoary-headed incubus that stands between the people and their sovereign will."

32. Russell, *My Diary*, pp. 106–7.

33. Alvy L. King, *Louis T. Wigfall: Southern Fire-Eater* (Baton Rouge, 1970), p. 102.

34. *CG*, pp. 112–14; Kirwan, *John J. Crittenden*, p. 377.

35. *CG*, pp. 115–20; *New York Herald*, Dec. 19, 1860.

36. David Detzer, *Allegiance: Fort Sumter, Charleston, and the Beginning of the Civil War* (New York, 2001), p. 28.

37. The flag from St. Louis was inscribed with the motto "We love the North; we love the East; we love the West; we love the South intensely." Coleman, *The Life of John J. Crittenden*, vol. 2, pp. 240ff.; Nevins, *Ordeal of the Union*, vol. 4, *Prologue to Civil War* (New York, 1947), pp. 392–93; Kirwan, *John J. Crittenden*, pp. 402–03; David M. Potter, *Lincoln and His Party in the Secession Crisis*, 2nd ed. (Baton Rouge, 1995), p. 198; Samuel Eliot Morison, "The Peace Convention of February, 1861," *Proceedings of the Massachusetts Historical Society*, vol. 73 (1961), p. 60.

38. Stampp, *And the War Came*, pp. 124–25; Philip S. Foner, *Business & Slavery: The New York Merchants & the Irrepressible Conflict* (Chapel Hill, 1941), pp. 215–16.

39. Foner, *Business & Slavery*, p. 208, quoting *New York Times*, Dec. 3, 1860, and *New-York Tribune*, Jan. 9, 1861.

40. *Philadelphia Inquirer*, Jan. 4, 1861; *Boston Daily Advertiser*, Jan. 19, 1861; Foner, *Business & Slavery*, p. 266, quoting *Journal of Commerce*, Feb. 6, 1861.

41. Stampp, *And the War Came*, p. 95; Henry Adams, *The Great Secession Winter of 1860–61, and Other Essays* (New York, 1958), p. 7. Adams was in the capital serving as secretary to his father, Rep. Charles Francis Adams, a Republican moderate.

42. Theodore Roosevelt, *New York: A Sketch of the City's Social, Political, and Commercial Progress from the First Dutch Settlement to Recent Times* (New York, 1906), p. 246; Foner, *Business & Slavery*, pp. 286–87, quoting *American Railway Review*, vol. 3, p. 345.

43. *New York Times*, Jan. 22, 1861; Wendell Phillips, *Disunion: Two Discourses at the Music Hall, on January 20th, and February 17th, 1861* (Boston, 1861), pp. 3, 25; *New York Herald*, Jan. 26, 1861; *Boston Daily Advertiser*, Jan. 25, 1861; *Philadelphia Public Ledger*, Jan. 26, 1861. "Carve him out," as a nineteenth-century colloquialism, meant something like "carve him up" or "cut his guts out."

Phillips himself may not have helped matters when he mocked the hecklers from onstage in terms that cast some doubt on his egalitarian principles: "I guess the Irish boys here will earn their holiday pretty well. Perhaps they are glad to be excused from sweeping out their masters' shops to come here and halloo." (*New York Herald*.)

44. *New York Herald*, Jan. 10, 1861; *Evening Patriot* [Madison, Wisc.], Jan. 31, 1861; Coleman, *The Life of John J. Crittenden*, p. 237.

45. King, *Louis T. Wigfall*, p. 104.

46. Allan Nevins and Milton Halsey Thomas, eds., *The Diary of George Templeton Strong: The Civil War, 1860–1865* (New York, 1952), p. 91.

47. Thomas Ricaud Martin, ed., *The Great Parliamentary Battle and Farewell Addresses of the Southern Senators on the Eve of the Civil War* (New York, 1905), p. 171; *CG*, pp. 485–87.

48. In Buchanan's time, it went without saying that only white citizens were welcome. That would change just a few years later. On January 2, 1864, *The New York Times* reported: "Years ago had any colored man presented himself at the White House, at the President's levee, seeking an introduction to the Chief Magistrate of the nation, he would, in all probability, have been roughly handled for his impudence. Yesterday four colored men, of genteel exterior and with the manners of gentlemen, joined in the throng that crowded the Executive mansion, and were presented to the President of the United States." The custom of the New Year's Day levee had been inaugurated by George and Martha Washington (while Philadelphia was the nation's capital) and was maintained by every subsequent president through Herbert Hoover.

49. David Herbert Donald, *Lincoln at Home: Two Glimpses of Abraham Lincoln's Family Life* (New York, 2000), pp. 8–9; Betty C. Monkman, *The White House: Its Historic Furnishings and First Families* (New York, 2000), pp. 111–23; Esther Singleton, *The Story of the White House* (New York, 1907), vol. 2, pp. 56–59; Pryor, *Reminiscences*, pp. 47–53.

50. Donald, *Lincoln at Home*, pp. 8–9; Michael Burlingame, ed., *At Lincoln's Side: John Hay's Correspondence and Selected Writings* (Carbondale, 2008), p. 118; Singleton, *The Story of the White House*, vol. 2, pp. 56–57; *Philadelphia Inquirer*, Jan. 2, 1861; *New York Herald*, Jan. 3, 1861; *Wisconsin Daily Patriot*, Jan. 16, 1861.

51. Pryor, *Reminiscences*, pp. 21–23.

52. Stampp, *And the War Came*, pp. 46–47.

53. Buchanan to Jackson, June 22, 1832, in George Ticknor Curtis, *Life of James Buchanan, Fifteenth President of the United States* (New York, 1883), pp. 142–43.

54. Singleton, *The Story of the White House*, vol. 2, p. 40; *Frank Leslie's Illustrated Newspaper*, March 14, 1857, quoted in Homer T. Rosenberger, "Inauguration of President Buchanan a Century Ago," *Records of the Columbia Historical Society*, vol. 57/59 (1957–59), pp. 104–05.

55. John B. Floyd, Diary, Nov. 7–13, 1860, in Edward A. Pollard, *Lee and His Lieutenants* (New York, 1866), pp. 790–94; Philip Gerald Auchampbaugh, *James Buchanan and His Cabinet on the Eve of Secession* (Lancaster, Pa., 1926), pp. 130–39; James Buchanan, *Mr. Buchanan's Administration on the Eve of the Rebellion* (New York, 1866), pp. 108–14; John Nicolay and John Hay, *Abraham Lincoln: A History* (New York, 1890), vol. 2, pp. 358ff.

56. Quoted in Nevins, *The Ordeal of the Union*, vol. 4, p. 353; Stampp, *And the War Came*, p. 56.

57. Floyd, Diary, Nov. 8, 1860, in Pollard, *Lee and His Lieutenants*, p. 791; "Narrative and Letter of William Henry Trescot, Concerning the Negotiations Between South Carolina and President Buchanan in December, 1860," *American Historical Review*, vol. 13, no. 3 (April 1908), pp. 528–56; Samuel W. Crawford, *The History of the Fall of Fort Sumter, and the Genesis of the Civil War* (New York, 1887), pp. 20–35; Nicolay and Hay, *Abraham Lincoln*, vol. 2, chap. 23, passim; Detzer, *Allegiance*, p. 70.

58. In a self-justification written afterward, Trescot justified his and Floyd's conduct with the rationale that the moment the Union, as a compact of independent states, began to dissolve, the federal government also dissolved. So, he continued complacently, "to apply the words treason and treachery therefore to the conduct of the Southern Members of Mr. B's Cabinet is to borrow a technical language from Foreign Governments which has no true application to the circumstances of our own." (Trescot, "Narrative and Letter," pp. 551–52.)

59. *OR* I, vol. 1, pp. 125–26.

60. Trescot, "Narrative and Letter," pp. 543–44. Not long after, Trescot finally left Washington for good, and stopped on his way out of town to bid farewell to Buchanan's attorney general, the Pennsylvania Unionist Jeremiah Black. As they talked over the events of the past two months, the attorney general admitted amiably that the Southerners had played their hand well until the news came from Sumter. "You nearly beat us," Black said, "but fortunately we had one card left and that was a trump so we beat you" (p. 549).

61. Russell, *My Diary*, pp. 33–34.

62. Dean R. Montgomery, "The Willard Hotels of Washington, D.C., 1847–1968," *Records of the Columbia Historical Society*, vol. 66/68 (1966/68), pp. 277–93. L. E. Chittenden, *Recollections of President Lincoln and His Administration* (New York, 1891), p. 23: "Willard's great hotel, like a parasitic plant, had then grown around and overtaken an old Washington church, which was then called Willard's Hall." Montgomery's article includes a period photograph of the church.

63. Robert Gray Gunderson, *Old Gentlemen's Convention: The Washington Peace Conference of 1861* (Madison, Wisc., 1961), p. 43. Clay, appropriately enough, had enjoyed many a mint julep at Willard's renowned bar.

64. L. E. Chittenden, *A Report on the Debates and Proceedings in the Secret Sessions of the Conference Convention, for Proposing Amendments to the Constitution of*

the United States, Held at Washington, D.C., in February, A.D. 1861 (New York, 1864), p. 14.

65. Henry Adams to Charles Francis Adams, Feb. 13 and 8, 1861, in J. C. Levenson et al., eds., *The Letters of Henry Adams, Volume I: 1858–1868* (Cambridge, Mass., 1982), pp. 229–31.

66. Gunderson, *Old Gentlemen's Convention*, pp. 73–74.

67. Klein, *Days of Defiance*, pp. 355–56; Earl Schenck Miers, *The Great Rebellion: The Emergence of the American Conscience* (New York, 1958), p. 59.

68. Gunderson, *Old Gentlemen's Convention*, p. 10; Nevins, *The Ordeal of the Union*, vol. 4, p. 340; Buchanan Papers, Library of Congress, passim; Chittenden, *A Report on the Debates*, pp. 32–33.

69. *CG*, Feb. 1, 1861, p. 669.

Chapter Three: Forces of Nature

1. *New-York Tribune*, Feb. 18, 1861; *Cincinnati Daily Commercial*, Feb. 13, 1861. See *The Crisis* [Columbus, Ohio], Feb. 14, 1861, for details of the weather and the state of the local crops.

2. James M. McPherson, *For Cause and Comrades: Why Men Fought in the Civil War* (New York, 1997), p. 180.

3. So were some of its most notoriously unsuccessful commanders: McDowell, McClellan, and Burnside.

4. *Ohio State Journal* [Columbus], Feb. 13–14, 1861; *Cincinnati Enquirer*, Feb. 14, 1861.

5. For Garfield's ideas on history, see, e.g., "Germany" (manuscript of undated lecture, circa 1858); Hiram College lecture notes, 1858–61, passim; *Oration Delivered by Hon. J. A. Garfield, at Ravenna, July 4, 1860*. For his purchase of Darwin's *On the Origin of Species*, see invoice to "Prof. Garfield" from J. B. Cobb & Co., Booksellers, Dec. 24, 1859–Mar. 27, 1860. All in James A. Garfield Papers, Library of Congress (hereafter, JAG Papers).

6. Garfield, Oration, pp. 7–8.

7. Margaret Leech and Harry J. Brown, *The Garfield Orbit: The Life of President James A. Garfield* (New York, 1978), pp. 97–98; Allan Peskin, *Garfield: A Biography* (Kent, Ohio, 1978), pp. 76–78; "Wigwam at Columbus, Oct. 5, 1860," partial manuscript of speech in JAG Papers. Garfield had also delivered a well-received, impromptu address at his party's state convention in June; that text has apparently not survived.

8. John Shaw, ed., *Crete and James: Personal Letters of Lucretia and James Garfield* (East Lansing, Mich., 1994), p. 99; "Cousin William" to JAG, Jan. 16, 1861; Mary Garfield Larrabee to JAG, Jan. 29, 1861; both in JAG Papers. *James A. Garfield Papers: A Register of the Collection in the Library of Congress* (Washington, D.C., 2009), p. 5. Not long after Garfield left its faculty, the Eclectic Institute was renamed Hiram College, as it is known today.

9. JAG to Hinsdale, Jan. 15, 1861; Hinsdale to JAG, Feb. 9, 1861; JAG to Lucretia Garfield, Apr. 7, 1861, all in JAG Papers.

10. F. M. Green, A.M., L.L.D., *Hiram College and Western Reserve Eclectic Institute, 1850–1900* (Cleveland, 1901), pp. 101–02; B. A. Hinsdale, A.M., *President Garfield and Education: Hiram College Memorial* (Boston, 1882), pp. 51–57, 126; Harry Rhodes to JAG, Apr. 18, 1859, JAG Papers.

11. "Wigwam at Columbus," JAG Papers; Harry James Brown and Frederick D. Williams, eds., *The Diary of James A. Garfield* (Ann Arbor, 1967), vol. 1, p. 350 (Nov. 6, 1860).

12. *Harper's Weekly,* Mar. 3, 1861; JAG to Burke Aaron Hinsdale, Jan. 15, 1861, in Mary L. Hinsdale, ed., *Garfield-Hinsdale Letters: Correspondence Between James Abram Garfield and Burke Aaron Hinsdale* (Ann Arbor, 1949), p. 54.

13. *New York Times,* Feb. 13, 1861.

14. *Daily Ohio Statesman* [Columbus], Feb. 8, 1860. The paper may have exaggerated in reporting that the three hundred legislators had consumed a thousand bottles of champagne (and it was actually sparkling Catawba wine).

15. Eric J. Cardinal, "The Ohio Democracy and the Crisis of Disunion, 1860–1861," *Ohio History,* vol. 86, no. 1 (Winter 1977), pp. 30–31; *Daily Ohio Statesman,* Jan. 11, 15, and 24, 1861. Confederate troops under General John Hunt Morgan did, in fact, invade Ohio in the summer of 1863, coming within about sixty miles of Columbus.

16. Robert Gray Gunderson, *Old Gentlemen's Convention: The Washington Peace Conference of 1861* (Madison, Wisc., 1961), p. 36.

17. JAG to Lucretia Garfield, Jan. 13, 1861, in Shaw, *Crete and James,* pp. 106–07. Garfield's roommate, Jacob D. Cox—the two young men actually shared a bed while the legislature was in session—would go on to become a prominent Union general, and eventually U.S. secretary of the interior under President Grant.

18. *Ohio State Journal,* Feb. 14, 1861; *New York Times,* n.d., reprinted in *Cincinnati Daily Commercial,* Feb. 20, 1861.

19. *Ohio State Journal,* Feb. 14, 1861; *New York Herald,* Feb. 14, 1861.

20. *Baltimore Sun,* Feb. 15, 1861; *Cincinnati Daily Enquirer,* Feb. 14, 1861; *Philadelphia Press,* n.d., reprinted in *Daily Ohio Statesman,* Feb. 16, 1861; *Cincinnati Daily Commercial,* Feb. 16, 1861.

21. JAG to Lucretia Garfield, Feb. 17, 1861, in Shaw, *Crete and James,* p. 107; *Ohio State Journal,* Feb. 14, 1861.

22. *Daily Capital City Fact* [Columbus, Oh.], Feb. 14, 1861; JAG to Lucretia Garfield, Feb. 17, 1861, in Shaw, *Crete and James,* p. 107.

23. *Daily Capital City Fact,* Feb. 14, 1861; JAG to Lucretia Garfield, Feb. 17, 1861, in Shaw, *Crete and James,* p. 107; JAG to Burke Aaron Hinsdale, Feb. 17, 1861, in Mary L. Hinsdale, *Garfield-Hinsdale Letters,* pp. 56–57.

24. *Albany Journal* [N.Y.], Feb. 15, 1861; *Philadelphia Inquirer,* Feb. 15, 1861.

25. Green, *Hiram College,* pp. 101–02; B. A. Hinsdale, *President Garfield and*

Education, pp. 51–57, 126; lecture notes headed "Alliance Nov 1859," JAG Papers.

26. Green, *Hiram College*, pp. 101–02; B. A. Hinsdale, *President Garfield and Education*, pp. 51–57; J. H. Rhodes in B. A. Hinsdale, p. 126.

27. Ironically, James Buchanan, too, had been born in a log cabin—though in his case, it failed to become part of his political persona.

28. The region was originally known as the Connecticut Western Reserve, since it was claimed by that state under colonial charters. Although Connecticut relinquished its jurisdiction to the federal government, it retained title to the land itself, which it sold to a joint-stock company in order to pay off Revolutionary War debts.

29. Clarence Walworth Alvord, *Governor Edward Coles* (Springfield, Ill., 1920), pp. 43–44. Coles (who inherited the slaves from his father) had been President Madison's private secretary, and tried unsuccessfully to persuade both Madison and Jefferson to emancipate their slaves. He later became governor of Illinois.

30. Frederic A. Ogg, *The Old Northwest: A Chronicle of the Ohio Valley and Beyond* (New Haven, 1919), pp. 98–99; Peskin, *Garfield*, pp. 3–6; J. M. Bundy, *The Life of General James A. Garfield* (New York, 1880), pp. 2–3; Robert I. Cottom, "To Be Among the First: The Early Career of James A. Garfield, 1831–1868" (PhD diss., Johns Hopkins University, 1975), pp. 3–4.

31. For thirty-three-year-old Abram Garfield, it was a case of "chills" brought on by exposure while fighting a late-autumn forest fire. The inept ministrations of a frontier doctor, who tried to draw out the evil humors by raising large blisters on Abram's throat, provided the coup de grâce.

32. David Van Tassel, *"Beyond Bayonets": The Civil War in Northern Ohio* (Kent, Ohio, 2006), p. 1; Frances Trollope, quoted in Andrew R. L. Cayton, *Ohio: The History of a People* (Columbus, 2002). Cayton's book is a fine social and cultural history of the state from statehood to the present, and I have drawn from it substantially in my descriptions of nineteenth-century Ohio.

33. Cayton, *Ohio*, pp. 75–76.

34. Peskin, *Garfield*, p. 9; Henry K. Shaw, *Buckeye Disciples: A History of the Disciples of Christ in Ohio* (St. Louis, 1952), pp. 13–14, 126, 140–44; Frederick Bonner, quoted in Cayton, *Ohio*, p. 39; Leech and Brown, *The Garfield Orbit*, p. 12; A. S. Hayden, *Early History of the Disciples in the Western Reserve, Ohio* (Cincinnati, 1875), pp. 39, 454. The early Disciples shunned the terms "sect" and "denomination," preferring to speak of "our communion" or "our brotherhood" (Shaw, p. 116).

35. Hayden, *Early History*, pp. 52–53. Campbell died on March 4, 1866—which his most loyal followers accepted as a fulfillment of the prophecy.

36. This is based on Smith's own detailed account. The Disciples disputed his version of events.

37. Peskin, *Garfield*, p. 13; Brown and Williams, eds., *The Diary of James A. Garfield*, vol. 1, p. 36. The Disciples, like many American evangelical

denominations, did not believe in infant baptism or "sprinkling," maintaining that Christian conversion must instead involve the conscious decision of a penitent believer.

38. W. W. Wasson, *James A. Garfield: His Religion and Education*, (Nashville, 1952), pp. 6–14; Shaw, *Buckeye Disciples*, pp. 21, 41, 72ff.

39. Wasson, *James A. Garfield*, p. 51; "Hiram Nov 29/60," lecture notes in JAG Papers; B. A. Hinsdale, *President Garfield and Education*, p. 71.

40. Cf. Daniel Walker Howe, *What Hath God Wrought: The Transformation of America, 1815–1848* (New York, 2008), chap. 5.

41. Shaw, *Buckeye Disciples*, p. 191; Wasson, *James A. Garfield*, pp. 56–61.

42. *Portage County Democrat* [Ohio], Mar. 5, 1862.

43. Horatio Alger, Jr., *From Canal Boy to President, or the Boyhood and Manhood of James A. Garfield* (New York, 1881). The future president was born in November 1831, the future novelist in January 1832.

44. JAG to Burke Hinsdale, Aug. 7, 1857, in Mary Hinsdale, *Garfield-Hinsdale Letters*, p. 22. For a carefully researched and sensitively written study of Garfield's early years, see Hendrik Booraem, *The Road to Respectability: James A. Garfield and His World, 1844–1852* (Lewisburg, Ohio, 1988).

45. Wasson, *James A. Garfield*, p. 41; "Lecture at Hiram Before Gents & Ladies, Sep 19, 1860," JAG Papers. For Emerson's extremely wide-reaching influence on young men in the antebellum years, see Thomas Augst, *The Clerk's Tale: Young Men and Moral Life in Nineteenth-Century America* (Chicago, 2003), chap. 3; David Leverenz, "The Politics of Emerson's Man-Making Words," *PMLA*, vol. 101, no. 1 (Jan. 1986), pp. 38–56. For the prewar Northern ideology of individualism, personal freedom, and egalitarianism, see Earl J. Hess, *Liberty, Virtue, and Progress: Northerners and Their War for the Union* (New York, 1997), esp. ch. 1.

46. See Booraem, *The Road to Respectability*, pp. 204–05.

47. Charles C. Cole, Jr., *A Fragile Capital: Identity and the Early Years of Columbus, Ohio* (Columbus, 2001), pp. 219–20.

48. JAG to Harry Rhodes, Sept. 22, 1858, and Feb. 3, 1859; Rhodes to JAG, July 1862; all in JAG Papers. Cotton's "To Be Among the First" pointed me to these letters. James and Lucretia Garfield did eventually develop a close emotional bond, although their marriage was tested in the mid-1860s when she discovered his affair with Lucia Calhoun, a young *New York Times* reporter.

49. JAG to A. H. Pettibone, May 3, 1859, JAG Papers.

50. JAG, draft editorial, March 1861, JAG Papers; *Sandusky Register*, Nov. 24, 1860; *Albany Journal*, Oct. 4, 1860; *Fall River News*, Feb. 14, 1861, quoted in *New-York Tribune*, Feb. 16, 1861.

51. Gerald Carson, "Hair Today, Gone Tomorrow," *American Heritage*, Feb. 1966; *Baltimore Sun*, Apr. 30, 1844; *Constitution* [Middletown, Conn.], Mar. 12, 1856; *The Congregationalist* (n.d.), quoted in *Charleston Mercury*, Feb. 27, 1857.

52. *Constitution* [Washington, D.C.], Apr. 7, 1860; *New Orleans Picayune*, Apr. 24, 1853; Christopher Oldstone-Moore, "The Beard Movement in Victorian Britain," *Victorian Studies*, vol. 48, no. 1 (2005), pp. 7–34; Susan Walton, "From Squalid Impropriety to Manly Respectability: The Revival of Beards, Moustaches, and Martial Values in the 1850s in England," *Nineteenth-Century Contexts*, vol. 30, no. 3 (Sept. 2008), pp. 229–45.

53. The classic account of this ideology and its rapid development is Eric Foner's *Free Soil, Free Labor, Free Men: The Ideology of the Republican Party Before the Civil War* (2nd ed., New York, 1995).

54. Foner, *Free Soil*, pp. 302–03; Eric J. Cardinal, "The Ohio Democracy," p. 29 note.

55. Booraem, *The Road to Respectability*, pp. 138–40. The sudden death of President Taylor in 1850 drew only a passing mention in Garfield's diary.

56. Peskin, *Garfield*, pp. 33–34; Cottom, pp. 63–64. Garfield, according to Cottom, was also influenced by an incident in November 1855 when a mob of Southern students attacked an antislavery meeting at a Disciple college in Virginia.

57. Allan Peskin, *Garfield*, pp. 60–61. His entry into electoral politics arose in a most unlikely way, with the sudden death of a sixty-two-year-old shop-keeper named Cyrus Prentiss. Until his inconvenient demise, the worthy Mr. Prentiss had been local Republicans' handpicked choice for the district seat in the Ohio Senate. But only three weeks before the nominating convention, the party chieftains of the 26th District were without a nominee. They settled on Garfield, who had won a degree of popularity with his sermons, lectures, and leadership of the college. Robert C. Brown et al., *History of Portage County, Ohio* (Chicago, 1885), p. 829; Charles J. F. Binney, *History and Genealogy of the Prentice, or Prentiss Family in New England Etc.* (Boston, 1883), p. 368.

58. JAG to Rhodes, Jan. 9, 1859, quoted in Brown and Williams, *The Diary of James A. Garfield*, p. xxviii.

59. In October 1860, the master's daughter had taken Bagby with her on a short trip across the Pennsylvania border; while there, Bagby managed to escape, first to Pittsburgh and then to Cleveland.

60. John E. Vacha, "The Case of Sara Lucy Bagby: A Late Gesture," *Ohio History*, vol. 76, no. 4 (Autumn 1967), p. 224; *Cleveland Herald*, Jan. 19, 1861, reprinted in *Cincinnati Daily Commercial*, Jan. 21, 1861; Judith Luckett, "Local Studies and Larger Issues: The Case of Sara Bagby," *Teaching History*, vol. 27, no. 2 (Fall 2002), pp. 88–89; *Anti-Slavery Bugle* (Salem, Ohio), Jan. 26, 1861. Rumor in the local African-American community held that Bagby had been betrayed by a black woman named Graves, who, for an unknown motive, had written to Bagby's master informing him of her whereabouts. (*Cleveland Herald*, Jan. 19, 1861.)

61. *Cleveland Herald*, Jan. 19, 1861, reprinted in *Cincinnati Daily Commercial*, Jan. 21, 1861.

62. *Cincinnati Daily Commercial*, Jan. 23, 1861; *Cleveland Leader*, Jan. 22, 1861, reprinted in *Anti-Slavery Bugle*, Feb. 2, 1861; John Malvin, *Autobiography of John Malvin* (Cleveland, 1879), pp. 37–38; Vacha, "The Case of Sara Lucy Bagby," p. 227; William Cheek and Annie Lee Cheek, *John Mercer Langston and the Fight for Black Freedom, 1829–1865* (Urbana, Ill., 1989), pp. 373–74.

63. *Cincinnati Daily Commercial*, Jan. 23, 1861; *Cleveland Leader*, Jan. 21, 1861, reprinted in *Anti-Slavery Bugle*, Feb. 2, 1861. After the affair was over, a group of abolitionist women sent thirty pieces of silver to the *Leader*'s editor, with a note identifying them as "Judas's Reward." Luckett, "Local Studies," p. 90.

64. *Cleveland Herald*, n.d., in *Anti-Slavery Bugle*, Jan. 24, 1861.

65. Vacha, "The Case of Sara Lucy Bagby," pp. 227–28. Spalding seems to have moderated his position of a few years earlier. At the 1856 Republican National Convention, he is reported to have said, "In the case of the alternative being presented, of the continuance of slavery or the dissolution of the Union, I am for dissolution, and I care not how quick it comes." *United States Review*, Oct. 1859, p. 207.

66. *Cleveland Leader*, Jan. 24, 1861, reprinted in *Anti-Slavery Bugle*, Feb. 2, 1861; Vacha, "The Case of Sara Lucy Bagby," p. 229; *Daily Capital City Fact*, Jan. 24, 1861.

67. *Cincinnati Daily Commercial*, Jan. 26, 1861; *Cleveland Leader*, Jan. 25, 1861, reprinted in *Anti-Slavery Bugle*, Feb. 2, 1861.

68. Booraem, "The Road to Respectability," pp. 130–31; Cottom, "To Be Among the First," p. 60, note; Brown and Williams, eds., *The Diary of James A. Garfield*, vol. 1, pp. 290, 344–45 (Oct. 6, 1857, and Dec. 2, 1859).

69. Peskin, *Garfield*, p. 58.

70. Dorothy Sterling, *Ahead of Her Time: Abby Kelley and the Politics of Antislavery* (New York, 1991), pp. 1, 14, 213–14; Douglas Andrew Gamble, "Moral Suasion in the West: Garrisonian Abolition, 1831–1861" (PhD diss., Ohio State University, 1973), pp. 12–13; *The Liberator*, June 27, 1845; C. B. Galbreath, "The Anti-Slavery Movement in Columbiana County," *Ohio History*, vol. 30, no. 4 (Oct. 1921), p. 370. One of Kelley's companions on the journey, F. F. Stebbins, reported back to Garrison that he found among the Ohioans "far more candor, and less blinding prejudice, than farther east, and of course more willingness to discuss fairly, and arrive at the truth. . . . A willingness exists in the minds of the people to hear and investigate; and we find those who will, we trust, be true to the cause." (*The Liberator*, June 27, 1845.)

71. Sterling, *Ahead of Her Time*, p. 214. The full quotation on the masthead continued, "the alarm bell which startles the inhabitants of a city keeps them from being burned in their beds."

72. Gamble, "Moral Suasion," pp. 18, 24; Galbreath, "The Anti-Slavery Movement," p. 380 (citing the *New Lisbon Palladium*, n.d.), pp. 383–85. Abby Kelley Salem remained in town for many years to come.

73. Harriet Beecher Stowe, *Uncle Tom's Cabin* (New York, 1995), p. 73.

74. Francis Phelps Weisenburger, *Columbus During the Civil War* (Columbus, 1963), p. 4.

75. John T. Cumbler, *From Abolitionism to Rights for All: The Making of a Reform Community in the Nineteenth Century* (Philadelphia, 2008), p. 57; James Brewer Stewart, *Joshua R. Giddings and the Tactics of Radical Politics* (Cleveland, 1970), p. 275.

76. In the 1870s, Garfield remarked privately that he did not want to buy a house on Capitol Hill in Washington because the neighborhood was "infested" with Negroes and that he "never could get in love with the creatures."

77. Foner, *Free Soil*, pp. 265–66.

78. Susan-Mary Grant, *North over South: Northern Nationalism and American Identity in the Antebellum Era* (Lawrence, Kans., 2000), pp. 105–07.

79. *New-York Tribune*, April 12, 1865, quoted in Foner, *Free Soil*, p. 310.

80. Frank L. Klement, *The Limits of Dissent: Clement L. Vallandigham and the Civil War* (New York, 1998), p. 18.

81. "Lecture 11th, April 21st 1859: Contrast & resemblances between North & South," JAG Papers. In another lecture, Garfield suggested that the natural fault lines in the Old World ran between East and West, while those in the New World ran between North and South. ("Lect 2, Jan 27th 1859: Physical Geography," JAG Papers.)

82. Burke A. Hinsdale to JAG, Feb. 13, 1861; JAG to Hinsdale, Feb. 17, 1861; both in JAG Papers.

83. JAG to Hinsdale, Jan. 15, 1861, JAG Papers.

84. *National Anti-Slavery Standard*, Mar. 30 and Apr. 6, 1861.

85. Burlingame, *Abraham Lincoln*, vol. 2, pp. 15–35.

86. Ibid., pp. 36–7; *New York Times*, Feb. 26, 1861.

87. Margaret Leech, *Reveille in Washington, 1861–1865* (New York, 1941), p. 35; *Philadelphia Inquirer*, Feb. 23, 1861.

88. 36th Congress, 2nd Session, Report No. 79, "Alleged Hostile Organization Against the Government Within the District of Columbia," pp. 3–8; Leech, pp. 28–30.

89. Kirwan, *John J. Crittenden: The Struggle for the Union* (Louisville, Ky., 1962), pp. 405–06; *The Liberator*, Mar. 15, 1861. The humorist was Matthew Whittier (younger brother of the poet John Greenleaf Whittier), who wrote under the pen name Ethan Spike.

90. Klein, *Days of Defiance*, p. 273; Burlingame, *Abraham Lincoln*, vol. 2, p. 41.

91. Frederick Douglass, "The Inaugural Address," *Douglass' Monthly*, April 1861, in Philip Foner, ed., *The Life and Writings of Frederick Douglass* (New York, 1952), vol. 3, p. 71.

92. *Cincinnati Daily Commercial*, Feb. 26 and 27, 1861; David M. Potter, *The Impending Crisis, 1848–1861* (New York, 1976), pp. 562–63; Henry Adams, "The Great Secession Winter of 1860–61," in George Hochfield, ed., *The Great Secession Winter of 1860–61 and Other Essays by Henry Adams* (New York, 1958), pp. 25–29; Burlingame, *Abraham Lincoln*, vol. 2, pp. 98–99.

93. Francis Bail Pearson, *Ohio History Sketches* (Columbus, 1903), pp. 139ff.; Edward Deering Mansfield, *Personal Memories, Social, Political, and Literary* (Cincinnati, 1879), pp. 219ff.; "Ohio Governors: Thomas Corwin, 1840–1842," Ohio Historical Society website, www.ohiohistory.org; Potter, *Lincoln and His Party*, p. 37; "Thomas Corwin, of Ohio, by a Buckeye," *Holden's Dollar Magazine*, vol. 5, no. 2 (Feb. 1850), pp. 97ff.

94. Potter, *The Impending Crisis*, pp. 530–31; Stampp, *And the War Came*, p. 131. The actual Thirteenth Amendment, of course, would be the one that abolished slavery in 1865.

95. Since the Corwin amendment was passed by the House and Senate, it is still technically pending and could be ratified with the support of thirty-three states.

96. Klein, *Days of Defiance*, pp. 305–09; Burlingame, *Abraham Lincoln*, vol. 2, p. 47; *Philadelphia Inquirer*, Mar. 4, 1861; *New York Herald*, Mar. 5, 1861; *CG*, 36th Congress, 2nd Session, pp. 1375ff.; *Boston Daily Advertiser*, Mar. 6, 1861.

97. Burlingame, *Abraham Lincoln*, vol. 2, pp. 60–62; William Lee Miller, *President Lincoln: The Duty of a Statesman* (New York, 2008), p. 13.

98. The original draft of the First Inaugural is in the Library of Congress, and is reproduced on its website at www.loc.gov/exhibits/treasures.

99. Douglass, "The Inaugural Address," in Foner, *Life and Writings*, pp. 72ff.; Burlingame, unedited version of *Abraham Lincoln* (online at www.knox.edu/documents/pdfs/LincolnStudies), pp. 2230–01. Douglass continued: "Some thought we had in Mr. Lincoln the nerve and decision of an Oliver Cromwell; but the result shows that we have merely a continuation of the Pierces and Buchanans, and that the Republican President bends his knee to slavery as readily as any of his infamous predecessors." In chastising Lincoln on his pledge to enforce fugitive-slave laws, he also referred to the Bagby case: "The hunting down [of] a few slaves, the sending back of a few Lucy Bagleys [*sic*], young and beautiful though they be, to the lust and brutality of the Border States, is to the rapacity of the rebels only as a drop of water upon a house in flames."

100. *CG*, p. 1378.

101. Burlingame, *Abraham Lincoln*, vol. 2, pp. 69ff. Months later, just after the Battle of Bull Run, Lincoln would remark that the tussle over the Bloomington position had caused him more annoyance than any other event of his presidency so far.

102. Nelson D. Lankford, *Cry Havoc! The Crooked Road to the Civil War, 1861* (New York, 2007), pp. 35–36; Kirwan, *John J. Crittenden*, p. 425ff; Gunderson, *Old Gentlemen's Convention*, pp. 95–96.

103. *Daily National Intelligencer*, Mar. 6, 1861; Lankford, *Cry Havoc!*, p. 35.

104. Report of the Select Committee on Weights and Measures, April 10, 1861, in JAG Papers.

105. *Cincinnati Gazette*, n.d., quoted in *Ohio Statesman*, Feb. 28, 1861.

106. Jacob Dolson Cox, *Military Reminiscences of the Civil War* (New York, 1900), vol. 1, p. 2.

Chapter Four: A Shot in the Dark

Epigraph: "Rise, Lurid Stars" is a poem in fragmentary form, unpublished in Whitman's lifetime. The manuscript is at Yale, which dates it to 1881, but Ted Genoways, *Walt Whitman and the Civil War: America's Poet During the Last Years of 1860–1862* (Berkeley, Calif., 2009), more convincingly proposes a date in the early months of 1861 (pp. 89–90).

1. James Chester, "Inside Sumter in '61," in *Battles and Leaders of the Civil War* (New York, 1887), vol. 1, pp. 65–66; Abner Doubleday, *Reminiscences of Forts Sumter and Moultrie in 1860–'61* (New York, 1876), pp. 141–42; E. Milby Burton, *The Siege of Charleston, 1861–1865* (Columbia, S.C., 1970), pp. 42–43; Ron Chepesiuk, ed., "Eye Witness to Fort Sumter: The Letters of Private John Thompson," *South Carolina Historical Magazine*, vol. 85, no. 4 (Oct. 1984). For the firing of 10-inch mortar shells: *The Story of One Regiment: The Eleventh Maine Infantry Volunteers in The War of the Rebellion* (New York, 1896), p. 155; also videos of historic artillery fire posted on YouTube.com by Springfield Arsenal, LLC.

2. *OR* I, vol. 1, p. 211; Samuel Wylie Crawford, *The History of the Fall of Fort Sumter, and the Genesis of the Civil War* (New York, 1887), pp. 398–99.

3. SWC to A. J. Crawford, Jan. 17, 1861, Samuel Wylie Crawford Papers, LC.

4. Eba Anderson Lawton, *Major Robert Anderson and Fort Sumter, 1861* (New York, 1911), p. 9.

5. Doubleday, *Reminiscences*, pp. 128–29.

6. *OR* I, vol. 1, pp. 197–202; W. A. Swanberg, *First Blood: The Story of Fort Sumter* (New York, 1957), p. 214; SWC Diary, Feb. 28, 1861, SWC Papers.

7. *OR* I, vol. 1, pp. 198–200.

8. Crawford, *History of the Fall*, pp. 375–76; Thomas Barthel, *Abner Doubleday: A Civil War Biography* (Jefferson, N.C., 2010), p. 65; SWC Diary, Apr. 3, 1861, SWC Papers.

9. Edward McPherson, *The Political History of the United States During the Great Rebellion* (Washington, D.C., 1882), pp. 27–28; Bruce Catton, *The Coming Fury* (New York, 1961), pp. 226–29; Caroline Baldwin Darrow, "Recollections of the Twiggs Surrender," in *BLCW*, vol. 1, pp. 33–35; *OR* I, vol. 1, p. 191.

10. Crawford, *History of the Fall*, pp. 290–91; David Detzer, *Allegiance: Fort Sumter, Charleston, and the Beginning of the Civil War* (New York, 2001), pp. 206–07. While a young officer during the Mexican War, Beauregard had famously persuaded the senior generals to change their plans for capturing the citadel of Chapultepec, the climactic action of the war.

11. SWC Diary, Mar. 7, 1861, SWC Papers.

12. Detzer, *Allegiance*, p. 208; Swanberg, *First Blood*, p. 251; Doubleday, *Remi-*

niscences, p. 131; SWC Diary, Feb. 10, 1861; Anderson to Miss HL, Mar. 28, 1861, copy in SWC Papers.

13. Doubleday, *Reminiscences*, p. 99; Swanberg, *First Blood*, pp. 139–40; *Albany Journal*, Apr. 20, 1861.

14. The men did receive many letters from acquaintances and total strangers telling them what ought to be done. A long-lost boyhood friend wrote to Samuel Crawford in early April, expressing himself with a crude play on words: "For Heaven's sake don't evacuate! For my sake, for your Country's sake, don't evacuate! . . . The word evacuation should never be mentioned except in connection with the intestinal canal." (J. B. Dillingham to SWC, April 10, 1861, in SWC Papers.)

15. Doubleday, *Reminiscences*, pp. 34, 133; Crawford, *History of the Fall*, p. 295; Doubleday to Mary Doubleday, Mar. 29, 1861 (fragment), in Abraham Lincoln Papers, LC; Barthel, *Abner Doubleday*, p. 66; SWC Diary, Mar. 1, 1861, SWC Papers.

16. Crawford, *History of the Fall*, p. 297; Chester, "Inside Sumter in '61," pp. 53–55; Doubleday, *Reminiscences*, p. 122; SWC Diary, Mar. 9, 1861, SWC Papers; *OR* I, vol. 1, p. 273.

17. Barthel, *Abner Doubleday*, p. 64; SWC Diary, Feb. 28, 1861, SWC Papers; *OR* I, vol. 1, pp. 219–21. The previous summer, Sumter had been used as a temporary detention camp for hundreds of Africans captured by a naval patrol aboard an illegal slave ship.

18. See Edward M. Coffman, *The Old Army: A Portrait of the American Army in Peacetime, 1784–1898* (New York, 1986), esp. chap. 2; also John C. Waugh, *Class of 1846: From West Point to Appomattox: Stonewall Jackson, George McClellan, and Their Brothers* (New York, 1994); Detzer, *Allegiance*, p. 21.

19. *DAB*; Abner Doubleday to Ralph Walso Emerson, Aug. 16, 1845, Ralph Waldo Emerson Papers, Houghton Library, Harvard University.

20. For these and many of Doubleday's other after-dinner tales, see Joseph E. Chance, ed., *My Life in the Old Army: The Reminiscences of Abner Doubleday from the Collections of the New-York Historical Society* (Fort Worth, Tex., 1998).

21. Doubleday's father grew up in Cooperstown, but there is no evidence that his son ever even visited the town, which would have entailed a 125-mile journey over bad roads from Auburn. Abner was born in Ballston Spa, Saratoga County, and moved to Auburn with his family at the age of one. Throughout the time when he is said to have been in Cooperstown inventing baseball, he was actually at West Point as a cadet. The legend seems to have sprung up more than a decade after his death in 1893. When the millionaire sporting-goods magnate Albert G. Spalding hired researchers to "prove" that baseball had red-blooded American origins, they produced an old man in Colorado who told a vaguely recollected version of the Doubleday-at-Cooperstown myth. Spalding, and the general public, seized upon it immediately: what better origin for the national game? See Barthel,

Abner Doubleday, esp. chap. 25; and Joan Smith Bartlett, *Abner Doubleday: His Life and Times* (n.p., 2009), p. 17.

22. "The National Game. Three 'Outs' and One 'Run.' Abraham Winning the Ball," Prints and Photographs Division, LC; *New York Herald,* Jan. 23, 1857, and Oct. 16, 1859; Crawford Diary, Mar. 1, 1861, SWC Papers.

23. Within months, in fact, Crawford would trade his surgeon's insignia for the oak leaves of an infantry major, and would go on to be brevetted major general.

24. Richard Wagner, *For Honor, Flag, and Family: Civil War Major General Samuel W. Crawford, 1827–1892* (Shippensburg, Pa., 2005); Detzer, *Allegiance,* pp. 43–44; SWC to A. J. Crawford, Mar. 4, 1861, Dec. 12, 1860; both in SWC Papers. Crawford's book would not be published for more than a quarter century, but it remains an indispensible account of the Sumter crisis.

25. Detzer, *Allegiance,* pp. 41–42; Doubleday, *Reminiscences,* p. 22; *The Drawings and Watercolors of Truman Seymour* (Scranton, Pa., 1986), passim; William A. Ellis, *Norwich University: Her History, Her Graduates, Her Roll of Honor* (Concord, N.H., 1898), pp. 258–60; *Twenty-First Annual Reunion of the Association of Graduates of the United States Military Academy at West Point, New York, June 12th, 1890* (Saginaw, Mich., 1890), pp. 35–37.

26. Doubleday, *Reminiscences,* p. 126. Many years later, Doubleday wrote of Anderson, "Unfortunately, he desired not only to save the Union, but to save slavery along with it. Without this, he considered the contest as hopeless. In this spirit he submitted to everything, and delayed all action in the expectation that Congress would make some new and more binding compromise which would restore peace to the country. He could not read the signs of the times, and see that the conscience of the nation and the progress of civilization had already doomed slavery to destruction" (*Reminiscences,* p. 90).

27. Ibid., p. 126.

28. Barthel, *Abner Doubleday,* pp. 66–69.

29. Detzer, *Allegiance,* pp. 16–17; "A Scene at the Battle of the Bad Axe," *The New Yorker,* Mar. 23, 1839; Kerry A. Trask, *Black Hawk: The Battle for the Heart of America* (New York, 2006), pp. 270–71.

30. Barthel, *Abner Doubleday,* pp. 57, 66–69.

31. SWC to A. J. Crawford, Mar. 4, 1861. SWC Papers.

32. Barthel, *Abner Doubleday,* pp. 68–69; SWC Diary, Mar. 1 and 15, 1861, SWC Papers.

33. SWC Diary, Mar. 6, 1861, SWC Papers.

34. Ibid.

35. SWC to A. J. Crawford, Mar. 19, 23, and 30, 1861; *Report of the Sick and Wounded for the Quarter Ending March 31, 1861;* all in SWC Papers; AD to Mary Doubleday, Apr. 2, 1861, in Abraham Lincoln Papers, LC.

36. SWC to A. J. Crawford, Apr. 9, 1861; Foster to Capt. Lewis Robertson, Mar. 26, 1861; both in SWC Papers. *OR* I, vol. 1, p. 241; Michael Burl-

ingame, unedited version of *Abraham Lincoln* (online at www.knox.edu/documents.pdfs/LincolnStudies), p. 237. Lincoln apparently never saw action in the war, and left the militia some weeks before the Bad Axe massacre.

37. SWC Diary, Apr. 8, 1861, SWC Papers; Crawford, *History of the Fall*, pp. 382–83; Doubleday, *Reminiscences*, p. 140; Maury Klein, *Days of Defiance: Sumter, Secession, and the Coming of the Civil War* (New York, 1997), p. 400; Detzer, *Allegiance*, pp. 245–46.

38. SWC to A. J. Crawford, Apr. 9, 1861, SWC Papers.

39. SWC Diary, Apr. 9, 1861; *OR* I, vol. 1, p. 235.

40. Elizabeth Todd Grimsley, "Six Months in the White House," *Journal of the Illinois State Historical Society*, vol. 19, nos. 3–4 (Oct. 1926–Jan. 1927), p. 50; Russell, *My Diary*, pp. 41–45; William Seale, *The President's House: A History*, 2nd ed. (Baltimore, 2008), vol. 1, pp. 356–58; Margaret Leech, *Reveille in Washington, 1860–1865* (New York, 1941), pp. 51–52; William Seale, *The White House: The History of an American Idea* (Washington, D.C., 1992), p. 108.

41. Russell, *My Diary*, pp. 42–44. The full story of what happened that evening between Lincoln and Scott was carefully reconstructed for the first time by Russell McClintock in *Lincoln and the Decision for War: The Northern Response to Secession* (Chapel Hill, N.C., 2008), chap. 9.

42. Erasmus Darwin Keyes, *Fifty Years' Observations of Events, Civil and Military* (New York, 1884), pp. 377–79; McClintock, *Lincoln and the Decision*, pp. 201–03, 212; John S. D. Eisenhower, *Agent of Destiny: The Life and Times of General Winfield Scott* (New York, 1997), pp. 358–60.

43. McClintock, *Lincoln and the Decision*, pp. 205–19; David M. Potter, *The Impending Crisis 1848–1861* (New York, 1976), pp. 572–75.

44. Eisenhower, *Agent of Destiny*, p. 360; McClintock, *Lincoln and the Decision*, pp. 229–30; *OR* I, vol. 1, 201–02.

45. McClintock, *Lincoln and the Decision*, p. 230; Wendy Wolff, ed., *A Capitol Builder: The Shorthand Diaries of Montgomery C. Meigs, 1853–1859, 1861* (Washington, D.C., 2001), p. 776.

46. Scott had been close to Anderson for at least twenty years. In 1842, he stood in for Anderson's father-in-law by giving away the bride at Anderson's wedding to Eliza Clinch. Detzer, *Allegiance*, p. 24.

47. McClintock, *Lincoln and the Decision*, pp. 229–30; Keyes, *Fifty Years' Observations*, p. 378.

48. Russell, *My Diary*, p. 43.

49. Burlingame, *Abraham Lincoln*, vol. 2, pp. 108–09.

50. Potter, *The Impending Crisis*, pp. 571–72; *Wisconsin Daily Patriot*, Mar. 21, 1861; *The Argus* (Easton, Pa.), n.d., quoted in *Macon Daily Telegraph* [Georgia], Apr. 1, 1861.

51. McClintock, *Lincoln and the Decision*, p. 222.

52. Crawford, *History of the Fall*, pp. 348–49, 369–73; Detzer, *Allegiance*, pp. 226–29; *OR* I, vol. 1, 211, Robert Means Thompson and Richard Wain-

wright, eds., *Confidential Correspondence of Gustavus Vasa Fox* (Freeport, N.Y., 1972), vol. 1, pp. 3ff.

53. John G. Nicolay and John Hay, *Abraham Lincoln: A History* (New York, 1891), vol. 3, p. 443.

54. McClintock, *Lincoln and the Decision*, pp. 231–33.

55. Fox was, in fact, not as inept as his role in the Sumter crisis made him seem. He later served ably as Lincoln's assistant secretary of the navy. And, though his Sumter plan may have been misconceived, he would prove remarkably clear-sighted at least once in his life. In 1882, Fox, an avid amateur historian, undertook to locate the long-disputed landing point of Christopher Columbus in the New World, finally deciding on Samana Cay, an uninhabited islet in the Bahamas. Fox's theory was almost wholly ignored for more than a century, but in 1986, a *National Geographic* study found he was correct, and Samana Cay is now accepted by many historians as the site of Columbus's landfall.

56. Burlingame, *Abraham Lincoln*, vol. 2, pp. 108–09.

57. See Shenk, *Lincoln's Melancholy.*

58. Blair to AL, Mar. 15, 1861, in AL Papers; Blair to Fox, Jan. 31, 1861, in Thompson and Wainwright, eds., *Confidential Correspondence of Gustavus Vasa Fox*, vol. 1, p. 4.

59. Welles to AL, Mar. 29, 1861, in AL Papers; Chase to AL, Mar. 15, 1861, and "Salmon P. Chase, Opinion on Fort Sumter, March 29, 1861," both in AL Papers.

60. John G. Nicolay and John Hay, *Abraham Lincoln: A History* (New York, 1890), vol. 3, pp. 443–49; Seward to AL, Apr. 1, 1861, AL Papers.

61. Patrick Sowle, "A Reappraisal of Seward's Memorandum of April 1, 1861, to Lincoln," *Journal of Southern History*, vol. 33, no. 2 (May 1967), pp. 234–39; Klein, *Days of Defiance*, pp. 362–63.

62. AL to Seward, Apr. 1, 1861, AL Papers. It is unclear whether Lincoln ever sent his note to Seward. Nicolay and Hay thought he had, but other historians assert that he did not, since there is no surviving copy in Seward's papers. Undoubtedly, however, Lincoln did communicate those sentiments to his secretary of state, either orally or in writing.

63. Sowle, "A Reappraisal," p. 236.

64. Abner Doubleday to Mary Doubleday, Mar. 27 [?], 1861 [fragment], AL Papers.

65. Nicolay and Hay, *Inside Lincoln's White House*, vol. 4, pp. 64–65.

66. Stampp, *And the War Came*, pp. 87–90.

67. James L. Hill to AL, Mar. 14, 1861, AL Papers.

68. Carl Sandburg, *Abraham Lincoln: The War Years* (New York, 1939), pp. 233–34.

69. Burlingame, *Abraham Lincoln*, vol. 2, pp. 105–06.

70. Ibid., pp. 123–24; McClintock, *Lincoln and the Decision*, pp. 247–49.

71. Thompson and Wainwright, *Confidential Correspondence*, vol. 1, pp. 31–32.

72. SWC Diary, Apr. 11, 1861, SWC Papers; Chepesiuk, "Eye Witness," p. 275. Some of the hardtack that the army issued to troops in 1861 was reported to have been in storage since the end of the Mexican War in 1848. William C. Davis, *A Taste for War: The Culinary History of the Blue and the Gray* (Mechanicsburg, Pa., 2003), p. 41.

73. SWC Diary, Apr. 11, 1861, SWC Papers.

74. Stephen D. Lee, "The First Step in the War," in Doubleday, *Battles and Leaders of the Civil War,* pp. 74–75; A. R. Chisholm, "Notes on the Surrender of Fort Sumter," in Doubleday, *Battles and Leaders of the Civil War,* p. 82.

75. *OR* I, vol. 1, 13; Crawford, *History of the Fall,* p. 423.

76. Crawford, *History of the Fall,* p. 423; SWC Diary, Apr. 11, 1861, SWC Papers.

77. *OR* I, vol. 1, p. 103.

78. *OR* I, vol. 1, pp. 293–94; Crawford, *History of the Fall,* p. 111.

79. *Instruction for Field Artillery, Horse and Foot. Compiled by a Board of Artillery Officers* (Baltimore, 1845), pp. 16–17.

80. Hay Diary, May 9, 1861, in Burlingame, *Inside Lincoln's White House,* p. 21.

81. James Chesnut and Stephen D. Lee to Robert Anderson, Apr. 12, 1861, Robert Anderson Papers, LC.

82. Chester, "Inside Sumter in '61," p. 65.

83. Chepesiuk, "Eye Witness," p. 276; Chester, "Inside Sumter in '61," p. 66.

84. Doubleday, *Reminiscences,* pp. 141–44.

85. Ibid., pp. 143–44.

86. Ibid., pp. 145–46; *OR* I, vol. 1, pp. 18, 44.

87. Chester, "Inside Sumter in '61," p. 67; Doubleday, *Reminiscences,* pp. 146–47.

88. Doubleday, *Reminiscences,* p. 147; Chepesiuk, "Eye Witness," p. 276.

89. On April 5, 1861, the *New York Herald* published a letter from another Sumter private, who it said had dictated the missive to a sergeant who could write.

90. Coffman, *The Old Army,* p. 137–41; Doubleday, *Reminiscences,* appendix. I am grateful to Rick Hatcher, National Park Service historian at the Fort Sumter National Monument, for sharing with me his unpublished listing of the Sumter garrison's names, service records, and enlistment data (which include places of birth and physical characteristics).

91. Coffman, *The Old Army,* pp. 137–41. A former soldier wrote, "Two-thirds of those in the service are foreigners, generally of the lowest and most ignorant class. The few Americans to be met with are men who have led dissipated lives and incapacitated themselves for any respectable business, taking up the army as a last resource [*sic*]."

Enlisted men even looked physically different from their superiors. Although several of Sumter's officers—including Doubleday and Crawford—were over six feet tall, not a single private was, according to their enlistment records. The average height of the garrison's foreign-born privates was only 5 feet, 5¾ inches, fully three inches shorter than the average American male of the mid–nineteenth century. This was almost certainly a result of poor nutrition in childhood in many cases. The average

age of Sumter's enlisted men was twenty-nine, with several of the men in their forties.

92. SWC Diary, Apr. 11, 1861, SWC Papers; Coffman, *The Old Army*, p. 205. Several of the Sumter privates' enlistments expired during the siege, but they apparently insisted on remaining to defend the fort.

93. Chepesiuk, "Eye Witness," pp. 274–75. "I only wish we had a chance to give the rascals hell," wrote another enlisted man. "We are all right, if old Lincoln will only have the backbone to stand by us." *New York Herald*, Apr. 5, 1861.

94. *Instruction for Heavy Artillery, Prepared by a Board of Officers, for Use of the Army of the United States* (Washington, D.C., 1863), pp. 54–59; David Detzer, *Allegiance: Fort Sumter, Charleston, and the Beginning of the Civil War* (New York, 2001), pp. 260–64; Mike Ryan, "The Historic Guns of Forts Sumter and Moultrie" (National Park Service study, 1997); Oliver Lyman Spaulding Jr., "The Bombardment of Fort Sumter, 1861," *Annual Report of the American Historical Association for the Year 1913*, vol. 1, pp. 200–01.

95. Doubleday, *Reminiscences*, pp. 148–49.

96. *Baltimore Sun*, Apr. 16, 1861: F. L. Parker, "The Battle of Fort Sumter as Seen from Morris Island," *South Carolina Historical Magazine*, vol. 62, no. 2 (April 1961), p. 67; Doubleday, *Reminiscences*, p. 151, Chester, "Inside Sumter in '61," pp. 66–68.

97. *Boston Daily Advertiser*, Apr. 24, 1861; *Albany Journal*, Apr. 19, 1861. In describing the battle, I have used only newspaper reports that were based on descriptions by eyewitnesses and that accord with other accounts. The *Albany Journal* article, for instance, is based on a clearly authentic interview with Doubleday immediately after the surrender.

98. *Baltimore Sun*, April 16, 1861; Chepesiuk, "Eye Witness," pp. 277–78; Thompson and Wainwright, *Confidential Correspondence*, pp. 32–33.

99. SWC Diary, Apr. 12, 1861, SWC Papers; *OR* I, vol. 1, pp. 20–21.

100. Chester, "Inside Sumter in '61," pp. 54; 70–71.

101. Chepesiuk, "Eye Witness," p. 278.

102. *OR* I, pp. 21–22; Chester, "Inside Sumter in '61," p. 71; Doubleday, *Reminiscences*, pp. 156–57; *Albany Journal*, Apr. 19, 1861.

103. Doubleday, *Reminiscences*, p. 158.

104. *Charleston Courier*, Apr. 13, 1861, in *Baltimore Sun*, Apr. 16, 1861.

105. Thompson, pp. 278–79; Crawford, p. 439; Chester, "Inside Sumter in '61," p. 72; SWC Diary, Apr. 13, 1861, SWC Papers.

106. Crawford, *History of the Fall*, pp. 437–38; Doubleday, *Reminiscences*, p. 159; May Spencer Ringold and W. Gourdin Young, "William Gourdin Young and the Wigfall Mission—Fort Sumter, April 13, 1861," *South Carolina Historical Magazine*, vol. 73, no. 1 (Jan. 1972), pp. 27–33. While Wigfall and the other Confederate were distracted, the three slaves, quite sensibly, pushed their boat off and set out again for the relative safety of Fort Moultrie. The private, William Gourdin Young, noticed their departure just in time to order them back onshore at gunpoint.

107. Chepesiuk, "Eye Witness," p. 279.
108. Ibid., pp. 278–79; Crawford, *History of the Fall*, pp. 439–41; SWC Diary, April 13, 1861, SWC Papers; Chester, "Inside Sumter in '61," pp. 72–73. The separate accounts given by Thompson, Crawford (who recounted the story twice), and Chester, who all claimed to be present for Wigfall's arrival, coincide in most particulars but offer slightly different sequences of events and attribute somewhat different words to Wigfall, Anderson, and Thompson. My own account combines elements from all four versions but relies most heavily on Thompson's letter to his father and Crawford's diary entry, both written shortly after the surrender.

    Wigfall himself told a rather different version of the story several days later, when he led Russell of the London *Times* on a tour of the vanquished fort. Wigfall recounted that the Yankee private who had first spotted him—possibly Thompson—was "pretty well scared when he saw me, but I told him not to be alarmed, but to take me to the officers. There they were, huddled up in that corner behind the brickwork, for our shells were tumbling into the yard, and bursting like—" (here the senator inserted some "strange expletives"). "I am sorry to say," Russell noted, "our distinguished friend had just been paying his respects *sans bornes* to Bacchus or Bourbon, for he was decidedly unsteady in his gait and thick in speech." Russell, *My Diary*, p. 107.
109. Winfield Scott to AL, Apr. 13, 1861, AL Papers.
110. *Milwaukee Sentinel*, Apr. 13, 1861.
111. Walt Whitman, *Memoranda During the War* (Bedford, Mass., 1990), p. 78; *New York Herald*, Apr. 5, 1861; Alan Nevins and Milton Halsey Thomas, eds., *The Diary of George Templeton Strong* (Seattle, 1988), p. 182.
112. Whitman, *Memoranda*, p. 78; *New York Tribune*, Apr. 13–16, 1861; *New York Herald*, Apr. 15, 1861; Mark Neely and Harold Holzer, *The Union Image: Popular Prints of the Civil War North* (Chapel Hill, 2000), p. 3; *Brooklyn Eagle*, Apr. 15, 1861; Strong Diary, in Nevins and Thomas, p. 182.
113. *Brooklyn Eagle*, Apr. 15, 1861; *New-York Tribune*, Apr. 15, 1861; *New York Herald*, Apr. 13 and 15, 1861; Imogene Spaulding, "The Attitude of California to the Civil War," *Quarterly of the Historical Society of Southern California*, vol. 9, p. 122.
114. Nicolay and Hay, *Abraham Lincoln*, vol. 4, pp. 68–75; Burlingame, *Abraham Lincoln*, vol. 2, p. 132.
115. Isaac W. Hayne to AL, Apr. 13, 1861, and H. W. Denslow to AL, Apr. 13, 1861, both in AL Papers. Information on the identity of Homer W. Denslow of Savannah is from the 1860 Census. He would later go on to serve as a Confederate officer. Hayne, the attorney general of South Carolina, had been one of the state's commissioners to Washington during the secession crisis. Both telegrams are marked as having been received at the telegraph office in Washington on April 13, though there is no way to know when Lincoln saw them. Denslow's reads simply: "Fort Sumter has surrendered

there is nobody hurt." Hayne offered a few more (just slightly inaccurate) details: "Fort Sumter has surrendered unconditionally & not a Carolinian hurt the stars & stripes were hauled down & the white flag raised precisely at half past one (1) oclock."

116. *New-York Tribune*, Apr. 16, 1861; Reid Mitchell, *Civil War Soldiers* (New York, 1988), p. 17.

117. James A. Garfield to Harry Rhodes, Apr. 13/14, 1861, JAG Papers.

118. Mayer, *All on Fire*, pp. 517–18; *Liberator*, Apr. 26, 1861.

119. *Philadelphia Press*, Apr. 15, 1861, in Nelson Lankford, *Cry Havoc! The Crooked Road to Civil War, 1861* (New York, 2007), p. 92; Neely and Holzer, *The Union Image*, pp. 9–12.

120. Bruce Catton, *This Hallowed Ground: The Story of the Union Side of the Civil War* (New York, 1956), p. 20; Allan Nevins, *The War for the Union*, vol. 1: *The Improvised War* (New York, 1959), pp. 75–76.

121. Neely and Holzer, *The Union Image*, p. 8; Henry Ward Beecher, *Patriotic Addresses in America and England* (New York, 1887), p. 297.

122. "Civilization at a Pinch," Ralph Waldo Emerson Papers, Harvard University; Eduardo Cadava, *Emerson and the Climates of History* (Stanford, Calif., 1997), p. 28; James Elliot Cabot, *A Memoir of Ralph Waldo Emerson* (Boston, 1887), vol. 2, pp. 599–602.

123. Cf. Nevins, *The War for the Union*, vol. 1, pp. 72–73: "Once fully established, such political separations—like those of Southern Ireland from Britain, Norway from Sweden, Pakistan from India—have a way of making themselves permanent."

124. New York *Daily News*, n.d., quoted in *New-York Tribune*, Apr. 16, 1861.

125. Albert D. Kirwan, *John J. Crittenden: The Struggle for the Union* (Lexington, Ky., 1962), pp. 425–34, 446–48.

126. Lydia Maria Child to Mrs. S. B. Shaw, May 5, 1861, in *Letters of Lydia Maria Child* (Boston, 1883), pp. 150–51.

127. Russell, *My Diary*, p. 79.

128. Doubleday, *Reminiscences*, pp. 164–67.

129. *OR* I, vol. 1, pp. 23–24; Doubleday, *Reminiscences*, pp. 171–73; Detzer, *Allegiance*, pp. 307–10; Crawford, *History of the Fall*, pp. 447–48.

Chapter Five: The Volunteer

1. *New York Herald*, Apr. 19–21, 1861.

2. [John Hay], "Ellsworth," *Atlantic Monthly*, July 1861.

3. Luther E. Robinson, "Elmer Ellsworth, First Martyr of the Civil War," *Transactions of the Illinois State Historical Society for the Year 1923*, p. 112.

4. Ruth Painter Randall, *Colonel Elmer Ellsworth: A Biography of Lincoln's Friend and the First Hero of the Civil War* (Boston, 1960), p. 27.

5. Ibid, pp. 23–26. The painting is preserved in the Illinois State Historical Society.

6.	George and Sarah Ellsworth, New York, pension file W.19226, National Archives.

7.	See Glenn Wallach, *Obedient Sons: The Discourse of Youth and Generations in American Culture, 1630–1860* (Amherst, 1997), pp. 118–19.

8.	Randall, *Colonel Elmer Ellsworth*, p. 31; Newton M. Curtis, *The Black-Plumed Riflemen: A Tale of the Revolution* (New York, 1846).

9.	Mabel McIlvaine, ed., *Reminiscences of Chicago During the Civil War* (Chicago, 1914), p. 4, and *Reminiscences of Chicago During the Forties and Fifties* (Chicago, 1913), p. 13.

10.	Donald L. Miller, *City of the Century: The Epic of Chicago and the Making of America* (New York, 1997), pp. 112–13, 123.

11.	Randall, *Colonel Elmer Ellsworth*, p. 92.

12.	Ibid., p. 43.

13.	Ibid., p. 37.

14.	Daniel Walker Howe, *What Hath God Wrought: The Transformation of America, 1815–1848* (New York, 2007), p. 491; James B. Whisker, *The Rise and Decline of the American Militia System* (Selinsgrove, Pa., 1999), p. 331.

15.	Marcus Cunliffe, *Soldiers and Civilians: The Martial Tradition in America* (Boston, 1968), p. 226.

16.	Luther E. Robinson, "Elmer Ellsworth, First Martyr of the Civil War," *Transactions of the Illinois State Historical Society for the Year 1923*, illus. facing p. 111.

17.	W. J. Hardee, *Rifle and Light Infantry Tactics* (Philadelphia, 1855).

18.	[John Hay], "Ellsworth," *Atlantic Monthly*, July 1861.

19.	See, e.g. [Jeremiah Burns], *The Patriot's Offering; or, the Life, Services, and Military Career of the Noble Trio, Ellsworth, Lyon, and Baker* (New York, 1862), p. 9.

20.	Robinson, *Elmer Ellsworth*, pp. 112–13; Martha Swain, "It Was Fun, Soldier," *American Heritage*, vol. 7, no. 5 (Aug. 1956).

21.	See, e.g., *Chicago Press and Tribune*, June 6, 1859.

22.	*Chicago Tribune*, Feb. 2, 1896.

23.	*Chicago Tribune*, July 25, 1860.

24.	Quoted in *Frank Leslie's Illustrated Newspaper*, July 28, 1860.

25.	E. E. Ellsworth, *Manual of Arms for Light Infantry, Adapted to the Rifled Musket, with, or without, the Priming Attachment, Arranged for the U.S. Zouave Cadets, Governor's Guard of Illinois*, n.d., n.p. [Chicago, 1860], pp. 15–17.

26.	*Chicago Tribune*, July 25, 1860.

27.	Undated [1859–60] clipping in scrapbook, *History of U.S. Zouave Cadets, G. G. Military Champions of America, 1859–60*, n.p., Library of Congress General Collections, UA178.Z8.H6.

28.	Burlingame, *Abraham Lincoln*, vol. 1, p. 267.

29.	Cunliffe, *Soldiers and Civilians*, p. 71; Burlingame, *Abraham Lincoln*, vol. 1, pp. 272ff.

30.	Cunliffe, *Soldiers and Civilians*, pp. 97, 427; John J. McDonald, "Emerson and John Brown," *New England Quarterly*, vol. 44, no. 3 (Sept. 1971), pp. 386–87 n.

31. Cunliffe, *Soldiers and Civilians*, pp. 400–01.

32. Ibid., p. 356.

33. Ibid., pp. 90, 369.

34. Ibid., p. 348; Charles Ingraham, *Elmer E. Ellsworth and the Zouaves of '61* (Chicago, 1925).

35. Eighteen-year-old Edgar Allan Poe, in his first published poem, *Tamerlane* (1827), rang out a challenge to his elders that could have been a *cri de coeur* for the rising generation: "I was ambitious—have you known / The passion, father? You have not."

36. For the culture and experiences of young men in nineteenth-century America, see especially E. Anthony Rotundo, *American Manhood: Transformations in Masculinity from the Revolution to Modern Era* (New York, 1993); as well as Howard P. Chudacoff, *The Age of the Bachelor: Creating an American Subculture* (Princeton, 1999); and Michael S. Kimmel, *Manhood in America: A Cultural History* (New York, 2006).

37. Whitman knew personally what it was like to be a solitary young man—and boy—in the city. When he was only about thirteen, in the early 1830s, his struggling parents moved from Brooklyn back to rural Long Island, and Walt remained alone to seek his fortune.

38. Early-nineteenth-century Americans above the age of fourteen consumed an average of 6.6 to 7.1 gallons of pure alcohol each year. The average at the turn of the twenty-first century was about 2.8 gallons. Thomas R. Pegram, *Battling Demon Rum: The Struggle for a Dry America, 1800–1933* (Chicago, 1998), p. 7.

39. See Thomas Augst, *The Clerk's Tale: Young Men and Moral Life in Nineteenth-Century America* (Chicago, 2003), Introduction and chap. 1.

40. Emerson's lecture was reprinted in *The Dial*, April 1844.

41. *Cleveland Morning Leader*, n.d. [July 1860], Library of Congress scrapbook.

42. *Albany Evening Journal*, July 14, 1860.

43. *New York Herald*, July 15, 1860.

44. Unidentified clipping, n.d. [July 1860], Library of Congress scrapbook.

45. *New-York Daily Tribune*, July 16, 1860.

46. *Frank Leslie's Illustrated Newspaper*, July 28, 1860.

47. Randall, *Colonel Elmer Ellsworth*, p. 7.

48. "Our New York Letter: The Zouaves in New York," unidentified clipping in Library of Congress scrapbook, July 14, 1860.

49. Ingraham, *Elmer E. Ellsworth*, p. 94; misc. clippings in Library of Congress scrapbook.

50. "The Zouaves," clipping in Library of Congress scrapbook, n.p., n.d.

51. Charles Dickens, "Naval and Military Traditions in America," *All the Year Round*, June 15, 1861.

52. Cunliffe, *Soldiers and Civilians*, p. 245.

53. *New-York Tribune*, July 16, 1860.

54. [John Hay], "Ellsworth," *Atlantic Monthly*, July 1861.

55. *Frank Leslie's Illustrated Newspaper*, July 28, 1860.

56. The simile is John Hay's. See "Ellsworth," *Atlantic Monthly*, July 1861.

57. Ingraham, *Elmer E. Ellsworth*, p. 97; *Daily National Intelligencer*, Aug. 6, 1860; *Washington Star*, Aug. 6, 1860.

58. *New York Herald*, Aug. 5, 1860.

59. Randall, *Colonel Elmer Ellsworth*, pp. 4–5; Ingraham, *Elmer E. Ellsworth*, pp. 106–07.

60. "Springfield, Illinois," map drawn by A. Ruger, 1867.

61. Randall, *Colonel Elmer Ellsworth*, pp. 6–7.

62. Quoted by Ellsworth in a letter to his fiancée, Carrie Spofford, in Ingraham, *Elmer E. Ellsworth*, p. 54.

63. Randall, *Colonel Elmer Ellsworth*, p. 163.

64. Ibid., pp. 163–64.

65. Randall, *Colonel Elmer Ellsworth*, p. 174.

66. John Hay, "A Young Hero. Personal Reminiscences of Colonel E. E. Ellsworth." *McClure's Magazine*, March 1896, p. 354; Stephen Berry, *House of Abraham: Lincoln and the Todds, a Family Divided by War* (Boston, 2007), pp. 55–56.

67. Hay, "A Young Hero."

68. *Illinois State Journal*, June 3, 1861, reprinted in Michael Burlingame, ed., *Lincoln's Journalist: John Hay's Anonymous Writings for the Press, 1860–1864* (Carbondale, Ill., 1998), p. 69.

69. *Chicago Tribune*, May 29, 1887.

70. *Atlantic Monthly*, July 1861.

71. John Langdon Kaine, "Lincoln as a Boy Knew Him," *Century Magazine*, vol. 85, no. 4 (Feb. 1913), p. 558.

72. Kaine, "Lincoln as a Boy Knew Him," p. 557.

73. *Philadelphia Inquirer*, Apr. 13, 1861.

74. Randall, *Colonel Elmer Ellsworth*, pp. 221–26, citing an undated article in the *Chicago Times*.

75. Carl Schurz to his wife, Apr. 17, 1861, in *Intimate Letters of Carl Schurz, 1841 to 1869* (Evansville, Wisc., 1929).

76. Many Union regiments in these early days of the war, and throughout the months that followed, wore gray. It wasn't until the following year, after a few ugly incidents in which federal troops fired on their own comrades, that blue was adopted as the standard dress throughout the service. See chap. 8, *infra*, and Bell Irvin Wiley, *The Life of Billy Yank: The Common Soldier of the Union* (Indianapolis, 1952), p. 22.

77. Kenneth Stampp, *And the War Came: The North and the Secession Crisis, 1860–1861* (Baton Rouge, 1950), p. 291; *New York Herald*, Apr. 16 and 17, 1861; *New-York Tribune*, Apr. 16, 1861; Alan Nevins and Milton Halsey Thomas, *The Diary of George Templeton Strong* (Seattle, 1988), p. 186. Ben-

nett also published a news story denying all of the "false reports" in the local press about the riot, assuring readers that the only reason a crowd had gathered in front of the building was that New Yorkers were so eager for copies of the city's most trusted source of news.

78. Mary A. Livermore, "War Excitement in Chicago," in McIlvain, *Reminiscences*, p. 68.

79. John A. Page, "A University Volunteer," in McIlvain, *Reminiscences*, p. 84.

80. *Chicago Tribune*, Oct. 27, 1910; "The Original Zouaves," *Chicago Post*, n.d. [c. 1861], in New York State Military Museum clippings file, 11th New York Infantry, accessed at www.dmna.state.ny.us.

81. *OR*, series III, vol. 1, pp. 73, 106.

82. Wiley, *Billy Yank*, p. 18.

83. Michael Burlingame, ed., *At Lincoln's Side: John Hay's Correspondence and Selected Writings* (Carbondale, Ill., 2000), p. 120; *Official Records of the War of the Rebellion*, III, vol. 1, pp. 140, 77–78, 175–76. In his reply to Pug-o-na-ke-shick through a state official, Secretary Cameron cordially thanked the chief, but regretted that "the nature of our present national troubles, forbids the use of savages."

84. A. M. Green, "The Colored Philadelphians Forming Regiments," in *Letters and Discussions on the Formation of Colored Regiments, and the Duty of the Colored People in Regard to the Great Slaveholders' Rebellion* (Philadelphia, 1862), p. 3.

85. Harlan Hoyt Horner, *Lincoln and Greeley* (Westport, Conn., 1971), pp. 176–78.

86. James Nye, quoted in William Harlan Hale, *Horace Greeley: Voice of the People* (New York, 1950), p. 244.

87. Lincoln to Ellsworth, Apr. 15, 1861, in *The Collected Works of Abraham Lincoln* (New Brunswick, N.J., 1953), vol. 4, p. 333.

88. *New-York Tribune*, May 25, 1861.

89. *Harper's Weekly*, Apr. 11, 1857.

90. A. E. Costello, *Our Firemen: A History of the New York Fire Departments, Volunteer and Paid* (New York, 1887), pp. 559–702, passim.

91. Most fires broke out at night, when an overturned lamp or an unattended candle could set a building aflame.

92. Costello, *Our Firemen*, pp. 171–72; Paul C. Ditzel, *Fire Engines, Firefighters: The Men, Equipment, and Machines from the Earliest Days to the Present* (New York, 1986), pp. 65–69.

93. Costello, *Our Firemen*, pp. 610, 588.

94. Terry Golway, *So Others Might Live: A History of New York's Bravest* (New York, 2002), pp. 85–91.

95. Luc Sante, *Low Life* (New York, 1991), pp. 77–78.

96. Costello, *Our Firemen*, pp. 125–44.

97. *New-York Tribune*, Apr. 18, 1861.

98. Reprinted in *Milwaukee Daily Sentinel*, Apr. 22, 1861.

99. *New York Herald*, Apr. 18, 1861; *Brooklyn Eagle*, Apr. 20, 1861.
100. *New York Herald*, Apr. 19, 1861.
101. *Brooklyn Eagle*, Apr. 20, 1861; *New York Herald*, Apr. 18, 1861.
102. *New York Herald*, Apr. 30, 1861.
103. *New York Herald*, Apr. 21, 1861; James McPherson, *Battle Cry of Freedom: The Civil War Era* (New York, 1988), p. 327; John Hay, Apr. 20, 1861, in Michael Burlingame and John R. Turner Ettlinger, eds., *Inside Lincoln's White House: The Complete Civil War Diary of John Hay* (Carbondale, Ill., 1999), p. 5.

Chapter Six: Gateways to the West

1. See Mark Twain's famous firsthand description of a Pony Express rider passing in *Roughing It* (Hartford, 1872), pp. 70–72. For the landscape of the Carson Valley near Fort Churchill, see Sir Richard F. Burton, *The City of the Saints, and Across the Rocky Mountains to California* (New York, 1862), pp. 492–93; Horace Greeley, *Overland Journey from New York to San Francisco in the Summer of 1859* (New York, 1860), pp. 272–76. For details of the Overland Telegraph Company operations in the spring of 1861, see James Gamble, "Wiring a Continent," *The Californian*, vol. 3, no. 6 (June 1881), pp. 556ff; Carlyle N. Klise, "The First Transcontinental Telegraph," master's thesis, Iowa State University, 1937, esp. chap. 4.

2. National Register of Historic Places Inventory, Nomination Form, "Fort Churchill," 1978.

3. *San Francisco Daily Evening Bulletin*, May 27, 1861.

4. Christopher Corbett, *Orphans Preferred: The Twisted Truth and Lasting Legend of the Pony Express* (New York, 2003), pp. 87–88; Twain, *Roughing It*, pp. 70–71; *Daily Evening Bulletin*, May 29, 1861.

5. Southerners opposed the act's passage, fearing—correctly—that the line would take a northern rather than a southern route (Klise, "The First Transatlantic Telegraph," pp. 26–29).

6. Robert Luther Thompson, *Wiring a Continent: The History of the Telegraph Industry in the United States* (Princeton, 1947), pp. 318–58

7. Ibid., pp. 290–92; Klise, "The First Transcontinental Telegraph," p. 37.

8. Jeptha Homer Wade Papers, Western Reserve Historical Society, passim; Gamble, "Wiring a Continent." Wade acted as Sibley's agent in San Francisco.

9. "Across the Continent," *Continental Monthly*, vol. 1, no. 1 (January 1862); Tom Chaffin, *Pathfinder: John Charles Frémont and the Course of American Empire* (New York, 2002), pp. 210–19, 262; John D. Unruh, Jr., *The Plains Across: The Overland Emigrants and the Trans-Mississippi West, 1840–60* (Urbana, Ill., 1979), pp. 240–43, 300–01.

10. The projected Russian-American telegraph ended up reaching only as far northwest as Hazelton, British Columbia. Work stopped abruptly in 1867 after Sibley's rival, Cyrus W. Field, opened the first successful transatlantic

line. The project, however, was an important factor in the United States' acquisition of Alaska. Cf. John B. Dwyer, *To Wire the World: Perry M. Collins and the North Pacific Telegraph Expedition* (Westport, Conn., 2001).

11. Gamble, "Wiring a Continent." The actual work on the western portion of the line was undertaken by a new firm, the Overland Telegraph Company, in which various California lines participated but with Sibley as the controlling investor. As soon as construction was completed, the short-lived company—along with all the previously autonomous California ones—was absorbed into Western Union. Alvin F. Harlow, *Old Wires and New Waves: The History of the Telegraph, Telephone, and Wireless* (New York, 1936), pp. 311–12.

According to one account, President Lincoln met with Sibley early in 1861 and told him that the planned Pacific line was a "wild scheme" and that it would be "next to impossible to get your poles and materials distributed on the plains, and as fast as you build your line the Indians will cut it down." George A. Root and Russell K. Hickman, "The Platte Route, Part IV, Concluded: The Pony Express and Pacific Telegraph," *Kansas Historical Quarterly*, vol. 14, no. 1 (Feb. 1946), p. 66.

12. Klise, "The First Transcontinental Telegraph," p. 52.

13. Geoffrey C. Ward, *The Civil War* (New York, 1990), p. 17.

14. The 1860 census has been largely ignored by historians as a source of Southern anxiety during the secession crisis. For detailed early census results, see, e.g., *New York Herald*, Sept. 13, 1860.

15. *Philadelphia Inquirer*, Apr. 2, 1861 and Feb. 9, 1861; *New York Herald*, Nov. 1, 1860.

16. See David Haward Bain, *Empire Express: Building the First Transcontinental Railroad* (New York, 1999), esp. pp. 48–51, for Davis's role; Adam Arenson, *The Great Heart of the Republic: St. Louis and the Cultural Civil War* (Cambridge, Mass., 2010), p. 69.

17. Jessie Benton Frémont, "A Home Lost, and Found," *The Home-Maker*, February 1892; JBF to Elizabeth Blair Lee, June 14, 1860, in Pamela Herr and Mary Lee Spence, eds., *The Letters of Jessie Benton Frémont* (Urbana, Ill., 1993), pp. 229–30.

18. *Selections of Editorial Articles from the St. Louis Enquirer* (St. Louis, 1844), p. 5, quoted in Henry Nash Smith, "Walt Whitman and Manifest Destiny," *Huntington Library Quarterly*, vol. 10, no. 4 (Aug. 1947), pp. 378–79 n. Benton's vision, of course, did not account for the Spanish colonists, who had long since reached the Pacific—let alone for the Native American children of Adam who had been settled along its shores for millennia.

19. Elbert B. Smith, *Magnificent Missourian: The Life of Thomas Hart Benton* (Philadelphia, 1958), pp. 47–48, 63–64, 68–69; Tom Chaffin, *Pathfinder: John C. Frémont and the Course of American Empire* (New York, 2002), pp. 80–81.

20. It later turned out that the place where Frémont planted his famous flag—the

tallest peak in the Wind River Range—was not, in fact, the highest point of the Rockies, though he believed it to be at the time.

21. Sally Denton, *Passion and Principle: John and Jessie Frémont, the Couple Whose Power, Politics, and Love Shaped Nineteenth-Century America* (New York, 2007), p. xi; Pamela Herr, *Jessie Benton Frémont: A Biography* (New York, 1987), pp. 82–83, 110–11; Jessie Benton Frémont, *Souvenirs of My Time* (Boston, 1887), p. 186. The question of how large a hand Jessie Frémont had in her husband's books has been a point of contention almost since they were published. Many people believed then that she was the sole author. The most careful recent historians conclude that the reports were a joint effort but that Jessie was responsible for much of the color, style, and literary touch that won them a large readership.

22. Early in his career, Benton always placed "Southern rights" ahead of anti-slavery principles, but by the end of his life, his views shifted to the point where he wrote to Charles Sumner congratulating him on his inflammatory "Crime Against Kansas" speech. William Nisbet Chambers, *Old Bullion Benton: Senator from the New West* (New York, 1970), p. 419.

23. Allan Nevins, *Frémont: Pathmarker of the West* (New York, 1928), pp. 387–89; Denton, *Passion and Principle*, pp. 180–81; Leonard L. Richards, *The California Gold Rush and the Coming of the Civil War* (New York, 2007) pp. 57–59, 102–3.

24. David Grant, "'Our Nation's Hope is She': The Cult of Jessie Frémont in the Republican Campaign Poetry of 1856," *Journal of American Studies*, vol. 42, no. 2 (2008), pp. 187–213; Denton, *Passion and Principle*, pp. 243–48; Ruth Painter Randall, *I Jessie* (Boston, 1963), pp. 176–78. Colonel Frémont was such a popular figure that Southern Democratic leaders had previously offered to make him their party's standard bearer, on the condition that he pledge not to oppose the Fugitive Slave Law and the Kansas-Nebraska Act. This he refused to do—after a long discussion with Jessie—even though he knew that whomever the Democrats nominated that year would be almost certain to win the presidency. Nevins, *Frémont*, pp. 424–25.

25. Richards, *California Gold Rush*, pp. 93ff; Robert J. Chandler, "Friends in Time of Need: Republicans and Black Civil Rights in California During the Civil War," *Arizona and the West*, vol. 24, no. 4 (Winter 1982), pp. 319–21; Imogene Spaulding, "The Attitude of California to the Civil War," *Historical Society of Southern California Publications*, vol. 9 (1912–13), p. 106.

26. See Spaulding, "The Attitude of California," p. 105.

27. See Joseph Ellison, "Designs for a Pacific Republic, 1843–62," *Oregon Historical Quarterly*, vol. 31, no. 4 (Dec. 1930), pp. 319–42.

28. Spaulding, "The Attitude of California," p. 108; *San Francisco Herald*, Jan. 3, 1861.

29. *San Francisco Herald*, Apr. 25, May 1, and May 8, 1861.

30. Katherine A. White, ed., *A Yankee Trader in the Gold Rush: The Letters of Franklin A. Buck* (Boston, 1930), p. 183 (Jan. 22, 1860). In January 1861, on hearing that secession had begun, Buck wrote his sister again: "I wash my

hands of it. Let what will come, I am innocent. If you attempt to coerce the seceding states you will have all the slave states united and how a war would affect you! You had better scrape together what you can and all come out here."

31. *Los Angeles Star*, Jan. 5, 1861; J. M. Scammell, "Military Units in Southern California, 1853–1862," *California Historical Society Quarterly*, vol. 29, no. 3 (Sept. 1950), pp. 229–49; Percival J. Cooney, "Southern California in Civil War Days," *Annual Publications of the Historical Society of Southern California*, vol. 13 (1924), pp. 54–68. One early historian sniffed that San Bernardino's disloyal citizenry also included large numbers of "outlaws and English Jews" (Spaulding, "The Attitude of California," p. 117).

32. James H. Wilkins, ed., *The Great Diamond Hoax and Other Stirring Incidents in the Life of Asbury Harpending* (Norman, Okla., 1958), pp. 5–16.

33. Ibid., pp. 16–23.

34. See C. A. Bridges, "The Knights of the Golden Circle: A Filibustering Fantasy," *The Southwestern Historical Quarterly*, vol. 44, no. 3 (Jan. 1941), pp. 287–302; Benjamin Franklin Gilbert, "The Confederate Minority in California," *California Historical Society Quarterly*, vol. 20, no. 2 (June 1941), pp. 154–70; Ollinger Crenshaw, "The Knights of the Golden Circle: The Career of George Bickley," *American Historical Review*, vol. 47, no. 1 (Oct. 1941), pp. 23–50; Richards, *California Gold Rush*, p. 231; Frank L. Klement, *Dark Lanterns: Secret Political Societies, Conspiracies, and Treason in the Civil War* (Baton Rouge, 1984), chap. 1. One exchange of signs and countersigns by which the Knights in California recognized one another was recorded by an informer: "Do you know Jones?" "What Jones?" "Preacher Jones." "Where does he live?" "At home." "Where is his home?" "In Dixie." Cooney, "Southern California in Civil War Days," p. 58. Such details might seem to strain credibility, but in fact mid-nineteenth-century America was rife with secret political societies of all sorts—most famously the Know-Nothings and, later, the Ku Klux Klan—that drew on Romantic fantasies, the faddish appeal of medieval chivalry, and the general craze for fraternal organizations.

35. Hugh A. Gorley, *The Loyal Californians of 1861* (n.p., 1893), p. 4.

36. William T. Sherman, *Memoirs*, 2nd ed. (New York, 1887), vol. 1, pp. 196–97; William S. McFeely, *Grant: A Biography* (New York, 1981), pp. 74–75; John Y. Simon, ed., *The Papers of Ulysses S. Grant*, vol. 2: *April-September 1861* (Carbondale, Ill., 1969), pp. 25–28.

37. Christopher Phillips, *Damned Yankee: The Life of General Nathaniel Lyon* (Baton Rouge, La., 1996), p. 134.

38. See Jeffrey C. Stone, *Slavery, Southern Culture, and Education in Little Dixie, Missouri, 1820–1860* (New York, 2006); Louis Gerteis, *Civil War St. Louis* (Lawrence, Kans., 2001), pp. 37–38.

39. Charles Dickens, passing through in 1842, described the old French buildings "lop-sided with age" that "hold their heads askew besides, as if they were grimacing in astonishment at the American Improvements." *American Notes*, quoted in Arenson, *Great Heart*, p. 15.

40. Galusha Anderson, *A Border City in the Civil War* (Boston, 1908), pp. 1–3, 9.

41. Stephen Aron, *American Confluence: The Missouri Frontier from Borderland to Border State* (Bloomington, Ind., 2006), pp. 235–36.

42. Arenson, *Great Heart*, pp. 19–20; Steven Rowan and James Neal Primm, eds., *Germans for a Free Missouri: Translations from the St. Louis Radical Press, 1857–1862* (Columbia, Mo., 1983), p. 88; Don Heinrich Tolzmann, ed., and William G. Bek, trans., *The German Element in St. Louis: A Translation of Ernst D. Kargau's "St. Louis in Former Years: A Commemorative History of the German Element"* (Baltimore, 2000), pp. 42, 179–80.

43. Rowan and Primm, *Germans for a Free Missouri*, pp. 3–4; Lea VanderVelde, *Mrs. Dred Scott: A Life on Slavery's Frontier* (New York, 2009), pp. 320, 424.

44. Hans Christian Adamson, *Rebellion in Missouri: 1861* (Philadelphia, 1961), p. 72; Aron, *American Confluence*, p. 241.

45. Arenson, *Great Heart*, p. 111; Gerteis, *Civil War St. Louis*, p. 79; Walter Harrington Ryle, *Missouri: Union or Secession* (Nashville, 1931), pp. 179–80; Anderson, *Border City*, pp. 41–42; James Neal Primm, *Lion of the Valley: St. Louis, Missouri, 1764–1980* (St. Louis, 1998), p. 233.

46. A. A. Dunson, "Notes on the Missouri Germans on Slavery," *Missouri Historical Review*, vol. 54, no. 3 (April 1965), pp. 355–58; Walter B. Stevens, *St. Louis: The Fourth City, 1764–1911* (St. Louis, 1911), vol. 1, p. 165.

47. Ella Lonn, "The Forty-Eighters in the Civil War," in A. E. Zucker, ed., *The Forty-Eighters: Political Refugees of the German Revolution of 1848* (New York, 1967), pp. 186–87; Stephen D. Engle, *Yankee Dutchman: The Life of Franz Sigel* (Fayetteville, Ark., 1993), chaps. 1–2; Carl Wittke, *Refugees of Revolution: The German Forty-Eighters in America* (Philadelphia, 1952), p. 88; Lawrence O. Christensen et al., eds., *Dictionary of Missouri Biography* (Columbia, Mo., 1999), pp. 138–40; Henry Boernstein, ed., Steven Rowan and James Neal Primm, *Memoirs of a Nobody: The Missouri Years of an Austrian Radical* (St. Louis, 1997), pp. 4–6; Rowan and Primm, *Germans for a Free Missouri*, pp. 35–43; Ernest Kirschten, *Catfish and Crystal* (St. Louis, 1989), pp. 247–48.

48. *Anzeiger des Westens*, Dec. 17, 1860, in Rowan and Primm, *Germans for a Free Missouri*, p. 147; Kirschten, *Catfish and Crystal*, p. 245; *Missouri Republican* [St. Louis], Nov. 4, 1860. Confusingly, St. Louis's leading Democratic newspaper was called the *Missouri Republican*, while its leading Republican paper was called the *Missouri Democrat*.

49. Rowan and Primm, *Germans for a Free Missouri*, pp. 27–28; *Anzeiger des Westens*, May 24, 1860, in ibid., p. 113.

50. James Peckham, *Gen. Nathaniel Lyon, and Missouri in 1861* (New York, 1866), p. xiii.

51. *Anzeiger des Westens*, Oct. 29, 1860, in Rowan and Primm, *Germans for a Free Missouri*, p. 136; *San Francisco Bulletin*, Oct. 19, 1860; Bruce Levine, "Immigrants, Class, and Politics: German-American Working People and the Fight Against Slavery," in Charlotte L. Brancaforte, ed., *The German Forty-Eighters in the United States* (New York, 1989), p. 131.

52. Elbert B. Smith, *Francis Preston Blair* (New York, 1980), pp. 245–47; *Speech of Hon. Francis P. Blair, Jr., of Missouri, on the Acquisition of Central America* (Washington, D.C., 1858).

53. *Missouri Republican*, Dec. 25, 1860, Feb. 13 and 25, Mar. 2, 1861; Gerteis, *Civil War St. Louis*, pp. 79–80; Phillips, *Damned Yankee*, pp. 136–37; Boernstein, *Memoirs of a Nobody*, pp. 275–76; Engle, *Yankee Dutchman*, p. 52; Peckham, *Gen. Nathaniel Lyon*, pp. 36–38.

54. Gerteis, *Civil War St. Louis*, p. 85; Basil W. Duke, *The Civil War Reminiscences of General Basil W. Duke, C.S.A.* (New York, 2001), pp. 37–38; Boernstein, *Memoirs of a Nobody*, p. 269.

55. *Missouri Republican*, Nov. 4, 1860 and Jan. 20 and Feb. 13, 1861.

56. Herr, *Jessie Benton Frémont*, p. 312.

57. Ibid., pp. 310–15; Denton, *Passion and Principle*, pp. 484–85; Nevins, *Pathmarker*, p. 468; JBF to Elizabeth Blair Lee, June 14, 1860, in Herr and Spence, *Letters*, pp. 229–31; JBF, "A Home Found, and Lost."

58. Hershel Parker, *Herman Melville: A Biography*, vol. 2 (Baltimore, 2002), pp. 449–50; Gary Scharnhorst, *Bret Harte: Opening the American Literary West* (Norman, Okla., 2000), pp. 16–20; JBF to Thomas Starr King, Jan. 16, 1861, in Herr and Spence, *Letters*, pp. 233–34; Catherine Coffin Phillips, *Jessie Benton Frémont: A Woman Who Made History* (San Francisco, 1935), pp. 231–32; JBF, *Souvenirs*, pp. 204–05; Denton, *Passion and Principle*, pp. 280–81; Elizabeth B. Frémont, *Recollections of Elizabeth Benton Frémont, Daughter of the Pathfinder John C. Frémont and Jessie Benton Frémont His Wife* (New York, 1912), p. 119.

59. John D. Baltz, *Hon. Edward D. Baker, U.S. Senator from Oregon* (Lancaster, Pa., 1888), pp. 9–10.

60. *San Francisco Bulletin*, Oct. 18 and 27, 1860.

61. Herr, *Jessie Benton Frémont*, p. 316; Scharnhorst, *Bret Harte*, pp. 17–18. Scharnhorst also says that Harte was "waving the Stars and Stripes" during his outburst, although the newspaper account does not mention this.

62. Mrs. Frémont herself said as much in an 1864 letter, though many attributed the original quotation to Winfield Scott; others to Lincoln himself. It might not have been literally true (and if either Scott or Lincoln ever made the remark, no written evidence of it survives). See Edwin P. Whipple, *Substance and Show, and Other Lectures, by Thomas Starr King*, p. xviii, etc. (Lincoln); *Cincinnati Daily Gazette*, Nov. 6, 1876 (Scott).

63. Robert Monzingo, *Thomas Starr King: Eminent Californian, Civil War Statesman, Unitarian Minister* (Pacific Grove, Calif., 1991), pp. 32–33, 58; Herr, *Jessie Benton Frémont*, pp. 314–15; JBF, "A Home Found, and Lost."

64. Charles Wendte, *Thomas Starr King, Patriot and Preacher* (Boston, 1921), pp. 1–10; William Day Simonds, *Starr King in California* (San Francisco, n.d.), pp. 5–8.

65. Wendte, *Thomas Starr King*, passim; Richard Peterson, "Thomas Starr King in California, 1860–64: Forgotten Naturalist of the Civil War Years," *California History*, vol. 69, no. 1 (Spring 1990), pp. 12–21; Kevin Starr, *Americans*

and the California Dream, 1850–1915 (New York, 1986), pp. 97–105. King read *Walden* in an advance proof in 1855; he praised its concluding section for "being more weird and winding further into the awful vitalities of nature than any writing I have yet seen" (Wendte, p. 46).

66. King did not *entirely* leave New England behind: he crossed the steaming Isthmus of Panama laden with a monstrous baggage train that contained, among other things, overcoats, shawls, bottles of cider, pots of pickled oysters, and bundles of sermons. Wendte, *Thomas Starr King*, p. 78.

67. Ibid., p. 69.

68. Shortly after his arrival in California, he wrote: "Early in May, in New England, people hunt for flowers. A bunch of violets, or a sprig or two of brilliant color, intermixed with green, is a sufficient trophy of a tramp that chills you, damps your feet, and possibly leaves the seed of consumption. Here they have flowers in May, not shy, but rampant, as if nothing else had the right to be; flowers by the acre, flowers by the square mile, flowers as the visible carpet of an immense mountain wall. You can gather them in clumps, a dozen varieties at a pull. You can fill a bushel basket in five minutes." TSK, "Picture of California in Spring-Time—Around the Bay," in Oscar T. Shuck, comp., *The California Scrap-Book* (San Francisco, 1869), pp. 47–50.

69. Wendte, *Thomas Starr King*, pp. 84–85; TSK, "A Vacation Among the Sierras—No. 2," in John Adam Hussey, ed., *A Vacation Among the Sierras: Yosemite in 1860* (San Francisco, 1962); Denton, *Passion and Principle*, p. 282. Oliver Wendell Holmes and John G. Whittier both wrote to King in California to praise his *Transcript* letters.

70. JBF, "A Home Found, and Lost"; Phillips, *Damned Yankee*, p. 231; Denton, *Passion and Principle*, p. 282.

71. TSK, "Selections from a Lecture-Sermon After Visiting Yosemite Valley, Delivered in San Francisco, July 29, 1860," in *The California Scrap-Book*, p. 457.

72. See, e.g., TSK, *The Organization of Liberty on the Western Continent, an Oration Delivered . . . July 5th, 1852* (Boston, 1892), pp. 10–12; also Wendte, pp. 25–26.

73. Wendte, *Thomas Starr King*, p. 185; Herr, *Jessie Benton Frémont*, p. 316; JBF, "Distinguished Persons I Have Known: Starr King," *New York Ledger*, Mar. 6, 1875.

74. *San Francisco Daily Evening Bulletin*, Feb. 23, 1861.

75. *Sacramento Union*, Feb. 25, 1861; Monzingo, pp. 71–74; Wendte, *Thomas Starr King*, pp. 159–60.

76. TSK to Randolph Ryer, Mar. 10, 1861, in TSK Papers, Bancroft Library, University of California; Herr, p. 317.

77. Starr, *Americans and the California Dream*, p. 103; JBF, "Distinguished Persons I Have Known: Starr King"; Monzingo, *Thomas Starr King*, p. 74.

78. TSK, "Daniel Webster," in Whipple, *Substance and Show*, p. 302; Wendte, *Thomas Starr King*, p. 162; *New York Times*, May 13, 1861.

79. Charles P. Roland, *Albert Sidney Johnston: Soldier of Three Republics* (Austin, Tex., 1964), pp. 245–46; Wilkins, *The Great Diamond Hoax*, p. 24.

80. JBF, "Distinguished Persons I Have Known: Starr King"; Herr, *Jessie Benton Frémont*, p. 319.

81. Chaffin, *Pathfinder*, p. 453.

82. Starr, *Americans and the California Dream*, p. 99.

83. In their private correspondence as published by Herr and Spence, the two continued to address one another as "Mrs. Frémont" and "Mr. King." On the other hand, when Jessie—during her husband's lifetime—published an article about her friendship with King, she quoted a letter to her that he signed, "Believe me to be to the brim and overflowingly, Yours, T.S.K." Could the worldly Mrs. Frémont possibly have failed to consider what some readers might make of this? Was she flaunting his devotion in the faces of her husband, King's family, and the general public, perversely daring them to accuse her and the sainted clergyman of adultery? Or was this, in a sense, her own tribute to the chastity they had maintained despite the confluence of attraction and opportunity? We may never know. Herr and Spence, *Letters*, passim; JBF, "Distinguished Persons I Have Known: Starr King."

84. Edwin P. Whipple, ed., *Christianity and Humanity: A Series of Sermons by Thomas Starr King* (Boston, 1877), p. xlv; JBF to William Armstrong, June 10, 1861, Anderson Family Papers, Kansas State Historical Society; JBF to the Editors of the *Alta California*, Feb. 26, 1861, in Herr and Spence, eds., *Letters*, pp. 235–37.

85. JBF, "Distinguished Persons I Have Known: Starr King"; Ralph Waldo Emerson to TSK, Nov. 7, 1862, quoted in J. A. Wagner, "The Oratory of Thomas Starr King," *California Historical Society Quarterly*, vol. 33, no. 3 (Sept. 1954), p. 225.

86. Denton, *Passion and Principle*, p. 291.

87. *San Francisco Bulletin*, Apr. 20, 1861; *Sacramento Union*, May 4, 1861.

88. White, *A Yankee Trader*, pp. 187–88.

89. JBF to William Armstrong, June 10, 1861, in Anderson Family Papers, Kansas State Historical Society; Denton, *Passion and Principle*, pp. 290–91.

90. Duke, *Civil War Reminiscences*, p. 39.

91. William C. Winter, *Civil War in St. Louis: A Guided Tour* (St. Louis, 1994), pp. 31–32.

92. Peckham, *Gen. Nathaniel Lyon*, pp. 82–83; Winter, *Civil War in St. Louis*, p. 33; Duke, *Civil War Reminiscences*, p. 41.

93. Ryle, *Missouri*, p. 175; *Journal of the Proceedings of the Missouri State Convention, Held at Jefferson City and St. Louis, March, 1861* (St. Louis, 1861), p. 244; Phillips, *Damned Yankee*, p. 148.

94. The full rationale is revealed in Duke's *Civil War Reminiscences*, pp. 37–42. Duke was among the secessionist leaders inside the mansion.

95. Winter, *Civil War in St. Louis*, pp. 38–9; Gerteis, *Civil War St. Louis*, pp. 82ff.; Phillips, *Damned Yankee*, p. 138.

96. Phillips, *Damned Yankee*, pp. 88–89; *Last Political Writings of Gen. Nathaniel Lyon, U.S.A.* (New York, 1861), p. 192; Stephen B. Oates, "Nathaniel Lyon: A Personality Profile," *Civil War Illustrated*, vol. 6, no. 10 (Feb. 1968), pp. 15ff.; Franklin A. Dick, "Memorandum of Matters in Missouri in 1861," Franklin A. Dick Papers, LC.

97. William A. Hammond, "Brigadier-General Nathaniel Lyon, U.S.A.—Personal Recollections," *Magazine of American History*, vol. 12, no. 3 (March 1885), pp. 240–48; Oates, "Nathaniel Lyon," p. 15; Phillips, *Damned Yankee*, p. 133.

98. Gerteis, *Civil War St. Louis*, p. 87.

99. Frank P. Blair to Simon Cameron, Mar. 11, 1861; War Department Special Orders No. 74, Mar. 13, 1861; both in *OR* I, pp. 656–58; *Missouri Democrat*, Mar. 31, 1861.

100. Boernstein, *Memoirs of a Nobody*, pp. 268–72; *Missouri Democrat*, Apr. 15, 1861; Arenson, *Great Heart*, pp. 113–15.

101. Rowan and Primm, *Germans for a Free Missouri*, p. 179.

102. Phillips, *Damned Yankee*, pp. 132, 156; Gerteis, *Civil War St. Louis*, p. 93.

103. Mark Twain, "The Private History of a Campaign That Failed"; Susan Staker Lehr, ed., *As the Mockingbird Sang: The Civil War Diary of Pvt. Robert Caldwell Dunlap, C.S.A.* (St. Joseph, Mo., 2005), p. 19.

104. Susannah Ural Bruce, "'Remember Your Country and Keep Its Credit': Irish Volunteers and the Union Army, 1861–1865," *Journal of Military History*, vol. 69, no. 2 (April 2005), pp. 332, 338; "Excerpts from *The Autobiography of August Bondi (1833–1907)*," *Yearbook for German-American Studies*, vol. 40 (2005), p. 152.

105. "Die Fahnenwacht" was also the title of a song popular during the 1848 revolution. It was sung at the flag presentation in St. Louis: *"Der Sanger hält im Feld die Fahnenwacht, / Im seinem Arme ruht das Schwert, das scharfe"* ("The singer is the color guard in the field, / In his arms rests the sword, the sharp sword").

106. Engle, *Yankee Dutchman*, pp. 56–57; *Westliche Post*, May 8, 1861, in Rowan and Primm, *Germans for a Free Missouri*, pp. 195–7; *Missouri Democrat*, May 4, 1861.

107. Cyrus B. Plattenburg, "In St. Louis During the 'Crisis,'" *Journal of the Illinois State Historical Society*, vol. 13, no. 1 (April 1920), p. 19.

108. Francis Preston Blair, Jr., to Simon Cameron, Apr. 18, 1861, Blair Family Papers, LC; Simon Cameron to Nathaniel Lyon, Apr. 30, 1861, *OR* I, vol. 1, p. 675.

109. Gerteis, *Civil War St. Louis*, p. 94; Peckham, *Gen. Nathaniel Lyon*, p. 139; Arenson, *Great Heart*, p. 114; *Missouri Democrat*, April 27, 1861; Boernstein, pp. 284–85; Winter, *Civil War St. Louis*, p. 40.

110. Phillips, *Damned Yankee*, pp. 166–67; Boernstein, *Memoirs of a Nobody*, pp. 286–88; Franklin A. Dick to Benson Lossing, July 6, 1865, Franklin A. Dick Papers, LC; Anderson, *A Border City*, pp. 78–79. About 5,000 of the guns

soon ended up in the hands of Ohio state troops—thanks to the efforts of a newly appointed officer who was sent to procure them, Colonel James A. Garfield.

111. Sherman, *Memoirs*, vol. 1, p. 201.

112. Phillips, *Damned Yankee*, pp. 181–82.

113. Some later historians have questioned whether the story of Lyon's cross-dressing mission was a myth, like similar stories of Abraham Lincoln and Jefferson Davis disguising themselves in women's clothing at other points in the war. But while the Lincoln and Davis rumors were concocted in each case by enemies trying to make them look ridiculous, the Lyon story was attested to in two separate and detailed accounts by two of Lyon's own co-conspirators. One of these was James Peckham (in his 1866 book *Gen. Nathaniel Lyon and Missouri in 1861*, op. cit., pp. 139–40), and the other was Franklin A. Dick (in his 1865 manuscript "Memorandum of Matters in Missouri in 1861," LC).

114. Winter, *Civil War in St. Louis*, p. 44; Engle, *Yankee Dutchman*, p. 58; *Anzeiger des Westens*, May 9, 1861, in Rowan and Primm, *Germans for a Free Missouri*, p. 190.

115. *Westliche Post*, May 1 and 8, 1861, in Rowan and Primm, *Germans for a Free Missouri*, pp. 189, 202–03, 206. The following week, when the editors learned the full story of the artillery shipped to Camp Jackson, they were outraged that the steamer had not been intercepted on its way upriver by federal troops in Illinois, and blamed it on military disorganization: "Things are even worse here than with the Imperial Austrian Military High Command in Vienna."

116. Francis Grierson, *The Valley of Shadows: Sangamon Sketches* (Boston, 1948), pp. 229–30.

117. Ulysses S. Grant, *Memoirs and Selected Letters: Personal Memoirs of U.S. Grant* (New York, 1990), pp. 155–56; Sherman, *Memoirs*, vol. 1, pp. 200–01; Peckham, *Gen. Nathaniel Lyon*, p. 150; Anderson, *A Border City*, p. 96.

118. James W. Covington, "The Camp Jackson Affair: 1861," *Missouri Historical Review*, vol. 15, no. 3 (April 1961), p. 206; Peckham, pp. 150–51.

119. Peckham, *Gen. Nathaniel Lyon*, pp. 151–52; Dick, "Memorandum of Matters in Missouri in 1861."

120. Grierson, *Valley of Shadows*, p. 227; Arenson, *Great Heart*, pp. 191–92; *Missouri Democrat*, May 13, 1861; *Missouri Republican*, May 12, 1861; Peckham, *Gen. Nathaniel Lyon*, pp. 153–35.

121. *Missouri Republican*, May 11 and 12, 1861; Sherman, *Memoirs*, pp. 201–02; *Missouri Democrat*, May 13, 1861; Engle, *Yankee Dutchman*, p. 59.

122. Sherman, *Memoirs*, p. 202; *Missouri Democrat*, May 13, 1861; Dick, "Memorandum of Matters in Missouri in 1861."

123. Grierson, *Valley of Shadows*, p. 230.

124. Anderson, *A Border City*, pp. 106–07; Plattenburg, *In St. Louis*, pp. 19–20; *Westliche* Post, May 15, 1861, in Rowan and Primm, *Germans for a Free Mis-*

souri, pp. 214–17; Boernstein, *Memoirs of a Nobody*, pp. 303–04; *Missouri Republican*, May 11 and 12, 1861; *Missouri Democrat*, May 13, 1861; Peckham, *Gen. Nathaniel Lyon*, pp. 157–63; A. Fulkerson to Francis Preston Blair, Jr., May 15, 1861, Blair Family Papers, LC.

125. *Missouri Democrat*, May 13, 1861; Boernstein, *Memoirs of a Nobody*, p. 304.

126. James M. McPherson, *Battle Cry of Freedom: The Civil War Era* (New York, 1988), pp. 291–92.

127. Grant, *Memoirs*, p. 155. For a highly critical account of Lyon, see Phillips, *Damned Yankee*. For a fascinating perspective on the events in St. Louis as the "second Baden revolution," see Steven Rowan's introduction to Rowan and Primm, *Germans for a Free Missouri*.

128. *Sandusky Daily Commercial Register*, Oct. 31, 1861.

Chapter Seven: The Crossing

1. *Philadelphia Press*, n.d., quoted in *Milwaukee Morning Sentinel*, May 13, 1861.

2. David Hackett Fischer, *Liberty and Freedom* (New York, 2005), p. 299.

3. Emory Holloway, ed., *The Uncollected Poetry and Prose of Walt Whitman* (Garden City, N.Y., 1922), pp. 32–33.

4. *Washington Star*, May 6, 1861; *Philadelphia Press*, n.d., quoted in *Milwaukee Morning Sentinel*, May 13, 1861.

5. "A Letter from One of Our Boys," unidentified clipping ["The Leader," May 1861] in 11th Infantry Regiment Civil War Newspaper Clippings file, New York State Military Museum; Ernest B. Furgurson, *Freedom Rising: Washington in the Civil War* (New York, 2004), p. 87; Isaac Bassett, "A Senate Memoir," unpublished manuscript, U.S. Senate Historical Office.

6. *New York Times*, May 3, 1861; *Harper's Weekly*, May 25, 1861.

7. [Theodore Winthrop], "Washington as a Camp," *Atlantic Monthly*, July 1861.

8. George Alfred Townsend, *Washington, Outside and Inside. A picture and a narrative of the origin, growth, excellencies, abuses, beauties, and personages of our governing city* (Hartford, Conn., 1873), pp. 637 38.

9. *Daily National Intelligencer* (Washington, D.C.), May 4, 1861.

10. Hay, May 2, 1861, in Michael Burlingame and John R. T. Ettinger, eds., *Inside Lincoln's White House: The Complete Civil War Diary of John Hay* (Carbondale, Ill., 1999), p. 17.

11. Margaret Leech, *Reveille in Washington 1860–1865* (New York, 1941), pp. 61–62.

12. James McPherson, *Battle Cry of Freedom: The Civil War Era* (New York, 1988), pp. 284–85; Currier & Ives, "The Lexington of 1861," Prints & Photographs Division, LC.

13. Carl Sandburg, *Abraham Lincoln: The War Years* (New York, 1939), pp. 230.

14. McPherson, *Battle Cry of Freedom*, p. 325.

15. Mrs. Roger Pryor, *Reminiscences of Peace and War* (New York, 1904), pp. 3–4.

A stalemate was achieved when the senator grabbed his adversary by both horns. "Let go, Mr. Clay, and run like blazes," shouted one youthful onlooker. Clay heeded his advice, and sprinted up the avenue with the goat in hot pursuit.

16. Mary Clemmer Ames, *Ten Years in Washington: Life and Scenes in the National Capital, as a Women Sees Them* (Washington, D.C., 1873), p. 68; William Howard Russell, *My Diary North and South* (Boston, 1863), p. 36; Henry Adams, *The Education of Henry Adams*, Ernest Samuels, ed. (Boston, 1973), p. 99.

17. Leech, *Reveille in Washington*, ch. 1–3, passim.

18. *Washington Evening Star*, May 3, 1861.

19. Ruth Painter Randall, *Colonel Elmer Ellsworth: A Biography of Lincoln's Friend and First Hero of the Civil War* (Boston, 1960), pp. 239, 243.

20. *New York Herald*, May 4, 1861; Constance McLaughlin Green, *Washington: Village and Capital, 1800–1878* (Princeton, N.J., 1962), p. 215.

21. *Washington Star*, May 4, 1861; *Milwaukee Morning Sentinel*, May 8, 1861; Hay, May 7, 1861, in Burlingame and Ettinger, *Inside Lincoln's White House.*

22. *Cincinnati Press*, n.d., quoted in *Fayetteville Observer* (N.C.), May 20, 1861.

23. *Daily National Intelligencer*, May 4, 1861.

24. *Daily National Intelligencer*, May 10, 1861; *New-York Tribune*, May 10, 1861; *New York Times*, May 11, 1861; *Brooklyn Eagle*, May 9, 1861; *New York Herald*, May 12, 1861; *Philadelphia Press*, n.d., quoted in *Daily Cleveland Herald*, May 11, 1861; *Harper's Weekly*, May 25, 1861.

25. *New-York Tribune*, May 8, 1861.

26. [John Hay] *New York World*, May 10, 1861. In Michael Burlingame, ed., *Lincoln's Journalist: John Hay's Anonymous Writings for the Press, 1860–1864* (Carbondale, Ill., 1998), pp. 58–64.

27. Hay, "Ellsworth," *Atlantic Monthly*, July 1861; Hay, May 2, 1861, in Burlingame and Ettinger, *Inside Lincoln's White House.*

28. *New-York Tribune*, Apr. 30, 1861; Hay, May 12, 1861, in Burlingame and Ettinger, *Inside Lincoln's White House.*

29. Randall, *Colonel Elmer Ellsworth*, pp. 175, 233.

30. John G. Nicolay and John Hay, *Abraham Lincoln: A History* (New York, 1890), vol. 4, p. 314; William O. Stoddard, *The White House in War Times: Memoirs and Reports of Lincoln's Secretary* (Lincoln, Neb., 2000), pp. 9–10, 163–64.

31. The Mrs. Lincoln story appears in, among other sources, an interview with a Zouave veteran published many years later in the *Washington Post*, Sept. 22, 1907.

32. *Washington Herald*, n.d., cited in Charles A. Mills and Andrew L. Mills, *Alexandria 1861–1865* (Charleston, 2008), p. 16.

33. Furgurson, *Freedom Rising*, p. 92; Donald G. Shomette, *Maritime Alexandria: The Rise and Fall of an American Entrepot* (Bowie, Md., 2003), pp. 152–53.

34. [Winthrop], "Washington as a Camp"; *Philadelphia Inquirer*, May 25, 1861.
35. *New-York Tribune*, June 1, 1861; May 26, 1861; "Harry Lorrequer" (pseud.), "Letter from the Fire Zouaves," unidentified clipping, 11th Infantry Regiment Civil War Newspaper Clippings file, New York State Military Museum.
36. [Winthrop], "Washington as a Camp"; *New York Times*, May 26, 1861.
37. James L. Huffman, *A Yankee in Meiji Japan: The Crusading Journalist Edward H. House* (Lanham, Md., 2003), pp. 24–26.
38. *New-York Tribune*, May 28, 1861; May 25, 1861.
39. Lorrequer, "Letter from the Fire Zouaves."
40. *New York Times*, May 26, 1861; *New-York Tribune*, May 25, 1861.
41. *New-York Tribune*, May 25, 1861; Shomette, *Maritime Alexandria*, pp. 159–61.
42. *Philadelphia Inquirer*, May 25, 1861.
43. Randall, *Colonel Elmer Ellsworth*, pp. 256–57; *New-York Tribune*, May 25, 1861; interview with Henry Winser, *Boston Globe*, Jan. 6, 1884.
44. *Life of James W. Jackson, the Alexandria Hero, the Slayer of Ellsworth, Martyr in the Cause of Southern Independence* (Richmond, 1862), pp. 20–22, 12–13, 44.
45. Ibid., pp. 28–30.
46. *New York Times*, May 26, 1861; *New-York Tribune*, May 25, 1861.
47. *Boston Globe*, Jan. 6, 1884.
48. *New York Times*, May 26, 1861; *New-York Tribune*, May 25, 1861; *Boston Globe*, Jan. 6, 1884; Randall, *Colonel Elmer Ellsworth*, pp. 256–58.
49. David Homer Bates, *Lincoln in the Telegraph Office: Recollections of the United States Military Telegraph Corps During the Civil War* (New York, 1907), p. 8; *New-York Tribune*, May 29, 1861; *Philadelphia Inquirer*, May 25, 1861.
50. One such poetical effusion, in the *Tribune* of May 25, begins:

    > *Hushed be each sorrowing murmur,*
    > *And let no tear be shed,*
    > *As in slow march, with drooping standards*
    > *Ye bear back the gallant dead.*

    Unfortunately, this is typical of the Ellsworth mortuary genre.
51. Burlingame, *Abraham Lincoln*, vol. 2, p. 178.
52. *New York World*, May 27, 1861.
53. *Richmond Dispatch*, May 18, 1861.
54. *New York World*, May 27, 1861; *Richmond Enquirer*, May 25, 1861, quoted in George B. Herbert, *The Popular History of the Civil War in America* (New York, 1884), p. 102.
55. *Illinois State Journal*, June 3, 1861, reprinted in Burlingame, ed., *Lincoln's Journalist*, p. 69; *New-York Tribune*, May 28, 1861.
56. *Daily National Intelligencer*, May 27, 1861; *New York Herald*, May 26, 1861; Randall, *Colonel Elmer Ellsworth*, pp. 264–65.
57. *New York Herald*, May 27, 1861. In the days that followed, fire companies,

militia regiments, and patriotic societies vied with one another in showering Brownell with gifts: a gold medal, a silver-mounted pistol, a jeweled dagger.

58. I have arrived at the figure of twenty thousand using the 1880 Census (considered the most accurate one of the late nineteenth century), accessed via Ancestry.com. I keyword searched for Americans born during the Civil War years with the first names "Elmer," "Ellsworth," and "Elsworth," subtracting as baseline figures the counts of children with each of these first names born in 1859, the year before Ellsworth became famous. If anything, my figure is probably an underestimate, since nineteenth-century Censuses typically undercounted by considerable margins, while many more namesakes were likely lost in transcription, or were simply identified by their initials, a common practice. Nor does it account for the infant mortality rate of approximately 18 percent in the 1860s.

59. Drew Gilpin Faust, *This Republic of Suffering: Death and the American Civil War* (New York, 2008), p. 94; Glenna R. Schroeder-Lein, *Encyclopedia of Civil War Medicine* (Armonk, N.Y., 2008), pp. 99–100.

60. *New York World*, May 25, 1861; *New-York Tribune*, May 30, 1861.

61. Nathaniel Hawthorne, "Chiefly about War Matters," *Atlantic Monthly*, July 1862. Such artifacts are still in public circulation: in 2010, I purchased on eBay a sliver of wood wrapped in nineteenth-century notepaper with the inscription "A Trace of the Stairs that Elsworth stood on, when he was shot dead by Rebel at Alexandrya Va." (And Ellsworth's relics are still commanding hefty prices; the bidding on the sliver closed at $105.49.)

62. David Detzer, *Donnybrook: The Battle of Bull Run, 1861* (New York, 2004), pp. 357–68.

63. Stoddard, *Inside the White House in War Times*, p. 164; John G. Nicolay, *The Army in the Civil War*, vol. 1: *The Outbreak of Rebellion* (New York, 1885), p. 114; Hay, "A Young Hero. Personal Reminiscences of Colonel E. E. Ellsworth." *McClure's Magazine*, March 1896.

64. *Chicago Tribune*, May 28, 1861.

65. Burlingame, *Abraham Lincoln*, vol. 2, 177, quoting *New York Mail and Express*, Feb. 11, 1899.

66. Burlingame, *Lincoln's Journalist*, p. 356.

67. *Chicago Tribune*, July 16, 1872; *New York World*, May 25, 1861.

Chapter Eight: Freedom's Fortress

1. Details of the strange and fascinating story of the first slave voyage to Virginia have only recently been unearthed. See Engel Sluiter, "New Light on the '20. and Odd Negroes' Arriving in Virginia, August, 1619," *William and Mary Quarterly*, 3rd series, vol. 54, no. 2 (Apr. 1997), pp. 395–98; Tim Hashaw, *The Birth of Black America: The First African Americans and the Pursuit of Freedom at Jamestown* (New York, 2007); John Thornton, "The

African Experience of the '20. and Odd Negroes' Arriving in Virginia in 1619," *William and Mary Quarterly*, vol. 55, no. 3 (July 1998); Adam Goodheart, "Reaching Point Comfort," *The American Scholar*, Winter 2005. These accounts make it clear that, contrary to the conventional version of the story, the slaves arrived at Point Comfort and not Jamestown, that the captain was English and not Dutch, and that the Africans on board were definitely slaves and not indentured servants. For tobacco and labor in early Virginia, see Edmund Morgan, *American Slavery, American Freedom: The Ordeal of Colonial Virginia* (New York, 1975); and Russell R. Menard, "A Note on Chesapeake Tobacco Prices, 1618–1660," *Virginia Magazine of History and Biography*, vol. 84, no. 4 (Oct. 1976), pp. 401–10.

2. The official name was—and still is—Fort Monroe, but during the Civil War it was known almost universally as Fortress Monroe, which is therefore the name I use here.

3. Robert Anderson had also done a tour of duty at the fort, as had a young soldier who would not become famous for his military career: Sergeant Major Edgar Allan Poe.

4. Richard P. Weinert, Jr., and Robert Arthur, *Defender of the Chesapeake: The Story of Fort Monroe*, 3rd ed. (Shippensburg, Pa., 1989), chaps. 3–5; John V. Quarstein, "Union Bastion in the Old Dominion," *America's Civil War*, vol. 15, no. 4 (Sept. 2002). The order to reinforce Fortress Monroe was issued less than forty-eight hours after Secretary Floyd resigned from the War Department.

5. Benjamin Ewell to Robert E. Lee, May 16, 1861, in *OR* I, vol. 2, pp. 853–54; Clement Anselm Evans, ed., *Confederate Military History*, vol. 3 (Atlanta, 1899), p. 130; Lee Jensen, *32nd Virginia Infantry* (Lynchburg, Va., 1990), pp. 10–11. One of Mallory's volunteer cavalrymen, a local doctor, actually rode across to the fort to demand of its commander: "By what right, sir, does your army cross that bridge and invade the sacred soil of Virginia?" The Yankee colonel roared in reply: "By God, sir, might makes right!"

6. C. K. Warren to A. Duryee, May 31, 1861, in Benjamin F. Butler Papers, LC; *Philadelphia Press*, June 1, 1861; Charles Carleton Coffin, *Drum-Beat of the Nation: The First Period of the War of the Rebellion from Its Outbreak to the Close of 1862* (New York, 1888), p. 76.

7. [Edward Lillie Pierce], "The Contrabands at Fortress Monroe," *Atlantic Monthly*, November 1861; Benjamin F. Butler, *Butler's Book: Autobiography and Personal Reminiscences of Maj.-Gen. Benjamin F. Butler* (Boston, 1892), p. 265; William C. Davis et al., eds, *Virginia at War, 1864* (Louisville, Ky., 2009), p. 154.

8. Pierce, "The Contrabands at Fortress Monroe"; BFB to Winfield Scott, May 24, 1861, BFB Papers, LC. The wives and children are mentioned in these two sources. According to both Butler and Pierce, the wife of one of the men was a free black woman in Hampton. Other information derives from data on the three men in the 1870 and later federal censuses. According to these, Baker would have been about twenty-five years old in

1861, Townsend about thirty-six, and Shepard Mallory (whose birth date varies considerably across the different census years) probably in his late teens. These ages square roughly with those of three of Colonel Mallory's unnamed male slaves (out of a dozen or so total slaves) enumerated in both the 1850 and 1860 censuses, which possibly suggests that all three had been with Mallory for at least a decade. (Of the three, the data for Shepard Mallory are, again, the least conclusive.) Unfortunately, information on the Mallory household has not been located in the 1840 census. The 1860 census lists two nine-year-old boys and one seven-year-old boy among the Mallory slaves; the identities of their parents were not recorded.

9. Pierce, "The Contrabands at Fortress Monroe"; *Proceedings of the Virginia State Convention* (Richmond, Va., 1861). There are inconsistencies among the various accounts of how and whence the three fugitives arrived at Fortress Monroe. Butler states that they came at night by boat from Sewell's Point, while Pierce says they walked into the Union lines that afternoon. For the original texts, visit the website for this book, www.1861book.com.

10. Pierce, "The Contrabands at Fortress Monroe"; BFB, *Butler's Book*, p. 265; BFB to Scott, May 24, 1861. Butler's two accounts contradict each other slightly; in his 1892 autobiography, he recalls the slaves telling him that the Sewell's Point battery was "a trifling affair" that as yet held only two guns, while in his 1861 report to Scott, he describes the battery (without attributing this information to the slaves) as "a very strong one, mounting fifteen guns." Perhaps Baker, Mallory, and Townsend described only the portion of the rebel works that they had worked on personally.

11. Howard P. Nash, Jr., *Stormy Petrel: The Life and Times of General Benjamin Butler, 1818–1893* (Rutherford, N.J., 1969), pp. 99–101; BFB to Scott, May 24, 1861; *Boston Traveller*, May 28, 1861.

12. *OR* I, vol. 1, 195; Samuel W. Crawford Diary, Mar. 11, 1861, Crawford Papers, LC.

13. Fred A. Shannon, "The Federal Government and the Negro Soldier, 1861–1865," *Journal of Negro History*, vol. 11, no. 4 (Oct. 1926), p. 566; *OR* II, vol. 1, p. 593.

14. Nash, *Stormy Petrel*, chaps. 1–3; *Butler's Book*, pp. 75–77.

15. Murray M. Horowitz, "Ben Butler and the Negro: 'Miracles Are Occurring,'" *Louisiana History*, vol. 17, no. 2 (Spring 1976), pp. 159ff.; *Pittsfield Sun*, Oct. 20, 1859; *Boston Semi-Weekly Courier*, Oct. 10, 1859.

16. John G. Gammons, ed., *The Third Massachusetts Regiment Volunteer Militia in the War of the Rebellion, 1861–1863* (Providence, 1906), pp. 7–13; Theodore S. Peck, ed., *Revised Roster of Vermont Volunteers and Lists of Vermonters Who Served in the Army and Navy of the United States During the War of the Rebellion, 1861–1866* (Montpelier, Vt., 1892), pp. 5–9; *New York Times*, Feb. 3, 1885; James Parton, *General Butler in New Orleans* (New York, 1864), pp. 124–26; W. H. Russell, "Recollections of the Civil War—IV," *The North American Review*, vol. 166, no. 498 (May 1898), p. 623; William

Howard Russell, *My Diary North and South* (Boston, 1863), p. 411; Theodore Winthrop, *The Life and Poems of Theodore Winthrop* (New York, 1884), p. 284. Decades later, a soldier in the Third Massachusetts named Charles R. Haskins would claim that he had been the three contrabands' original savior, but most contemporary accounts mention the Vermonters.

17. Nash, *Stormy Petrel*, pp. 38–39; BFB to Mrs. Winthrop, n.d. (June 1861), BFB Papers, LC.

18. My description of the antebellum landscape of Hampton and its surrounding area is drawn from Pierce, "The Contrabands at Fortress Monroe"; Marion L. Starkey, *The First Plantation: A History of Hampton and Elizabeth City County, Virginia, 1607–1887* (n.p., 1936); Gene Williamson, *Of the Sea and Skies: Historic Hampton and Its Times* (Bowie, Md., 1993); [George W. Curtis], "Theodore Winthrop," *Atlantic Monthly*, August 1861; G. P. Lewis, "Virginia Lands," *American Agriculturalist*, vol. 4 (1845), pp. 118–19; Jacob Hellelfinger, *Kecoughtan Old and New; Or, Three Hundred Years of Elizabeth City Parish* (Hampton, Va., 1910); Lyon Gardiner Tyler, ed., *History of Hampton and Elizabeth City County, Virginia* (Hampton, Va., 1922); J. Michael Cobb and Wythe Holt, *Images of America: Hampton* (Charleston, S.C., 2008); Robert Francis Engs, *Freedom's First Generation: Black Hampton, Virginia, 1861–1890* (New York, 2004), esp. chap. 1; James T. Stensvaag, ed., *Hampton: From the Sea to the Stars* (Norfolk, Va., 1985); Parke Rouse Jr., ed., *When the Yankees Came: Civil War and Reconstruction on the Virginia Peninsula, by George Benjamin West, 1839–1917* (Richmond, Va., 1987); Jane Eliza Davis, *Round About Jamestown: Historical Sketches of the Virginia Peninsula* (n.p., 1907); Thomas P. Southwick, *A Duryee Zouave* (n.p., 1930); Sarah Shaver Hughes, "Elizabeth City County, Virginia, 1782–1810: The Economic and Social Structure of a Tidewater County in the Early National Years," (PhD dissertation, College of William and Mary, 1975); as well as reports from the spring and summer of 1861 in the *Boston Traveller, New York Times, New York World, New-York Tribune,* and *Philadelphia Inquirer.* See also two detailed topographical maps of the vicinity by R. K. Sneden of the U.S. 3rd Army Corps, Mar. 8 and 10, 1861, Geography and Map Division, Library of Congress.

19. Rouse, *When the Yankees Came*, p. 22. In 1857, a lecturer at the Academy assailed *Uncle Tom's Cabin*, telling the students that since Southerners were "taught from youth to believe, and being better assured of it from the studies of our manhood, that the institution of slavery is divine in its origin," it was their responsibility to create a new body of American literature to counter Mrs. Stowe's book.

20. Henry Reed Mallory, *Genealogy of the Mallorys of Virginia* (Hartford, Conn., 1955); Robert Alonzo Brock, Virgil Anson Lewis, *Virginia and Virginians,* vol. 1 (Richmond, 1888), pp. 689ff.; "F.M." [Francis Mallory], "Colonel Mallory," *The Virginia Historical Register, and Literary Companion,* vols. 3–4 (1850), pp. 24ff; *Memorial, Virginia Military Institute: Biographical Sketches of the Graduates and Élèves . . . Who Fell During the War Between the States* (Philadelphia, 1875), pp. 352ff.

21. Mallory, *Genealogy of the Mallorys*, p. 15.

22. Walter Minchinton et al., eds., *Virginia Slave Trade Statistics 1698–1775* (Richmond, 1984), passim; Starkey, pp. 34–36; U.S. Census data, Elizabeth City County, Virginia, 1790–1860. One interesting case of a transition from slavery to freedom was that of Caesar Tarrant, a slave who served during the Revolution as a pilot for the Virginia Navy, aboard vessels with names like *Patriot* and *Jefferson*. Some years after the war, the General Assembly rewarded his valuable service by passing a special bill to purchase his freedom—with state funds, no less. Tarrant and his children went on to become fairly substantial landowners in the county.

23. Engs, *Freedom's First Generation*, chap. 1, passim; Starkey, *The First Plantation*, p. 38; WPA interview (1936) with Moble Hopson (born near Hampton in 1851) in George P. Rawick, ed., *The American Slave: A Composite Autobiography* (Westport, Conn., 1972), series 1, vol. 16, Virginia Narratives, pp. 31ff. Despite the persistent literary convention of writing blacks' spoken words as "Negro" dialect, recent historians have suggested that at least in antebellum Virginia, the dialect of enslaved blacks was quite similar to that of poor whites. See Melvin Ely, *Israel on the Appomattox: A Southern Experiment in Black Freedom from the 1790s to the Civil War* (New York, 2004).

24. Shepard Mallory census data, 1870–1920.

25. Engs, *Freedom's First Generation*, chap. 1, passim; Robert Seager II, *And Tyler Too: A Biography of John & Julia Gardiner Tyler* (New York, 1963), p. 442.

26. *New York World*, June 11, 1861.

27. *American Agriculturalist*, vol. 11, no. 7 (July 1850), p. 203.

28. I'm grateful to Ned Sublette for permission to borrow his idea of the Chesapeake as America's slave coast, the subject of an important book now in progress.

29. Thomas Jefferson to John Wayles Eppes, June 30, 1820. For the Virginia trade, see Frederick Law Olmsted, *A Journey in the Seaboard Slave States* (New York, 1861), pp. 49–59; Steven Deyle, *Carry Me Back: The Domestic Slave Trade in American Life* (New York, 2005), esp. chap. 4; Robert Edgar Conrad, ed., *In the Hands of Strangers: Readings on Foreign and Domestic Slave Trading and the Crisis of the Union* (University Park, Pa., 2001), esp. part 2. For more on Jefferson's views, cf. Susan Dunn, *Dominion of Memories: Jefferson, Madison, and the Decline of Virginia* (New York, 2007), pp. 45–48.

30. Pierce, "The Contrabands at Fortress Monroe."

31. L. C. Lockwood, "Decennial Report," *The American Missionary*, vol. 15 (1871), pp. 196–97; former slave William Roscoe Davis in the *New York Times*, Jan. 14, 1862.

32. Elizabeth City County, Va., Minute Book, June 23, 1859 (Library of Virginia).

33. Elizabeth City County, Va., Minute Book, Nov. 26, 1859.

34. Ibid.

35. David S. Reynolds, *John Brown, Abolitionist: The Man Who Killed Slavery, Sparked the Civil War, and Seeded Civil Rights* (New York, 2005), pp. 329–33;

see also Adam Gopnik, *Angels and Ages: A Short Book About Darwin, Lincoln, and Modern Life* (New York, 2009), pp. 55–56; Barton Haxall Wise, *The Life of Henry A. Wise of Virginia, 1806–1876* (New York, 1899), p. 150. Wise would go on to be a Confederate general.

36. C. Vann Woodward, ed., *Mary Chesnut's Civil War* (New Haven, 1981), pp. xxxvi, xlvi–liii, 29, 153; *DAB* vol. 2, p. 57.

37. Dunn, *Dominion of Memories*, pp. 49–56; Elizabeth City County, Va., Minute Book, Jan. 24, 1861.

38. Federal troops from Fortress Monroe were sent to keep order in Southampton during the rebellion's aftermath. (Personal communication with J. Michael Cobb, Hampton History Museum.)

39. Scot French, *The Rebellious Slave: Nat Turner in American Memory* (Boston, 2004), introduction and pp. 279, 280–82; Russell, *My Diary*, p. 132. Turner's skull was also kept as a local relic. It ended up in a museum at the College of Wooster in Ohio in 1866. After disappearing for several decades in the twentieth century, it was rediscovered in 2002 and donated to the Civil Rights Hall of Fame in Gary, Indiana.

40. Pierce, "The Contrabands at Fortress Monroe"; *Harper's Weekly*, June 29, 1861.

41. Jensen, *32nd Virginia Infantry*, p. 10. In response to the earlier message carried under flag of truce, Butler had arranged to meet the Confederate envoy at 3:30 that afternoon.

42. *Butler's Book*, p. 258. According to the 1860 Census, Mallory's real estate was worth $20,600 and his personal property $29,750, making him one of the wealthiest men in the county.

43. Portraits of both men are in the collections of the Virginia Historical Society.

44. *Butler's Book*, p. 256. Butler and Cary each left two accounts of their parley, one contemporary and one written several decades after the fact. Cary's are, respectively, a brief report to Col. J. B. Magruder, dated 7:15 p.m., May 24, 1861, immediately after the meeting (*OR* II, vol. 1, p. 753); and a letter to Butler, Mar. 9, 1891 (Butler, *Letters*, vol. 1, pp. 102–03). Butler's accounts are in his report of May 24–25, 1861, to Winfield Scott (BFB Papers, LC); and *Butler's Book*, his 1892 autobiography, pp. 256–66. These four versions substantially corroborate one another, and I relied on all of them for my account of Butler and Cary's conversation. The dialogue where quoted directly is from *Butler's Book*.

45. Pierce, "The Contrabands at Fortress Monroe."

46. Nathaniel Morton to "Dear Friend," May 29, 1861, quoted in J. Michael Cobb, "Rehearsing Reconstruction in Occupied Virginia: Life and Emancipation at Fort Monroe," in Davis et al., *Virginia at War*, p. 141.

47. *Chicago Tribune*, June 5, 1861.

48. Quoted in James M. McPherson, *The Struggle for Equality: Abolitionists and the Negro in the Civil War and Reconstruction* (Princeton, N.J., 1964), p. 41.

49. *New York Herald*, May 5, 1861.

50. McPherson, *The Struggle for Equality*, p. 58.

51. Sermon at Zion's Church, April 27, 1861, in *Douglass' Monthly*, June 1861.

52. Frederick Douglass, *My Bondage and My Freedom*, in *Autobiographies* (New York, 1994), p. 452.

53. John Stauffer, *Giants: The Parallel Lives of Frederick Douglass and Abraham Lincoln* (New York, 2008), pp. 215–19; *Douglass' Monthly*, May 1861.

54. *Douglass' Monthly*, June 1861.

55. Ibid., May 1861.

56. *New York Times*, May 27, 1861.

57. *New York World*, May 29, 1861; Montgomery Blair to BFB, May 29, 1861, BFB Papers, LC.

58. Montgomery Blair to BFB, May 29, 1861, BFB Papers, LC.

59. John Hay Diary, May 7, 1861, in Michael Burlingame and John R. T. Ettinger, eds., *Inside Lincoln's White House: The Complete Civil War Diary of John Hay* (Carbondale, Ill., 1999), pp. 19–20.

60. Orville H. Browning to AL, Apr. 30, 1861, AL Papers, LC.

61. Hay Diary, May 7, 1861, in Burlingame and Ettinger, *Inside Lincoln's White House*.

62. For an eloquent discussion of Lincoln's "cult of the law," see Adam Gopnik, *Angels and Ages: A Short Book About Darwin, Lincoln, and Modern Life* (New York, 2009), pp. 57–60.

63. *Richmond Dispatch*, May 29 and June 1, 1861. Those "patriotic yellow men" in New Orleans switched sides to the Union Army, more or less en masse, after Benjamin Butler's troops occupied the city in 1862.

64. Ervin L. Jordan, Jr., *Black Confederates and Afro-Yankees in Civil War Virginia* (Charlottesville, Va., 1995), esp. chap. 10; Hopson interview in Rawick, *The American Slave*.

65. Woodward, *Mary Chesnut's Civil War*, p. 48.

66. *New-York Tribune*, February 20, 1861.

67. Woodward, *Mary Chesnut's Civil War*, p. 44.

68. William H. Lee to Jefferson Davis, May 4, 1861, in Ira Berlin et al., eds., *Freedom: A Documentary History of Emancipation, 1861–1867*, series 1, vol. 2: *The Wartime Genesis of Free Labor: The Upper South* (New York, 1993), p. 282.

69. Steven Hahn, *A Nation Under Our Feet: Black Political Struggles in the Rural South, from Slavery to the Great Migration* (Cambridge, Mass., 2003), p. 67.

70. Armstead Robinson, "In the Shadow of Old John Brown: Insurrection Anxiety and Confederate Mobilization, 1861–1863," *Journal of Negro History*, vol. 65, no. 4 (Autumn, 1980), p. 285.

71. John T. Washington and John H. Stuart to Daniel Ruggles, May 7, 1861, and Daniel Ruggles to R. S. Garnett, May 8, 1861, both in *OR* I, vol. 2, p. 820.

72. *New York Herald*, May 30, 1861; *Springfield Republican*, June 1, 1861; "The (Fort) Monroe Doctrine," Prints & Photographs Division, LC. The car-

toon circulated as a "patriotic cover"—a decorative envelope often used by soldiers sending letters home from the front.

73. Rev. J. D. Fulton, "Funeral Sermon Commemorative of the Death of Colonel Elmer E. Ellsworth . . . Before the New York State Volunteers," *Albany Journal*, May 28, 1861.

74. Montgomery Blair to BFB, May 29 and 31 [*sic*], 1861, BFB Papers, LC; *New York World*, June 4, 1861. Since newspaper accounts all confirm that the meeting occurred on May 30, it is likely that Blair misdated his second letter. The next day's *New York Times* summarized the meeting thus: "The Cabinet adjourned without disposing of Sambo—not a surprising fact, considering that Sambo has been on hand so long."

75. BFB to Winfield Scott, May 27, 1861, BFB Papers, LC; Montgomery Blair to BFB, May 29 and 31 [sic], 1861, BFB Papers, LC; *New York Herald*, May 30, 1861.

76. Montgomery Blair to BFB, June 8, 1861, BFB Papers, LC.

77. Curtis, "Theodore Winthrop," *Atlantic Monthly*, August 1861.

78. *Butler's Book*, pp. 246–49; Russell, pp. 405–06; *Boston Traveller*, May 1, 1861. For Scott on seafood, see *Butler's Book* and *Boston Traveller*, June 18, 1861.

79. My description of the activities at Fortress Monroe is drawn from reporting in the *Boston Traveller*, *New York Times*, *New York World*, and *Atlantic Monthly*, as well as the BFB Papers and *Butler's Book*. For Professor La Mountain, see Frederick Stansbury Haydon, *Aeronautics in the Union and Confederate Armies* (Baltimore, 1941). For the mosquitoes: *New York Times*, July 28, 1861.

80. *New York Times*, June 4 and 14, 1861; Alfred Davenport, *Camp and Field Life of the Fifth New York Volunteer Infantry (Duryee Zouaves)*, (New York, 1879). Winslow Homer's painting "The Briarwood Pipe" shows the Duryee Zouaves later in the war, sporting the red fezzes that they sometimes wore under their turbans. The Turner Rifles' name came from the *Turnverein*, the German young men's clubs that combined culture, nationalist politics, and physical fitness; the movement had come to America after 1848 and its adherents composed the bulk of the regiment's recruits.

81. *Boston Traveller*, July 10, 1861; *New York Times*, June 2, 1861; BFB to Lewis Tappan, Aug. 10, 1861, *Letters*, vol. 1, pp. 200–01; *The Independent*, Aug. 8, 1861. Quite a number of Union accounts compared the "low white laboring class" unfavorably with the blacks. Major Rutherford B. Hayes wrote in his diary in January 1862, while stationed in western Virginia: "Two more contrabands yesterday. These runaways are bright fellows. As a body they are superior to the average of the uneducated white population of this State. More intelligent, I feel confident. What a good-for-nothing people the mass of these western Virginians are! Unenterprising, lazy, narrow, listless, and ignorant. Careless of consequences to the country if their own lives and property are safe. Slavery leaves one class, the wealthy, with leisure for cultivation. They are usually intelligent, well-bred, brave, and high-spirited. The rest are serfs." Charles Richard Williams, ed., *Diary and Letters of Ruth-*

erford B. Hayes, Nineteenth President of the United States, vol. 2, (Columbus, 1922), p. 188.

82. *New York Times*, June 9, 1861; Kate Masur, " 'A Rare Phenomenon of Philological Vegetation': The Word 'Contraband' and the Meanings of Emancipation in the United States," *Journal of American History*, vol. 93, no. 4 (March 2007), p. 1051; *Philadelphia Inquirer*, July 1, 1861.

83. Eric Foner, *The Fiery Trial: Abraham Lincoln and American Slavery* (New York, 2010), p. 171.

84. Engs, *Freedom's First Generation*, pp. 15–16; Rouse, *When the Yankees Came*, p. 54; Pierce, "The Contrabands at Fortress Monroe."

85. *Trenton Daily State Gazette and Republican*, June 5, 1861; *Frank Leslie's Illustrated Newspaper*, June 8, 1861; *Douglass' Monthly*, July 1861.

86. BFB to Montgomery Blair, June 6, 1861, Blair Family Papers, LC; BFB to Winfield Scott, May 27, 1861, BFB Papers, LC.

87. Theodore Winthrop to Laura Winthrop Johnson, May 31, 1861, in Winthrop, *Life and Poems*, pp. 288–89. Parton, *General Butler in New York*, pp. 131–32, gives a similar version of the story as recollected several years later by some of the other officers present.

88. Winthrop, *Life and Poems*, passim; Curtis, "Theodore Winthrop," *The Atlantic*, November 1861.

89. *Butler's Book*, p. 203; Curtis, "Theodore Winthrop."

90. Curtis, "Theodore Winthrop."

91. Lewis C. Lockwood to "Dear Brethren," April 17, 1862, American Missionary Association Papers, Fisk University.

92. Blair to BFB, May 29, 1861, BFB papers.

93. C. K. Warren to A. Duryee, May 31, 1861, BFB Papers.

94. Lockwood to "Dear Brethren," Mar. 26, 1862, AMA Papers; Pierce, "The Contrabands at Fortress Monroe"; Ervin L. Jordan, Jr., *Black Confederates and Afro-Yankees in Civil War Virginia* (Charlottesville, Va., 1955), p. 28; *Boston Traveller*, July 6, 1861; Lewis C. Lockwood, *Mary S. Peake, the Colored Teacher at Fortress Monroe* (Boston, n.d.), p. 56. Vermont in 1860 had just 709 black inhabitants, or less than one quarter of one percent of its population (1860 census).

95. *New York Times*, June 15, 1861; *Philadelphia Inquirer*, July 16, 1861; Davenport, *Camp and Field Life*, pp. 76–80.

96. Eugene Goodwin, Civil War Diary, July 22, 1861, online at www.iagenweb .org.

97. Engs, *Freedom's First Generation*, pp. 18–19; M. F. Armstrong and Helen W. Ludlow, *Hampton and Its Students* (New York, 1874), pp. 109–14.

98. Gammons, *Third Massachusetts Regiment*, p. 194; *New York Times*, Sept. 8, 1897; *Boston Traveller*, May 10, 1861. Pierce wrote a series of dispatches to the *Traveller* between April and July, parts of which he eventually adapted into his article on the contrabands in the *Atlantic*.

99. Pierce, "The Contrabands at Fortress Monroe"; *New York Times*, Oct. 4, 1861; *Boston Traveller*, July 15, 1861.

100. *Boston Traveller*, July 10, 1861.

101. *New York Times*, June 13, 1861; Charles P. Poland, Jr., *The Glories of War: Small Battles and Early Heroes of 1861* (Bloomington, Ind., 2004), p. 208; Winthrop, *Life and Poems*, p. 291; *Springfield Republican*, June 29, 1861; E. W. Pierce to BFB, June 12, 1861, *OR* I, vol. 2, p. 83; Benjamin Quarles, *The Negro in the Civil War* (Boston, 1953), pp. 78–79.

102. *Weekly Anglo-African*, Aug. 17, 1861; Winthrop, *Life and Poems*, p. 291; *New York World*, June 14, 1861; Poland, *Glories of War*, pp. 208–09.

103. *New York World*, June 14, 1861.

104. Poland, *Glories of War*, pp. 211–224.

105. Pierce, "The Contrabands at Fortress Monroe."

106. BFB to Simon Cameron, July 30, 1861, in *Letters*, vol. 1, pp. 187–88.

107. BFB to Pierce, Aug. 15, 1861, in *Letters*, vol. 1, p. 216.

108. As just one example of Butler's fan mail, an old college classmate wrote to him on May 31: "Do you recollect how often, when planning for the future in my room at college, you used to remark *'Well Gray if you & I live, you will hear from me by & by?'* Your prophecy seems to be rapidly fulfilling. . . . You have already made several 'happy hits'—but none that has met with more hearty response & indeed *electrified* the whole nation, like your *nigger 'contraband goods' doct..!!* Why shdnt the darkies dig trenches & throw breast works for *us*, as well as for the rebels? To know how best to dispose of them, when they come rushing to you by the 1000s, is the question. But you struck the right chord! Two or three such brilliant strokes, will put you in sight of the *White House!* The man who does the most towards removing the *cause* of this war, will be the next President of the U.S.! Mark the prophecy!" (E. H. Gray to BFB, May 31, 1861, BFB Papers.)

109. Pierce, "The Contrabands at Fortress Monroe."

110. Michael Meyer, *The Year that Changed the World: The Untold Story Behind the Fall of the Berlin Wall* (New York, 2009), pp. 5–8, 166–67.

111. John G. Nicolay and John Hay, *Abraham Lincoln: A History* (New York, 1904), vol. 4, p. 387.

112. Media, Pa., *Advertiser*, n.d., in *Weekly Anglo-African*, Aug. 10, 1861; *Boston Traveller*, May 2 and June 1, 1861; *Sandusky Register*, June 28, 1861; Harvey Brown to E. D. Townsend, June 22, 1861, *OR* II, vol. 1, p. 755; *Harrisburg Union*, June 27, 1861, in *Washington Evening Star*, July 3, 1861; Pierce, "The Contrabands at Fortress Monroe." Some slaves even crossed the Potomac from Washington, D.C., to Virginia in search of troops that might harbor them. (Nicolay and Hay, *Abraham Lincoln*, vol. 4, p. 390.)

113. George McClellan to "The Union Men of Western Virginia," May 26, 1861, *OR* II, vol. 1, p. 753; Harvey Brown to E. D. Townsend, June 22, 1861, *OR* II, vol. 1, p. 755.

114. *Boston Traveller*, July 13, 1861; J. H. Lane to S. D. Sturgis, Oct. 3, 1861, *OR* II, vol. 1, pp. 771–72. Lane had served as a U.S. senator from Kansas, which is probably how he got away with sending such an extraordinary note to his commander.

115. Simon Cameron to BFB, Aug. 8, 1861, in BFB, *Letters*, vol. 1, pp. 201–03; Pierce, "The Contrabands at Fortress Monroe."

116. *Trenton State Gazette*, June 12, 1861.

117. Allan Pinkerton, *The Spy of the Rebellion* (New York, 1886), p. 194; *Albany Evening Journal*, n.d., in *Weekly Anglo-African*, Aug. 17, 1861.

118. *New York World*, June 4, 1861.

119. *New-York Tribune*, July 25, 1861.

120. *Douglass' Monthly*, June 1861; *Boston Traveller*, June 4, 1861; John Cimprich, *Slavery's End in Tennessee, 1861–1865* (Tuscaloosa, Ala., 1985), pp. 12–13; Pinkerton, *Spy*, p. 177.

121. *New-York Tribune*, n.d., in *National Anti-Slavery Standard*, May 18, 1861; *New York Herald*, n.d., in *National Anti-Slavery Standard*, June 15, 1861.

122. Jessie Frémont to John Anderson, May 11, 1861, Anderson Family Papers, Kansas State Historical Society.

123. Robinson, "In the Shadow of Old John Brown"; Mary Elizabeth Massey, *Ersatz in the Confederacy: Shortages and Substitutes on the Southern Homefront* (Columbia, S.C., 1993), p. 7; John Eaton, *Grant, Lincoln, and the Freedmen* (London, 1907), p. 2.

124. Donn Piatt, *Memories of the Men Who Saved the Union* (New York, 1887), p. 150.

125. Burning of Hampton: BFB to Winfield Scott, August 8, 1861, and J. Bankhead Magruder to George Deas, Aug. 9, 1861, in *OR* I, vol. 4, pp. 567–72; *Philadelphia Inquirer*, Aug. 10, 1861; H. K. W. Patterson, *War Memories of Fort Monroe and Vicinity* (Fort Monroe, Va., 1885), pp. 30–33; *Boston Globe*, Aug. 7, 1911; Cobb and Holt, *Images of America*, pp. 33–39; Williamson, *Of the Sea and Skies*, pp. 181–82; Cobb, "Rehearsing Reconstruction in Occupied Virginia," p. 144; William H. Osborne, *The History of the Twenty-ninth Regiment of Massachusetts Volunteer Infantry* (Boston, 1877), pp. 78–81; Starkey, *The First Plantation*, pp. 81–2; Rouse, *When the Yankees Came*, p. 99.

Chapter Nine: Independence Day

1. Cometary observations: *Daily National Intelligencer*, July 4, 1861; *Astronomical and Meteorological Observations Made at the United States Naval Observatory, During the Year 1861* (Washington, D.C., 1862); *Washington Star*, July 2 and 5, 1861; "The Comet As It Appeared to the Eyes of a Common Man," *Scientific American*, vol. 5, no. 2 (July 13, 1861), p. 27; "The Great Comet of 1861," *The Friend: A Religious and Literary Journal*, Aug. 3, 1861, p. 34; *Littell's Living Age*, Oct. 19, 1861; *New York Herald*, July 3 and 4, 1861; *Cincinnati Daily Commercial*, July 6, 1861; *New York Times*, July 8, 1861; *Boston Traveller*, July 8, 1861; Alfred Davenport, *Camp and Field Life of the Fifth New York (Duryee's Zouaves)* (Boston, 1879), p. 84; Thomas Starr King, *Christianity and Humanity* (Boston, 1877), p. 325.

2. *Washington Star*, July 5, 1861; *New York World*, July 10, 1861; Eugene Goodwin Civil War Diary, July 4, 1861.

3. *New York Tribune*, July 10, 1861; Robert F. Durden, "The American Revolution as Seen by Southerners in 1861," *Louisiana History*, vol. 19, no. 1 (Winter 1978), pp. 33–42; *New Orleans Daily Picayune*, July 4, 1861.

4. Durden, "The American Revolution," pp. 40–1.

5. *Philadelphia Inquirer*, July 4, 1861; *The Crisis* (Columbus, Ohio), July 4, 1861.

6. Allan Nevins, *The War for the Union*, vol. 1: *The Improvised War* (New York, 1959), p. 188; *Washington Star*, July 3, 1861; *New York Times*, July 7, 1861; *Report of the Commissioner of Public Buildings*, Nov. 8, 1861.

7. Nevins, *War for the Union*, vol. 1, p. 189; *Washington Star*, July 2, 1861; *Philadelphia Press*, July 5, 1861; [Theodore Winthrop], "Washington as a Camp," *Atlantic Monthly*, July 1861; Thomas U. Walter to Amanda Walter, May 3, 1861, quoted in William C. Allen, *History of the United States Capitol: A Chronicle of Design, Construction, and Politics* (Washington, D.C., 2001), p. 314. "These are nasty things to talk to a lady about," Walter added, "but ladies ought to know what vile uses the most elegant things are devoted to in times of war."

8. Robert W. Johannsen, *Stephen A. Douglas* (New York, 1973), p. 867.

9. *Cincinnati Daily Commercial*, July 8 and 9, 1861; *Congressional Globe*, July 4, 1861.

10. Michael Burlingame, *Abraham Lincoln: A Life* (Baltimore, 2008), vol. 2, pp. 133–34.

11. William J. Cooper, *Jefferson Davis, American* (New York, 2001), p. 353.

12. John Hay Diary, May 7, 1861, in Michael Burlingame and John R. T. Ettinger, eds., *Inside Lincoln's White House: The Complete Civil War Diary of John Hay* (Carbondale, Ill., 1999), pp. 19–20.

13. AL to the Regent Captains of San Marino, May 7, 1861, in Roy P. Basler, ed., *Collected Works of Abraham Lincoln*, vol. 4 (New Brunswick, N.J., 1953), p. 360.

14. Burlingame, *Abraham Lincoln*, vol. 2, p. 168; *New York Times*, June 20, 1861; Nicolay to Therena Bates, July 3, 1861, in Michael Burlingame, ed., *With Lincoln in the White House: Letters, Memoranda, and Other Writings of John G. Nicolay, 1860–1865* (Carbondale, Ill., 2000), p. 46.

15. Douglas Wilson, *Lincoln's Sword: The Presidency and the Power of Words* (New York, 2006), p. 74. The context of Emerson's remark makes it clear that it was meant as a criticism: cf. Linda Allardt, et al., eds., *The Journals and Miscellaneous Notebooks of Ralph Waldo Emerson* (Cambridge, Mass., 1982), vol. 15, p. 520.

16. Wilson, *Lincoln's Sword*, pp. 94–95; Charles Sumner to Francis Lieber, June 23, 1861, and Sumner to Richard Henry Dana, Jr., June 30, 1861, in Beverly Wilson Palmer, ed., *The Selected Letters of Charles Sumner* (Boston, 1990), vol. 2, pp. 71–72; David Herbert Donald, *Charles Sumner and the Coming of the Civil War* (New York, 1960), pp. 382–83; John Lothrop Motley to Mary Motley, June 23, 1861, in George W. Curtis, ed., *Complete Works of John Lothrop Motley* (New York, 1900), vol. 16, pp. 158–59; Nicolay to Therena Bates, July 3, 1861, in Burlingame, *With Lincoln in the White House*,

p. 46; Burlingame, *Abraham Lincoln*, vol. 2, p. 166. Wilson's *Lincoln's Sword* offers a careful and informative analysis of the document's several surviving drafts and how they reflect the evolution of Lincoln's thought during the writing process.

17. Burlingame, *Abraham Lincoln*, vol. 2, p. 170. Although dated July 4, Lincoln's address was not actually read aloud in the House and Senate until July 5.

18. Wilfred Buck Yearns, *The Confederate Congress* (Athens, Ga., 1960), p. 35.

19. Wilson, *Lincoln's Sword*, p. 79.

20. Burlingame, *Abraham Lincoln*, vol. 2, p. 172.

21. *Baltimore Sun*, July 20, 1861.

22. AL, "Message to Congress, July 4, 1861," handwritten draft, May or June 1861, in AL Papers.

23. George W. Curtis to John J. Pinkerton, July 9, 1861, in Edward Cary, *George William Curtis* (Boston, 1896), p. 147.

24. Burlingame, *Abraham Lincoln*, vol. 2, p. 171.

25. *Washington Star*, July 7, 1861 (italics in original).

26. *Sandusky Daily Commercial Register*, July 19, 1861; Nicolay to Therena Bates, May 31, 1861, quoted in Helen Nicolay, *Lincoln's Secretary: A Biography of John G. Nicolay* (New York, 1949), p. 106. Although George Washington freed his own slaves in his will, the so-called dower slaves at Mount Vernon—the Negroes and their descendants who had come into the estate as part of his wife's dowry—remained the property of Martha Washington, and passed to her Custis heirs at her death.

27. *Philadelphia Inquirer*, July 5, 1861; *Illinois State Journal*, July 9, 1861.

28. *New York World*, July 4, 1861.

29. *Philadelphia Inquirer*, July 5, 1861; William Milmine to Alf Milmine, July 8, 1861, private collection.

30. Margaret Leech, *Reveille in Washington, 1860–1865* (New York, 1941), p. 85; *Harper's Weekly*, July 27, 1861; *Washington Star*, July 5, 1861; *Philadelphia Inquirer*, July 5, 1861; *New York Times*, May 26 and July 5, 1861; Nicolay to Therena Bates, July 7, 1861, in Burlingame, *With Lincoln in the White House*, p. 47; James G. Randall and Richard Nelson Current, *Lincoln the President*, vol. 4: *The Last Full Measure* (Carbondale, Ill., 2000), pp. 77–78.

31. *Philadelphia Inquirer*, July 5, 1861.

32. C. Vann Woodward, *Mary Chesnut's Civil War* (New Haven, 1981), p. 94.

33. *Christian Examiner*, July 1861.

34. Julia Taft Bayne, *Tad Lincoln's Father* (Lincoln, Neb., 2001), pp. 30–31.

35. *New York Herald*, July 4, 1861.

Postscripts

1. *New York Times*, Apr. 18, 1865; Debby Applegate, *The Most Famous Man in America: The Biography of Henry Ward Beecher* (New York, 2006), pp. 1–15; E. Milby Burton, *The Siege of Charleston 1861–1865* (Columbia, S.C., 1970).

2. *DAB*, vol. 2, pp. 213–14; Elbert B. Smith, *The Presidency of James Buchanan* (Lawrence, Kans., 1975), pp. 193–98.

3. *DAB*, vol. 10, p. 92; LeRoy P. Graf et al., eds., *The Papers of Andrew Johnson*, vol. 11 (Knoxville, Tenn., 1994), pp. 525–26 n.

4. Albert D. Kirwan, *John J. Crittenden: The Struggle for the Union* (Lexington, Ky., 1962).

5. Dorothy Sterling, *Ahead of Her Time: Abby Kelley and the Politics of Antislavery* (New York, 1991), pp. 339–56.

6. John E. Vacha, "The Case of Sara Lucy Bagby: A Late Gesture," *Ohio History*, vol. 76, no. 4 (Autumn 1967), p. 231; Charles M. Christian and Sari Bennett, eds., *Black Saga: The African American Experience: A Chronology* (Boston, 1995), p. 185; Judith Luckett, "Local Studies and Larger Issues: The Case of Sara Bagby," *Teaching History*, vol. 27, no. 2 (Fall 2002), p. 97.

7. Margaret Leech and Harry J. Brown, *The Garfield Orbit* (New York, 1978); Allan Peskin, *Garfield: A Biography* (Kent, Ohio, 1978); Frank Holcomb Mason, *The Forty-Second Ohio Infantry; A History of the Organization and Services of That Regiment, in the War of the Rebellion* (Cleveland, 1876).

8. Alvy L. King, *Louis T. Wigfall: Southern Fire-Eater* (Baton Rouge, 1970), pp. 205–31.

9. Pamela Herr, *Jessie Benton Frémont: A Biography* (New York, 1987), pp. 324–450; Jessie Benton Frémont, *The Story of the Guard: A Chronicle of the War* (Boston, 1863), pp. 222–24; *Out West*, January 1903.

10. Sally Denton, *Passion and Principle: John and Jessie Frémont, the Couple Whose Power, Politics, and Love Shaped Nineteenth-Century America* (New York, 2007), p. 341; Jessie Benton Frémont, "A Home Lost, and Found," *The Home-Maker*, Feb. 1892; *San Francisco Chronicle*, July 4, 2010.

11. Robert Monzingo, *Thomas Starr King: Eminent Californian, Civil War Statesman, Unitarian Minister* (Pacific Grove, Ca., 1991), pp. 133–239; *Los Angeles Times*, May 29, 2009.

12. Hans L. Trefousse, *Ben Butler: The South Called Him Beast* (New York, 1957), passim; Benjamin Quarles, *The Negro in the Civil War* (Boston, 1953), pp. 115–18; *Norfolk Virginian-Pilot*, July 25, 2010.

13. Robert Francis Engs, *Freedom's First Generation: Black Hampton, Virginia, 1861–1890* (New York, 2004).

14. Henry R. Mallory, *Genealogy of the Mallorys of Virginia* (Hartford, Conn., 1955), pp. 24–26.

15. C. Vann Woodward, ed., *Mary Chesnut's Civil War* (New Haven, 1981), p. 746.

16. *Inside Business: The Hampton Roads Business Journal*, June 11, 2010; *Hampton Roads Daily Press*, Aug. 9, 2010; *Norfolk Virginian-Pilot*, Jan. 10, 2010.

17. U.S. Census data, 1870–1920; Engs, *Freedom's First Generation*, pp. 145–46. The census worker in 1920 recorded Mallory's age as seventy, but other records make it clear he was approximately a decade older than that.

The total number of books published on the Civil War since 1861 roughly equals the total number of soldiers—both Union and Confederate—who fought the First Battle of Bull Run. Sending my own off into that fray, I have of course benefited enormously from the work of those who went before, including trailblazing research during the past two decades that has done much to open new fields of inquiry and correct past imbalances.

Surprisingly, there are still some topics that remain too little explored, such as the presidential campaigns of 1860 (especially the Wide Awake phenomenon); the transcontinental telegraph; the distinctive roles of Germans and other white ethnic groups; and the story of the contrabands at Fortress Monroe and elsewhere during the opening year of the war.

Space does not permit a full listing of every source that I drew upon; the bibliographical essay below touches on a few highlights for each chapter, especially the secondary sources. A much more complete bibliography can be found on the website for this book, www.1861book.com.

The Civil War era is, of course, also incredibly rich in visual images. The technology of the printed page cannot do full justice to the astonishing detail captured in a glass-plate photograph, but that of the Internet can: zooming in bit by bit is like entering the vanished moment itself. High-resolution versions of the photographs in this book are available on my website. Readers will also find there the full texts of poems quoted as epigraphs.

In referring to African-Americans, I have used the terms "Negro" and "colored," in keeping with the usage of the time. Unfortunately, giving a full sense of the period also compels the historian to quote racist rhetoric that is often quite ugly. But this was so much a part of the political culture of the Civil War era, in both North and South, that it cannot and should not be avoided. In providing verbal quotations from African-Americans themselves as reported by whites, I have, reluctantly, preserved the "dialect" versions used in almost all the original sources, even though some of the conventional spellings (e.g., "wuz" for "was") served no conceivable phonetic purpose, and were as characteristic of Southern whites' speech as of blacks'. Trying to correct this would have required bowdlerizing the original sources, and I believe that the voices of the original speakers ring through eloquently despite the white writers' reflexive habits of belittlement.

Period newspapers are essential sources for the Civil War era, but must be used with caution, since objectivity was an alien concept in the 1860s, and most editors cared more about providing sensational coverage than about being accurate. (For example, many Northern papers originally described the disasters at Big Bethel and Bull Run as magnificent Union victories.) On the other hand, the concept of eyewitness journalism was just coming into its own, and when a reporter was actually on the scene, he often recounted details quite vividly and usually with reasonable accuracy. Even "second-tier" papers such as the *Cincinnati Daily Commercial* and the *Philadelphia Press* often provide a surprising amount of valuable firsthand reporting by those papers' national correspondents.

It is considerably more difficult to hear the voices of ordinary Americans from the months that this book covers than from later in the war. Eventually, of course, the long struggle would generate a tremendous outpouring of letters and diaries written by enlisted men and their families back home, papers that (unlike most routine correspondence during peacetime) would be treasured and preserved by them and their descendants. But there were simply far fewer soldiers in the early months of 1861, and even those who did serve were perhaps less likely to send as many letters, since most were on three-month enlistments and believed they would soon be home to recount their experiences in person. Perhaps, too, families were less likely to preserve the soldiers' letters than they would be later, once it became clear to everyone that the war was going to be both a long struggle and an epochal event in the nation's history. So far, I have been able to locate only two letters from an enlisted man at Fort Sumter during the siege. There are very few surviving letters or diaries of African-Americans from this period.

General Sources

James M. McPherson's *Battle Cry of Freedom: The Civil War Era* (Oxford University Press, 1988) has been justly hailed as the best contemporary one-volume history of the war. I would go further and call it the best one-volume history of the conflict ever written: it is astonishing how much narrative detail, period color, subtle analysis, and topical breadth the author is able to fit into a single (admittedly thick but never ponderous) book. Older accounts continue to provide fresh insights and are written with an elegance and wit, a sense of irony and a subtle appreciation of the complex (often contradictory) nature of the past, that are too rarely found in recent scholarship. Allan Nevins's eight-volume *The Ordeal of the Union* (New York: Scribner, 1947–71) remains a monument of American historiography. Bruce Catton has gone somewhat into eclipse in recent decades, but his books—especially, for the purposes of my own work, *The Coming Fury* (New York: Doubleday, 1961)—are inspiring examples of how an author can write history as literature without sacrificing accuracy.

Russell McClintock's *Lincoln and the Decision for War: The Northern Response to Secession* (University of North Carolina Press, 2008) is an invaluable recent addition to the historiography, meticulously reconstructing the events leading up to the fall of Sumter and illustrating the relationship between Northern public opinion and the inner councils of the Lincoln administration.

The compendious collection published by the War Department, *The War of the Rebellion: A Compilation of the Official Records of the Union and Confederate Armies* (Washington, D.C.: U.S. Government Printing Office, 1880–1901) is an indispensable resource for anyone studying almost any aspect of the conflict.

Michael Burlingame has done more than perhaps any other single scholar to assemble exhaustive information about Abraham Lincoln's life and presidency—in the process also casting light into many other corners of nineteenth-century America. His two-volume *Abraham Lincoln: A Life* (Johns Hopkins University Press, 2008) is a true gold mine, and Burlingame has further earned the gratitude of researchers and readers by posting an unabridged version of the already almost two-thousand-page biography (including his full footnotes) on the website of Knox College's Lincoln Studies Center.

Philip Paludan's *A People's Contest: The Union and Civil War, 1861–1865* (New York: Harper & Row, 1988) is a revealing account of how the Civil War transformed the identity and society of the North. Scott Reynolds Nelson and Carol Sheriff's *A People at War: Civilians and Soldiers in America's Civil War* (Oxford University Press, 2007) lucidly portrays the various roles of ordinary American men and women. George M. Frederickson's *The Inner Civil War: Northern Intellectuals and the Crisis of the Union* (New York: Harper & Row, 1965) remains one of the most thoughtful and subtle treatments of American intellectual life in the Civil War era, and of the complicated relationships among poetry, philosophy, and politics.

Prologue: A Banner at Daybreak

Two of the Union officers besieged at Fort Sumter during the winter of 1860–61 left vivid accounts of their experience. Samuel Wylie Crawford's *The History of the Fall of Fort Sumter* (New York: C. L. Webster & Co, 1887) not only recounts the events in Charleston Harbor but also puts them in their larger political context, based on information he diligently gathered after the war from both Northern and Southern participants. Crawford's letters and diary in the Library of Congress provide even more detail. Abner Doubleday's *Reminiscences of Forts Sumter and Moultrie in 1860–'61* (New York: Harper & Brothers, 1876) is another valuable source, colored somewhat by the author's own cantankerous personality; it provides the fullest description of the move from Moultrie to Sumter. The first volume of *Battles and Leaders of the Civil War* (New York: The Century Company, 1887) contains other, briefer, eyewitness accounts. The Robert Anderson Papers in the Library of Congress offer many clues to the enigmatic commander's experience at Sumter, as well as his earlier career, including fan letters, poems, and testimonials that he received from Northerners (and a few Southerners) during the siege.

The story of the Sumter crisis has been narrated many times by later historians. Among the best and most authoritative accounts, Maury Klein's *Days of Defiance: Sumter, Secession, and the Coming of the Civil War* (New York: Alfred A. Knopf, 1997) is notable for its richness of detail and deft interweaving of events in Washington and Charleston. David Detzer's *Allegiance: Fort Sumter, Charleston, and the Beginning of the Civil War* (New York: Houghton Mifflin Harcourt, 2001), a fast-paced narrative, provides especially rich portraits of the various participants in the Sumter standoff. W. A. Swanberg's *First Blood: The Story of Fort Sumter* (New York: Charles Scribner's Sons, 1957) offers another well-researched account. Nelson D. Lankford's *Cry Havoc! The Crooked Road to the Civil War, 1861* (New York: Viking, 2007) is especially strong in its treatment of the political struggles in the border states during the secession crisis.

For the changing meanings of the American flag, see especially Mark E. Neely and Harold Holzer's *The Union Image: Popular Prints of the Civil War North* (University of North Carolina Press, 2000), as well as Scot M. Guenter's *The American Flag, 1777–1924: Cultural Shifts from Creation to Codification* (Fairleigh Dickinson University Press, 1990) and Michael Corcoran's *For Which It Stands: An Anecdotal Biography of the American Flag* (New York: Simon & Schuster, 2002).

Chapter One: Wide Awake

For Ralph Farnham, see C. W. Clarence, *A Biographical Sketch of the Life of Ralph Farnham, of Acton, Maine, Now in the One Hundred and Fifth Year of His Age, and the Sole Survivor of the Glorious Battle of Bunker Hill* (Boston, 1860); as well as contemporary newspaper accounts. George B. Forgie's *Patricide in the House Divided: A Psychological Interpretation of Lincoln and His Age* (New York, W. W. Norton, 1979) is a provocative and important book that has unfortunately fallen somewhat out of favor; it offers an ingenious interpretation of the complicated feelings that the Civil War generation bore toward its antebellum parents and Revolutionary grandparents.

A magisterial survey of America's transformation during the first half of the nineteenth century (although it stops a dozen years before the story in this book begins) is Daniel Walker Howe's Pulitzer Prize–winning *What Hath God Wrought: The Transformation of America, 1815–1848* (Oxford University Press, 2008).

There are surprisingly few good secondary sources on the presidential campaign of 1860, especially treating the Lincoln campaign as a grassroots cultural phenomenon rather than simply a product of machinations among Republican leaders. Burlingame's Lincoln biography, cited above, offers some useful details. Gil Troy's lively chronicle of American presidential campaigns, *See How They Ran: The Changing Role of the Presidential Candidate* (Harvard University Press, 1996), includes a chapter on Lincoln's two campaigns. See also Wayne C. Williams, *A Rail Splitter for President* (University of Denver Press, 1951) and William E. Gienapp, "Who Voted for Lincoln?" in John Thomas, ed., *Abraham Lincoln and the American Political Tradition* (University of Massachusetts Press, 1986). Henry Mayer's magnificent *All On Fire: William Lloyd Garrison and the Abolition of Slavery* (New York: St. Martin's, 1998) portrays not just the great abolitionist himself but also the larger movement of which he was a part.

A superb recent article by Jon Grinspan, "'Young Men for War': The Wide Awakes and Lincoln's 1860 Campaign," *Journal of American History*, vol. 96, no. 2 (September 2009) is, rather amazingly, the only in-depth treatment that the Wide Awakes have ever received.

Donald E. Reynolds's *Texas Terror: The Slave Insurrection Panic of 1860 and the Secession of the Lower South* (Louisiana State University Press, 2007) offers an important (though horrifying) account of racial violence in the Lone Star State and throughout the South in the summer and fall of 1860, a pivotal but hitherto almost ignored factor in fueling the secession crisis.

Chapter Two: The Old Gentlemen

Seven decades after its original publication, Margaret Leech's *Reveille in Washington, 1860–1865* (New York: Harper & Bros., 1941) is still a paragon of historical writing, unsurpassed as an account of the nation's capital just before and during the war. The London *Times*'s William Howard Russell arrived in Washington just before the attack on Sumter and recorded his impressions (both there and throughout the country) in *My Diary North and South* (Boston: T.O.H.P. Burnham, 1863), a delightfully wicked book. Mrs. Roger Pryor's gossipy *Reminiscences of Peace and War* (New York: Macmillan, 1908) vividly recalls antebellum Washington's social and political circles from the viewpoint of a congressman's wife. Constance McLaughlin Green's several books on Washington are rich in detail, with *The Secret City: A History of Race Relations in the Nation's Capital* (Princeton University Press, 1967) ahead of its time in its portrayal of the local African-American community. Ernest B. Furgurson's more recent *Freedom Rising: Washington in the Civil War* (New York: Alfred A. Knopf, 2005) is another good account.

The only full-scale modern biography of John J. Crittenden is Albert D. Kirwan's sympathetic *John J. Crittenden: The Struggle for the Union* (University Press of Kentucky, 1962). The senator's papers in the Library of Congress are an invaluable resource.

Among the many fine books on the run-up to the war, two have particularly shaped my own account. The first of these is Kenneth Stampp's *And the War Came: The North and the Secession Crisis, 1860–1861* (Louisiana State University Press, 1950); the second is David M. Potter's equally classic *The Impending Crisis, 1848–1861* (New York: Harper & Row, 1976). For the Peace Conference, see Robert Gray Gunderson's *Old Gentlemen's Convention: The Washington Peace Conference of 1861* (University of Wisconsin Press, 1961). Gabor S. Borritt, ed., *Why the Civil War Came* (Oxford University Press, 1996) offers a number of enlightening essays.

Chapter Three: Forces of Nature

For Abraham Lincoln's journey to Washington and his activities and political strategy throughout the interim between his election and his inauguration, Harold Holzer's *Lincoln President-Elect: Abraham Lincoln and the Great Secession Winter 1860–1861* (New York: Simon & Schuster, 2008) is an authoritative, deeply researched source.

The standard biography of James Garfield is Allan Peskin's *Garfield: A Biography* (Kent State University Press, 1978). Margaret Leech was working on a biography at the time of her death in 1974, focusing on the social and political world within which her subject lived; she had gotten as far as the Civil War. The book was finished posthumously by Harry J. Brown (unfortunately in a perfunctory fashion) and published as *The Garfield Orbit* (New York: Harper & Row, 1978). The best source on Garfield's early political career is Robert I. Cottom's "To Be Among the First: The Early Career of James A. Garfield, 1831–1868" (PhD dissertation, Johns Hopkins University, 1975). W. W. Wasson's *James A. Garfield: His Religion and Education.* (Nashville: Tennessee Book Co., 1952) and Hendrik Booraem's *The Road to Respectability: James A. Garfield and His World, 1844–1852* (Bucknell University Press, 1988) are useful as well. *The Diary of James A. Garfield* (Michigan State University Press, 1967), edited by Harry J. Brown and Frederick D. Williams, is a window into Garfield's intimate thoughts from his teenage years until the end of his life, although unfortunately he did not maintain the diary consistently during the late 1850s and early 1860s. The best published collection of his writings during that period is Mary L. Hinsdale, ed., *Garfield-Hinsdale Letters: Correspondence Between James Abram Garfield and Burke Aaron Hinsdale* (University of Michigan Press, 1949). The Library of Congress's immense collection of Garfield's papers, along with another significant deposit at the Western Reserve Historical Society, contain more information about the twentieth president than almost any historian has ever wanted to know.

The fascinating cultural history of nineteenth-century Ohio (I am aware that this phrase may strike some readers as an oxymoron) unfolds elegantly in a book by Andrew R. L. Cayton, *Ohio: The History of a People* (Columbus: Ohio Historical Society, 2002). For the Civil War in Ohio, see David Van Tassel, *"Beyond Bayonets": The Civil War in Northern Ohio* (Kent State University Press, 2006); as well as Eric J. Cardinal, "The Ohio Democracy and the Crisis of Disunion, 1860–1861," *Ohio History*, vol. 86, no. 1 (Winter 1977). The most thorough sources on the Disciples movement are Henry K. Shaw, *Buckeye Disciples: A History of the Disciples of Christ in Ohio* (St. Louis: Christian Board of Publication, 1952); and A. S. Hayden, *Early History of the Disciples in the Western Reserve, Ohio* (Cincinnati: Chase & Hall, 1875).

For the prewar Northern ideology of individualism, personal freedom, and egalitarianism, see Earl J. Hess, *Liberty, Virtue, and Progress: Northerners and Their War for the Union* (2nd ed., Fordham University Press, 1997). The classic treatment of the growth of free-soil republicanism and the birth of the Republican Party is Eric Foner's *Free Soil, Free Labor, Free Men: The Ideology of the Republican Party Before the Civil War* (2nd ed., Oxford University Press, 1995). The cultural underpinnings of the Union cause are explored in James M. McPherson's *For Cause and Comrades: Why Men Fought in the Civil War* (Oxford University Press, 1997) and in Susan-Mary Grant's *North over South: Northern Nationalism and American Identity in the Antebellum Era* (University Press of Kansas, 2000), which is especially incisive in its analysis of how Northerners contrasted their culture to that of the South. Also see Melinda Lawson, *Patriot Fires: Forging a New American Nationalism in the Civil War North* (University Press of Kansas, 2002).

The abolitionist movement in Ohio is chronicled in William Cheek and Annie Lee Cheek, *John Mercer Langston and the Fight for Black Freedom, 1829–1865* (University of Illinois Press, 1989). Dorothy Sterling's *Ahead of Her Time: Abby Kelley and the Politics of Antislavery* (New York: W. W. Norton, 1991) is the best biography of that fiery crusader.

Chapter Four: A Shot in the Dark

For sources on Fort Sumter, see under Prologue, above.

Thomas Bartel's *Abner Doubleday: A Civil War Biography* (Jefferson, North Carolina: McFarland & Company, 2010) and JoAnn Smith Bartlett's *Abner Doubleday: His Life and Times: Looking Beyond the Myth* (Bloomington, Indiana: Xlibris Corporation, 2009) are the only two biographies of baseball's noninventor. Richard Wagner's *For Honor, Flag, and Family: Civil War Major General Samuel W. Crawford, 1827–1892* (Shippensburg, Pa.: White Mane Books, 2005) treats Sumter's surgeon. Edward M. Coffman's *The Old Army: A Portrait of the American Army in Peacetime, 1784–1898* (Oxford University Press, 1986) is a vivid and well-analyzed portrayal of that institution.

John G. Nicolay and John Hay's multivolume *Abraham Lincoln: A History* (New York: The Century Company, 1890) traces events leading up to and during the war from the perspective of the two men closest to the president throughout that period.

Joshua Wolf Shenk's thoughtful and empathetic *Lincoln's Melancholy: How Depression Challenged a President and Fueled His Greatness* (Boston: Houghton Mifflin, 2005) opens a new window into the soul of the sixteenth president, shedding light on almost every aspect of Lincoln's life and decision making. William Lee Miller's *President Lincoln: The Duty of a Statesman* (New York: Alfred A. Knopf, 2008) traces its subject's moral and political evolution.

In reconstructing the difficult chronology and interlocking events of the secession crisis, I was aided greatly by Russell McClintock's recent *Lincoln and the Decision for War: The Northern Response to Secession*, cited above.

Chapter Five: The Volunteer

The only relatively modern biography of Elmer Ellsworth is Ruth Painter Randall's lively *Colonel Elmer Ellsworth: A Biography of Lincoln's Friend and First Hero of the Civil War* (Boston: Little, Brown & Co., 1960), which is carefully researched and well written but unfortunately not footnoted. Charles Ingraham, *Elmer E. Ellsworth and the Zouaves of '61* (University of Chicago Press, 1925) and Luther E. Robinson, "Elmer Ellsworth, First Martyr of the Civil War," in *Transactions of the Illinois State Historical Society for the Year 1923*, both contain useful information and lengthy passages from period sources.

On the cultural history of youth in nineteenth-century America, see Glenn Wallach, *Obedient Sons: The Discourse of Youth and Generations in American Culture, 1630–1860* (University of Massachusetts Press, 1997); Anthony Rotundo, *American Manhood: Transformations in Masculinity from the Revolution to Modern Era* (New York: Basic Books, 1993); Howard P. Chudacoff, *The Age of the Bachelor: Creating an American Subculture* (Princeton University Press, 1999); Thomas Augst, *The Clerk's Tale: Young Men and Moral Life in Nineteenth-Century America* (University of Chicago Press, 2003); and Michael S. Kimmel, *Manhood in America: A Cultural History* (New York: Free Press, 2006).

Marcus Cunliffe's *Soldiers and Civilians: The Martial Spirit in America, 1775–1865*, (Boston: Little, Brown, 1968) is a subtle, learned, and colorful exploration of Americans' ambivalent attitudes toward war and the military. See also James B. Whisker, *The Rise and Decline of the American Militia System* (Susquehanna University Press, 1999).

Michael Burlingame, in *Lincoln's Journalist: John Hay's Anonymous Writings for the Press, 1860–1864* (Southern Illinois University Press, 1998), collects a number of articles that provide glimpses of Washington during the first weeks of the war, from someone close to both Lincoln and Ellsworth. Burlingame also edited *At Lincoln's Side: John Hay's Correspondence and Selected Writings* (Southern Illinois University Press, 2000) and, with John R. Turner Ettlinger, *Inside Lincoln's White House: The Complete Civil War Diary of John Hay* (Southern Illinois University Press, 1999)—both offer further accounts by Lincoln's voluble private secretary—as well as *With Lincoln in the White House: Letters, Memoranda, and Other Writings of John G. Nicolay, 1860–1865* (Southern Illinois University Press, 2000).

Chapter Six: Gateways to the West

For the building of the transcontinental telegraph, see James Gamble, "Wiring a Continent," *The Californian*, vol. 3, no. 6 (June 1881); also Carlyle N. Klise, "The First Transcontinental Telegraph," (master's thesis, Iowa State University, 1937); the growth of Western Union is covered in Robert Luther Thompson's *Wiring a Continent: The History of the Telegraph Industry in the United States* (Princeton University Press, 1947). The most reliable account of the Pony Express is Christopher Corbett's myth-busting *Orphans Preferred: The Twisted Truth and Lasting Legend of the Pony Express* (New York: Broadway Books, 2003). See also John D. Unruh, Jr., *The Plains Across: The Overland Emigrants and the Trans-Mississippi West, 1840–60* (University of Illinois Press, 1979).

Pamela Herr provides the best account of Jessie Frémont's life in *Jessie Benton Frémont: A Biography* (New York: Franklin Watts, 1987). Herr also edited, with Mary Lee Spence, *The Letters of Jessie Benton Frémont* (University of Illinois Press, 1993), a lively collection of correspondence. For John C. Frémont's life and career, see Tom Chaffin's fine biography, *Pathfinder: John Charles Frémont and the Course of American Empire* (New York: Hill and Wang, 2002), along with Allan Nevins's classic *Frémont: Pathmarker of the West* (University of Nebraska Press, 1992; originally published 1928). Sally Denton's *Passion and Principle: John and Jessie Frémont, the Couple Whose Power, Politics, and Love Shaped Nineteenth-Century America* (New York: Bloomsbury, 2007) is an engaging joint biography.

For California and the Civil War, see Leonard L. Richards, *The California Gold Rush and the Coming of the Civil War* (New York: Alfred A. Knopf, 2007), as well as Kevin Starr's compelling *Americans and the California Dream, 1850–1915* (Oxford University Press, 1973). Thomas Starr King's life and career have been covered most recently in Robert A. Monzingo's *Thomas Starr King: Eminent Californian, Civil War Statesman, Unitarian Minister* (Pacific Grove, California: Boxwood Press, 1991) and in Richard Peterson's "Thomas Starr King in California, 1860–64: Forgotten Naturalist of the Civil War Years," *California History*, vol. 69, no. 1 (Spring 1990). Among several earlier biographies, Charles W. Wendte's *Thomas Starr King: Patriot and Preacher* (Boston: The Beacon Press, 1921) is the most valuable. Some of King's sermons were published posthumously in volumes of his collected work; hundreds more are preserved as manuscript drafts at the Boston Public Library. His personal correspondence is in the Bancroft Library, University of California.

Adam Arenson's recent book *The Great Heart of the Republic: St. Louis and the Cultural Civil War* (Harvard University Press, 2010) convincingly treats the city as a fulcrum of the national crisis. The most thorough blow-by-blow account of the war there is Louis S. Gerteis's *Civil War St. Louis* (University of Kansas Press, 2001). The only modern biography of Nathaniel Lyon is Christopher Phillips's *Damned Yankee: The Life of General Nathaniel Lyon* (Louisiana State University, 1996), a book that, as its title suggests, betrays so little sympathy for its subject that one wonders how the author managed to get through writing it. Steven Rowan has done important work bringing to light the early history of the city's German community, including *Germans for a Free Missouri: Translations from the St. Louis Radical Press, 1857–1862* (University of Missouri Press, 1983), coedited with James Neal Primm; and his edited translation of Henry Boernstein's autobiography, published as *Memoirs of a Nobody: The Missouri Years of an Austrian Radical, 1849–1866* (St. Louis: Missouri Historical Society Press, 1997). For the Forty-Eighters, see A. E. Zucker, ed., *The Forty-Eighters: Political Refugees of the German Revolution of 1848* (New York: Russell and Russell, 1967) and Carl

Wittke, *Refugees of Revolution: The German Forty-Eighters in America* (University of Pennsylvania Press, 1952). William E. Smith's *The Francis Preston Blair Family in Politics* (New York: Macmillan, 1933) traces the various schemes of Frank Blair and his ambitious kinsfolk.

Chapter Seven: The Crossing

See chapter 5, above, for sources on Ellsworth and the Fire Zouaves, and chapter 2 for sources on Washington, D.C. The scene of the troops in the Capitol and the general sights of Washington in the first weeks of the war are captured beautifully in Theodore Winthrop's essay "Washington as a Camp," published anonymously after his death in *The Atlantic Monthly* (July 1861). Drew Gilpin Faust's *This Republic of Suffering: Death and the American Civil War* (New York: Alfred A. Knopf, 2008) puts Ellsworth's death into a larger, tragic, context.

Chapter Eight: Freedom's Fortress

An essential source for the story of the Hampton Roads fugitives is Edward Lillie Pierce's largely firsthand account, "The Contrabands at Fortress Monroe," published anonymously in *The Atlantic Monthly* (November 1861). Pierce also sent regular dispatches (signed "P.") to the *Boston Traveller* throughout his three-month stay at Monroe (April–July 1861); these frequently include material that did not make it into the *Atlantic* essay. Dozens of other newspaper and periodical correspondents converged upon Hampton Roads in the spring and summer of 1861, largely because people thought the first major battles of the war would be fought there—and when such battles failed to materialize, many of the reporters sent back copy about the contrabands. The archives of the American Missionary Association (housed at Fisk University, Nashville, Tennessee, and also available on microfilm) include letters from the missionaries who began arriving at Fortress Monroe in the autumn of 1861, some of which recount various contrabands' life stories—although these should be used with care, since some of the missionaries were clearly seeking dramatic or shocking testimonies rather than representative ones.

The two best modern biographies of Benjamin F. Butler are Hans L. Trefousse, *Ben Butler: The South Called Him Beast* (New York: Twayne Publishers, 1957), and Howard P. Nash, *Stormy Petrel: The Life and Times of General Benjamin F. Butler, 1818–1893* (Fairleigh Dickinson University Press, 1969). The general's own memoir, *Butler's Book: Autobiography and Personal Reminiscences of Maj.-Gen. Benjamin F. Butler* (Boston: A. M. Thayer & Co., 1892) is a small masterpiece of self-aggrandizement, certainly not without its charms. The general's letters are collected in *Private and Official Correspondence of Gen. Benjamin F. Butler During the Period of the Civil War* (Norwood, Massachusetts: The Plimpton Press, 1917). Butler's papers in the Library of Congress include far more extensive material from the war years, and provide virtually a day-by-day picture of his activities at Fortress Monroe.

For nineteenth-century Hampton, see Robert F. Engs, *Freedom's First Generation: Black Hampton, Virginia, 1861–1890* (Fordham University Press, 2004). Marion L. Starkey's *The First Plantation: A History of Hampton and Elizabeth City County, Virginia, 1607–1887* (n.p., 1936) offers a surprisingly honest, nuanced, and sympathetic (for its place and time) account of black life there during slavery, along with the recollections of the last few surviving people who remembered the antebellum town.

Other works give a broader picture of society and race relations in antebellum Virginia. Frederick Law Olmsted's *A Journey in the Seaboard Slave States* (New York: Dix & Edwards, 1861) is the best analysis of Virginia's economy and society by a period observer. Melvin Patrick Ely's *Israel on the Appomattox: A Southern Experiment in Black Freedom from the 1790s Through the Civil War* (New York: Alfred A. Knopf, 2004) is a valuable community study. Steven Deyle's *Carry Me Back: The Domestic Slave Trade in American Life* (Oxford University Press, 2005) situates often horrifying details within a larger context. Susan Dunn's *Dominion of Memories: Jefferson, Madison, and the Decline of Virginia* (New York: Basic Books, 2007) provides a subtle analysis of evolving racial attitudes amid rapid changes in the economy and society of the Upper South. Scot French's *The Rebellious Slave: Nat Turner in American Memory* (Boston: Houghton Mifflin, 2004) disentangles truth and myth.

For the larger picture of racial dynamics during and after the war, Ira Berlin et al., eds., *Freedom: A Documentary History of Emancipation, 1861–1867* (Cambridge University Press, 1985–) provides a distillation of voluminous material uncovered by the Freedmen and Southern Society Project. David Brion Davis's *Inhuman Bondage: The Rise and Fall of Slavery in the New World* (Oxford University Press, 2006) offers an enlightening treatment of the contrabands within the larger story of slavery's end in the Western hemisphere. James M. McPherson's groundbreaking *The Struggle for Equality: Abolitionists and the Negro in the Civil War and Reconstruction* (Princeton University Press, 1964) traces the battle over race and slavery throughout the course of the war; Benjamin Quarles's *The Negro in the Civil War* (Boston: Little, Brown, 1953) remains a valuable resource. Steven Hahn's *A Nation Under Our Feet: Black Political Struggles in the Rural South, from Slavery to the Great Migration* (Harvard University Press, 2003) does much to correct mistaken impressions of black passivity. Interviews with ex-slaves conducted in the 1930s under the auspices of the Works Progress Administration are collected in George P. Rawick, ed., *The American Slave: A Composite Autobiography* (Westport, Conn., 1972–79).

Surprisingly, few studies specifically treat the contrabands in any depth. One of these, Armstead Robinson's *Bitter Fruits of Bondage: The Demise of Slavery and the Collapse of the Confederacy, 1861–1865* (University of Virginia Press, 2005), is a provocative and compelling book, persuasively arguing that Southern blacks played a major role in undermining the rebel war effort. An encouraging sign of further interest in the subject is Kate Masur's article "'A Rare Phenomenon of Philological Vegetation': The Word 'Contraband' and the Meanings of Emancipation in the United States," *Journal of American History*, vol. 93, no. 4 (March 2007). See also Stephanie McCurry, *Confederate Reckoning: Power and Politics in the Civil War South* (Harvard University Press, 2010).

Many books, on the other hand, have examined the contested subject of Lincoln and slavery. Two of the best are Richard Striner's *Father Abraham: Lincoln's Relentless Struggle to End Slavery* (Oxford University Press, 2006) and Eric Foner's *The Fiery Trial: Abraham Lincoln and American Slavery* (New York: W. W. Norton, 2010).

Chapter Nine: Independence Day

Harry V. Jaffa's *A New Birth of Freedom: Abraham Lincoln and the Coming of the Civil War* (Lanham, Md.: Rowman & Littlefield, 2000) includes an in-depth analysis of the history and political philosophy undergirding Lincoln's July 4, 1861, message to Congress. Douglas Wilson, in *Lincoln's Sword: The Presidency and the Power of Words* (New York: Alfred A. Knopf, 2006) meticulously reconstructs Lincoln's composition of the document by examining its various drafts. Adam Gopnik's stimulating *Angels and Ages: A Short Book About Darwin, Lincoln, and Modern Life* (New York: Alfred A. Knopf, 2009) speaks eloquently of Lincoln and the concept of the rule of law, while Richard Striner's *Lincoln's Way: How Six Great Presidents Created American Power* (Lanham, Md.: Rowman & Littlefield, 2010) proposes Lincoln as a figure embodying both the progressive and conservative traditions in American politics.

For the Comet of 1861, see David A. Seargent's *The Greatest Comets in History: Broom Stars and Celestial Scimitars* (New York: Springer Science, 2009).

ACKNOWLEDGMENTS

I would especially like to thank two people: my friend and colleague Ted Widmer and my friend and student Jim Schelberg.

Ted has made so many good things happen: bringing me to the Eastern Shore of Maryland and to Washington College; introducing me to the joy of teaching; and, through countless conversations over the past nine years, opening my love of American history in new directions. (Not to mention some memorable nights in Chestertown with him and his family, dancing to 1970s rock in a 1730s house.) Ted's work as a writer and public intellectual sets a high standard indeed. I am grateful to him as well for reading my entire manuscript and offering insights on subjects from beards to baseball, as few but he can.

Jim was present throughout the creation of this book. If not for his interest in the Civil War during his freshman year of college, we never would have come across those letters in the attic that rekindled my own curiosity about 1861. One year later, Jim deployed to Afghanistan as a U.S. Marine fighting in a twenty-first-century conflict; his experiences there gave me a new understanding of how—as he wrote to me in a letter from far-off Helmand Province—"strange and unpredictable things occur in politics and war." After Jim's return, he generously assisted with research, during which we had many conversations about both the present and the past. The book truly would not have been the same without him.

Abbie Kowalewski, gifted and passionate student of the past, constantly reminded me that history is a story of people, not abstractions. Our regular breakfasts before my research sessions at the Library of Congress sent me sailing into the nineteenth century with the wind at my back.

Birch Bayh, Kitty Bayh, Richard Ben Cramer, and Joan Smith—cherished friends all—helped me through a rough patch and extended many other kindnesses (and meals) throughout the course of this project. Birch embodies the kind of statesmanship our country sorely needed, and finally got, in 1861—not to mention the kind that it could use in 2011. Richard is one of the snazziest writers I know. Kitty and Joan are two of the most thoughtful and civilized readers I know; moreover, Joan provided invaluable help with my illustrations and bibliography. For offering inspiration and encouragement (not least by example) when I needed it most, I also thank my friends Marc Pachter, Joshua Wolf Shenk, and especially Robert Wilson.

I am proud to be a member of Washington College's extraordinary community of teachers and students. I feel especially fortunate to work with a superb group of colleagues at the C. V. Starr Center for the Study of the American Experience, each of whom brings to bear his or her own perspective on history, and who made my life both easier and happier throughout the course of this project: Jill Ogline Titus, Jenifer Emley, Michael Buckley, and Lois Kitz. My colleague in the History Department, Richard Striner—author of important scholarship on Lincoln and the Civil War era—read my manuscript and offered helpful suggestions. Mitchell Reiss, Baird Tipson, and Christopher Ames were all generous with their encouragement. For their support of my work at the Starr Center, I am also grateful to Jay Griswold, the Hodson Trust (especially the late Finn M. W. Caspersen), the Starr Foundation, the late Margaret Nuttle, and Margaret Melcher. Toasts to Mary Wood, the late Howard Wood, James Wood, and Olivia Wood (as well as their thirteen generations of voluble and colorful ancestors) for the adventure at Poplar Grove that led me into 1861.

For assistance, support, and camaraderie of many kinds during the writing of this book, I thank Jeffrey Akman, Julianna Andrews, Adam Arenson, Richard Beeman, Felicia Bell, Ira Berlin, Dianne Brace and Bob Lynch, Clayton and Masha Black, Bill Bodenschatz, Jack Bohrer, Jennifer Brathovde, Wanda Brogdon, Elizabeth Broun, Elizabeth Clay, J. Michael Cobb, Thomas and Virginia Collier, Jasper Colt, Christian D'Andrea, Steven Dick, Murray and Mary Drabkin, Robert and Louisa Duemling, Kaity Edwards, Lennart Erickson, Ralph Eubanks, Dennis Fiori, Charles Francis, Meredith Davies Hadaway, Eleanor Harvey, Richard Hatcher, Brian Hecht and Douglas Gaasterland, Barbara Heck, Lesley Herrmann, Gerri Hollins, Harold Holzer, Tony Horwitz, Maria Hynson, Mary Jackson, the Jefferson Institute, Karl Kehm, Donald Kennon, Jamaica Kincaid, Bruce Kirby, Chip and Linda Knight, Michael Lai, Diane Landskroener, Charles King Mallory III, James Martin, Carla Massoni, Kitty Maynard, Davy McCall, Donald and Ann McColl, Alex McDowell, Maurice Meslans and Margaret Holyfield, Michael Meyer and Suzanne Seggerman, Ken Miller, Marla Miller, Megan Nelson, Scott Reynolds Nelson, the Newell family (Sam, Ilana, Isaac, and Eli), Susan O'Donovan, Andrew Oros and Steven Clemons, Eric Paff, Edward Papenfuse, Atiba Pertilla, Leslie and Vince Raimond, Mary Rhinelander, Vincent Robinson, Ted Rose, Jeremy Rothwell, Richard Schmidt, Helen Schneeberg, Ivan Schwartz and Mary van de Wiel, John Sellers, Gregory Shelton, Scott Shumaker and Barry Halvorson, Janet Sorrentino, Ben Soskis, Jacob and Katherine Spencer, David O. Stewart, Scott Stossel, Ned Sublette, Martin Sullivan, Regina Thielke, Kathy Thornton, Phillip Todd, John Ulrich, Carol van Veen, Thomas Watson, Freddy Widmer, Felicia Wilson, Laura Wilson, Martha Wilson, Kate Wiltrout, Matt Winters, and Koethi Zan.

I am grateful to Natasha Leland, Sylvain Bellenger and Jean-Loup Champion, Gary Tinterow and Christopher Gardner, Robert Hicks, Justin Stelter, Kate Livie and Ben Ford, the Worth family, Trevor Potter and Dana Westring, and Max Blumberg and Eduardo Araujo for relieving my labors with idyllic interludes in their various corners of the eighteenth and nineteenth centuries—as well as for their love and friendship. The late Ted Phillips and Janet Hopkins gave me a memorable introduction to Charleston and the South Carolina lowcountry. Allan Gurganus and I began a conversation about history in Hillsborough, North Carolina, that has continued among the named and nameless ghosts of Rapa Nui and Washington, D.C.

They say that writing is solitary work, and I suppose that's true, but it helps to have friends who toil at lonely keyboards of their own. For comradeship-in-arms (or in aching wrists), I salute Ben Anastas, Louis Bayard, Casey Cep, Sewell Chan, Trey Graham, Emily Kaiser, Donna Lucey, Thomas Mallon, Stephen Metcalf, Jonathan Rauch, Hank Stuever, Eric Tipler, David Vine, and Henry Wiencek. *Tanti abbracci* to my peerless *compare* Robert Worth, to Alice Clapman, to Felix Worth—and especially to Zack Worth.

I have been lucky to write for, work with, and learn from, some of the most gifted editors in journalism, many of them also friends: John Bethell, Robert Wilson, Stephen Smith, Nelson Aldrich, John Rosenberg, Glenn Oeland, Alex Star, Alida Becker, Nathan Lump, Katy Roberts, Mary Suh, Regan Solmo, Dennis Drabelle, Tom Frail, and Elizabeth Hightower. Sam Tanenhaus has pushed me hard, in the best way possible. David Shipley, George Kalogerakis, and Clay Risen turned me, surprisingly, into a blogger. Anne Fadiman continues to be my literary *beau ideal*, as well as a treasured friend and loyal mentor.

At the Wylie Agency, I thank Andrew Wylie, Sarah Chalfant, Scott Moyers, Jacqueline Ko—and especially the indomitable, indefatigable Jin Auh. Zoe Pagnamenta guided me expertly to a publisher. At Knopf, I have been lucky indeed to work with George Andreou, who wields his editorial rapier with the elegance of a Carolina duelist, and with his trusty second, Lily Evans. Thanks, too, to designer Michael Collica for his role in putting my words onto these pages.

Last of all, but actually first of all, the Goodhearts—Mom, Dad, Harry, Mark, Danielle, Avery, Logan, Herb, Karen, and David, as well as the no-less-good-hearted Lauren Krenzel and Natalie Levant—I love you more than words, printed or otherwise, can say.

•

I feel privileged every time I walk into the Main Reading Room of the Library of Congress, a room that Henry James said "crowns itself with grace." James—who found little else to admire in Washington—is no longer there, but the room is, little changed, and it's where I wrote much of this book. I owe a debt to those who have preserved its splendor and its soul in the midst of this most un-Jamesian age.

Outside, much has changed in Washington, and in the rest of the country, even since I began to write. I remember leaving the library late one afternoon in January 2009, a week or so before Inauguration Day. I walked down the front steps, and right in front of me, lit by the setting sun, was the Capitol: the dome with its statue of Freedom that a slave forged, the steps where Lincoln spoke of mystic chords of memory, the wide expanse where the Zouaves played baseball on the grass beneath the chestnut trees. The grass is gone now, and the chestnut trees: the historic landscape was replaced several years ago by a sterile and soulless plaza, and by a visitor center that allows people to "experience" our great national edifice without actually going inside. But I'd like to think that the old place is still there, somewhere beneath.

Index

Page numbers in *italics* refer to illustrations. Page numbers beginning with 385 refer to endnotes.

ILLUSTRATION CREDITS

Larger versions of these images can be found on this book's website, www.1861book.com.